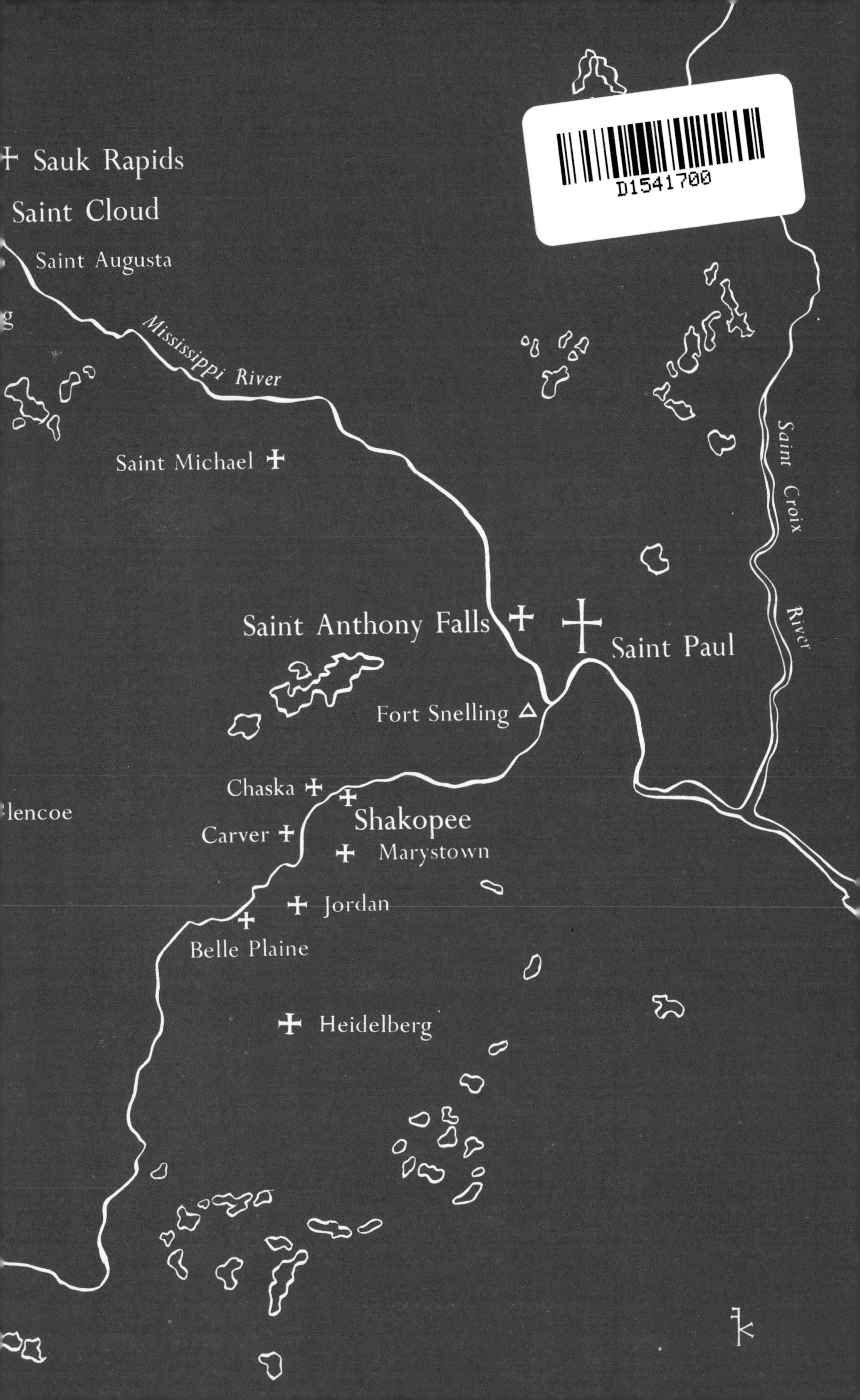
Sauk Rapids
Saint Cloud
Saint Augusta
Mississippi River
Saint Michael
Saint Croix River
Saint Anthony Falls
Saint Paul
Fort Snelling
Chaska
Shakopee
lencoe
Carver
Marystown
Jordan
Belle Plaine
Heidelberg

WORSHIP AND WORK

SAINT JOHN'S ABBEY AND UNIVERSITY 1856–1956

SAINT JOHN'S ABBEY AND UNIVERSITY 1856–1956

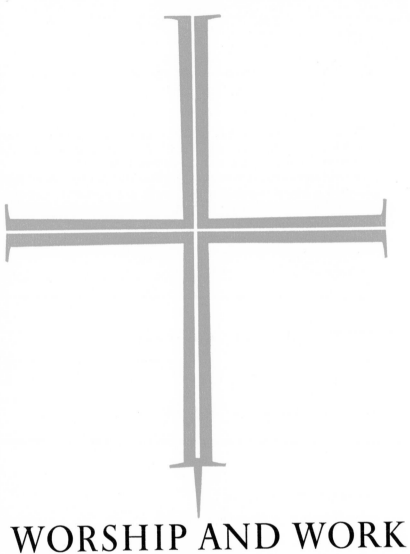

WORSHIP AND WORK

COLMAN J. BARRY, O.S.B.

SAINT JOHN'S ABBEY

COLLEGEVILLE, MINNESOTA

1956

AMERICAN BENEDICTINE ACADEMY

HISTORICAL STUDIES NUMBER II

Library of Congress Catalog Card Number: 56-10530

Printed in St. Paul, Minnesota
by the North Central Publishing Company

TABLE OF CONTENTS

Page VII LIST OF ILLUSTRATIONS

3 MONTE CASSINO, METTEN AND MINNESOTA

25 GO WEST YOUNG MONKS

56 THE FORMATIVE DECADE

93 ABBOT OF INDIANBUSH

131 SOWING WITH GRANITE

163 RESIGNATION AND REFORM

222 AND THE ROCK WAS PETER

255 NO TASK REFUSED

328 SERVICE NOT RECOGNITION

345 APPENDIX

379 FOOTNOTES

385 INDEX

LIST OF ILLUSTRATIONS

BETWEEN PAGES 38 AND 39

1   The Right Reverend Abbot Boniface Wimmer, O.S.B.
2   Archabbey of Monte Cassino.
3   Abbey of Metten.
4   St. Vincent Abbey, 1855.
5   The Most Reverend Joseph Cretin.
6   The Reverend Francis Xavier Pierz.
7   First Cathedral of St. Paul.
8   The Very Reverend Demetrius di Marogna, O.S.B.
9   The Reverends Cornelius Wittmann, O.S.B., and Bruno Riess, O.S.B.
10 The Very Reverend Othmar Wirtz, O.S.B.
11 The Very Reverend Benedict Haindl, O.S.B.
12 The Reverend Clement Staub, O.S.B.
13 The Right Reverend Abbot Rupert Seidenbusch, O.S.B.
14 The St. Cloud Priory, 1856.
15 Ruins of the St. Cloud Priory, 1907.
16 The Honorable John L. Wilson.
17 St. Germain Street, St. Cloud, 1860's.
18 The Original Collegeville Road.
19 The Indianbush Priory, Collegeville.
20 Candidates for the Monastery, 1886.
21 The Old Stone House.
22 The Old Stone House and First Brick Buildings.
23 St. Louis Abbey on the Lake, 1867.
24 The Future St. John's as Envisioned in 1873.

BETWEEN PAGES 70 AND 71

25 Assumption Church, St. Paul.
26 Holy Angels Procathedral, St. Cloud.
27 St. Joseph's Church, St. Joseph.

28   Celebration at St. John's Church, Meire Grove.
29   First *Stella Maris* Chapel, Lake Sagatagan.
30   *Stella Maris* Chapel, 1916.
31   The Most Reverend Rupert Seidenbusch, O.S.B., and Some Diocesan Clergy.
32   The Old Watab Mill.
33   Harvest Time in Early Stearns County.
34   District School at Farming.
35   The Gertken Family.
36   St. John's and a Brick Kiln, 1880's.
37   Indians at White Earth, 1878.
38   St. John's Community, 1886.
39   The Most Reverend Martin Marty, O.S.B.
40   The Right Reverend Abbot Alexius Edelbrock, O.S.B.
41   The Most Reverend John Ireland.
42   The Poplar Walk, 1890.
43   Lake Sagatagan, 1886.
44   Boating on the Watab.
45   First Communion Class of Indian Boys.
46   Students and faculty, 1880.
47   The Bells of St. John's.
48   St. John's from Cemetery Hill, 1886.
49   Croquet Court.
50   Picking Potatoes behind the monastery.

BETWEEN PAGES 150 AND 151

51   St. Alexius Priory, West Union.
52–53 White Earth School and Mission.
54   Abbot Alexius Edelbrock and the Reverend Aloysius Hermanutz, O.S.B., with White Earth Indians.
55   Second St. Mary's Church, St. Cloud.
56   St. Clement's Parish, Duluth.
57   Original St. Alexius Hospital, Bismarck.
58   Old St. Mary's Parish, Bismarck.
59   The Right Reverend Abbot Bernard Locnikar, O.S.B.
60   Abbot Bernard and Community at Caesar's Bay.
61   The Most Reverend Otto Zardetti and His Clergy.
62   American Cassinese Abbots, 1891.
63   View from Lake Sagatagan, 1887.
64   Aftermath of Tornado, 1894.
65   Funeral of Abbot Bernard Locnikar.
66   St. Francis Xavier School, Nassau, Bahama Islands.
67   The Reverend Chrysostom Schreiner, O.S.B.
68   The Reverend Peter Engel, O.S.B., in His Science Laboratory.
69   The Right Reverend Abbot Peter Engel, O.S.B.
70   St. John's Observatory.
71   The Apostolic Delegate, the Most Reverend Giovanni Bonzano, at St. John's.
72   The Fish Hatchery.
73   Motoring on Lake Sagatagan.
74   The Reverend John Katzner, O.S.B., and His Alpha Grape.
75   Lake Sagatagan, 1910.
76   Coach Edward J. Flynn.
77   Ice Skating on Lake Sagatagan.
78   Football Champions of 1901.

BETWEEN PAGES 230 AND 231

79   A Baseball Diamond of 1915.
80   Early Radio Experiments.

81   Track and Field, 1909.
82   The Reverend James Hansen, O.S.B.
83   Dedication of World War I Memorial.
84   The Right Reverend Abbot Bruno Doerfler, O.S.B.
85   Original St. Peter's Priory, Saskatchewan.
86   Abbots in Canada.
87   The Right Reverend Abbot Michael Ott, O.S.B.
88   St. Peter's Abbey, Saskatchewan, from the Air.
89   St. Martin's Priory, Olympia, Washington.
90   The Right Reverend Abbot Oswald Baran, O.S.B.
91   St. Martin's Abbey from the Air.
92   The Most Reverend James Trobec.
93   An Air View, 1924: Campus and Lakes.
94   Campus and Woods, 1924.
95   The Future St. John's as Envisioned in 1925.
96   The Right Reverend Abbot Alcuin Deutsch, O.S.B.
97   The Apostolic Delegate, the Most Reverend Pietro Fumasoni-
     Biondi, at St. John's in 1928.
98   The Apostolic Delegate, the Most Reverend Amleto Giovanni
     Cicognani, Visiting in St. Cloud.
99   The Abbots of the American Cassinese Congregation in 1946.
100 The Most Reverend Peter W. Bartholome, Coadjutor Bishop
     of St. Cloud, Welcomed to St. John's, May, 1942.
101 The Most Reverends Joseph F. Busch, Bishop of St. Cloud,
     John Gregory Murray, Archbishop of St. Paul, and Abbot
     Alcuin Deutsch, O.S.B.
102 The Reverend Virgil Michel, O.S.B.
103 The Reverends Oliver Kapsner, O.S.B., and Alexander Korte,
     O.S.B.
104 The Reverends Walter Reger, O.S.B., and Theodore Krebsbach,
     O.S.B.
105 The Reverend Gilbert Winkelmann, O.S.B.
106 The Fathers' Recreation Room.
107 The Reverends Roman Homar, O.S.B., and Thomas Borger-
     ding, O.S.B.
108 The Reverends Innocent Gertken, O.S.B., and Anthony Unter-
     hofer, O.S.B.
109 The Reverend Placid Wingerter, O.S.B.

     BETWEEN PAGES 278 AND 279

110–14 Brothers at Work.
115 Brothers of St. John's Abbey, 1956.
116 Blessing of the Right Reverend Abbot Baldwin Dworschak,
     O.S.B.
117 Ordination Day.
118 Coach Joseph Benda and Players.
119 Mr. Theodore Schreiner.
120 Lowering Old Glory.
121 Air Force Cadets of World War II.
122–25 St. John's Seminary of the Diocese of St. Cloud.
126–28 Puerto Rico: San Jose School; Church of the Holy Name of
     Jesus, Humacao; Monasterio San Antonio.
129 Colegio del Tepeyac, Mexico City.
130 Faculty and Students, Colegio del Tepeyac.
131 Benedictines in Civilian Garb.
132 Candidates for the Mexican Foundation.
133–35 St. Maur's Priory, South Union, Kentucky.
136 Abbot Baldwin Dworschak and Tokyo Benedictines.
137–40 St. Anselm's Parish, Tokyo.

BETWEEN PAGES 310 AND 311

141 Indian Congress at Grand Portage.
142 Indian Congress at Cass Lake.
143 Holy Family Church, Cloquet.
144 Assumption Shrine, Cold Spring.
145 Seminarians at St. Maur's Seminary, Kentucky.
146 Benedictines at Red Lake.
147 Red Lake Indian Mission.
148 The Priory, Nassau, Bahama Islands.
149 Benedictines in the Bahamas.
150 His Eminence, Patrick Cardinal Hayes, and the Most Reverend John Bernard Kevenhoerster, O.S.B.
151 The Right Reverend Abbots Vincent Taylor, O.S.B., and Alcuin Deutsch, O.S.B.
152 St. Benedict's Hall, Bahama Islands.
153 Consecration of Bishop Bernard Kevenhoerster.
154 Bishop Bernard Kevenhoerster Visiting Bahama Missions.
155 Bishop Bernard Kevenhoerster at Grave of the Reverend Chrysostom Schreiner, O.S.B.
156 The Most Reverends Stephen Donahue, Auxiliary Bishop of New York, and Paul Leonard Hagarty, O.S.B., Vicar Apostolic of the Bahama Islands.
157 Laying Cornerstone of St. Augustine's Monastery, Bahamas.
158 Hermitage of Fra Jerome Hawes, T.O.S.F., Bahama Islands.
159 Bishop Bernard and Abbot Alcuin with Missioners.
160 Blessing of St. Augustine's Monastery and School, Bahamas.
161–62 Bahama Islands Sisters.
163 At Monasterio San Antonio, Humacao, Puerto Rico.
164 Chapter Assembled to Elect the Sixth Abbot of St. John's.
165 Congratulations to Abbot-elect Baldwin Dworschak, O.S.B.
166 The Franciscan Sisters of Collegeville, Minnesota.
167–68 The Community of St. John's, 1956.

BETWEEN PAGES 334 AND 335

169 American Cassinese Abbots in Austria.
170 Benedictine Abbots Received by Pope Pius XII.
171 American Abbots in France.
172 Old Timers' Alumni Reunion, 1955.
173 Blessing of St. Mary's Hall, 1951.
174 Graduation Day at St. John's.
175 Homecoming at St. John's.
176 North American Benedictine Abbots in Rome, 1953.
177 Novices and Clerics of St. John's, 1956.
178 Clerics from Several Parts of the World.
179 Community of St. John's, 1956.
180 Lourdes Grotto in Winter.
181 Breaking Ground for New Monastery Wing, May, 1954.
182 St. John's Branch General R.O.T.C. Unit.
183 Stairway of New Monastery Wing.
184 Main Lobby of New Monastery Wing.
185 Interior Model of Proposed Abbey Church.
186 New Monastery Wing Completed in 1956.

BETWEEN PAGES 362 AND 365

Map of St. John's Parochial and Mission Work in Minnesota.
Map of St. John's Parochial and Mission Work in North Dakota.

WORSHIP AND WORK

SAINT JOHN'S ABBEY AND UNIVERSITY 1856–1956

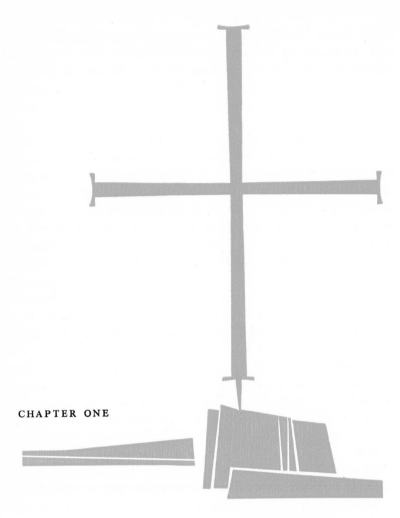

CHAPTER ONE

MONTE CASSINO, METTEN AND MINNESOTA

The history of one abbey does not have major importance in terms
of the thousands of monastic families that have followed the rule of
religious life established by St. Benedict. Nor is 100 years of community observance particularly striking in over fourteen centuries of
Benedictine tradition. The first centennial of St. John's Abbey does
have significance, however, if the proportions and contribution of
this New World house are considered. Its development is an evidence
of the Benedictine revival of modern times. The story of St. John's
is also a manifestation of the vitality of the Catholic Church on the
frontier and in general American society during the period of its
growth and maturity.

St. John's Abbey stands as an integral and living part of a distant
and definite past. Its roots extend far beyond the Mississippi River
Valley, the State of Minnesota, or the national boundaries of the

United States. The Collegeville community has truly identified itself with the locality in which it was established, as older Benedictine monasteries have consistently done. At the same time it has been the means of transplanting one of the main currents of European civilization to the West. August Krey noted this phenomenon when he said:

Monte Cassino, Metten and Minnesota

"To the historian of early European history it is peculiarly interesting to watch the growth on Minnesota soil of an institution whose work he has so often followed in those earlier years of European civilization. It is amazing to find repeated here so much of what occurred around Monte Cassino, or at the monastery of the Venerable Bede in Anglo-Saxon England, or at Fulda in western Germany, or at Metten in eastern Bavaria. Only the names and dates are different. The successful qualities of those earlier monasteries, particularly in England and Germany, where the work was of a pioneer character, reappear in the Minnesota community. Like them, the Minnesota monastery was peculiarly fitted to cope with pioneer problems." [1]

The life of Benedict of Nursia, the nature of the rule for monks which he wrote, and the long history of his followers during 1,400 years is well known. "Like a star in the darkness of the night," Pope Pius XII declared, "Benedict of Nursia brilliantly shines, a glory not only to Italy but to the whole Church." In his encyclical letter on the occasion of the fourteenth centenary of the death of St. Benedict, the Holy Father sketched the evolution of the Benedictine institute and he said:

"All who are not blinded by prejudice but examine events in the light of history and judge fairly, must recognize what a beneficial influence the power and strength of the Benedictine Order had in that early period, and how many great benefits it conferred on succeeding generations. . . . The sons of Benedict were almost alone in that dark age of profound ignorance and turmoil, in preserving the codices of literature and learning, in translating them most faithfully and commenting on them; they were also among the pioneers in practicing and promoting the arts, science and teaching. . . . The Benedictine Institute and its flourishing monasteries were raised up not without divine guidance and assistance, in order that, while the Roman Empire was tottering, and barbarous tribes goaded by warlike fury were attacking on all sides, Christian civilization might make good its losses." [2]

It was the establishment of his monastery at Monte Cassino in 529, as well as the beginning there of life according to his *Rule*, which inaugurated the broad influence of St. Benedict upon European events of which Pius XII spoke. Benedictine literature concerning that European monastic life is voluminous and thorough.[3] From Monte Cassino a chain of religious families, for both men and women, spread across

4

the world to form the oldest religious body in the western Church. The link which connects St. John's with Monte Cassino, and brings 529 in touch with 1856, is the ancient Abbey of Metten on the Danube in lower Bavaria.

Metten was established in 792 during the period when Charlemagne was sponsoring Benedictine houses throughout the territories under his jurisdiction. This abbey was never one of the larger or more renowned Benedictine centers, but it carried on the same type of missionary, educational, and cultural activity as the monasteries of St. Boniface. Located on the border of Bohemia, Metten throughout the years suffered from invading tribes, in turn converted and Christianized successive peoples from the East, and from the tenth century on served the region as a typical Bavarian institution. It was at different times known for its properties, its learning, art, illuminated manuscripts, and its influential position in ecclesiastical affairs of Bavaria. It survived the Protestant Revolt but became a victim of the secularization laws which followed in the wake of Napoleon's conquests.

Bavarian Origins

Since Bavaria had led the way in assisting Napoleon, Maximilian I of that kingdom was rewarded handsomely and made king. Through the efforts of his Francophile chief minister, Count Maximilian Montgelas, all spiritual principalities and ecclesiastical possessions were confiscated in the Bavarian secularization decrees of 1802 and 1803. Metten was suppressed, its possessions secularized, and its twenty-three monks scattered by virtue of the thirty-fifth article of the *Reichsdeputationshauptschluss* of 24 March 1803.[4] For the Abbey of Metten it was the end of almost a thousand years' existence. For practically all other Benedictine houses throughout Europe the Napoleonic depredations held a similar fate. By 1814 scarcely thirty Benedictine monasteries remained as a disorganized and, for the most part, tottering remnant of the armies of monks which had once Christianized and civilized Europe.

Liberals and advanced prophets of scientific progress had relegated monasticism to mediaeval times as atavistic and out of harmony with the ideals of the nineteenth century. Yet within a generation the Benedictine institute launched one of its most striking revivals. It was at Metten that the first indications of this revival took shape, and it was through the noble efforts of one of the new sons of Metten that organized Benedictine life was brought to American shores.

Upon the death of Maximilian in 1825 his son the crown prince succeeded to the throne of Bavaria as Ludwig I. He was then in his fortieth year, highly cultured, and determined to reverse the short-sighted policies which he had witnessed during the previous reign. Ludwig dreamed of creating a union of political liberalism and traditional Catholicism. He supported the reforming work of Josef Michael Sailer, Bishop of Ratisbon, and the struggle for the Church's freedom undertaken by the Ultramontane Party under the leadership of Graf Karl August von Reisach, archbishop of Munich and later cardinal. The new King Ludwig I strove to attract Catholic scholars to the University of Munich, rejoiced in the scholarship and action of Josef von Goerres' 'Round Table' in that city, and lent his support to movements which would restore to Bavaria what he considered its pure Christian and German traditions.

The restoration of Benedictine life in Bavaria was at the heart of Ludwig's plans. He had a deep personal attachment to the sons of St. Benedict for religious, educational, and cultural reasons, and he set about immediately to purchase back Metten's properties as the first step in the restoration of the Bavarian Congregation. Within five years all was in readiness. The two remaining monks of Metten, who had been serving in parishes since the secularization, gratefully returned to their cloister. These two aged priests, Ildephons Nebauer and Roman Raith, began their humble conventual life in 1830, and two years later a class of five novices came to Metten. Among them was Gregor Scherr, to become the community's new abbot in 1840 and afterward archbishop of Munich, and Boniface Wimmer, the future patriarch of Benedictinism in North America.[5]

At this time Sebastian Wimmer was twenty-three years of age, and a priest of the diocese of Ratisbon who had served one year as curate of the shrine of the Blessed Virgin at Altoetting before deciding to apply for admission to the priory of Metten. He chose the name of Boniface and here gave the first indication of the dominant passion of his life, to spread the kingdom of God through missionary labors as had the patron of Germany. His earlier studies under Ignatz Doellinger at the University of Munich, at a time when Doellinger was still an ardent Catholic, had filled him with love and veneration for the Benedictine monks who had converted the fatherland. From the very beginning of his monastic life Father Boniface wanted to be a Benedictine missionary, but for ten impatient years he was obliged to assist in the work of Bavarian restoration. He suggested to his abbot that Metten expand, that a mission house be established in Munich, and he even acquired the former monastery of Mallersdorf which he desired to make into a missionary school. But King Ludwig was making demands upon the small community for new monasteries, educational ventures, and parish activity. Father Boniface was accordingly sent by Abbot Gregor to the newly restored monastery of St. Stephen in Augsburg, next assigned as pastor of Stephansposching, then as procurator of the Abbey of Scheyern, and finally as professor of Latin and Greek in the Ludwigs-Gymnasium, a state college in Munich. Simultaneously he served as prefect in the Hollandeum, a boarding school under royal patronage connected with that college.[6]

It was while Father Boniface was stationed at the Hollandeum in

Munich that his ardent expectations began to take shape. The Reverend Edward Hipelius, O.S.B., a future secretary of the St. Vincent chapter, recorded the anxiety of the young Bavarian monk at that time. He said:

"He was moved partly by a strong desire to propagate the Christian religion and partly by reading the annual reports of Mission Societies. He was roused to enthusiastic ambition especially when he saw that Benedictine monks, while members of other religious institutes were zealously laboring for the propagation of the faith, were doing almost nothing in this regard and were, so to speak, looking on with folded hands. Thus he began to encourage and persuade the monks of Metten to enlist in this glorious enterprise, and devote themselves to the work of preserving and spreading the Christian religion in the United States, especially among the Germans. For a number of years he discussed the matter frequently and seriously, and as happens in the case of great and arduous undertakings encountered considerable opposition. While some approved, others ridiculed and criticized. Not even his superiors were at first inclined to give his proposals serious attention." [7]

Abbot Gregor called Father Boniface his "plan maker," and with reason. In 1838 the Bavarians had established their own independent mission society, called the *Ludwig Missionsverein*, separate from the older French Society for the Propagation of the Faith. There was much discussion in Catholic journals and papers how missionaries for the needs of German immigrants could be adequately provided, and Wimmer entered the debates with zest. Ludwig I and the *Ludwig Missionsverein* had authorized the establishment at Altoetting of a seminary, which never developed, for the training of German missionaries to the United States. It was proposed that the Redemptorists conduct the seminary, and no one, except Father Boniface, thought of the Benedictines. He entered an anonymous article in the columns of the Augsburg *Postzeitung* on 8 November 1845,[8] which the Reverend Felix Fellner, O.S.B., biographer of Wimmer, has called the charter of the American Benedictines.[9]

This debate, which waxed strong both among the Germanic peoples in Europe and in the Church of the United States, was another manifestation of the growing nationalistic tensions of the time. German Catholic immigrants were protesting that they were not being properly cared for by American bishops, that monies sent from Europe for their missionaries and churches were being channelled into non-German projects, and that they were not adequately represented in the hierarchy of the United States. The Very Rev. Friedrich von Held, C.Ss.R., provincial of the Redemptorists' Belgian province, to which their American missions were subject, journeyed to the United States to examine conditions at firsthand, as did Canon Josef Salzbacher of Vienna. The latter was the representative of the *Leopoldinen Stiftung*, the Austrian

Father Boniface Wimmer

mission society which had been established in 1829. Both priests were in Munich about this time, both wrote letters and reports of their impressions, and it was in answer to Salzbacher's conclusions that Wimmer wrote his celebrated letter.[10] Wimmer felt that the best way German immigrants in the United States could be aided was to establish a Benedictine monastery there, rather than anywhere in Europe. There, united with the monastery, a permanent and indigenous Benedictine school could be established. Only in this way could success and permanency be assured. The immediate need of immigrant care could be met, and gradually, as the Germans became adapted to their new homeland, the sons of the immigrants would continue the same work for religion and society.

Monte Cassino, Metten and Minnesota

It was a farsighted vision and it took courage to urge it. Years later, when Wimmer had more than realized these first designs, he was acclaimed as one of the greatest of nineteenth-century missionaries. But he would scarcely have achieved recognition or permission to undertake his project if several influential persons had not backed him. Ludwig I, after discovering who the author of the article in the Augsburg *Postzeitung* was, supported the plan; the Apostolic Nuncio to Bavaria, Archbishop Carlo Morichini, gradually confirmed the proposal, and Josef von Goerres encouraged him. The central committee of the *Ludwig Missionsverein,* through the instrumentality of its director, the court chaplain, Ferdinand Josef Mueller, who was Wimmer's perennial defender, approved the idea as the most practical one, and gave 6,000 florins ($2,560) to implement the proposal. The scales had been tipped, and before long an exultant Wimmer was on his way to the New World.

Few volunteers could be found, for the expedition was considered to be a risky undertaking and not sufficiently matured. But this did not deter Father Boniface. The Reverend Peter Henry Lemke, missionary from Carrolltown, Pennsylvania, was in Munich in 1845 trying to arouse interest in the American missions. He met Wimmer and offered him land in Carrolltown, which was in the recently erected See of Pittsburgh. With this incentive, Wimmer wrote to Michael O'Connor, first bishop of Pittsburgh, for permission to establish a monastery in his diocese. O'Connor willingly gave his consent, but the letter did not reach Wimmer. Meanwhile, the bishop of Chicago, William Quarter, had heard of the project, wrote to Wimmer inviting him to his diocese, but this letter also miscarried. Wimmer, without ecclesiastical invitation in hand, nevertheless bought the Carrolltown farm which Lemke had proffered. Four students and fourteen young laborers had volunteered to accompany him, and this was the party which gathered around Bishop Karl von Reisach in St. Michael's Church, Munich, at five o'clock on the morning of 25 July 1846, to assist at Mass before de-

8

parting across the seas. Not one of Wimmer's volunteer party was a Benedictine, nor had any received previous monastic training.

Two months later the strange little group arrived in New York. Father Boniface sought the advice of several German priests in the New York area: Vicar General John Stephan Raffeiner of St. Nicholas Parish, Williamsburg; the Redemptorist, Gabriel Rumpler, on Third Street; and the lone Benedictine missionary in Newark, Nicholaus Balleis from Salzburg. They were anything but encouraging and looked upon the project as a most precarious one, making clear to Wimmer how every other attempt to establish such an institution had failed during the previous years. The unsuccessful efforts of the Trappists during the time of Bishop John Carroll, of the Redemptorists' seminary in Baltimore, of the scholasticate of the Jesuit Fathers Anthony Kohlman and Benedict Fenwick in New York, of Bishop John Dubois' seminary project in New York, of Bishop Benedict Joseph Flaget's institute for Brothers in Kentucky — all were detailed.

Yet Wimmer was not to be turned back. Two of the prospective Brothers became ill, but the rest of the party moved on to Carrolltown. In a short time Wimmer realized that the location was not favorable for a monastery and school and that the land there was poor. Then Bishop O'Connor took him to Mount Saint Vincent in Westmoreland County, forty miles east of Pittsburgh, and only a half mile off the Cumberland Turnpike. He offered him the parish located on the site of Sportsman's Hall, the pioneer parish of western Pennsylvania. Wimmer was to take charge of the parish temporarily and to divide its revenues with the Reverend Michael Gallagher who was then stationed there. The congregation was composed of Irish and German Catholics, and Father Gallagher was to stay on until the Bavarian party could acquire some English. The bishop also promised to give him 315 acres of land attached to the parish for his proposed monastery. This land had been purchased by the Franciscan, Theodore Brouwers, on 16 April 1790, and he had willed the property to the pastor of St. Vincent. Both Bishops Carroll and O'Connor had experienced difficulties with some of the priests who claimed the land, and with trustees of the parish who asserted the right of appointing pastors. O'Connor was thus anxious to solve this problem by giving the place to the Benedictines. Wimmer also felt the opportunity was not to be neglected, and so he accepted. The following year the bishop of Pittsburgh granted the parish and property to Wimmer in perpetuity, and Pope Pius IX ratified the land conveyance, while raising the colony to the rank of a monastery.[11]

It was a humble beginning, with poverty on all sides, but it was in the full spirit of St. Benedict. The buildings included the Church of St. Vincent de Paul, a one-story school house, an old log cabin in which the

9

tenant of the church farm lived, and a dilapidated log hut used as a barn. The parish rectory housed Sisters of Mercy until their new convent of St. Xavier, one mile to the south of St. Vincent, was completed in the spring of 1847. So Father Boniface and his community moved into the small school house, divided it into two rooms: one for dining room, kitchen and space for the prospective brothers; the other for Fathers Gallagher and Boniface and the four students. The revenues from the parish were slight, and had to be divided with Gallagher; the harvest of the first year belonged to the tenant of the farm; cash on hand after the expenses of the voyage was insufficient to buy horses or farm implements, the buildings were in bad condition and, as Wimmer wrote back to Bavaria, "we froze even under the woolen coverings," [12] on thin straw sack beds in the school house attic.

As soon as he had transferred his party from Carrolltown to St. Vincent, 'Superior' Wimmer proceeded to invest his four young clerics and twelve brother candidates with the Benedictine habit. There were only six habits available, but they were joyfully handed on from one to another on that morning of 24 October 1846, as all prepared to begin life together in the New World according to the *Rule* of St. Benedict. The Benedictines were beginning stable community life rather late in the United States, but there was no one around the altar who did not fervently pray that in God's providence they were here to stay. Wimmer at once introduced the traditional horarium of the Bavarian Benedictines for his new family of students, carpenter, farmer, blacksmith, stone mason, cook, teamster, tanner, miller, locksmith, and baker. The monastic schedule included:

A.M.	3:45,	Rising, Matins and Lauds of the Divine Office in the Organ Loft of the Church; Brothers recited the Rosary in the nave of the Church
	5:00,	Meditation
	6:00,	Prime, Conventual Mass, Breakfast
	7:00,	Classes for Clerics; Manual Labor for Brothers
	9:00,	Terce and Sext of the Divine Office
	10:45,	Examination of Conscience in Church
	11:00,	Dinner with Reading During the Meal; Adoration of the Blessed Sacrament; None of the Divine Office; Recreation
P.M.	1:00,	Study for Clerics; Manual Labor for Brothers
	3:00,	Chanted Vespers of the Divine Office; Study for Clerics
	5:00,	Explanation of the Holy Rule
	6:00,	Supper with Reading; Recreation
	7:30,	Compline of the Divine Office; Rosary
	9:30,	Bed

The next two years were filled with much hard work and accomplishment at St. Vincent. When the Sisters of Mercy left for their new convent, the rectory was made into a monastery by the large number of hard-working Brothers; crops were planted and harvested; bricks were burnt, wood cut and construction begun on a monastery building; classes were taught to the clerics. None of this would have been possible without a continued flow of money from the *Ludwig Missionsverein* in Munich. Director Mueller also strove to arouse interest in Wimmer's foundation among Bavarian priests, students, and Benedictines. In 1847 the Reverend Peter Lechner, O.S.B., a doctor in theology, arrived from the Abbey of Scheyern bringing with him sixteen Brother candidates; two Benedictine priests, one from Metten and one from Augsburg, also came. Wimmer's old friend, Archbishop von Reisach, president of the *Ludwig Missionsverein* and now a cardinal, allowed the monastery 2,000 florins ($860) annually for twenty years. Most of these funds went toward the purchase of books, vestments, art works, etc. Other donors were the venerable bishop of Linz, Gregor Ziegler, O.S.B., the abbots of Metten, Abbot Rupert of Scheyern, and King Ludwig I.

With the foundation itself secured, Father Boniface moved to implement other phases of his plan. As priests were ordained he and they began to care for Catholics of the region, the German immigrants primarily, but gradually for Czech, Slovak, Polish, and Irish Catholics as well, scattered throughout the counties of western Pennsylvania. Land was purchased in Pennsylvania at Carrolltown, Indiana, St. Mary's, and Chestnut Ridge, all with the view of possible future monastic establishments. Some of the monks lived at different mission stations, while others travelled many miles throughout the Allegheny Mountains to serve small congregations or colonies.

At St. Vincent school work was likewise vigorously pursued. Besides the novitiate for the monastery there was a scholasticate for Benedictine candidates studying classics, a clericate for young monks studying philosophy and theology, and a Latin school for boys studying to be priests for the dioceses as well as for the monastery. The great majority of the students were from Germany or of German descent. In 1852 English-speaking students were accepted as well as young men intent on receiving a liberal arts training. In this way a traditional Benedictine school gradually took shape. Wimmer was able to preserve his primary aim of establishing a monastic center in which a large number of young men would be trained for the American priesthood. At the same time, quite naturally and consistently, the beginnings of a Benedictine academy and liberal arts college evolved.

Wimmer carried on all these enterprises, wrote a vast number of letters to friends and benefactors, travelled to and from Europe, and all the while continued his planning and designing. His motto was "Al-

11

ways go ahead," and his German thoroughness, combined with remarkable apostolic zeal, accomplished surprising results. Court Chaplain Mueller told John Martin Henni, bishop of Milwaukee, that he was confident of the success of the Benedictines in America. Mueller considered his life's ambition accomplished in the assistance he had given in bringing the religious orders to the United States, such as the Benedictines, Redemptorists and Norbertines. He felt that the complaints he had lodged in Rome, and with the mission societies, against the Irish and French bishops in the United States had been well founded. He wrote:

Monte Cassino, Metten and Minnesota

"Why are there now so many German parishes? Why do bishops now so eagerly ask for Redemptorists; yes, one of them even accused the Redemptorists in Rome, why? Because they do not cost anything and the bishops may not give them anything. Formerly, however, they paid everything and then they did not have any money for them. And yet the German parishes were very well taken care of and supported, so they said. I have always said that only through the Orders would the Germans be taken care of best, and it has been proven, although the Redemptorists also made many mistakes, especially in their building program. . . .

"Now as for Father Boniface, his idea can only be welcomed with joy in America. God Himself has thus far, so to speak, guided the undertaking. For who would believe that all the ill advice given by the most experienced and well meaning priests should redound precisely to his success. They were surprised in New York when he came with so many men and called it a foolish venture; but this was precisely to Father Boniface's greatest advantage. Without his men he could never have taken over St. Vincent's, nor begun his work.

"In no more than two years he is able to support and educate from fifty to sixty boys and thus prepare a native clergy. Thus finally will be realized what you had in mind. That this is best done through an Order I am sure we are agreed. If the Benedictines in Europe who want to go would be allowed to leave, half of them would emigrate; but their abbots are opposed." [13]

The German question was moving into the area of controversy at this time, as Mueller's letter testified, and Wimmer, unfortunately — and quite unconsciously — became a part of it. As German immigration increased, stronger demands were being made on the American bishops for German parishes, German-speaking priests for those parishes, and more German representation in the hierarchy. When Father Boniface made moves during these years for canonical erection of his foundation as an independent house, Bishop O'Connor of Pittsburgh took exception. He did not favor the idea of an exempt monastery in modern times, and he also felt Wimmer's move was precipitous. There were two further points of difference.

12

The first concerned the nature of the seminary at St. Vincent. O'Connor desired that Wimmer should have a seminary independent of the monastery, of which the bishop himself would be rector. He also wanted no distinction made between German and English-speaking seminarians, with both receiving equal grants-in-aid and scholarship assistance. Wimmer, for his part, insisted that the seminary should be part of the monastic school in which students for the diocesan clergy, especially German boys, would be accepted. It was for this purpose that he had come to the United States, and he would not be deflected from his original plan. He insisted that no distinctions were to be made on the basis of nationality.[14]

The second point of difference was, perhaps, even more acute. Wimmer, following the century-old custom of European religious, had entered into a brewery enterprise about thirty miles from the abbey at Indiana, Pennsylvania. His nephew had emigrated with $800 belonging to Father Boniface, and with the money had purchased a brewery in Indiana and lost the business. It was in order to recover his money that Wimmer bought the property, and the brewery was then operated by its original owner on Wimmer's account. Temperance advocates, both non-Catholic and Catholic, took strong exception to this practice. Catholic temperance people, whom Wimmer always looked upon as fanatics, felt that the Church was being harmed by this German custom of brewing beer, that student morale was being impaired by such activity, and that it was a clear indication of lack of understanding of the dominant Puritan mores of the nation. Irish Catholic leaders also felt a keen need for a strong total abstinence program, and Bishop O'Connor was sympathetic with its necessity. There was never a brewery at St. Vincent during these years, however, and Wimmer discontinued the Indiana enterprise even before a decision was obtained from Rome.[15]

In December, 1854, Wimmer drew up a long petition to the Holy See requesting independent abbey status for St. Vincent, and in February of the following year he departed for Rome to push the petition personally. Both he and Bishop O'Connor sought the aid of friends and agents to explain their contrary positions. O'Connor asked the Reverend Bernard Smith, O.S.B., curial official and Roman agent for several members of the American hierarchy, to present his views before the Congregation of Propaganda, the curial agency under which the Church in the United States, as mission territory, was then directed. He was particularly incensed that Wimmer should have sought the offices of King Ludwig I, who was in Rome at the time, and those of his ambassador to the Holy See, Graf von Spaur. Bishop O'Connor informed Smith:

"I hope that instead of a mitre and a crozier he (Wimmer) will get what he wants much more badly, a good lesson on the shameful manner in which he has acted, disregarding all I could say to him. It would be a poor encouragement for us to stand out for defending the liberty of the Church from secular power to find out that we are only exposed by our independence to the interference of foreign secular powers. If seculars are to dabble in our affairs it would be much better for us to have to deal with those we know and whom we could call to an account, than to have German princes dabbling in our affairs. If I were but to apply to our Secretary of State he would be only too glad to be asked to write a letter to Rome that would rebut this gentleman's interference; but thank God I would scorn to do so no matter how it ends." [16]

On the other hand, Wimmer presented his viewpoint to King Ludwig when he said:

"The ecclesiastical condition of America is still in its infancy; the will of the bishop is the only law. The bishops can expect no support from the state against refractory priests, and much less from the Protestant, or better, atheistic state and the democratic inclinations of its citizens. Accordingly they are naturally mistrustful of every attempt to deprive them more or less of their unrestricted power, or to insure oneself against their arbitrariness." [17]

Wimmer sought the advice and aid of Abbot Angelo Pescetelli, O.S.B., former abbot of Farfa, and then abbot of St. Paul's Outside the Walls. Pescetelli was also procurator general in Rome for the Cassinese Congregation, and in this capacity he submitted a report on Wimmer's petition to Filippo Cardinal Franzoni, prefect of Propaganda. O'Connor had recommended as possible candidates for abbot of St. Vincent the Reverends Benedict Haindl, O.S.B., Demetrius di Marogna, O.S.B., both monks of the monastery, and in last place Wimmer himself. Wimmer suggested as his candidate for abbot di Marogna, who was his prior.[18]

After studying the matter at length the Congregation of Propaganda recommended to the Holy Father that St. Vincent be made an independent abbey. Pope Pius IX consented to this petition on 24 August 1855, and at the same time created the American Cassinese Congregation of Benedictines while affiliating it to the Cassinese Congregation of Italy. The new American congregation was to be self-governing and was to be permitted to observe the statutes of the Bavarian Congregation. Father Boniface was appointed president of the congregation and named abbot of St. Vincent for a three-year period, although he had requested from the pope that the monks be allowed freely to elect their abbot. Wimmer was disappointed at this latter decision, which was an obvious result of the previous controversy. After his first term expired, the monks were to elect an abbot. In 1858, in accord with the papal brief, the election was held, and Wimmer was elected; in 1862 he was again returned to office, and the Holy See then confirmed the election for an indefinite time. Finally in 1865 Wimmer was named abbot for

14

life by Pius IX. Abbot Wimmer never received the abbatial benediction. The Holy Father, according to one report, gave Father Boniface his personal blessing before he left Rome, saying, "Now you are abbot; you need no further blessing."

In regard to the two points at issue between the new abbot and O'Connor, who by this time had resigned his see and joined the Society of Jesus, the Holy See decided in favor of Wimmer and his supporters. The seminary was to continue as before, an integral part of the monastic establishment, with the students of the bishop of Pittsburgh being admitted at their or his expense. The bishop had the traditional right to watch over the education and morals of these students. As for beer, in 1852 it was granted that it could be distilled and sold wholesale in barrels, but not retail. Wimmer later explained in his shaky English to Mathias Loras, bishop of Dubuque, what had transpired:

"It may seem a laughable affair to bring such a question before the Apostolic See; but for us it was truly important. We are now ten years in this country; all of us have been used to drinking beer; here we have it not; it is too high in price to buy it for so many (we were at that time 100 men; now we are 150, not accounted 100 scholars); but it is cheap, if we would distill it ourselves; however, if we dare not sell any, we can not afford either to brew it for our own use, it being yet too costly; and always being obliged to drink fresh water and nothing else, is a thing which no religious orders, even not the Trappists, Carthusians and Paulans are obliged to do. Therefore all religious orders, except Capuchins and Franciscans, were allowed everywhere to sell the *wine* of their own vineyards, or the beer of their own distilleries, in order to have from profit of the sale their own drink gratis, and not only in barrels, but (of course not in the monasteries and by their own friars) even in retail in taverns kept for that purpose. . . .

"When I was in Rome last summer, even the Holy Father plagued me a little in an audience I had with him, about the beer-affair. I replied: 'Holy Father, you have good saying about your Benedictines brewing and selling beer; but you forget that we don't drink any these nine years, and that we have no brewery.' 'Germans and not drinking beer,' he replied, 'that is much.' 'Yes indeed,' I said, 'until now we could do so, being young; but when we grow older, we will probably be in necessity to make beer.' 'Of course,' he said, 'S. Paul also wrote to S. Timothy he should take a little wine for his weak stomach, and so you must have something' — and he laughed heartily.

"This is the fact Right Rev. Bishop, of which six years ago many a joke was made by Temperance-men, who indeed brew no beer, but drink strong ales, spirits and wines, and preach temperance to the hard working classes.

"I may have been imprudent in getting my hands into that business, but I could hardly help it, and from the notions I have of that business

First American Benedictine Abbey

I could positively not foresee any difficulty or scandal, except from the Temperance-men; and with regard to these men, I only say, I divide them into two classes — in fools and in hypocrites; and I could easily defend this thesis. The Apostolic See has at different times and repeatedly declared against this temperance system, which is of no Catholic character." [19]

After his visit to Rome was completed in 1855, Abbot Wimmer moved up through Switzerland and Germany toward Munich, all the while pouring out his gratitude and joy to Prior Demetrius di Marogna and the community back at St. Vincent over the decision of the pope and the cardinals. He was acclaimed wherever he went as the first American Benedictine abbot, but he warned his religious family back home not to rejoice in the decision as if it were a triumph. He repeated anew that no bishop would ever have to fear them because of their new independence, an independence which the Holy See had been granting monastic establishments for centuries. Characteristically he ordered his monks to make him a simple wooden crozier because, as he reminded them, Pope Alexander VII had decreed that the pontificals of an abbot should be simpler than those of a bishop. Wimmer's directives were pointed toward good discipline, fraternal peace and happiness, love of worship and work.

The new abbot then turned at once to their obligations to spread the faith. Even before he had returned home he was writing to Prior Demetrius:

"We are now well enough established at St. Vincent's, also at St. Mary's and Carrolltown. Now we go West, and when it is possible, I will give you the opportunity, as you desire, to undertake something there. H. Roehrl, who is here, thinks he has a very good place in Wisconsin for us. It could be, now that we are exempt, that no Bishop will want to receive us." [20]

On the contrary, several bishops were most anxious to have him make a monastic foundation in their dioceses. Bishop Henni of Milwaukee had invited him to Wisconsin in 1846, the very first year that Wimmer was in this country, and Henni never ceased hoping that he would be able to come. He kept telling Wimmer, as well as the Swiss Benedictines at Einsiedeln, that the Benedictines would be able to accomplish their utmost only if they established themselves in the West, "the real home of German life and German missions." Wisconsin offered the best opportunity, he claimed, because of its climate, rural beauty, and the wide field of endeavor among the numerous immigrants in the interior and northern sections of the state. Henni's cherished ideal was to establish a seminary for the training of priests for German immigrants, a plan which he realized when he established his famed St. Francis Seminary at Milwaukee in 1856. But at first he had wanted the Bene-

16

dictines to found such an institution. He told them he could buy land for them in Milwaukee or on one of the four beautiful lakes of Madison, the capital of the state, and that he was on the point of asking the Jesuits to come for that purpose if the Benedictines should refuse. But Wimmer's foundations and commitments in Pennsylvania kept him in the East for ten years, and when the Swiss monks did arrive in 1854, they settled in southern Indiana and began there the development of the future St. Meinrad Archabbey.[21]

At this same time Bishop Joseph Cretin of St. Paul appealed to the *Ludwig Missionsverein* for German priests to care for the growing number of German Catholics who were immigrating to Minnesota Territory. The Bavarian mission society, in turn, suggested that he inquire at St. Vincent in Pennsylvania and he sent a plea there for assistance. After Wimmer returned to the United States, therefore, the Wisconsin project was no longer mentioned, and the idea of a Minnesota mission gradually gained the ascendancy in his plans.

Those plans had never changed from the days of the Bavarian beginnings: the Benedictine Order was to spread in the United States while dedicating itself to the salvation of souls and the education of youth. Wimmer held that tradition in the order, as well as the *Rule* of St. Benedict, should exert an influence on the choice of location for a monastic institution. The spread of the order was a natural development of the living principles active within the order itself. This was evident in all religious communities in the Church. Each one, he maintained, grew, prospered, and spread to the degree that, according to its nature, it felt responsible for and responded to existing religious and social conditions. A religious order could not stand still or limit itself in time, place, or numbers. No foundation can stand alone. "We must seize the opportunity and spread," he said, "even before we have had time to become thoroughly rooted in one place." [22] He explained to King Ludwig I why this was especially true in the United States. Here the people were 'go-getters,' not afraid to risk, to attempt new things, to depend on credit, and Wimmer felt that spirit should permeate Catholic life. It must spur the Benedictines on, as he wrote:

"Among such people, your Royal Majesty, and in such a country, one must act differently from the way he would act in good, loyal Bavaria. Whoever has intelligence must use it. There is no standing still; one must keep on going, must risk, must hazard something, but in such a way that if it proves a failure, not everything will be lost, and no one else will suffer injustice. In the province of religion there is the same active life as among the people in America. Everywhere cathedrals, seminaries, hospitals, and orphanages, convents, educational institutions, churches and schools are being erected. And, truly, we Catholics yield to none of the other parties. In fact, we surpass them if our more limited means are taken into consideration. Everything depends upon this one question, namely, to whom will the young generation belong. . . ."[23]

It was precisely this 'go-getting' spirit of Wimmer's which startled many of his European confrères, friends, and supporters, not to mention those who had never agreed with his efforts. He was often called a 'visionary' or an 'ecclesiastical adventurer' who was too progressive, too reckless in accumulating debts from land speculation, and too much influenced by the materialism of the United States, all of which was retarding the spiritual development of his subjects by such excessive activity. Wimmer's friend Mueller warned him repeatedly to go more slowly; the archbishop of Munich was displeased; Father Lemke, now a Benedictine, opposed him in the Augsburg *Postzeitung;* he was several times reported to Rome, even by some of his own monks, but each time he was exonerated. These very same charges would be repeated years later in Minnesota when his spirit was infused there by the second abbot of St. John's. In all this, however, Wimmer was not slow to defend himself, for, as he told Mueller:

". . . These newly founded missions will not become abbeys like Metten, Scheyern or other Benedictine houses in Europe which have more well defined activities. Here every abbey must become the mother of other abbeys. This 'call for the missions' cannot have its limits and knows no rest. Our efforts, therefore, have to be greater because the supreme aim of the Catholic Church is to render everything subject to Christ. After the Benedictine Order awakens from this century-old lethargy, it must become conscious of adapting itself to present conditions, to unfold its banners in the field of battle, where one half of the earth is the price of victory. . . . The stream of immigration is tending westward. We must follow it."[24]

He responded even more forcefully again, and in this letter he summarized his driving spirit so well that it warrants quotation in full:

"I really should not reply to these objections, that I am undertaking too much, or starting too many expensive enterprises, because I am of the opinion that I am doing too little. At times I feel sad because our work is not progressing fast enough in the construction of buildings, in the cultivation of the soil or in the education of youth, especially when members who worked with us for years are leaving the Order. No one who sees how a bad and non-Catholic press is systematically maligning and reviling the Church can find fault with my work. Moreover, who would not be compelled to warn the younger generation, when under various names the Secret Societies, notably the Know-Nothings, are spreading their nets of infidelity, to catch the unwary. Or who could be indifferent, when the spiritual ignorance of Catholics, and more so of non-Catholics is daily increasing. Anybody who realizes that the condition created by such influences must bring ruin in the

18

future, ought to be anxious to help in making the Catholic Church strong enough to permeate this indifferent society with the unchanging principles of law and liberty, authority and obedience, fidelity and conscience. All this does not require an extraordinary zeal for the honor of God or the spiritual and temporal welfare of one's fellowmen. Therefore, any sincere Catholic and patriotic American will do his utmost to promote the welfare of his country, and the defense of the Church against these evil tendencies. This result can only be achieved, if our immigrants who are moving into new regions, which are now the hunting grounds of Indians, are not neglected or forgotten by the Church, but cared for and educated before the infidels and heretics can gain influence over them. It is true, these foundations demand many expenses, but if these properties which are donated or purchased, are well managed, they must become valuable rallying points for Catholics. Therefore, as the military posts in these territories protect these people against the wild Indians, these spiritual centers will be the bulwarks of their faith against their spiritual enemies." [25]

It was a vision and a determination such as this which caused Abbot Angelo Pescetelli, O.S.B., to exclaim of the founder of the American Benedictines:

". . . I have great admiration and enthusiasm for the person of Wimmer. He is a man of mind and heart who conceives a grand project and has the firmness, constancy, and courage to complete it, overcoming obstacles in every manner. I see in him a type of the Middle Ages, illumined by faith, strengthened by hope, and filled with charity, a Champion of the Church and of the Order of St. Benedict. These sentiments have increased in time." [26]

Abbot Wimmer returned to the United States in December, 1855, and within a month had assembled the first general chapter of the American Cassinese Congregation, held at St. Vincent on 10–12 January 1856. Before the capitulars of St. Vincent dispersed, they had discussed the possibility of accepting the pressing requests from a number of bishops to send a Benedictine colony into the West. Documentary evidence is not extant to identify all of the bishops who asked Wimmer for Benedictines at this time. From correspondence and references it can be inferred, however, that they might have included Archbishop Peter Richard Kenrick of St. Louis; Bishop Loras of Dubuque; Frederic Baraga, Vicar Apostolic of Northern Michigan; Henni of Milwaukee; and Cretin of St. Paul.[27] During the discussion the capitulars had agreed that within a short time they would have more priests than they could employ at St. Vincent, and thus they voted to send a small colony west as soon as possible. Wimmer and his monks, characteristically, decided that they would go where the need was greatest, and they determined, therefore, to answer the urgent invitation from the missionary bishop of St. Paul, in the Territory of Minnesota. The abbot described

19

the locality as "in the most western part of the United States where the 'Father of Waters,' the Mississippi, has its source." He explained to the King of Bavaria:

Monte Cassino, Metten and Minnesota

"A few years ago Minnesota was an unknown wilderness, through which the uncivilized Indians roamed. It was visited only by daring hunters. Now it has eighty thousand inhabitants, among whom are many German Catholics. For twenty thousand Catholics the Bishop has only twelve priests, an altogether insufficient number because the people are scattered throughout the territory. Without doubt many of our Catholic countrymen, as elsewhere, will succumb to the Methodist sect if they do not soon receive spiritual leaders and protectors. The distance of the foundation from the motherhouse is great, too great, even though it can be reached by train in five days. But since the older dioceses are better supplied with priests, I thought that help should be nearest to the place where the need is the greatest, and decided in favor of Minnesota." [28]

If anyone had striven to convince Catholics both in the United States and Europe that the need was greatest in Minnesota, it was the veteran Indian missionary, the Reverend Francis Xavier Pierz. It was he who had encouraged his ordinary, Bishop Cretin, to appeal to the *Ludwig Missionsverein* for missionary priests; he had also interceded there himself. His numerous letters and reports, both picturesque and moving, which were printed in several Catholic newspapers, were a major influence in attracting German Catholic settlers to Minnesota.

In his own right Pierz had pioneered on a grand scale before opening the way for Benedictine missionary efforts. At the invitation of his countryman Baraga, Father Pierz had come to America in 1835 at the age of fifty years to work among the Indians of the Midwest. He labored zealously at La Croix, Sault Ste. Marie, Grand Portage, Fort William, along the North Shore of Lake Superior, and among the Ottawas at Arbre Croche. Then he answered the call of the first bishop of the newly erected Diocese of St. Paul to work among the Chippewa and Sioux, who far outnumbered the whites in the area. At the age of sixty he began anew in 1852 to preach the gospel and administer the sacraments among the Indians along the upper waters of the Mississippi. He established his mission center at Crow Wing, an Indian trading post near the present city of Brainerd, Minnesota, and traversed wide areas embracing Mille Lacs, Leach Lake, Red Lake, Long Prairie, Belle Prairie while evangelizing not only the Indians but also French Canadians and half-breeds.[29]

Then after word went abroad that the Sioux treaties of 1851 were signed, white settlers began to move into the Minnesota territorial lands west of the Mississippi river. The Indians had nearly all retreated from the 'Suland' by the end of 1853, but the lands were not legally opened to settlement until late summer of the year following. Land transactions were based on the pre-emption laws of 1841 which permitted occupation only of surveyed lands. Although these new Minnesota lands were not surveyed until 1853, and not opened for sale until 1855, settlers had no scruples over 'squatting' on lands of their choice.[30] Immigration really began in earnest during the summer of 1854 after the Chicago and Rock Island Railroad extended its tracks into Rock Island on the east bank of the Mississippi. Settlers could then move from there up the Mississippi on the numerous steam boats operating along the river as far north as St. Paul. In the spring of 1855 the flood of immigration was on, and unlike earlier settlers in Minnesota who came in great part to speculate, these new peoples moved across the rich lands of the Territory, the first nucleus of solid communities and stable family life on the land. Most of the settlers were transplanted Yankees, descendants of earlier pioneers from New York, New England, Ohio, Indiana and Illinois; a number were from northern European nations, especially the vanguard of the great Viking migration from Scandinavian countries which was soon to follow.

Father Francis Xavier Pierz

Prominent among these new Minnesota peoples were German immigrants. Catholic Germans settled after 1850 along the Mississippi and Minnesota rivers in Scott, Carver, Ramsey and Hennepin counties. Others, soon to be more numerous, moved up the Mississippi from St. Paul toward Sauk Rapids, and then out into the rich, fertile farm lands of the Sauk River valley. Bishop Loras had pursued immigration promotion vigorously in Iowa, but Bishop Cretin had been hesitant at first to encourage Catholic settlement of Minnesota until he was certain that all of the promises of speculators concerning the advantages of Minnesota were sound and true. After 1853 he began a policy of endorsing Catholic colonization, as he obtained a few more priests, and Father Pierz then began actively to invite colonizing. He wanted the good farm lands of Minnesota and its healthful climate to be enjoyed by Catholics. After trying to interest his Slovenian countrymen, he turned to the Germans, and urged them to come before it was too late to obtain these rich prairie and timber lands where Catholic life could be inaugurated and sustained. He wrote private letters, he entered public letters and articles in the columns of German Catholic newspapers such as the *Wahrheitsfreund* of Cincinnati and the New York *Katholische Kirchenzeitung,* as well as numerous Catholic periodicals and journals of Germany. He incorporated a brochure in his work *Die Indianer in Nord Amerika,* which he entitled *Eine kurze Beschreibung des Minnesota-Territoriums.*[31] Here he described the location and geography of Minnesota, its waterways and natural resources, towns, climate and produce. He quieted fears concerning Indian dangers and continued with some poetic license:

". . . Our winter, indeed, is somewhat longer, but not more severe than in the southern states; it usually begins in the early part of Novem-

21

ber and continues until the end of April. During the three years I have spent here I have not seen more than one foot of snow, and with the exception of some fifteen or twenty cold days the weather was generally so pleasant that one could work outdoors. During the past winter I have seen German settlers at work in their shirt sleeves, cutting their wood for building and fencing. . . .

*Monte Cassino,
Metten and
Minnesota*

"The summer in Minnesota is more favorable for human health and for the growth of farm and garden produce than in any other country in the world. Rains are not frequent and rainfall seldom continues for more than a day, and yet we are not troubled by drouth and we have not experienced crop failure. For the countless lakes and rivers in this territory give rise in the warm weather to great clouds of vapor, which become charged with electricity and alkaline particles and are precipitated on clear nights in the form of heavy dew, thus furnishing to soil and vegetation an amount of moisture equal to a gentle rain, after which the warm sunshine effects a chemical fermentation in the earth which nourishes the vegetation and promotes its rapid growth. Thus, though the sowing is late, Minnesota's crops ripen in good time and we have finer and more abundant harvests than any other region.

"In the past year I saw very fine oats cut at Belle Prairie on the first of August and it had been sown at the end of May. We have cucumbers an ell in length, melons weighing twenty-eight pounds, cabbages of twenty-four pounds, and eighteen-pound rutabagas; winter wheat yields forty-two bushels to the acre; and one can infer that the rest of the crops are equally good. The abundance of water in Minnesota also maintains throughout the summer a pure and wholesome air, for our numerous lakes and rivers create currents in the air which purify and refresh the atmosphere and make the long summer days quite bearable.

"In the southern states of North America the climate, air and health of the people are quite different. There the winter is much shorter, but it is very changeable and damp and hence injurious to health; the long autumn and dry spring, for the above-mentioned reasons, are unfavorable for the development of vegetation. During the hot summer days a host of noxious miasmas and poisonous gases arise from the marshes and mineral-charged soil and hang like heavy fog and taint the air and the crops. Thus serious fevers, cholera and other epidemics appear and fill the hospitals with patients and the cemeteries with corpses; and especially the German immigrants, who are not accustomed to such air, fall victims in great number. . . . But the like does not happen in Minnesota. . . .

"Hasten then, my dear German people, those of you who have in mind to change your abode, and settle in Minnesota. Do not delay joining the stream of immigration, for the sooner you come the better will be your opportunity to choose a good place to settle. Several hundred families can still find good claims along the Sauk River, and in the sur-

22

rounding country no doubt several thousand families can find favorable places for settlement.

"I do wish, however, that the choicest pieces of land in this delightful Territory would become the property of thrifty Catholics who would make an earthly paradise of this Minnesota which heaven has so richly blessed, and who would bear out the opinion that Germans prove to be the best farmers and the best Christians in America. I am sure that you will likewise do credit to your faith here in Minnesota; but to prove yourselves good Catholics, do not bring with you any free thinkers, red republicans, atheists or agitators." [32]

Germans did respond to these glowing invitations. More than fifty German families were in central Minnesota by early 1854 and 1855, and began staking claims on both sides of the Sauk River. Pierz passed among them when he could, offered Holy Mass in private homes, and began erecting mission stations at Sauk Rapids, at St. Joseph, and purchasing properties for future church locations. He searched out settlers along the Sauk River, all the while appealing to his bishop and to German aid societies for priests, preferably a religious order, to supply the stable spiritual care which he, primarily and ever the Indian missionary, could not furnish.

It was for these peoples, accordingly, that Cretin applied to Wimmer, and it was for these peoples that the Benedictines first came to Minnesota. Abbot Wimmer placed the expedition in the hands of his prior, Demetrius di Marogna, who had longed to undertake a monastic settlement. With him came two young Benedictine clerics not yet ordained priests, Cornelius Wittmann and Bruno Riess, and two Benedictine Brothers, Benno Muckenthaler and Patrick Greil.

The entire community at St. Vincent prepared with joy during that spring of 1856 for the first monastic departure to the West. Vessels and vestments for liturgical worship were packed in wooden crates made by the Brothers. Three missals, a fine ostensorium, ciborium, three chalices, and breviaries for the *Opus Dei,* the recitation of the Divine Office in common by the community. One of the chalices was Father Demetrius'; the other two would be used by the clerics when they were ordained in Minnesota. Wimmer also supplied the departing band with two trunks of books and furniture valued at $1,500. He was able to send these objects along because he had just returned from Bavaria with numerous gifts. The new prior was given $540 for travelling expenses, and two land warrants with which he was to secure title to federal lands if possible. [33]

The little party received the last blessing of their abbot and the kiss of peace from their brethren in the gray dawn of Saturday morning, the Feast of St. Benedict, 5 April 1856. After reaching Pittsburgh by rail they offered Holy Mass, and remained two days until the steamboat 'Paul Anderson' set off down the Ohio for St. Louis.

Abbot Boniface summarized simply the momentous endeavor: "The foundation should be a center from which we will be of service to both the civilized and uncivilized people of Minnesota." [34] From that day forward the aim of his family in Minnesota has been to implement and develop this service which their founder envisioned.

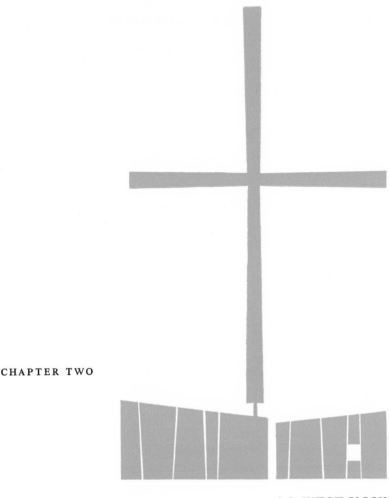

CHAPTER TWO

GO WEST YOUNG MONKS

Travelogues of visitors to the United States in the nineteenth century, as well as memoirs and letters of early settlers in the West, have supplied valuable insights into American economic and social developments. The diaries and letters of Minnesota's pioneer band of Benedictine monks, recording their impressions and movements during that spring of 1856, offer further data on the importance of religion as an integral part of frontier society.

Abbot Wimmer's five Benedictines found themselves moving down the Ohio river with about two hundred other settlers, in great part farmers, who like themselves were heading westward. It took the 'Paul Anderson' ten days to reach St. Louis, and the boat was so crowded that the five monks had only a single cabin with two berths, which meant that three of them slept on the floor. These hardships were, however, but a foretaste of what awaited them in Minnesota.

There could scarcely have been any person on board whose background was more varied or whose family ancestry was less adapted to the responsibilities ahead than the prior of these Benedictines, Demetrius di Marogna. He was born at the Villa Lagarina in the diocese of Trent on 17 September 1803, a scion of the patrician family di Marogna of Verona. In his early boyhood Conte Carlo Giuseppe di Marogna served as a page at the court of the archduke of Tuscany in Florence. When his father moved the family to Germany in 1809 Carlo did not attach himself to the Bavarian court, as did other members of the family, but entered the diocesan seminary of Mainz where he studied theology under the renowned Benno Liebermann. Ordained for the diocese of Augsburg on 31 March 1826, he first served as curate in the diocese of Mainz, and then as pastor in the Allgaeu, a territory at the foothills of the Alps, in the diocese of Augsburg. But moved by a desire to care for German Catholic emigrants, he determined in 1847 to leave for America, as Boniface Wimmer had done the year before. He served as pastor in St. Joseph's parish, Chicago; St. Theodore's parish, Germantown, Illinois; and St. Henry's parish, Hanover, Illinois, during the years 1848–52. His name was a household word among the German Catholics of southern Illinois, but Father di Marogna found himself in conflict with several Irish priests of the diocese of Chicago over parochial jurisdiction, and he decided to apply as a novice at St. Vincent monastery. He felt that "the secular priest seems like a skiff coursing upon high sea amid angry billows, and in constant danger of being wrecked on some hidden rock."[1] Wimmer accepted him and gave him the religious name of Demetrius in honor of the Reverend Demetrius Gallitzin, nobleman and pioneer priest of western Pennsylvania. He was appointed prior at St. Vincent only a few months after taking his vows, both because of his attainments and because Father Boniface needed an older priest with experience to assist him during those critical years before abbey status was achieved. Prior Demetrius was in charge of St. Vincent during the protracted absence of Wimmer at Rome in 1855, amassed a number of debts by building, and did not escape the criticism of several members of the community. Bishop O'Connor of Pittsburgh favored him as a possible candidate for the office of first abbot of St. Vincent, and it is not surprising that he was eager to lead a monastic colony into the West, nor that Wimmer chose him for the task. Besides, his previous pastoral experience in Illinois seemed at that time to fit him for a western expedition.

With him as nucleus of the new community were the two young clerics, Bruno Riess and Cornelius Wittmann, and two Brothers, Benno Muckenthaler and Patrick Greil, all natives of Bavaria.[2] In his first letter to Abbot Boniface while en route to St. Louis, the prior of the Minnesota foundation wrote in the name of the group:

". . . Our striving will henceforth be to obtain an ever deeper insight into the spirit of the *Holy Rule,* always to observe it more exactly, and to act in such a way as to be recognized as true sons of St. Benedict." [3]

All involved, as well as Wimmer himself, would have cause to recall this determination of the little group in the trials and differences which awaited them.

At St. Louis, Archbishop Peter Richard Kenrick entreated the colony to stay in his diocese, as he thought they had come in answer to his appeal to Wimmer for a Benedictine monastery. Father Demetrius and the two clerics stayed with an old acquaintance, Vicar General Joseph Melcher of the diocese, who was later to be bishop of Green Bay and a firm friend of St. John's. The prior found residence for the Brothers, who were in charge of the luggage, with, as he said, "a trustworthy Plattdeutsch family." The prior offered Mass for the Ursuline Sisters in St. Louis who were of Bavarian origin and patronized by King Ludwig I, visited his former parish at Germantown, Illinois, and assisted at St. Mary's Church, St. Louis, over the weekend. From all sides no efforts were spared to detain the monks, but true to their purpose, they found passage on the 'Minnesota Belle,' first steamer taking passengers north, and left for St. Paul on April 22. At Davenport, Iowa, the 'Minnesota Belle' had difficulty in passing under the Chicago, Rock Island railroad bridge which crossed the Mississippi at an oblique angle and was a serious obstacle to navigation, especially during spring floods. The cleric Bruno Riess recorded what ensued:

". . . Our steamer struggled for nearly an hour trying to effect a passage between the piers of the bridge. Fat and pitch were thrown into the furnace to raise steam pressure to the utmost. We passed safely. Not so the steamer that ran in our wake. Its boilers exploded and its passengers were hurled to destruction. Two other steamers came up to offer assistance; but they also burned and hundreds of lives were lost. The good priest at Dubuque was not informed on what steamer we had embarked and was deeply grieved as he supposed that we were lost. The next day he mailed a Davenport paper to St. Vincent's where we were also believed to have perished and mortuary services were celebrated for us, while we were slowly but cheerfully nearing our port of destination." [4]

The cleric Bruno Riess was not exaggerating the danger of the voyage. The Dubuque *Herald* reported that the river had not been so high in many years and was raising white caps which left the appearance of "a lake of which a storm spirit had taken possession and was lashing into subjection." [5] The Minnesota *Pioneer and Democrat* also recorded that it looked like "all booms in Christendom had broke loose" from the number of logs floating past St. Paul. [6] The 'Minnesota Belle,' after a slow and dangerous journey, edged up to the levee at St. Paul at ten o'clock on the evening of May 2, a day which had brought the muddiest streets in years to the thriving river city at the end of the steamer route.

The Benedictines came to Minnesota while the first notable tide of immigration was moving into the territory. This movement had begun the year previous, and continued for a three year period until the panic of 1857 interrupted it for a time. In 1854 there were about 32,000 people in the territory; by 1857 there were 150,037. These new settlers were, as William Watts Folwell wrote:

". . . a solid nucleus of industrious, reputable citizens, around which later accessions were to crystallize. . . . In every neighborhood schoolhouses were built, often of logs or sods, and in them the neighbors gathered for their gospel meetings until churches were erected. Within a few years the churches in the cities and towns were self-supporting, and not long after they were contributing not only to weaker societies in the territory but also to foreign missions. Literary and library associations sprang up in every town, and agricultural societies in every organized county." [7]

During the week that the monks came to Minnesota several colonies arrived: three hundred Yankees from New York state moved to Mankato while another group headed for a settlement east of Elk River and St. George's Prairie; two colonies from Pennsylvania arrived bound for Crow River and Glencoe; another from Ohio moved up the Rum river; while settlers arrived at Lake Minnetonka to take over the town named after the Hutchinson family. [8]

The *Pioneer and Democrat* claimed with hasty optimism that this movement to Minnesota was unparalleled in the history of territories and states, with the exception of that to California, which was not lasting. It would require the utmost effort, the editors continued, to find a "returned Minnesotan" in the East. In 1855 settlements fanned back from the western bank of the Mississippi river up to the Falls of St. Anthony. In 1856 the rush was to the Minnesota river valley and up the Mississippi to Sauk Rapids. Two steamers, scarcely equal to the demand, were already running between St. Anthony Falls and Sauk Rapids, while the river business at St. Paul in the first two months of spring, 1856, equalled all of the former year, with two hundred steamers coming into port during April and May alone. [9]

The passengers of the 'Minnesota Belle' remained on board overnight on May 2, and at four o'clock the next morning Prior Demetrius and the cleric Bruno Riess struck out to find the bishop's residence, while the others remained to guard the luggage. They had little difficulty in locating the three story brick dwelling on the corner of Wabasha and Sixth streets, and as Holy Mass was being celebrated by Bishop Cretin in his 'cathedral' on the second floor of the building, they first assisted at the Mass, and then sought out the gentle and holy missionary ordinary of their frontier home. Cretin was overjoyed that they had come, received them most kindly, put two rooms in his dwelling on the third floor at their disposal and, as di Marogna recorded, "in characteristic French style fetched our belongings with his own horses." [10]

It was arranged that the Benedictines would remain with Bishop Cretin for two weeks until the spring Ember Days at which time he would ordain the two clerics to the priesthood. There were language difficulties since the bishop and his clergy conversed in English or in French which the prior could manage, while the two clerics refused to speak except in German. The bishop and his vicar general, Augustine Ravoux, were amazed that Wimmer would send but one priest and two unordained clerics, and Father Demetrius began at once to entreat Abbot Boniface to send another priest who could speak English. These petitions for more help were never-ending, and carry through the correspondence of these early years like a constant refrain.

Bishop Joseph Cretin

The two Brothers went to work at once for the bishop, helping around the gardens, repairing the building, and doing carpentry work for the Sisters of St. Joseph at their new hospital directly across the street from the German church of the Assumption which was then being constructed by the Reverend George Keller, sole German priest in the entire diocese. The only mishap that occurred was on one warm spring day when Brother Patrick, who did not have any beer at hand, drank too much water and became sick. The bishop was very pleased with the industry and generosity of the Brothers, while the monks were deeply impressed with the kindness and holiness of the bishop's household:

"The bishop and his household lead a cloistered existence, in which we can see our own mirrored beforehand. He is in everything an example from early morning (4:30) until evening (9:00). Frugality bordering on poverty reigns in the whole house. The clergy, church helpers and school teachers are all French. The kitchen, stables and workshops are in the hands of the Irish. English is the ordinary language of the house. The French here all speak fluent English, but with a miserable accent. An English sermon in this church is ear-splitting. The bishop is easiest to understand. Last Sunday evening, after May devotions, the bishop gave a eulogy on the Benedictines. He announced our arrival and purpose to the congregation, and urged them as well as all good Catholics to give us a helping hand. I had Benediction afterwards, and as we were going in he remarked that he considered our arrival as a wondrously quick response to the prayers he had been sending to Mary and her Son. Not long before he had requested the congregation to implore Mary for workers in the Lord's vineyard; and now more had come in one group than he had dared to hope for either in the present or future.

"At this point, Father Abbot, I must not conceal from myself the difficulties of our project! Will we be equal to these hopes which the people have for us? Will we meet these expectations? Will we, in a word,

29

measure up? I trust in Him who dwells in my innermost being, and who knows how I fear Him. With the *Rule* and the *Statutes* in our hand, while holding fast to the course charted therein, we shall succeed, if our plan is from God: we are, after all, only tools in the hands of the Craftsman." [11]

In this way was begun the reciprocally friendly and understanding relationship between the diocese of St. Paul and its first monastic foundation which has continued and developed to the present time. In time St. John's would be separated from St. Paul when new dioceses were formed from the original mother diocese. But it would never be forgotten that Minnesota's monastery was nurtured in Bishop Cretin's household, and that its first priests ordained in the territory were sent forth from his cathedral.

Prior Demetrius made an especially good impression on Bishop Cretin and his clergy. His cultivated manners, command of languages and priestly zeal marked him as an exceptional acquisition to the diocese. He preached to the congregation of the cathedral parish as well as to the German Catholics of the other parish in the city, that of the Assumption. He gave conferences and heard the confessions of the Sisters of St. Joseph, and the bishop gave him the faculties of the diocese which were to be valid until revoked.

The two young clerics, however, did not fare so well. Prior Demetrius explained to Abbot Wimmer what happened when the bishop examined them in theology preparatory to ordination:

". . . The bishop has given them one examination already. The results were mediocre, and their clumsy manners were still more disturbing. The bishop was so disturbed that he perspired. In the goodness of his heart he excused them as well as he could. He excused their clumsiness, but let us know that they were made too much of. I promised him that I would continue their instruction, and protected them, offering as excuses their distraction caused by travel, their different manner of speaking, etc." [12]

Bruno Riess, in turn, offered his interpretation of the examinations:

". . . We had to take two examinations, and if the bishop had more time he would have given us three, namely one examination for each order since he is very strict in observing the rubrics. The first was in English and the second one was in Latin. The Most Rev. Bishop, who is himself the examiner, took through practically all the branches of theology, and all this briefly and without any order. First there was a question of Moral Theology, then in Church History, Dogma, Canon Law, Holy Scripture of the Old and New Testament, and especially Liturgy. He demands quick answers, for he has hardly given the question before he wants the answer. If the first word of the answer doesn't hit the last word of the question, then he answers himself. He is quite a strict moralist and especially strict in liturgy. I am writing this for the benefit of those clerics who may perhaps be sent later on so they may know what kind of examination to prepare themselves for." [13]

Here was clean-cut evidence of the difference in attitude between Cretin and di Marogna on the one hand, both European trained, and the young immigrants, trained in one of America's first missionary seminaries where academic standards were at first, understandably, not so rigid. The clerics Bruno and Cornelius did not do so badly during the second examination, which Prior Demetrius also considered much more successful. They received their major orders on the Ember Days preceding Trinity Sunday, and were ordained to the priesthood on Trinity Sunday, 18 May 1856. Bishop Cretin expressed the wish that he might be able to ordain five Benedictines every Ember week for five years. He felt that he could best provide for his diocese in this way. Father Cornelius celebrated his first Holy Mass in the cathedral at nine o'clock for the German congregation, and Father Bruno had the late morning Mass for the congregation. Bishop Cretin gave them faculties for two years, and immediately put them to work, as Father Bruno recorded:

". . . On the afternoon of their ordination day they were ordered to taste the sweets of their vocation in the confessional. The same duty was assigned them on the morning of the Sunday on which they were to celebrate their first Holy Masses. After Mass a marriage was solemnized and several baptisms administered. Hardly had they sat down for dinner when one was ordered to accompany a funeral to the cemetery but to be back, unmistakably, by three o'clock for the celebration of Vespers. In the evening there were May devotions and Benediction of the Blessed Sacrament, and the bishop jokingly regretted that no sick call had been announced, which he certainly would have entrusted to me. So passed our first day in the active exercise of the priesthood." [14]

The Benedictines were now ready to establish their monastery. During their sojourn in St. Paul several new locations had been suggested to them by Bishop Cretin and the clergy as possible fields for settlement, such as Shakopee, Stillwater or Crow River. Catholic settlers were moving into these areas rapidly, and the bishop and his eleven priests would have welcomed a monastic establishment and parochial assistance in the region of St. Paul and the Minnesota river valley. Bishop Cretin wanted them to settle in St. Paul, and offered the thirty acres then laid out for a cemetery, the site where the Sisters of St. Joseph later built their convent. But the monks did not want to settle in a city. After three days of prayer, and because they were not acquainted with the other suggested locations, the Benedictines decided to choose the place first suggested by Father Pierz and Bishop Cretin to Abbot Wimmer, and they made preparation to move north toward Sauk Rapids. It was a happy decision. The organized Church in Minnesota was in its infancy, and there were pressing needs for missionary work in the southern and more densely populated section of the territory. But by moving nothwest into the central section of the territory, the Benedictines entered a virgin area where they had wide latitude for needed labors, freedom of movement for peaceful Christianizing and colonizing efforts, unhampered until a much later date by misunderstandings over jurisdiction. It is evident as well that Bishop Cretin eventually and wisely desired such a development.

On Monday, May 19, the party set forth accompanied by the bishop. They travelled in two sections; Father Bruno with the Brothers and the supplies went over to St. Anthony Falls where they boarded the steamer 'H.M. Rice' for Sauk Rapids, while Bishop Cretin and Fathers Demetrius and Cornelius made the seventy-eight mile journey by stage coach by way of Itasca, Elk River and Clear Lake. The bishop's party arrived in Sauk Rapids the next day, sought out Father Pierz's small log chapel, and moved in. Meanwhile the 'H.M. Rice' got as far on the first evening as the juncture of the Mississippi and Crow Rivers. The next morning fifty more passengers were taken on, despite the fact that it was a freighter with no passenger accommodations, no meals, not even chairs. For two days and one night Father Bruno and the Brothers sat on the trunks and other freight, all the while exposed to "ferocious attacks of mosquitoes and with nothing to eat." The boat landed about two miles below St. Cloud on the afternoon of May 20 where the Benedictines understood that all freight was to be unloaded, while the passengers were to land at St. Cloud. Father Bruno explained what then happened:

". . . About half of the freight was unloaded. Father Bruno and one of the Brothers were on shore attending to their baggage and the other Brother remained on board keeping guard over our cask of Mass wine for the little cask was an attraction to the deck hands. Before we who were on shore could realize our situation, the boat pushed off and made for Sauk Rapids. Now find a human habitation or even St. Cloud without roads or guides! The Brother remained with the baggage and Fr. Bruno set out to explore. To find St. Cloud was then a rather more difficult task than it would be today, comprising as it did one house and four less dignified edifices and these far apart. On the prairie Fr. Bruno met a Catholic German, a Mr. Lodermaier, who showed him the direction in which he would find St. Cloud and stated that he now stood upon the land intended for a monastery, the property or claim of two brothers by name of Rothkopp. At last he succeeded in engaging a vehicle which transferred the poor Brother and the baggage to St. Cloud. And so it occurred that the Benedictines made their entrance into St. Cloud on the evening of May 20." [15]

Father Bruno and the Brother found lodgings the first night with Joseph Edelbrock who had come to St. Cloud the year before and had opened the village's first general store. The next morning Prior Demetrius offered Holy Mass in the log chapel at Sauk Rapids. A note had been left there by Father Pierz for his expected Benedictines. In it he again revealed his simplicity and greatness of soul:

"Your Reverence!

St. Cloud
Arrival

"I leave to the Church in Sauk Rapids, first, four altar pictures; the Child Jesus, St. John the Baptist, Mater Dolorosa and Christus Coronatus, presented by a benefactor. I moreover leave of my personal property, as a present to Fr. Prior: 1 altar picture of the Assumption, 1 altar cloth, 2 altar hangings, 2 candle sticks, 1 altar bell, 1 Mass vestment, alb with amice and cincture, 2 Mass cruets.

Your Friend,
F. Pierz"

After Mass the prior crossed the Mississippi to St. Cloud. The ferry boat was rowed by a boy of thirteen years, Anthony Edelbrock, son of Anton Edelbrock, first German settler in St. Cloud. This same boy was one day to be the second abbot of St. John's. In St. Cloud Prior Demetrius contacted Father Bruno and the Brother at Joseph Edelbrock's place, and since the next day was the Feast of Corpus Christi, the Benedictines made arrangements to hold their public services for the first time in St. Cloud. The attic of Joseph Edelbrock's two-story frame building at the Mississippi end of the village's main street was prepared for the occasion, and Father Bruno again records the precious memoirs of that event of 22 May 1856:

". . . the altar was placed at one end under the apex of the gable to enable the celebrant to stand upright, but it was necessary, especially at the Elevation, to look upward lest he strike the roof. The narrow space could not contain all who had come for the services and so many were compelled to remain on the lower floor and that was fortunate. In the course of the solemnities they noticed that the ceiling — our floor — was giving way and improvised supports with fence rails. Otherwise we might have had a sad accident." [16]

These Catholics of central Minnesota thus met the Benedictines for the first time at holy Mass, and worshipped with them as they would so often and in so many places in the next hundred years. News had spread rapidly that the monks had come, and that they were there to stay. To the German Catholic on the American frontier there was no more important news than that a priest had arrived and that stable, orderly religious life was assured.[17] Bruno Riess explained, with considerable exaggeration, how the German Catholics of the St. Cloud area reacted:

"Up to the date of our arrival St. Clouders had not dreamt of making land claims — all looked so hopeless. But our appearance turned the tables and that very night the inhabitants of St. Cloud claimed and staked out the entire prairie between St. Cloud and the crossing of the Sauk River not leaving a single spot in the vicinity for us to locate upon." [18]

Who were these pioneer people of central Minnesota, what was their background and from where had they come?

The large majority of early settlers to the region moved into and around Sauk Rapids, a stopping place on the St. Paul–Fort Ripley mail route. It was on the left bank of the Mississippi opposite the junction of the Sauk and Mississippi rivers. The United States Land Office was located there, and its neighbor hamlet, St. Cloud, was not platted until 1854, a year before Stearns County was organized. The earliest settler was Ole Bergeson, a government surveyor, who located his claim in 1852. John L. Wilson, a native of Maine, who had been moving with the westward tide of immigration, building saw and flour mills, had erected a sawmill and house in Sauk Rapids during the same year as Bergeson's claim was made. He purchased this claim from the Norwegian squatter on the western bank of the Mississippi, platted a town site, and, as he told Bishop Otto Zardetti later, named the projected city in a way that was characteristic of his romantic and optimistic nature:

"It was, as he told us, some time in July or August, 1853, that he had hired two young Frenchmen to put up a fence inclosing what thereafter became the plat of the town of St. Cloud. The weather at this time being very unsettled and cloudy. Mr. Wilson, who had always taken great interest in literature, spent his lonely leisure hours in reading of the campaign of Napoleon Bonaparte in Russia. The edition of the work was an English translation. He arrived at the point when an official messenger from Paris had reached Napoleon before Moscow, conveying to the emperor official state news. After having listened to him, Napoleon was anxious to hear something of his wife, the Empress Marie Louise, then residing in the imperial palace at St. Cloud (a suburb of Paris). Napoleon, therefore, turning to the messenger, said: 'How are things in St. Cloud?' Mr. Wilson had just read this passage when the two hired men put in an appearance and he jokingly repeated what he had just read and also addressed them as Napoleon had addressed the messenger: 'Boys, how are things in St. Cloud?' The two men found the name euphonic (Mr. Wilson pronounced it as if it were English) and furthermore being French themselves, found in its French origin some attraction. They often, when meeting Mr. Wilson, would ask: 'Mr. Wilson, how are things in St. Cloud?' This finally induced Mr. Wilson to give this townsite the name of St. Cloud, and so had it registered in the Benton Co. courthouse, Stearns County not yet existing." [19]

Wilson was eager, as thousands of other town platters on the frontier, to have his site develop, and he gave lots away to the first German settlers attracted to central Minnesota by Father Pierz. Some of these early Germans were craftsmen and preferred business instead of farming, or part-time work along with farming. In this way St. Cloud gradually grew

34

and became the center of trade and organized life in the area. It was picturesquely located high on a bluff overlooking the Mississippi, and served as the gateway to the northwest. There was not an organized county west of Stearns County as far as the Rocky Mountains, and Red River cart caravans moved through St. Cloud, county seat of Stearns County, toward the rich Red River valley. According to a map in the first issue of the St. Cloud *Advertiser* on 1 January 1857, the city's location was excellent as an extensive distributing point. There were not only the two rivers and the cart trails, but also Territorial roads which extended from St. Cloud in all directions: on the west side of the Mississippi to Minneapolis, on the east side to St. Anthony; toward the east to St. Croix Falls; to the north toward Lake Superior; one on each side of the river to Crow Wing, one northwest to Breckenridge and Dakota; one southwest to Fort Ridgely, where it interesected with the Government road to California; and one toward the south to Traverse des Sioux, or St. Peter in the Minnesota River valley.

The first Catholic to settle in St. Cloud was Joseph Keough, a native of County Wexford, Ireland, who came to Sauk Rapids in 1849 and established his homestead in 1853 within the present limits of St. Cloud. Then Anton Edelbrock and his family arrived in the fall of 1854 from Evansville, Indiana. German Catholics around Evansville had read Pierz's articles in the *Wahrheitsfreund,* and had delegated John W. Tenvoorde to journey to central Minnesota and to test the veracity of the missionary's descriptions. Apparently Tenvoorde gave a good report of the region since German Catholics began to move in from Indiana, and then from other Eastern states during the years 1854–57.[20] Tenvoorde returned with his family in the summer of 1855, fortified by a gift of lots from Wilson and bringing him a stock of goods for a store. He later replaced his original log cabin store with a large frame building which was the city's boarding hotel and restaurant. Anton Edelbrock's brother Joseph also came in 1855, and like the other two Indiana Germans, opened a store, while obtaining the government contract for postal service in the new city. Other early German settlers included Henry and Baltasar Rosenberger who opened a hardware store; John Metzroth, tailor; Xavier Braun, John Rengel and John Schwartz, farmers; Joseph Emmel, carpenter and church painter; Nicholas Lahr, blacksmith; and Wolfgang Eich, carpenter. These Germans settled in and around Wilson's 'Middle St. Cloud' and, as the German immigrants patronized the merchants there, the older Yankee or southern settlement lost out, and those establishments moved up from Lower Town. This did not mean that the new German Catholics gained control of the economy of central Minnesota by any means. Organized credit, position and power were and remained in the hands of the earlier 'Yankee' minority which included among others such shrewd business pioneers as Nehemiah P. Clarke, Lewis and William T. Clark, Charles A.

35

Gilman, Freeland H. Dam, Josiah E. West, General Henry Z. Mitchell, and Stephen Miller, later governor of Minnesota.[21]

Two brothers, Louis and Wilhelm Rothkopp, had come to central Minnesota from the Prussian Rhineland with the first group of German immigrants in 1854. They had made two 160 acre claims along the Mississippi river about two miles south of Wilson's town, and had declared that they would give these claims to the Benedictines when they arrived. These elderly brothers were deeply religious and generous, but at the same time eccentric, impractical recluses who were unacquainted with American legal procedures, as the monks were to learn to their sorrow. Their claims, however, were strategically located on a bend in the river which was the levee for St. Cloud river traffic. Of the 320 acres, 140 were rich bottom land, ten were wooded islands in the Mississippi directly out from the claims, and the rest was sandy prairie soil lying on a terrace thirty feet above the bottom land. This half section ran a half mile along the river and a half mile inland.

Father Bruno visited the Rothkopp brothers in their two small huts on the claims, and discussed with them their offer to transfer ownership. They had been offered $3,000 for their claims by St. Cloud 'Yankees,' but they wanted to donate them to the Church. The two brothers asked only, in return for their gift, that they be allowed to live with the community as charges of the monastery until death, receiving during that time board, room and clothing. They promised to do what work they could, and in addition requested that the monastery accept the responsibility of educating their nephew and niece. Prior Demetrius agreed to this arrangement on May 27, and Wilhelm gave a quit-claim deed for his 160 acres to the prior, while Louis gave his to Father Cornelius, and both deeds were entered in the clerk of court's office in St. Cloud. The Benedictines were to pay the government $400 for these claims at $1.25 an acre when the government decided to sell the land. During the following week the five Benedictines moved in with the Rothkopp brothers.

The Rothkopps had erected two small log cabins on their claims; one was 12x12, barely six feet high to the eaves, and contained a single pane of glass rudely inserted between the logs; the other cabin was of similar dimensions and stood a short distance away. Seven people had to live in these two primitive cabins until the monks could cover the intervening space between the buildings with wooden rafters on which they packed straw and hay. This addition was to be their first chapel. Brother Benno did the carpentry work, Brother Patrick served as cook and domestic, and the three priests helped throughout that first summer whenever they returned from the missions. Gradually, with help from St. Cloud Catholic men, they completed a kitchen and a frame building to extend their structure to a frontage of seventy-two

36

feet along the river bank.[22] It looked like a warehouse or a boarding house. Both immigrants and river hands often had to be fed. They came up the sixty feet from the river to the monastery for accommodations since boats could move no farther north than the levee at their property.

Prior Demetrius was exultant at first and considered the property to have been set aside for them by Providence. He decided to name the site 'Morning Star' in honor of Mary the Mother of God, and to dedicate the chapel to St. Boniface as a tribute to Abbot Wimmer. The people of the region called it the 'Priester Wald.' Di Marogna caught the fever of the expanding frontier from the very beginning, as he told Abbot Boniface: "Here everything is not in a hurry but at a storm pace. Whoever does not keep up with the storm appears unimportant, is ridiculed and loses the golden opportunity which never returns."[23] He planned to construct a warehouse for river freight on their levee, the first tannery in Minnesota, and a mill. This could be done, he entreated Wimmer, if only more Brothers would be sent, and at once. Their wood could be turned into cash by the sale of fence poles. More than this, he entered with an almost frenzied intensity, to his later regret, into plans for platting their land as a town site or addition to St. Cloud.

Father Bruno was equally optimistic. He reported to St. Vincent on Independence Day, 1856:

". . . As far as the location of the land is concerned, it could not be better. It lies for a mile along the river which is so studded here with islands that the place is called 'Thousand Islands,' and protected against floods. The river is navigable for five months and the boats pass through and land at our place, since they can only go up the river when the water is high. What could be more pleasant and desirable? We have lime, clay, and a granite quarry on our land. The cattle here are large and wonderful, and I haven't seen any nicer. Briefly, I am not exaggerating when I say that everything thrives that is planted and sown. We miss only one thing, and that is the bedbugs. These do not thrive, for although we brought enough luggage along for them to settle down here, it did not help. The climate does not suit them. They do not last a month. They all die. . . . But we do not even have the prospect of improving the land for the next year if we do not get a few Brothers immediately. We have pasture enough here for sixty head of cattle and are not able to have one cow because we have no fence material and cannot buy hay even though we have a hundred acres of pasture land. The same holds true for hogs. We have not even one hen, so we are, in spite of the richness of the land, in dire poverty and cannot make any progress as long as we have to buy the necessities of life."[24]

The first year was, indeed, one of dire poverty. Prior Demetrius, with little business acumen, paid out their precious money at exorbitant rates for hired helpers on his surveying, platting and improving projects. Meanwhile the Benedictine household was living on a little wheat and corn for bread, coffee, a few strips of bacon now and then, and potatoes every day. All of these items had to be purchased at first.[25]

The prior lacked the aristocrat's sensitivity for finding just the proper note. He was a severe disciplinarian with the members of the community, exacting in religious exercises, and ever conscious of his responsibility to instill Benedictine ideals. But he could not engender fatherly love and respect. His Benedictine apprenticeship had been too brief, his rise too abrupt. He was ever the individualist, conscious of his ability and background, suspicious, impractical and aloof. At the same time, while not loved, he was highly respected on all sides as an extraordinary acquisition in frontier society. From the very beginning a flood of letters continued to reach Abbot Boniface Wimmer from his Minnesota monks concerning the differences of opinion at the priory. Relations were particularly difficult between the prior and Father Bruno. The latter was young, headstrong and influenced by the spirit of freedom of the open plains. Father Alexius Hoffmann, O.S.B., first historian of St. John's, characterized Father Bruno as a good priest *sans reproche* who was at the same time most energetic. Abbot Wimmer would often be criticized for sending his young monks forth to engage in widely diversified missionary responsibilities before they had matured sufficiently for spiritual leadership. His old friend, Father Benedict Haindl, who was one of the first to volunteer for his American experiment, and who would later come to Minnesota as one of the priors of these years, warned Wimmer of this danger:

". . . The fact is that we young priests on the parishes and missions will soon gain contact with the worldly and it will be impossible for us to conform to the *Holy Rule* as we should. The case with the religious clergy here in America is not the same as in Germany. When one of the Fathers in Germany goes out of the monastery in order to do business, he is always able, after two or three hours, to return, and then has the remainder of the week to catch up with his monastic life. He has to do so whether he wants to or not. We, however, in this country have to move around for days and weeks in the world, and when we come home, what incentive is there at home to comply with the *Holy Rule* when there are pastors and missionaries together? Each one will be his own boss and get up and retire whenever he wants to. Doesn't the Providence of God amount to anything any more? Does not Our Lord say that not a hair of our head falls without the knowledge and will of God? Doesn't the good God perhaps know and take into consideration the work which you have started with such great effort and have continued up to the present? Do you not think that God does not perhaps know how you started all this? I am living in the firm conviction that from the very beginning it was the will of God and that it still is. Therefore I think that this work should be continued as it was begun." [26]

38

1 *Abbot Boniface Wimmer, founder of the American Cassinese Benedictines.*

2 *Monte Cassino, cradle of the Order of St. Benedict.*

3 *Metten Abbey on the Danube,*
where Wimmer's life as a Benedictine began.

4 *St. Vincent Abbey in 1855.*

5 Bishop Joseph Cretin
invited the Benedictines to Minnesota.

6 Father Francis Pierz, Minnesota Indian missionary.

7 The two pioneer Benedictine clerics
were ordained in St. Paul's first cathedral.

8 *First prior of Minnesota's monastery,*
Demetrius di Marogna.

9 *Fathers Cornelius Wittmann and Bruno*
Riess, companions of Prior Demetrius.

10 Prior Othmar Wirtz.

11 Prior Benedict Haindl.

12 Father Clement Staub.

13 Rupert Seidenbusch,
St. John's first abbot.

St. John's near St. Cloud

*14 St. Cloud Priory
on the Mississippi River, 1856.*

*15 1907: ruins of the priory
in St. Cloud.*

*16 John L. Wilson,
founder of the city of St. Cloud.*

*17 Looking west toward the first St. Mary's
Church on St. Germain Street, St. Cloud.*

*18 Brother 'Taddy'
on the Collegeville Road.*

*19 Indianbush farm and priory,
at present Collegeville station.*

*20 Monastic candidates
'at work' in the fields, 1886.*

*21 Old Stone House,
first building on present site.*

22 *Old Stone House and two buildings still in use.*

23 *Frame structure moved from Indianbush and Old Stone House.*

24 *The monastery's future expansion as envisioned by Abbot Rupert.*

Here was the central problem of missionary Benedictinism that would develop only with the years. It was a struggle for souls, in response to the needs of the Church, and for their own Benedictine principles. The problem of the founding fathers of Benedictinism in America lay in their very firstness. They had to make all initial decisions. They had the major task of establishing monastic life in the wilderness, first in Pennsylvania, then in Minnesota and Kansas. Not only did they have to establish a monastery, but at every step they had to consider the crucial problem of establishing precedents for the future in regard to mission work, education, and active life. Differences of opinion were, accordingly, inevitable. They were confronted with the dilemma of preserving their traditions and serving the needs of the Church on a fluid frontier in modern times. Each had to meet the problem head on, and at St. John's the problem continued throughout the nineteenth century.

Yet these same men achieved virtually both ideals, for they firmly established their cloister while accomplishing notable work for Church and society. These first Benedictines made no mistakes of a serious nature. A kind of monumental obviousness about their assets appears. Their accomplishments emerge more distinctly as the years go on. They managed the debut of St. John's, solved its first concrete problems, gave content to Benedictinism on the frontier, and made it stable and institutionalized. This was their true contribution.

But at first the problems were many. Bishop Cretin had transferred the six mission stations of central Minnesota from Father Pierz to the Benedictines. Their jurisdiction embraced six hundred square miles, and in case of sick calls two thousand four hundred square miles. The first and largest mission was in St. Cloud. Here, on 17 August 1855, Father Pierz had arranged for the purchase of nineteen lots from Wilson for $500, and Catholic men of the community had half completed a church before the arrival of the Benedictines. In June of 1856 Father Bruno conducted the first Sunday services there which included Confessions, High Mass, Sermon, Catechism, Vespers. Father Cornelius first cared for St. Augusta and Sauk Rapids, while Prior Demetrius offered Mass for the Brothers and any settlers who wished to come to the rude chapel at the monastery. In July, Father Bruno began to visit the missions at St. Joseph, St. James Prairie and Richmond, while Father Cornelius took over at St. Cloud, finished the church, formed a congregation, and cared for St. Augusta and Sauk Rapids as missions.[27] A correspondent in the New York *Katholische Kirchenzeitung* of 7 August 1856 wrote that there were already two hundred Catholics in St. Cloud.

In St. Joseph, St. James and Richmond all did not go so smoothly at first. At St. Joseph a log church and house were already erected and the people had set aside land for the parish; a log chapel stood in St.

39

James or Jacobs Prairie; and Richmond had a similar structure not under roof. But some of the people of these places, especially in St. Joseph, were disturbed that the Benedictines were coming, and feared the latter would impose community ownership in their hard-won missions. These people did not want the monks to acquire title to the best land of the area and establish farm tenancy as had happened in Europe. Father Bruno, who had to face their first coldness, records succinctly:

". . . a few turbulent spirits agitated against the expected monks and went so far as to send a petition to the bishop of St. Paul, begging him not to inflict the monks upon them, and not to permit them to come to St. Joseph. In consequence, the misguided hotheads had no services until August. . . . At St. James and Richmond both congregations had no services during that summer for the same reason." [28]

This was merely a passing phenomenon, and not typical in any way of the Catholics of the area, or of St. Joseph itself. In a short time Father Bruno was speaking of St. Joseph as "a very active, entirely German and entirely Catholic settlement. It is a little town which promises to be something." The young missionary informed Wimmer:

". . . New settlers arrive here daily and all are German Catholics who come from other states where they lived among non-Catholics without a church and without a priest. They came here because they heard that they will find here what they missed so greatly there. The great majority of these are good, practical Catholics. How happy they were when they heard that I would give them my services regularly. They covered not only my hands but even my religious habit with kisses and tears of joy. Old men come to me with their difficulties even on the street and beg me with tears to remain with them saying: 'Father, stay with us. We poor sinners do not deserve this grace in any way, but have pity on innocent children.' What will happen to them if they are without a priest and grow up without any instruction?" [29]

The Benedictines decided that before organizing the parishes they would prepare the people spiritually and at the same time inform them that the monks had no intention of taking over large sections of the good land in the area. To accomplish their purpose they invited the well-known and saintly Jesuit missionary of that time, Francis Xavier Weninger, to conduct missions in all their parishes. He was an ardent and magnetic preacher from Austria who carried on a ceaseless apostolate of giving missions in German, French and English-speaking parishes across the United States for some forty years. He had been at St. Vincent, was known to Prior Demetrius from his Illinois days, and could help the Benedictines inaugurate regularized Catholic life. Infrequent services and instructions, irregular procedures by Father Pierz in the ownership of Church properties, and the general irreligious atmosphere of nineteenth century America all combined to point up the wisdom of this decision.[30] Weninger was a major influence in uniting especially the German Catholics on the frontier. He gave them a Catholic sense and determination where before they were separate and dissonant. His system of carefully planned missions with four sermons a day, erection of a mission cross in each station, inaugurating of processions with songs and prayers in the mother tongue, all did much in spreading the kingdom of God in the United States.

When Weninger arrived in St. Cloud he spoke with praise of the Benedictine establishment, of Prior Demetrius' firmness of character, which he considered a God-send for St. Cloud and all the surrounding country, and of the organized religious life which a stable monastery could supply. He said:

". . . I visited the Fathers in their frame cabin, quite a contrast with the splendid abbeys of Europe. . . . Not even the Prior's cell had a door. Mosquitoes and all kinds of vermin had free admittance. Yet all the members of the community were cheerful and busy." [31]

Father Bruno accompanied Father Weninger as he conducted missions in St. Cloud, St. Augusta, St. Joseph, Jacobs Prairie and Richmond. The mission at St. Joseph was especially successful, and Prior Demetrius proceeded to appoint Father Bruno resident pastor there, with Jacobs Prairie and Richmond as missions. Father Weninger preached the sermon at Father Bruno's installation on the Feast of the Assumption, a day which brought the first serious test of the settlers' faith and courage:

"The 15th of August, on which day Fr. Weninger preached a sermon in St. Joseph, was the beginning of a two years after-mission sent by Divine Providence. During the discourse of the missionary a heavy darkness set in, accompanied, as we thought by a tremendous hail storm, the clatter of which drowned the voice of the preacher. But it was something worse than hailstones, for when we left the church our eyes beheld nothing but greedy grasshoppers, which had darkened the sun and in their descent had struck so heavily upon the roof of our church.

"This small, voracious, yet invincible monster had in a short time devastated all that grows and blooms upon the face of the earth. Within about two or three days the fields presented the appearance of having been newly plowed. Then indescribable misery entered the homes of the poor settlers of Stearns County. The entire harvest was a dead loss for those settlers who had taken their abode in this region during the previous year (1855); those, of course, who had settled during the year of the famine, had no crop to lose, as they had not planted any. The first terrible winter was at hand. The few victuals that remained were soon consumed, prices rose enormously, because the nearest market was St. Paul, and it required a full week to make a trip with an ox-team. Still hope did not die. What would man be without hope? Spring came; seed wheat stood at $2.00 a bushel, but it was bought

41

and sown. But the new brood of grasshoppers suffered nothing to grow except peas. Everything else became their prey. They found their way into the houses and destroyed what clothing they could reach. In the church not a shred of cloth remained exposed; everything was locked up in presses. Even the priest at the altar was not secure from their attacks; before Mass the hoppers had to be swept from the altar. The priest had to vest hastily, place the altar linen upon the altar and be careful to keep the Sacred Host covered with the paten, and at the elevation had to leave the pall upon the chalice. During Mass the altar boys were kept busy driving away the insolent insects with whips from the vestments of the priest.

Go West
Young
Monks

"For another year the poverty-stricken farmers had to live upon their own substance and that was little. . . ."[32]

This first plague of Rocky Mountain locusts or grasshoppers was a severe blow to the struggling Benedictine house on the Mississippi river below St. Cloud as well as to their hard-hit missions. Prior Demetrius had to borrow money for the monastery food, and he considered himself fortunate to find cash at 36% interest. If he had borrowed from the St. Cloud 'Yankees' he would have had to accept interest rates from 50% up. Corn in the husks went at $2.00 per bushel, as did frozen potatoes. At the monastery corn was ground in coffee mills to prevent waste, and then boiled together with frozen potatoes for the ordinary meal. There was an abundance of game, but the Benedictines had no money to purchase powder or shot. They once succeeded in capturing a few owls which they found delicious, and as they could always fish in the river, they did not starve.

In the meantime the chapel at the monastery in St. Cloud was finished and dedicated on the Feast of St. John the Baptist, 24 June 1856. Prior Demetrius changed his mind about the names 'Morning Star' or 'St. Boniface' and, in memory of the fact that St. Benedict had dedicated his first chapel on Monte Cassino to John the Baptist, the monks decided to name their little house of prayer after St. John, patron of the missions. Father Bruno said that "as the tidings of salvation were first preached from the banks of the Jordan, now they were to spread westward from the banks of the Mississippi." The Minnesota monastery never completely lost this name of St. John's in the following years, despite the fact that the foundation received several official titles as it changed locations. The pioneers always referred to the foundation as St. John's and in the end this name and patron prevailed.

As soon as the chapel was finished the prior began common, public recitation of the Divine Office, official prayer of the Church. St. Benedict had called this daily praying together by his monks of the psalms, lessons, hymns and collects in their age-old liturgical cycles, the 'Work of God' to which nothing else was to be preferred in the monastery. If any one distinctive activity characterizes the Benedictines in the history

42

of the Church it is this prayer life in common. From the very beginning, as soon as there was a chapel, the Minnesota monks began their traditional work, and they continued it from that 24 June 1856, at great sacrifice and for the love of God, whenever there were two or more of them together in the monastery. In his old age Father Bruno reminisced about the place of the Divine Office in the history of St. John's:

". . . Although we were but three priests, worked hard throughout the day and had poor fare, choir was never intermitted, even if only two priests were at home. And this exertion, I must confess, did not shorten the life of any of us. Two of us are still alive, and Father Demetrius, in spite of the effort choir attendance cost him, reached a venerable age. Let the rising generation remember that the service of God does not shorten life." [33]

Letters continued to come to Abbot Wimmer from his Minnesota foundation begging him to come West and discover at first-hand what conditions were like. Those whom he had sent as missionaries wanted to see him again, to feel his indomitable spirit, and wanted especially to receive additional manpower which they were entreating him to bring along. The Minnesota monks stated many times that they did not want monetary assistance from St. Vincent, that they would provide for their needs as best they could. But they did need more Brothers to improve the buildings, the farm and the claims; even more they needed several priests to undertake urgent missionary labors. Abbot Boniface set forth on his first of many trips to the West in the late fall of 1856, and brought with him the Reverend Alexius Roetzer, O.S.B., newly ordained; Frater Paul Stenger, O.S.B., a theologian; and four Brothers: Wolfgang Beck, O.S.B., Vincent Hoermann, O.S.B., Roman Veitl, O.S.B., and Veremund Erhard, O.S.B. The party arrived in St. Cloud on the mail stage after midnight, and made their way to the monastery, reaching it at five o'clock in the morning of October 23. Prior Demetrius had passed them unknown on his way to St. Paul where he was forced to go to purchase winter provisions since the controlling group in St. Cloud had demanded prices that were exorbitant. Again it is Father Bruno who preserved the precious memory of Wimmer's entrance to the priory at St. Cloud:

". . . he arrived at 5 o'clock in the morning, to visit us for the first time and entering our house while we were in choir, he was greatly pleased and edified at the disposition and religious zeal which prevailed. He did not interrupt our prayers, but patiently waited behind the curtain-door of our chapel, until we had finished our Office, and the two Brothers had recited the Rosary in the kitchen." [34]

Wimmer was overjoyed at the developments and prospects of the foundation. In fact, he became deeply attached to Minnesota from the very beginning, and declared to both Abbot Utto Lang, O.S.B., of Metten, and to his Roman agent, Abbot Angelo Pescetelli, O.S.B., that he

43

liked Minnesota best of all his houses. If he were not re-elected again in 1858 he planned to come to Minnesota to start another abbey there, or be a missionary to the Indians. Bishop Josue M. Young of Erie, realizing this attachment of Abbot Boniface, told him: "I fear Minnesota will have more attraction for you than Pennsylvania." [35]

Go West Young Monks

The main reason why Wimmer had personally come to Minnesota was to look at the claims Father Bruno wanted to establish on land four miles out of St. Joseph. Father Bruno had never been convinced that their St. Cloud site was suitable for a monastery because it lacked both wood and pasture land. He felt the seminary and college should be started there, but that the monastery should be near St. Joseph, along the Watab river where a thousand newly surveyed acres could be claimed. Prior Demetrius would allow Father Bruno only one day a week to explore these prairie and wooded lands, and the latter spent each Monday tramping through the territory with a parishioner as companion.

While Wimmer was awaiting the return of Prior Demetrius from St. Paul he went with Fathers Bruno and Cornelius to St. Joseph and thence into the Watab lands. This area was called the 'Indianbush' because it had but recently been the hunting grounds of Sioux and Chippewa Indians, who still made occasional forays through it. They walked Indian fashion through the area, badly scratching themselves on the dense underbrush, but becoming more excited each hour over the excellent timber and beautiful meadow of wild hay which grew higher than their heads. Wimmer, practical and far-seeing as always, determined then and there that this land must be obtained. Eight claims were to be made, four in the names of the new Brothers from St. Vincent, and the other four in the names of Father Alexius, Frater Paul, Brother Benno and Brother Patrick. Father Bruno also had claimed another 240 acres near St. Joseph, 160 acres of prairie and 80 acres of forest, which he felt would be ideal for a convent of Benedictine Sisters when they would arrive in Minnesota.

It is to the foresight and shrewdness of Bruno Riess primarily that St. John's owes its permanent location. He it was who first saw the possibilities of the 'Indianbush,' who pressed for permission to obtain it, and who directed the work of erecting claim shacks on each 360 acres. When Prior Demetrius returned to the monastery he strove to convince the abbot of the necessity of obtaining additional wooded land on the Mississippi islands. Wimmer authorized this venture as well because he could never resist the temptation to obtain land, which he ever maintained was a monastery's natural life blood. When the Rothkopp claims were contested and the monks were in danger of losing everything, it was the 'Indianbush' claims along the Watab, Bruno Riess' claims, which saved the community.

Wimmer purchased a cow and a pig for the community, left them a little money, and prepared to return East. He visited Bishop Cretin in St. Paul and received written authorization from him to establish the monastery as soon as possible. Not only was this Cretin's ardent desire, but he also asked Wimmer to consider establishing another monastery at Crow Wing, eighty miles north of St. Cloud, which would care for the Indians. Pierz was growing old and could not care for the Indians of the northern waterways, and the bishop desired to arrange for stable spiritual ministration there such as the Benedictines had supplied in central Minnesota. Wimmer welcomed this second proposal, told the bishop his monks must first care for the German immigrants, but if there were enough recruits, the monks would seize the opportunity of working among the Indians. This was the beginning of Indian missionary dreams which the second abbot of St. John's would realize.

The young Benedictine missionary, Alexius Roetzer, relieved Father Bruno of the congregations at St. James and Richmond, and Father Bruno took up residence in his parish at St. Joseph. Under his direction Brothers Vincent, Wolfgang, and Roman began during that first winter to erect their claim cabins and to take up residence in them. With the coming of spring Father Bruno and the three Brothers continued their exploration of the 'Indianbush' and the north Watab basin which Brother Wolfgang christened 'Schoenthal' or beautiful valley. It was in this way, and because they were so convinced of the worth and advantage of their cherished holdings, that they came upon and claimed the present site of St. John's. In St. John's literary lore its beauties have been the object of tributes in prose, verse and song. The qualities of this location for monastic and educational life have been acclaimed with undiminished enthusiasm for one hundred years. Father Bruno described their exploration and discovery of the Sagatagan site:

". . . In the course of this survey, we one day arrived on the shores of the beautiful lake, near where the University now stands. I was bound to acquire this sheet of water for the monastery. But how? Of course I must claim it. But how could I claim it? There were not enough of us to establish a legal claim besides those we already held. Eight men were required and we were but six. All, however, insisted that the lake must be ours. I might have easily sacrificed the two quarter sections of Sec. 31, because most of the woods had been badly scorched; but in that case the section would have to be broken, we would have lost an approach to the meadows and probably some undesirable neighbor might have wedged between our possessions. I was unable to lose hold of Sec. 6, on account of the timber on it. This put me in a quandary. Moreover, how was all this land to be paid for? We had no money on hand, debts enough on account of our provisions, and could expect nothing of the grasshopper-stricken congregations.

"In later years I was frequently reproached for not claiming more land west of the lake. Nowadays the eggs are always wiser than the hen.

45

At this juncture, a solution of this puzzle occurred to me. I had a personal friend in Washington, whom I requested to submit to Congress a petition for land for a monastery and a college, for the foundation of which Fr. Demetrius had already acquired a charter. At the same time I put up about twenty signs in different parts of the land I intended to claim, with the inscription: 'Application for this land is made to Congress for Saint John's College.' These signs effectively kept off intruders. My application to Congress was unsuccessful but we were no longer disturbed by land-sharks." [36]

Go West Young Monks

Meanwhile the Benedictines began at once to establish schools as they had traditionally done wherever they colonized. After Mass on the Feast of the Immaculate Conception, 8 December 1856, Father Cornelius, pastor of St. Cloud, opened the first school of that city in a small frame building owned by Joseph Edelbrock. It was a parish elementary school which at the same time inaugurated free public education in central Minnesota, as William A. Boerger, a superintendent of schools in Stearns County, testified:

"About a Roman Catholic priest, a zealous, devoted and self-sacrificing man, centers the history of the Stearns county schools. In the days when the city of St. Cloud was but a pitiful little string of shanties and equally unpretentious places of business, anchored against a high bank overlooking the Mississippi river; where the pioneers crossed rutty and unpaved roads on slabs laid at intervals in the mud, and all the rest of Stearns county was an uninhabited wilderness, the settlers found in their midst — for he was among the first to come — a young priest, the Reverend Father Cornelius Wittmann, O.S.B. He had come to minister to the wants of a number of Catholics who hailed from various eastern states, and had scattered widely over the territory newly ceded to the Government by the Indians. It is needless to say that his hands were of the proverbial fullness!

"However, despite his large missionary field and innumerable duties, this zealous young man, observing the utter absence of institutions of learning, added to his already long list of strenuous labors the hard task of teaching school. It was in the dwelling of Joseph Edelbrock, who, with the openhanded generosity of pioneers, cheerfully donated the use of one of the rooms, that Father Cornelius, in the early fall of 1856, taught the first school within the present boundaries of Stearns county. It was thus a free school in the fullest sense of the word, for no tuition was asked, and the teacher received no pay!" [37]

Twenty-five sons and daughters of the pioneers were his pupils, and Father Cornelius conducted this school while acting as pastor and missionary. Father Bruno at St. Joseph in the same way established the second school, acting as schoolmaster himself at first, and then securing the services of Nicholas Hoffmann. The Benedictine missionaries of Minnesota followed this pattern for years: the first pastor was the first

46

schoolteacher, and as the parish developed a man teacher was employed, in the German tradition, for the District School, which was usually built near the church, if the original log church structure itself was not used as a school.

But it was the task of Prior Demetrius to put into effect Wimmer's plan, namely, to establish a school in connection with the monastery, and to begin at once a liberal arts seminary program for training native vocations. This task stands out as the major pioneering accomplishment of these years. Here the educational attainments and background of di Marogna proved to be an enduring contribution to the new foundation and to Minnesota. He was successful in obtaining a charter for the first Catholic institution of higher education in Minnesota, which at the same time is the oldest Minnesota institution of higher education that has enjoyed uninterrupted existence. If the first prior had accomplished nothing else his significance would be marked.[38]

John L. Wilson, 'the father of St. Cloud,' was one of the three representatives from the Fifth Legislative District to the Minnesota Territorial Legislature in 1857. Prior Demetrius and he worked together in drawing up a proposed bill to incorporate the Order of St. Benedict in Minnesota, and to petition for a charter for St. John's Seminary. At the same time they planned to submit another bill for the incorporation of their cherished town plan as the 'Rothkopp Addition to the City of St. Cloud.' Wilson, who was a Democrat, introduced their petition for a charter as Bill Number 70 on 22 January 1857, and he championed it throughout the turbulent struggle ahead. Meanwhile Prior Demetrius had been called to St. Paul by Bishop Cretin, who was critically ill and had requested to see the prior. Father Demetrius gave the dying bishop general absolution and was with him during his last illness. At the same time he contacted Territorial Governor Willis A. Gorman, who was a baptized Catholic, sought and obtained his support of the charter for the first Catholic seminary and institution of higher learning in Minnesota. Prior Demetrius also moved among the members of the Legislature and Council lobbying for the charter, and, as he told Abbot Boniface, talked with so many members that the bill became generally known.[39]

It was not long before the struggle over St. John's charter was on. The bill was tabled on February 5 and placed in the general files by the controlling Republican majority of the legislature. Then when the bill was brought before the Committee of the Whole, on a straight party vote, the last sentence of Section Two of the bill was amended. This sentence originally had read: "that also good talented boys of the poorer classes may enjoy the benefit of said institution." It was altered to read: "no student shall be required to attend the religious worship of any particular denomination, except as specified by the student, his parent or guardian."[40] On February 9 a motion on the floor of the

47

House to reconsider the committee's amendment was defeated by a tie vote of fourteen Democrats for and fourteen Republicans against. Wilson records that the charter was "fought desperately" in the House by three Protestant Ministers in the Republican camp. They were the Reverends Wentworth Hayden from Champlin in the Eleventh District, Warren J. Howell of Canton who had initiated the amendment to Section Two, and Edward Thomas from the Eighth District. Three Democratic Catholic lawyers, in turn, defended the bill. The first was Francis Baasen whose Luxemburger father in Milwaukee was a patron and friend of the Benedictines. Francis Baasen was a lawyer from New Ulm who later became first secretary of state of Minnesota. The second was John J. McVey of the Sixth District. The third, Friend J. Whitlock from Belle Plaine, was most active in defense "and spoke up in favor of his religion with great fire," Prior Demetrius declared.[41] Whitlock adduced precedent, constructions of the Constitution and opinions of Chancellor Kent in support of his position. Other legislators who spoke in defense of the proposed charter for a Catholic institution of higher learning were Judge Luther M. Brown of Shakopee; Joseph R. Brown, publisher of the *Minnesota Pioneer;* William Pitt Murray, St. Paul lawyer, who had sponsored Hamline University's charter three years previously, and in whose honor Murray County was named.

The opposition to St. John's charter on either political or religious grounds is difficult to understand in view of the earlier charter voted without such amending to Hamline University, which was operated under the direction of the Methodist Church. Yet such opposition did exist and was supported by such individuals as Charles Powell Adams, M.D., later mayor of Hastings; Lucas Kingsbury Stannard, Taylor Falls lawyer; Thomas A. Thompson of Plainview, superintendent of schools in Wabasha County for three terms; Mahlon Black, postmaster of Stillwater; and Elam Greeley, sawmill operator in that same city. It was an obvious effort, under the guise of a so-called religious latitudinarianism, to keep legal status from any Catholic educational effort. Such movements were not new in American history. Its eventual failure on Minnesota soil is a tribute to the sound understanding by the charter's defenders of true principles of religious and educational liberty as established in the American Constitution. The defense by members of the Democratic party was also another indication during these years of that party's support of immigrants and their interests. Abbot Wimmer was a staunch Democrat, as were the early Benedictines in Minnesota and the large majority of German Catholic immigrants of Central Minnesota.

The charter bill, with its controverted religious amendment attached, had passed the House on February 13, and went to the Council of the Minnesota Territorial Legislature. Here the amendment was struck out and the bill quickly passed with seven of the eleven members supporting. Support came from John Ball Brisbin, president of the Council and mayor of St. Paul; William W. Wales, pioneer from St. Anthony Falls; Joel Bean Bassett, pioneer lumberman from Minneapolis; Henry George Bailly, Hastings; Lewis Stone, Langola; B. F. Tillotson, Oshawa; and the famed Joseph Rolette of Pembina, who notoriously, during this same session of the legislature, carried away the bill to remove the seat of government to St. Peter, and thus saved the state capitol for St. Paul. Against the charter in the Council were Henry Nolan Setzer, warden of the state prison at Stillwater; Alonzo D. Balcombe of Jordan; Samuel Dooley of Sand Creek; and P. P. Humphrey of Oshawa.

When the bill was returned to the House the fight was resumed, except for a slight interruption when members of the legislature attended the funeral of Bishop Joseph Cretin, who died on 22 February 1857. The Council's action in striking out the House's amendment added further complication to the issue. For now it was a question of preserving the honor of the House, and the bill was moved back and forth between the two bodies. Prior Demetrius let it be known that he would ask Wilson to withdraw the bill if the amendment were retained. Meanwhile Wilson was working to exchange votes among his friends who served with him on standing committees. He gained one vote from each of these three committees, namely: William Branch, St. Paul contractor, from the Committee on Territorial Expenditures; John McDonogh Berry, a lawyer from Faribault, from the Committee on Science and Literature; and Jonathan Chase, Minneapolis lumberman, from the Committee on Ferrys. Justus C. Ramsey, St. Paul, brother of Minnesota's first Territorial governor, also indicated that he would vote for the charter on final passage. The whole proceeding would have ended much earlier if it were not for the opposition of the Republican speaker of the House, Joseph W. Furber from Cottage Grove, who was the marshal of the Territory. He not only was against the charter from the very beginning, but carried his opposition to an unusual extreme. When Wilson was able to turn the tide, the House concurred in the Council amendment to strike out the controverted amendment, and the bill passed as originally drawn on 27 February 1857 by a vote of 24–12.[42] Speaker Furber then omitted to tear off the slip attached to the original charter and it became enrolled with the proviso although the bill had passed without it.

Wilson, the sole representative from Stearns County, was not able to gain legislative consideration of incorporation for the 'Rothkopp Addition to the City of St. Cloud' at this Eighth Session of the Legislature. This proved in time to be a fortunate development. But he obtained satisfaction to the end of his life over the St. John's Seminary Charter, which he considered to be the most important bill for Stearns County during the 1857 Legislative session.[43]

The signature of Governor Gorman was assured for two reasons.

First, he had stated to Prior Demetrius he would support the measure. Secondly, in his message to the legislature on 14 January 1857, he had spoken out not only in support of public schools but also favorably concerning private seminaries and colleges. He signed the act authorizing St. John's Seminary on 6 March 1857, and Wimmer could exclaim to his Roman confrere Pescetelli: "The banners of St. Benedict are now unfolded in the middle of the United States on the great Mississippi River." [44] Prior Demetrius, however, did not inaugurate the educational institution whose charter he obtained. St. John's Seminary and College was not set in motion until eight months after its charter was secured, and then it was by a new prior. During that spring and summer of 1857 the prior worked hard, however, at two further projects, one of which failed completely, while the other became in time one of the major influences in the development of Catholic life in the upper midwest.

The first of these two projects was the abortive Rothkopp city plan or addition to St. Cloud. Although Prior Demetrius' and Wilson's Bill to incorporate the site did not come before the Territorial Legislature, the prior all the while moved ahead with surveying and platting. The Rothkopp land at the public levee opposite Boom Island was divided into sixteen blocks, with ten lots to each block. Projected thoroughfares were laid out and picturesque names such as College, Boniface, St. Louis and Bavaria were given to the streets. The prior felt that sale of these lots would provide a steady source of income to meet current expenses, and afford them the opportunity of beginning construction of their monastery and college buildings. They could not spend another winter in their draughty wooden shelter with two stoves. It is difficult to understand why the prior was willing to have a city addition almost at the door of the monastery. Perhaps it was the only source of income he could foresee, since the Benedictines received only small offerings from the struggling congregations of immigrants. The first collection in St. Cloud, Sauk Rapids, and St. Augusta totaled $2.15, $1.00, and $1.13 respectively. Stipends for Holy Masses were offered at $.50. Request upon request kept pouring into the monastery for spiritual care in new missions while the bills mounted. At the same time there were many demands for the Rothkopp lots, and Prior Demetrius began to sell them at $100 to $200 a lot. First purchasers included Frank Schlick Sr. of St. Paul, the Reverend George Keller, pastor of the Assumption Church, St. Paul, and Frederick Kemper of St. Cloud.[45]

But all of this effort was in vain, and the community had to return every dollar received for lots. For Prior Demetrius and the pioneer Benedictines had entered into their agreement with the Rothkopp brothers before the latter had secured title to the land which they claimed. They acted precipitously, without legal advice and without knowledge of American legal procedures. Abbot Boniface pressed the Rothkopp brothers to apply for entry of their claims, and to comply with the pre-emption laws, but to no avail. They vacillated, agreed and then retracted, all the while obstinately convinced, in their ignorance, that they were somehow being duped. They delayed so long that finally everything was lost.

When Wilhelm and Ludwig Rothkopp had come to Minnesota in 1854 they claimed land which was still Winnebago Indian possession. Such land, however, could later be purchased, according to the pre-emption laws, if buildings or improvements had been made upon it. The Rothkopp brothers proceeded on 27 May 1856 to transfer their improved claims by quit-claim deeds as a gift to the Minnesota Benedictines, and these were registered in the Stearns County courthouse on 11 August 1857. The first mistake was made here, for the Rothkopps could in law sell improvements made on their claim before they obtained title, but they could not transfer untitled claims. If the Benedictines had bought the Rothkopp's improvements, they then would have had the status of pre-emptors and could have filed the claims in their own names. As soon as the prior unwisely registered the claims which the community believed the Rothkopps had transferred to them, the transaction was made public.

This error, and the resulting advantage that it offered was perceived by George F. Brott, a pioneer wagon maker of Dutch and Yankee ancestry from New York. He was at the same time a realtor, and the organizer of the townsite company of Lower St. Cloud. Brott contracted to carry mail from Minneapolis to St. Cloud on 6 September 1855, and was allowed by law to select free lands as compensation for his services. In 1858, as Henry C. Waite stated, Brott's "cupidity naturally led him" to file a claim to the very tract occupied by the Rothkopps.[46] He did this because the Rothkopp claims lay adjacent to his townsite of Lower St. Cloud and to a claim made by his brother-in-law, Newton N. Smith, who had relinquished that claim to Brott, choosing to obtain his rights under Brott's mail contract. In this way Brott hoped to obtain title to the entire Mississippi river lands from lower St. Cloud through the Rothkopp claims.

As soon as the Benedictines were informed of the invalidity of the Rothkopps' quit-claim gift, they restored the three hundred and twenty acres to the brothers on 3 July 1858. Perhaps the Rothkopps' obstinacy in refusing to file their claims as they then could so easily have done can be explained by the fact that Brott shrewdly prevailed upon Sebastian Wimmer, nephew of Abbot Boniface, to explain to all concerned that they could obtain their lands much easier through Brott and his mail contract privileges than through their own pre-emption rights. Brott said he would reconvey their claims to them when these claims had been entered in his name. Abbot Boniface made two trips to Washington, D.C., to see what could be done to save the lands, and friends of his there obtained an interview for him with J. M. Edmunds, U.S.

Land Commissioner. He was told that if the Rothkopp brothers and the Benedictines would cancel their previous agreements, and if the Rothkopp brothers would then in turn file their claims, there would be proof of their prior rights, through witnesses and in equity.

But the question dragged along for six years, and Prior Demetrius retained Judge E. O. Hamlin of St. Cloud as the community's first lawyer in the case. The imminence of loss of everything, as well as the collapse of his frontier development plans, broke the spirit of the first prior. He began to think of resigning his office into the hands of Abbot Boniface. But before he did this he performed one last service to the establishment of Benedictinism in the West. This service consisted in receiving, directing and supporting the first convent of Benedictine Sisters in that region.

Prior Demetrius did not agree with that group of German Catholics who tried, in Minnesota and elsewhere in the United States, to transfer the German idea of state schools to America. He agreed with the majority of the German Catholic immigrants who eventually prevailed and went on to take the leadership throughout the country in establishing and defending the parochial school system. Some of the German Catholics in and around St. Cloud and St. Joseph wanted to hire Catholic male teachers for their schools, which would then become the public or district schools and at the same time Catholic schools. Prior Demetrius denounced this as "two incompatible ideas," and if his example had been followed more consistently in the years following, the educational problems of the Church in central Minnesota would not have developed.

The prior supported that group of Catholics who desired a parochial school, and began to look around for possible teaching Sisters. He was interested first in inviting the Notre Dame Sisters from Milwaukee, but then turned to the Benedictine Sisters in St. Mary's, Pennsylvania. These Benedictine Sisters had been brought to the United States in 1852 by Abbot Wimmer from the ancient convent of St. Walburga, in Eichstaett, Bavaria.[47] Wimmer had, with the permission of Bishop O'Connor of Pittsburgh, installed them in a monastery which his community had constructed at St. Mary's in Elks County, Pennsylvania. From the beginning Wimmer acted as though he had jurisdiction over the Benedictine nuns. He attempted in 1855 to obtain canonical status for the Sisters of St. Mary's and to affiliate them with the American Cassinese Congregation, but he failed in this effort and the Benedictine Sisters remained a diocesan institute. Nor did the motherhouse of St. Walburga wish the nuns to be independent. The American bishops had consistently desired that nuns in the United States be under their diocesan jurisdiction, that they make simple vows and not be cloistered, so as to serve the educational and charitable needs of the Church in the New World.

Prior Demetrius wrote to Sister Benedicta Riepp, O.S.B., superioress at St. Joseph's Convent in St. Mary's, Pennsylvania, and invited her community to consider a Minnesota foundation. Sister Benedicta, one of the pioneers, was a far-seeing and courageous woman who at first was on good terms with Abbot Boniface, relied on his judgment and advice, but who gradually began to differ with him over procedure. Wimmer believed that the Sisters should firmly establish their own community and school at St. Mary's before making moves to take over city schools. Sister Benedicta was moved by that same expanding spirit which Wimmer himself manifested, but in this case could not encompass. She determined to establish new foundations in both Erie, Pennsylvania, and St. Cloud, Minnesota, because St. Mary's, in her opinion, presented few possibilities for the development of the community. Wimmer, in turn, felt that she should rather consider the invitation of Bishop James Roosevelt Bayely to come to Newark, where Wimmer had himself decided to send monks to work among German immigrants.

Benedictine Sisters

In the spring of 1856 Sister Benedicta established her second convent in Erie, and in June of 1857 she decided to go to Minnesota herself with a colony of Sisters. Wimmer objected because he felt his monks were not fully established there, nor did Prior Demetrius expect that the Sisters would come for another year. The settlers in Minnesota had just undergone a financial panic as well as a second invasion by the dreaded grasshoppers in that spring of 1857 and were in no position to assume the added financial burden of supporting the Sisters.[48]

In Wimmer's mind there was a cloud over the Minnesota foundation of Benedictine Sisters from the very beginning. He had threatened to depose Sister Benedicta from office as difficulties increased between them in Pennsylvania, and she had begged instead to be allowed to lead a band of thirteen religious to Minnesota. Wimmer, happy to find a solution to the problem, consented on condition that both Prior Demetrius and the Bishop of St. Paul be notified, and that only half of the Sisters be taken. Mother Benedicta did not comply with these conditions, and with their annual allotment from the *Ludwig Missionsverein* in hand, she and her followers left St. Mary's for Erie. From there a vanguard of seven Sisters set out for Minnesota, while the remainder of the group was to follow later. When the prior took Father Cornelius to St. Paul on June 28 to apply for his citizenship papers he was informed that the Benedictine Sisters had arrived and were housed with the Sisters of St. Joseph at their hospital. Prior Demetrius cried out "Precipitous," and the administrator of the diocese, the Very Reverend Augustine Ravoux, was equally surprised and annoyed. He told the prior that he must take the four Sisters and their three postulants with him to St. Cloud and care for them.[49] This he did, first housing them for eight days with Wendelin Maertz family, and then renting John Tenvoorde's boarding house, where they lived and conducted a school for almost a year. Meanwhile the St. Cloud congregation raised a frame building for them near the church, and the Sisters lived here in their Convent of St. Joseph for six years, while teaching the children of both Catholic and non-Catholic settlers in elementary grades, music, and domestic science. Tuition charges were listed at $2.00 a year, but the Sisters seldom collected any money for their services.[50]

The Benedictine Sisters suffered much from poverty at first, but they soon won the hearts of all the community, as di Marogna wrote:

". . . The Sisters are honored, respected and loved; they edify the people by their modest behavior. The Americans are amazed and wonder how it is possible to live such a mortified life. They admire the Sisters and cannot help respecting them.

"The Sisters now have six girls in school and under their supervision. Needlework is sent to their convent. People bring them things to eat. Sometimes when the Sisters get up in the morning they find vegetables, etc., at the kitchen door. Some bring them chickens and young pigs. It seems to me that this, humanly speaking, overhasty coming of the Sisters was in reality in the eyes of the good heavenly Father a providential permission from Him who likes to transcend and cross over the ideas and plans of men. The Sisters barely manage in St. Cloud. As soon as the contract of the teacher has expired, they will take over the boys' school. God grant that the Sisters may always remain as united and loving among themselves as they are now. Here in Minnesota good, model Sisters are indeed necessary." [51]

Prior Demetrius not only aided the Sisters, but also interceded with Wimmer to forgive them, which Abbot Boniface did, and on the occasion of his second visit to Minnesota in the fall of 1857 he expressed his joy at their progress. Later developments and the growth of this Benedictine community of women on Minnesota soil more than proved the correctness of Mother Benedicta Riepp's hopes for this foundation, and the support which St. John's first prior gave them. Abbot Wimmer's difference with Mother Benedicta was one of the few unfortunate developments of his life, for it prevented the organization of the monks and nuns in one American congregation and kept the Sisters for too many years in the status of diocesan institutes.

During 1857 Prior Demetrius began to look toward St. Paul as a possible field of activity which would relieve him of his office and enable him to devote his energies entirely to the care of souls. At the same time he was being mentioned and advanced as a possible successor to Bishop Cretin. The growing number of German Catholics would have welcomed a bishop of their nationality, but the prior never seriously considered these rumors and stated that Administrator Ravoux and the Reverend Anthony Pelamourgues had advanced his name to divert attention from themselves. He also felt that in God's providence he would

54

never be chosen and declared: "The Lord may certainly in this instance remain as calm as I am." [52]

Di Marogna was interested, however, in working among the Germans who were, so he said, fairly swarming into the St. Paul area. The German parish of the Assumption, recently completed, was growing rapidly and already had a larger congregation than the cathedral itself. The Assumption parish was too heavy a burden for Father Keller, and the diocesan priests were encouraging Prior Demetrius to come to St. Paul, where his talents could be of great use. The administrator of the diocese, Father Ravoux, offered the parish of the Assumption to the Benedictines, which meant he wanted Father Demetrius as pastor, and he called the prior to St. Paul during August to take up residence with Father Keller. The change was made gradually with Father Keller going to New Trier, thirty-five miles south of the city, during December, and Father Demetrius assuming pastoral charge on 29 December 1857. When Abbot Wimmer came West in October he had not been slow to realize that the prior wanted to be relieved of his office. At the same time he saw the rich possibilities of bringing Benedictine influence to the capital of the Territory. He accordingly granted permission for this development and appointed Father Cornelius Wittmann as second prior. This was obviously a temporary arrangement, as Father Cornelius had been a priest for little more than a year and was then only thirty years old. He was the logical choice, however, because his educational interests best fitted him to open St. John's Seminary which needed to be established during that autumn. Abbot Wimmer had sent two additional priests to Minnesota in April, Benedict Haindl and Clement Staub, and had in mind to appoint his old friend and first volunteer, Father Benedict, as prior in Minnesota. But Haindl had not been in the territory long enough and had furthermore moved into the Minnesota River Valley, where he was doing mission work among German Catholics. His appointment would follow during the coming year.

Assumption Church

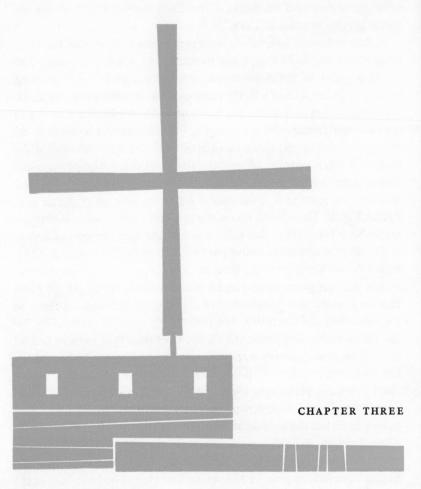

CHAPTER THREE

THE FORMATIVE DECADE

With the charter in hand, and little else materially, Father Cornelius set about organizing a Benedictine school in Minnesota. Spiritually and intellectually, however, the community was rich. For there were thirteen centuries of educational tradition to draw upon, and such examples to follow as Reichenau, Jarrow, York, St. Denis, Fulda, Corbie, Bec, and St. Gall. Abbot Wimmer and his Benedictine family in America were fully conscious of this tradition, and considered their educational effort as central to the revival and restoration of Benedictine life in nineteenth century society. Like Augustine or Boniface they strove to respond to the challenge of vigorous, new peoples. In this consisted their strength and durability which was essentially practical. They faced the facts as sons of St. Benedict had always done when they flourished. They were willing to act, not on emotion or prejudice, but realistically and imaginatively. The Church needed educational in-

56

stitutions in America, especially seminaries and colleges, and the Benedictines quickly accepted the challenge.

Abbot Wimmer had hardly left Minnesota three weeks when St. John's Seminary was opened at the Rothkopp claims on 10 November 1857. The beginnings could scarcely have been more humble. Father Cornelius Wittmann was at the same time, prior, president, sole professor, and pastor of St. Cloud, while Father Alexius Roetzer was to assist him whenever he was free from mission work. The first students were five in number, all from the region, and included Henry Emmel and Anthony Edelbrock from St. Cloud; Joseph Duerr of St. Joseph; Henry Klostermann of Richmond; and Andrew Stahlberger of Lake George. There was no publicity or formal announcement of the opening. The five young men merely moved in with the monks, as students had often done in centuries past in hundreds of monasteries. None of the students could have been aware that they had by this act become members of Western civilization's oldest educational family.

The curriculum was that of a liberal arts Latin school with instruction in history, English, German, Latin, Greek, astronomy, rhetoric, and mathematics. The first curriculum was thus based on the mediaeval discipline of the *trivium* and *quadrivium*. Anthony Edelbrock, who later became second abbot of St. John's, recorded his memories of those first days at 'Old St. John's' on the Mississippi river:

"We were frontier lads, accustomed to ample elbow-room; broad prairies, little restraint and good meals suited us first rate. We had been largely our own bosses and to enjoy life was not at all the last or least of our aspirations. When therefore the reins were slowly but firmly put on to us, sour faces became visible, one or the other even doubted whether he ought not at once to bid a long, lingering adieu to Apollo and the Muses. The College regulations were read to us. We had to rise at 5 o'clock, say our morning prayers, attend daily Mass, then study and 7 o'clock breakfast; i.e. a cup of coffee — if such it could be called — and dry bread, no butter or molasses or sugar there. After breakfast free for one half hour, at 8 o'clock classes began and lasted until eleven; then dinner. At dinner a watery black soup with plenty of bread in it invariably made its appearance, presumably an *edition seconde* of the soup prepared by Lycurgus for the boys of Sparta. After soup came potatoes and meat — never more than one kind — then bread. Our drink was water. We never had pie or delicacies — in fact there is serious doubt whether our culinary lord ever knew of these agreeable items. After dinner, free time until one o'clock, then classes resumed. At three we received a piece of dry bread. This, with fresh water, was relished with a gusto. From 4 to 6 we had to study, at 6 o'clock supper. The first dish was again the indispensable soup, the rest usually as at noon. From 7½ to 8½ study time, then night prayers and to bed. After night prayers silence reigned supreme, no talking whatever was allowed. There was poverty everywhere; a poor and miserable house, poor and scanty food; poor and bad lights. The tallow candle was the only light in those days. Then nobody knew anything of kerosene, gas, or electric light, the indispensable requisites of the modern school room. Must it not be a surprise to some people of our days that in the centuries gone by such great luminaries arose, illuminated only by the tallow candle? Yet such is the truth. The greatest men the world ever saw, were surrounded by poverty and poor light. 'Superasque evadere ad auras, hoc opus hic labor est,' was truly said of the pious Aeneas by Virgil. We too experienced it. To be confined to the class room for hours when the sun was bright and the weather pleasant for outdoor sports, was not a small trial. To be checked and corrected and hemmed in convinced us that our play grounds did not extend as far as our horizon. One of our number had only entered the college as a day scholar, he invariably brought his own dinner along in a pail, he considered it impossible to eat the college soup, when one day requested to do so by the Professor. 'Well,' said the Professor laughingly, 'you will learn to eat the soup in due time.' And sure enough the time came even when this young man could eat the soup. 'Probieren geht ueber studieren,' nothing like trying. We had few books. The Professor lectured, we had to write. Yes, we were started in on the European plan. Those were hard days for the book makers; they could not then fleece the scholar and drain the parents' pockets as at present. The proverb holds good: 'every question has two sides.' The first few months seemed half a 'saeculum' to us, it took time to break us in. However some three months did the work; we were tamed and felt at home in our 'Alma Mater.' The result could not be otherwise. Rev. Father Cornelius Wittmann, our professor, although firm in enforcing discipline, bore patiently with us. We began to understand that the rules and regulations of the college were for our own good, that if we observed them they would elevate and ennoble our lives. The fine and strict order of the house made a deep and an indelible impression upon us. One day the same as the other, every hour had its duty affixed, every thing moved as regularly as clockwork. This was the time for prayer that for work. Such regularity and punctuality inspired us with love and awe. We had not seen it before. The sun pursues his course, deviating neither to the right nor to the left and our youthful days at St. John's firmly and equally balanced. Mallock asks: 'Is life worth living?' Our answer is: 'Yes, our life at St. John's was worth living.' " [1]

The students of the first ten years spoke of themselves as alumni of 'Old St. John's.' From the original five, the annual enrollment reached twenty in number during the period from 1857–67, but fluctuated during the Civil War and Sioux Indian War. St. John's was known as a seminary primarily, but from its inception Catholic immigrants sent their sons to the Benedictines for a Catholic higher education which would at the same time fit them for secular life. Thus teachers, farmers, professional and business men are found among St. John's first alumni of this period.[2] All students pursued the same courses during these years, namely a liberal arts program similar to the classical *gymnasium* curriculum of Germany which the Fathers themselves had experienced. A course in philosophy and theology was also offered for cleric members of the community who made their novitiate in the motherhouse at St. Vincent, but returned to St. John's for seminary training.

Old St. John's

The Rothkopp land litigation continued during all of this time and and the community never knew from one month to the next if they would retain anything. Prior Cornelius, influenced by Father Bruno who never liked the St. Cloud site, determined to move both monastery and educational institution to St. Joseph, and there begin anew. This was the first of several moves which the community would make, and it was effected on 5 March 1858. The moving did not present much of a problem as St. Joseph was only eight miles away, and the few belongings of the community, along with the students, were carried there by carts in a single day.

At St. Joseph the school was conducted in a log structure, 25 x 30, located in the vicinity of the church. Prior Cornelius, Fathers Bruno, Alexius and Clement, along with the Brothers, lived in the parish rectory. Father Cornelius cared for St. Cloud from here, while Father Bruno continued as pastor of St. Joseph, and Father Alexius did missionary work in the other missions and stations throughout the area. Determined to concentrate more fully on the general affairs of the community, Prior Cornelius appointed Father Alexius as professor of the college. The latter taught until the end of June, 1859, while continuing to function as a missionary.

St. John's second teacher has been described by Alexius Hoffmann as:

". . . a man of imposing physical stature, with an emaciated countenance from which beamed a bright intellect; he was zealous and amiable, pious and talented, kind yet strict. He carried into the class-room the same zeal with which he had visited the missions and enjoyed the love and confidence of his class. He was an excellent professor, still the number of students did not increase during his regime. The times were too hard and the settlers too poor. He worked faithfully until June 1859 when his rapidly failing health compelled him to resign. He felt that he was doomed and returned East; on 25 February 1860 he expired (from Tuberculosis) at St. Vincent's at the age of twenty-eight."[3]

Father Alexius attracted people to God wherever he moved in his short life. His instruction and example were held in special memory throughout the area. It was he also who inspired the high-spirited Anthony Edelbrock, his frequent companion on mission trips, to become a Benedictine and study for the priesthood. When Edelbrock was admitted to St. John's he asked for and received the name in religion of his youthful ideal.

During these first ten years several Benedictines were sent to the Minnesota foundation by Abbot Wimmer, and they alternated in teaching at the school and serving in the ever-growing mission stations. Thus Father Alexius was succeeded by the Reverend Anschar Frauendorfer, O.S.B., who taught for one year, from September 1859 to November 1860, and was best remembered by the students for his scholarly attainments in Greek. From 1860–61 the Reverend Magnus Maria Mayr, O.S.B., ably directed the school with the assistance of John Daxacher, a student of theology from Austria. Daxacher at first received the Benedictine habit, but later decided to become a diocesan priest, and served until his death in 1904 in the diocese of Omaha, Nebraska. After Father Magnus' term, Father Anschar returned to the school until the Reverend Wolfgang Northmann, O.S.B., took over as professor and disciplinarian in 1862. Cleric members of the community helped in teaching whenever possible. The community was moved four times, the Sioux Indian outbreak reduced the student body for a time, but the little frontier school, unique among Minnesota's pioneer educational institutions, never closed its doors and survived its embryonic decade intact.

The Benedictines had not only branched into Minnesota from St. Vincent during these years, but had also moved along the Missouri river in the Kansas Territory. The Reverend Henry Lemke, O.S.B., had made a new foundation there in 1855, with the permission of John Baptist Miège, S.J., Vicar Apostolic of the Indian Territory. He settled at Doniphan City between St. Joseph and Leavenworth. This was one of the many colonizing projects headed by Lemke during his life, and Wimmer, after leaving Minnesota in the fall of 1857, went to Doniphan to examine the possibilities of the project. Despite the crying need for men and money in Minnesota, Abbot Boniface decided to support this promising venture. He evidenced here again his determination to move in the spirit of ninth century Benedictinism. The mother abbey was to be a cell, a viable and dynamic living organ serving as a feeder for new monasteries. Accordingly, when he sent Fathers Benedict Haindl and Clement Staub to Minnesota he sent the Reverend Augustine Wirth, O.S.B., and a cleric, Casimir Seitz, O.S.B., to Kansas to take over from Lemke who returned to St. Vincent. In 1858 after the frontier real estate boom of Doniphan did not develop, Father Augustine moved the foundation to the new river town of Atchison, Kansas, where it was established under the title of St. Benedict.[4]

Wimmer wanted both the Kansas and Minnesota foundations elevated to the rank of independent priories as a first step toward abbey status because it was difficult for him, especially during the winter

60

months, to administer these remote regions and to make immediate on-the-scene decisions. Both Miege and Cretin had clearly evidenced their desire for abbeys in their jurisdictions. Wimmer could have prudently delayed this move, but he never acted in that manner. Within ten years he had solidly established a growing community at St. Vincent, supervised the building of a large physical plant there for over 200 persons, opened a college and seminary, accepted parishes in seven dioceses, and begun his first two foundations. With them independently launched, he could turn to the many intriguing ventures he dreamed about.

With this in mind Wimmer assembled in September 1858, the Second General Chapter of the American Cassinese Congregation of Benedictines at St. Vincent. Fathers Cornelius and Benedict attended from Minnesota and participated in the decisions which raised the foundations in Kansas and Minnesota to independent canonical priories. Novices and clerics, however, were to be sent to the motherhouse for their training. The Congregation's chapter was to elect the priors, while Abbot Boniface had power to change the monks in the priories according to his considered judgment. Father Benedict was elected prior for Minnesota with sixteen of twenty-seven votes on the second ballot.[5]

When Prior Benedict and Father Cornelius returned to Minnesota they found two members of the community waiting for them in St. Paul. Abbot Wimmer had sent the Reverends Eberhard Gahr, O.S.B., and Anschar Frauendorfer, O.S.B., to Minnesota, and the new prior assigned them at once. Father Anschar was to be assistant to Father Demetrius di Marogna at Assumption Church, St. Paul, and Father Eberhard went with the former Prior Cornelius to Shakopee, the new Benedictine mission center for Scott and Carver counties, where Prior Benedict had moved the year before.

Prior Benedict arrived at the monastery in St. Joseph on October 16 and that evening delivered his inaugural conference to the community. It was based on the Scriptural text: "Seek first the kingdom of God, and all these things shall be added unto you" (Luke 12:31). He could not have characterized his own spirit better. This first Benedictine invested in the United States was a deeply spiritual man who had suffered and was yet to suffer many hardships in the following of Christ. Alexius Hoffmann, O.S.B., characterized him exactly:

". . . as a fairly tall man, erect, slow of speech and movement, mild of voice, wearing a long beard that recalled traditional pictures of St. Benedict. He was a quiet man, and perhaps a disappointed man, for Abbot B. Wimmer had made him Prior at St. Mary's, Pa., but had to recall him because he was not a financier; moreover, he had been Bp. O'Connor's (Pittsb.) candidate for the mitre at St. Vincent as against B. Wimmer and Demetrius Marogna. . . . He always seemed to be at rest, placid, silent, only interrupting his meditations by taking a pinch

61

of snuff, which somewhat discolored his beautiful white beard. . . . He is described as a man distinguished for piety, learning and prudence. He may have been pious; he was not learned and prudence sometimes is identified with mistrust, reticence and irresolution." [6]

The new prior was primarily a missionary, and his name was held in esteem along the Minnesota river valley. He was anxious to establish the community on a sound spiritual basis, but did not know how to administer an institution nor to win the support of his confreres. His term was consequently troubled and indecisive.

Prior Benedict feared from the beginning of his superiorship that the community's move from St. Cloud to St. Joseph could create difficulties for the college because St. Cloud had been designated as the institution's site in its 1857 charter. He resolved, without consulting the other members of the community, to return to the Rothkopp claims below St. Cloud, and the removal was effected on 15 March 1859. In the course of the same year he and the Brothers built a 20 x 30 log house in the Indianbush outside St. Joseph.[7] There, with the help of neighboring farmers, they first broke and cultivated part of these Indianbush claims of Father Bruno Riess in section 31 of St. Wendel township. Prior Benedict spent much time developing a farm on the Indianbush claims, left the operation of the college outside of St. Cloud in the hands of its various directors, and seemed to find internal tranquility in this place of withdrawal. The Rothkopp land litigation continued during his three year superiorship and the prolonged insecurity of this controversy moved him to prepare the way for a place where Benedictine life could be pursued on a more stable basis.[8]

Abbot Boniface was also becoming more worried over the outcome of the Rothkopp controversy. At this time, as the case dragged along, an occasion presented itself to Wimmer to secure title to the Indianbush lands, and he decided to seize the opportunity. In his sincere and eager desire to obtain land for his Minnesota monks he made, perhaps, what was one of the most auspicious faux pas of his life. This act served at the same time to deepen the misunderstanding between him and Mother Benedicta Riepp while securing St. John's present location.

Wimmer had written to Court Chaplain Mueller and asked why other Bavarian nuns such as the Ursulines were receiving donations from King Ludwig while the Benedictine nuns in the United States had received no assistance. Mueller recommended these Benedictine nuns to the king and Ludwig gave 6,000 florins ($2,560) which Mueller wanted to divide equally between the Benedictine convents in Erie and St. Cloud and the monastery in Doniphan. But Ludwig asked which of the convents was the newest and poorest, and Mueller described the Sisters' St. Cloud foundation to the king as Wimmer himself had detailed their poverty and needs in an earlier letter. Ludwig decided that the money was to be divided between the St. Cloud convent and the Kansas monastery, and the money was forwarded to Wimmer. He sent 3,000 florins ($1,280) to Doniphan, but failed to send the other 3,000 florins to the St. Cloud Sisters whose status he questioned and whose independent decision to come West he resented. He decided instead to send their 3,000 florins to Prior Benedict with the instructions to secure title to the Indianbush claims in Minnesota. The Sisters protested to the king who was at first displeased. He ordered Wimmer to repay the money by September of 1859 or the *Ludwig Missionsverein* would withhold its yearly allotment from him. Mueller also warned Wimmer that he had no right to use this money and that he was losing the confidence of the king and other Bavarian benefactors. Wimmer hastened to explain his actions to King Ludwig:

Indianbush Property

". . . There are Benedictine Sisters there (St. Cloud), but it is very uncertain if they can remain there. Their case has been reported to the Apostolic See and a decision is still pending. Under these circumstances I did not deem it advisable to send the 3,000 fl. to them for fear that they might spend it contrary to the purpose for which it was sent. But inasmuch as I did not want it to lie idle, I bought eight Government Land Warrants with the money, that is government patents which in the year 1812 were given to soldiers who served in the war. Each soldier who received such a patent or land security had the right to occupy 160 acres of land free of charge. Many of these land warrants were sold by these soldiers and they became a sort of government paper in the hands of different owners. These papers have, according to demand, a higher or lower price. Their true value is $200 because one gets 160 acres of Congress land for one warrant which would otherwise cost $1.25 an acre — $200. In the stock market there is a constant fluctuation from .85 to $1.05 an acre. I bought them in New York for .86 an acre. Therefore, one warrant for $137.60 and the eight of them for $1,100.80. I sent these eight land warrants directly to Fr. Benedict Haindl, the first independent prior of St. Cloud, with the instruction that the land occupied by the Brothers, but not yet paid for, should be bought immediately, so that a solid basis for *St. Louis Monastery* might be assured. The prior received 1,280 acres of land for these warrants or two square miles (English) in one piece — a magnificent possession!" [9]

Wimmer described how discouraging the prospects were for Minnesota because, as he put it, of the inexperience of di Marogna, first prior. The abbot desired to erect a lasting memorial to Ludwig in Minnesota, but he could not obtain the money to buy the land, nor would the Bavarian mission society give him the money for speculation. So he sent the money to Haindl with the instructions that if the Benedictine Sisters should be recognized he would have to be ready to restore the

3,000 florins or $1,280. He told the king that he would have Prior Benedict send a receipt to that effect, asked the king, in several letters, to forgive him, and declared:

"While both a priest and a monk, I am by no means so inconsiderate of the other sex that I would enrich men to the detriment of women; and under ordinary circumstances I would sooner have laid sacrifices upon my brethren in order to have given relief to our Sisters. Nevertheless, in this instance, an extraordinary advantage would undoubtedly develop for the monks on the one hand, which never could be gained later on or only by the heaviest sacrifice; on the other hand it would be most certain that the Sisters would derive little or no lasting advantage from the donation of Your Serene Majesty. I believed that I could not have acted differently than I actually did. . . . Perhaps never was there better use made of a sum of money than in this instance. This is only possible in the far West of our continent. The 1,280 acres of land are already worth $12,850 and will be worth ten times as much within a few years. St. Louis Abbey has with this a foundation like Scheyern, but of course without buildings. The next task will be to build a steam mill. Then the establishment of a numerous congregation there is assured. At present the four priests and ten brothers there have about 100 acres fenced and under cultivation.

"The Prior writes me that everything is prospering, since through the acquisition of the 1,280 acres they have established a solid footing. He has already begun a school for boys. It is quite certain that these two priories in Kansas and Minnesota, whose independence has been acknowledged by the Apostolic See, will within a short time become abbeys and the source of many other Benedictine foundations. I especially hope for this from St. Louis which is surrounded by a numerous Catholic population, mostly German immigrants, and extensive stretches of most fertile land, which is at this time still occupied by the wild Indians. The Whites are, however, following fast upon their heels. The immigrants are relying upon the spiritual benefits of the monastery whose priests, without a doubt, are following them, step by step, to seek and find suitable place as new centers for their activity.

"I am somewhat proud of the fact that Bavarian Benedictines, supported by their great Ludwig are arrayed there as pioneers of civilization and religion to undertake a foundation which will have the richest, lasting blessings. At the same time this foundation will have the most extensive effect, and will weave about the brow of Your Kingly Majesty a laurel crown of glory, the like of which not even the best and most noble rulers will be able to display." [10]

Ludwig must have been impressed for he informed Wimmer on 1 June 1859 that he would not be under any obligation to pay the 3,000 florins to the St. Cloud Sisters until a decision was obtained from Rome

64

concerning jurisdiction over the Benedictine Sisters in the United States.[11]

It was in this way that the Minnesota Benedictines obtained clear title to the Watab meadow, the Indianbush, and the rolling hills of timberland with two beautiful lakes which the St. John's family came to call 'the landscape paradise.' Prior Benedict and his successor, as well as the first two abbots of St John's were most conscious of the Benedictine Sisters' prior claim to the money that had secured the land for the monks. They would repay this 'loan' in several ways during the years ahead. Wimmer's original intention to place his Minnesota foundation under the title of St. Louis in honor of the king of Bavaria appears again in this transaction. It is one of the anomalies of these first years that Wimmer and the community of St. Vincent held to the name of St. Louis Monastery, while in Minnesota the Benedictines called their foundation several names, such as St. Cloud Priory, St. John's Priory, the Monastery at St. Joseph, and later even Subiaco Abbey. It was a problem which lasted for twenty-five years. Nor did King Ludwig, as was claimed for years, establish St. John's directly by his personal munificence. Ludwig had been forced to resign his throne eight years before the Benedictines came to Minnesota.[12] The only money obtained from the ex-king of Bavaria by the Minnesota monks was this grant which had been originally intended for the Benedictine Sisters. Ludwig's generosities were rightly directed to his friend Boniface Wimmer and the Pennsylvania foundation, only indirectly to Wimmer's foundations in whatever ways Abbot Boniface so liberally used them for his projects.

King Ludwig 1

The acquisition of title to the valuable new lands did not secure monastic life immediately, nor were the problems of Prior Benedict solved. Opinion was sharply divided among the missionary Benedictines in Minnesota, drawn roughly along lines between the pioneers and those who were yearly coming from St. Vincent. There was no common agreement on where to locate and the proper emphasis to be given to the different activities they were pursuing. It was far from definite, furthermore, who were the members of the chapter of their independent priory, and who intended to transfer their original vow of stability from the motherhouse in Pennsylvania to the Minnesota foundation. In order to relieve Prior Benedict of these difficulties and to bring about a speedy decision, Abbot Wimmer, as president of the American Benedictines, came West and assembled the monks in chapter at Assumption Church, St. Paul on 30 October 1860. Present were Prior Benedict, Fathers Demetrius, Bruno, Cornelius, Clement and Frater George Scherer, O.S.B., a cleric in minor orders who had arrived just in time to take part in the chapter. Frater Pius Bayer, O.S.B., had also come West with Frater George, but he was not a chapter member since he had taken only simple vows.

Wimmer told his assembled confreres that those who wished could transfer their vows of stability to the Minnesota priory. Of those present all agreed except, strangely, the prior himself who was not decided whether he wished to remain. Such indecision on his part could hardly contribute to the stability and common purpose so badly needed in the foundation. Nor did Fathers Eberhard, Anschar and Magnus attend the chapter because they could not decide whether they should transfer their stability.[13]

Thus, within six months, divergence in opinion over procedure crystalized again, and this time in a most singular manner. On 11 April 1861, the day on which the first shot was fired at Fort Sumter, opening the War Between the States, four of the Fathers took matters into their own hands and proceeded to call themselves together in chapter at St. Joseph. The younger monks were not invited, and Prior Benedict, to say the least, was not sympathetic with the move. He did not attend this meeting of the original pioneers, Fathers Demetrius, Cornelius, Bruno and Clement. On this one occasion these four monks were able to reach a common agreement. It was based on their so-called by-laws for the corporation which had been drawn up by Father Cornelius. After Father Demetrius was chosen chairman and Father Cornelius secretary, they drew up ten articles, signed the document, and forwarded it and the minutes of their meeting to Abbot Boniface.

Besides naming provisional officers, a president and a secretary, the members of this quasi-chapter attempted to legislate concerning acceptance of new missions, support of pastors, preservation of chapter secrecy, and admittance of new members. In the latter instance they decided to accept the petitions of Father Anschar; of the Reverend Louis Fink, O.S.B., then stationed in a dependency of St. Vincent at Covington, Kentucky; and of the controversial visionary cleric, Paul Maria Keck of St. Vincent. Approval for these transfers were to be obtained from Abbot Boniface.

The main concern, however, and the reason for this assembly, was to decide once and for all where their Minnesota monastery and college were to be located. They selected the Indianbush as the locality for the monastery. In regard to the college, which they said was imperatively necessary, they determined that not more than $3,000 annually was to be drawn from monastery funds for the building of the institution. If the community did not receive a favorable legal decision in the Rothkopp litigation by the middle of May, their college should be moved to Shakopee and built there.[14]

Shakopee was chosen for the college because Father Cornelius Wittmann, after taking over Prior Benedict's missions along the Minnesota River, had become completely convinced of the possibilities of a Benedictine school in that region of rich land where German Catholic immigrants were settling so rapidly. Father Demetrius now favored the idea of establishing the college closer to St. Paul, and Father Bruno, who was now also doing mission work along the Minnesota River, had never liked the St. Cloud site from the very beginning. Father Cornelius had actually begun spending money on the construction of the first building for this proposed St. John's in Shakopee, and plans were being made to have the bishop lay the cornerstone.

When Abbot Boniface received these curious resolutions, he of course immediately repudiated the entire transaction. Father Cornelius was advised to discontinue the unauthorized work begun in Shakopee, and a church was later built upon the foundations laid in this strange excursion along the Minnesota River. Wimmer wisely did not impose any penances for this unwarranted chapter. For the indecision of Prior Benedict, as well as the indefinite status of the community's future development, had combined to urge these missionaries toward their precipitate action.

He wrote instead to the new bishop of St. Paul, Thomas L. Grace, O.P., who had been consecrated for that see on 24 July 1859.[15] Wimmer stated that he was ready to allow Prior Benedict to resign as he wanted to do, that he would prefer to recall Fathers Eberhard, Anschar and Magnus, or if the bishop needed these priests, have them together in one station, preferably at St. Cloud or Shakopee, making them responsible to Wimmer directly. He felt Father Bruno must be recalled if the community was to live in peace. He recognized that the majority wanted a new prior, and suggested that if the above mentioned Benedictines did not return home, they might constitute another monastic family under Father Benedict to be directly connected with St. Vincent. Here was another evidence of the resiliency of Abbot Wimmer; from the very disagreement which could have discouraged him, he was ready to solve the problem by beginning a second monastery right on the scene. Perhaps he had in mind to begin with this contingent the monastery he contemplated for the Indians at Crow River, or even in the Indianbush. He then declared to Bishop Grace:

"I send here the Rev. Wendelin Mayer, Master of Novices, to give a retreat for all our Fathers in your Diocese, from which I hope a happy result, as Fr. Wendelin is a very able man for such purposes. . . .

"Fr. Wendelin has for particular events particular authority from me; if his measures should not be agreed upon, I would feel compelled to make use of your offer to lend me your arm for restoring order, if necessary. I hope, though, it won't come to that. . . .

"I am ashamed and sorry that we give you such an unfriendly picture of internal discord. I trust nevertheless, that in a short time things will give a better aspect with God's help and your assistance."[16]

Father Wendelin, a preacher, missionary and writer, thus came to Minnesota during November in the capacity of visitor and retreat master. He conducted a ten day retreat at the monastery near St. Cloud which was attended by the entire community. A chapter was then held on November 14 in which Father Wendelin, as visitor, detailed several disciplinary regulations and accomplished some good in calming the troubled waters. The six Minnesota missionary monks voted to discontinue, in obedience, the proposed college at Shakopee. Prior Benedict wished to resign, but Wimmer asked him to retain his office even after it had expired, until another prior could be elected. To solve the obvious ineptitude of Prior Benedict in temporal affairs, Father Clement was appointed procurator, or manager of the business of the community, with the title of subprior.

In this way Wimmer and his delegate were able to forestall any serious rupture, if not to settle existing problems. In the time obtained by this delay, Wimmer planned to move ahead rapidly toward having the Minnesota priory erected as a fully independent abbey. He felt throughout his lifetime that foundations should be advanced to abbey status at a rapid pace. Priors, owing to a certain want of authority, could not succeed in bringing about unity of action and conformity of discipline, as had been well evidenced in Minnesota. With an abbot elected for life, long-range plans for future development could be carried out.

With these aims in mind, Wimmer within a year's time assembled the Third General Chapter of the American Cassinese Congregation. Prior Benedict and Father Cornelius, again representing Minnesota, attended the sessions at St. Vincent from 15-18 September 1862. There it was agreed to petition the Holy See for abbey status for the house in Minnesota. The very next month Wimmer returned to Minnesota and assembled the chapter members who proceeded to elect a successor to Prior Benedict. The second prior was to take charge of the Minnesota foundation at once and if the Holy See granted abbey status to the foundation, this prior was to succeed automatically as the first abbot of St. John's. All present agreed to this carefully designed, if rather unusual plan of Wimmer's, and they proceeded on the second ballot to elect the prior at St. Vincent, the Very Reverend Othmar Maria Wirtz, O.S.B., to the position.[17]

Wimmer was not able to carry out these plans as quickly as he wished. The War Between the States dragged on and prevented his taking passage for Europe. It was not until three years later, in 1865, that he was able to arrive in Rome and present his petition for a first daughter abbey of St. Vincent. And in Minnesota itself, even before his successor could arrive, Prior Benedict was faced with one last crisis.

The War Between the States seemed far distant to the little band of Benedictines deep in the timber wilderness and along the waterways of Minnesota. The state of Minnesota had been admitted to the Union in 1858, two years after their arrival, but not many of the St. John's community were Americanized enough at this early date to become involved in any way in the momentous struggle for federal survival then

68

taking place. The Minnesota Benedictines were too busy caring for the German immigrants who had moved West before the war began and had their own domestic difficulties to cope with. Several members of the priory were not yet citizens, and the possibility of sending any priest as chaplain to the army was out of the question because of shortage of man power and excessive demands for spiritual care.[18]

But the famed Sioux Indian outbreak in 1862, the most serious of the Indian uprisings against the Whites, did have immediate and terrifying effects upon the community. Sioux problems had not been resolved by the treaties of 1851–53. The Indians nurtured resentment, in great part justified, over unfulfilled money payments, land adjustments, and cession of reservation lands, not to mention the unbelievable injustices heaped upon them by unscrupulous traders and government agents who were political schemers. Tribal integrity, traditions, and customs were being constantly undermined by contact with the so-called civilizing influences of the White man. On 17 August 1862 the bitter Sioux nation of about 7,000 united in the uprising, and 1,500 braves took to the warpath. Since Governor Ramsey had been the first from any state to send troops in support of the Union cause, the Sioux realized that they would never have a more opportune occasion for striking than when so many soldiers of the First Regiment were out of the area.

From the Lower Sioux Agency near Redwood Falls the Indians charged across the Minnesota River, scalping settlers, ambushing a company from Fort Ridgely, and killing over 400 Whites within a few days. The Indians were met at the German settlement of New Ulm by valiant defenders who broke the momentum of the uprising at great cost of life and property. But over 600 persons had been killed within a week, eighteen counties ravaged and 30,000 people, one tenth of the state's population, were temporarily left homeless.

The Chippewa chiefs assembled in a council of war near Crow Wing in answer to a summons sent out by the Sioux Chief, Little Crow, to cooperate with him. The venerable Indian missionary Father Pierz had been resting for a few weeks with the Benedictines in St. Cloud when the Sioux outbreak occurred. He was informed by a Catholic Indian courier of the council being held. Pierz started out immediately for the Chippewa camp in order to dissuade Chief Hole-In-The-Day, who, surrounded by his braves in war paint, was resisting the efforts of government officials to conclude a treaty with the Red Lake Chippewas. Indian sentinels were stationed near the camp, and Father Bruno relates a little-known incident which had major influence on the Indian danger:

". . . Pierz was already within a quarter of a mile of the spot, when he was confronted by a sentinel who drew a line on the ground and told him, no stranger could be permitted to pass. The zealous priest asked the guard, who was a Catholic:

" 'Am I a stranger? Am I not a friend of the red man? Have I not always been with you?'

"The child of the wilderness found no reply and permitted the priest to pass.

"But they had not proceeded far, when other marks on the ground, and sentinels were at hand who informed him, that they must shoot every stranger, even an Indian who went beyond this inner line. Now his wits were at an end; all persuasion was in vain. No protestations, that he must see the chiefs, were of any avail. The guards had strict orders to allow no one to pass. But God's help was not distant.

"One of the Indian guards, a Catholic, took recourse to a ruse.

" 'We have orders,' he said, 'to allow no man to go beyond this line; now the black-robe says he must see the chiefs. There is no way of evading orders; we must carry the black-robe into the council. He thus does not go, but is carried, and that has not been forbidden.'

"The other sentinel seemed satisfied, and Father Pierz was carried into the encampment. It must be ascribed to his priestly zeal, and eloquence, inspired by God that he succeeded in dissuading the Chippewas from entering alliance with the Sioux against the Whites. Peaceful attitude on the part of the Chippewas was thus secured and the chiefs returned to their homes. How noble is the example of this heroic priest who braved death to spare many of his fellow men, Indians and White, from the terrors of the war!" [19]

If the Chippewas and Winnebagos had joined the Sioux, as everyone feared, the whole state could have been laid waste.

The counties along the Minnesota River were not the only ones ravaged, although they received the brunt of the Sioux blow. McLeod, Kandiyohi, Stearns, Meeker, Otter Tail, Douglas and Sibley were all overrun in whole or part. J. Fletcher Williams summarized the activity in central Minnesota:

"Western and southern Stearns county, however, suffered severely from the depredations of the red foe. About August 23rd, they committed murders and other crimes near Paynesville. The people of that town erected a strong stockade, and the citizens and refugees from points further west, sheltered themselves therein. A part of the town was burned, but no attack was made on the post. At Maine Prairie, St. Joseph's, Sauk Centre, Clear Water, Little Falls and other places, similar stockades were built, and held by a few determined citizens. At St. Cloud, which was filled with refugees, strong fortifications were built, and preparations made to defend the place to the utmost, but no foe ever appeared, fortunately. A number of persons were murdered in the western and southern part of Stearns county, and houses burned." [20]

Most of the settlers around St. Cloud fled to that town for protection. Father Bruno records again the intimate details of Benedictine contri-

70

25 *Assumption Church, St. Paul.*

26 *Holy Angels Procathedral, St. Cloud.*

27 *First consecrated church
in Minnesota at St. Joseph.*

28 *Bishop Rupert Seidenbusch and Abbot Alexius
Edelbrock with parishioners at Meire Grove.*

29 Original Stella Maris Chapel on Lake Sagatagan.

30 Stella Maris Chapel as altered in 1916.

31 Bishop Rupert Seidenbusch, vicar apostolic of Northern
Minnesota, with some of his diocesan priests.

32 The old Watab mill.

33 Harvest time in early Stearns County.

34 Schoolmaster Theodore Lobmiller
and pupils at Farming.

35 The Gertken family of Stearns County.

36 *On the spot manufacturing: St. John's front yard brick kiln in the 1880's.*

37 *Abbot Alexius Edelbrock and Father Aloysius Hermanutz*
at White Earth with Indians in 1878.

38 *St. John's community at the dedication of the new quadrangle in 1886:*

L. to R. First row: Fathers Severin Gross, Bernard Locnikar, Valentine Stimmler, Prior Norbert Hofbauer, Abb
Alexius Edelbrock, Subprior Peter Engel, Cornelius Wittmann, Meinulph Stuckenkemper, Joseph Buh (Dulut
Vicar General Francis Xavier Stemper (St. Cloud). Second Row: Fathers Vincent Schiffrer, Alexius Hoffman
John Katzner, Chrysostom Schreiner, Alphonse Kuisle (hand on chair), Edward Ginther, Martin Schmitt (ha
on chair), Timothy Vaeth, Henry Borgerding. Third row: Fathers Roman Homar, Rupert Kiefer, Francis Mers
man, Paulin Wiesner, Bartholomew Rajglj, Gregory Steil, Othmar Erren, Xavier White, Ildephonse Molitc
Wolfgang Steinkogler, Oswald Baran, Jerome Heider. Fourth row: Fathers Benno Ferstl, William Eversman
Conrad Glatzmaier, Isidore Siegler, Cyril Zupan, Paul Rettenmaier. Fifth row: Fathers Lawrence Steinkogl
Meinrad Rettenmaier, Ulric Northman, George Scheffold, Simon Lampe, Herman Bergmann, Corbinian H
manutz.

39 *Martin Marty, first bishop of the Vicariate of Dakota.*

40 *Alexius Edelbrock, St. John's second abbot.*

41 *St. Paul's archbishop: John Ireland.*

42 *'Poplar Walk' in front of monastery: 1890.*

43 *Lake Sagatagan: 1886.*

44 *Student body 'afloat': 1887.*

45 *Indian boys of St. John's Industrial School on First Communion day.*

46 *Family portrait, students and faculty: 1880.*

47 *The bells of St. John's enroute to twin towers.*

48 *Students of '86 on cemetery hill
overlooking present seminary site.*

49 *Abbey intramural croquet champions of '71.*

50 *Picking potatoes in the '80's.*

bution to regional defense and how the people gathered around their priests:

"The Benedictines in Stearns County did what was in their power to protect the individual settler as well as their congregations. Classes at the college in St. Cloud were dismissed, the director, a civil engineer and zealous priest, was stationed at Richmond (Torah) to reside there in a log hut near the church. Father Clement and myself were in St. Joseph; Fathers Benedict, Anschar and Eberhard in St. Cloud. We invited families to leave their homesteads and to establish temporary residence in the church, schoolhouse, stables, etc. As St. Cloud had grown to the proportions of a town, there was room for the farmers of that congregation. The village of St. Joseph consisted of five houses and could not give shelter to the eighty families of the vicinity. We therefore placed our extensive stablings, schoolhouse and even the church at the disposal of the fugitives. The men capable of standing under arms patrolled the vicinity during the night with orders to fire a shot as soon as an Indian was noticed. The church bell was then to give the alarm and the townsfolk were to place themselves in defense. Occasionally a timid or imaginative militiaman mistook a stump for an Indian; a sharp report resounded through the quiet night and who might describe the agony and shrieks of the terrified women and children? My pen is inadequate. In such occasions there might have been twice our number of priests at hand to calm and console the terrified settlers.

Defense Measures

"At Richmond Father Magnus distinguished himself as an engineer The settlers with their families, cattle, provisions, and utensils occupied the church, schoolhouse, and stables. The priest's house, a log hut 16x20 was inhabited by the priest who occupied the attic. Father Magnus caused the prairie about the church, school, etc., to be plowed and earth-banks seven feet high to be thrown up. Loopholes were pierced at intervals in the ramparts; two wooden pump shafts were metamorphosed into fieldpieces, having been well hooped by the blacksmith. Luckily they were never put to use; they would have been more harm than use to the artillerists.

"These preparations however primitive, allayed the terror of the frightened settlers who thought, they were now perfectly safe. Father Magnus was recalled to the monastery and I was sent to Richmond. There was a lack of arms and ammunition and I drew up a list of all available fighting men, had officers chosen and reported to the Governor that I with these constituted homeguard, with the request to furnish us arms and ammunition. The request was willingly granted, and we were furnished with a quantity of muskets — with the Austrian Coat of Arms on them — also several casks of powder and shot. This infused new courage." [21]

71

When news of the raids on the so-called Norwegian and Yankee settlements around Paynesville reached St. Cloud, a force of thirty men, accompanied by Father Eberhard as chaplain, set out in rigs to bury the dead and to rescue those they could find. The settlers in the fortified towns suffered from lack of food, and no one dared to leave the barricades to bring in the fall harvest. After Little Crow and his Sioux warriors were defeated at the battle of Wood Lake on 23 September 1862, and they had fled into Dakota, the danger subsided. The people were than able to return in October to their homes and pick up their lives again. The settlers of central Minnesota had much to be thankful for when they considered how much worse their condition might easily have been.

The Sioux uprising was the last storm Prior Benedict had to weather. He re-established community life at the priory during October, and to his great relief, prepared to hand over his office to the new prior, Othmar Maria Wirtz, who arrived on November 17.

There were, however, still a number of unsolved problems and bitter days remaining before the Minnesota community would safely pass through the formative years of its development. All hoped for able leadership from Prior Othmar. His background had been varied from the days of his early upbringing in the Calvinist faith. His parents were prosperous Zurich bourgeois who sent their son to the best Swiss schools. But the young boy felt that studies did not contribute much to the solution of life's problems. He consequently abandoned an academic career and apprenticed himself to a watchmaker, immigrated to the United States in 1848 at the age of seventeen and worked at his trade in New York City, Johnstown, and Altoona, Pennsylvania. In the latter city he came in contact with Benedictine Fathers from St. Vincent, and was converted to the ancient Catholic faith of his fatherland.

Wirtz, who was of a serious and religious disposition, resolved to become a Benedictine and was aided in this resolution by his countryman Father Clement Staub, at that time procurator of St. Vincent. He made his solemn vows in 1854, was ordained in 1857, and two years later was made director of St. Vincent College, and subsequently prior of the abbey in 1860. He was a medium sized man of slight build with dark complexion and beard. His serious disposition, slow yet gentle speech, did not make him too approachable. But his piety and zeal were all the more marked by his determination to promote the ideals of the monastic life among his confreres at St. Vincent and later at the Minnesota priory. The knowledge that he was supposed to succeed automatically to the abbotship of the Minnesota priory as soon as possible aided him in inaugurating a spiritual program.

For two months the new prior carefully studied the problems of missionary Benedictinism on the Minnesota frontier. He was eager to resolve the accumulated difficulties of the previous years such as regulation of missionary activity, appointment and transfer of the Benedictines from one mission to another. Most important, he faced the task of insuring a religious, monastic spirit among Minnesota's active Benedictines who were constantly exposed to secular influences.

By late January of the new year he was ready to act, and the members of the community were assembled in chapter at the St. Cloud priory on 22–23 January 1863. During those sessions a single horarium for the daily ordering of life both at the priory and on the missions was established. It was the first partial adjustment of Wimmer's monastic schedule which he had brought to St. Vincent from Bavaria. It was, furthermore, an indication of Wirtz's rigoristic tendencies, especially in regard to hours of rising and retiring. This schedule could be readily followed in the priory itself, but could scarcely be adjusted to migratory life on the missions. For this reason it would have to be altered again in the future. It represents clearly the decisions which faced these first American Benedictines. They had to adapt the mature and stable communal monastic life of Europe to the demands of the Church in a new, expanding society where immigrant people were beginning parish life. Settlements were remote and separated from one another by distances unrelated in every way to Europe's geography. Furthermore, the supply of priests was never adequate to these demands throughout the whole period. At the same time Prior Othmar felt strongly that monastic ideals could not be lost in the midst of such work. His schedule was an attempt to achieve both aims:

Prior Othmar Wirtz

A.M. 3:45, Rising, Matins and Lauds of the Divine Office; Half Hour of Meditation; Masses.

6:00, Prime, Terce, Sext of the Divine Office.

10:45, Particular Examination of Conscience; Dinner and Adoration of the Blessed Sacrament.

11:45, None of the Divine Office.

P.M. 4:30, Vespers and Compline of the Divine Office.

5–6, Spiritual Reading.

7:30, Silence.

The annual retreat was to begin on the Wednesday after the second Sunday of October, while a chapter of faults and a conference were to be held monthly during summer, and every second month of the winter season. These gatherings were to be held simultaneously at the priory for the Benedictines of central Minnesota, and at Assumption Church, St. Paul, for those active in the region of the Mississippi-Minnesota river valleys.

Then the assembled members of the priory endeavored to coordinate their expanding mission activity. They decided to have two priests and a Brother at St. Cloud, with one of the priests visiting the missions of St. Augusta and St. Wendel at Luxemburg. St. Joseph would likewise have two priests and a Brother, and all western missions were to be visited from this point. But they realized the inadequacy of this arrangement and resolved to establish a new western missionary center, also with two priests and a Brother, as soon as possible. The Assumption parish in St. Paul was to have two priests and a Brother. Along the Minnesota River valley, their mission station was to be located in Shakopee, and from there the Benedictines would care for Marystown, Chaska, Benton (Cologne), Waconia, St. Victoria, Watertown, Spring Mount, St. Bonifacius, Glencoe, French Settlement, Cedar Lake and Young America. In St. Anthony, commonly called St. Anthony Falls during these years, and later to be named Minneapolis, the Benedictines cared for St. Boniface Church, and the missions of Crystal Lake, Jordan and Lexington Station. The chapter was willing to remain in charge of St. Boniface Church which Bishop Grace had been encouraging them to maintain, but they requested that the bishop of St. Paul also assign the Church of St. Anthony in the same place to the Benedictines. Bishop Grace did not agree with this proposal, however, and the Benedictines discontinued care of St. Boniface Church from April of 1865 until 1873 when they again accepted responsibility. In each of these places the annual support for a Benedictine priest was to be $400; $100 a year for service at a mission once a month, and $5 stipend for a visit and divine services on a weekday.[22]

Such were the community's first comprehensive enactments aimed at regularizing the ever-expanding demands of mission activity. They would be revised and amended often in the future as spiraling requests came in from every side for spiritual care. But a good beginning had been made by Prior Othmar, and during his term of office additional personnel came West to assist the overburdened pastors, missionaries, educators and laborers of the priory. They included two new priests. The Reverend Meinulph Stuckenkemper, O.S.B., became pastor in St. Cloud, and the Reverend Matthew Stuerenburg, O.S.B., did mission work at St. James and Sauk Centre. Wimmer sent with them Brother Clement Wirtz, a brother of Prior Othmar, who was a good cook and was, therefore, deeply appreciated at the priory. The clerics Wolfgang Northman, O.S.B., Anthony Capser, O.S.B., and Joseph Vill, O.S.B., also came during these years, helped in the school while studying theology, and after their ordination remained in the community until death.[23] Late in 1864 Prior Othmar was able to send the first Minnesota candidate for the priory to St. Vincent to make his canonical novitiate. On 6 January 1862 Prior Benedict had invested five of the pioneer students with the Benedictine habit. Their names were Fratres Benedict M. Duerr, Boniface Emmel, Willibald Michel, Augustine Marshall, and Valentine Stimmler. They attended college classes with the other students while preparing gradually as scholastics for monastic life. The community was proud of these first candidates for their priory, and thanked God that so many of the first students had chosen to follow St. Benedict's age-old way of life. But the indecision, differences and instability of the Minnesota Benedictine pioneers militated against instilling the virtues and ideals that these candidates needed. Accordingly, only one, Valentine Stimmler, persevered in his original determination by the time of Prior Othmar, and it was he who was sent to St. Vincent for the novitiate. He completed his training, took solemn vows and was ordained in 1869, thus becoming the Minnesota priory's first candidate who persevered. Prior Othmar saw in this large loss of scholastics another pressing reason for ordered monastic life.

The welfare and progress of the Benedictine Sisters was also a part of the new prior's program. They had been carrying on convent life and teaching in their quarters next to the church on Eighth Street in St. Cloud for five years. Their sacrifices and efforts were not fully appreciated, it appears, by some of the people of St. Cloud. Bishop Grace expressed his regret that the congregation there was giving the Sisters continual trouble, and added: "Such people are not worthy of having Sisters to draw down blessings upon them." That minority element among German Catholic immigrants who looked upon Sisters and the Catholic parochial schools which they maintained as an unnecessary burden, felt that state schools with Catholic teachers, as they had known them in Germany, were the practical solution of frontier conditions. This could be especially the case where a Catholic enclave, like the one developing in central Minnesota, could by majority vote and by control of the school boards obtain Catholic men teachers. These teachers in turn would be paid by state funds and thus spare thrifty Germans from supporting parochial schools. In 1863 a plan was advanced to do just this in St. Cloud by leasing a portion of the church property for a public school. Bishop Grace and Prior Othmar were quick to realize the implications of this move, as Grace stated:

". . . We cannot be too cautious in yielding to others' claims and privileges over the property of the Church, especially in such cases as the one in question in which there is reason to suspect that the congregation demand as a right that such lease shall be made. The mere probability that a Catholic teacher may be appointed, does not change the character of the school which remains essentially a school in which no religion is allowed to be recognized; and it would seem strange that a School System which the Church has denounced as God-less, should have a local habitation on ground dedicated to church purposes. We cannot consistently lend such countenance to a system to which the whole spirit of the Church is opposed." [24]

In this way the movement for district schools with Catholic teachers was averted in St. Cloud at an early date. It was not halted throughout the region, however, as future developments in a large number of communities attest. Nor was Grace's successor as bishop of St. Paul, John Ireland, of the same opinion as his two predecessors, as his hotly debated Faribault-Stillwater school experiment of three decades later evidences.

There is further indication that St. Cloud's pastor, Father Meinulph, had difficulty with the St. Mary's congregation at this time over control of the church property. Bishop Grace was adamant in this regard also.

He insisted that church property be administered by ecclesiastical authorities according to the law of the Church, that title to all the land be secured legally by the Benedictines, and the deed for the church lot itself be transmitted into the bishop's hands. The Benedictines and the people of St. Cloud were planning a larger and more worthy church structure at this time, to replace the original frame building which had grown inadequate in every way. They chose a new site at the corner of Ninth Avenue and St. Germain Street, and planned their church to face on St. Germain Street across from the original church which faced on Ninth Avenue. Throughout the whole transaction Grace wanted ecclesiastical control enforced. For the perennial problem of early nineteenth century American Catholicism, namely Trusteeism, was clearly being manifested again in Minnesota. This early vigilance prevented lay domination or control from developing as a serious problem of the Church in the area.

Motivated, no doubt, by the ungrateful treatment given the Sisters in St. Cloud, Prior Othmar determined to prepare a new convent for them in St. Joseph. It was felt that this place offered a more suitable and advantageous location for a Benedictine convent. The Sisters had also opened a parish school in St. Joseph in 1862. The scholastic Valentine Stimmler and Brother Placidus Brixius did most of the carpentry work on the modest frame building, 30x56, which was raised on the main street of St. Joseph village, about a half block west of the parish house. Here the Sisters moved in 1863, and this building remained their convent for eighteen years until the first wing of the present structures was finished in 1881.

Prior Othmar and the community were not acting purely out of charity in giving this assistance toward the establishment of St. Benedict's Convent at St. Joseph. Everyone was conscious of the fact that their valuable Indianbush lands had been purchased with money originally intended by the king of Bavaria for the Minnesota Benedictine Sisters. This assistance in establishing them at St. Joseph was, accordingly, looked upon as the first of several indemnities to be effected during the coming years.

The Sisters had scarcely removed their convent from St. Cloud, when the monks found themselves in a position where they were forced to abandon their entire development outside the same city. They then turned to those precious Indianbush lands for a new and secure beginning. As the War Between the States dragged on, the question of ownership of the Rothkopp claims on the Mississippi River had remained

76

unsettled through a series of court decisions, reversals and appeals. The Benedictines retained at different times, Henry C. Waite, St. Cloud's first lawyer, along with Judge E. O. Hamline, and W. L. Stevens, while George F. Brott's case was pleaded by Colonel M. Thompson. Waite was particularly active in advancing the case of the Rothkopp brothers' prior claim to the lands which they had donated to the Benedictines. While informing Cyrus Aldrich, Minnesota's representative in Congress, of the nature of the case, Waite stated, concerning the Rothkopps: "Their great misfortune seems to be that they came here early and settled upon valuable tracts of land adjoining St. Cloud and thus placed themselves in a position to excite the covetousness of their neighbors." [25] Waite felt that although the Rothkopp brothers had erred in filing their claims, the prior efforts of pioneer settlers in developing land should be recognized over the claim of Brott who used their mistake in filing to claim land on the basis of a congressional grant to mail carriers.

The Benedictines had relinquished their useless quit-claim deed to the Rothkopp brothers as soon as title to the lands was challenged. One of the Rothkopp brothers, Wilhelm, died in May of 1859, and willed his supposed half ownership to the remaining brother, Louis. The Register and Receiver of Deeds at St. Cloud reported against the Rothkopp claim on 30 November 1860 and it was also rejected by Commissioner Joseph S. Wilson of the U.S. General Land Office in Washington, D.C., on 15 March 1861. A new commissioner, J. M. Edmunds, reversed this decision however, and Brott and his lawyers then appealed Edmund's decision to Caleb B. Smith, Secretary of the Interior. Here the case pended for another year. Brott went to Washington to push his cause and was well received, as Sebastian Wimmer reported, in the Department of the Interior. Another observer and friend of Abbot Boniface, John Dowling of Washington, D.C., warned the Minnesota Benedictines that all the leading men in that department were "abolitionists and Republicans," and strongly suggested that they request the good offices of one of Minnesota's senators or representatives to give their claim a candid and favorable consideration. Waite proceeded to do this in his letter to Congressman Cyrus Aldrich, who pressed for a favorable decision, but to no avail. For on 25 April 1862 Secretary Smith reversed the decision of Commissioner Edmunds, and ruled in favor of Brott. Of the 320 acres in question only 75 acres were ultimately adjudged to Louis Rothkopp.

It was a major blow to the community. Although this litigation had gone on for six years and the danger of loss was ever imminent, the community had preserved the hope that somehow all of the labor, improvements and buildings there might be salvaged. Abbot Alexius later declared that "seventy-five acres was little enough in return for all the annoyance which the land has caused, and when it is remembered that the Fathers had spent $2,000 to secure a home there." Louis Rothkopp proceeded to convey this parcel of land to the monks, and they in turn supported him as they would a member of the community for twenty-eight years until his death on 22 October 1890.[26]

A hard decision now faced the community. They could attempt to find suitable land along the Mississippi near St. Cloud, or look elsewhere. The good land around St. Cloud had been occupied by this date, and the Benedictines could not afford to purchase available tracts. The possibility of a move to St. Paul or especially Shakopee in the Minnesota River valley again was advanced, but the contemplative inclinations of Prior Othmar influenced the final decision. He wanted the monastery to be removed from town life and into a solitude where he might follow the bent of his religious and ascetical disposition. The Indian-bush lands just out of St. Joseph offered such a possibility, and Prior Othmar imagined that by locating there they would be so far from the movements of urban life that a locomotive whistle would never wake the echoes of the forest. Yet within a few years the St. Paul and Pacific Railroad lines were being laid across the monastery property. The Indian trail out of St. Joseph was already giving way to the state road between St. Cloud and Breckenridge, or Fort Abercrombie. It passed a short distance from the projected priory, and although the nearest mail station was St. Joseph, then known as Clinton P.O., it would not be many years before the monastery would have its own mailing address. The ever-expanding march of settlement was closing in on the Indian-bush. But in 1864 it was still on the edge of the frontier.

In that year, with disaster facing the priory, it was to the woods west of St. Joseph, out to Father Bruno Riess' farsighted and ingenious claims, that the community migrated. Under Prior Benedict the valley had been partially cleared and opened to cultivation, while the Brothers had erected a frame shack. So in the spring of 1864, the monks and students, with their humble belongings in a few carts and wagons, lumbered away from the river bank through St. Cloud toward St. Joseph, as they had done once before in 1858. But this time they passed beyond the frontier village and wound along the Watab Creek to the clearing on a knoll a short distance northwest of the present Collegeville station.

There was water and fuel nearby, but the frame house, actually no more than a claim shack, was a poor substitute for the buildings which had been erected with such devotion and sacrifice on the Mississippi River bank at St. Cloud. The priests, Brothers and students set to work at once to raise a two-story frame building which would serve as monastery and school, while the small house they found on their arrival was adjusted to serve as single chapel for the community's public recitation of the Divine Office, Brothers' spiritual exercises and students' religious services. The cleric, Wolfgang Northman, directed the school and was professor of music. Gradually the order of Benedictine life was established, and for three years, from 1863–66, the search for God and knowledge was pursued deep in the Indianbush.[27]

It was, however, the peace before a storm. Their calm and uneventful life was shortly shattered by what was, perhaps, the most bizarre event of the community's formative problems. Its origins extend back to St. Vincent Abbey where in 1859, Abbot Wimmer admitted a young man, George Keck, then twenty-four years old, into the clerical novitiate. Wimmer, ever generous and big-hearted, opened the doors of his monastery to men who professed an interest in the religious life. At the same time he was most interested in obtaining personnel for his spiraling projects. A closer investigation of the background of Keck, who received the name of Paul in religion, would have prevented many future difficulties and one of the major crosses of Wimmer's life. Keck, as it was later discovered, had been a professional actor, a talent which he was not slow to utilize at St. Vincent. While sick in the infirmary he first began to speak of supposed visions he was privileged to have concerning the future of the community and its members. He was effective enough to attract a group of supporters, including the master of novices, Wendelin Mayer, and the prior of St. Vincent at that time, Othmar Wirtz. Keck advocated several reforms such as wearing a rosary on the belt and affixing the name of Mary as a second name for each monk, a suggestion which both Wirtz and Mayer, as well as several others, adopted. The Keckites looked upon themselves as a reforming element working for spiritual deepening in the midst of Wimmer's too-active developments. It was at this point that his fantastic influence converged on the Minnesota foundation.

Prior Othmar Wirtz was by this time in Minnesota as superior, and on 19 January 1863 Paul Maria Keck came to the St. Cloud Priory, where he was harbored by Prior Othmar for a month. This development was not entirely the work of Prior Othmar, for one of the enactments of the unauthorized chapter of 12 April 1861 had been to accept Keck for the Minnesota priory. It is thus apparent that he had sympathizers in the West. Keck did not have much opportunity at the priory to create reforms through his pretended visions, for his presence was reported to Wimmer by those Minnesota monks who opposed Keckism. He was ordered to move on and he went to New York City where he disappears from the history of American Benedictinism.

His influence did not fade away so easily, however. Wirtz continued to have faith in Keck and declared that "He who humbled him will also exalt him again." Father Wendelin left St. Vincent for Rome with proposals to be submitted to the Curia petitioning for a more spiritual emphasis in American monastic life. Wirtz carried on correspondence with him, encouraged him to persevere in their ideals, invited him to come to the Minnesota priory where they would work out the proposed reform that would make it unnecessary for Mayer to join a European

79

abbey. Wirtz aimed at establishing a novitiate in Minnesota where their own candidates could be trained, thus eliminating the necessity of sending them to the motherhouse at St. Vincent. He wrote to Mayer:

". . . Let us trust in God and patiently wait for the time He has appointed for us all. Even though Minnesota will not be raised to the status of an abbey, and if we have no Cluniac statutes as yet, do not let this discourage you. Do not be afraid and deceived. Come to Minnesota gladly and quietly and help me in my difficult position which I am to maintain.

"Only be patient; we are not at the end yet even if the Abbot may think so. Not I, however, oh no. We have not even started yet. For our further progress God will have to help us, and will do so despite all opposition." [28]

Here was manifested for the first time in the New World that reforming spirit which is such an integral part of monastic history. Repeatedly, in Benedictine development, splinter groups, opposed to the emphasis and trends of a successful movement in the Order, have broken off and established a new house. There those ideals of St. Benedict's *Rule*, which the reformers see undeveloped in the mother movement, have often been reaffirmed successfully to supply new vigor to Benedictine life at a particular time. Such reforming movements have not only manifested the perennial vitality of St. Benedict's way of life, but also the broad liberty of spirit inherent in Benedictine tradition. They further indicate that the original movement from which the reform sprang can in time peacefully continue side by side with the new development, as each stresses aspects of Benedictine life needed by the Church in her mission to mankind.

Wirtz apparently looked upon his priorship and eventual abbotship in Minnesota in such a light. His reference to the famed mediaeval monastery of Cluny indicates that he considered the house deep in the Indianbush as a new reforming center where emphasis on contemplation, interior spiritual life and stress on the public recitation of the Divine Office could be brought to America. But at this time the reform did not succeed for several obvious reasons. Wirtz, so recently a convert from Calvinism, showed spiritual immaturity and lack of balance in his attachment to Keck. It was Wimmer's defect and even more his misfortune, that he was forced by shortage of trained personnel to entrust important positions to monks, like di Marogna and Wirtz, whose monastic apprenticeship had been so short.

Wimmer was fortunately in Rome at this time petitioning for a number of decisions concerning the American Benedictines. He learned of Mayer's and Wirtz's activities, and proceeded to explain his side of the story to the Curia cardinals and congregation officials. Wimmer was deeply hurt that such a movement was developing which would, as he judged it, splinter the young American branch of the Benedictines and tear asunder the infant congregation which he was struggling to establish. He wanted cooperation in reform within the congregation rather than secession, which, because it was based on support of Keck, bordered on religious fanaticism. The Congregation of the Holy Office on 16 September 1865 handed down a decision condemning the opinions which Keck had been spreading, and Wimmer informed the communities at St. Vincent and in the Indianbush that all were expected to disavow such opinions as false and dangerous. His letter reached Minnesota about December 8 and by its contents ended abruptly the nascent reform movement. As early as October 17 Wimmer informed Prior Othmar, in a general letter to the community, that since his term in office had come to an end, he was to be retired from office. Wimmer was at that time also petitioning Rome for abbey status for his Minnesota priory. But since it was still uncertain whether the monastery of St. Cloud was to remain a priory or be raised to an abbey, and also because it was impossible for him to conduct an election in Minnesota, no new election was to be held at that time. Wimmer, accordingly, appointed the senior of the monks in Minnesota, Benedict Haindl, as temporary prior until such a time as an election could be held.

Wirtz, to his credit and as an indication of his basic monastic sincerity, immediately complied with Abbot Boniface's orders. He wrote to Wimmer, submitted to his decisions, and informed Mayer that he wished to comply entirely with the repudiation of Keckism. He then went to St. Paul to serve as assistant to his old friend and countryman, the pastor of the Assumption Church, Father Clement Staub. Here he remained for nine years until his death, serving quietly and humbly in the capacity of a parish assistant. Father Othmar, by his heroic example of obedience, made his final and greatest contribution to the Minnesota priory. By his action he prevented any serious breach from developing, admitted the precipitous nature of the whole movement, and secured the establishment of Wimmer's first daughter abbey.[29]

In this way Wimmer's first Benedictine, Father Benedict Haindl, again found himself, against his personal inclinations, heading the Minnesota foundation from 11 December 1865 until 22 December 1866. It was the final period of the difficult first decade.

While Wimmer remained in Rome pushing for the advancement of the priory to abbey status, the monks in Minnesota made the final move of the community's history. During the year and a half spent in the Indianbush near the present Collegeville station it was discovered that the location was not entirely desirable. The land was not too hilly, the soil was fair, and there was no lack of wood for fuel and building. But the water supply was inadequate for institutional life. A mere creek, bearing the imposing name of North Fork of the Watab River, flowed through the section, while the few ponds in the vicinity were fast disappearing as the forest was levelled and the ground turned by the first plows.

Prior Benedict and his confreres began exploratory excursions across their nearly 2,000 acres, reminiscent of Father Bruno's initial treks through the rolling woods in 1856. Inevitably they paused on the shore of the delightful and large lake, set like a jewel in the forest about a mile southwest of the first farm where the priory stood. This body of water covered three hundred and sixty acres, was fed by springs and creeks, teemed with several varieties of fish, and was hemmed in on all sides by wooded shores. Directly behind the high wooded shores on the north side of this lake lay another winding body of water. As the Benedictines stood on the elevation between the two scenic bodies of water, their thoughts carried them back to the beautiful lakes and rivers of Europe on whose banks great abbeys like Metten, Scheyern, Subiaco, Solesmes or Melk had taken shape. Here were water, woods, seclusion, and natural surroundings that could not but elevate the mind and heart to God. St. Benedict defined a monastery as a school of the Lord's service. In that year of 1865, as peace finally came to the divided nation, Minnesota's Benedictines decided once and for all to build on that spot where all nature seemed to combine in securing the development of the Benedictine tradition of peace.[30]

During the winter of 1865–66 a primitive road was cut through the maple forest from the old farm to the new building site. In April, as soon as the spring thaws set in, the Benedictines, with a few hired laborers, began cutting down trees where the monastery, school and stables were to stand. The frame house was moved up from the Collegeville farm to serve as lodging for the laborers. Then excavations for foundation walls were made, a well dug, and on 28 May 1866 Brother Thaddaeus drove up the winding road with the first wagon load of boards from the saw mill in St. Cloud. As he came over the hill Fathers Prior, Meinulph, Joseph, Wolfgang and Valentine chanted the *Salve Regina,* seasonal hymn in honor of the Blessed Virgin Mary.

The most intriguing aspect of this move was the type of building the monks decided to erect on the lake shore. In St. Cloud, St. Joseph and the Indianbush they had rushed ahead with frontier frame structures indicative of the pressures of their first ten years. Now, clearly convinced that they had made their last move, and with abbey status soon to become a reality, they chose to build with stone. They could scarcely have chosen a better medium to express the stability and security they were seeking. Large boulders were hauled from the hill tops and smaller rubble stones collected along the lake shore. Many of these native field stones of the region lay exposed on the surface, and as clearing and plowing proceeded, they were more than sufficient for any building or fencing desirable. The Benedictines and the settlers of central Minnesota used these boulders often during the early years for their homes, churches and schools. Although irregular in appearance, these stones gave to their buildings a certain air of permanence, strength and color variation. They were the first evidence of man's victory over nature in central Minnesota.

The first monastic building of 1865–66, later called the 'Old Stone House,' was 46x50 feet, with basement, two levels and attic. Facing the east, and placed two hundred feet from the lake shore, this Old Stone House was a frontier adaptation of the simple colonial stone houses and Pennsylvania Dutch gabled structures which the Minnesota monks had known around St. Vincent in the foothills of the Alleghenies. Although the building was unadorned, its severe austerity was functional and blended with the natural surroundings of frontier life. Father Valentine painted a picturesque sundial with baroque corona in bright Bavarian colors on the south wall. It soon became a favorite target for stones, aimed with curves or straight on, by students, until the style gave way before the onslaught of pioneer student recess periods. On the ridge of the roof was an open stylized turret in which Brother Benno's bell was hung. This bell, a gift from relatives in Germany, had arrived at the St. Cloud Priory in 1857. It accompanied the community in all its wanderings, and now announced, in the key of C, the hours of the Divine Service and the school schedule from early morning Matins until Compline officially ended the day's worship and work.[31]

Old Stone House

This quaint and practical structure contained cellars, kitchen and dining room in the basement; monks' rooms, study and class rooms on the first and second floors; and dormitory for students in the attic. The transplanted frame house, about forty feet to the southwest, housed the chapel, Brothers' quarters, three private rooms, and the carpenter and tailor shops. Bishop Grace laid the cornerstone of the priory's Stone House on 19 July 1866, and by the end of the year it was ready for occupancy.[32] If there was any temptation to consider a return to the river bank south of St. Cloud it had been cut off on 20 February 1866, when the group of five original buildings, then partially occupied by Herman Stoeckling, an organ builder, were totally destroyed by an early morning fire. They were not insured and this loss was the final act of the community's bitter experience in land development during the first decade.

In June of that year the long-awaited decision concerning abbey status for the Minnesota foundation was announced. Abbot Wimmer informed Prior Benedict that the cardinals of the Congregation of the Propagation of the Faith had held their *concursus* on June 4 dealing with the petitions submitted by Wimmer concerning the American Benedictines. The question of erecting the St. Cloud Priory as an abbey was weighed carefully pro and con, with the main objection being that the buildings were not adequate. Wimmer held that if the abbot were elected for life this deficiency would soon be supplied, since the foundations had been laid and there were no debts. The cardinals decided that the St. Cloud Priory should be advanced to abbey status, and that the abbot of the new abbey should be elected for life. This was a major accomplishment in Wimmer's life, for Rome had decreed ten years before that he at first was to be appointed and then successively elected as abbot for a limited period of three years. Now as his first foundation was at the point of canonical maturity, he secured for his American Cassinese Congregation the principle that abbots be elected for life. In this way the old European tradition of lifetime abbots was transferred to the New World as a basic means, in Wimmer's mind, of supplying stability. Here was a clear-cut example of traditional European practice penetrating the distinctively democratic practices of nineteenth century America. When the English Benedictines established their revived congregational life in the nineteenth century, the influence of Anglo-Saxon democracy was evident in their decision to have term abbots in that body. In the United States, on the other hand, both the Bavarian and Swiss Benedictines adhered to the age-old structures. Neither the conditioning factors of the frontier nor American social forces altered the strength of ancient European usage and the determination of Abbot Wimmer's forceful personality.

In an audience granted to Monsignor Capalti, Pope Pius IX approved the decree of Propaganda, and it was promulgated in an Apostolic Brief of 3 August 1866. Pio Nono stated:

"The Chapter of the American Congregation has humbly petitioned that the priory of St. Cloud in the diocese of St. Paul, Minnesota, be adorned with the honors of an abbey. After duly considering the request of our Venerable Brethren the cardinals, and finding that this priory, both by reason of the number of religious belonging to it, who have also served faithfully in the diocese of St. Paul, and by reason of the adequacy of its resources . . . deserves to be honored with the abbatial dignity, which will serve to give greater strength to monastic discipline, we have resolved to meet the wishes of the said chapter. Hence . . . we raise the Priory to the rank of an Abbey." [33]

Wimmer rushed the good news to Bishop Grace and informed him that he was leaving Rome immediately. After short stops in France and Bavaria he planned to return to the United States as soon as possible and come west to preside over the election of Minnesota's first abbot. He told Grace:

"It affords me great pleasure to give your Lordship these news, as I am quite sure you take the greatest interest in the welfare of our Order and especially of that branch of it which is in your Diocese. The Benedictines are at present in 11 American Dioceses; we stand and always will stand on the best terms to the respective Rt. Rev. Bishops, because we did our best to give them all aid and assistance possible in the care of souls and to comply with their regulations. Possibly our Fathers have all ways tried to do the same in your Diocese, and I trust, they will do it more effectively, after they will be better settled among themselves.

"Before finishing this letter I beg leave to recommend your Lordship my confreres in your Diocese, to beg pardon for our shortcomings, and to accept of my sincere assurance, that we shall endeavor to make ourselves worthy of your protection and confidence." [34]

Here in this simple letter, with its quaint and halting English, Wimmer revealed anew the humility and sacrificing spirit which he nurtured. On the threshold of the establishment of his first daughter abbey he hastened to assure the local bishop that exempt status would not alter the tradition of service which existed. The Benedictine stream, now spreading out across the country, was to blend with the main currents of American religious life. The Church needed missionaries, pastors, and educators; his abbeys would not remain aloof. The monks would strive to be at the same time true sons of St. Benedict and active missionaries in the struggling American Church.

Such a challenge was not only difficult but sometimes a danger to sound monastic development, as the events of the first decade in Minnesota testify. The needs of Catholic settlers pressed in upon the monastery, forcing immediate solutions. But at the same time the large demands of frontier life brought out the best in the American Benedictines. These new horizons eliminated the equally dangerous possibility of stagnation taking hold in a New World house. Their response to the challenge and needs of American frontier society brought forth and revived a vitality not unlike that which Benedictines had evidenced from the seventh through the twelfth centuries on the European continent.

Wimmer's Benedictines thus proceeded to realize two ideals simultaneously. In the formative decade the establishment of a monastery carrying out a full Benedictine horarium gave way before the valid pressures of a missionary frontier. However, priors like Benedict Haindl and Othmar Wirtz did not allow the active missionaries to lose sight of their Benedictine heritage, and their endeavors in time proved to be effective. For from the obedience and sacrifices of active life the vigor and endurance of the monastery itself took root. The virtues and courage of these early monk missionaries actually laid the foundation for the growth of a monastery beyond the most optimistic dreams of any Benedictine at the start of the nineteenth century.

It was the enthusiasm and devotion of the first decade's pioneers which dominate the beginnings of St. John's. Their stalwart and rugged qualities stand forth as they proceeded to make the first permanent religious impact on the region from 1856 to 1866. Primitive Indian life had passed away in Minnesota before the pioneer farmers appeared on the scene. The trading frontier had taken over, and the first waves of German mechanics, farmers, and small retailers were moving along

85

the water arteries, trade routes and Red River cart trails. The missionary Benedictines followed the people along these arteries, constantly
being drawn to more remote settlements by urgent pleas for spiritual
care. It was a period of small steps: visits to private homes, erecting
mission stations, buying acres for the first log church, erection by priest
and people of their hard-won house of God, bartering in wood or produce, and finally the taking up of residence by the missionary to sow the
seed of the gospel. Where the noble Indian missionary, Father Pierz,
had passed through the forest and over the lakes in search of souls, the
Benedictines now brought the first stable Catholicism to the area and
made deep inroads on the religious isolation of the region. The churches
and schools they built on the original Indian trails contributed to the
broadening and interweaving of the complex pattern of civilization. For
settlers, especially in the period after the Civil War, came to places
where they heard that a church might be maintained by the Benedictines. The role of these pioneer monks in consolidating communities is
accordingly an important factor in upper midwest history. The earlier
French missionaries had moved from fort to fort; the mid-century
Benedictines settled and began their well-tried methods of cultivation
and civilization. Everyone knew they had to come to stay. These monk
missionaries carried the stability of their monastery over into every
church and mission as they moved out from the Indianbush.

It was the number of these religious missions and stations established
during the first decade which is particularly striking. The Benedictine
priests were never more than eleven in number, counting those priests
stationed in the monastery and college as well as those on missions.
Ordinarily they were no more than eight. Yet in this period they cared
for fifty-three parish and mission stations. They operated two of the
largest parish centers in Minnesota, that of the Assumption in St. Paul
and of St. Mary's in St. Cloud, while moving through a dozen counties
of central and southern Minnesota. They maintained three centers of
operation: the priory itself, St. Paul and Shakopee. From the monastery
eighteen missions were served; from Shakopee, twenty-nine; and from
St. Paul, three.[35] It is apparent what major assistance the Benedictines
supplied to Bishops Cretin, Grace and the diocese of St. Paul. When
Grace came to his diocese in 1859, in an area embracing roughly the
present states of Minnesota, North and South Dakota, there were twenty-seven priests caring for thirty-one parishes and ninety missions.
The Benedictines had come to Minnesota only three years before, under his predecessor Cretin. Yet at this time these eight to eleven Benedictines were caring for fifty-three of those parishes and missions.

Nor did they confine their spiritual activity to German Catholic immigrants. Although that was their original and continuous purpose,
they soon were answering the calls of French along the Crow River, and
of Irish, Polish, Scotch and Italian settlers in the Minnesota River val-

ley. Some of these settlements, like the Irish on Cedar Lake beyond Jordan, had not been visited by a priest from the time of their arrival three years before, until Father Benedict came to them in July of 1857.[36] All the while the moving entreaties of the Chippewa Indians to the north beckoned the monks into that work, and within a few years they would be in a position to respond.

Father Bruno left a vivid description of the missionary methods of these few Benedictines, and of the difficulties they encountered. He wrote:

"The secret of attending each of these many places once a month lay in the fact that we celebrated Sunday wherever we held services. . . . Our calendar was prepared two months in advance in order that the larger congregations might have services on Sunday at least twice a month. According to the arrangements I was free to return to Shakopee every two weeks. For two years I made all these trips afoot, for in the first place I had no horse, and if I had been so fortunate, I could not have used it on those roads. The backwood settlers generally had no need of roads as they had neither horses nor oxen nor wagons. Perhaps one or two yoke of oxen could be found in a settlement. For this reason also it was difficult to erect log churches unless the material was close at hand. After the log structure had been completed as far as the roof, whence to obtain materials for the roof? The shingles were homemade, there were no boards except far distant along the river — but how carry them to the settlement without a road, without a wagon, and, which was paramount, without money? At many places I was obliged to show the settlers how to cut boards with a log saw, in order that I might have boards for a church door and an altar table. For the purchase of nails I applied the results of three Sunday collections. The floor of these structures was mother earth.

"Now it was necessary to procure vestments for the divine service. Here we had a means of helping ourselves. We had an outfit. Whenever we set out on a trip we stowed away in the fathomless depths of a carpet bag one altarstone, a missal, a book of Gospels, a breviary, vestments for Mass, candles, crucifix, altar wine for two weeks, altar breads — in fact all that was needed; moreover, some linens and — snuff. When all had been packed away, this baggage weighing some sixty pounds was fastened to the end of a substantial stick; this was slung over the shoulder and we plodded over hills and through swamps, in every season, exposed to biting cold and vexatious mosquitoes, from station to station for six-to-eight and occasionally twelve-to-fifteen miles a day. Arrived at a station, the morning was spent hearing confessions, celebrating Mass, preaching, baptizing, instructing until one or two o'clock in the afternoon. Every day we had different fare, different water, different lodgings infested with all kinds of vermin; then after a short rest we moved on to the next station. Such was pioneer missionary life." [37]

The most interesting and important aspect of this Benedictine missionary activity was the quality of the Catholicism they strove to impart. The interior life or spiritual growth of Christianity in the New World has been the most elusive factor and undeveloped topic of American religious history. There are few extant records of such developments and, more important, no living tradition among American historians of the significance of such realities. A growing consciousness of the importance of this basic aspect of American life is gradually emerging, however, and with it a more mature approach to the actual development of American society. The Benedictines of the upper midwest give evidence from the very beginning of an eagerness to transplant the full life of the Church as they had experienced it in Germany. Coming from Bavaria where the Church had enjoyed an uninterrupted tradition of Catholic culture, these missionaries were conditioned to spread the full liturgical and public life of the Church wherever they moved. In their parishes and missions they worked at once to inaugurate as intense and complete a spiritual program as was possible. Their letters are filled with references to this ideal. They requested missals of the best quality from friends in Europe, as well as altar stones, relics, worthy monstrances and chalices. They made their own church furniture with devotion and care from the best wood available. Father Meinulph travelled East in the early sixties to solicit funds to embellish his new parish church under construction in St. Cloud. The St. Cloud *Journal* for 14 July 1864 described in superlatives this imposing and substantial brick structure, 60x120 feet, with a 150 foot tower. It was the second church building of St. Cloud, replacing the original frame structure. This church seated 1,000 people and cost $20,000. It was dedicated on 14 December 1865, and was characterized by the St. Cloud *Democrat* on September 20, as "the largest and finest structure of its kind in the state." Father Cornelius had prepared the people of St. Cloud ten years before to make sacrifices on the frontier for such expression of their religious faith. He had written to Abbot Wimmer at that time:

". . . I am ardently longing for church utensils, and especially for the ciborium because it really is a terrible situation here, especially at Easter time. I don't suppose they will be too expensive.

"About fourteen days ago we obtained a nice cheap organ for $300. A number of people naturally said, when it came to paying, that this was not so necessary. Nevertheless, they paid for it, and in two days we had the entire amount collected. We brought it over from Sauk Rapids. Mr. Brocker, who studied theology in Germany, plays it remarkably well, and with this began a new era in St. Cloud. Next spring, as soon as the first steamboat runs, we will also get a church bell. Mr. Anton Edelbrock gave us two lots which on the 25th of March will be raffled off. Mr. Burkhard, a native of Munich but raised in Miesbach, is an artist and is working on a painting of 'The Resurrection of Christ.' A larger cross for the church will also be made by him because the Indians have left nothing like this behind." [38]

The general cultural effect of these efforts on the people of the region was pronounced. The fact that the Benedictines encouraged craftsmanship, endeavored to secure art from Europe, introduced church music, all kept before the consciousness of the people the heritage that was theirs. The hardships of frontier life were softened by these familiar symbols of Western civilization. The pioneers did not have to abandon the hope of acquiring the finer things of life, but through joint effort acquired them for daily use through their churches. When they could not at first afford an organ or provide an organist they improvised, and one of the community would accompany at Mass on a violin. Meanwhile the Sisters were giving music lessons to their children.

The constant attention given to altar vessels, church decoration and furniture, bells and organs, was, moreover, an exterior expression of the traditional customs these Catholic people were in the process of transplanting intact from Europe to America. Their chapels were as tasteful and beautiful as possible; their shrines, which began to appear across the countryside, were objects of daily devotion. The grasshopper-plague shrine to the Blessed Virgin, under the title of her Assumption, in the Sauk valley outside of Jacobs Prairie was the best known throughout the region. Processions were made to these shrines by pioneer Catholic peoples who held outdoor processions on important feasts and Rogation Days as an ordinary manifestation of their religious faith. It is not unusual, accordingly, to find Father Benedict declaring that he and his congregation at Shakopee held the first Corpus Christi procession in Minnesota through the woods around their clearing in 1857. [39]

Nor were the monks alone in this liturgical endeavor. As soon as a parish was organized these German Catholics of the region immediately formed their cherished and traditional societies. Throughout the area in each new parish the well-known social, fraternal and insurance groupings were formed: *Bonifatius Verein, Josephs Brueder, Unterstuetzungs Verein, Kindheit Jesu Verein, Benedictus Verein*. These societies began at once in each congregation to receive monthly Holy Communion in a body, to make vestments for divine service, and to hold fairs in order to collect money for religious improvements. Such fairs were important community events anticipated for months by parents and children who prepared crafts, clothing, food and drinks for the occasion. Then, gathered around the church after worshipping together, they auctioned, raffled and sold their goods to one another, ate and drank, sang and danced, all in a spirit of ageless Christian joy from early morning until time for evening chores. Sometimes the fairs were extended over several days, like the one sponsored by the ladies of St.

Mary's Parish in St. Cloud on 13–14 November 1861 which netted
$215 in receipts for their church.[40] These celebrations were always in-
formal, and were not limited only to fairs but were held also on Christmas, New Year's Eve, *Fastnacht* or Shrove Tuesday, and at the end
of the harvest season, *Kirchweih Fest*, the time when they first had
dedicated their hard won churches to God. The pastors always attended,
and favorite characters of the community were called upon to do stunts
or recite poems of their childhood days in Europe. Some of the men
would recall fire and brimstone mission sermons of former years and
even repeat them. Always there was the beer, and when the tempo
slowed down there was ever someone on hand to take up the old
lustige Lieder. Then the woods re-echoed with "Muss ich denn,"
"Haidenroeslein," "Du, du liegst mir am Herzen," "O du lieber Augustin," and of course the hoary Napoleonic "Ich hatt' einen Kammera-
den," which was harmonized with gestures and dramatic pauses for appropriate names to be supplied.[41]

Celebrations were in this way intimately associated with the Church
year, as had been done for centuries in Europe. There was no thought
of separating culture from cult. Their very communities were named
after the saint under whose title their church was erected, except in
those settlements where the New Englanders or 'York Staters' had arrived before them and established title. This geo-religious phenomenon
is apparent by a glance at the Minnesota map wherever the Benedictines
moved during these years. There are such place names along the Minnesota, Mississippi and Sauk River valleys as Assumption, St. Benedict, St. Victoria, Marystown, St. Bonifatius, St. Scholastica (Heidelberg), St. Michael, St. Henry, St. Walburga (Fletcher), St. Augusta,
St. Joseph, St. James Prairie, St. Martin, St. Stephen and St. Wendel.
Each of these was a Catholic community, deep in faith and family culture, free on the land. Around these parish churches, whose steeples
raised the cross into the Minnesota sky, were the rapidly increasing
Catholic families.[42]

The most characteristic tradition which these peoples carried with
them from Europe was their attachment to the Mass and official worship of the Church. In the German tradition they participated at Mass
especially by singing. B.H.F. Hellebusch's *Katholisches Gesang und
Gebet Buch* was prominent in every parish, and the half dozen *Sing
Messen* found therein were known by heart and sung by all. These
simplified and popular Masses were used until the Ratisbon style of
Gregorian Chant was introduced in the 1880's. The entire congregation also often sang other vernacular hymns at low Masses, but these
hymns were not haphazard selections. Each hymn fitted the spirit and
mood of that part of the Mass during which it was sung, and expressed
sentiments in turn of penance, offering, sacrifice or union with God.

The Benedictines offered High Masses in these parishes on Sundays.

After participating at them the people drove home for dinner, and then returned to their churches at three o'clock in the afternoon for Vespers and Benediction of the Blessed Sacrament. These Sunday afternoon Vespers were a cherished institution of the community. Two or three men of the congregation with the best voices held the respected position of psalm intoners. When the priest came into the sanctuary and took his place, these men, standing in the front pew on the Gospel side bravely intoned the *Dixit Dominus Domino meo,* opening verse of Psalm 109, the first psalm of Vespers. It was taken up by the men on the Gospel side, and the women on the Epistle side answered with the second verse. Here was congregational singing in the nave of the church from the very beginning as a common practice of the whole community. After Sunday worship concluded with the evening song of the Church's prayer, the families gathered in the church yard or at each other's homes for visits before the heavy work of the next week began.

There was intense competition among these parishes over the quality and excellence of their choirs. All had as large a choir as possible, and in the first decades St. Mary's parish in St. Cloud and Sts. Peter and Paul parish in Richmond led the field. They sang special Masses on major feasts, but it was the old and treasured vernacular German hymns which never lost in popularity. They sang to the Holy Ghost, "Erleucht' O Schoepfer, den Verstand"; to the Sacred Heart, "Dem Herzen Jesu, singe"; in honor of the Blessed Virgin, "Maria zu lieben," and "Wunderschoen praechtige, hohe und maechtige." These choirs were usually directed by the men schoolteachers whom the pastors had obtained for the schools which they were beginning to establish in their settlements. The Benedictines first wrote to Germany for available *Lehrer Seminar* graduates who might be interested in emigrating to the United States. Then in 1871 St. Francis Seminary in Milwaukee began a normal or training school for young men where students could maintain the high standards expected of these male schoolteachers, and at the same time learn the English language. Professor John Singenberger came from Germany to this institution, called Pio Nono, and taught Church music to prospective teachers. He was the first to introduce Catholic Church music and organ instruction in the United States as an integral part of teacher training.

The names of the male schoolteachers who came forth, first from Germany and then from Pio Nono and St. John's itself, are held in affectionate memory among the people of these early communities even to the present day. These *Kirchen Vaeter,* as they were called, not only acted as organists and choir directors, with little financial compensation, but also taught catechism, acted as sacristans, directed dramatics, and helped around the church. They formed a *Katholischer Lehrer Verein* among whose pioneer members were Lucas Gertken of Rich-

91

mond, Louis Wieber of St. Cloud, Lucas Lambech and Gotthard Haaren of Freeport, and Theodore Lobmiller of Farming. Other well-known teachers included Theodore Ortmann, August Kapsner and Anton Zimmermann of Pierz; Nicholas Bohnen and Jacob Hohmann of Meier Grove; Michael Mainz, John Wocken and John Glass of Cold Spring; Bernard Torborg, Nicholas Weber and John Conrad Diekmann of St. Martin; John Maus of Watkins and Spring Hill; Michael Lutgen of Albany; Michael Loesch of St. Nicholas; Hermann Ricker of Freeport; Joseph Himsl, Simon Gretsch, Albert Eich and Conrad Marshall of Collegeville; Simon Blum and Franz Xavier Statz of Jacobs Prairie; William Boerger, who taught in several Stearns County communities before becoming county superintendent of schools; and Peter Brick and Peter Kaiser of St. Cloud. The latter two in 1874 founded the German Catholic paper, *Der Nordstern,* which had a major influence on the northwest.

From the families of these men many sons and daughters entered the monastery at St. John's, the convent at St. Joseph, the diocesan clergy and other religious institutes, while descendants of these pioneer schoolteachers continue to do so at the present time. Other children of these families became artists, such as Carl Bohnen of St. Paul and Aloysius Bohnen of New York, as well as businessmen, craftsmen and teachers. The entire area has, accordingly, benefited from these cultured and self-sacrificing pioneer teachers who brought the first formal education to communities of the region.[43]

In these several ways the Benedictines began to fulfill their duties as pioneer missionaries and as religious. Early efforts were made to carry out the worship of God with devotion and care. An opportunity was offered for these communities to unite their prayer and work in the liturgical life of the Church. As a result the Christian faith was firmly established by these pioneer Catholics deep in the Minnesota woods of the middle United States.

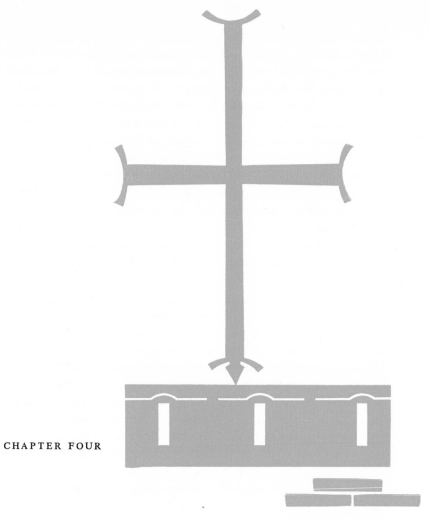

CHAPTER FOUR

ABBOT OF INDIANBUSH

The first election of a Benedictine abbot in the United States was held on a cold winter day of 12 December 1866 at the Indianbush farmhouse. Abbot Wimmer returned from Europe with authorization from the Holy See to preside at the election of a life-time abbot for his first daughter abbey. After attending the II Plenary Council of Baltimore he hastened to Minnesota with his secretary, the Reverend Edward Hipelius, O.S.B., for the event he had long anticipated. Minnesota's Benedictines had been notified of the election and nine capitulars were there in person, while three were represented by proxy vote. They were about to exercise an ancient right, handed down for centuries in the Benedictine family, of electing a spiritual father to govern their religious community.

Prior Benedict Haindl, administrator during the interim between priory and abbey status, had made arrangements for this chapter, with

93

the help of Frater Joseph Vill, solemnly professed deacon, who was going to make his first decision as a capitular that day. Fathers Meinulph Stuckenkemper and Anthony Capser came out from St. Cloud, picking up Father Wolfgang Northman at St. Joseph; Fathers Cornelius Wittmann, a former prior, and Anschar Frauendorfer drove over from Richmond and St. Augusta; another former prior, Othmar Wirtz, assistant at Assumption Church in St. Paul, carried delegation to act as proxy for the pastor, Clement Staub. With Father Othmar came Father George Scherer of Waconia. Father Eberhard Gahr at Shakopee had appointed a proxy, as had Demetrius di Marogna, the community's first prior, who had gone to Florida for the winter because of rapidly failing health.

Prior Benedict was celebrant of a Solemn High Mass *coram abbate* at 9 o'clock on that morning in the stark and bare chapel. Abbot Boniface then led his nine monks into the main room of the frame farm house and opened the chapter meeting according to the ancient forms of the Bavarian Benedictine Ritual. Abbot Wimmer gave an opening address on the importance of the occasion and the achievements of the last ten years which they had accomplished in spite of trials and hardships. He admonished his assembled sons to choose as abbot one who was outstanding in wisdom and virtue as well as zeal for the advancement of the kingdom of God and the good traditions of the Benedictine Order. Then he stated that if Minnesota's Benedictines could not arrive at a choice of one of their own members, they were free to elect any monk of the American Cassinese Congregation, and in particular any member of the motherhouse at St. Vincent.

Wimmer knew well what he was suggesting by this pointed recommendation. It had long been apparent that an abbot would not likely be elected from among the Minnesota Benedictines. Father Alexius Hoffmann records the reasons why. Each of the first three priors had eliminated himself from serious consideration; di Marogna because he had chosen to become pastor of the Assumption Church in St. Paul rather than continue among the difficulties of his St. Cloud ventures which had failed, and also because of his advanced age and poor health; Wirtz because of the unforgettable Keck incident; and Haindl because of his retiring and reticent nature, as well as his opposition to the building of a college at Shakopee, which had alienated several of the missionaries. The Fathers themselves were divided into two groups along lines of their missionary work in the southern and northern sections of the state. Neither group wished a representative of the other to head the new abbey. Father Cornelius Wittmann was not seriously considered because he had presumed to head the proposed college in Shakopee. Fathers Anschar, Eberhard, Anthony, Clement and George were missionaries by talent and inclination, Father Wolfgang was needed in the school, and the deacon, Frater Joseph Vill, was too young. This left

94

for serious consideration only Father Meinulph, the pastor of St. Mary's parish, St. Cloud. However, he let it be known that he would be in favor of returning the monastery to St. Cloud, despite the unhappy moves of the past, the excellent Indianbush property now available, and their newly erected 'Stone House,' which was almost ready for monastic life.[1]

Abbot Rupert Seidenbusch

Father George stated unequivocally that he would be content with anyone but a Minnesota monk, and it was opinions such as these which moved Wimmer to make this preliminary remark. After that the actual proceedings of the election did not take long. On the very first vote all twelve ballots were cast for the prior of St. Vincent, the Very Reverend Rupert Seidenbusch, O.S.B., and Abbot Boniface solemnly proclaimed him to be canonically elected. The acts of the chapter were subscribed and prepared to be sent to Rome for approval. Prior Rupert was informed of his election, and the missionaries were able to begin returning to their stations early in the afternoon of the same day.[2] A week later Prior Rupert had a neat little Latin note to the Minnesota Benedictines in the mail formally signifying his willingness to accept. He wrote:

"I have today received the letter dated December 12 in which you officially notify me of my election as your abbot. Although I am fully aware that I am unworthy of the honor and unqualified to bear the burden imposed upon me, I feel assured by your confidence that I may hope to accomplish with your help what I will not be able to achieve by my own strength. Moreover, hesitation on my part was overcome by the hope that God never abandons those who place their trust in Him. Therefore, while I accept the election, I thank you for the confidence shown me and commend myself to your prayers." [3]

The prior of St. Vincent was thirty-six years old when he was elected by the monks of the Minnesota priory as their first abbot. A native of Bavaria, he was born in Munich on 13 October 1830, studied in the common schools of that city and entered the diocesan seminary at Freising, where he pursued classical and philosophical studies. The reports which Wimmer kept sending back to Bavaria about the American mission filled young Seidenbusch with a desire to consecrate his life to that same work. Court Chaplain Ferdinand Mueller, director of the *Ludwig Missionsverein,* arranged admission for him into the St. Vincent community, and in 1850, after obtaining his bachelor's degree in philosophy, Seidenbusch left for the United States. His companion on this journey was a newly ordained priest, the Reverend Franz Xavier Krautbauer, who was going to Wisconsin to work among his countrymen in Bishop Henni's diocese. The two young men became fast friends, and in later years as bishops of Northern Minnesota and Green Bay respectively, continued in close association with each other. Seidenbusch received the name of Rupert in religion, made his novitiate,

95

and after his solemn vows in 1852 was, like so many others under Wimmer, immediately put in command. He was director of St. Vincent College during the school year 1852–53 while still a theological student. After his ordination on June 22 of that year he worked for two years on small missions around the abbey before being appointed pastor of St. Mary's parish, Elk County, Pennsylvania, where he finished the church begun by his predecessor. In 1857 he was transferred to St. Mary's parish, Newark, New Jersey, where Wimmer's Benedictines were working among German Catholics, and here again he completed the church which had been begun earlier. This church, which was dedicated on 20 December 1857, today serves as the abbatial church of St. Mary's Abbey of Newark. After serving at Butler, he was recalled in 1863 to St. Vincent as claustral prior, and skillfully discharged this responsibility during the critical years of the War Between the States. After the war Wimmer was in Rome for over a year, and during this time Seidenbusch directed the community with general satisfaction.

His election did not come as a great surprise to him, as Wimmer had been considering such a possibility for some time. All of the time that Wimmer was in Rome rumors to this effect came through to Seidenbusch. His confrere, Edward Hipelius, who was studying in Rome, informed him as early as 1865 that he would be the abbot if the priory at St. Cloud became an abbey. Hipelius said it was "un fatto compiuto," and again wrote him from Bavaria that his mother was saying she would buy him the finest ring she could find in Munich if he should be elected abbot.[4]

Seidenbusch was a man of moderate stature and rather stout, a tendency which in later life became a serious physical handicap, as his obesity definitely limited his activity and harmed his health. He was good natured, popular, understanding of human nature and thoroughly *gemuetlich* in the best Bavarian tradition of that word. He did not have Wimmer's drive, although Abbot Utto Lang of Metten told Wimmer he thought the abbot-elect was much like Abbot Boniface himself. Surprised at this comparison, Wimmer answered:

"And so you think Abbot Rupert is my alter ego. Is that possible? Strange to say, Herr Lebling [treasurer of the *Ludwig Missionsverein*] has said the same thing, while I certainly believe that our two characters are quite different. Undoubtedly he is much better than I; but on the other hand, after his close contact with me of several years — I am in the habit of taking my priors as confessors — he might have assimilated certain things from me, as Lebling thinks, perhaps some of my mistakes. But I hope that he has at least adopted the one good trait of mine, that of not looking narrow-mindedly only at his own abbey, but in everything to be concerned with the true welfare of the whole congregation. He has often enough seen that I have always done this in my activities and plans; because such an attitude never brings any reward, often not even thanks." [5]

In another letter Wimmer was even more magnanimous toward the new abbot and his frontier abbey:

"I think I may confidently hope that Father Rupert will make a much better abbot than I have been (although that wouldn't be much), and that his monastery will accomplish more for the Northwest than St. Vincent has done for the East. He is young, energetic, pious, chaste, good-natured, conciliatory and honest. In advance he has already gone through my experiences. God bless him." [6]

*St. Louis
on the Lake*

Meanwhile Abbot Boniface had returned to St. Vincent and all waited for the official confirmation of the election to come from Rome. Five months later, on 14 May 1867, the document reached America. On 15 March 1867 Pope Pius IX had confirmed the election upon the recommendation of the cardinal members of the Congregation of the Propagation of the Faith, the missionary curial body which had jurisdiction over the religious affairs of the Church in the United States down to 1908.[7] Two days later, on 17 March 1867, the Holy See had also officially changed the name of the St. Cloud Priory to the Abbey of St. Louis, in recognition of the missionary support of Ludwig I of Bavaria. The words 'On the Lake' were authorized to be added to the new abbey's title because it was to be located near a lake. Abbot Wimmer was highly pleased at this development, as he had never abandoned his cherished ambition to name the Minnesota foundation after his friend Ludwig I. Although the king had been forced into retirement by this time, Abbot Boniface felt that the former Bavarian monarch's contribution to the bringing of Benedictinism to America should be immortalized in a worthy tribute. Now Ludwig's name had been brought into contact with his first daughter abbey.

As nearly six months had gone by since the election, and Prior Benedict was anxiously waiting for the new superior to assume leadership, Abbot-elect Rupert determined to receive his abbatial blessing as soon as possible. Ascension Thursday, May 30, was set as the date, and the place, his home abbey of St. Vincent. This left only half a month to make preparations, and Bishop Grace, upon being invited to be the officiating prelate, had to decline because of shortness of time. Bishop Michael Domenec, C.M., local ordinary of Pittsburgh, was at that time sailing for Rome to assist at the eighteenth centenary commemorating the death of St. Peter, so Wimmer and Seidenbusch decided to ask the Most Reverend George A. Carrell, S.J., neighboring bishop of Covington, Kentucky, in whose diocese the Benedictines were also laboring. He willingly accepted, and Abbot Boniface and Prior Benedict from Minnesota were designated as assistants to the abbot-elect.

That 30 May 1867 was a memorable day at St. Vincent as the community's first monastic foundation was given a son of the motherhouse as its abbot.[8] A large crowd of dignitaries, clergy and laity assembled at 10:30 a.m. in the abbey church, which had been especially adorned for the occasion. Outside, the abbey grounds were graced with triumphal arches and festoons according to the custom of nineteenth century celebrations. Slowly and solemnly the old and beautiful Roman ritual for the blessing of an abbot was enacted. Before the pontifical Mass the brief from Rome approving the election was solemnly proclaimed; the ring and crozier were conferred on Abbot Rupert before the gospel; at the offertory the new abbot offered the bishop two burning tapers, two loaves of bread and two miniature casks of wine. Together the two sons of St. Ignatius and St. Benedict, the one a bishop and the other an abbot, renewed the Sacrifice of Calvary. The final investiture of the new abbot followed the last blessing of the Mass. To the chanting of the *Te Deum* the mitre was placed on Abbot Rupert's head and gauntlets presented. Then a solemn procession was formed, and the abbot of St. Louis on the Lake in Minnesota's Indianbush, in full pontificals and carrying his crozier, passed through the crowd giving his first blessing. Beside him, with tears of joy streaming down his face, strode the little immigrant missionary, Boniface Wimmer the abbot, whose hour it unquestionably was.

Abbot of Indianbush

A festive banquet was held at St. Vincent that afternoon at which time Bishop Carrell gave Abbot Rupert his own ring as a souvenir of the occasion, a ring which would be handed down from abbot to abbot in Minnesota, and worn at the present time by the first abbot's fifth successor. Speeches, toasts, music and good cheer abounded. But the guests who had assembled for the event had not all departed before Abbot Rupert had set out for the 'far West.' He in his practical way could see no reason for further delay; St. Louis Abbey and the pressing problems of the future were awaiting him in Minnesota. He went to Pittsburgh the very next day, to Allegheny and Newark for short visits with former congregations, and then was off for Chicago by train. This rail journey was quite a contrast to the first Benedictine journey to Minnesota eleven years earlier. From Chicago he came to St. Paul on a Sioux City train, and entered the West St. Paul depot toward evening of June 10.

Fathers Clement and Othmar had prepared a public reception by the people of the Assumption parish. When the little train came into the depot, however, Abbot Rupert stepped out at the rear of the last car with his valises, and stood there unrecognized, tired and surprised that no one had come to meet him. Father Alexius explained what happened:

"Among the men sent down to the Sioux City depot was my father, John Hoffmann, Sr., a member of the St. Peter's *Unterstuetzung's Verein*. Years later he told me the following: 'I took you with me (you were then four and a half years old) and carried you on my left arm most of the way from East 10th St. to Bridge Square, across the bridge down to West St. Paul where the depot was and where Abbot Rupert was supposed to arrive in the evening. I held you on my arm, and stood waiting there: at last the train came in and stopped. The escort waited at the front of the first passenger coach, but no one looking like an abbot came out; so they were puzzled and marched back to Assumption Church where Father Clement Staub told them to wait as the abbot was surely coming. A messenger came up to Assumption rectory, saying that the abbot was waiting — doubtless for a carriage — at the RR Station in West St. Paul. Then someone procured a carriage, a delegation was sent to the station and His Lordship was carried to the priests' house on W. 9th Street." [9]

Everyone had a hearty laugh over the comedy, and Abbot Rupert proceeded to acquaint himself with his abbey's and Minnesota's largest parish, commonly called 'The German Cathedral of the Northwest,' since it served as the German national parish of the state capitol. On June 13 Seidenbusch arrived at St. Cloud, visited St. Mary's parish there, and was then driven out to the Indianbush by Father Meinulph. As they struggled along the narrow, rough wagon track through the woods toward the lake shore, Prior Benedict and the community stood in the clearing before the Stone House waiting to receive him.

What a panorama stretched out before him when he came over the hill. There was the Stone House on the lake shore; behind it were the frame house and chapel which had just been moved up from the farm in the pasture. No more of the bush had been cleared away than was absolutely necessary; the ground was uneven and hundreds of stumps bore eloquent witness to the labors of the last fifteen months. All around was a dense forest of oaks and maples hiding the rippling lake to the south and the river behind. Around the edge of the clearing were clustered a few rude log stables for the animals. Nothing in the new abbot's previous experiences offered a point of contact; his past stood out in stark contrast to this primitive scene before him. Life in Munich, in the seminary at Freising, at St. Vincent or the parishes of the East where he had served could never have embraced the cold realism, the vastness and ruggednes of this region. He had volunteered for mission work in the United States, and now indeed he would have his opportunity.

The place had in all its primitiveness, however, an air of contemplation and quiet beauty that was enchanting. On all sides was the quiet of the forest, and above, the great, blue dome of heaven. There was no apparent possibility of intrusions upon this hard-won retreat. But Abbot Rupert was not a romantic man. As the monks led him around the clearing he began at once to point out things that were crying to be done: the Stone House was too small, barns were needed, a garden must be planted, a dam and mill begun at once. The community realized from that hour that they at last had a leader with a purpose and the authority to carry through a project.

The new abbot began to function in a room twelve feet square on the first floor of the Stone House. The building was not entirely plastered and lacked even necessary furniture. The only monks at home were Prior Benedict, Father Joseph Vill, who had been ordained by Bishop Grace in February, Frater Valentine Stimmler, a cleric in minor orders, and six Brothers. The other nine priests and two Brothers were stationed on the missions. Abbot Rupert could, however, take consolation in the fact that he had been chosen by a full majority of the capitulars. He knew at the same time that his choice had been motivated by the forces of misunderstanding among the pioneers, and that his basic task was to achieve harmony by sincere and sympathetic guidance. He must quicken a consciousness of the monastic ideal in spite of the all-absorbing demands of pastoral work; he must begin at once to develop a strong religious spirit by establishing a monastic family which would supply future native missionaries and trained laity for the American Church.

He was genuinely delighted with the work before him and eager to cope with the difficulties that lay to hand. His distinguished appearance, a robust frame bespeaking power, a fine black beard and clear, searching eyes, all combined to leave the impression of firmness. Beneath a gruff exterior, capable of being misunderstood, his men came to discern a simple, kindly nature and deep piety. Nor could anyone have asked for more prudence or inspiration then he supplied during his nine years as abbot.

The first problem which he faced was that of the school. Now that stability of place had been achieved, and a stone building erected, the new abbey could concentrate more consistently and thoroughly on that educational effort which Wimmer's Benedictines held to be so central. They had come to the United States and won support primarily on the grounds of caring for the large influx of German settlers through missionary endeavor and training of a native clergy on the scene. Seidenbusch had been director of the school at St. Vincent, and prior of the abbey. He shared Wimmer's ideal of reviving Benedictinism in the nineteenth century according to the solid and traditional norms of seventh, eighth and ninth century Benedictine effort. At that time, in the service of the Church, the sons of St. Benedict had worked for the conversion of Europe, established their distinctive school of spirituality wherever they moved, and flourished to a marked degree. Seidenbusch wrote in this vein to the archbishop of Munich and the *Ludwig Missionsverein*:

"When I came to my abbey in Minnesota after my blessing, I was met with much rejoicing, but I also had great cause for sorrow. I found the monks full of love and affection, zealous in the monastic life as well as in the care of souls, persevering in all pain and hardship which they have to endure due to the great privations and lack of priests in these isolated missions. I was also very happy to find the Christ-life so deeply imbedded among German Catholics. This indeed brought me great consolation. The great shortage of priests caused me deep sorrow. In Stearns County, where the Abbey of St. Louis on the Lake is situated, there are only five priests to care for ten widely scattered parishes. In view of this great need for priests and the advancement of Catholic higher education, I have taken it upon myself to build up our minor seminary. From this seminary we hope to draw many vocations to the priesthood and also offer an opportunity for higher education to all German youths.

Indianbush Seminary

"Only poor youths come to us for education. Since this state has only recently begun to be colonized, we cannot expect much help from parents. The erection of a seminary and its maintenance entail many debts for us. From the very beginning, we must give the majority of the boys, especially those studying for the priesthood and the Order, not only instruction, but food and clothing as well.

"What we have begun is, unfortunately, still on a very small scale. Since this seminary is the only one of its kind in Minnesota, and the only German one for miles, I am of the opinion that this undertaking should not be discontinued. However, in the near future this seminary will need a new building. We are able to accommodate twenty or thirty boys for the present, and are able to do this by crowding closely together, thus causing ourselves extreme inconvenience." [10]

Seidenbusch pointed out that over thirty thousand Germans had already come to Minnesota, that Irish were moving into the region in large numbers, and that their school was the only Catholic institution of higher education available. He asked for a yearly grant from the *Ludwig Missionsverein* to help build an addition so that monastery and school could be separated, and monastic order and silence enforced. The generosity of the Bavarian mission society now was directed to St. Louis Abbey, as St. Vincent and so many Catholic institutions across the country had previously benefited. A yearly stipend of 2,000 florins ($860) was promised to the Minnesota Benedictines, and Abbot Rupert began plans for a two-story brick building, one hundred by forty feet, to be begun in the spring of 1868. During the year of building the society even gave an extra $750 to speed along the construction. [11]

With this heartening support the new abbot pushed ahead with his plans. The Watab river was dammed and a saw mill erected so that lumber would not have to be purchased at St. Cloud, eleven miles distant. A brick yard was laid out early in 1868 in the hollow west of the present cemetery, since a decision had been reached to take advantage of the abundant clay of central Minnesota. It would be both cheaper and less laborious to build with bricks, and the pressing need for room could more quickly be met. Thus it happened that the tradition of building at St. Louis Abbey with native granite and field stones was abandoned before it was hardly established.

Abbot of Indianbush

But the new addition was both functional and substantial. All joined in the work, and their home-made red bricks had a soft, natural color as well as excellent durable qualities. Architects have characterized this first addition as the best of the brick buildings at St. John's. It was far enough completed by the fall of 1868 for occupancy, and the student dining room was placed in the basement with its walls of granite boulders. The first and second floors were divided into study halls and class rooms, while the attic served as a dormitory. The Stone House could then be used exclusively for the monastery.

This physical expansion was but one aspect of the first abbot's program. The second activity, and the reason for the first effort, was the integration and development of the abbey's educational apostolate. Now that their monastic home was stabilized, the itinerant and primitive school work of the first decade could be improved. Father Wolfgang Northman was called home from St. Joseph to serve as director of the school, and four weeks after Abbot Rupert's arrival, two new members of the community came West from St. Vincent to augment the staff. They were the Reverend Augustine Burns, O.S.B., and the cleric, Alexius Edelbrock, O.S.B. Father Augustine was a native of Tipperary, Ireland, educated in the Irish Seminary at Paris, who had emigrated to the United States to serve in the Pittsburgh diocese where his brother Edward was also a priest. After sixteen years mission work as a diocesan priest, he felt convinced that he had a religious vocation, entered the monastery at St. Vincent in 1866, and after taking his vows volunteered for the new abbey in Minnesota.

Frater Alexius, on the contrary, was no stranger to the area. In fact, his family headed the first German settlers to St. Cloud, and he was among the first five students to register at St. John's Seminary in 1857. He was a native of Duelmen, Westphalia, where he was born on 12 September 1843, and as first son, received his father's baptismal name of Anthony. The Edelbrock family immigrated to the United States in 1850 and settled first at St. John's, Indiana, where his mother died the following year. Anthony, Sr., married again, moved to New Vienna, Iowa, and then to St. Cloud in the fall of 1854. The elder Edelbrock was a dynamic and enterprising pioneer. He established a general store in St. Cloud, and Anthony, Jr., helped in this business place during the winter, while operating John L. Wilson's ferry across the Mississippi in the summer months.

After two years of schooling with the Benedictines south of St. Cloud, and inspired by his boyhood ideal, Father Alexius Roetzer, he determined to become a Benedictine himself. Here he clashed head-on

102

with his father, who was determined to have his son in the store. Both father and son were rugged and spirited individualists, and the conflict was resolved only by Anthony, Jr., running away from the family home at St. Joseph, where they were then living, in the middle of the night on 2 June 1859. He walked the nine miles to the St. Cloud priory, but his father was soon in hot pursuit. The boy then hid in the house of St. Cloud friends for a few days before taking a steamboat for St. Anthony. From there he walked to St. Paul and visited his old friend Father Demetrius, who encouraged him to go to St. Vincent as he desired. The sixteen-year old worked his way down the Mississippi toward St. Louis as a steamboat hand; there several priests offered to place him in the diocesan seminary, but Anthony was determined to be a Benedictine.

His savings were sufficient to get him to Latrobe, Pennsylvania, where he was kindly received and continued his classical studies. During the year 1862–63 he was sent to Assumption College at Sandwich, Ontario, then conducted by the Benedictines from St. Vincent. When he returned to the monastery he was admitted into the novitiate. Following this he acted as teacher and prefect at St. Vincent for three years. Abbot Boniface had decided to send him to the College of St. Elizabeth in Rome for advanced study. This house of studies had been established by Wimmer in 1866 as residence for an American Benedictine Roman agent, as well as a center for young monks studying at Roman universities. But then the news of Prior Rupert's choice as abbot of St. Louis arrived, and Frater Alexius felt drawn to return to Minnesota. Eight years earlier he had resolved never to go back, but he volunteered for the new abbey, and Abbot Boniface sent him with Father Augustine Burns.[12]

During that summer of 1867 the largest faculty in the ten years of St. John's Seminary and College was assembled. Prior Benedict was to teach dogmatic theology; Father Wolfgang, Church history, Latin, Greek, mathematics, bookkeeping and music; Father Augustine, moral theology, religion, rhetoric, English grammar and composition; Father Alexius, philosophy, Latin, Greek, history, English and German; Father Valentine, religion and arithmetic, and to serve as prefect of students with the imposing title of 'chief disciplinarian.' A theological student, Nicholas Dreher, taught German, and two diocesan priests, the Reverends John F. Kearney and Dr. James P. Aylward, who were residing in the abbey for a time at the request of their bishops, also helped with classes.[13] Andrew Schiffrer was the first student to register on August 13, and his artistic talent was employed also in the capacity of drawing instructor. This Andrew Schiffrer was called 'the Baron,' and not without reason. He came from a noble Austrian family, and had determined to emigrate to America in order to go on to Mexico and there fight for his prince, the unfortunate Archduke

103

Maximilian who had been placed over Mexico as emperor of that country by the legitimate monarchs of Europe. But while young Schiffrer was en route across the ocean, Maximilian was shot. So he decided to enter the United States and locate in Minnesota, where he had friends. He then enrolled at St. John's, and a year later entered the abbey as a novice, received the name of Vincent in religion, and continued as a member of St. John's until his death in 1929.

This first faculty under Abbot Rupert had a cosmopolitan character quite distinctive for the West of the 1860's. There was one further faculty member who cannot be passed over. He went by the name of 'Mr. Stein,' and supplied the final dash of color to this interesting staff. He came to St. Louis Abbey as a theological student, was, strangely, accepted, and also assigned classes which he taught most ably. It was not until Abbot Rupert while he was in Europe obtained information of his background, that he learned the full story of 'Mr. Stein.' He was in reality Dowiat, one of the leading spirits of the famed 'German Catholic Church.' This religious body had been established as an attempt by the Prussian government to undermine the strength of the Catholic Church through the establishment of a substitute national body which would enlist the support of ardent Germans. Dowiat had originally been a Lutheran preacher at Danzig who became a Catholic and began preparations for the priesthood at the diocesan seminary in Pelplin. He left the Church before ordination, participated in the 'German Catholic Church' movement until it was abandoned by the Prussian government, and then emigrated to the United States. He abjured his error at Buffalo, New York, in 1864 and moved on to St. Louis Abbey. When Abbot Rupert identified 'Mr. Stein' and dismissed him, the abbey's annals record that "he left for a northern country."

The first faculty of the school under abbey auspices thus totalled the surprisingly ample number of eleven in the ratio of one faculty member to five students. In every succeeding year a losing battle would be waged to keep the faculty total at this initial ratio. During the summer of 1867 advertisements were entered in the columns of several newspapers announcing that St. John's College would open at its new location on September 2.[14] It is interesting to observe that the Benedictines were already calling their institution St. John's College, though it had been given the title of St. John's Seminary in the charter. During these years they consistently stated that since the institution was popularly known at St. John's College, it was being called such for the sake of convenience.

Meanwhile Abbot Rupert prepared to make his first trip to Europe to solicit vocations, funds and aid for the new abbey. Poverty prevailed on all sides; there was a critical lack of books, sacred vessels, vestments and money both in the abbey and on the missions. His begging tour, which extended from August, 1867, to March, 1868, took him

104

across Europe from Spain to Austria. He had interviews with Ludwig I in Munich, told him about conditions in the abbey which bore his name, and left convinced that he would be a major benefactor, but Ludwig died soon afterwards, in 1868. He also saw officials of the *Ludwig Missionsverein,* as well as several prelates and religious superiors in each country. He found to his disappointment that his abbey and its work would have to be better known before he could hope for substantial help and financial grants. The case of an unknown abbot from unknown Minnesota was quite different from the well-established interest of Bavaria in their popular Abbot Boniface Wimmer. While obtaining only $2,500 in financial help, Abbot Rupert did receive substantial quantities of goods which he shipped back to Minnesota from Europe. These books, vessels, vestments and furnishings were important aids to the frontier Benedictines who were striving to transplant to America their monastic institute with its traditions and way of life intact.[15]

Most important of all, Seidenbusch returned with five student volunteers for St. Louis Abbey. He placed three of them at once in the novitiate at St. Vincent, and brought the other two back to the abbey for further classical training. These five candidates were the first of a long line of recruits from Europe during these years. Most of them were from German and Austrian provinces, and had, with few exceptions, attended first-class schools in their native countries. They came accordingly with a solid academic background and were well prepared for philosophical and theological studies, as well as teaching assignments in the future. They constituted the nucleus for the formation of the monastic community during its first half century. The increase during Abbot Rupert's administration was far from phenomenal, but it was consistent and determined. Twenty-four members joined the community under Seidenbusch, of whom only two, the Reverends Placidus Watry, O.S.B., and Francis Mershman, O.S.B., were born in the United States. Ten were ordained priests during his term, one died as a cleric, and one discontinued his studies.[16]

The enrollment of the school began to increase slowly. Classes were begun in the fall of 1867 with twenty-eight enrolled. After the harvest season was over, and a few of the homesteaders could spare their sons on the farms, eight more came. By the end of that first academic year at the new location a total of fifty-one students had entered St. John's. The first brick addition was scarcely completed before it became apparent that another unit for living and working quarters would have to be added. Although the first debts were still in great part outstanding, the community determined to begin building again, as cheaply as possible, as small as possible, with as many materials and as much labor supplied by the community as possible. The second addition was to be also of home-made bricks, 100x50 feet, four stories high, adjoined to the north end of the first brick wing and set at right angles with it. The first diggings were made in the summer of 1870, but so many difficulties were met in securing the foundations in the clay and sand that the building could not be occupied before the autumn of 1871. For years it was known as the middle or main building, since the administration offices were located there.[17]

Abbot Rupert struggled throughout his administration to meet the financial demands of the growing community and of these building projects. He not only continued to beg for donations, but also tried in his own way to borrow money and obtain credit wherever he could. He was successful in obtaining a few loans from individuals such as C. V. Vandenburg of Minneapolis, M. A. J. Baasen of Milwaukee and the Benziger Brothers publishing house in New York. Franz Von der Verlung of Munich, Archbishop Franz Albert Eder of Salzburg and Provincial Albert Schmidt of the Altoetting shrine in Bavaria sent gifts of money. Apart from the yearly stipend received through the *Ludwig Missionsverein* from the people of Bavaria, these donations and loans were irregular and inadequate. Seidenbusch was incapable, both by temperament and inclination, of organizing a forceful program of fund raising. One of his monks, Father Alphonse Kuisle, perhaps best summarized the situation when he stated that "good Abbot Seidenbusch was naturally satisfied with anything . . . and was so indulgent in many things."[18] During this period stable income came only from the activities which Abbot Rupert found when he became superior. These were first and most important of all from the parish and mission labors of the priests. Since the Benedictines, as religious, had made vows of poverty, their personal incomes and salaries were always turned into the common treasury, while parish monies remained in the accounts of each parish unit. Other sources of income for the monastery, such as they were, included in decreasing order: stipends from weekend assisting in various mission stations; student fees, which, however, never sufficiently covered school expenses; and sale of goods whenever there was any produce remaining after the needs of the entire group had been served. Early cash books of the community show sales in the first years of wheat, cattle, horses, hides, tallow, and flour from the abbey's grist mill. The wheat of the settlers in the area was also ground at the monastery mill, and goods bartered or exchanged for this service. When the farmers could not afford to pay in money or goods, as was often the case, the monks donated this service.[19]

Under the first abbot there was, accordingly, no definite plan of financing. The community lived from day to day and were thankful to keep their religious, educational and monastic program operating. One service which a number of the monks made to the region cannot be passed over. It not only supplied quite substantial amounts of money

106

to the monastery, but also was a picturesque example of the practical social services traditionally given by a Benedictine establishment. This was the practice during the pioneer years of giving medical advice and aid to those who sought it. Because of the shortage of professional medical service in the beginning, several of the Benedictines, such as Fathers Clement Staub, Martin Schmitt, Meinulph Stuckenkemper, Adrian Schmitt, and Chrysostom Schreiner offered medical assistance in time of need. It was a monastic family heritage that was learned, passed on and practiced in the missions. The monks were received with open arms by the poor settlers who could afford only in extreme cases to go considerable distances for a doctor. Although priests were prohibited by canon law from practicing medicine, the abbots obtained permission from Rome during the first years for some of their monks to offer homeopathic remedies as long as pioneer conditions continued.

The most noted of these Benedictine medicinal advisors was Father Clement Staub. He had acquired a knowledge of herbs and drugs in his native Switzerland, and as pastor of the Assumption Church succeeded in bringing his countryman, Doctor Justis Ohage, to St. Paul. Ohage was a prominent doctor of that city with a large practice, and he and Father Clement worked together. Father Clement is especially remembered for his famed 'Philopaidia,' commonly called 'St. John's medicine.' The students irreverently named it 'fill-up-and-die,' although they and generations of other early settlers in the region never found its high alcoholic content difficult to take. It could be either swallowed or gargled, and used for anything from diphtheria to the common cold. Other ministrations of the Benedictines included herbs, teas and imaginative compresses, as well as generous application of the 'Kneipp Cure' of the Reverend Johann Kneipp of Bavaria.[20] The early cash books are filled with exotic names of drugs and mixtures purchased for these ministrations, such as mercurinus vivus, arsenicum album, glonium, arnica, chammomilla, phosphorous, pulsatilla and belladonna. The sale of Father Clement's admixtures customarily brought in an average of $50 a month, and they did not lose in popularity until after World War I. When the WPA historical survey of Stearns County was made during the depression years, it was concluded that "among those to be remembered with the early medical history is Father Clement, a holy man, a physician to souls who did much to help the physician relieve the sufferings and alleviate the fears of the pioneer families." [21]

The demands for buildings, money, education, as well as the needs of the settlers, were not the only matters of concern for Abbot Rupert during these years. He fully realized that his first obligation was to establish a sound monastic observance and spiritual orientation in the young Benedictine community. Abbot Wimmer reminded him of this responsibility when he wrote: "Try to have choir and everything that

107

constitutes an abbey in good order . . . for you well know that you are bound under serious sin to have one." [22] Thus when the new buildings were finished no time was lost in arranging a 30 x 15 foot choir chapel on the first floor of the middle unit. Here, from four o'clock in the morning until nine o'clock in the evening, Brother Benno's bell called the small community of monks to chant the Divine Office at stated hours. A plain home-made altar stood at the southern end, while eight 'kneelers' with a moveable bench for a seat served as choir stalls. The monks all faced the altar and were divided into two choirs by a strip of wood nailed across the middle of the long prie-dieus. The abbot's chair was in the back of the chapel next to a large wood stove which on the Feast of St. Benedict, 21 March 1873, fell over during the chanting of Prime. Light came from four oil lamps suspended above the heads of the choir. During the week all priests and clerics gathered here with the abbot according to the St. Vincent horarium, to worship and praise God publicly and as a community. This action was the most important work of their day, as St. Benedict their founder had established thirteen centuries earlier. On weekends, only the abbot and clerics were at home since the priests had to assist in the missions. But the Divine Office never ceased, and at the end of the monastery's first century, no other contribution of the community stands forth in comparative value or significance before God or society.

No mitigation was made in the Bavarian-St. Vincent monastic schedule despite the severity of Minnesota's climate, especially in winter months, and the demands of the monks' active life. The majority of the monks were Europeans and never considered adjusting their treasured religious horarium to the American continent or temperament. It was unfortunate that the first abbot separated the choir chapel from the frame church, and thus withdrew the public worship of God by the community into the cloister. Little did he realize that his action would establish a tradition in the monastery which persisted over fifty years. It was not until the stirrings of the liturgical movement at the abbey that the Divine Office would again be restored to its proper and central place around the altar in the abbey church. Seidenbusch had separated the choir chapel from the main church primarily because of limitations of space, the perennial problem of the pioneers. For their 'church' was the old frame chapel brought up from the Collegeville farm. Although they had hoped to have a good-sized church on the third floor of their second brick addition, the pressing obligations of candidates and students always delayed them. Thus both community and students worshipped God in a 50 x 20 foot building that was 12 feet high. No communion rail separated a plain wooden altar from the people, and a three foot passageway led through the congregation to the sacristy. The simple pews were home-made; there was neither picture nor statue to break the dead whiteness of the walls, and the abbot's throne was a

108

massive, high-backed chair which was placed on the gospel side for the rare pontifical ceremonies.

The early chronicles and diaries record in detail the few ceremonies which were bravely enacted under these conditions on major feasts of the Church year. In Abbot Rupert's time this humble series of observances was made a part of the permanent traditions of the house. Only Christmas, New Year's, Holy Week, Easter, and the feasts of the Immaculate Conception, St. Benedict, St. Boniface and St. Patrick were solemnized.[23] The two celebrations especially cherished by the student body were on March 17 and June 6, the patronal feast days of the Irish and German races. Since the majority of the students were of German ancestry the school year was always extended through June 5 when a full day of festivities was enacted. After Solemn Mass with panegyric in the morning, the whole community would adjourn to the lake area around Boniface Bay where a giant picnic with traditional German foods, speeches, games, songs and good fellowship filled out an unforgettable day. On St. Patrick's Day the same procedure would be enacted, again after Solemn Mass and sermon, at an all-afternoon indoor picnic. The Irish students, who came mostly from the the southern sections of the state, would take up a special collection, go to St. Cloud, purchase distinctive foods and cigars, and return to orate and sing their songs into the night. In this way the first generation sons of the two major American Catholic immigrant groups of this period began to learn to live together and to respect each other's heritage in the melting pot of their frontier school.[24]

The number of students continued to increase steadily. By 1870 attendance exceeded eighty, and during 1875, the last year of Abbot Rupert's administration, a total enrollment of one hundred and thirty was reached.[25] The faculty in turn had been enlarged from eleven to twenty-two. The priest members of the faculty remained constant during these years, while the growing number of capable teachers among the Benedictine clerics and diocesan seminarians supplied this faculty increase. In reports to the Minnesota superintendent of public instruction Father Wolfgang stressed this faculty continuity and emphasized that it could be increased from the clericate any time the board of directors deemed it necessary.

The academic program of St. John's Seminary, commonly called St. John's College, comprised three divisions: the elementary school, the classical course, and the theological course. In the elementary division of the institution, where most of the clerics and seminarians taught, instruction was given in spelling, reading, penmanship, arithmetic and religious doctrine. In this grammar school the abbey was making a typical Benedictine adjustment to the needs of the area where it was located. In the country schools of the day most students passed through four readers, and then went to work. St. John's offered a continuation

109

of this elementary training consisting of three years of preparation for 'college.' Actually, when the students had gone from the fifth to the eighth reader, they were ready for secondary or high school work.

This high school and junior college work, called collegiate or classical course, and comprising the second division of the institution's curriculum, was strict *gymnasium* orientation. During these years there was no provision for specialized study, but rather a general cultural course designed, after the manner of European schools, to prepare students for admission to a university. It comprised six classes, two of elements on the lowest levels, and one each of humanities, poetry, rhetoric and philosophy. There was a striking similarity to the mediaeval disciplines of the *trivium* and *quadrivium,* which Benedictines had been teaching for centuries. The branches in the two lowest classes of this course were Latin, German and English grammar, Bible history, geography, arithmetic and penmanship. The Latin course was finished in five years, as were the courses in English and German. History was a subject throughout. Arithmetic was finished in the second year, algebra in the fourth. Geometry and trigonometry were the highest branches of mathematics taught and occupied the fifth year. Greek was introduced in the third year, rhetoric in the fourth. In the last year eight divisions of philosophy, along with astronomy and chemistry, were studied. For students who did not intend to prepare for the priesthood there was training in bookkeeping.

The Benedictines quickly began to realize that while this system might suit the aristocratic temper of European society, or the traditional upper-middle class schools operated by Benedictines on the continent, it was not wholly satisfactory in democratic America where growing numbers were going to school expecting to find their needs consulted. Members of the community like Father Alexius Edelbrock wanted their educational program to spring from the roots of society, to be in intimate contact with the ideals and needs of the workers and farmers, the Catholic immigrants on the lowest levels of American society. The students came from two distinct American institutions, the western frontier and the laboring immigrant groups. St. John's was a meeting place where the ideas of Europe were applied to the lives of young Americans as a permanent influence on the country's development. Immigrants sent their sons to the cloister for that very purpose, and in this way the cloister in turn made its contribution to the shaping of American society according to the ideals of Western civilization. But there was the further need of associating the basic social activities of the American West with their institution as an intimate part of its educational ideal.

A second adjustment was accordingly made in the institution's program. The classical course was modified, first by providing a scientific course. Secondly, in response to the demand for secondary instruction

110

in business and bookkeeping, St. John's organized a commercial department in 1872. It was grandiloquently styled the Commercial College and offered a three year course. Students were supposed to be admitted only after they had completed eight grades, but young immigrants who could neither read nor write were sometimes admitted, and for the most part they more than justified this trust.

A distinct program was organized for young Catholic men to receive a business training that would enable them to take advantage of the growing demands for trained accountants and bookkeepers in the expanding towns of the region. This commercial sequence included instruction in bookkeeping, actual business practice, commercial arithmetic, commercial law and business correspondence. In addition, courses were taught in religion, English, German, French, elocution, rhetoric, penmanship, geography, history, chemistry and natural philosophy. By the early 1870's the department had been built up to the point where a special Master of Accounts diploma was offered. Father Norbert Hofbauer was sent to the Iron City Commercial College in Pittsburgh for specialized training, and he headed the commercial department with energy. In succeeding years others of the faculty attended Smith Business Institute in St. Louis, and such Benedictines as Alfred Mayer, Oswald Baran and Jerome Heider also became well-known among the instructors in this field. When Father Jerome later became pastor of the Assumption Church in St. Paul he put his training to good use by organizing a markedly successful banking account in that parish for poor immigrants.

To provide each student with both theoretical and practical knowledge of business, the staff employed a method based on the operation of a model emporium and bank. As each student began his work in the department he received from the principal his capital in college currency with which he transacted a regular business. He bought and sold goods, drew checks, notes and drafts, deposited money and discounted notes at the bank, opened and closed his books according to the different forms of bookkeeping. In this way he became thoroughly familiar with the chief business and accounting practices. A course of twelve lectures on commercial law by some of the outstanding lawyers in the state, and four on banking by bankers also formed part of the program.

This commercial department at St. John's quickly acquired an excellent reputation, and students came from all parts of the northwest to enroll.[26] The first degrees were awarded in 1872 to eight students who had completed the three year program. They included Frank Schlick and William Hamm of St. Paul who went on to distinguish themselves in department store and brewery business in that city; J. J. Byrnes of Faribault; Peter Fehn of St. Michael; Thomas Young of Arlington; Adam Steffes of Old Mission, Iowa; William Eversmann of St. Augusta and Francis Cotter of Winona. Five hundred and twenty-two commercial students had taken work in this department by 1897. Merchants, enterprisers and bankers in many communities received their training at St. John's.[27] In this way the Minnesota Benedictines began early in their educational effort to assist Catholic immigrants and their sons to enter the mushrooming American business world with solid and recognized training.

The third division of the institution was the ecclesiastical or seminary department. The clerics of the house had been receiving philosophical and theological training at St. John's since 1857, for the institution was primarily inaugurated as a seminary, with charter under that title. A formal seminary sequence to include students preparing for the diocesan clergy was not, however, set in motion until 1868. Abbot Rupert was intent on preparing both religious and diocesan priests, first for German Catholic parishes, and then for any bishop in need. The closest seminary was that of St. Francis in Milwaukee, and there was no seminary institution to the west of St. John's.

The curriculum was of three years duration, one of philosophy and two of theology. The first diocesan seminarians to enroll were Joseph B. Cotter, Ralph Haase, James Hesse, John Holzer and James McGlone; the Benedictine clerics included Boniface Moll, Simplicius Wimmer, Alphonse Kuisle, Edward Schwarz, Vincent Schiffrer, Bernard Locnikar and Louis Salzeder. The enrollment soon began to increase. Bishop Grace of St. Paul, who was unable to realize his dream of establishing a major seminary, rejoiced that the Benedictines had begun the training of diocesan priesthood students in his diocese. He sent students to the institution each year, and soon requests were coming in from other ordinaries such as Archbishop John Baptist Purcell of Cincinnati, and Bishops James Roosevelt Bayley of Newark, Joseph P. Macheboeuf of the Vicariate of Colorado and Utah, John Hennessy of Dubuque, Thomas P. Foley of Chicago, Joseph Melcher and Franz Xavier Krautbauer of Green Bay, and Michael Louis Fink, O.S.B., of the Vicariate of Kansas. Enrollment fluctuated between twenty and thirty in the seminary department during the 1860's and 1870's. The regular yearly tuition for diocesan seminaries was decreased from $180 to $125 as a policy of St. John's to assist the American bishops to prepare much needed candidates for the priesthood. From 1868 to 1956 St. John's Seminary furnished instruction to a total of 1,678 priests, of whom 1,206 were diocesan priests and 472 Benedictine priests. It also provided the Church with ten archbishops and bishops, and seven abbots.[28]

There was a close relationship from the very beginning between the students in these departments of the school. Those students who were studying elementary or classical courses in preparation for the priesthood had separate halls and distinct schedules for spiritual exercises. But they were neither removed from the ordinary student life of the

112

institution nor isolated from the lay students. They did not wear a cassock during their predivinity years. While the Benedictine clerics and the diocesan seminarians in the upper division each had separate schedules, and wore ecclesiastical dress, they too joined in the common life of the institution. In this way a wholesome family association was generated, with future clergy and laymen of the Church in the United States enjoying together those ageless academic pursuits of a collegiate community. The basic social form of the school was patterned after the synthesis of the monastery itself where abbot, priests and Brothers worshipped and worked together. In the same way as the early mediaeval abbey schools were the forerunners of the first university communities, the identical process was begun in miniature at St. John's. The educational program was not artificially secular, nor was theological and philosophical discipline divorced from science, classics and the humanities. The Benedictines aimed at creating a stable, happy community, simple in daily life, and as rich as possible under pioneer conditions, in culture and thought. Their educational emphasis was on the love of God, reverence for persons and social solidarity. If this could be accomplished to any degree in the family of their frontier monastery and school, there would be, they were convinced, a carry-over to daily life, both generous and helpful, so that in all things God would be glorified. The *Northwestern Chronicle* of St. Paul commented on this endeavor in its columns for 27 June 1868:

"Too much credit to Abbot Seidenbusch and the learned faculty of St. John's cannot well be given — their efforts in the cause of Catholic education in our nascent State will one day be testified to in its records, — and St. John's, growing with their growth and strengthening with their strength, will one day treasure their memories as the 'Mountaineers' guard zealously that of a 'Dubois and Brute.' " [29]

St. John's is not mentioned in the annual reports of the Minnesota superintendent of public instruction before 1872. At that time twenty-four private schools on all levels of instruction were listed, of which ten were Catholic. Three of these ten schools were operated by Benedictines: at the abbey, at Assumption parish in St. Paul, and at St. Boniface Academy in Hastings. Two private collegiate institutions are mentioned, Carleton College in Northfield with 119 students, and St. John's with 106 enrolled. The University of Minnesota by this time had an enrollment of 331. [30] In 1874 Superintendent H. B. Wilson termed the instruction at St. John's "very thorough," and in the next year's report the institution, "conducted by the Benedictine Fathers, so celebrated in the history of education as guides of youth and directors of studies," was accounted as rapidly growing in reputation, importance and numbers. The Reverend Wolfgang Northman, O.S.B., professor of English at St. John's, also entered a description of the site of the institution. He characterized it as scarcely rivalled in the northwest and then continued with a description, all in one sentence, typical of nineteenth century florid promotion material:

"By a placid lake, whose limpid waters gently lave a slowly receding shore; encircled by congenial hills whose verdant sides lend beauty to the scene, or raise their snow-crowned tops to stay the winter's withering blast; in a noble forest cultured by nature's generous hand; whose towering tree tops cast refreshing shades in summer's heat or animate weary hope in winter's cold; near the lonely Watab, that gently glides amid hills and through vales to busier scenes of bustling life; amid silence undisturbed save by the sylvan zephyr's gentle murmur, Nature planned a home for science and spread round beauties with lavish hand, inspiring thoughts of beauty increate, in whose mysterious ways the human mind delights to wander, on whose hidden but unerring laws finite intelligence delights to dwell." [31]

In March of 1869 the Minnesota legislature had authorized the institution to confer college and university degrees and academic diplomas. The first six degrees were conferred on 24 June 1870, and included a master of arts to the Benedictine, Boniface Moll, and bachelors of arts to Joseph B. Cotter and John Nealis of St. Paul, Fratres Simplicius Wimmer, Alphonse Kuisle and Bernard Locnikar. These early commencement days also served as 'exhibition days' at which, according to the fashion of the time, impressive demonstrations of student achievement on all grades were prepared for the general public. At first an outdoor Grecian theatre was prepared to the south of the buildings on the lake shore, and elaborate programs of declamation, drama, music and awards were presented. From five hundred to seven hundred people would attend these yearly events which lasted for five hours from nine o'clock in the morning. By 1874 a unique, large frame exhibition hall had been erected to the northeast of the buildings especially for these occasions. The Minnesota authoress, Minnie Mary Lee of Sauk Rapids, was a frequent visitor on exhibition days and sent reports to newspapers, of which the 26 June 1872 account in the *Northwestern Chronicle* is characteristic:

"St. John's, where it is, is a happy surprise. You may have heard its name called frequently — have heard that it was prospering, that it had many students — that it was situated some three or four miles from St. Joseph, a small town of little note — but you have no great expectations about it — the people all around about are a farming community, how can anything very astonishing in the educational line have arisen in their midst? Can any good come out of Nazareth? You receive a card invitation to the exhibition. You wonder if it is really worth your while to go. Were it a hundred miles away, you would be more inclined. But right here at home? Still, there is so little of other entertainments, and you start. It is a fine road leading to St. Joe (from St. Cloud) through fine farms. White houses with green blinds have taken the place of many a primitive shanty and log-house. Leaving St. Joe, you take the college road which is up and down hill through a magnificent forest. The way does not seem so long, because it is so unusual a one for our State. You admire the tall, graceful trees, as do evidently the squirrels and birds, whose twitter and music fill the air. There is a long line of carriages winding over the hills in front of you and a stream behind as far as you can see. Carriages? Most of them are farm wagons, loaded to the brim with whole families. . . .

"I had thought to tell you something of the exhibition. After all, what is a school or a college exhibition that may be particularly described? Plays and dramas in English and German, well selected and creditably acted; orations in Greek, Latin, French, German and English, and oh! such music, both plaintive and lively, and all sweet and beautiful.

"No marvel the Germans turn out in crowds: they are proud of St. John's, their sons' Alma Mater. Though they may not go elsewhere, save to Mass, for all the year, they gather up their children and make the pilgrimage. They have something to look forward to and something to remember." [32]

This observer's enthusiasm for musical achievement at St. John's was indicative of the reputation the institution had for emphasizing music from its inception. Since most of the monks were of Germanic origin, they combined native talent and interest with the treasured Benedictine tradition of music as integral in religious and community life. The carry-over to their educational program was instinctive and spontaneous. During the struggles of the school's first ten years, vocal and instrumental instruction was never abandoned. When Abbot Rupert arrived at the abbey an instrumental group was waiting for him in the belfry of the Stone House. With two violins sent from Bavaria, a baritone horn and trumpet, the first instrumental group at St. John's was born, and Abbot Rupert came up the walk to the strains of "Home Sweet Home." In 1868 a small set of second hand brass instruments was obtained in Minneapolis, and the school catalog announced the formation of a band under the direction of the Northmans, Wolfgang and Ulric. Beginning with twelve members, this organization was the pioneer band of the region, and by 1900 had grown to twenty-five musicians.

The monks also fervently desired to form an orchestra, and during the year after the band was established, Father Norbert Hofbauer took the first step by organizing a string quartet, dedicated to the playing of chamber music. At first the group played mostly Hayden, but were soon including others of the classical and romantic masters in their repertoire. Father Norbert, who had received lessons in his native Bohemia, was an accomplished violinist and in great demand as a soloist. The same Minnie Mary Lee describes his solo at the exhibition of 1874 as follows:

"The St. John's band has become so famous for its excellence that it need not be dwelt upon in praise. Good judges who before never listened to it were surprised and delighted. The violin performer (Father Norbert) may be regarded simply as a prodigy: one of those geniuses, which now and then arise, gifted for astonishing and entertaining us every-day mortals.

"While Norma was being played, a certain lady remarked to her husband: 'There, *that* is the part I never get right.' 'That! You never play *that!*' was the answer. This suggested to me that we might all aver of the music generally — we never heard *that* before." [33]

Practice conditions were far from ideal. One small room with one piano sent up from St. Paul by Father Clement was the entire music department. In 1872 Michael Esch of St. Paul gave a piano to cover board, room and tuition for his sons Peter and Jacob, and then there were two. Practice schedules were not regular, and time had to be snatched from over-crowded days whenever possible. The Reverend John Katzner, O.S.B., was the first full-time instructor, and gave lessons in piano, violin, flute, clarinet, guitar, cornet and other instruments. Father Ulric helped with piano and cornet; Father Norbert with violin. The stock of available music was meager, and there was no money for purchases. So Father John proceeded to harmonize most of the music himself since he had only to hear the melodies to jot down the harmonization. Abbeys and friends in Europe soon sent music, however, and by the 1880's real progress had been made.

Vocal and choir work was more advanced. Every ecclesiastical student had to learn at least one instrument, and was also required to take singing lessons at the rate of twenty-five cents an hour. In this way the faculty hoped to instill respect for beauty and art in public worship conducted by these future priests of the American Church. Cecilian music was cultivated at this time, and elaborate preparations were always made for major feasts. Fathers Ulric (bass), Wolfgang (baritone), Simplicius and Louis (tenors) possessed good voices, chanted the Holy Week Passions and Lamentations, and sang for parish events. Both the monks and the students had choirs, and on special occasions would combine in Masses by Witt, Schweitzer, Thaumann, Mozart, Concone, Lambilotte or Zangl. The brass band would play for the entrance processional, and then the string ensemble would take over the accompaniment for the sung Mass. Both were stationed in the choir loft. The monastery choir would often sing at various church functions in neighboring parishes during these years, and the brass band would accompany them to assist at church blessings, public functions and funerals. At the abbey funerals the brass band always accompanied the corpse to the cemetery while rendering Chopin's funeral march.

Literary organizations also received emphasis during these years, and were along with musical groups the popular source of recreation.

116

In 1869 the senior students organized the Grace Literary Association, named after the bishop of the diocese. Its avowed purpose was to assist its members in mastering English and providing opportunities for oratory and debate. Public disputations were held on such topics as capital punishment, the primacy of St. Peter, the marks of the Church and its infallible teaching authority. The following year a similar organization, the St. Boniface Literary Organization, was founded for the cultivation of German Letters. Both of these organizations sponsored a private library, and engaged in a considerable amount of dramatics. Programs by these clubs were given on every possible occasion since the students were forced to provide their own entertainment.

In these days students were under strict supervision, and were not free to leave the grounds or go "out of bounds" without permission. A comprehensive set of rules regulated all of their activities, and these rules were enforced, including those against smoking and trips to town when the motive was anything but dire necessity. The parents of the students agreed with these regulations, and in many cases sent their boys to the Benedictines because they knew the character of St. John's regime. The faculty regarded these rules not in a narrow or restrictive way but as an indispensable means of character formation. The institution's prime concern was to develop Christian gentlemen endowed with both intellectual and moral virtues. Religion held a central place in student life; all were required to assist at Holy Mass daily and attend other religious exercises as well. In 1871 the Sodality of the Holy Name was organized on the campus and for many years proved to be a valuable means of fostering piety.

St. John's was not creating its own disciplinary pattern by these procedures, but was only reiterating ideals associated with Benedictine educational experience. Derived from a family philosophy, this educational emphasis on Christian cultural formation was rooted in development of both moral and intellectual virtues as equally important. The norm was St. Benedict's rule of life. These monks could not accept the assertion, being advanced steadily in the nineteenth century, that habits of searching for truth, goodness and beauty were either in conflict or separated realities. Father Wolfgang summed up their position:

"The code of general regulations is adopted on what a lengthened experience has tested and proved most efficient to advance students in the practice of virtue, and in the acquiring of useful knowledge and graceful accomplishments. The direction is always firm, yet decidedly paternal. Noble, generous character is always duly aided; resolute and continued effort to improve, strongly and perseveringly assisted; but any display of degenerate passion is promptly corrected, and, if habitually repeated, is considered an evil which must be eradicated, even if resort must be had to the severest measure — the expulsion of the student." [34]

117

As the school was a boarding institution in a remote, rural area, students were necessarily creative and self-sufficient in their leisure pursuits. Nor did religious exercises, classes and long hours of supervised study eliminate time for recreation. Charles J. Williams of St. Paul, a student in 1868, described these conditions:

"Things were primitive in those days at that temple of learning. I remember this because on the morning after my arrival I heard of an Indian encampment along the lake shore, some half mile distant from the college and being of an investigating mind, resolved to visit it forthwith, which I did. On my return I was informed that I had been out of 'bounds.' In the guilelessness of my childish nature, I asked where the line ran. As it was as imaginary as a parallel of longitude and much harder to find, and as it was easier for the authorities to forgive me than to answer my question, I was excused.

"Our baseball grounds were at the college gate. They were constructed like an angry porcupine's back. The frantic efforts of a fielder to chase down a ball in its crazy career through the array of maple stumps with which the diamond was studded, would be a revelation to the champions at St. John's today. The multiplicity of caroms was appalling. There was some relief for the outs in the rule which retired a base runner hit by a batted ball, for the man whose prowess at the home plate had sent the sphere on its wild course, was apt to find it going toward him before he got very far on his journey. The woodman's axe has changed the face of nature in that locality now. I am reminded that John Pendy of the St. Paul police, used to handle that implement very artistically and effectively. When the boys discovered a particularly obnoxious monarch of the forest, John's Celtic brawn and genius was called into requisition, and like his ancestors in the old land, he cleared the way." [35]

There were other outdoor sports like hockey, horseshoe and football, but the latter was not the modern version of that game. It was played in winter and on ice, and from available accounts it seemed to resemble present day soccer much more than football. Neither baseball nor football was on an organized basis. The first baseball team was not organized until after 1873, and football did not come until 1900. The students of this period were rather informal and nonchalant about their sports. There were no varsity teams to make, and no championships to win. They played for fun and relaxation, since the great wave of organized athletics had not as yet captured American society. After 1900 quite another spirit prevailed.

Students took advantage of all the enjoyments nature offered them on the scene. They took hikes through the woods, hunted, studied nature, built some rather elaborate shrines and memorials to different classes. But it was the lake that especially fascinated them. The institution was proud owner of a long line of sailing barges which always

118

appeared on early prints. Boating, swimming, snaring of small fish and night spear-fishing were especially popular.

The lake was called St. Louis at first, then St. John, and in 1896, after attention was called to its original Indian name by Father Alexius Hoffmann, it became Lake Sagatagan. Sagatagan was the Chippewa name for a group of lakes of the region near which the Indians gathered punk or spunk and of which the institution's lake formed a part. The Indian name for spunk was sagatagan. The shore and inlets of this lake gradually acquired distinctive names commemorating events or members of the faculty. An integral part of the St. John's tradition are such hallowed spots as Hell Gate Rock, British Isles, Meier's Bay, Horseshoe Bend, Ulric's Island, Chapel or Doctor's Island, Boniface Bay, Caesar's Bay and Pickerel Point.

The administration of the school was, in the Benedictine spirit, unencumbered and practical. The charter had established a board of trustees, composed of president, procurator and secretary, and the abbot from the beginning filled the office of president, while the other two positions were interchanged between members of the community. Except for the abbot, these officers of the corporation had no necessary relation to monastic officials. While the abbot was president of the corporation, there was also a president of the school during Abbot Rupert's entire administration. From 1867–73 Father Wolfgang served in that capacity, but the guiding force and energy of the young Alexius Edelbrock emerges distinctly. In 1873 Abbot Rupert proceeded to appoint Father Alexius as president, and he continued as head of the school until the end of the abbot's administration.

It was Father Alexius who gradually and definitely took control. The most pressing need was for efficiency in operation. An unusually large number of students could not pay established fees, while the proportion of scholarships and grants-in-aid was necessarily unbalanced. In those days board, room and tuition were often paid through bartering, especially by the farm students. Aloysius J. Schwinghammer, '87, was brought to St. John's with a team of oxen which his father left at the institution to cover expenses. When students from the towns would ask a boy from the country what he was studying for, the reply would be: "For two pigs and a cow." It was not long before Father Alexius became well known for driving a shrewd bargain, a talent he had acquired from his merchant family and his early St. Cloud associations with Yankee business men. He often stated that he had saved Abbot Rupert $5,000 during his days as head of the school. He was economical in every detail, careful of the money he paid out, checking all bills for accuracy, and ordering everything personally and by hand. The constant refrain throughout his letter books of these years is: "Our terms are cash, but very moderate." In many cases he did not get this cash, as students would leave the institution with bills unpaid. Edelbrock

119

was not slow to remind them of their obligations and to tell them repeatedly: "We are in great need of money," or, as on one occasion: "We are dead broke."

At the same time he had a deep sympathy and affection for poor students. When John Stariha of St. Paul came to him in tears in 1874 telling him he had no more money and would have to discontinue studying for the priesthood, Father Alexius wrote to the Reverend James Trobec, pastor of St. Agnes Church, St. Paul, and asked him to take up a collection in his parish for the boy. He stated:

"I think that if it be meritorious to support the poor, an act of charity towards a mendicant student will not pass without a reward. Do you not also think so?" [36]

Trobec did as requested, and Stariha continued his studies for the diocesan priesthood. In the same way Father Alexius was most generous in his recommendations for future teachers, and did all in his power to place graduates in good positions. The beginnings of a characteristic St. John's tradition is also apparent in his letters. If a bishop sent a student to St. John's to be trained for his diocese, such a student was always reminded of his obligation to his future ordinary. Nor did he direct undecided priesthood students towards a Benedictine vocation, but was conscientious in pointing out their obligation to pray and meditate over the question of whether they were called to the religious or diocesan priesthood. To a predivinity student who could not decide which state of life he wished to enter, Edelbrock wrote:

"There is a vocation to the priesthood, and there is a vocation to religious life, and these two vocations are not opposed to each other, but the latter is the perfection of the former, and a good secular priest will also make a good religious priest." [37]

Abbot Rupert more and more turned the direction of affairs over to Father Alexius, whom he trusted implicitly, and gave himself to the growing demands of the abbey's parishes and missions. He explained to the *Ludwig Missionsverein* how his abbey had extensive care of souls and continued:

"Although we have worked and labored here for sixteen years, we are still beginners at our task. However, if we had the support that a well-established monastery in Germany has, so that the abbot would only have to care for the administration of his abbey, it would be somewhat easier. But here, where we have to do everything ourselves, we do not have a bed of roses. We have the thorns, but perhaps our successors will enjoy the roses as well." [38]

The first major parochial decision Abbot Rupert made was to withdraw the Benedictines from parish and mission work along the Minnesota River and in the southern part of the state. As Bishop Grace was slowly obtaining more diocesan priests, the first abbot decided to curtail the monastery's far-flung missionary work of the first ten years. Although Catholic settlers throughout the southern half of the state were begging the Benedictines to work among them, Abbot Rupert felt that the abbey's first obligation was to the settlements in the immediate region of the monastery. A more effective deploying of personnel would achieve greater efficiency in operation.Concentration of effort in the central and northern parts of the state was the more natural and pressing demand.

There was one exception to this decision. The abbey continued to take charge of the state's largest and most important German parish, that of the Assumption in the capital at St. Paul. Abbot Rupert increased the number of priests from two to five at the Assumption Church, established priory life, and agreed to care for the two missions of Hastings and Oakdale on Hudson Road from St. Paul. Because the original Assumption Church was too small and beginning to deteriorate, plans were made to build a large stone edifice. The pastor, Father Clement Staub, never did things by halves. Joseph Reidl, court architect to the ruling Wittelsbach family in Bavaria, was asked to design the church, which he did, and its corner stone was laid with ceremonies on 10 June 1871. Abbot Boniface came to Minnesota for the occasion and was somewhat alarmed at the size and cost of the proposed structure. It was in every way a pretentious undertaking, and for many years the debts accumulated in building the Assumption Church harrassed the parish and the St. John's community. But the vision evidenced in this undertaking was quickly justified. The beautiful Romanesque building, 185 x 85 feet, not only served the state's largest parish, but also, located as it was in the business district of St. Paul, met the needs of transients. It stands today as a memorial to the architectural pioneering of the German people of St. Paul, and their early Benedictine pastors. George N. Shuster noted this contribution as recently as 1953, when he wrote:

"In downtown St. Paul you will find the old church of the Assumption, dwarfed by the grandeur of the new cathedral erected on the hill above it, but still in many respects more significant. For the Assumption came right out of the heart of the German Rhineland, is as close as the builders could come to the score of small minsters in which the glory of Mainz or Maria Laach was scaled down to meet the needs and desires of lesser towns like Andernach. It belongs where it was put up, because at the time it was the Catholic Rhineland which moved into Minnesota." [39]

In St. Joseph the congregation was faced with the same building decision that was met at Assumption parish. St. Joseph's parish had grown from eight to one hundred and eighty families, and a new church structure had to replace the old frame building. After much consultation it was decided to build a Rhineland Gothic church, 150 x 66 feet, from field stones and native red granite. Father Anthony began and the pioneer, Father Cornelius, continued the direction of this community endeavor. During the winter of 1869 farmers hauled boulders from the fields and quarries along the Sauk River, and construction was begun the following spring. Local craftsmen who used their talents to build 'their church' included the masons Martin Fielder, Andrew Fuchs and his son Baltasar; the carpenters, Ferdinand and John Danzl, Sr.; and the artisans Andrew Schwegel, Michael Roth, and the local strongman, Peter Adam, whose feats of strength with these boulders became legendary. The congregation decided to await more prosperous years for the completion of the church tower, and made plans to have their church consecrated on 29 June 1871. Their church was to be the first consecrated church in Minnesota; Abbot Rupert pontificated and Bishop Grace performed the consecration rites before a happy throng.[40] Within the twenty-five mile radius of the abbey, where Abbot Rupert had doubled the number of priests from four to eight, churches were also built during these years in St. Michael, Melrose, Sauk Centre, Albany, St. Wendelin, St. Augusta, and enlarged at St. Nicholas. New parish houses were erected in St. Paul, St. Cloud, St. Joseph and St. Augusta.

Abbot of Indianbush

This building activity grew out of the rapidly increasing movement of new settlers into Minnesota. During the years after 1870 there was a quick extension of railroads throughout the state with direct social and economic advance on all sides. Duluth was connected by rail with St. Paul in 1870, thus opening the northern area of the state as settlers began to develop that 'city of unlimited potential.' For Duluth, the 'Head of the Lake,' was now the natural terminus of a continual waterway to New York for outgoing midwest grain and lumber and incoming eastern coal and merchandise. In the following year the main line of today's Great Northern Railroad, then called the St. Paul and Pacific, was extended to Breckenridge on the Red River of the North, and the Northern Pacific united Duluth with Moorhead, also on the same Red River. Then in 1872 the Milwaukee and St. Paul line was extended through Winona to LaCrescent at the southern end of the state, bringing Minnesota's railroad lines to 1,906 miles, of which seventy percent had been constructed in four years. It was during that same year of 1872 that the St. Paul and Pacific rails were completed from St. Cloud to Melrose, and new stations at St. Joseph, Avon, Albany and Melrose were opened on this thirty-five mile extension. Life at St. John's and in the region was altered dramatically by this advance. St. Joseph now became the post office as well as the passenger and freight station for the institution, and would remain so until 1879 when the Collegeville station was established. Now the laborious trips to St. Cloud with heavy springless wagons, over ill-kept roads, through mud in summer and snowdrifts in winter, were a thing of the past. The station was only three miles distant, and labor as well as carrying expenses were cut considerably.

But more important was the large number of new settlers who followed the railroad lines into the region. The settlement about the Spunk Lakes five miles northwest of the abbey was called Avon. Albany, first known as Two Rivers or Schwinghammer's Settlement, was seven miles further on, while Freeport, then Oakdale in Oak township, developed between Albany and Melrose. These stations did not have resident priests at first. Prior Benedict organized the parishes of Avon and Albany, and visited them on weekends from the abbey; Melrose was visited from New Munich. One of Abbot Rupert's main concerns was to obtain more resident priests for this new area north of St. Joseph.

Settlers at the same time continued to pour into the entire region. According to a Minnesota legislative survey of 1875, the state had a total population of 597,407, of whom 376,000 were native American, 205,949 being from such eastern states as Pennsylvania, New York, Indiana, Illinois, Ohio and Wisconsin. There were 217,429 foreign-born people in the state, of whom the largest segment were 88,325 Scandinavians, who had been coming into the area in large numbers. Germans and Austrians were next with 67,030, and would in time become the largest single nationality in Minnesota. English-speaking immigrants from Britain and Ireland numbered 52,932, and there was a scattered 9,142 from other countries.[41] Minnesota had grown in twenty years from lowest in population to twenty-eighth among thirty-seven states. It was a typical American commonwealth with a diversified populace of transplanted Easterners and foreigners. The foreign-born people made up thirty-seven percent of the total residents.[42] The main body of the population resided roughly south of St. Cloud and east of New Ulm, but a pronounced movement into the northern and western areas of the region had begun. The two main industries were lumbering and milling of wheat, Minnesota's chief crop. With the extension of the railroads, settlers had the courage to move out into the free prairie lands, and soon the Dakotas would be opened. Settlers were now moving past the older river counties of the state out into the back counties.

It was because of this new economic and social development that the Benedictines, located in the center of this expanding frontier, were called upon to supply pastoral care where it was needed. The first movements were made by Abbot Rupert throughout central Minnesota. Under his successor the second Catholic missionizing effort would be extended to the northern part of the state, and then out into northern Dakota.

German Catholics continued to be the main colonizing force of central Minnesota. Immigrants came in a steady flow during the four decades after the War Between the States. The movement of these

123

Germanic peoples through central Minnesota was not haphazard. They headed for Stearns, Morrison, Benton, Todd, Sherburne and Pope counties because they had friends there already, had heard of the available farm lands, or had received reports that the Benedictines were creating Catholic communities in that region. Abbot Rupert and individual Benedictine pastors continually made direct contact by mail with various people and advertised in German papers for Catholic settlers.[43] Thus gradually separate areas of the region began to take on distinctive characteristics. The Cold Spring, Jacobs Prairie, Collegeville area was called the Bavarian settlement; Albany was *Nieder-Bayern*, or as these people liked to be called, *Grober-Bayern*; Freeport and Meier Grove were Plattdeutsch; St. Augusta was Westphalian; and the Luxemburgers moved into the community of Luxemburg. The Irish who came to central Minnesota settled in the farming communities of St. Wendel and Maples around their churches of St. Wendelin and St. Columbkille, and included such families as the Barretts, Meaghers and Murphys. Other Irish railroad workers settled in Melrose and started their church of St. Patrick there. Some Irish and English-speaking settlers came to St. Cloud, as did Polish peoples. Austrians, or more specifically Krainers, settled in the townships of Brockway and Krain. These Krainers were Slovenes from the ancient Austrian crownland of Carniola, and came into the area at the call of their missionary countrymen Fathers Pierz, Ignatius Tomazin and Joseph Buh, all of whom were working among the Indians in the northern part of the state.[44]

While efforts were being made to bring the sacramental life of the Church to these peoples, and to aid them to advance in Christian virtue and perfection, movements were formulated to strengthen ecclesiastical organization in the area. Minnesota at this time was a part of the ecclesiastical province of St. Louis, and as early as 1869 Bishop Grace had intended to propose a division of his diocese if a provincial synod could be called. But since there was no prospect of one being held, Archbishop Kenrick had advised Bishop Grace to write to the other bishops of the province advancing the idea of a division of the diocese of St. Paul. He proceeded to do this in 1871, and described the great increase in Catholic population. Land was being rapidly taken up and increasing in value so that Grace felt no time should be lost in securing good property for the interests of religion. Finding it impossible to attend to the spiritual and material interests of his extensive territory, he recommended the division of the diocese north of the southern boundary of Chisago, Isanti, Sherburne, Stearns, Pope, Stevens and Traverse counties in Minnesota, as well as Richland, Ransom, La Moure, Logan and Burleigh counties in North Dakota. Such a division would extend from the Mississippi and St. Croix on the east to the Missouri and White Earth rivers on the west; from his proposed southern boundary to Canada on the north. This area would include about two-thirds of the original area of the diocese of St. Paul, and the new bishop could reside in St. Cloud.

Grace stated that the work of the Church in this area was mostly in charge of the Benedictines, and he placed the name of Abbot Rupert first on his proposed *terna* of recommended names for bishop. In second and third order he suggested two priests of his diocese, the Reverends Joseph Buh, Slovenian missionary, and Alexander Berghold, German pastor in New Ulm. He added that he felt it was desirable for a Benedictine to be appointed, and urged the bishops of the province to express their opinions by letter to the Congregation of the Propagation of the Faith in Rome.[45]

Vicariate of Northern Minnesota

Bishop Heiss of LaCrosse did not entirely agree with Grace. He felt that such a diocese could not support a bishop who was not a Benedictine, as nearly all of the priests in the district were Benedictines; St. Cloud was small with no future; and the northern sections along the shores of Lake Superior would not offer much support for a bishopric especially during the long winters. He preferred Winona, rival city to LaCrosse, as site for a new Minnesota diocese, thus placing St. Paul as the center of a northern and southern division of the state. Heiss also felt that more important than a new diocese for Minnesota was the necessity of dividing the St. Louis province itself and of making Milwaukee a provincial see for the northern area of the Mississippi valley.[46]

Each of the ten suffragan bishops of the province expressed his opinions concerning this and other provincial matters to Rome. On 1 March 1874 Archbishop Kenrick announced that a provincial synod would be held in St. Louis on March 11 for formal discussion and voting to be forwarded to Rome. Bishop Joseph Melcher of Green Bay had died in the interim and his successor must be recommended. Also under discussion was the possibility of new sees in Peoria, Davenport, Kansas City, and a coadjutor for the Vicariate of Nebraska. All of these recommendations were made, as well as the advancement of Milwaukee and Chicago to provincial status. On 12 February 1875 the Holy See, by papal brief, proceeded to divide the province of St. Louis by establishing the province of Milwaukee, but delayed the establishment of the province of Chicago for five more years, and the division of the diocese of Dubuque for six years. The new province of Milwaukee was to include the suffragan sees of Green Bay, LaCrosse, Sault Ste. Marie, St. Paul, and a new Vicariate of Northern Minnesota divided along the lines recommended by Bishop Grace. Abbot Rupert was named first bishop of the new vicariate, his friend, Franz Xavier Krautbauer, second bishop of Green Bay, and the Reverend John Ireland, priest of the diocese of St. Paul, was named to succeed Bishop James O'Gorman, O.C.S.O., as vicar apostolic of Nebraska.[47] As

125

further indication of the growth of the Church not only in the Mississippi valley, but throughout the country at large, the Holy See established during this same year three other new provinces — Boston, Philadelphia and Sante Fe.

Abbot of Indianbush

The news of this honor bestowed on the abbey community and its first abbot was received with joy on all sides. It was both a recognition of the work of the Benedictines in the upper midwest, and stimulation for further participation in the Church's mission of spreading the kingdom of God. The new vicariate in Minnesota, which Bishop-elect Seidenbusch was to head, extended 250 miles north and south, and 500 miles east and west. The Holy See had designated this district as a vicariate apostolic, a canonical division of an ecclesiastical territory which was not a diocese but rather a provisional arrangement to last until such a time as the area's population warranted the establishment of a diocese. Abbot Rupert was to be consecrated a bishop, however, as head of this new vicariate, and he was designated titular bishop of Halia, a former Armenian diocese in Asia Minor that was no longer actively organized. Father Edward Hipelius of St. Vincent, the American Cassinese Congregation's canonist of those days, while congratulating Seidenbusch on his new position, pointed out that he could take consolation in the fact that his titular diocese at least was not pagan but only schismatic, since it was located in territory under the control of the Greek Orthodox Church. In a more serious vein, Hipelius went on to inform Seidenbusch of procedures to be employed in the consecration of a Benedictine bishop. He was informed that he was not to wear the violet cassock of a bishop, but retain his black cassock with no violet trimming. When he left the monastery he was to leave with the community everything he had as abbot, and could take only such things as the chapter presented to him as a gift.[48]

Abbot Rupert proceeded on March 7 to make provision for the immediate future of the abbey by appointing Father Alexius Edelbrock as prior and Father Bernard Locnikar as subprior. By these prophetic choices Abbot Rupert placed in office the two monks who would be his successors as abbot of the monastery. He formally submitted his own resignation as abbot to the chapter on 4 May 1875. The capitulars then elected Prior Alexius as vicar of the chapter, and Father Cornelius Wittmann as administrator of the institution's temporalities, both offices to continue until an abbatial election could be held.

It was first announced that Abbot Rupert was to receive episcopal consecration at the Assumption Church in St. Paul. But since he had selected St. Cloud for his residence, the people of St. Cloud successfully prevailed upon him to hold the ceremonies in St. Mary's, the mother church of that city. He chose for the date of his consecration May 30, the same date on which, nine years previous, he had received the abbatial blessing.

126

Abbot Wimmer came west to witness the elevation of his first foundation's abbot. It was the second episcopal consecration in five years of one of his Benedictine sons. In 1871 Prior Louis M. Fink, O.S.B., of his second foundation, St. Benedict's Priory at Atchison, Kansas, had been appointed coadjutor bishop of the Vicariate of Kansas and the Indian Territory. Bishop Fink had just the year previous, on 18 November 1874, succeeded Bishop John Baptist Miège, S.J., as bishop of this vicariate. For Wimmer these appointments were major consolations of his life. Although he never was to become a bishop himself, he rejoiced in these honors received by his monastic family, and saw in them confirmation of his dreams of the last thirty years. He had first brought organized Benedictine life to the New World, established it firmly, and was now watching it become again an integral part of the life of the Church as it had been for centuries, before dissolution, revolt and revolution in Europe had all but destroyed the Benedictine Order. A colony of French Benedictines had gone to the present state of Oklahoma and during the year following Abbot Rupert's consecration, Abbot Isidore Robot, O.S.B., had been appointed prefect apostolic of the Indian Territory. The Swiss Benedictine foundation established at St. Meinrad, Indiana, in 1854 had also flourished in the United States, and three years after Abbot Rupert's consecration, the first abbot of St. Meinrad's, Martin Marty, O.S.B., was, because of his devotion to the spiritual care of the Dakota Indians, appointed bishop of the newly erected Vicariate of Dakota. In this way, one American prefecture and three vicariates were placed in charge of the Benedictines during the decade of the 1870's. There was no better evidence that the sons of St. Benedict had recaptured their original missionary spirit established by their founder. To Wimmer there was a further satisfaction in the fact that Benedictines were charged with the spiritual care of missionary vicariates and a prefecture, not with well-established dioceses.

Bishop Grace was absent in Rome at this time, so Bishop Michael Heiss of La Crosse consecrated Bishop-elect Seidenbusch, assisted by Bishops Joseph Dwenger of Fort Wayne and Louis Fink, O.S.B., of the Kansas vicariate. Bishop John Hennessy of Dubuque delivered the sermon, and Bishop Rupert's old friend, Bishop-elect Franz Xavier Krautbauer of Green Bay, was present in the sanctuary. Special trains brought societies, dignitaries and clergy to St. Cloud from all parts of the region for the ceremonies. Predominant on the scene, however, were the farm wagons and buggies of the Catholics of central Minnesota who were on hand to welcome their first bishop.

Bishop Seidenbusch decided to make St. Mary's Church his procathedral, and took up residence in the rectory there. During the following year he bought Joseph Broker's brick residence near the corner of Sixth Avenue and Third Street North as his residence, and began making plans for the building of Holy Angels Procathedral and parochial school. This plant would not be finished until 1884, however. In the meantime the new bishop began confirmation and visitation tours of his vast vicariate. His first confirmation tour took him into parts of Minnesota where the sacrament had never been administered. He visited Duluth, Brainerd, White Earth, Moorhead, Pembina, as well as Fort Trotten, Jamestown and Wahpeton in Dakota Territory. He dedicated the new church of St. Wendelin in the town of St. Augusta, selected a site for a church in Fargo, and began extensive plans for the spreading of Catholicism in northern Minnesota. Twenty-one Benedictines and eight diocesan priests comprised Bishop Seidenbusch's clergy. There were forty-two churches in the vicariate, thirty-six stations, one college at St. John's and three orders of Sisters : Benedictines at St. Joseph, Franciscans at Belle Prairie, and Sisters of Charity at the Devils Lake Indian Agency, Fort Trotten, Dakota. The total Catholic population of this area included 14,000 Whites and 25,000 Indians.[49]

Abbot of Indianbush

Four days after the consecration of Bishop Seidenbusch the chapter of St. Louis monastery was assembled by Abbot Boniface Wimmer, in his capacity as president of the American Cassinese Congregation of Benedictines, to elect the community's second abbot. Twenty-four capitulars were present, and it was a stirring session from the first moment. There was tension in the air, and Abbot Boniface sensed it. He did not, as in 1866, recommend that a competent monk from St. Vincent be considered. Such a suggestion was not necessary in actuality, for a majority of the electors had already decided that they were going to choose the prior of St. Vincent, the Very Reverend Innocent Wolf, O.S.B.

Father Alexius Hoffmann again recorded the background of this decision. He pointed out that the monks were divided along lines of nationality. Nine were Bavarian, seven Westphalian, three Wuerttemberger, three Krainer and two Swiss. The Bavarians were the founders and pioneers of the monastery, and outnumbered the Westphalians or Plattdeutschers. The Swiss favored the advancement of a Bavarian, while the Krainers were aligned with the Westphalians. Although all of these capitulars were of Germanic origin, yet there were distinct regional ties and traditions which had been carried over into America, and were vital realities at this time to those involved. Now that there was a possibility of one group gaining control of the monastery, the pioneers and older parish priests had decided to turn again to a prior of St. Vincent. They held this position also because they felt an older monk should be elected, one who was learned and who also had been a pastor and a builder. The younger monks, who were already being called 'Amerikaner,' had been building up the school during Abbot Rupert's administration. The older Benedictines on the missions and parishes had not been a part of this development, and felt that directors,

128

professors and prefects should continue in that capacity where they were needed.

When Abbot Boniface finished announcing the first ballot which returned Prior Innocent Wolf of St. Vincent with 13 of 24 votes, he became excited and exclaimed: "No, no, that cannot be. I will not release my prior." Some of the Fathers remonstrated with him and pointed out that he did not object to their chosing Prior Rupert in 1866. He replied that this was a different matter; that he had sent Father Innocent to Rome for several years to study theology and canon law; that he had been teaching the same at St. Vincent for the past five years, and was needed in his seminary. He stated that they must ballot again and choose someone else. On the first ballot Father Alexius Edelbrock had received 8 votes, Father Benedict Haindl 2 and Father Clement Staub 1. The capitulars then proceeded to the second ballot as ordered, and this time the totals read: Fathers Alexius 11, Innocent 8, Benedict 2, Clement 1, and Aegidius Christoph of St. Vincent 1.

Abbot Alexius Edelbrock

Now Abbot Boniface declared that there would be one more vote, and he urged the capitulars to chose one of their number or he would have to exercise his right as president of the congregation and appoint an abbot. This statement was not well received by some, and on the third ballot a few handed in blank votes which were disqualified by Abbot Boniface. The returned votes were: Fathers Alexius 11, Innocent 8, and Benedict 1. Abbot Boniface then announced that he was appointing Father Alexius Edelbrock as second abbot, and that he would account to the Holy See for his action. With this he closed the chapter. As the capitulars were moving into the corridor one of the monks said as Father Alexius sadly and with tears in his eyes passed by: "Now the Plattdeutscher takes over." [50]

Father Alexius did not want to accept the office of abbot, and begged Abbot Boniface to release him. But Wimmer was adamant, and prepared the acts of the chapter along with his own explanation of the proceedings, and forwarded them to Rome for confirmation. Two of the younger and one of the older monks insisted that he enter their protests against the way he had proceeded with this election, which he did. They wanted to report that the election had, in their opinion, not been free. In the meanwhile an anonymous article appeared in the columns of *Der Wanderer* on 12 June 1875 in which the election was discussed, and here it was publicly asserted that Father Alexius had not been elected. Father Edward Hipelius, canonist of the congregation, answered this charge in the following issue, and stated that the voting had been regular and the procedure canonical.

While everyone waited for over two months to hear Rome's decision, Father Alexius headed the monastery. This period, to say the least, was not pleasant for him. The open opposition as well as public and private discussion of the election throughout the country left him with a heavy heart and deep qualms for the future. This was not the case with Abbot Wimmer, however. He was personally convinced that he had proceeded correctly, and wrote a complete account of the election to his Roman agent, Abbot Angelo Pescetelli. It was this act perhaps more than any other which assured the outcome of the matter. For Pescetelli actively defended Wimmer's report in the Congregation of the Propagation of the Faith where it was held up for a time. The Secretary of Propaganda, Monsignor Giovanni Battista Agnozzi, in audience with Pope Pius IX on the Feast of the Assumption, 15 August 1875, received papal confirmation of the election, and Pescetelli cabled the news immediately to America.[51]

Abbot of Indianbush

Abbot-elect Alexius could then take preparatory steps for his blessing. While all the monks of his monastery complied sincerely and immediately with the decision of the Holy See, Father Alexius could not but realize that he was entering upon his office with serious disunity in the ranks. It would be fourteen years before this opposition could finally coalesce and create St. John's most serious crisis. Before that happened, however, the monastery, under the second abbot's direction, had its most representative hour.

CHAPTER FIVE

SOWING WITH GRANITE

It was apparent that the small chapel at St. Louis Abbey could not accommodate the clergy, alumni and friends who wanted to participate in the abbatial benediction of Father Alexius. Not only was he widely known personally, but the pioneer monastic institute which he was to head was an integral part of north central American society, directing a large segment of the religious life of Minnesota. Accordingly, the Church of the Immaculate Conception in the abbot-elect's home town of St. Cloud was chosen for the occasion. St. Cloud, in turn, was well prepared for the event as the episcopal consecration of Bishop Seidenbusch had been held in the same church five months earlier. Special trains carrying guests into the city on the evening of October 23 were received with cannon salutes, and the college band led parades of delegates through the town. The next morning Bishop Seidenbusch conferred the abbatial benediction on his successor in the presence of

131

Bishops Grace of St. Paul and Krautbauer of Green Bay. Abbot Wimmer delivered the first eulogy in German, and Bishop-elect John Ireland, who would be consecrated coadjutor bishop of St. Paul two months later, followed with a sermon in the English language. The fascinating careers of Minnesota's two ecclesiastical 'empire builders' were thus initiated in that same autumn of 1875. Little did anyone realize the complicated crosscurrents of religious and social developments about to be released as a result of these events.

Felicitations and good wishes poured in upon the new abbot.[1] He was thirty-two years of age, in the prime of his manhood, with a good understanding of the character of the community and its work. His years in the school, his intimate acquaintance with the region, his position as president and prior, had, along with personal abilities, fitted him for this responsibility. And yet in the midst of these manifestations of joy his heart was heavy beneath the pontifical raiment. Nor was he slow to inform Abbot Wimmer of these feelings when he wrote: "For the abbatial dignity or rather burden I do not thank you because I have not as yet perceived any good that has come to me on account of it, and whether I will get to heaven in spite of it."[2]

Abbot Alexius entered upon his office in this spirit not only because of the opposition evidenced at his election, but also because of the precarious financial condition of the community bequeathed him by Bishop Seidenbusch. The monastery's cash balance was $277.49 when Abbot Alexius took over, and he soon discovered that debts outstanding from the building program of previous years totalled $30,000. He informed Wimmer:

". . . You know what the situation of our monastery is. The income in Minnesota is meager. Money cannot be obtained anywhere. I am so short of priests that I cannot even take care of our missions without sending out the professors on weekends. I would not be able to take care of the college if I did not have diocesan priests staying here. I am not exaggerating. Anybody can tell you the same thing if you ask them. . . . I want to tell you, Father Abbot, that if your spiritual sons in Minnesota want to keep your name intact, it will mean that we must work and be watchful. I do not even have anybody to run the college and the whole task devolves upon me. I am hoping against all hope that it will get better especially if you will not withdraw your helping hand."[3]

While these problems were serious enough, they were insignificant compared to the critical situation facing him from the first moment at the Assumption parish in St. Paul. There debts on the elaborate church just erected, along with mismanagement and jumbled bookkeeping, placed the abbey's most important parish in a precarious position. The new abbot's first act was to withdraw the good but ineffectual pastor, Father Clement Staub, and call him back to the abbey where he was

132

appointed claustral prior. Father Valentine Stimmler was given the unenviable responsibility of taking charge at the Assumption, and Father Meinrad Leuthard was sent from the Commercial College to audit the parish books. By December the full picture was clear; the total indebtedness of the parish was $151,000, and for years one of the new abbot's main concerns was to liquidate this debt while maintaining peace in the parish itself. It was eventually accomplished through the efforts of successive pastors and the good will of the German Catholics of St. Paul. Fairs were held, drives made, and the pioneer missionary, Father Bruno Riess, came back to Minnesota for a few months to help collect money. These accumulated debts were a serious drawback for a new administration. But with a characteristic zeal and energy which would soon be the talk on every side, Abbot Alexius declared "it is never too late to do a thing well." With a mixture of felicitous ingenuity and frontier practicality, he moved toward positive results. Yet such uncertainties were to continue to plague him throughout his administration.

First
Problems

He immediately began a complete visitation of parishes and missions in charge of the Benedictines of the abbey. This entailed considerable personal hardship and inconvenience, but he was determined to discover at first-hand the spiritual condition of these parishes, missions and stations; to ascertain their financial status; and gain an exhaustive picture of the full mission work of the house. He planned to develop the resources of the community to their fullest capacity, place priests only where they were needed, and then accept new tasks as soon as possible.

Bishop Seidenbusch at this time requested that the abbey turn over to him the Church of the Immaculate Conception in St. Cloud, where he was then residing, so that it could become his cathedral. Abbot Boniface counselled that the Minnesota chapter accede to this request, but the capitulars would not surrender their first parish, the one which they had struggled to establish and bring to its existing condition. The new abbot agreed with the chapter, and proceeded to ask Bishop Seidenbusch what he would do of he were still in the abbatial position. The vicar apostolic replied that in such a case he would not relinquish the parish. Seidenbusch then purchased Henry Broker's brick residence in St. Cloud as a bishop's house, and began making plans to establish an English-speaking parish there, dedicated to the Holy Angels, which was to serve as his procathedral. The bishop also asked Abbot Alexius to serve as his administrator whenever he was absent in the East raising money or trying to obtain priests for his vicariate. Seidenbusch was not offended that the abbey had not relinquished the Immaculate Conception parish to him, and remained on friendly terms with his former monastery throughout his life. However, if the monks of St. Louis Abbey had turned over the mother parish of St. Cloud to the first bishop of the area, as he had requested, the unfortunate differences of opinion preceding the eventual acquisition of this parish as his cathedral by the fourth bishop of St. Cloud could have been averted.

The new abbot soon realized, as he often stated in later years, that he did not have the credit of a sack of flour in Minnesota. He accordingly determined to go to Milwaukee, Chicago, St. Louis and through the East looking for lower rates of interest on his debts, possibilities of refinancing and new sources of income. He had a calling card prepared for himself, and included a short description on the reverse side of who and what an abbot is. Here in his characteristic prose of strong and rather exaggerated cadences, he announced that an abbot was a prelate in his own right, with accompanying dignity and prestige. Years later he would laugh about this card, which became so celebrated an example of his exaggerations and imprudence in the opinion of his opponents, and declare: "That was tossing a bone among the dogs." On this trip he did make several new business transactions, such as obtaining money at a lower rate of interest from the Northwestern Life Insurance Company in Milwaukee, and a loan from the New York Catholic Orphange.[4]

When he returned he inaugurated a policy of economizing that sometimes bordered on frugality. If any characteristic of the new abbot stood out in bold relief to the previous regime, it was punctiliousness in details. Nothing escaped his close surveillance; nothing was allowed to be wasted. He personally set an example of rigorous observance of the vow of poverty. He asked for and obtained passes on the railroads, would always walk from the depot to a rectory in a city rather than take a streetcar, and wore his clothes until they sometimes were frayed and torn. His big old tattered hat became a familiar landmark of the area as he moved from parish to parish, increasing services where they were needed, establishing uniform stipend rates, working for efficiency in operation, demanding and obtaining salaries for his priests from congregations accustomed, too often, in their loosely organized missions, to take such parochial services for granted. Abbot Alexius demanded careful bookkeeping from his priests on the missions, had his prior check parish accounts each year, and if all was not in order as he judged it should be, he would personally appear in a parish pulpit on a Sunday to remind the people of their obligations. If his priests did not comply with his regulations, they were removed.

Edelbrock also determined to sell properties accumulated by the Benedictines during the previous twenty years. In quick succession he sold lots in Shakopee, St. Joseph, Sherburne County, and Broker's brick block in St. Cloud. Then he approached individuals throughout the area to lend money to the abbey, or to accept annuity agreements in which they would entrust their money to the monastery while receiving the yearly interest rates from the principal. Among such individuals who cooperated with Abbot Alexius in these projects were Bishop Seidenbusch, Alois Tschumperlin, Henry Broker and Peter Gotten of St. Cloud; John H. Linnemann of St. Joseph; John Preimesberger, Joseph Deimel and the Dawson Lumber Company of St. Paul. He petitioned for gifts from the *Ludwig Missionsverein* and the *Leopoldinen Stiftung,* and received generous grants, especially for the Assumption Church in St. Paul, and for his new enterprises.[5]

At home he worked for greater production totals on the farm, cleaned up the grounds around the institution, and sketched plans for new utility buildings. The stables were outmoded; the blacksmith shop was a small log hut near the Watab; the carpenters were housed in dingy quarters in the frame house; while unsightly stables and pens were still scattered about the main buildings. So Abbot Alexius had a brick blacksmith shop raised on the site of the present science hall, a new slaughterhouse near the Watab, and a two-story laundry on the shore of the Sagatagan. New machinery which he purchased in Pittsburgh and an improved sawmill were also added. Then he turned to the problem of supplying adequate water, which was much needed both for domestic use and for protection against fire. The four main buildings, one of stone, the rest of brick, housed two hundred persons, and there was a constant danger of fire from kerosene lamps and wood stoves. A new cistern or reservoir capable of holding seven hundred barrels of water was erected on the crest of the hill east of the house, and an accompanying steam pump station placed on the lake shore. This was a farseeing move and a valuable asset two years later when fire broke out in the old stone house on a winter night.[6] Abbot Wimmer, amazed and pleased at these lightning-like enterprises, told Abbot Alexius: "Now you are ahead of us with your waterworks; but wait a little, then I will get ahead again of you."[7] Next he ordered that the hill lying a quarter of a mile south of the monastery be cleared of timber, and a worthy monastic cemetery laid out on its eastern slope. The eight bodies of the deceased pioneers were then removed from St. Joseph and from the first cemetery in front of the abbey itself, and reinterred around a large white cross at the new location on 2 and 9 November 1876.

These general improvements bettered appearance and efficiency. The new abbot insisted that the monastery be self-supporting, as St. Benedict had desired in his *Rule.* Lasting, ample shops and outbuildings were the first step in this program of supplying food and physical necessities at home. Throughout his life he held to the principle that whatever could be self-made should not be purchased. Generally in those days this worked out successfully. It had questionable results later on with larger undertakings, however.

In the midst of all these activities the abbot made his first trip to Europe as companion of Bishop Seidenbusch in April of 1877. They intended to assist at the golden episcopal jubilee of Pope Pius IX, visit

135

monasteries, solicit vocations and funds. After a Roman sojourn, Abbot Alexius visited Benedictine houses in Italy, Austria, Bavaria, and took diary notes on different monastic horariums, traditions and discipline. Although he returned through France and England, he did not visit Benedictine houses in either country. This was particularly unfortunate in the latter case since the English Benedictines were wrestling with problems at this time which might have considerably broadened his perspective had he come in contact with them. There was a strong movement among English Benedictines of Abbot Alexius' generation, such as Priors Aidan Gasquet and Edmund Ford of Downside, to build up the full monastic life of their houses and to outgrow the mission character which was holding them back from developing along traditional Benedictine lines. Shane Leslie in his recent memoir biography of Cardinal Gasquet writes of this development:

"Gasquet found himself in an Ancient Order scattered in old-fashioned missions through Victorian England. They represented the famous black monks, who once served the Abbeys of Glastonbury and Westminster and built the great Minsters, since wrecked or appropriated to the State. Gasquet took the lead in bringing back the modern monks from isolated missions and forlorn Priories. His gentle zeal enabled him to stand between the restorers of the real mediaeval life and the old-fashioned monks, who lived like parish priests, as it was said 'served by a housekeeper and a cat,' instead of multiplying communities of Benedictine life. His influence prevailed and the change was really settled after the visitation of the same Cardinal Persico who had courageously visited the Irish Hierarchy in the 'eighties. Persico had seen in a moment that monastic strength was being dissipated into the dioceses while the imagination and knowledge of England showed that the country had never forgotten the Benedictines in their proper surroundings. Great choral and educational Abbeys, mighty Minsters and modernized schools filled Gasquet's dream. Incidentally, it was necessary to break down the prickly prejudice which Protestant historians had taken four centuries to sow." [8]

If the young Abbot Alexius could have met Benedictines like Gasquet, he might have been tempered in his activistic inclinations and influenced by their ideals to build his monastic community from the very beginning equally as strong internally and at home as it was to be in the many parochial tasks of the growing Church in the United States.

On this European journey Abbot Edelbrock and Bishop Seidenbusch must have discussed the conditions of the Chippewa Indians on the reservations of northern Minnesota, which were within the territory of the vicariate. For on his return the abbot immediately began making plans to accept the invitation which the bishop offered his former community to go into the missionary field among these Indians. This was

136

a most significant move to make, and one of his first policies that met with misgivings and questions in some quarters. The older Minnesota Benedictines especially felt that it was an untried activity and that care of German settlers was more than enough for the abbey to carry. Abbot Alexius was not slow to point out that St. Benedict himself had missionized the pagan natives around his monastery, as had St. Boniface in eighth century Germany. The Bavarian St. Ottilien Benedictines were doing missionary work among the natives of East Africa, as were the English Benedictines in Australia, while the Swiss-American Benedictines, under the leadership of Abbot Martin Marty, O.S.B., had already been working for ten years with marked success among the Sioux Indians in Dakota Territory.[9] Abbot Wimmer agreed wholeheartedly with the project. Since Father Pierz had asked the Benedictines twenty years earlier to help him among the Indians, Wimmer had wanted to establish a Minnesota monastery for such work at that time, and even dreamed of heading it himself. But the monks had been fully occupied in the central and southern sections of the state. Now with the entrusting of northern Minnesota to the spiritual direction of Bishop Seidenbusch, the expansion of the Benedictines into Indian work was logical and imperative.

Father Pierz had first cared for the Chippewa Indians at the Crow Wing Reservation, principal Chippewa reservation of Minnesota.[10] In 1859 he obtained the assistance of his countryman, the Reverend Lawrence Lautischar, but this young priest froze to death in a blizzard on the ice of Lower Red Lake only four months after being taken to the Red Lake area by Father Pierz. When the Federal Government eased the Chippewas out of their lands along the Mississippi River in 1867, these Indians in great part moved to a new reservation of 36 x 36 miles at White Earth on 14 June 1868. Father Pierz again worked alone for a period of six years until he was joined by two more of his countrymen, the Reverends Joseph Buh in 1864 and Ignatius Tomazin in 1868. The veteran missionary returned to his native land in 1873, leaving his two youthful confreres in possession of the entire field.

Father Tomazin came up to White Earth, visited the transplanted Indians, and there erected a small log church, which was blessed on 30 June 1874. However, there was as yet no really organized Catholic mission activity at White Earth. Father Tomazin was occupied in visiting distant Indians as well as white settlers along the Northern Pacific Railroad from Duluth to Moorhead. Bishop Grace yearly became more convinced that he was in no position to provide adequately for the Indians in his far-flung diocese, and this was one of the chief reasons which moved him to petition for the erection of the new vicariate in 1875. In this he was not disappointed. Bishop Seidenbusch confirmed seventy-nine Indians at White Earth on 22 August 1875, and on this first visitation tour realized that Father Tomazin, the only

Indian missionary west of the Mississippi in Minnesota, could not carry the burden alone, and was immature and erratic in his public relations. It was then that the bishop turned to the Benedictines to sponsor this mission endeavor. Bishop Seidenbusch wished to keep Tomazin at White Earth, but was forced to remove him. The bishop wrote a strong letter in support of Tomazin to the Catholic Indian Bureau, protesting the action of the bureau against Tomazin.[11]

Abbot Alexius chose one of his most promising young monks, then teaching in the school, who was talented in languages and who had volunteered for the project, as the monastery's first Indian missionary. He was the Reverend Aloysius Hermanutz, O.S.B., who was sent to White Earth on 4 November 1878 and remained fifty-one years among his adopted Chippewa people until the day of his death on 4 September 1929. Abbot Alexius understood from the very beginning that the abbey would have to carry the financial burden of this new enterprise. No aid was given by the government and the Indians themselves were almost destitute. To gain a firsthand knowledge of Indian affairs the abbot decided to accompany Father Aloysius on his trip north, and the young missionary records how they arrived in the Chippewa country:

"At St. Joseph we were joined by Sisters Lioba and Philomena, who were to conduct the school on the mission. At Brainerd we chanced to meet Bishop Seidenbusch, who gave us his blessing. At Perham we were joined by Father Buh. At 6 p.m. we reached Detroit (Lakes).

"On Tuesday the 5th of November at 9 a.m. we left Detroit by wagon and arrived at White Earth at 2:30 p.m. It was a fine, warm November day. Father Abbot left us at 3:00 p.m., November 6th, but Father Buh remained with us over Sunday and gave us a number of valuable hints. On the Second Sunday in November I read the Gospel in Chippewa for the first time." [12]

Such was the beginning of St. Benedict's Mission at White Earth Reservation. Father Aloysius and the two Sisters found the mission buildings, two miles from the agency, in a wretched condition. They consisted of a rude log cabin serving as a chapel, and two other cabins for school and residence. The 2,872 Chippewa Indians attached to the reservation were members of the Mississippi, Ottertail and Pembina tribes. Tomazin estimated 1,000 were Catholics, with 800 more Catholic Indians living adjacent to the reservation proper. This figure was somewhat exaggerated and Father Aloysius in 1881 placed the Catholic total on the reservation as closer to 800. Perhaps Tomazin included French half-breeds in his total, and then his calculation would be accurate, for a large number of French, along with some Irish, had married Indians and settled on or about the reservation.

The Protestant Episcopal Church, which had been given charge of White Earth Reservation under Grant's Peace Policy, had on the other hand an imposing array of two churches, two rectories for seven preachers, and a hospital.[13] Under the vigorous and noble leadership of Bishop Henry B. Whipple, the Episcopalians had contributed much to the welfare of the Chippewa Indians since 1859.[14] Their permanent missionary at White Earth was the Reverend Joseph A. Gilfillan, who always worked harmoniously alongside the Benedictines during these years.

During the first two years, Father Aloysius gained sufficient mastery of the Chippewa language to preach to the Indians, while visiting numerous small Indian settlements where he began to make large numbers of converts. The Benedictines and their flocks desired to have churches and schools. There was an existing government school on the reservation directed by non-Catholics, but the Catholic Indians wished to have their children instructed in the Catholic faith. During the first winter the log school house was destroyed by fire, and that made it imperative to build a church and school. It was then that Abbot Alexius organized the abbey's Indian work with a wonderful enthusiasm, while expending $20,000 in the following years erecting the imposing mission buildings which stand today. The story of his efforts here, of the robust building venture itself; of his widespread contacts with governmental and Catholic Indian officials; of his frequent trips to the reservation and to Washington to plead the Indian's case; of his effective association with Minnesota's Senator Henry Rice and Congressman Knute Nelson to obtain government grants for religious Indian work — are too detailed for treatment in a general history of St. John's.[15] The history of the Benedictine effort for the Chippewa Indians still awaits adequate treatment, and is worthy of comprehensive analysis. Collected memoirs of the missionaries, reminiscences, and archival records attest to the need of this study as an aid toward a more complete understanding of actual Indian realities in nineteenth century American life.[16]

Father Aloysius visited the Indians on the Red Lake Reservation some eighty miles northeast of White Earth, but there was no permanent resident priest stationed at this point. The Indians of the Red Lake area petitioned Bishop Seidenbusch for a priest, and the White Earth agent at that time, Major T. J. Sheehan, who was the first Catholic appointed to that position, also wanted a Catholic priest working there. In 1886 Abbot Alexius wrote to Katherine M. Drexel, Philadelphia Catholic heiress, who along with her sister, Mrs. Edward Manell, was generously supporting Indian and Negro missions in the United States.[17] He invited them to extend their charity to the Minnesota Indian missions, and they responded in several ways. They sent donations to him personally, while Katherine Drexel began planning for a boarding school at White Earth, which was dedicated on 11 June 1892. But before this was accomplished, the Drexel girls, in company with the Most Reverend James O'Connor, bishop of Omaha, Agent Sheehan and Father Aloysius journeyed to Red Lake to examine the possibilities of opening a church and school. The Drexels promised to aid the mission by erecting a church and school. Abbot Alexius then submitted the project to the abbey chapter, and on 11 November 1888, ten years to the month after Father Aloysius first went north to the Indians, two more priests were sent into this work. They were Reverends Thomas Borgerding, O.S.B., and Simon Lampe, O.S.B., both of whom had volunteered. Abbot Alexius accompanied them, and immediately began making plans for a church, school, rectory and convent. Of the 1,124 Red Lake Indians at that time, one-third were Catholics, and within three years, the Catholic population had been increased to one-half of all Indians belonging to that reservation. Two Benedictine nuns from St. Benedict's Convent in St. Joseph again joined the monks on this new mission, and by 1889 a parish house and a small log school for forty children was built. On 29 September 1893 Katherine Drexel's new church was dedicated.[18]

Thus in ten years the second abbot directed the energy of Minnesota's Benedictines into this field which had been neglected far too long by American Catholics. He had enlisted the sons of St. Benedict in that Indian religious and sociological work which had been the glory of Jesuits and Friars during the three previous centuries. By this step, he followed Abbot Marty in restoring Benedictine participation in the missionary life of the Church in the New World. It was a clear indication of the new vigor which the Order was experiencing and positive proof that the Benedictine restoration, begun only fifty years earlier, had advanced another step. Abbot Wimmer was overjoyed and wrote him: "I like to hear that you engage so much for the Indians. It seems that both the Black and Red men will and must become the object of particular attention and care of the Sons of St. Benedict." [19] Wimmer during these years was expanding into Kentucky, Texas, Virginia, North Carolina, Alabama, Georgia, Florida and Skidway Island with foundations which he believed would be of major influence upon the religious development of the South.[20] He felt that Edelbrock's efforts in the Northwest would have a similar effect. Both abbots, as well as Bishop Marty, had to work within the legal framework of the narrow nationalistic Indian and Negro policy of the Federal Government, influenced far too often by economical exploitation, as well as the accumulated prejudices toward racial and minority groups on the part of nineteenth century White, Anglo-Saxon society. Accomplishments were accordingly never major in character, but a religious foundation was laid for an eventual realization of the true potential of democratic ideals.

While these Indian efforts were being undertaken, the abbot was busy at home with another of the major projects of his administration. For years everyone had realized that the small center room in the old

140

frame house which the community was using as a chapel was all too inadequate for monastic worship and the growing student body. The ceremony and beauty of the Church's liturgy had to be drastically curtailed, and divine services were limited to bare essentials despite the best intentions.[21] In 1876 Abbot Alexius had started a parish, dedicated to St. John the Baptist, for settlers around the abbey, and this congregation also was using the facilities of the chapel. In late 1878 the abbot began to talk about plans for a worthy abbey church to be built on the north side of the existing buildings. Buildings were needed in every department, but the church was given priority. On this project he received whole-hearted support, as all realized that the community had never had an adequate church of its own. Twenty-three years had been given to constructing parish and mission churches throughout the area, and the time had now come for the abbey church itself.

On 3 December 1878 Abbot Alexius attended the celebration of the patronal feast of the diocese of Green Bay, and while there he saw the plans for the new cathedral then being erected by his friend, Bishop Krautbauer. He felt that this church would be a suitable model for the proposed abbey church, and proceeded to send the Reverend Gregory Steil, O.S.B., and Brother Andrew Unterburger, O.S.B., both of whom had had some architectural experience before joining the monastery, to study this church. They were given the Green Bay cathedral plans, which Father Gregory later discovered were of the bishop's home town church in Bruck, Bavaria, and an adaptation of the abbey's own Assumption Church in St. Paul. Everyone had a good laugh at this discovery. Father Gregory then worked at remodeling the plans until they were adopted by the community chapter.

The story of the building of the abbey church is again one of originality, farsightedness, determination and boundless energy. Legend has it that the abbot stepped off the one hundred and forty-four foot length of the proposed church, then turned north sixty-four paces and commanded: "Dig here." The Reverend Xavier White, O.S.B., kept an exact chronicle of the erection of the abbey's first church, and gives careful documentation of the difficulties the abbot had to encounter from an incompetent contractor, bad workmanship and difficult itinerant laborers hired to assist the Fathers, clerics and Brothers who worked on the building. The first contract for the building was let on 14 March 1879, and excavations were begun in early April. Progress was slow as building materials could not be brought in as promptly as desired. Father Gregory was boss-contractor, and the abbot was out on the job with the workers whenever he was free and at home, excavating, hauling and rolling stones. One day he worked in a drenching rain to erect sand barriers as protection for an uncompleted wall and caught a severe cold. The basement walls were laid with natural granite boulders found on the grounds, and the water table was of St. Cloud granite. In the spring of 1880 a brickyard was laid out northeast of the proposed church and operated by the Brothers and hired workmen. Abundant clay of good quality was found on the lands and in the woods around the abbey, and an average of 15,000 bricks a day were soon coming forth from the kilns, which were operated around the clock. These months were the only time in the first century of St. John's that the institution's grounds were adequately lighted at night, as the red glare from burning kilns illuminated the Collegeville countryside.[22]

Abbot Alexius placed the cornerstone in the base of the south tower on 24 September 1879, and the whole structure was under roof by October of the following year. On the ninth day of that month a sad and only accident of this building undertaking occurred. One of the ablest Brother artisans, Brother Leo Martin, O.S.B., superintendent of carpenters and himself a master carpenter, was struck by a falling plank while removing some boards from a tier of scaffolding above his head, and hurled fifty feet to the floor of the transept. He was carried to the infirmary and the abbot was summoned. The Brother was distressed, and when Abbot Alexius asked him what was troubling him, Brother Leo said his triennial vows had expired on September 29 and he had not as yet made final profession. "I guess I'm going home, Father Abbot," Brother Leo commented. The abbot administered Viaticum and Extreme Unction, and about 5:30 received the Brother's perpetual vows. He was then at peace and died shortly after six o'clock. The abbey chronicler records that Abbot Alexius felt Brother Leo's death keenly.

On 24 October 1882 the church was consecrated by Bishop Seidenbusch.[23] It was a momentous and happy day for the community. They were now in possession of a worthy church, built along traditional Benedictine Romanesque lines. Its portals were flanked by twin towers one hundred and fifty feet high, which became with the years a symbol for the institution itself. The ground plan was in the form of a Latin cross with choir transept floor built four feet higher than the nave.[24] The church stood for many years with only the barest necessities because the altars had cost $6,000 and there was no more money available. A few large oil lamps supplied doubtful light; a parlor organ wheezed from the far-off balcony, and two box stoves in the sanctuary constituted the sole source of heat until 1888. The community continued to chant the Divine Office in the choir chapel within the cloister, and the church was used only on rare occasions and major feasts. But a superstructure was there, and a major step had been taken. Actually Abbot Alexius intended the entire north arm of his main quadrangle of buildings to be the abbey church. But the necessity of economy and demands for school space forced him to wall off the apse as it now is. As so often happens in institutional development, such temporary adjustments become, in time, permanent traditions. Where he had conceived a church for a community of 1,200 worshippers, the institution

142

from the day of that temporary adjustment used his abbreviated structure, which admitted only 400 persons at one time. If he had been given enough time to complete his structures as originally conceived, St. John's would have been in possession of an adequate church and would not have been faced with the problem of solving the church congestion which vexed the community in recent decades.

During this building activity, the inconvenience of hauling materials from the railroad station at St. Joseph three miles away became more and more evident. Furthermore, visitors, students, mail and daily freight had to be carried via Brother 'Taddy's' springless wagon over the unforgettable bush road to the institution. In the spring of 1879 Abbot Alexius completed arrangements with the St. Paul, Minneapolis and Manitoba Railroad Company, formerly the St. Paul and Pacific Railroad Company, to have a station erected at the point closest to the abbey. This railroad crossed the monastery's east pasture near the old farm, and here the company erected a small, neat passenger and freight house, while the abbot arranged with the government for a post office there. A large sign was attached to the building announcing that this new stop was known as Collegeville. That name had been used unofficially perhaps for the first time when the Reverend Bernard Locnikar, O.S.B., took charge of the local parish on 25 February 1877. Now that the place name of the monastery was fixed, the abbot proceeded to end the confusion over the name of the institution itself to which he had previously added. The abbey was under the patronage of St. Louis under the title of St. Louis on the Lake; the college had always been called St. John's; the new parish and church were likewise dedicated to St. John the Baptist. Then the abbot added to the jumble by beginning in 1880 to call the abbey 'Subiaco' on the occasion of the fourteenth centenary of the birth of St. Benedict. When a second Babel resulted, he untangled the entire perplexity by returning to the first name given the monastery at St. Cloud, and asked Rome for permission to place the abbey, school and parish under the patronage of St. John the Baptist. When this was officially granted, he again aroused resentment among older Benedictines in Minnesota and at St. Vincent who held to the myth that Ludwig I of Bavaria had been the benefactor of the Minnesota foundation, when in actuality the king's benefactions had gone to Abbot Wimmer. It was true that Wimmer's desire had always been to name his first foundation after his friend Ludwig, and he had achieved this at the time the monastery was raised to abbey status. The name 'St. Louis on the Lake' was unquestionably appropriate and beautiful, but the ever-practical second abbot had little choice in making a final change of name.

In his eagerness to add prestige to St. John's, Abbot Alexius, while in Rome, had petitioned for the rather pretentious privilege of conferring pontifical major degrees on members of his monastic family,

143

in theology, canon law and philosophy. This right was granted by papal brief on 16 June 1878, and he exercised it for the first time on 1 June 1879, when after examinations three monks were promoted to doctorates. They were the Reverend Peter Engel, O.S.B., doctor of philosophy, and the Reverends Francis Merschman, O.S.B., and Bernard Locnikar, O.S.B., doctors in sacred theology. The institution was scarcely possessed of sufficient academic stature to confer these titles, and the second abbot was only inviting ridicule and sarcasm by such a procedure. Nor was it long in coming. An anonymous article appeared in the columns of the Baltimore *Katholische Volkszeitung* on 16 August 1879 caricaturing these degrees, and listing the recipients under the fanciful names of Barnabas, Thaddeus and Alexander, which were in actuality the names of three of the oldest Brothers of the community. In quick succession other satires appeared in the August 23 issue of the same paper and in the August 20 issue of the St. Louis *Herold des Glaubens*, signed by a certain "F.A." of Trenton, Illinois.

Father Bernard Locnikar, who had been serving as prior since 1875 after the short term of Father Clement, requested on August 20 during the time these events were transpiring, to be relieved of his office. He had reluctantly participated in the doctoral ceremonies, and was not in agreement with the abbot's policies. He felt that development should be internal, consisting in perfection of monastic discipline rather than in external growth. Since he was also suffering from poor health and nervous tension, Abbot Alexius granted his request, and appointed him assistant at the Assumption Church in St. Paul. There he remained, first as assistant, and after 1888 as pastor, until his election as Abbot Alexius' successor eleven years later. The Reverend Norbert Hofbauer, O.S.B., was then named as prior, and Father Peter Engel, Father Bernard's successor in turn as abbot, was appointed subprior. Both of these latter members of the community were strongly in sympathy with the regime.

Undismayed by these developments, Abbot Alexius pressed forward. With Horace he felt that his whole life was a series of incidents which could be characterized as *laudatur ab his, culpatur ab illis*. His favorite expression, reminiscent of his earlier days on the Mississippi, was "Go ahead, steamboat," or as he told Father Peter, "Put on all steam the boiler is capable of holding." In this spirit he requested his friend, State Senator Henry C. Waite of St. Cloud, to introduce a bill into the Minnesota legislature amending the original charter and changing the name of the school from 'St. John's Seminary' to 'St. John's University.' This act was passed by both houses and approved by Governor Lucius Hubbard on 17 February 1883.[25] Previous to this change, it had been decided to open a minor elementary department in the school for boys between the ages of nine and fifteen years. The teachers in the lower classes felt that students were too often insufficiently prepared in elementary branches in the existing state schools. Brother Nicholas Kirsch, O.S.B., who had received a classical education in Luxemburg, was placed in charge of this department in 1879, but he soon proved himself incapable in this work. He subsequently left the community and later published a pamphlet, *Das Luxemburger Vehmgericht* (St. Paul, 1884) in which he held the institution up to scorn. As a result of this diatribe Abbot Alexius wanted to sue, but his lawyer, John W. Arctander of Minneapolis, persuaded the abbot to ignore the incident. As a result the name stuck, and those who felt Abbot Alexius was moving precipitously in obtaining the title of university for the abbey school, persisted in referring to St. John's as the Luxemburger University. This was not the case with Abbot Wimmer, however. He wrote: "I congratulate you on the grade of University to which your College has been raised. Always go on! Must I style you now *Rector Magnificus* of St. John's University? Minnesota flourishes, but always as elsewhere through hard work." [26] Here as in every advance during these years, Wimmer was solidly behind the young abbot who was so much like himself. Edelbrock had received his training at St. Vincent and was filled with the same ideals that moved the founder of the American Benedictines. Throughout the years they carried on a voluminous correspondence which reads like the letters of a father and his son, and when Abbot Boniface decided to give up some of his many duties, he willingly turned over the presidency of the American Cassinese Congregation to Abbot Alexius.

During his years as president of the school, and now as abbot, Edelbrock was overflowing with a vast energy spreading in many directions, his enormous enthusiasms finding expression in heaped-up adjectives and adverbs. He was impatient with the stagnation and helplessness to which many European Christians appeared to him to have resigned themselves in the nineteenth century; he resented the charges of backwardness and lack of adaptation levelled against the Church. His was the typical *sturm und drang* spirit of the youthful German American frontier. He wrote: "The Benedictine Order still lives and is destined to thrive even in northern Minnesota. Of course the winds are pretty rough in this far northern region, storms come and pass away, but the tree planted by St. Benedict is strong enough to stand the blast." [27] Slowly he gathered around himself a group of young Benedictines who shared these same ideals, and worked robustly with him to achieve them. They included Fathers Norbert Hofbauer, Peter Engel, Alexius Hoffmann, John Katzner, Francis Mershman, Chrysostom Schreiner, Gregory Steil, Ulric Northman and Xavier White. Their new spirit at St. John's found expression in the fourteenth annual catalogue of the institution in 1880:

"It is evident that St. John's has passed the days of its infancy, and that it is rapidly approaching a bright and glorious future. Its Alumni are to be found everywhere; they occupy noble and exalted positions; they look back to their Alma Mater and bid her 'God speed.' Besides conducting the College the Fathers of St. John's Abbey labor to advance the interests of religion, and keep divine faith aglow in the hearts of a population sparsely settled over a large extent of country. As in the days of yore, in the countries of the old world, religion and science were cultivated in the populace by the Sons of St. Benedict, so it is now in our young Northwest: — Religion and science are extending over the country through the zealous labors of the same Sons of St. Benedict and the generous assistance of a grateful and appreciative people." [28]

Three official patrons of the institution were enlisted: Bishops Grace, Seidenbusch and Marty; references were obtained from seventy-five prominent people of the Northwest; and testimonies and commendations of forty clergymen and business leaders were printed annually. The traditional major seminary, classical college and commercial college courses were strengthened, and bachelors and masters degrees awarded annually. Besides the new minor or preparatory department, special sequences were developed in science, telegraphy, typewriting, photography, drawing, painting, and music. Abbot Alexius by 1883 had initiated three-year programs, with visiting lecturers, in law and medicine and there is every indication that he was considering developing these departments along professional lines as soon as it was possible. Farm boys from the region were given special tutoring on a monthly basis adjusted to the planting and harvest seasons.

Perhaps the most intriguing of all his educational experiments was the opening of an industrial school at St. John's for Indian students. Edelbrock had been working unsuccessfully through the instrumentality of his friend, Congressman Knute Nelson, later governor and senator, to obtain federal grants for the two Benedictine schools at White Earth. Nelson then suggested in 1884 that funds could be made available for training Indian boys at Saint John's and Indian girls at St. Benedict's Academy in St. Joseph. He successfully pushed such an application with Indian Commissioner H. Price, and on 1 January 1885 Abbot Alexius came over the hill at Collegeville with fifty Indian boys. He placed them under the charge of Fathers Chrysostom and Meinrad and Brother Philip Kilian, in the old stone house. The government contract allowed for fifty Chippewa boys to be trained at St. John's, and fifty girls to be trained at St. Benedict's, with $167 yearly allowance supplied for each student.

The Reverend Joseph A. Stephan, director of the Catholic Indian Bureau, arranged another government contract for St. John's in August 1886 for fifty students, and for another fifty students sponsored by the Catholic Indian Bureau at an allowance of $108 a year. Up to 1890 the average enrollment was ninety-five at St. John's, but from 1890 to 1896, under the superintendency of the Reverend Roman Homar,

O.S.B., who searched out Chippewa children along the north shore and into Wisconsin, a total of 150 was maintained.

Through a program of granting support to off-reservation schools for a period of three years' training of Indian children, the government's Indian Bureau hoped that these children would learn to adopt the customs of the country. The pupils were from nine to fifteen years old, and were to be taught elementary academic courses along with a trade. At St. John's the situation was ideal for such a program. Classes were held for half a day, and then the boys were distributed in the printing, tailor, shoemaker and carpenter shops, garden, kitchen, barns and power house. A religious program was also followed. This Indian Industrial School was a sound application of original Benedictine educational practice, although at the outset the school encountered many difficulties. The children were selected under the supervision of the Indian agent at White Earth, and although the parents had consented, they soon regretted their decision, as the Indians were deeply attached to their children. A few months after the school opened, several unhappy boys ran away and spread alarming reports. Other parents immediately came down to the abbey and spirited off a number of the boys. The boys were frequently sick, and in the first five years, five Indian children died. All of them found indoor life in an institution difficult to take, and each spring when the sap began to run in the trees, a number inevitably disappeared over the hill. But gradually boys who completed this program were apprenticed to tradesmen, others went to work on the abbey farm or other farms throughout the area, while more returned to the reservation where they continue today, according to the Benedictine missionaries, as leaders in their communities.[29] The first fears and prejudices of parents vanished when the fruits of this endeavor to uplift their race became evident. The program was short-lived for several reasons: the concerted policy of building government schools on the reservation, President Cleveland's policy of cutting such appropriations to off-reservation schools by twenty percent, and at St. John's itself the demands for more space to accommodate a growing number of students in the other departments.

In these undertakings Abbot Alexius and his faculty were fostering an education program which they believed was indigenous to the American West. In their plain, strong, rural society, the democratic levelling process of the frontier influenced their educational planning. They aimed at balancing classical and technical culture, while gradually and consistently extending their original seminary and classical training to include scientific, commercial, agricultural, professional and craft programs for White and Indian Catholic laity. This adaption was a response to the trend of the age when Americans, amid struggles of frontier life, looked upon education as the best means of advancement. The young monks now coming into the community had been reared

St. John's Industrial School

147

in Catholic immigrant families from the farms of the West, or from middle-class homes of Western towns. They wanted to build a Christian society in the region, and full education of both clergy and laity was the first step.

The main weakness of this effort was an obvious lack of means to achieve such ends. The average yearly faculty for all of these programs numbered twenty-two members, of whom two had earned masters degrees, while the student body grew to two hundred and twenty-five. Cleric members of the community prefected and taught courses in the lower divisions as a common practice during their theological and philosophical course. This activity would be one of the most serious and just indictments made shortly against Abbot Alexius. Nor were the courses taught as competently and completely as public bulletins and catalogues described them. The abbot's friend, Father Edward Hipelius, O.S.B., of St. Vincent Abbey, criticized the courses of study, the granting of advanced degrees, the exaggerations enthusiastically made in public, and told him: "When I read the report of your Abbey and College the fable of the ox and the frog came to my mind. *Cavete Magniloquentiam!*" [30]

Despite the validity of these criticisms, the large-scale innovations which the abbot continued to put into practice were invariably those projects most needed for the development of the institution. They were as well the projects which stood the test of time, and came to be accepted as significant and integral aspects of St. John's life. He, for instance, began at once to insist on a thorough understanding and universal use of the English language in monastery and school. Older members of the house never became reconciled to this program, and held to the German origin and character of Benedictine beginnings in the United States.[31] *Bei uns drausen* was a common expression used by this group in classroom and monastery to signify their attachment to the German educational system, Bavarian monastic practices, German customs and especially the German language. But Abbot Alexius struck out vigorously against this emphasis. By 1878 he had pushed through chapter a resolution to discontinue the former custom of serving beer to the students at various times throughout the year. He would walk into the community recreation room and say, "Now you speak English in here." He made a practice of writing his letters in English whenever possible, and wrote to Abbot Frowin Conrad, O.S.B., of Conception Abbey, on 3 March 1886, "Excuse my answer in English; I am almost a Yankee!" It was for this reason he gathered around him such American-born young monks as Fathers Alexius Hoffmann, Francis Mershman, Chrysostom Schreiner, and the Canadian diocesan priest, Xavier White, who had obtained a master's degree in English literature before joining the community. An official publication of the school, *The Record,* was started by Father Chrysostom in 1888 to

148

stimulate writing among the students. Carleton College had started a similar publication in 1875, and these two journals were the pioneer student papers of the area. The abbot also had the initials of the traditional Benedictine motto *In Omnibus Glorificetur Deus* set in stone on the college entrance of his new quadrangle. It was handed down for years in student lore that he was never seen to be more angry than the time he asked a group of students standing before this entrance what the initials IOGD signified, and received the reply: "Independent Order of Green Dutchmen."

As abbot, Edelbrock continued his earlier policy of building up the standards of the school. He kept the presidency himself when he became superior and appointed a vice-president as head of the school. Father Chrysostom held this position and was an influential advisor of the abbot. Their personalities were strikingly similar, and in pursuing the aim of efficiency and standards in the school, Father Chrysostom was not popular with members of the community at home or in the parishes, nor with the students. He was authoritarian, exact, and demanding. He insisted that scheduled classes be taught, and that Fathers who assisted in parishes on weekends be back on Sunday evening for Monday morning classes. Student disciplinary regulations were rigorous and the insignia of a prefect was a spare rein from Brother Andrew in the barn.

When German-American priests were organizing on a national scale in the late 1880's to preserve German customs and language among their congregations, the Reverend John Conway, editor of Bishop Ireland's organ, *The Northwestern Chronicle,* wrote to the leading German ecclesiastics of the region asking them whether they felt there was growing discontent among Germans there. Abbot Alexius answered this query straightforwardly:

"Though a German by birth I have lived in this country since a child and admire and love its institutions. The question of nationality should not enter into God's Church. Unquestionably Catholics should have every opportunity to practice their religion in their own language, and in mixed congregations no matter how small any particular nationality may be, those who are best acquainted with a foreign tongue should have the advantage of hearing the Gospel read and sermons preached to them in their own language. I always instruct our Fathers [the Benedictines] to carry out this idea. Unfortunately, it is not always done in congregations where the German-speaking portions of the congregation are in a minority and hence some dissatisfaction and grumbling. But there is no widespread ill feeling between Catholics on account of national differences and priests and religious are respected by all irrespective of where they were born." [32]

Here again if Abbot Alexius had sufficient time to carry out these ideals in the numerous parishes of the abbey, the developments of the nationality problem with its resulting impact on central Minnesota might have been quite different.

Other projects initiated at this time included the founding of an alumni association in 1882, and the establishment of an archives at St. John's. With devotion he collected and preserved the papers and correspondence of the early years, began making carbon copies of his own letters, and kept several diaries. He wrote a manuscript history of the Benedictines in Minnesota in a style similar to his preaching. He favored strong Victorian rhythms and long formal periods amply interspersed with classical quotations and references to Greek and Roman mythology. He purchased a printing press in 1889 and fostered the publishing art in the community. Before that time printing for the institution was done by the Wanderer Printing Company in St. Paul, or the Times Publishing Company in St. Cloud. The first publication emanating from St. John's, apart from the yearly catalogues, was a seven-page pamphlet composed in both German and English by Abbot Alexius in 1877 to foster the institute of Oblates of St. Benedict among students, parishioners and friends of the abbey.[33] Then in 1880 he wrote a commemorative pamphlet on the life of St. Benedict and a summary history of the Order down to the present. This publication also appeared in German and English, with Father Xaxier translating the original German text into English and subjoining a centennial ode dedicated to Abbot Alexius. These two pamphlets were the first works printed at the abbey.[34]

During his first trip east he purchased a complete new set of instruments for the brass or cornet band. Music continued to be promoted in both monastery and school, and in 1885 an orchestra of seven musicians began practice. Father John Katzner directed the group which included Father Isidore Siegler, John Gans, Jason Howard, Leopold Brunner, Max Dick and Victor Quale. They played two violins, a flute, cornet, trombone, viola and piano, and included in their repertoire the Blue Danube, Zidwicka Polka, Shower of Gold and solos for individual instruments. This was the pioneer orchestra of the Northwest, and continues to the present time with a personnel drawn as originally from both monastery and school. It was first called the 'Alexian Philharmonic Society,' but when an auxiliary student orchestra was formed in 1891 for those who did not have the necessary technique for the senior group, the orchestra was called the 'University Orchestra.'[35]

Benedictines throughout the world commemorated the fourteenth centenary of the birth of St. Benedict in 1880, while abbots gathered at Monte Cassino Abbey, their founder's monastery, for solemn celebrations. Abbot Alexius attended these festivities with Father Peter Engel as companion and was inspired by the evident signs of the Benedictine restoration that was gaining momentum not only in Europe, but

150

51 *St. Alexius priory and farm, West Union.*

52 *White Earth: School.*

53 *White Earth: Indian Mission.*

54 *Abbot Alexius and Father Aloysius with Indians.*

55 The second St. Mary's Church, St. Cloud.

56 First St. Clement's Parish, Duluth.

57 Original St. Alexius Hospital, Bismarck.

58 Old St. Mary's, first Catholic Church
in North Dakota's capital city.

59 *Bernard Locnikar,*
St. John's third abbot.

60 *Abbot Bernard and community picnicking*
at Caesar's Bay.

61 *Bishop Otto Zardetti*
with his diocesan priests of St. Cloud.

*Front: Innocent Wolf (St. Benedict's), Bishop Leo Haid (Belmont). Back:
Andrew Hintenach (St. Vincent), Hilary Pfraengle (St. Mary's), Bernard
Locnikar (St. John's).*

62 *American Cassinese Congregation abbots, 1891.*

63 *The sturdy bark 'Lone Star' and passenger Peter Engel.*

64 Aftermath of 1894 tornado.

65 After an administration of only four years: Abbot Bernard Locnikar's funeral, 1894.

66 Father Chrysostom Schreiner, Sisters of Charity, and students of first mission school.

67 Father Chrysostom Schreiner offering first holy Mass on Columbus' landfall at San Salvador.

68 *Father Peter Engel in his science laboratory.*

69 *Peter Engel, St. John's fourth abbot.*

70 *St. John's Observatory.*

71 *The apostolic delegate to the United States, Archbishop Giovanni Bonzano, visiting at St. John's.*

72 *The fish hatchery, a 'must' for a double lake campus.*

73 *Motoring on Lake Sagatagan.*

74 *Father John Katzner and his Alpha grape.*

75 *Lake Sagatagan from cemetery hill in 1910.*

76 Coach Ed Flynn:
immortalized in 'city' north of St. John's.

77 For a St. John's winter, ice skates were essential student gear.

78 St. John's first football champions of 1901.

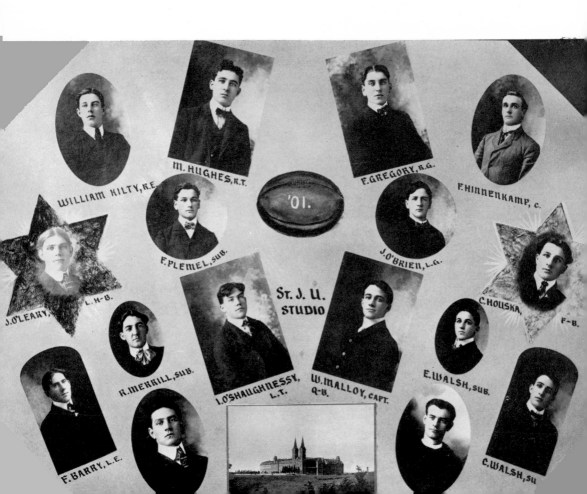

throughout the world in Australia, Africa, North and South America. In the half century since the first stirrings of this movement, a new development of the Benedictine way of life had taken root for the first time since the Protestant Revolt. Monks were again worshipping God and working for society as an integral part of the life of the Church, and he thanked God that he had the opportunity to share in this modern renewal.[36]

He then went to Austria to arrange for an examination of his throat, which for years had so troubled him that he had almost lost the use of his voice. On 6 September 1879 he had told Abbot Wimmer:

"I don't believe that I will carry on very long any more. My health is poor; hardly a morning passes that I do not expectorate a great quantity of blood. My hoarseness is likewise so bad that I have periodic intense pains when I want to utter a word. If my health does not improve soon, it will certainly be necessary for me to resign. Such a step would be most desirable for me since I could better prepare myself for eternity. I am not afraid of work but I hate to be at the head of things. In the meantime 'patientia.'"[37]

Dr. Schroeller, internationally known throat specialist in Vienna, advised removal of a polyp which was lodged in his throat, and promised him he would "regain full voice, be able to sing, preach and live a hundred years." Another doctor, Dr. Feroni of the same city, advised that he go to Gleichenberg to "inhale salt, alumina and sodkali from ten to fifteen minutes a day." Fortunately Dr. Schroeller prevailed upon him to disregard this suggestion as well as the advice of several ecclesiastics who warned him not to undergo an operation. The operation was performed and he did regain the use of his voice, although he continued for years to suffer from bronchitis and inflammation of throat and nasal passages.

He was back in Minnesota by August 5 of the same year, and nearly four hundred pieces of fireworks and fifteen pounds of powder were used in the welcoming ceremonies at the monastery. These detonations could have been at the same time a foreboding of other explosions soon to follow. But the abbot was brimming over with several new ideas and enterprises. He appears to have been newly inspired after each trip to Europe, for upon returning in 1877 and 1880 he began a series of foundations. In 1880 he expressed an interest in establishing a farm priory in Todd County forty miles northwest of the abbey. As land around the monastery was well known for its inferior quality, he wanted to obtain arable land on which cereals, produce, and cows could be raised for the institution. Next to a team of young horses, good rich land was the abbot's delight.[38]

Abbot Boniface advised him to break and cultivate four hundred new acres of land across the Watab, but Abbot Alexius purchased six hundred and forty acres of rich land near the village of West Union

151

instead, and with additional purchases soon owned a thousand acres of this prairie land. He made this move also because from his reading of the history of the Order and observations in Europe he saw how land had been confiscated from monasteries. He felt that when a man joined a monastery he had a right to security for his last days. If such anti-Catholic movements as the Nativists or Know-Nothings would spring up in the West, he imagined that his monks would have a refuge in West Union. The Reverend William Eversmann, O.S.B., his right-hand man in business affairs, was placed in charge as prior, and Brothers Thomas Adam, O.S.B., Louis Schaefer, O.S.B., Roman Poppler, O.S.B., and Gabriel Detzel, O.S.B., tilled the farm and raised stock there with the help of hired laborers. By 1884 this prairie priory was producing 2,200 bushels of wheat, 3,000 of oats, 250 tons of hay and was feeding 128 head of cattle. Abbot Alexius was much attached to the place and visited it whenever possible; he even saw it as a possible future abbey. In 1881 a spacious brick priory was erected of St. John's bricks by Fathers, Brothers and those scholastics who had no homes to go to during vacations. All candidates for the monastery were called back from vacation early to help on this farm which was called St. Alexius Priory. Benedictine sisters from St. Benedict's Convent did the cooking. In a few years a frame church was erected, called St. Alexius Church, and Father William served as pastor of a parish for the settlers. This church of West Union was moved into the village in 1897. For twenty years this enterprise continued, but his successors did not share Edel-brock's enthusiasm for the place, and when it was not deemed to be an economic success it was sold in 1901. Then Abbot Alexius declared: "St. John's has lost its security." Perhaps St. John's actually lost a much more significant opportunity for developing an agricultural school at this priory which could have served the farmers of the area.

Next on the agenda was a breathtaking plan for new monastery and school buildings. To appreciate the extent of his conception it must be remembered that the existing buildings, standing contiguous to one another, had a frontage of three hundred feet and were three stories high. These four buildings, one of stone and three of brick, housed over three hundred persons. Now plans were made for three wings, three hundred and seventy feet in length, fifty-five feet wide and five stories high. They were to be placed in a traditional monastic quadrangle with the church as north wing of the unit when it was completed. In one move he planned to double the buildings by these additions.

The story of the construction of these new brick wings was the same as that of the church. The abbot loved to be on the job as the buildings were going up. He wanted personally to see, as Goethe said, that they stood on the right spot, were securely founded and successfully executed. The foundations were as usual laid with granite field boulders.

152

Sixty workmen were employed on this construction project, but the Fathers and clerics helped whenever possible. The Brothers of the community were the main carpenters and masons. Some cut and felled trees, sawed lumber and hauled it to the building site; others dug clay and hauled it in two-wheeled carts or wagons to the kilns. There it was mixed by hand and baked into bricks, as the Brothers stood watch over the fires.[39] While the Brothers were working on this project they were also continuing their ordinary tasks and duties in the daily schedule of the house. Father Alexius Hoffmann described activities on the construction scene:

The Monastic Quadrangle

"Everyone worked, and many of us did work we were not fitted for. For instance not everybody can stand on a scaffolding fifty feet high above the ground, nor can everybody sit on the roof of a five-story building and lay shingles near the cornice. I could not and was not asked for that matter as I was a priest. But the clerics and scholastics did go up there to work, and the Abbot clad in a long linen 'duster' would clamber out on the roof as if he had been used to that sort of thing from his cradle days and 'speed them up.' Some of them were too slow for him and he ordered them down." [40]

Father Gregory Steil was as before architect and supervisor of these buildings, and Hoffmann continues with some details of Father Gregory's experiences:

"People used to say he drew the plans after the building was up. Not so. He worked under peculiar difficulties . . . and had few of the worries of modern architects. He built only the shell, including of course, doors, windows and chimneys; he was not required in most cases to provide for ventilation, toilets, water supply, heating apparatus, etc. And yet he never knew if he were meeting the wishes of his Superior. So he kept on planning and drawing as the suggestions or orders from his Superiors came to him. Abbot Alexius had no idea of a builder's worries. He would often make surprising changes that would nonplus Fr. Gregory. You are supposed to tell an architect just what you want and he will draw a plan in accordance. But the Abbot was not so disposed. 'Draw me a plan!' How could Fr. Gregory divine what sort of plan the Abbot had in his head? Abbot Peter Engel was almost equally simple minded. 'Get a plan of the Library and then we will discuss it.' One plan after another was considered and when one was finally adopted, and the work begun, some Superior wanted this and that changed, and confusion and error resulted. . . . Poor Fr. Gregory suffered much from 1877 to 1890. And yet he always remained submissive, and threw the blame (as he had a right to do) on others. . . . He had been trained to be an architect. That is, he was trained according to Luxemburg ideas. The houses that he built are all very simple; you will note the frequency of the Mansard roof. That is a French detail. Germans do not favor it. Besides drawing, or architecture, he

153

also knew French and taught it, though he always insisted he was German, as his name would suggest." [41]

The building was solemnly blessed in 1886, although portions of it had been occupied since February of 1885. Now available were accommodations for guests, rooms for monks, new dining room and kitchen, classrooms, gymnasium, study halls and auditorium. Abbot Alexius' new quadrangle was built for six hundred students when the school enrolment was but three hundred. Consequently there were vacant rooms for many years. But, as always, he built big because he foresaw that the monastery and school were growing and would continue to grow. The men of St. John's used his building for over seventy years, and for two-thirds of that time this quadrangle served all needs which he originally provided for. They were not particularly attractive structures, and the main facade presented a blunt appearance unbroken by any graceful line or alternating contours. For the time, however, they were an accomplishment. He had raised in Minnesota's Indian-bush the largest institutional physical plant, as the catalogue yearly heralded, in the West. When Archbishop Ireland visited St. John's in 1888, he said: "Abbot, your buildings! They are simply gigantic, simply gigantic." Bishop Leo Haid, O.S.B., of North Carolina, spoke of his "famous home." Abbot Frowin Conrad of Conception Abbey told him he was "almost drawn to follow you in expanding our monastery," while Abbot Wimmer praised him and told him "you let me far behind you in building (and everything indeed)." Wimmer also jokingly asked him if he had a direct pipeline to the Black Hills where he obtained his treasure to do such building.[42]

During the years that Abbot Alexius had been building the abbey, Bishop Seidenbusch had labored to spread the Church in the great expanse of his Vicariate Apostolic of Northern Minnesota. In his yearly reports to the *Ludwig Missionsverein,* he detailed the difficulties of establishing spiritual outposts in this area.[43] He began with twenty-nine priests, of whom all were Benedictines except eight. He searched constantly to find volunteer diocesan priests and candidates in Europe and America. As a result during his fourteen years as vicar apostolic, he increased his diocesan clergy from eight to thirty-seven in number. But this was not done without some serious difficulties which eventually broke the bishop's health.

The large majority of these new priests were self-sacrificing and zealous missionaries, such as his secretary, the Reverend Franz Xavier Stemper, or the veteran missionaries, Joseph Buh and William Wilkins. The diocesan priests worked in parishes and missions outside of Stearns County, and began Catholic churches in such communities as Red Lake Falls, Crookston, Rush City, Fergus Falls, Browerville, Wadena, Brainerd, Belle Prairie, Long Prairie and Little Falls. Settlers were rapidly establishing homes in the 1870's and 1880's along the railroad lines in the northern sections of the state, and continuing to move into the rich prairie lands stretching towards the Dakotas.

Bishop Seidenbusch had only three localities with a resident priest in the whole of the Dakota section of his vicariate, Pembina, Bismarck and Grand Forks. He visited the area, but was unable to contribute much to its spiritual development. In 1879, after making several entreaties to the Holy See, he was relieved of this area, when the Dakotas were erected as a vicariate. Abbot Martin Marty, O.S.B., who had been working among the Dakota Sioux Indians, was named the first vicar apostolic and consecrated on 1 February 1880. Now Seidenbusch had spiritual jurisdiction extending from Grand Portage to Fargo, and from Stearns County to the Canadian border, a region which today embraces the dioceses of St. Cloud, Duluth and Crookston.

He established his procathedral at the parish of the Holy Angels in St. Cloud, and had the church completed by 1884. It and the school which was immediately begun were constructed of St. John's bricks. The Benedictines cared for the steadily growing parishes of Stearns County, and both the bishop and the abbot continued to encourage migration to this section and to invite German Catholic colonists. Bishop Seidenbusch often stated during these years that he lived and gained his support from Stearns County, the only Catholic segment of his jurisdiction. The Catholic colonizing effort of the Benedictine pioneers was already becoming evident. New Stearns County parishes were started by the Benedictines at Pierz, Cold Spring, Holdingford, Farming, Freeport; at the same time Abbot Alexius was accepting Bishop Grace's invitation to take charge of Stillwater and of St. Joseph's parish in Minneapolis. Then the abbey aided the vicar apostolic by taking charge of Millerville, Alexandria and Osakis in Douglas County, the two missions to the Chippewa Indians, and Moorhead on the western border of the state.

In other sections of the vicariate Catholics of several nationalities, including Irish, French-Canadians, Poles, and Slavs, lived as minority groups in typical American mixed communities. Priests working among them had to know at least three languages and sometimes as many as five. If Bishop Seidenbusch could find a diocesan priest with such talents, he usually incardinated him into his vicariate without delay. This practice, combined with the bishop's natural kindness and tendency to view all men in the most favorable light, led to a series of major crises.[44] When such priests did not move on to new and even more pioneer areas further west where they could operate in unrestricted freedom, they clashed with the vicar apostolic over much-needed divisions of their missions, and questioned his clergy appointments. French-Canadian missionaries, such as former Oblates of Mary Immaculate, moved across the northern section of the state caring for widely separated Catholic settlements, and Bishop Seidenbusch used

155

their services to his later regret. These French priests found it difficult to work under a German-born superior, and there can be no question that nationality conflicts played a part in the troubles ahead.

Then in the spring of 1885 Bishop Seidenbusch had a serious heart attack from which no one expected him to recover. He had worn himself out at the age of fifty-five, and his growing obesity had been a detriment to his health. On 20 April 1885 he appointed Abbot Alexius administrator of the vicariate. To everyone's surprise, the bishop did recover sufficiently to be sent by his doctor to St. Vincent's Sanitarium in Los Angeles, where he was forbidden to assume responsibility. Bishop Seidenbusch never recovered his health, and continued as a semi-invalid for the rest of his life. He did return to Minnesota in 1886, then was off to Europe for treatment in 1887. It is difficult to understand why he did not voluntarily submit his resignation at this time, as it was clear that he could not carry the burden of his position. As administrator during half-year periods in 1885 and 1886, Abbot Alexius tried to move circumspectly, innovating nothing and visiting the far-flung missions of northern Minnesota. He summed up his impressions to Abbot Wimmer:

"Bishop Seidenbusch is slowly improving again. His vicariate is in a deplorable condition and if the good Bishop will live many years he will see hard times ahead. . . . The administration of the vicariate causes me plenty of trouble; things are in a queer condition and unless there is a change for the better soon, our good Bishop Seidenbusch will not be able to stand at the helm very many more years. He is now in Los Angeles, California, and as far as I know his health is again improving. He cannot stand troubles. He has only a few priests, but one is worse than the other and he is in fights with nearly all. I have settled some troubles for him, yet there are enough yet on hand." [45]

While in the midst of performing this additional work as administrator of the vicariate, Abbot Alexius struck out on his final Western venture. It was during those last three years from 1885 to 1888 that the full force of his program took shape. Yearly the possibilities of development in the upper midwest seemed to become ever more unlimited to him. He wanted religion to be alive in that region. He told Abbot Bernard Smith, O.S.B., procurator of the American Benedictines in Rome, that immigrants were pouring into the area by the trainload. He wanted the Church to be an essential organ of the area, not away from the people, but close to them, leading, guiding, a very part of this new society. He and his supporters were filled with the buoyant feeling of their times, that they were creating something new and good, monastic establishments built on the adjustment of interests and circumstances of a new continent. He insisted that labor and effort should be expended in this apostolate which was waiting to be developed.

Such an effort had borne real fruit in central Minnesota during the

156

first thirty years of St. John's. Then followed the permanent and stabilized missionary indentations among the Indians of the area in the early 1880's. Now he turned to the new movement of immigrant peoples into the Dakota Territory, which followed the advent of railroad development. [46]

Plans for a northern transcontinental line had taken shape during the closing days of the Civil War with the granting of a federal charter to the Pacific Railroad Company. The projected route ran from Duluth at the head of the Great Lakes, across Minnesota to the Red River Valley and then westward to the Pacific coast. There was much speculation about the potential of the Dakota Territory. At first, evident skepticism existed. During the middle sixties General William T. Sherman commented dismally about the Dakota Territory to Philadelphia financier, Jay Cook, who had decided to promote the projected Northern Pacific:

". . . That part of the country is almost inaccessible during seven or eight months of the year, and is barren and worthless, especially the Dacota [*sic*] Territory extending about four hundred miles in width. From Fort Abercombie at the Red River of the North to Fort Stevenson on the Missouri, about 500 miles, the country is as bad as God ever made or anybody can scare up this side of Africa." [47]

But as the possibilities of prairie land were realized, these earlier pessimistic views soon changed. Charles Carleton Coffin, newspaperman on the Northern Pacific inspection tour of the region, dispatched a glowing report to the Boston *Journal*:

". . . Lay a ruler on your map. Draw a line from the Mississippi at St. Cloud to Pembina on the Red River close to the boundary line and you have west of that line a region which to my mind comes nearer to the Garden of Eden than any other portion of the earth. There are no mountains, but there are undulations, gentle swells, parks, groves, lawns, lakes, ponds, pellucid streams — a rare combination of beauty and fertility which will make it in coming years one of the fairest portions of the earth." [48]

The Northern Pacific directors followed the second school of thought, and launched public land sales as the transcontinental line advanced toward the Missouri country. The company's original charter secured federal lands which amounted to more than 22,000 acres for each mile of rail laid. This government bounty eventually procured a total land grant to the company which was ten times the size of the state of Massachusetts. It was this land which settlers began to buy in the seventies on an eight-year credit plan. By 1873 the Northern Pacific had reached the Missouri River where the city of Bismarck was platted. This frontier town was named in honor of the German Chancellor in the hope that German investors and colonists would be induced to take an interest in the road.

During the next decade the railroad line was pushed westward, and through service between the Twin Cities, Duluth and Tacoma, Washington, was now available. Indian treaties opened a three-hundred by two-hundred mile Dakota strip to settlers, while the 'Empire Builder' James J. Hill, and his associates, were pushing forward in the direction of Minot another transcontinental line, the St. Paul, Minneapolis and Manitoba Railroad Company, or the Great Northern as it was eventually called. Then 'Dakota fever' became the talk of the nation in the eighties as these freight facilities pointed up the possibilities of developing large wheat crops and cattle grazing in the area. The lure of spring wheatlands now drew settlers further westward from the river valleys and timberlands.

It was as a result of this new development that Bishop Seidenbusch's vicariate had to be divided, and Abbot Marty Martin became vicar apostolic of the rapidly developing Dakota Territory. Abbot Marty had left his community at St. Meinrad's Abbey, Indiana, in 1876 to begin a zealous career in the interests of the Sioux Indians of Dakota. In this work he was assisted at first by the Reverend Chrysostom Foffa, O.S.B., Swiss Benedictine from the Abbey of Einsiedeln, and Brother Giles Laugel, O.S.B., of St. Meinrad's.[49] Now as vicar of the vast expanse of the Dakota Territory, Bishop Marty fixed his residence at Yankton. He had few priests, and found it especially difficult to supply missionaries for the fast-growing Catholic settlers along the Northern Pacific lines and the Missouri River in northern Dakota Territory. Then, just as he and his Benedictines from St. Meinrad's had helped Bishop Seidenbusch in 1876 by working among Indians and scattered Whites in the southern Dakota section of the Minnesota vicariate, now Abbot Alexius and the Benedictines of St. John's came to Bishop Marty's assistance in the northern section of the new vicariate of the Dakota Territory.

In November of 1878 Abbot Alexius had made a trip to Bismarck to look over the possibilities of a monastic foundation in that area. The monastic chapter had approved such an undertaking on 22 October 1878. He was overjoyed at the prospects of this new railroad frontier and began thinking of establishing a monastic center which would contribute to northern Dakota, through a monastery, college, convent, hospital, and parishes, what St. John's and St. Benedict's had accomplished in central Minnesota. After talks and tours with Father Chrysostom Foffa, O.S.B., who was then stationed in Bismarck, he decided to have articles of incorporation drawn up for establishing the Order of St. Benedict in Dakota Territory, and began encouraging Catholics to immigrate to the Dakotas. They examined possible sites on the outskirts of Bismarck and engaged a lawyer to draw up an act of incorporation for a projected St. Rupert's College, named after Bishop Seidenbusch. Foffa told Edelbrock: "Words cannot express what your

158

visit meant to me. I feel ten years younger." By 29 August 1879 the legal document for incorporation was ready, with the board of trustees to include Abbot Alexius as president, Father Bernard as secretary and Father Chrysostom Foffa as treasurer. Apparently Foffa contemplated joining this projected venture, for he wrote to Edelbrock from Bismarck on 25 August 1879:

"Bishop Marty was very much pleased with his visit to St. John's especially with the basement of your church and very much with your laundry. . . . I spoke to him about the Incorporation of our Order in Dakota and recommended him very strongly to give to your Abbey the whole line of the Northern Pacific RR which he said he would do with the greatest pleasure." [50]

Bishop Marty stated that he was grateful for Abbot Alexius' overtures in Dakota, and that he would be only too happy to entrust to St. John's the entire area between Fargo and the Missouri River. Incorporation of the projected St. Rupert's College at Bismarck was never submitted to the Dakota Territorial Legislature, although Abbot Alexius had contacted Senator McNeider and Colonel Lownsburg and obtained their support. But as a first step in the realization of his project, Abbot Alexius accepted the invitation of Bishop Marty to send a priest to Bismarck. Father William Eversmann was recalled from West Union Priory and set out for Dakota on 10 January 1881, while the pastor of the Immaculate Conception parish in Bismarck, the Reverend Bernard Bunning, came to St. John's to enter the novitiate. He had previously been a monk in simple vows at St. Meinrad's, and now with Bishop Marty's encouragement wanted to enter religious life again. He discontinued, however, during his novitiate at St. Vincent.

The Reverend Jean Baptiste Marie Genin, O.M.I., who would be heard from often during these years, had started this Bismarck parish in 1874. Father William stayed there until November, when he was succeeded by the Reverend Paul Rettenmaier, O.S.B. Next the Reverend Martin Schmidt, O.S.B., was sent to Mandan in 1884, and he undertook the spiritual care of all Catholic peoples west of the Missouri River. From Father Martin's account book, it appears that he followed the railroad across the river from Mandan to visit settlers in Dickinson, Taylor, Glen Ullin, Marmot, South Heart, Little Missouri, Antelope, Eagles Nest, Fort Lincoln, Fort Buford, Hensler, Stanton, Medora, Blue Grass, Sims, Richardton, Sully Springs, Sedelia, Belfield, Newlon, Knife River, Sweet Briar, Gladstone, Sentinel Butte and Curlew, all in Dakota, and Glendive and Wibaux in Montana. Abbot Alexius noted in his diary for 2 August 1884 that Father Martin was tending forty-four stations along the railroad line and added: "Each station had several Catholic families — almost all the railroad workers are Catholic. He also attends Fort Abraham Lincoln and several places in Mandan. Too much for one priest." Father Paul was at the same time making regular visits to stations at Dawson, Williamsport, Painted Woods, Burnt Creek and Fort Stevenson along the Missouri. In January of 1885 he was joined by the Reverend Bede Northman, O.S.B., who became pastor at Bismarck in August when Father Paul went over to Mandan to assist Father Martin.[51]

Now that the two parishes at Bismarck and Mandan were functioning, and mission work was being done throughout the area, Abbot Alexius initiated the second step in his plans for a Benedictine center at Bismarck. In these enterprises, Abbot Alexius had the assistance and support of Mother Scholastica Kerst, who had been elected superior at St. Benedict's Convent in 1880. She came from the Assumption parish in St. Paul and was the daughter of the prominent businessman, Peter Kerst, of that city. Similar in temperament and ideals to Abbot Alexius, she worked with him during these years in establishing several foundations. On 14 April 1885 Edelbrock purchased the Lamborn Hotel in Bismarck, a formidable three-story brick structure with a two hundred foot frontage, for the Benedictine Sisters of St. Joseph. He paid $2,000 down and gave a note for the remaining $20,000 to Alexander McKenzie and Richard B. Mellon of Bismarck. The Sisters later reimbursed the monastery for this loan. It was heralded as the only first-rate hospital between St. Paul and Portland. The impressed local newspaper editor, upon making a tour of inspection of the new institution, went even a bit further when he wrote:

"There is a natural prejudice against hospitals accountable only by the disrepute into which the word has fell [*sic*] in connection with county and corporate institutions which are too often operated for political plunder rather than with a view to the relief of the suffering. But the Lamborn is such a bright, inviting structure, its rooms so admirably arranged and the management so kind and considerate, that in time it must become the most popular hospital in the northwest. There is nothing in St. Paul and Minneapolis to compare with it as a hospital, and it is the most creditable institution with which Bismarck has been blessed." [52]

The citizens appreciated the policy of not operating the hospital as a strictly Catholic institution. Its doors were open to all creeds. Patients were free to receive the advice of ministers from whatever denomination they desired. Another development which received public approval was the novel hospitalization plan which the Sisters fostered. Hospital admission tickets at an annual cost of $10 for use in their Bismarck hospital, as well as in their new hospitals in St. Cloud and Duluth, were available. In this early hospital care and insurance plan, each purchaser of such a ticket obtained care and treatment should illness overtake him at any time during one year from the date of the ticket.[53]

The Benedictine Sisters also undertook the direction of St. Mary's

Academy in Bismarck at this time. Then in May of 1887 Abbot Alexius purchased sixteen lots in Bismarck, three blocks from the Lamborn Hospital. He entered in his diary: "It was a splendid bargain, they say." Now the Benedictine parish, hospital and school existed; a draft of a charter was on hand for a college; and monks were doing mission work in the area as a preliminary step toward a monastic establishment. Sebastian Wimmer wrote the abbot on 9 June 1886 that the "Empire Builder," Jim Hill, "thinks the world of you." [54] But the end of the adventure was approaching rapidly. Nor did the Benedictine monastery which he contemplated ever materialize. However, in 1947 when St. Benedict's Convent established an independent motherhouse in Bismarck, the Benedictine convent was achieved sixty years after it was first planned.

*Duluth
Foundations*

Abbot Alexius conceived and brought into existence one more monastic enterprise in these years. It was exactly the same type of elaborate endeavor as had been undertaken in Dakota Territory. This time he turned to the new movement of immigrant peoples, Slavic, Polish, Italian, Irish and German, into the range area of northern Minnesota. These undertakings in Dakota and Duluth were in fact simultaneous, and the pattern of operation appears to have been taken from the same blueprint.

The magic of iron had touched Duluth and its surrounding area during the 1880's, when the precious ore deposits of the Mesabi range were first tapped. Within one decade, 1880–1890, the population jumped from 3,000 to 33,000. The increasing numbers of Catholics in this area required additional priests and nuns who would care for them, and then build up native vocations from among the people through a monastery and convent, rather than by importing priests from Europe. One church, that of the Sacred Heart, had been erected in Duluth in 1870. Bishop Seidenbusch had organized and dedicated a second parish to St. Mary in November 1883, and a French church of St. Jean Baptiste was started in August 1885 for the numerous French-Canadians who moved into the northern area after 1870 with the building of the St. Paul and Duluth Railroad. As the city expanded, the Catholics of the west end petitioned St. John's to consider the establishment of a parish in that district, and Bishop Seidenbusch encouraged the abbey to take on this responsibility. The chapter agreed, as during these years vocations had been steadily increasing. Abbot Alexius took the Reverends Timothy Vaeth, O.S.B., and Edward Ginther, O.S.B., and set off for Duluth to investigate the situation. The people and the Benedictines felt that Rice's Point was the ideal spot for development, and organizational work was begun at Garfield Avenue.

Abbot Alexius was not thinking of a parish only. He grasped the full significance of Duluth's future importance at the head of the lakes, and planned again that from this parish would spring a monastery,

161

college, convent and hospital. It would be another spiritual, educational and charitable center and, at the same time, a natural monastic center for their Indian missionary work in the same area. The Duluth *Tribune* even spoke of the Benedictines "invading Duluth," and there were letters pro and con in its columns.[55]

While parish services were being held in the basement of a building at 1806 West Superior Street, Abbot Alexius, toward the end of April 1887, organized and sent up to Duluth a crew of carpenters, bricklayers and helpers, both Brothers and workmen. Father Gregory was in charge again, and at home in Collegeville the kilns were fired anew for bricks which were shipped from the abbey by rail to Duluth. Over a thousand stumps were grubbed from the parish block, with a sick Abbot Alexius assisting. Work was begun on the first building, a hospital to be staffed by the Benedictine Sisters from St. Joseph, as Mother Scholastica was cooperating with him again on this project.

While workmen were raising the brick hospital, the decision was reached to construct a frame church, rectory and school in the same block. On 11 September 1887 Abbot Alexius blessed the new church and placed it under the patronage of St. Clement, in memory of Father Clement Staub, O.S.B., the Minnesota pioneer who had died the previous year. The Duluth *Tribune* on the following day commented on this achievement and fixed the total cost of the buildings when completed at $70,000, while the Milwaukee *Catholic Citizen* for August 27 stated that the undertaking would be "a great credit to the Catholics in Duluth." The new St. Mary's Hospital was dedicated the following spring on 3 April 1888.

In this way the parish, school and hospital were initiated at Duluth. When Mother Scholastica began the Benedictine community at St. Scholastica at Duluth in 1892 and established a motherhouse there, the fourth aim of the undertaking was achieved. Abbot Alexius' proposed monastery never became an actuality as time was running out and his Minnesota career was about to be abruptly terminated. In fact, crushed in spirit and on the verge of physical collapse, he entered the Sisters' new hospital as their first patient. When he was released from St. Mary's Hospital, it was to leave Minnesota for Rome and resignation.

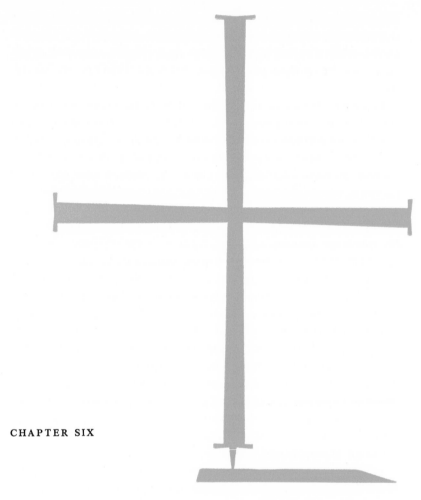

CHAPTER SIX

RESIGNATION AND REFORM

Abbot Alexius never realized that his program would result in a clash among the members of the community. He was young, forceful, and intent upon building up a strong establishment without being aware of the consequences. For fourteen years he worked at a feverish pace, and with an industry that overcame desperate obstacles. Beginning with a religious community of fifty-two members, by 1889 he was heading a Benedictine family of fifty-seven priests, ten clerics, thirty-seven Brothers and thirty-two scholastics. Enrollment in the school had increased from 183 to 350. The monastery was caring for forty-five missions of which he had inaugurated thirty-five.

In 1888 he was but forty-five years old, yet his health was failing. As early as 1885 he had exhausted his strength, and the Fathers living in the monastery petitioned him to take a rest. The abbot was moved by this expression of interest in his health and willingly obeyed. But in

163

1887 he was ill again. Constant travelling was hard on him, and he was troubled with recurring bronchitis, headaches, and colds. He often recorded in his diary after a long day's trip: "I feel sick, have a bad cold," or "my bronchia pained me so much that I did not feel like living."

Resignation
And Reform

Much harder on him was the steadily increasing crescendo of criticism directed against himself personally, his projects and his activities. It had begun immediately in 1875 after his indecisive election as abbot, and persisted among a hard core in the community for fourteen years. No one questioned his ability to govern or maintain what he had established. But the older members of the house, especially the missionary Benedictines in the German parishes of central Minnesota, felt the diversified undertakings of the 1880's militated against the purposes for which the Benedictines had originally come to Minnesota. They viewed St. John's as a monastic training center for the spiritual care of German Catholics of the region. These were the men who had been living in parishes and missions for all of their mature years, for the most part in small parish priories, but also alone in separated mission stations. The community chapter was always consulted by the abbot concerning each new undertaking, and they steadily supported him throughout his administration. But the pioneer missionaries outside of the monastery, who did not attend these chapters, looked upon the decisions of the junior members of the community as another indication that their young abbot had surrounded himself with youthful supporters. The unfulfilled abbatial ambitions of such pioneers as Fathers Cornelius Wittmann and Meinulph Stuckenkemper also played a part in such criticisms. Abbot Alexius admitted that *de jure* all monks should be present for policy-making chapters, but *de facto* he explained that the distance of many missions, expense in coming and going, as well as the necessity of immediate decisions often made it impossible. A closer observance by the abbot of the congregation's statutes on this point could have prevented such resentment, however.[1]

Much more significant in this matter were the obvious monastic difficulties arising from monks being stationed for long periods in permanent parish units. While Abbot Wimmer and the abbots of his new monasteries continued to take up other missionary endeavors, such as those among Indians and Negroes, the original German missionary endeavor developed into permanent parish work attached to the motherhouses. As Abbot Alexius reported to Rome, a split in his community had formed between those monks stationed in the parishes and those at home in the monastery. His new projects of starting monastic foundations and entering into new mission fields were looked upon by the Fathers outside the monastery as innovations.

Another small segment of the community believed that excessive stress was being placed on external growth at the expense of monastic spirit. A former prior and a former novice master, Fathers Bernard Locnikar and Alfred Mayer, were the most outspoken in this regard. This group felt that monks were too often moved from one mission to another to the detriment of the mission and the discouragement of priests, that a retreat master was not obtained for annual retreats, that the abbot was absent from the monastery about half the time, that money matters were given too much attention, that insufficient attention was paid to spiritual matters, and that the active life of mission and charitable work militated against monastic development.[2] Abbot Alexius answered these charges in detail. He stated that he moved members of the community only when prudence or necessity compelled him to do so. The abbot explained that no retreat master was obtained from 1886 to 1888 for the community retreat because the statutes permitted such a procedure.[3] As to his absence from the monastery, Abbot Alexius stated:

"I have been in the monastery whenever my duties permitted me; when duties of monastery called me away from home, and when the missions required my presence, then I yielded. I have never been absent from my monastery when not forced by duty. I have made no vacation trips. Very few Bishops in America are permitted to be home half of their time: duties call them away. The same must be said of many superiors of religious houses. They go whenever duty compels them to go. In my abbatial life I have felt nothing so hard as to be away from home. I have often thought that an abbot has no home, and this same thought makes me feel sad many a time. I always remained home as long as my outside duties permitted. And now, after having performed my duties, I am censured for it."[4]

In money matters the abbot believed that he was obliged to insist on observance of the vow of poverty, and that he had not asked for any money that did not justly belong to the monastery. Churches and buildings had been erected on the Indian reservations, donations had been made to missions and poor people, a convent had been built for the Sisters at St. Joseph, money obtained for parishes in Minneapolis, St. Paul, and Moorhead at low rates of interest, and with chapter consent $20,000 had been donated to the Assumption Church in St. Paul. In fact the General Chapter had advised him he was too liberal with parishes under the monastery's care.[5]

The final accusation of the 'monastic reformers,' that missionary work was militating against the Benedictine spirit was answered by the second abbot as follows:

". . . St. Benedict himself started his men on missions. Of course, it is not best for *one* or *two* to live alone on missions, yet it would appear that such is almost the history of our Order. At least, such appears to have been the beginning of our Order in every country wherever its members worked. Our American life has thus far been, and will for

165

some years to come be a missionary life — certainly to a big extent. Thousands of souls have reached Heaven because the Benedictine Fathers were there to help them in: had the Patres remained in the monasteries those souls would not be in Heaven now. The four walls alone will not sanctify the monk, as we all know. Yet some can only reach Heaven by remaining within the four walls. . . . I do not entirely approve of the way we conduct Missions, yet it could not have been otherwise in the past. We have no congregations as in Europe having 40,000, 50,000 and 60,000 souls; it takes time to form such large congregations. Ergo, here our forces must of necessity be divided, at least for a time. The transition period will come and is near at hand. Besides, did not other religious communities — Jesuits, Redemptorists, Franciscans, etc. — follow the same course? Even at the present day such is the case. . . . I am sorry that we must have our forces scattered, yet I don't see how such a course can be prevented." [6]

The accusation of this second group, that spiraling, external, material activity excluded the possibility of developing Benedictine piety and ascetical life, bore the most weight of all attacks. The abbot's dominant concern was intense external growth, as is apparent from his fourteen year rule. But it was not so obvious that religious spirit, as it was asserted, was essentially weakened. Community discipline was good, choir was regularly attended, vocations to the religious life increased in large numbers. The speed-up, force and vision in the monastery as a result of Abbot Alexius' leadership tended to unite the majority and create a true community consciousness rooted in an evident spirit of self-sacrifice for religion and society. There was lacking, however, a consciousness of distinct Benedictine liturgical traditions, of a first interest and development of spiritual life centered in divine worship. The active life, with an emphasis on the moral virtues, which was the dominant spirit of nineteenth century American religious life, was also evident at St. John's. It was the heritage of Abbot Wimmer's spirit. Concentration on internal spiritual development was ardently desired by Father Bernard, but was scarcely the motive force of the large majority of the 'reformers.' [7]

The two groups of critics were given surprising and unauthorized support in 1887 by two former Benedictine abbots. The first was the former abbot of St. Mary's Abbey, Newark, the Right Reverend James Zilliox, O.S.B., who had resigned on 2 November 1886 as first abbot of that monastery after serving nineteen months. As master of novices at St. Vincent he had earlier induced several young monks to leave that abbey, and had himself thought of joining the newly organized monastery of Beuron in southern Germany. "Had I let Father James go to Beuron," Abbot Wimmer stated, "then all unquestionably would not have happened." [8] Instead, as Wimmer often did, he magnanimously appointed his critics to key positions to give them an opportunity of carrying through the reforms they advocated. With this in mind Father James was appointed prior at St. Vincent and entrusted with preserving the discipline he had been asserting was weak. By 1881 Zilliox and Father Mauritius Kaeder, O.S.B., professor of moral theology at St. Vincent, had entered a memorial at the Congregation of the Propagation of the Faith in Rome stating that discipline was suffering at St. Vincent because of excessive external activity. Cardinal Simeoni investigated the charges, and on 25 February 1882 declared them to be exaggerated and circumstantial. Abbot Alexius was acting as first visitator of the congregation at that time, and he vigorously supported Wimmer, while declaring that he had visited many European abbeys and found the discipline at St. Vincent, to say the least, comparing favorably with them. Abbot Alexius had been a friend of Father James for years, and in this case defended the prior and claimed the fault was more Father Mauritius', while Bishop Seidenbusch was convinced that Zilliox, whom he called 'poor, simple James,' should be removed from office. Wimmer eventually did this in October of 1882. When Abbot Boniface obtained permission from Rome to have St. Mary's Priory in Newark elevated to the status of an abbey, Father James was elected first abbot. Both because of poor health and a constitutional inability to cope with situations, Abbot James soon resigned and was succeeded by the Reverend Hilary Pfraengle, O.S.B.

Abbot James Zilliox

Then Abbot Alexius kindly invited his old friend, the resigned abbot, to come out to Minnesota for the sake of his health, sent him clergy fare coupons for the trip, told him to stay as long as he wished, and to visit some of his former novices who were by this time priest-monks at St. John's. The leading critics of Abbot Alexius among the young Benedictines came from two classes that had made their simple and solemn vows in 1879, and included the Reverends Othmar Erren, O.S.B., Ambrose Lethert, O.S.B., and Bede Northman, O.S.B., of one class, and Alfred Mayer, O.S.B., Jerome Heider, O.S.B., Martin Schmitt, O.S.B., Conrad Glatzmeier, O.S.B., and Urban Fischer, O.S.B., of another class. Two of this latter class, Edward Ginther, O.S.B., and Thomas Borgerding, O.S.B., had no part in the opposition.

Abbot James first visited at St. John's, then after a trip to Red Lake moved from parish to parish in Stearns County for two months. His former novices, as well as the older Benedictine missionaries, gathered around him at these places, and within a short time the identical pattern which had formed at St. Vincent five years before began to take shape. Zilliox gave ear to the criticisms and was soon writing long alarming letters to Archabbot Wimmer, who by this time had celebrated his jubilee, received the title of archabbot from Rome, and was in his last illness. At the end of his tour of inspection Abbot James also wrote a letter to Abbot Alexius, who was unaware of what had transpired, and stated:

". . . It is in the attitude of a friend I write the following, and if I reflect on defects, whilst I omit reference to all the good I saw, it is not, as if this were insignificant, but because I need not praise what speaks for itself.

"It is my own observation, that the guiding spirit in St. John's Abbey is one of intense external activity, expanding materially and embracing as much as possible of things external. I believe, your own person is the best representative both of the monks and the nuns in this regard. The sincere praise, that is given you is, that you are a first-class business manager, farseeing in your schemes and simply irresistible in executing them. That the nuns, in particular, have advanced materially, very much is your *merit*; also that they have assumed an undue external activity, which combines the spheres of 2 or 3 distinct Sisterhoods is due to you, as preparing, advancing and encouraging them to their present mode of life. Whatever may be said of all this external activity, as actually existing, or also as to the correctness of principle in it, I will only say that *too much of it harms,* and that it seems that there is too much of it to be consistent with monks and nuns of the Rule of St. Benedict, and that the spiritual advancement of all parties concerned seems at present to be more than questionable. This point is fundamental.

"Added to the general spirit, there are some circumstances, which influence activity noticeably, but in the end adversely. As far as you are personally concerned, one of the circumstances is your natural impetuousness. That this is natural to you, no one denies, that it (barring God's special help) has been one of the natural causes of your success in business thus far, is plain. But I believe this impetuous (quick, radical, severe) method of controlling the men, whom you have in your special spiritual charge, has been the cause of dissatisfaction as much as anything else may have been. Your piercing look, pointed words, indiscriminately used, whether speaking or writing, the severe alternatives you often place — all manifest the strength of your determination, which is not strength alone, but impetuousness, that hurts those to whom it is directed.

"I almost identified impetuosity with severity, though they are far different. Without wanting to be methodical I keep them apart now, in order to say, that I am impressed, that you are in various things too severe and make use of the power, which you have, beyond the measure that circumstances warrant." [9]

The two divergent groups of missionary and monastic critics had a common emotional response to Abbot Alexius which Abbot James expressed in the last part of the visitation report he had decided to make. Abbot Alexius possessed a certain stiffness, an inconsiderate and irritable attitude which he acquired with his office. He was not easy, genial, and lacked a large, good nature to go with his broad vision. He had lost the cheerfulness of his early years. If there had been more willing sympathy and generous treatment of those he controlled, the difficulties might have been resolved. He was eminently just in all his relations, and he had a deep affection, in his own characteristic way, for his community, or his 'folks,' as he was accustomed to say. He wrote to the Jesuit John Lawler in this regard:

"Justice goes a good deal further with some people than common sense. I submit my views for what they are worth. I am always inclined to mercy, but hate to see men abuse religion for their own base ends. Some people can only be checked by force." [10]

There existed the paradox in his personality that often made him harsh and quick with his ordinarily good and faithful monks. At the same time he showed a parallel sympathy and softheartedness toward monks and priests in trouble, whom he often harbored, even against the advice of the community.

The visit of Abbot Zilliox to Minnesota was the occasion for one of his former novices, now a priest at St. John's, to crystallize the opposition he had been waging against Abbot Alexius for six years. This was the Reverend Othmar Erren, O.S.B., who saw in Abbot James' encouragement of the rebels an opportunity he had sought to assume leadership among the missionary monks outside the monastery. Abbot Alexius himself gave the best concise description of Father Othmar's career when he informed Abbot Bernard Smith, O.S.B., procurator of the American Benedictines in Rome:

"The Reverend Othmar Erren is the son of poor parents, his father is now dead and his mother sick abed. His two brothers have fallen away from the faith. He was taken to our college by myself in 1870; here he was fed and educated *gratis* for nine years and after his solemn vows on August 15, 1879, he was in April, 1881, ordained a priest. Our chapter was much divided about admitting him to his final vows because his sharp and unbridled tongue had been the cause of enmity among the Fratres more than once. After his ordination he became more aggressive and made himself intolerable to the other Fathers at home. To have peace at home I placed him on a mission called Moorhead. Here he continued his uncharitable talk; he actually had a good word for nobody. . . . The Moorhead mission subsequently requested his removal; I put him to another mission called Millerville. Whilst here he published articles in the New York *Freeman's Journal* and in *Der Wanderer* of St. Paul, Minn. — making me Bishop of Dakota, — thus ridiculing me before the people; he also has opposed in the same papers the temperance movement of Bishop Ireland. Besides whilst on this last mission he has frequently absented himself, running about *ad libitum*. I concluded to transfer him to St. Paul as assistant, but when he had called upon Bishop Ireland for the faculties of the Diocese the Bishop refused him because of the objectionable newspaper articles. I was forced to take him home for at least some time. After his sojourn here for a few weeks I gave him charge of the mission called Albany. From this place he made weekly and often bi-weekly excursions. . . . As much as I regretted these his excursions, I did not check them at once but I became fully convinced of the mischief he was doing. I forbade him in the early spring of 1887 to visit in the future. This restriction weighed heavily upon him and he waited for an opportunity for revenge." [11]

The newspaper articles Abbot Alexius referred to were written by Father Othmar under the pseudonym of 'Aurora Borealis,' and consisted of sarcastic essays on the abbot's undertakings, as well as ridicule of the temperance movement among Catholics which Bishop Ireland was championing so ardently.[12] Worn down by such persecution, and sick with typhoid fever, Abbot Alexius entered the hospital at Duluth after the dedicatory ceremonies of the new Benedictine parish, school and hospital there. Prior Norbert was appointed administrator of St. John's by Abbot Alexius, and the community members at the monastery encouraged their abbot to remain in the Duluth hospital for a rest until the difficulties could be terminated. Abbot Alexius had also been forced to bring disciplinary action against three other of the young monks at the same time, namely, Fathers Ambrose Lethert, O.S.B., Vincent Schiffrer, O.S.B., and Bede Northman, O.S.B. Thirty-three chapter members of the community signed the following document prepared by Prior Norbert supporting Abbot Alexius:

"We, the undersigned sons of St. Benedict and your subjects believe that duty calls upon us to express in unmistakable terms, our most profound sympathy with you, to assure you of our unbounded confidence in you, and to pledge you our entire support, all of which we do by these presents.

"We condemn in the most unqualified manner the conduct of some of our brethren who have trampled under their feet solemn vows, spat upon your forbearance, your charity and your zeal, scandalized the people at large, degraded the brotherhood and disgraced themselves.

"Moreover we heartily approve your action toward these misguided brethren, and we will strenuously sustain you in it.

"We pray God in His mercy to change the hearts of these fallen brethren and to bring them to a knowledge of the wickedness of their ways.

"We earnestly beg God to sustain you, to strengthen you, to give you victory in this struggle you are making for virtue, for religion, for God." [13]

This memorandum had been prepared because Abbot Alexius had had sent a document of resignation to Prior Norbert from Duluth, and had asked him to forward it to Rome. The monks in the monastery rallied to their abbot's support and begged him not to consider such a

170

move. Prior Norbert informed Abbot Innocent Wolf of the abbot's despondency, and the abbot of St. Benedict's rushed a letter to Abbot Alexius on 30 April 1888 which deterred him from resigning:

"Father Prior told me his trouble about your resignation, which you sent him to be forwarded. I wrote him that he would do wrong if he sent it to Rome. Now, do not get angry at me for interfering in this matter, but since Father Prior asked me to write to you about it, I cannot help but trouble you in regard to the resignation. I do not know how it came about, but it seems that some agitated against you, and Abbot James had no small part in it. Suppose, you would resign, would that not be acknowledgment of the justice of their agitation? The good Archabbot was in a similar position, and *just then* he would have acted wrong by resigning. Again, suppose you resign, and another becomes Abbot, will that mend matters? No, it would only encourage those agitators to continue their nefarious work. Once more, suppose you resign, will you thus do the will of God? Is it not rather shunning the cross he has sent you? Have a little patience. *Non sunt condignae passiones huius temporis ad futuram gloriam quae revelabitur in nobis.* I beg you to read the last chapter of the second book of the *Imitation of Christ,* where you will find consolation and encouragement."

From Albany, however, Father Othmar continued to spread accusations against Abbot Alexius which also included the criticisms discussed with Abbot Zilliox. Abbot Alexius appointed a committee of three community members, which the Congregation's Visitators called completely impartial, to examine the charges against himself. This committee was composed of Prior Norbert Hofbauer, Father Peter Engel and Father Severin Gross, pastor of St. Mary's Church, St. Cloud, and vicar-general of Bishop Seidenbusch. The committee concluded after thorough study that "the accusations were made up for the purpose of having the abbot removed or of making him resign." [14] Father Othmar was cited before the committee. He came, adhered to his position, and was suspended by Abbot Alexius on 23 March 1888. Erren then became a fugitive religious and left his monastery without permission. He went to Bishop Martin Marty, O.S.B., at Yankton, Dakota Territory, who not only listened to his story but also encouraged the fugitive monk and gave him the faculties of the vicariate.

It is difficult to understand Bishop Marty's action in this matter. For nine years previous his relations with Abbot Alexius had been most cordial. Marty had welcomed him in the northern expanses of his jurisdiction, turned over parishes and missions, spoke of a future foundation from St. John's in that area, and sent several of his theological students to St. John's for their seminary training. But now like Abbot Zilliox he felt, as he told Abbot Wimmer, that although he regretted having to sadden him greatly, "the welfare and honor of our holy Order demands quick and decisive action. For some time there has been a disturbance in family life at St. John's Abbey, Minn. A number of the Fathers come to me with their complaints." Marty told Wimmer that Father Ambrose had reported this, and he asked Wimmer to investigate and take whatever steps he considered necessary. Wimmer replied that Lethert should not even be honored with the recognition of investigating his charges, and just as the large majority of the community at St. John's had supported Abbot Alexius after learning the full story, so did he.[15] Although Bishop Marty then stated that he did not consider it wise to admit Father Ambrose into his vicariate, he nevertheless sheltered him and placed him at Dickinson to attend the missions west of Morton County as long as he would keep his good resolutions. Father Othmar, the suspended monk, was also harbored. Abbot Alexius was deeply hurt that these two former abbots, Zilliox and Marty, should give support to such insubordination. Bishop Marty had served as abbot of St. Meinrad's for only two years before resigning to devote himself to Indian work in the Dakota Territory. Abbot Alexius was surprised that Bishop Marty should consider that he was too harsh in administration since, as he stated twice in Rome during subsequent months, Bishop Marty's unusual number of suspensions was known throughout the country.

These happenings, however, were but the prelude to the final drama. In August of 1888 the community at St. John's learned to their astonishment that Father Othmar had departed for Rome as a delegate of the missionary and monastic faction opposed to Abbot Alexius. Erren left from Yankton with the approval of Bishop Marty, with letters of recommendation, an introduction to his brother, Monsignor Martin Marty, chaplain of the Swiss Guards at the Vatican, and direction to contact Monsignor Denis J. O'Connell, rector of the American College, and Roman agent for a number of American bishops. The delegate also received letters of recommendation from Abbot James Zilliox, who said he "wished success to truth and justice, which I am convinced is on your side," and from the Reverend Otto J. Zardetti, vicar-general and secretary of Bishop Marty. With this backing Father Othmar planned to lay the whole case against Abbot Alexius before Cardinal Simeoni, prefect of the Congregation of the Propagation of the Faith. He intended to request that an apostolic visitation of St. John's be ordered by the Holy See because of Abbot Alexius' tyrannical handling of his religious and his expenditure of large amounts of money without chapter consent. When reports of this development were spread abroad Abbot Innocent Wolf of St. Benedict's Abbey wrote to Abbot Bernard Smith, Roman agent of the American Benedictines:

"What seems strange to me is, first that Bishop Martin Marty, O.S.B., could give a run-away monk faculties; second, that he can encourage a monk to go to Rome without having tried to have the ordinary means

172

used to settle such matters first in law, then, if the party may feel dissatisfied, appeal to Rome, without going personally; third, that Fr. Othmar Erren goes to Rome with the purpose of having his Abbot, Alexius Edelbrock, removed, not dreaming about proving his accusations; fourth, that he is recommended to stop at the American College instead of stopping at San Callisto with his own brethren." [16]

Bishop Marty explained his position as follows. He first stated in May that he would see to it that Father Othmar's case would be prosecuted according to the statutes of the American Cassinese Congregation. But in July he became convinced that Father Othmar's censures were dubious and unjust, that Archabbot Wimmer would not consider them, and that Abbot Alexius as president of the Congregation could not judge the case because of the moral principle that no one is a judge in his own case. He then gave Father Othmar faculties and a testimonial letter for his Roman journey in which he stated that Erren was not under censures "in as far as we know." Bishop Marty advised Father Othmar:

"*Alea jacta est.* Since the President you ought to appeal to is the culprit, you are bound to appeal to Rome, *ad Sedem apostolicam, ad quam etiam semper et quandocumque liber potest accessus.* It seems to me that your best course would be to go yourself in person to consult Rt. Rev. Abbot Krug and arrange with him the best form to lodge your complaint and that of your confreres with the S. Congregation.

"Their conduct at the Visitation should also be agreed upon. We can settle those things when you shall come here." [17]

Meanwhile Abbot Alexius, as president of the Congregation, requested that the regular triennial visitation of St. John's be held as soon as possible. The two visitators, Abbots Innocent Wolf and Hilary Pfraengle, came to Collegeville on 5 September 1888 and for two days carefully examined all phases of the charges. In their report, a copy of which they forwarded to Abbot Smith in Rome, who was a consultor of the Congregation of the Propagation of the Faith, they declared that the accusations were from hearsay and rumors traced back to Fathers Othmar Erren and Ambrose Lethert:

"If Father Othmar Erren had been sincere, he would have reported his complaints to the Visitators, and if he thought them not competent, to the General Chapter, which was in session on July 6th, 7th and 8th. The Fathers of St. John's Abbey had a retreat at the end of June, and after it elected, according to our Statutes, a Procurator to the General Chapter, but that Procurator, the Rev. Cornelius Wittmann, did not get any instruction to bring charges against the Abbot, as we enquired particularly about this. . . .

"Had Rt. Rev. Bishop Marty been sincere, he would have notified some Abbot of the Congregation about the matter, so that it could have been dealt with according to our Statutes, but instead of this he harbored a fugitive monk and priest, and encouraged him to act against our Statutes, and, for that matter, against all law, to go to Rome. . . .

"In regard to the accusations we enquired no more than to satisfy us, that they were made up solely by Father Othmar Erren, that the Abbot had satisfied the monks by appointing as a committee three of them, who were beyond suspicion of connivance, to call witnesses, etc. We saw all these documents, and know that they were sent to you. Hence we did not think it necessary to do more in the matter, being satisfied that the accusations against the Abbot were made up for the purpose of having him removed or of making him resign.

"In regard to the vow of poverty we found that some of the monks were under the impression that the Rt. Rev. Abbot and his Prior held property in their own name without any security for the Abbey; this impression though was dispelled by the fact, which those parties did not know, that there is provision made by deeds kept in the safe of the Abbey for the transfer of such property at any time, without a will being necessary. This matter was discussed in the General Chapter." [18]

Before Father Othmar set out on his mission to Rome he stopped in St. Paul and asked for a recommendation from Bishop John Ireland. Because Bishop Ireland had previously quarrelled with Father Othmar over the temperance question, and had refused him the faculties of the St. Paul diocese, the bishop was placed in a peculiar position. His action in the case, and the reason for so proceeding, place the whole undertaking in its full setting. Ireland sent a letter concerning Erren's arrival in Rome to his close friend and advisor, Monsignor Denis O'Connell at the American College:

"A Benedictine priest from Northern Minnesota, Father Othmar Erren, will arrive in Rome about as soon as this letter. I told him I would inform you of his coming. His business is to enter complaints against Abbot Edelbrock. I am keeping out of the trouble, and refused to give Erren a letter to Cardinal Simeoni. Bishop Marty is supporting him strongly and will introduce him to the Cardinal. Without implicating yourself in his business you can show him some kindness and, if occasion offers, and prudence permits, give him some advice.

"The fact of the case is that this Benedictine Order in Minnesota is all torn up. The majority are dreadfully opposed to the Abbot, whom they accuse of fearful things. Some Fathers have run off in disgust. Religion suffers more than writing can tell. I am afraid the matter will get out into the papers. Bishop Marty thinks that nothing will do, but an appeal to Rome. I believe so myself, and, at any rate, I let the Benedictines judge. In my opinion a severe check is needed to their incursions over Northern Minnesota.

"The case brings in Bishop Seidenbusch, as, if he had been doing his duty, the difficulties never would have arisen. Propaganda has written

174

to me to find out why Bishop Seidenbusch does not resign. He says he will not resign unless asked to do so, again and in clearest terms. I have sent my report to Cardinal Simeoni — intimating that in my own judgment a resignation is very desirable. I am placed in a very difficult position. I cannot take openly part against Bishop Seidenbusch and the Benedictines and yet in my soul I know that religion under them is perishing. Bishop Seidenbusch says he will not accept a coadjutor. Better than nothing, but best yet, if he would return to the monastery. I outlined for Propaganda my plan — which is — resignation of present vicar, and two new dioceses, one at St. Cloud, and another in Duluth.

Bishop John Ireland

"The German question is reviving a little — but nothing to alarm." [19]

Bishop Ireland had succeeded Bishop Grace in the diocese of St. Paul after the latter's resignation on 31 July 1884. St. Paul was a suffragan see of the province of Milwaukee which included besides St. Paul, the dioceses of LaCrosse, Green Bay, Marquette, and the vicariates of Northern Minnesota and Dakota Territory. Bishops Ireland and Marty felt that the rapidly growing region of Minnesota and Dakota should be separated from the Milwaukee province, and a new archdiocese erected in St. Paul. The distance from Milwaukee often delayed unified action, and the predominantly German make-up of the province of Milwaukee did not find sympathetic response from these two bishops. While in Rome in 1887 for discussions concerning the establishment of a Catholic University of America, Bishops Ireland and John J. Keane of Richmond had actively opposed a petition brought from Milwaukee by the Reverend P. M. Abbelen for equal rights between German and English-speaking parishes.[20] During this stay in Rome Bishop Ireland and his close friend and advisor, Monsignor O'Connell, also made overtures at the Congregation of the Propagation of the Faith for the erection of a new province of St. Paul with four suffragan sees in Minnesota and Dakota. Twenty-six years later, after Ireland and O'Connell had worked together in the celebrated series of controversies of the 1890's which included the questions of Cahenslyism, the Faribault-Stillwater school plan, erection of a Catholic University of America, and Americanism, O'Connell recalled that their careers had begun in 1887 with "the *piccoli congressi* wherein we urged the cutting away from Milwaukee and the creation of the Metropolitan See of St. Paul." [21]

Cardinal Simeoni informed Archbishop Heiss of Bishop Ireland's request, and of the fact that Bishop Marty concurred with the same petition. The prefect asked that a meeting of the bishops of the Milwaukee province be called to discuss this matter.[22] Archbishop Heiss then assembled a provincial synod at Milwaukee at which new decrees were enacted, and the Holy See was petitioned to erect a new metropolitan see of St. Paul. On 4 May 1888 Pope Leo XIII, upon recommendation of the Congregation of the Propagation of the Faith, established the archdiocese of St. Paul and named Bishop Ireland as first archbishop. The vicariates of Northern Minnesota and Dakota were to constitute the suffragan sees of the new province.

Archbishop Ireland had desired that four new suffragan sees be simultaneously erected in the new province, but Monsignor O'Connell informed him that Cardinal Simeoni at the Propagation of the Faith had decided that Bishop Seidenbusch should first resign: "Bishop Seidenbusch's resignation is contemplated and has been suggested to him by letter from the Propaganda, and then you and Bishop Marty would be left alone." O'Connell also informed Ireland that the plans for the St. Paul province recommended to the Congregation were:

". . . identically the ones you recommended to me. I put in a good many papers on the matter. Let me be the first to congratulate you, and believe no congratulations will be more sincere. There will be no trouble about Bishop Seidenbusch's resignation, but say nothing about it yet." [23]

Archbishop Ireland replied to this information:

". . . Ten thousand thanks for your kind offices in favor of the archdiocese of St. Paul. You managed things with most wondrous dexterity, so that everything has come out just as I wished. 'A friend in Rome' is a very useful auxiliary. The Pallium ceremony will take place sometime in September, after the cool weather has come. There will not be much of a display. After the ceremony we will send on names for the new sees. Bishop Seidenbusch is home. He tells me that Cardinal Simeoni asked him to resign. He took care, he adds, not to go up that stone stair-way a second time: he saw no other official of Propaganda. Now he declares he will not resign. I have written to Cardinal Simeoni, asking why the See of St. Cloud was not erected — and thus opening the way for some declaration as to the intentions of the Propaganda." [24]

Monsignor O'Connell, in turn, answered as follows:

". . . Possibly the matter could be forced, but I do not see what you could gain by it just now. You might stir up the Brotherhood, and then! If you cannot gain the resignation at once without strong and risky pressure, why not use the matter as a means of carrying through your other plans of putting the right men in Dakota — and the new dioceses of St. Paul, and then you can command the future as long as you live. The Vic. Ap. of Northern Minnesota would yield to you on those points. They say they did not want to erect the new diocese of St. Cloud before the resignation. They suspect over here that it is the Brotherhood that is principally opposed to the Vicar's resignation." [25]

O'Connell's reference to 'the Brotherhood' obviously meant the Benedictines of St. John's Abbey. This correspondence was being exchanged at the very time that Father Othmar set out on his mission to

176

Rome, and the above letter of Archbishop Ireland to O'Connell on 4 August 1888 announcing Erren's arrival, explains how the mission against Abbot Alexius coalesced with the movement for new sees in the province of St. Paul and the desired resignation of Bishop Seidenbusch.

Unquestionably Bishop Seidenbusch's poor health, as well as his protracted absences from his vicariate, were not conducive to efficient administration. While in Europe for his health in 1887, Seidenbusch did visit Cardinal Simeoni in Rome, as Ireland stated. At that time the cardinal prefect suggested to the bishop that he resign. It is difficult to understand why the sick and aging prelate did not follow this recommendation, as he was obviously not able to continue the active and consistent direction of his spiritual charge. The insurrection of the three recalcitrant French priests in the Vicariate of Northern Minnesota, which Simeoni had asked Cardinal Gibbons to investigate in 1887, undoubtedly also influenced the cardinal prefect's pointed suggestion. The recommendations which Ireland and O'Connell were making to Simeoni for Seidenbusch's resignation were a further influence in the matter. These recommendations were directed in the Congregation of the Propagation of the Faith by Canon Donato Sbarretti, an assistant in that congregation whom Ireland and O'Connell were cultivating in several ways.

When the news became known that Cardinal Simeoni had again in a letter of 30 September 1888 requested Bishop Seidenbusch to resign, and that the bishop was about to comply, Abbot Alexius, in the midst of his own troubles, did not delay to support his old friend who had backed him at every turn of his career, and with whom he had worked for fourteen years in the vicariate. Abbot Alexius prepared a petition to Pope Leo XIII, which was supported by fifty-one capitulars of St. John's, and forwarded to Abbot Smith for presentation to the Holy Father. It read:

"Prostrated at your feet we express our grief over the intended resignation and removal of Bishop Rupert Seidenbusch, Vicar Apostolic of Northern Minnesota. We were informed that His Eminence Cardinal Simeoni had requested Msgr. Seidenbusch to tender his resignation, and that the Bishop is about to comply with said request. We feel aggrieved that such a demand should have been deemed necessary or even expedient and we believe in all sincerity that the resignation of our Bishop will not be *in bonum religionis*.

"Bishop Seidenbusch is a pious man, good and charitable. He has given no offense or scandal to the best of our knowledge; he drinks a glass of beer or wine, but never to excess and, in truth, no charge of any serious nature can be brought and maintained against him.

"Of late years his health has been somewhat impaired, yet he was in his place wherever and whenever duty called and we believe his

177

episcopal career will compare very favorably with that of many others in the hierarchy. His Vicariate is dotted with fine churches and Catholic schools; in it are a Seminary and University and two Hospitals. His clergy are zealous and attached to their Ordinary. The few bad priests and rebels, who have caused much trouble in this Vicariate, were not of this Vicariate. They had been admitted on probation and out of mere charity; when other Bishops had closed the doors against them, Bishop Seidenbusch at least gave them a trial and endeavored to raise them out of the mire. They should not have complained against their benefactor and their complaints should not — we believe — have been of any weight, even with Cardinal Simeoni.

"If the work is considered too hard or too much for him, would not Your Holiness assign him a co-adjutor? Such an appointment would please all and would remove the gloom which is now hanging over the Vicariate in consequence of His Eminence's letter and request.

"It is an undeniable fact that this Vicariate has been built up under Msgr. Seidenbusch and his removal at the present time forebodes evil results. If at all possible we would beg Your Holiness most humbly and earnestly not to accept his resignation, but to leave us our dear Bishop until God sees fit to call him to his reward. All the Benedictine Fathers — 51 in number — capitularies of St. John's Abbey support the above petition." [26]

Members of his diocesan clergy also requested the bishop not to resign. Typical of these sentiments of support was one from the Reverend Arthur Lamothe, pastor of St. Joseph's Church, Little Falls, who wrote:

"With regret I heard of the important decision Your Lordship has taken to lay down the pastoral charge of this vicariate. I ignore the motives which have called for this step, and though convinced that your personal happiness might gain by it, I regret however to lose a Superior who has been a tender father to me for years.

"As a mark of my devotion to your person, I gladly join my name to those already written on the petition to Rome." [27]

Bishop Seidenbusch, however, sent in his requested resignation on 30 October 1888, the day after Lamothe's letter. At the Propaganda the resignation was accepted, and a coadjutor was not named for the bishop. For years Abbot Alexius had been spoken of for such a position, or as a future bishop of St. Cloud, Duluth, or Bismarck where he had done so much to build up Catholic life. His critics had even maintained that his extensive developments in those areas had been, as Father Alfred Mayer stated, for his "contemplated episcopal property." But under attack as the abbot was at this time, such an eventuality was remote to say the least.

Cardinal Simeoni informed Archbishop Ireland that Bishop Seidenbusch's resignation had been accepted by Pope Leo XIII on 15 November 1888, and that the archbishop of St. Paul was appointed administrator of the vacant vicariate. Simeoni recommended that a fitting pension should be assigned to the retired bishop, and that this could be arrived at by a friendly agreement between Ireland and Seidenbusch. Bishop Seidenbusch left St. Cloud and retired to St. John's where he lived in a room in the monastery during the summer months. In the winter he went to Catholic rest homes or hospitals in California and Florida until the day of his death, 3 June 1895, six years later.[28]

While the events leading up to Bishop Seidenbusch's resignation were transpiring, Father Othmar was busy in Rome. With his recommendations in hand, he was petitioning Cardinal Simeoni and Archbishop Domenico Jacobini, through personal visits and memorials placed at Propaganda, that an apostolic visitation of St. John's be ordered. Father Othmar was in Rome before O'Connell returned from his summer vacation, and while waiting for action Erren lost heart a bit and at one stage wrote: "I am nearly sorry that I offered to take the chestnuts out of the fire for the rest. — Well, I can't change matters now." [29] Erren tried to enlist the support of Prior Adalbert Mueller, O.S.B., monk of St. Benedict's Abbey, Atchison, Kansas, and then prior of the Collegio di Sant'Anselmo, international Benedictine house of studies in Rome. Abbot Innocent rushed information to Prior Adalbert about Father Othmar and his mission to Rome. Mueller informed his abbot that he felt Abbot Alexius would emerge gloriously vindicated, and added:

"Yesterday morning I received your telegram. I almost believe that you were afraid that I would abet the cause of P. Othmar. You consider my sensitive nose very incapable if you think that I couldn't detect P. Othmar's situation at first sight. . . . Abbot Smith thinks that if P. Othmar doesn't abandon his intentions there will be a visitation (probably Archbishop Ireland) called for at St. John's. . . . It would perhaps be very disagreeable if the Propaganda would entrust the investigation to an enemy. In my postcard I just wanted to remark that the American Benedictine Congregation itself should undertake the investigation, send in a detailed report and so take the foundation from P. Othmar and his accomplices. It is always disagreeable when strangers stick their noses in everything, especially when they are unsympathetic as probably Archbishop Ireland. You seem to believe that Archbishop Ireland is in favor of Abbot Alexius and against P. Othmar and his accomplices. However, I must have entirely misunderstood P. Othmar if he didn't tell me that Archbishop Ireland is supporting him, and I thought I understood Monsignor O'Connell that two bishops had given recommendations to P. Othmar. One of them is in all events Bishop Marty and the other is undoubtedly Archbishop Ireland. . . . Concerning the obnoxious affair of P. Othmar I do not want to say anything more today. Would that P. Othmar were where the pepper grows

179

or in Hongkong or in one of the most distant settlements in Northern Minnesota." [30]

But when Monsignor O'Connell had taken up his cause, Erren had no intention of returning to the outposts of northern Minnesota before his purpose was achieved. He stated to the officials at the Propaganda that the formal visitation of St. John's held during September by Abbots Wolf and Pfraengle had been negative in its results, and he and O'Connell pressed for an apostolic investigation before Bishop Seidenbusch's successor should be named.[31] In a series of letters O'Connell kept Archbishop Ireland abreast of events:

Resignation And Reform

"I met Fr. Erren who was awaiting my return, and who is now rather sick. I had time at the Propaganda for only a few words on the business, but they were very opportune. . . . I never mentioned your name in the matter of the Benedictines. . . . Fr. Erren has his case ready for presentation. Your name is not mentioned except to ask for your appointment as 'Investigator.' . . . Abbot Smith returned a short time ago from the East and took up Abbot Alexius' side, but I think he can effect nothing. Up to the present he made nothing out of the Cardinal nor anything out of Erren. He tried to buy Erren out, and made fine promises. Erren would not sell out, nor did the Card. Prefect recommend him to accept the fair terms. . . . I did not allow Erren to say one word about himself here, and maybe his case must be heard at home." [32]

Abbot Smith, Prior Adalbert and Monsignor O'Connell were correct in their surmises that an apostolic visitation of St. John's would be held, and that the new archbishop of St. Paul would be named the visitator. Cardinal Simeoni informed Archbishop Ireland on 20 December 1888 that several reports had been given to the Congregation of the Propagation of the Faith about the manner in which business in the monasteries of the Benedictines in the Vicariate of Northern Minnesota was conducted, and that the archbishop was asked to search out the truth of the matter. As administrator of the vacant vicariate and apostolic visitator of the Benedictines within the vicariate, Archbishop Ireland was given all the faculties he had as an archbishop. Even before this official deputation, Monsignor O'Connell had rushed a note to his friend:

"It seems big changes are in store for Northern Minnesota. It seems you are to be not only *Deputatus Apostolicus ad Visitandum Monasterium*, but also Administrator of the Vicariate.

"Father Erren leaves tomorrow. He is just like a child, nothing wicked or bad in him. As far as I could see, talks out just as he thinks, open and brave, and meaning well. His case must now be heard in Minnesota." [33]

Archbishop Ireland proceeded to this investigation, with several interruptions, from 15 February to 10 May 1889. He visited, in company

180

with the Reverend John Shanley as secretary, St. John's Abbey, St. Benedict's Convent, the Indian missions and the main parish centers in charge of the Benedictines. All monks and nuns were heard, and a set of questions asked of each. Cardinal Simeoni had sent Archbishop Ireland copies of the documents which had been submitted at different times to the Propaganda against Abbot Alexius and his administration. The questions asked by Archbishop Ireland in his capacity as visitator were strikingly similar to the charges Abbot Zilliox had made during his visit to Minnesota in 1888. At Red Lake Father Shanley told Father Aloysius, after the latter had finished an ardent defense of the abbot, that he "felt sorry for Abbot Alexius and that no Benedictine would be a bishop of the new province, he believed, under the circumstances." When the archbishop arrived at the abbey, Fathers Chrysostom, Francis, Valentine and Gerard headed a petition which they requested the visitator to forward to Rome with his own papers. In the protest they stated that "the Rev. Othmar Erren is a *fugitivus* and as such excommunicated. Msgr. Marty could not legally receive him into his Vicariate, could not give him Faculties and having done so in violation of Canon Law, the Msgr. Marty has also fallen into censures. He is an abettor of bad monks and a danger to all monastic life." [34]

Archbishop Ireland informed Father Chrysostom, vice-president of the school, "that the whole visitation would amount to nothing except the two points: 1) spiritual and 2) intellectual training." The questions asked by the visitator of the abbey were, as Abbot Alexius recorded:

". . . How is the order or Rule kept? Does the Abbot — Alexius Edelbrock — attend choir? Does the Abbot run around much? Is the Abbot cruel and tyrannical? Is the Chapter free? How many Fathers were expelled? How many ran off? Is the Abbot after money? Why have you so many missions? Have the clerics time to study? Do they teach classes? He placed great stress on the time allowed the clerics for studying; he thought the clerics ought not to teach, they ought to have *five* years in the clericate and should not be Prefects, should stand under strict obedience. The *intellectual* and *spiritual* training at St. John's Abbey and University was by him considered too low. Yet it is a fact that no secular clergyman up to the present time has received as much spiritual training as our folks, and very few secular clergy have gone through a five years' classical and three years' theological course, such as all our men O.S.B. have had. Of course, a longer and more thorough course would be very desirable, yet as long as the priest is for the people, and as long as people are going to destruction for want of priests, so long would it be cruel not to have priests ordained when they possess *sufficient knowledge*. We must first look to what is necessary, then to what is merely desirable. . . . An improvement in these two points may be desirable, yet has the time for a change arrived? Our present period may be fairly considered as quasi-transition period, and it will be wise not to forget the *festina lente*." [35]

Abbot Alexius, characteristically, chafed under the imposed delay and indefiniteness of the visitation procedure. Archbishop Ireland said he was moving slowly so that his visits to the various Benedictine places in Minnesota would not excite attention and bring the matter into the papers. Cardinal Simeoni had also informed the visitator that the visitation could be prolonged until minds and spirits were more settled. Abbot Innocent Wolf tried to encourage Abbot Alexius:

"I do not wonder that the Visitation of Abp. Ireland made you nervous. After I read your letter, I got so nervous that I could not do anything anymore that morning. The thought never left me; I tried to sleep and dreamt of it. If the news affected me so much, I can have some idea, how it affects you. Well, it must be borne, and so it is best to have recourse to our Lord. I pray hard, but alas! my prayers are no good: I offer up all my works for you, so that God may give you strength to bear this heavy cross according to His holy will. I prayer that God might take away this heavy cross from you: but he wills it otherwise; so we must say: *Fiat voluntas tua*. It also is a cross for all of us. Let us pray as the Church prays on the Feast of St. Gregory II: *largire nobis quaesumus ut omnia adversa pro nominis tui gloria humili corde sustinentes, aeternitatis gloriam consequamur. . . .*

"Since Cardinal Simeoni ordered the Visitation, I think you should lodge a complaint against Bishop Marty for encouraging fugitive members of your Abbey, even giving them faculties. Then I would propose too that a protest be given by you, that any monk can have a Visitation ordered nothwithstanding the fact that he did not use the ordinary way of bringing his complaints to the Visitators and the General Chapter: that thus any mean person can make such disturbance, and if, after the Visitation, such a monk is even secularized, he does not get the punishment due to such a malicious way of acting. We are all interested in this Visitation. . . . Such proceedings weaken discipline and will at least break up communities. Had Fr. Othmar any show of being a member of good standing, a good religious, and had he followed the ordinary way of applying to the Visitators and General Chapter, I would not protest, for then there would be a show of some reason. As it is, the wickedest man is encouraged to be more wicked: and against this I protest. I would still insist on P. Vincent being expelled, for he never showed a spirit of prayer, etc., just as little as P. Othmar: you must show them up as they are, men who always followed their own will, did not care for prayers, etc., read novels, etc.: then ran away when brought to terms." [36]

The correspondence files of Abbot Alexius are filled with similar letters of encouragement and testimony. Members of the community such as Prior Norbert Hofbauer, Fathers Peter Engel, Chrysostom

Schreiner, Xavier White, Francis Mershman, Gregory Steil, John Katzner, Alexius Hoffmann, Ulric Northman, Gerard Spielmann, Oswald Baran, Timothy Vaeth and Henry Borgerding strongly supported him. Other monks such as Fathers Martin Schmitt, Vincent Schiffrer, and Stephen Koefler admitted the mistake of their former opposition. The diocesan priests residing at the abbey for disciplinary reasons told him he had always been their friend and they now wished to voice their sympathy. But from Fathers Othmar Erren, Ambrose Lethert, Alfred Mayer, Bernard Locnikar, Cornelius Wittmann, Meinulph Stuckenkemper, Conrad Glatzmeier, Placid Wingerter, and Isidore Siegler there was only silence.

Support of the Abbots

The American Cassinese abbots unanimously backed Abbot Alexius. Edelbrock's old and loyal supporter, the founder of American Benedictinism, Archabbot Boniface Wimmer had died on 8 December 1887, and was not on hand to direct and advise his Minnesota protégé as he had done so often in the past. In his second last letter to Bishop Seidenbusch he had said of Abbot Alexius' troubles: "Now it seems the devil is loose in St. John's Abbey. . . . I should help. I fear the Abbot will hardly come through the trouble without great personal harm. I can't judge because I don't know the entire case. But certainly P. Othmar has erred." Wimmer's successor, Archabbot Andrew Hintenach, O.S.B., immediately came to Edelbrock's support and told him it was only a few who could not harmonize, while Abbot Hilary Pfraengle, O.S.B., of St. Mary's Abbey, Newark, declared: "Barring some indiscretions on the part of the Abbot, the whole affair manifestly showed itself to be a premeditated revolt brought about by some sore headed do-as-you-please monks, who could not brook the idea of being corrected and brought to duty." Bishop Louis Fink, O.S.B., of Leavenworth told Abbot Alexius: "There is nothing as straight as a straight line which I believe you have endeavored to follow," and Bishop Leo Haid, O.S.B., abbot-ordinary of Belmont, North Carolina, pleaded with the abbot:

". . . Your resignation would certainly not benefit your Abbey for which you toiled so hard and successfully. I feel that you will be amply vindicated and then continue your good work in the Northwest. I am sure the Visitators' report will help to put matters in the proper light also. I can well appreciate your feelings; but nothing brings out the strong elements of character so well as trials. . . I referred your affair to Cardinal Simeoni, expressing my hope that you would be relieved honorably from the petty persecutions of a few of your people. . . . I can well imagine your feelings — however good a whole community may be, there are always mistakes made, as in the best regulated families — a person naturally does not wish such matters to be made public. It is a shame that our Visitators, elected by the General Chapter, were not allowed to settle everything. I am confident they could and would do so. I can only counsel patience and resignation now. This great trial will soon be over and I trust it may be a lesson to all our Abbeys. I will certainly join in the glad Alleluia on Easter Day with you. May your happiness be the greater for the trials undergone." [37]

As the visitation dragged on and Archbishop Ireland did not grant Abbot Alexius the interview he had promised him for a discussion of the points obtained during the visitation, Edelbrock asked on 26 May 1889 for an opportunity to meet him in St. Paul. He finally had an interview with Ireland on June 14, but by that time, pressed by the monks at the abbey, he had determined to go to Rome and there personally defend himself. As to his talk with Archbishop Ireland, he recorded:

"I had a long talk with Msgr. Ireland today, he promised to give me a letter to Rome. He is puzzled over my trip, says he is friendly disposed to me, assures me of the perverse course of my Fathers, the men acted double-faced. Is partly of the opinion that the whole affair was begotten and reared in iniquity, yet he seems doubtful of the result. 'You have suffered on account of Msgr. Seidenbusch's resignation, and it seems to be the intention of having you also resign. At any rate don't resign in Rome, but only after being back here. If Rome does not uphold you strongly you will not be able to fill your position and you might as well not return here. I see that you have been wronged, yet if you stay some 8 or 10 Fathers said they would leave. You are the Jonas on the boat — so it is claimed by them. I am satisfied that the growlers did not build up St. John's Abbey and your position is more difficult than that of a Bishop, etc., etc.' " [38]

The abbot of St. John's, with Father Chrysostom Schreiner as travelling companion, left that same evening for Europe. Abbot Alexius naively believed that he could be back in America within three months with his troubles resolved. After stopping at the Paris Universal Exposition he was in Rome by July 6 and was welcomed by Abbots Bernard Smith and Leopold Zelli at San Callisto Abbey. He was soon informed by the two abbots and Abbot Anselm O'Gorman, procurator of the English Benedictines, that a resolution of the issues raised by the visitation would take months, and could extend over some years. Abbot Anselm O'Gorman had already been in Rome for three months together with Abbot Augustine O'Neill, president of the English Benedictines, trying to resolve the difficulties between the English Benedictines in the monasteries and those on the missions. Bishop Bernard J. McQuaid of Rochester had just left Rome after spending eight months in controversy with one of his priests, the Reverend Louis A. Lambert. On Tuesday, July 8, Abbot Smith took the abbot of St. John's to the Propaganda for his first visit with Cardinal Simeoni. Abbot Alexius reported hastily:

"He was very kind and friendly: was glad to see me. He asked about our Abbey, the number of monks, the College, and missions. I answered his questions — told him the Benedictines had built up the diocese: that they were most numerous there now, etc. He inquired after Bishop Seidenbusch — is he content? Where is he? I told him the Bishop was content, and would reside in our Abbey. He told me of the resignation of the Bishop when in Rome, etc., said his health was poor, etc., and that he could now spend his days in peace. He spoke well of Bishop Seidenbusch. After Bishop Seidenbusch had *resigned in Rome* and failed to send in his papers: Msgr. O'Connell said to Prior Adalbert that the Bishop had promised to forward his papers but did not keep his word. Abbot Edelbrock had perhaps dissuaded him — the Bishop — and the Propaganda did not like it. *Sic*! There is possibly Msgr. Ireland behind Msgr. O'Connell's saying. At any rate they are very willing to have me out of the way. Had I known of such stuff before, my advice to Bishop Seidenbusch would certainly have been different. I am not a diplomat; certainly don't understand enough of hypocrisy. Cardinal Simeoni next asked whether the Visitation had been satisfactory, and here Abbot Edelbrock arose like a lion and dissected the whole *Modus agendi* of Msgr. Ireland; he imitated even the gestures of Msgr. Ireland to perfection and told His Eminence of the wrong done me and our Order. The Cardinal listened attentively and asked about that priest — Erren — was he suspended? I answered yes. — *Quis eum absolvit*? he again asked. I answered that I was not consulted at all: that Mgr. Marty gave him faculties, etc. The Cardinal will give the case close attention; surely Mgr. Marty will get into trouble. Abbot Smith then inquired whether any report regarding the Visitation had come to hand. His Eminence said: No. Even your documents were with the Cardinal yesterday evening. The Cardinal said: before I can say anything, I must see the report, — and we agreed with him. He promised to inform us as soon as the report would come to hand. And I said, then I would like to discuss the report and see the documents. The audience lasted quite a while and was very satisfactory. Apparently I will get a fair hearing here. The case will be settled in the Propaganda, no appeal. Abbot Smith assured me confidentially that Cardinal Simeoni did not like Mgr. Ireland. This sounds differently from Minn. talk. Cardinal Simeoni will not resign his position, the report of the *N. W. Chronicle* notwithstanding. Abbot Smith places full confidence in Cardinal Simeoni. Well, we will see." [39]

Abbot Smith, understanding Rome's careful procedure in such cases, and realizing that the whole matter would be delayed, petitioned the Congregation of the Propagation of the Faith for a pass for Abbot Alexius and Father Chrysostom from Brindisi to the Holy Land. This favor was extended, and the two Benedictines began a two month tour of Egypt, the Near East and Palestine. Abbot Alexius was scarcely on board the steamer 'Ettore' before he entered into religious discussions with the Jewish passengers and began giving religious instruction to

Abbot Alexius in Rome

185

three Arabs who knew German: "I will hardly be as successful as St. Paul in these waters, but sure it is, the ignorance is great, the field for instruction ever so big." He was also penning travelogue articles of the journey to be published in the German paper of St. Cloud, *Der Nordstern*. When Abbot Alexius returned to Rome he was informed that Archbishop Ireland's visitation report had arrived at the Propoganda and that the case would most probably be heard in November. Although urged on all sides to stay on, and treated kindly wherever he visited, the abbot had lost heart, as he said:

Resignation And Reform

". . . I am between Scylla and Charybdis: if I win the battle over here, I have to meet hostile men among my subjects, and if I lose — well, that will please all the rebels, but above all, it will please myself, because it will afford me a chance of living once more. It is needless to assure you of the gall and bitterness prepared for me by the very persons for whom I offered a big portion of my life. No doubt, God will judge between me and them in due time, yet when that judgment comes, I may be buried. Even then shall I be satisfied, but my patience is not great, and I feel the wrong the more, the longer it lasts. . . . The result, whether pro or con, is entirely indifferent to me, and this is not because I am a great or even a little Saint, but because I have tasted enough of public life, public gratitude, public *Vivats,* etc. The *Hosanna* and the *Crucifige* are too closely connected for my liking, in the abbatial life. *Dixi.* Let us leave this matter with God and abide by His decision. I am grateful to you and all my friends: you must not blame my course and considering my motives, you will not. . . . I shall certainly resign, yet may not do so whilst in Rome, but if at all bothered, I intend to make short work of it. The next few weeks ought to determine my future. I could remain in Europe and spend my days agreeably, yet I cannot very well give up the idea, that I am an American citizen and that I ought to end my days on American soil." [40]

Nor was Abbot Alexius pleased with Abbot Smith's handling of his case. This veteran consultor of the Congregations of the Index, Holy Office and Propaganda was undoubtedly doing everything he could, but Edelbrock's impetuous nature was not satisfied with his constant refrain of "It will take time! It requires a long time." All of the American Cassinese abbots continued to direct a steady stream of supporting letters to Abbot Alexius and begged him to remain firm. They suggested that the case be transferred to the Congregation of Bishops and Regulars or else an appeal be made directly to the Holy Father, but Abbot Smith assured them that such procedures would not be allowed and that the trial must be held in the Congregation of the Propagation of the Faith.

Meanwhile O'Connell kept Archbishop Ireland abreast of developments:

"Alexius, aided by his companion Father Chrysostom, has put in a defense based on the summary of charges he learned from you. There must be a great deal of silliness about the man, or unacquaintance with the ways of Rome, because he looked for a decision on the matter from the congregation of yesterday. . . . Sometimes, I understand, he is overcome by disgust at the slowness of the proceedings and threatens to throw up the whole case. The threat however, I am informed, is not very sincere, and that his determination is to fight it out to the end. Still there seems to be some shaking along the lines of his brethren in his regard, and some of the Abbots advise him to resign. Abbot Leo Haid is, I heard, foremost among them, and is deeply concerned in the matter. The Benedictines now blame the two Visitors that passed the matter over, and they now admit that the General Chapter that was said to have examined the matter did not examine it at all, and contented itself by saying that it did not come under its sphere. I am watching Abbot Smith, and I can discover no great signs of zeal in him for the Praes. [Abbot Alexius]. However, only the future can bring out the colors truly. Prior Adalbert informs me on the authority of Prior Norbert, that in the Abbey all was peace and love, and that the trouble was stirred up only by a few envious fellows on the Mission. He was also informed by Chrysostom as follows: 'I know on certain authority that I cannot reveal that the Praes. [Abbot Alexius] is innocent and that the attack was begotten & fostered by hate.' . . . Zardetti is in a hot hurry for the Congregation to act on St. Paul affairs. . . . He would rather Edelbrock were set aside. . . . He writes me continually. He feels as you toward the Abbot." [41]

Monsignor Denis O'Connell

O'Connell knew exactly what he was saying concerning "some shaking along the lines of his brethren in his regard," for it was the monsignor himself who had contacted Abbot Leo Haid on his 1889 summer's trip to the United States and suggested precisely that idea. Haid then wrote to Edelbrock:

". . . Mgr. O'Connell told me it would be a fight with Mgrs. Ireland, Marty and Province and a part of your monastery against the American Cassinese Congregation. He had but one advice to give: Compromise! Don't let this matter go before the Roman Curia with its 50 consultors — danger of publicity, etc. Victory for either side would be an injury to religion, etc. He referred me to your willingness to resign, etc. I told him of the evil effect on discipline in general and especially the evil effect of a triumph for those who brought this affair about. But — he insisted on the wisdom and prudence of compromising. I asked him what compromise he would suggest: he said nothing definite, but intimated that a way out to save your honor and personal integrity could be found — also to admonish, etc., the evil doers in the Order. . . . Really I don't know what is best. Mgr. O'Connell says Ireland assures him your case is much against you, and now that Ireland has gone into the business I fear he will fight to the end. What, if after

187

all in spite of what I know and feel to be true, the decision should be against us? . . . If you see fit, Mgr. O'Connell can stay proceedings before the matter gets before the Congregation proper. He can then — after hearing from you — fix upon a satisfactory compromise." [42]

Within three days Bishop Haid realized what had happened and he rushed another letter to Abbot Alexius retracting his previous wavering letter, attesting to his fullest confidence in the abbot personally and in the justice of his case:

". . . I do hope the unflinching devotion of the 2 Rev. Visitors [Wolf and Pfraengle] — both Doctors — to Religion and the Holy See — and the memory of our late Archabbot's devotion to the Church and its head — a devotion the Benedictines in America inherit in many ways — will not go for nothing and that the whole Congregation will not be treated as if its spiritual life was gone. We look to Rome for justice and the maintenance of religious discipline. If we have made mistakes we are certainly more than ready to correct our conduct — and the actual history for years shows our sincerity. But we do not wish to see everything undermined and unruly members rendered ungovernable by a decision in favor of those who are most adverse to religious discipline and order." [43]

But the damage had been done. The carefully planted suggestion of Monsignor O'Connell had reached an Abbot Alexius worn down by two years of attack and now struggling alone among strangers for his name and reputation. The day before Abbot Alexius received Bishop Haid's letter Abbot Smith had told him that Archbishop Ireland wanted him to resign and that this fact had been known to Smith for five months. Smith told him: "I am glad your monastery is not in his diocese: the documents which he (Mgr.) put in against you are crushing: he does not mean well with you." For Abbot Alexius that was the *coup de grace*. He now learned that what the archbishop had told him personally concerning the conclusions of the visitation before he left for Rome was quite different from what the archbishop forwarded to the Propaganda. Abbot Alexius wrote:

". . . If anybody still had any doubt about Ireland's disposition, the above will lift the veil fully. An archbishop, a bishop, and two-thirds of the fathers against a poor abbot! Well, the result cannot be doubtful to any intelligent person: there is no use to blindfold oneself! My diagnosis taken some months ago was correct. Time will justify my suspicion. The brothers of Joseph had to clear themselves — therefore they sold him. *Semper idem*. . . . Surely he has not written here in my favor: he has undoubtedly submitted that lying report of his so-called Visitation to the Cardinal and besides made some suggestions to proceed slowly, for if I were removed soon, he might appear before the world as the cause of my removal, and even such an appearance might not benefit His Grace. I almost feel convinced that Ireland's plan is

188

to keep me at a distance: to have Mgr. Zardetti well installed meanwhile, and thus by the time that my head is to drop, the responsibility at least before the public, can also be shared by the Bishop of St. Cloud. A German killed off a German: the Irish will regret this: it will appear as if Zardetti killed me. I feel and will feel very sorry. Diplomacy. . . . Well, it was the Bishop of Beauvais, who falsely accused and judged the unfortunate Jeanne d'Arc as a sorceress in 1431. A false priest betrayed her secrets, and 24 years was needed by Rome to ascertain that after all she was not a sorceress." [44]

Abbot Alexius referred in his letter to the Reverend Otto J. Zardetti, who along with the Reverends John Shanley, Joseph B. Cotter and James McGolrick had been appointed to the new sees of St. Cloud, Jamestown, Winona and Duluth on 16 September 1889. These dioceses, along with the new see of Sioux Falls, to which Bishop Marty had been transferred, were to constitute the suffragan sees of the province of St. Paul. Throughout the entire period following the creation of the archdiocese of St. Paul negotiations had been going on toward this end. The three priests, Shanley, Cotter and McGolrick, were from the archdiocese of St. Paul, and Zardetti was vicar-general and secretary to Bishop Marty. Zardetti had been in Europe for one year previous to his appointment keeping careful contact with the Propaganda concerning the erection of new sees in the province of St. Paul. His interest in being advanced to the episcopacy was common talk in Europe at the time. O'Connell told Ireland:

". . . I have given a great deal of thought before receiving your letter to the new sees and Zardetti. I believe he expects one of them, and I suppose Marty would urge him. My opinion is this, that tho he may not be absolutely the best man, he is the best compromise you can find, maybe the solution of many problems and many inconveniences for you might follow his setting aside." [45]

Father Zardetti was consecrated by Archbishop William H. Gross, C.Ss.R., of Oregon City, at the monastery of Einsiedeln on 20 October 1889, while Archbishop Ireland, assisted by Archbishop Grace and Bishop Marty, consecrated the other three appointees on December 27 of the same year in St. Paul. O'Connell had told Ireland: "Allow me first of all to congratulate your Grace on the consummation of your wishes. Never, perhaps, in the history of the Church, has a new province bloomed as rapidly as St. Paul's. Its growth is typical of the American Church." [46]

The erection of the new dioceses with incumbents of Archbishop Ireland's choice, the unfavorable St. John's visitation report the archbishop was reputed to have submitted, the O'Connell suggestion that a favorable compromise could be found — all these factors merged in time and emphasis to convince Abbot Alexius he must step aside. He was shocked that the visitation report had placed two-thirds of the Fathers against him. The Duluth document of April, 1888, and the vote of confidence by the community chapter after the annual retreat in June, 1888, had both indicated just the opposite, namely that over two-thirds of the capitulars supported their abbot. Nor does any extant document of the entire proceeding indicate such a total of opponents. From the day of his election there had existed a hard core of opposition, but an opposition by two-thirds of the capitulars of the community is nowhere in evidence before the questions of the visitation were asked.

Abbot Alexius informed the prior of St. John's:

". . . I have fully made up my mind to resign. I don't wish to be the superior of those men. I mentioned my determination to Abbot Smith: he advised me not to hasten this matter. Having listened to his advice, I shall wait with my resigning until I hear from the Abbots in Baltimore. I trust they will consent and thus free me from an odious position. . . . Nobody here has said an evil word to me. Card. Simeoni has always been friendly — also the Secretary, Mgr. Jacobini, of the Propaganda, has shown me his good will. Even Abbot Smith has expressed his disapproval of my resignation; also P. Adalbert Mueller, O.S.B., yet my mind is fully made up, and the act will be published in a short time, within two weeks. . . . Understand me well, I have not been asked to resign, nor has any intimation to that effect ever been indicated to me, and if such had been the case, then I would fight to the end. I have been assured of success in my case by a good authority. My resignation shall be my own free and voluntary act and I shall get a receipt to that effect from the Propaganda. I cannot be the superior of men who are opposed to me and this after the innumerable sacrifices which I brought for them. I don't intend to permit an Apostolic Visitation to hang over St. John's on my account. True, others caused this, yet they claim they did so on account of my unworthiness. And how long will this Visitation last, if I don't resign? Nobody knows, nobody can tell. My resignation will end it, must end it. If I continue to urge the fight, all the documents thus far submitted to the Propaganda will have to be printed, each Consultor (there are some 50 Consultors) will get a copy of the whole affair; secrecy is impossible, and the first thing one knows there will be public scandal. The affairs of the English Benedictines, as you well remember, got into the newspapers last year. The affairs of Bishops also thus were brought before the people. If all the documents of this Visitation were brought before the public, there would and could be only a scandal. A victory for either side would be dear, dear indeed. A second such victory would kill off any man!! The effect for our monastery and even for our Order in America would be sad. Better prevent it. The true mother did not want her child cut in two even by Solomon. Ergo prudence: the welfare of our monastery and even religion induce me to say: So far no further! Those who

190

have caused this upheaval must also answer for the consequence. My blood will be asked of their hands. *Videant ipsi.* I shall do my duty." [47]

Moved, accordingly, by unwavering attachment to his monastery, Abbot Alexius urged an unwilling Abbot Smith for ten days to submit his resignation. From every side he was told not to take such a step. The archivist of the Vatican, Dom Gregory Palmieri, O.S.B., joined the ranks of supporters, told the abbot that he had been cruelly treated and that he must not tender his resignation.[48] Abbot Innocent Wolf wrote him that he had just been at St. Vincent and had there examined the documents of the celebrated controversy between Abbot Wimmer and Bishop O'Connor of Pittsburgh in the 1850's: "I never knew what a hard stand Padre Bonifacio had until I read those documents. In 50 years they can be published and then the world will admire the charity, courage, patience, humility, but also the prudence and fortitude of the founder of our Order in America. . . . I wish they could be published now." [49] If Wimmer were still living he would unquestionably have been on the scene with Edelbrock, directing and encouraging him to be patient and showing him that the case had not even come up for discussion in the Congregation.

Abbot Alexius did not at first submit a formal, written resignation. Smith told Simeoni that the abbot wanted to resign on condition that the case would be ended, that he receive a document stating that he had freely and voluntarily resigned, that the refractory monks be punished, and that the visitation be ended immediately. After some deliberation the cardinal prefect said the conditions could be fulfilled and that he would present the resignation to the Holy Father at his first audience which was scheduled for November 21. Because of the pope's weak condition Cardinal Simeoni had not been granted an audience for fifty days. In the meanwhile Abbot Alexius went out to the Abbey of St. Paul Outside the Walls to return a book to Abbot Zelli. He and Zelli discussed the case and Edelbrock stated that he was resigning. Zelli, who had himself undergone an attack and accompanying investigation for over a year, asked to see all the papers of the proceeding. When he had read them he informed Edelbrock unequivocally that justice was on his side, and that he would help in any way possible. A resignation would be an injury to the abbot's name and to the other abbots. After prayer and meditation on the matter Abbot Alexius went back to Abbot Smith on November 22 and told him he did not wish to resign immediately. He would wait until he had heard from the American Cassinese abbots who were to assemble in Baltimore after the centennial celebrations commemorating the establishment of the hierarchy in the United States, and the dedication of the Catholic University of America at Washington, D.C. Abbot Smith said:

". . . 'But if the Holy Father yesterday [Nov. 21] accepted your resignation, then the thing is done. I cannot undo it.' By and by he said: 'You can fight the case until the end, even if your resignation has been presented. You did not hand in your resignation officially — you did no official act. Well, I shall try to see the Cardinal as soon as convenient, possibly next Monday.' I said that would be too late, better see him today. He did not like this. I left his room, but soon met him in the hall. He said: 'I am going to Propaganda.' About 1 p.m. he returned from the Propaganda; he had not seen the Cardinal, who had a *congressus,* but had ascertained that Cardinal Simeoni had had an audience with the Holy Father on Thursday (21st) and that my resignation had in all probability been presented to the Pope by the Cardinal. The thing was done.

"In the afternoon of Nov. 22 I mentioned the whole proceeding to Prior Adalbert Mueller, O.S.B., who disapproved of my course. He thought, I should have waited, should have fought to the end. *Fiat voluntas Tua sicut in caelo et in terra.* I am fully satisfied with the way in which God may dispose of me. My case being thus far, I may as well write my resignation and thus make it legal or official. This done I can leave for — where?" [50]

On 27 November 1889 Abbot Alexius formally resigned as second abbot of St. John's, and Abbot Smith handed the papers to Cardinal Simeoni the next day. The abbot then addressed a letter to his religious community at St. John's announcing this action and bidding farewell to his brethren.[51] Then he proceeded on November 30 to make a general confession to the Reverend Cyril, O.F.M., at the Lateran. He entered in his diary afterwards: "I hope our dear Savior has forgiven me all the sins of my past life, especially those of my official life. *O pretiosa crux, te complector, te osculor, in te cupio ut vitam aeternam inveniam.*"[52] On December 7 Cardinal Simeoni informed Abbot Alexius that Pope Leo XIII had accepted his resignation. The cardinal prefect also told the abbot that he should continue in his position as president of the American Cassinese Congregation of Benedictines. Since there was no ruling against it in the Congregation's statutes, and as his case was the first in the United States, the cardinal wanted him to retain this honorary position.

The abbot's friends were shocked when the news of his resignation reached America. They all felt it was a hasty and imprudent move, and as his friend and supporter Abbot Innocent Wolf declared: "Abbot Alexius was surely too impatient and this was also the principal cause of the dissatisfaction of the monks."[53] The ex-abbot returned to the United States in mid-January of 1890 and was warmly welcomed at St. Mary's Abbey, Newark. There he met his fellow abbots and spent long hours with them discussing all aspects of the events which had transpired. Abbots Hilary and Innocent then accompanied him to Belmont, North Carolina, for the official visitation of that abbey. Invitations came in from all sides to ex-Abbot Alexius. The American Cassinese abbots, Andrew, Hilary, Leo and Innocent, as well as Prior Nepomucene Jager, O.S.B., of St. Procopius Priory in Chicago, told him he would be welcome to stay at their houses if he should so desire. The abbots also offered him the position of becoming their procurator at Rome since they were dissatisfied with the services of Abbot Smith. The abbot of Metten invited him to live permanently at Metten, and Bishop Leo Haid invited him to take over Belmont's dependent priory of St. Leo near San Antonio, Florida, which had just been established the year previous. A college was being developed there and Haid wanted Edelbrock to assume charge of the foundation and in time build it up so that it could become an independent abbey with himself as first abbot. Abbot Alexius visited the foundation in Florida but decided against accepting this offer. The several diocesan priest friends of the ex-abbot in New York, who had either spent some time at Collegeville or had cooperated with Abbot Alexius in former years to assist their brother New York priests who had been temporary disciplinary problems, assured him that he would find a welcome place in the archdiocese of New York. At the head of this group of New York priests was the Reverend John Edwards, pastor of Immaculate Conception Church, who had financed several such retreatants at Collegeville and who was himself a benefactor of St. John's for several years. But Abbot Alexius was close to a physical collapse and decided not to accept any of these offers immediately. He preferred to journey from one eastern Benedictine abbey and parish to another for four months, alone and despondent.

Return from Rome

In the meanwhile the American Cassinese abbots had moved rapidly to petition Cardinal Simeoni for an immediate termination of the apostolic visitation at St. John's. Since the entire proceeding had rested with the cardinal prefect personally, and had not come before the full body of the Congregation nor to the attention of the Holy Father, the abbots asked Simeoni to expedite their request. They submitted a memorial to that effect on 12 February 1890 in which they expressed their regret that Abbot Alexius had resigned, listed and praised his labors and efforts for religion and the spread of the Church. They stated that the good of religion would be endangered and all the advances he had made would be lost if peace and tranquility were not restored to his abbey. The abbots finally requested that a new abbot of St. John's be elected according to the constitutions of the American Cassinese Congregation.[54]

Three days later Cardinal Simeoni issued formal instructions to Archbishop Ireland that the visitation was officially closed and that the monks should proceed to elect a new abbot according to their constitutions. The archbishop did not communicate this information to the capitulars of the abbey, as he was instructed to do. He rather wrote back to Cardinal Simeoni after half a month's delay, on 3 March 1890, and stated that it would not be prudent to permit the chapter of St. John's to elect their abbot according to their constitutions because Abbot Alexius as president of the Congregation would preside and he would favor a party. Ireland then asked if the present superior were to preside. Cardinal Simeoni turned to Abbot Smith for advice on this matter and the consultor, anxious that the election proceed freely according to Benedictine tradition, with an abbot and not a bishop presiding, recommended that Abbot Innocent Wolf, as first visitator, be named. Abbot Hilary was also in Rome at the time and he likewise petitioned Simeoni for Abbot Innocent's appointment.

News had reached America from Abbot Smith that the visitation had been lifted, but that Archbishop Ireland had not promulgated the papers. It was generally known in clerical and lay circles in Minnesota, and rumors circulated among all concerned. Some Benedictines of St. John's Abbey, who represented the group of outspoken opponents of Abbot Alexius, had been alerting Archbishop Ireland to the dangers of Abbot Alexius' presiding at the election, and the missionary Benedictines prepared a petition asking Pope Leo XIII to appoint an abbot. The monks in the monastery were equally concerned that the archbishop himself should not preside and have the visitation lifted only after an abbot satisfactory to himself had been elected. They also telegraphed Cardinal Simeoni and begged that they be allowed to proceed to an election according to their constitutions.

On March 28 Cardinal Simeoni informed Archbishop Ireland:

"After having received your letter of March 3, I diligently examined the question of the election of the new abbot of the Benedictine monastery of St. John in the diocese of St. Cloud. Having weighed the matter thoroughly, I thought it would be satisfactory that the Right Reverend Innocent Wolf, abbot of St. Benedict's in Atchison, should preside over the Chapter, even more so because according to the Constitutions at present in force in the aforesaid Benedictine Congregation, if the President of the Congregation is impeded, the first Visitator ought to exercise the duty of presiding over the Chapter." [55]

Archbishop Ireland issued a circular, upon receipt of this directive, to all the Benedictines of St. John's to the effect that the apostolic visitation of their abbey was ended. The capitulars immediately assembled to elect a vicar of the chapter and an administrator of temporalities. On 1 April 1890 Father Bernard Locnikar was elected vicar with eighteen votes to Father Peter Engel's eleven. Father Peter was then elected administrator with twenty votes to Father Norbert Hofbauer's nine.

Father Peter had been appointed superior of St. John's on 26 November 1889 by Archbishop Ireland to replace Prior Norbert, and he had acted in that capacity up to the election of a vicar of the chapter. Archbishop Ireland had come up to St. John's, in company with Bishop Marty, convened the chapter on November 26 and removed Prior Nor-

194

bert because the latter had ordered a change in personnel at White Earth. He had sent Father Simon Lampe to assist Father Thomas Borgerding at Red Lake. Father Aloysius, who did not want Father Simon changed, sent the prior's letter to Archbishop Ireland. The apostolic visitator immediately removed the prior because he had exceeded his jurisdiction while the abbey was under apostolic visitation. Father Peter wrote at once to Abbot Alexius:

". . . Pity me, Father Abbot, for being forced into such a position, and believe me that in spite of all I will stick to you and pray God more earnestly than before to grant you victory and a speedy return. Come back to us Father Abbot, for what shall become of us if you do not? Everything now looks discouraging — if I could only show my loyalty to you otherwise than by words alone. I will use this authority only when it is absolutely inevitable. . . . I consider it my duty to thank you sincerely, not only for the many favors shown me personally during these many years, but also for what you have done for our Order in general. It is true, I can never pay the debt I owe you; but I earnestly hope never to prove myself ungrateful. May God, who alone can adequately reward you, yet permit you to enjoy the fruits of your labors in the midst of the children you have reared, and for whom you have toiled so much. I see you wronged and suffering, and it pains me to feel myself so little able to help you. I might have acted more resolutely on some occasions, but I certainly did nothing to bring about, or even to hasten the calamity that has befallen you and us.

"Now all I can do is to extend to you, dear Father Abbot, my heartfelt sympathy and to offer up to God earnest prayers, that he may give you grace and strength to bear patiently these severe trials, and that he may turn them to your greater glory and reward in heaven, and even here, to your full vindication before men. I entreat you, do not give up the fight, not when victory is well nigh won, for victorious you shall be in any case, even if the decision of the Congregation should (which I hope not), favor your opponents. Appearances may mislead human judges, but not Him who searcheth the depth of the heart." [56]

Abbot Alexius preferred Fathers Peter, Norbert and Chrysostom, in that order, as his successor. But Father Peter's adherence to Abbot Alexius, as well as his youth and inexperience on the missions, worked against his candidacy. This was especially evident in the election of Father Bernard as vicar of the chapter. Father Gregory Steil reported that the parties of the right and left, that is, the missionary monks and those who desired monastic development, had united their separate causes in the person of Father Bernard. Abbot Alexius felt Father Bernard was "a good man, but would make a poor Abbot." Father Peter, however, told his retired superior that Father Bernard's intentions were undoubtedly good and now he would have the opportunity "to make good the pain he may have caused you in the past."

". . . This election plainly showed that the externals [outsiders] are too well organized. They will have their man, and they will certainly carry their point. P. Bernard will be our next abbot. I am not in the least surprised at this. I had some chances, but I have forfeited them. Yes, if I had shown myself as opposed to you, Norbert and Chrysostom, especially the latter, I might have been elected. I could not stoop to such meanness. Moreover, you can believe, not only am I not anxious to become Abbot, but I am ever so glad to see that my chances of becoming one are gone. For I never considered myself fit for such an office, and don't think I will ever deem myself fit. We must be prepared for a defeat. It may be humiliating indeed to some, yes to all that remained true to you, to see men of Othmar's stamp boast of a complete victory, but I trust none of us will prove a coward — we have nothing to be ashamed of." [57]

The date of the abbatial election was fixed for 7 May 1890. Abbot Innocent journeyed from Atchison to Collegeville, asking all to pray that God would guide them to select the best abbot under the circumstances, and determined that the entire proceeding would be conducted peacefully. Abbot Innocent announced at the opening of the voting that only discussion of matters pertaining strictly to the election would be allowed. He was asked at one point in the proceedings if he would accept the abbotship of St. John's if elected. Abbot Innocent, whose election at St. John's in 1875 had been refused by Abbot Boniface, and who also had been offered and had refused the abbotship at St. Vincent in 1888 after Wimmer's death, responded:

". . . Please excuse me for using a very strong expression. I must say that is an impudent question, for it tempts me to answer yes or no. If I should say yes, it would be a bid for votes, ambition; if I say no, it would indicate that I expected votes. My answer was the hardest word that was spoken. I begged pardon of the Father for having used it. The question made me very angry. In regard to accusations or allegations I must say that they were brought up against the eligibles, but decently, and were also answered or passed over if all knew that they were true. . . . Yes, it was a great pleasure at St. John's that the election went off so well. Everybody is satisfied. The election was practically unanimous because the few who voted differently were not against P. Bernard. One of them received one vote, and a number said that he voted for himself because otherwise nobody else would have voted for him." [58]

There was no contest at the election when it came to voting; all had been decided previously. Father Bernard received forty-three votes; Father Peter, four; Abbot Alexius a token of six, and Father Meinulph, one. Father Bernard broke down, wept, and did not want to accept the office. Abbot Innocent was afraid to urge him too much but said: "You can hardly refuse."

Abbot Innocent wrote to Abbot Alexius to report on the election, and told him that Father Bernard was elected on the first ballot in the morning session. After dinner Abbot Innocent assembled the monks and read a statement to them:

". . . 'Abbot Alexius was told by the Procurator General that the Visitation might last for years and that many had lasted ten years: if he would resign, it would end sooner; Abbot Alexius then said he would resign under the condition that the Visitation would end at once; that those monks who were to be punished, should be punished by Rome: that the Cardinal give him some official testimonial that he, the Abbot, remained in good standing: the answer to the resignation was, that it was accepted and his good work done as Abbot praised: besides, the Cardinal told him to remain Praeses until his term was up, i.e., to the next election or General Chapter. . . . Missions are not essential, as a College is not essential, but both can be carried on by Religious: by and by we will be forced by Rome to give up the small missions, because Rome does not want so many Religious to live alone and outside the monastery. We must be good monks, then we can do anything. Our Order converted nations, and instructed them in arts, sciences, agriculture and industrial pursuits.

Abbot-elect
Bernard
Locnikar

" 'Now, hold together: each one hold his own opinions, and let him have that right as you claim it for yourself: hence respect each one for his sincerity, and do not chide him for it: but do not be false to one another, but work together. Appeals to external authority are disliked by the Church. We should not act against ourselves. Had the case of Abbot Alexius been brought up in the General Chapter, it would have been taken up. But no, it was brought directly to Rome, and thus our Congregation could do no more. When the Visitation was ordered, your monastery was practically cut off from our Congregation: hence, no one can say that such a Visitation is a benefit. Whatever the opinions of each about the past may be, in the future hold together: speak to one another and you will soon get to an understanding, and all will live together then as Brethren. Let the outside know nothing of our affairs: and especially now, until the Abbot is confirmed, try to do your very best for the honor of God, the good of the Order and your monastery.'

"After having read the above, I left: and then the Fathers had a lively, good-natured time as much as I could judge from their hearty laughter. The next day I visited the Bishop [Zardetti], who seems to be all kindness in conversation: but they say he is terrible when he wields the pen. They have found out already that it pays to travel and see him rather than write to him." [59]

At four o'clock in the afternoon of May 9 Abbot Innocent and Abbot-elect Bernard visited Archbishop Ireland in St. Paul. He was delighted with the result of the election, as Abbot Innocent reported:

197

". . . His Grace, Archbishop Ireland said to the Abbot-elect Father Bernard: 'You will live to let those go who will not be satisfied, no matter to what side they belonged. Otherwise you will not have to disencumber or change, except perhaps to improve the instruction of the young, to give up some small places where the monks live like secular priests. There is no one to look after except P. Othmar whose case will soon be settled.' There you have it! Nothing important to change! And yet so much agitation! The new abbot will therefore, in case he insists on order and discipline, have the same opponents. They will naturally expect that they can now do as they please, and if the abbot wants them to do what he thinks best, he is then a tyrant. I also have been branded as a tyrant, but did not allow it to go so far, and did what I suggested to Abbot Alexius earlier; i.e., brought the matter before the chapter. After the chapter the instigator had no more followers even though he had many sympathizers before. The abbot is supposed to be responsible for everything and yet say nothing. He should see to it that all observe the Holy Rule and yet allow each to do what he considers suitable. He is not supposed to expend unnecessarily and yet be sure not to see to it that others spend foolishly. Should he demand what is left over for the monastery, then he is a 'money grabber.' He should give up all the missions and yet build, educate, send money here and there. If we would not have had the missions, nothing would have come out of St. Benedict's and St. John's Abbey. St. Vincent's itself would not be as far as it is. We will not keep the missions for all eternity, but now we cannot make ends meet and get through without them. In Minnesota the missionary priests were against the abbot because he didn't support them and demanded only money from them. The Anselmianum got its money from America through the missions. Now they always want money, money and more money." [60]

But Abbot-elect Bernard, even before the confirmation of his election arrived from Rome, indicated that he would not tolerate critical discussions of monastery affairs. When he came upon a group of the missionary Benedictines carrying on such a discussion in the rectory of St. Mary's Church, St. Cloud, he left the gathering without saying a word. The Holy See approved the new abbot's election on July 6 and his blessing was held in the abbey church on August 27, with Bishop Zardetti, first bishop of St. Cloud, officiating, assisted by Archabbot Andrew Hintenach and Abbot Innocent Wolf. During the pontifical Mass the monastery choir, with a fifteen piece orchestra, produced Zangl's Mass *in honorem S. Joannis Cantii*. An alumnus of St. John's, Bishop John Shanley of Jamestown, N. Dak., delivered the sermon. Abbot-elect Bernard had asked Archbishop Ireland to be his preacher, but the latter had replied that because of circumstances it would be better if he was not. At the banquet for 1,200 people following the ceremonies Judge D. B. Searle of St. Cloud, Bishop Shanley and another alumnus, Bishop Joseph B. Cotter of Winona, gave testimonials to Abbot Alexius in their speeches, and praised what he had accomplished in fourteen short years. However, when Archbishop Ireland rose to speak he said: "You have heard much of what the Order has done in the past. I don't care for that. We will look to its future and to what it can do now." [61]

Those who expected the new abbot to change Abbot Alexius' personnel immediately and install his opponents in positions of authority soon learned that Abbot Bernard, in pursuit of peace, was determined to act in every case magnanimously and toward all charitably. His first act was to have the letters PAX placed over the main entrance to the abbey. Then he called Father Severin Gross back to the monastery from New Munich and named him prior. Prior Severin, who had no part in the previous controversies, was a fellow countryman of the new abbot, and as a diocesan priest in Carniola, had been a benefactor of Locnikar during his student days. Abbot Alexius' old friends and supporters, Fathers Peter and Norbert, were appointed subprior and procurator respectively, while Father Chrysostom was retained as vice-president of the school despite strong pressure on Abbot Bernard to remove the former abbot's forceful and controversial defender.

Next on the agenda was the solution of the case of Father Othmar Erren. Following the division of ecclesiastical authority in Dakota, Erren had come under the charge of Bishop Shanley of Jamestown and Shanley desired his case settled at once. Erren was assisting Father Vincent Wehrle, O.S.B., at Devils Lake, but Wehrle wanted Father Othmar recalled to the abbey. Father Othmar came back to St. John's after the election with promises of good behavior if reinstated. Abbot Bernard refused to deal with him in any way until he received instructions from Rome. Cardinal Simeoni informed Abbot Bernard on 30 July 1890 that Father Othmar could be absolved from his ecclesiastical censures by his superior. Abbot Bernard and his senior council then decided that Father Othmar was to go to Conception Abbey, Missouri, where he was to make a strict four-week retreat under the new abbot's close friend, Abbot Frowin Conrad. Abbot Bernard also ordered Erren to write a letter of apology to Abbot Alexius. In this letter Erren wrote:

"Please kindly excuse the liberty I take in writing to you who must have thought me, at least in the past his bitter, relentless and ungrateful opponent. . . . In how far I may have been right and where my culpability began it would at this date be useless to argue. Doubtless concerning some matters you, Father Abbot, and I will never agree. My conscience accuses me in some points. Yet I cannot but think that my conscience and your opinion it is under to plead guilty in many regards would never agree — neither on the number of offenses or their gravity.

"It would be useless therefore to enter into past history — for evident reasons. As regards myself personally I shall try very hard to do what is right before God, in the future, — and am perfectly willing to live on a footing of brotherly amity with all my confreres at St. John's.

*Resignation
And Reform*

"If you should desire to return to the monastery for which you have worked so perseveringly and successfully — I will do my best to show you proper respect and due deference and will take very good care that no old wounds be reopened through my fault. In conclusion — for all my transgressions toward you, conscious and voluntary — as also for those unknown to me, but of which yourself or others may have judged me guilty, I humbly and sincerely beg your pardon and forgiveness.

"May our monastery continue and progress in the spirit it is at present exhibiting — which is — a spirit of charity, with a desire for harmony and the extinction of all old feuds and troubles. I do not know whether you intend to make St. John's your home anew, but if so I am sure you will find the portals wide open and a cordial welcome from all." [62]

Erren sent a copy of this letter to Abbot Bernard who was not pleased with its contents, its obvious qualified admission of guilt, and the old-time spirit of passing judgment on extraneous matters. Abbot Alexius considered the missive another insult from Erren and ignored it. The new abbot then ordered Erren to send a second letter in which he simply and humbly begged pardon of Abbot Alexius, as he was asked to do originally, and to send his former superior a copy of Rome's decision in his case. Then Erren wrote:

"In reconsidering the contents of my former letter which was written rather hurriedly and I fear, without sufficient forethought, I have come to the conclusion that they could not have been satisfactory to you.

"Having now, however, finished my retreat, I take this opportunity to beg of you, therefore, to consider my former letter as never having been written, and herewith to receive my unqualified apology and humble petition for pardon — of which I will try, with God's grace, to prove myself not all unworthy in the future." [63]

With this act the most turbulent and needless crisis of St. John's first century was terminated. The repercussions of the train of events set off by Father Othmar Erren and his abettors would not be forgotten for many years. But Erren himself was effectively preserved from any future activity of a like nature by both Abbots Bernard and Peter who informed him that any expression of his opinions in the future would be unwelcome in every way. Abbot Bernard first assigned him to Hastings after his reinstatement, and after a pastorship of fourteen years there, Abbot Peter appointed him pastor of St. Joseph's Church, Minneapolis, where he died on 11 September 1923.

The new abbot was determined to heal all the wounds of 1889, the *annus miserabilis,* as Father Alexius Hoffmann liked to call it. It is difficult to see how anyone else could have pointed up spiritual values and pacified the community as effectively as Abbot Bernard did. The perennial problem of an historian of the Church is to discover and strive to evaluate objectively the reality of God's providence operating in events. It can be seen more plainly in the advancement of Father Bernard than, perhaps, in any other single development in St. John's history. And toward no one did Abbot Bernard evidence his charitable spirit more than toward his retired predecessor Abbot Alexius. For years the two men, so different in temper and sympathy, had not seen eye to eye on administration and policy. Abbot Alexius' burning energy and predilection for building stood out in strong contrast to Abbot Bernard's love of quiet and contemplation. It was in some ways like a New World clash between Cluny and Citeaux. Both as novice master and vice-president Father Bernard had felt that there was not a deeply rooted monastic spirit at the abbey. "What we need most among us is men of prayer," he stated as early as 1878. Later he told Abbot Frowin: "I think what is lacking with us is a firm foundation, firmness of good aspirations and resolves which come from inner conviction and determination." [64] Nor had he hesitated to write such sentiments to Bishop Grace of St. Paul, nor to give ear and sympathy to the opponents of Abbot Alexius. During his years as pastor of Assumption Church in St. Paul, the rectory was a sympathetic center of anti-Alexian dissatisfaction. Yet Father Bernard never assumed leadership of the movement, although it was frequently proferred to him. Father Peter for a time had listened to the criticisms, but, unlike Father Bernard, soon realized the proportions the movement had assumed and dissociated himself from its course. The defenders of Abbot Alexius reminded Abbot Bernard after his election that he, even if unwittingly, had abetted the revolt and would now have to resolve the problems it had created.

It would appear that for this reason especially Abbot Bernard was anxious to make immediate overtures to his predecessor, who was equally desirous of restoring peace. In fact, Abbot Alexius made the first move in March of 1890 after Father Bernard had been elected vicar of the chapter. He sent him a ring from St. Leo's Abbey which a Frank Gerner of Florida wanted delivered to his brother Otto in Assumption parish. This transaction had a figurative meaning also, as Abbot Alexius wanted Father Bernard to realize:

". . . I offer you my good wishes in your present position. I wish you well. I suppose you will be my successor. It looks that way. I certainly have no objections. I always did my best for you, meant well, and the balance we may safely leave in God's hands. . . . I am satisfied that you meant well towards me. I do not believe that you wronged me intentionally. If you are elected Abbot you shall have my support. I am certain you don't desire or even wish the mitre. Yet if elected, I desire you to accept the burden and bear it. God has given you the shoulders and He will also give you the necessary strength. I do not ignore your good qualities. You possess many of them. With God's grace you will be able to fill the abbatial position in an able manner. Surely prayers are necessary: God must select the man. And the man when elected must say: *Ecce adsum*. Yes, fifteen years ago we worked together and *Deo volente* we may yet work together in the future. You were mainly instrumental that then I accepted the *onus*. . . . That you will practice, when elected, what you then preached to me, is my earnest desire, my sincere wish and even my command as far as it goes. I repeat that if elected you shall have my full support. Let green grass grow over the past. Bear up bravely. I thank you for your prayers. I do not fail to make a daily *memento* for you, differences or no differences." [65]

Resignation And Reform

After the election Abbot Alexius wrote congratulations and then mentioned that he might consider taking a Minnesota mission such as Duluth. Abbot Bernard answered immediately:

"I was glad to hear from you and thank you from my whole heart for your kind wishes and especially for the prayers. . . . I wish to have a clear understanding with you before any other thing. You were my superior for so many years, and worked so hard for our community that I could not but consider it my first duty to be in a clear understanding with you, and this so much more, because I know now your wishes are only for the best of our monastery. Now you started the question and I am glad you did it. Rt. Rev. Father Abbot, I can assure you every one of your wishes shall be considered with due and true respect on my part. Of course as I am a green-horn I will make mistakes by the wholesale but I can say sincerely I don't intend to hurt anybody and to work only for and in the interest of peace and harmony in our community and as far as possible for a higher standard of religious life, and I am sure you will help us along for that purpose." [66]

Abbot Bernard agreed that Abbot Alexius could go to Duluth if he wished to, and have an assistant of his own choosing. Locnikar suggested they talk it over more at length when they met. After the benediction ceremonies were over Abbot Alexius came out to Minnesota for two months, staying most of the time with friends in St. Cloud, but also visiting the abbey and several of the missions he had established. With Abbot Bernard setting the tone, Abbot Alexius was received kindly by his confreres, and welcomed by his large number of friends in the area. For instance, Governor Knute Nelson of Minnesota, an old friend of St. John's, wrote the resigned abbot after this first return visit to Minnesota:

". . . I have missed you very much, and so have your friends. I often think of you and I never go to St. Cloud but what I enquire for you among your friends. When I slowly and by degrees learned of the injustice that had been done you I was as angry as I could be and my

202

heart turned into stone against the men who led in the crusade. I have had a little of such experience myself and so I can feel these things keenly. But my dear Abbot, you have shown, are showing and will show these men that you are superior to their wiles and that 'truth crushed to earth will rise again.' The local argon of your traducer is hostile to me, also, but I am proud of the fact that I too am distasteful to your enemies. They belittle me as they did you. I have heard of the good work you are doing and I feel that you will meet with great success." [67]

Abbot Alexius did not remain in Minnesota, as he had originally intended, but returned to New York where Archbishop Michael J. Corrigan had made him several offers. Abbot Alexius had been recommended to the archbishop by his New York priest friends, John Edwards of Immaculate Conception parish, Anthony Kessler of St. Joseph's parish, Anthony B. Schwenninger of Assumption parish and Joseph F. Mooney of St. Patrick's parish in Newbury. During these years Archbishop Corrigan was the leader of the so-called conservative group of American Catholics which stood in opposition to the so-called liberalizing tendencies of Cardinal Gibbons, Archbishop Ireland, Bishop Keane and Monsignor O'Connell. Corrigan received Edelbrock most cordially on 27 September 1890, told him he had heard of his Minnesota experiences, and said he would be happy if he would remain in New York. He wanted to appoint him vicar-general of New York for the Germans of the archdiocese, allow him to organize a parish for German Catholics, appoint him spiritual director of all religious communities in the archdiocese, and finally turn over ecclesiastical control of the Bahama Islands to his charge. The ex-abbot was overwhelmed by these offers, especially as Archbishop Ireland had so recently asserted that religion had suffered more than writing could tell and was perishing under the Benedictines when he was abbot. Abbot Alexius asked to be excused from again assuming command as a vicar-general for German Catholics or for religious, but Archbishop Corrigan insisted that he should fill some responsible position. Edelbrock then told Corrigan he would like to be an instrument in God's hand for establishing Benedictines in the archdiocese of New York, and the archbishop replied that he would be most pleased if this came about. On 9 January 1891 the archbishop and his consultors authorized the abbot to begin a parish on the West Side between the Assumption parish on 49th Street and St. Joseph's parish on 125th Street, and to assume charge of the Bahama Islands. After several unsuccessful attempts to start at this first location because of undetermined borders, Archbishop Corrigan told him to go further out into the country, to the township of Morrisania, and he was given forty lots as a gift on 160th Street and Boston Avenue. At first the abbot held services in a hall over a tobacco factory, but the pastor of St. Augustine's parish, Thomas F. Gregg, considered a new parish unnecessary

in that area. Then the Reverend John Hughes, pastor of St. Jerome's
Church, gave him a chapel of ease on Concord Avenue and 151st Street
which belonged to St. Jerome's parish. It was 75 x 30 feet and held
300 people. This was the beginning of 'the abbot's parish,' as it was
called in New York. He placed it under the patronage of the Benedictine doctor, St. Anselm. The parish was seven miles from downtown
New York, entirely out in the country and embraced a mile and a half
of territory, including Hunt's Point.[68]

Abbot Bernard was very pleased with the project and told Abbot
Alexius he was for it with his whole soul:

". . . I am sure that after a short time, we might get different Fathers free — as the Bishop [Zardetti] would like to have some of our
missions as soon as he gets priests of his own for them, and in New
York — how much could be done, if say half a dozen or so could be
there, conduct a monastic life and tend to a large congregation, especially as it is known that people have a preference for Religious, if
these try to do their duty as such. And besides you have so many inducements and encouragements on the part of your friends among the
clergy of New York. . . . I would also like to have a clear understanding between us two regarding that affair, and this from the beginning. Now do you intend to have it — on your own name independently from St. John's — or is it to come on the name of St. John's
Abbey, as you often told me. If the last is the case, then I must state as
I did before in writing and verbally, that I do not consent, not by any
means, that the Bahamas be put to our name and such a burden be
placed on our Abbey. If you intend to run it independently on your
own name and account, without any risk to St. John's Abbey, then of
course you may do so, I will have nothing to say then, and also have
no responsibility, in that regard. I suppose you will understand that
whatever help St. John's gives or will give you, is more for your own
personal regard than for any practical use for the Abbey itself. Hoping
that you will not take these remarks amiss — they were written only in
view of the better interests of our common home. . . ."[69]

Abbot Alexius unquestionably wanted the new enterprise to be under St. John's, and he expected assistance from his abbey since he
had been given no pension by the chapter after his resignation and was
left to find a place for himself. Abbot Alexius looked upon St.
Anselm's parish as a step in the establishment of a Benedictine monastery in New York, just as he had planned previously in West Union,
Bismarck and Duluth. When he began to build the parish buildings
they were of the same character and architectural style as his other
foundations. Within a year he had purchased twenty lots for $16,744
on Tinton Avenue and 155th Street, a short distance from the original
chapel, and begun construction of a four story, thirty-one room rectory. Here was the familiar pattern of broad-visioned planning for

the future. This rectory was ready to become a monastic priory at once, and an abbey eventually. His plans for the church were similar. It was to be 171 feet long, 72 feet high, 86 feet wide with a 210 foot steeple, and when completed would be one of the largest churches in the city. This was one structure he did not see through to completion, however. The basement was built and used as the parish church until 1916, and an aging but impatient Abbot Alexius was forced to use it to the end of his days.

From the beginning the other abbots of the American Cassinese Congregation looked upon this New York foundation as a future abbey. Bishop Leo Haid especially pressed Abbot Alexius to begin full monastic community life there and take up command again. It would be, these old friends maintained, the final vindication. But while insisting that this was his aim, and building toward that end, the abbot dissimulated and put off a decision whenever pressed. His bitter experience in the past with what he considered a community's ingratitude dampened his ardor. Now that he had again built up a thriving establishment he was loathe to endanger his hard-won peace, and as the years rolled by such a decision became all the more impossible to make.

Abbot Alexius asked Abbot Bernard to send him three assistants from St. John's, two for the parish and one to go to the Bahama Islands. Locnikar could only spare two men, but gave them graciously in 1891. They were the resigned abbot's choices, and included Father Chrysostom Schreiner, vice-president, and Father Gerard Spielmann, professor in the college. It was a sacrifice for Abbot Bernard to give up the versatile and talented head of the abbey's school, but Father Chrysostom was anxious to work again with his friend and confidant. He never felt at home under the new administration, and the reformers in turn looked upon him with his forceful personality as a source of future difficulties. Father Gerard assisted Abbot Alexius at St. Anselm's parish, and Father Xavier White, professor of English and Abbot Alexius' unwavering supporter, was also allowed to go to New York as a second assistant in July of 1891. But he was in the parish less than two months when he became ill and doctors informed him he had a malignant cancer of the stomach. He began his homeward journey to St. John's but could not go on when he reached Buffalo. He was taken to Tanawanda, six miles west of Buffalo, and died at the home of his sister on 26 September 1891.

Meanwhile Abbot Alexius had sent Father Chrysostom to the Bahama Islands. Archbishop Corrigan had given Abbot Alexius a New York parish with the stipulation that the Benedictines take over the ecclesiastical charge of the Bahama Islands which were then under the jurisdiction of the archdiocese of New York. Corrigan wanted two priests and two Brothers sent there at once. The parish in New York was to be a source of income and contact for the work in the Bahama

Islands. The archbishop promised $1,000 a year donation from the archdiocese for the work, and freedom to collect for the Bahama mission in the parishes of New York. But Abbot Bernard and the chapter at St. John's would not even consider the possibility of such an undertaking. For years the community had grown accustomed to the breathtaking projects of their resigned abbot which somehow or other always flourished. But now they had to refer to a map to discover the geography of this latest proposal of Abbot Alexius, who only a short time previously had been under attack for just such moves. Besides there was a new administration at St. John's. The new abbot was interested in religious and monastic deepening at the abbey itself, not in more active commitments on Caribbean corals 1800 miles from home.

To Abbot Alexius, as would be expected, the Bahamas offered a new opportunity for the Benedictines to convert another nation, as they had brought thirty-three nations to Christianity before. The blessing of God would be assured, he said, if the Order would seize the opportunity to work anew for the spread of Christianity and social improvement. To Abbot Bernard it was going to another world, and he told Abbot Alexius he would not submit the project to a chapter scrutiny because it would not receive six votes.

Father Chrysostom went to the Bahama Islands because Abbot Alexius' agreement with Archbishop Corrigan had been made, and Abbot Bernard felt that the abbey was obliged to assist the resigned abbot in every possible way. St. John's for years, however, had no official association with the project. It was a case of nonrecognition in theory and cooperation in practice. In practice, perhaps this was the best procedure. For as members of the community were able to visit the islands and slowly come to understand the need and potential of this mission field, the work became an integral part of the abbey's life. Abbot Alexius had broadened the community's vision during fourteen previous years and led it from an initial apostolate among German Catholic immigrants into new efforts in several fields. These included an expanded educational endeavor in an American mold, service to Catholic immigrant peoples of other national origins than German, Indian mission activity, and vigorous application of Wimmer's New World renewal of the vital Benedictine principle that an abbey must be constantly in the process of establishing new daughter abbeys. Now he was lifting St. John's out of its regional origins by establishing a center in the country's largest city. And finally the community was being drawn outside the national boundaries of the United States and presented with the challenge of working for the spiritual and temporal advancement of the Negroes.

The Bahama Islands, windfall of Christopher Columbus' first voyage to the New World, embrace nearly 700 islands and more than 2,000 cays and rocks lying off the eastern coast of Florida. Only twenty-one

206

of these pieces of land have permanent settlements, however. The Arawak Indians Columbus found there, and called 'Lucayans,' disappeared under the pressures of European colonization and were gradually replaced in the eighteenth century by the many tribes of African slaves deposited in the Bahamas to grow cotton, sisal for rope making, pineapples and tomatoes. When England replaced Spain as an American empire builder the islands passed under the control of Britain. Ecclesiastically also the islands were transferred by the Holy See from the vicariate of Trinidad to Jamaica, and then to London. After the American Revolution England retained possession of the Bahama Islands, but Catholic life in England during the eighteenth and early nineteenth centuries was so precarious that nothing could be done for such a small affiliate of the mother country as the Bahamas. Anglicans and Protestants were active in the Bahamas during this period, however. Accordingly, Rome in 1858 placed the Bahamas under the ecclesiastical jurisdiction of the diocese of Charleston, S.C. But Charleston in the post-Civil War period was in no position to spare priests for the Bahama Islands. During seventeen years under Charleston no clergyman had been sent to reside on the islands. Since the main water routes originated in New York, one of the handful of Catholics in Nassau, capital of the islands, a Major Ayde-Curran, surgeon of the British army post here, suggested to Archbishop Corrigan on a visit to New York that priests be sent from that archdiocese to the Bahamas. Previously Bishop Henry P. Northrup of Charleston had relied on the aid of his friend Archbishop Corrigan for the priests who irregularly visited the Bahamas to administer the sacraments and offer Holy Mass. In February of 1885 Corrigan sent one of his New York priests who was sickly, the Reverend George O'Keefe, to the Bahamas to reside and organize the small Catholic population in Nassau. On July 28 of that same year Cardinal Simeoni of the Propaganda transferred the Bahamas to the ecclesiastical jurisdiction of New York. O'Keefe began a subscription drive for a Catholic church in Nassau and on 14 February 1887 Archbishop Corrigan travelled to Nassau to dedicate, under the title of St. Francis Xavier, the first Catholic church built on the islands. Besides Father O'Keefe three other New York priests, the Reverends D. P. O'Flynn, J. Ryan and J. Reilly, served at Nassau during the years 1885–90.

First Bahama Missions

During this five year period Archbishop Corrigan became convinced that his diocesan priests could not supply permanent spiritual direction to the far-flung mission needs of the islands as effectively as a religious order. He accordingly made overtures to the New York Capuchins and the New Orleans Jesuits, but neither group was in a position at that time to supply personnel. The provincial of the New Orleans Jesuits, Ignatius O'Shanahan, told Corrigan that the Bahamas appeared to be suited for a Benedictine development since it was believed at that time

207

that a mission there could be maintained by cultivation of the land. Corrigan first asked Archabbot Andrew Hintenach of St. Vincent, who could not accept, and then Abbot Hilary Pfraengle of St. Mary's Abbey, Newark. Pfraengle was interested and visited the Bahamas in October of 1889 in company with Mother Ambrosia and a group of Sisters of Charity from Mount St. Vincent on the Hudson, whom the archbishop had interested in the project. These four Sisters, with a dynamic Sister Marie Dolores of the New York Van Rensseleer family as superior, opened their free school of St. Francis Xavier Academy in Nassau on November 6.

Abbot Hilary returned to New York with much enthusiasm for the undertaking, thought of going there himself, and made plans on his 1890 trip to Europe to contact European Benedictines, especially in England, with the intention of obtaining volunteers for a Bahama undertaking. Corrigan and his council wished to retain title to Bahama church property for a three year period until such a mission proved successful, and on this point he and Pfraengle could not reach an agreement. It was then that Abbot Alexius entered the picture, accepted the archbishop's three year stipulation, and sent Father Chrysostom to examine the possibilites at Nassau. Schreiner arrived on 2 February 1891, took over from Father Reilly on March 1 and reported to Archbishop Corrigan:

"As to the condition of the mission, I have the pleasure of submitting the following: There are about 50 practical Catholics here, children included. The number of apostate Catholics is about 20, of whom I think, some can be reclaimed. These figures are not thoroughly reliable. During the month I will see every Catholic here and will then give your Grace the exact numbers. The mission has lately grown by the acquisition of several Catholic families and the prospects of further increase by immigration are good. Increase from conversion, especially from Anglicanism, is not at all improbable and I look hopefully to good results from this source. The main source of increase however will be the schools. The venerable Sisters are doing most excellent work in the schools and I cannot speak too highly of their work and their spirit of patience and self-sacrifice. . . .

"Next year is the centenary year of the discovery of America. I learn that a squadron representing many nations will gather at San Salvador in October, 1892. Ought not the Catholics of the U.S. do something for the occasion? I propose that they build a monumental chapel there and that your Grace come down to dedicate it October 13, 1892. Secondly, I propose that the clergy of the archdiocese furnish a memorial bell for the church here and that your Grace consecrate it on the same occasion.

"Will your Grace give me permission to take steps in the matter?

208

If so, I will write a circular, submit it to your approval, and then hand it to the Catholic press of the states. . . .

"Next Saturday (Vigil of Pentecost) I will receive into the Church two colored persons, one a married woman whose husband is a Catholic, and the other a 14-year-old boy who attends the Sisters' school. Everything there progresses nicely and the Sisters and myself are well.

"We have May devotions and the Governor (Sir Ambrose Shea) and family, Secretary Jackson and family and a few others are daily attendants. Every Thursday evening during the month I preach a sermon and the attendance there is quite large.

"Abbot Alexius has promised to send down a pump and hose, which I will place in the garden adjoining the church. I started in gardening a few days ago, and hope to be able soon to furnish convent and my own house with vegetables." [70]

Father Chrysostom had taught history at St. John's before going to the Bahamas, and his imagination was quickened by the thought that he was now a missionary on the very islands first touched by Columbus when he brought Catholicism to the Americas. Abbot Bernard had sent the Reverend Paul Rettenmaier, O.S.B., to the Bahamas as a possible assistant to Father Chrysostom. Schreiner chartered a schooner and made arrangements for a party to visit some of the out islands while at the same time touching the points historically and traditionally associated with Columbus' voyage. Also in the party were the Reverend M. J. Duffy, who was visiting from New York, and Dr. Sterling of Sag Harbour, New York. The priest first offered Holy Mass and preached at Eleuthera and Cat Island, where Duffy and Sterling left the party. Then the schooner headed for San Salvador, or Watling Island as it was called by the British. On 4 April 1891 at ten o'clock in the evening the boat ran onto a rock one-half mile off the reef running north of Conception Island, and sank within two minutes. The two priests and crew of six were able to jump into a life boat. Schreiner described what followed:

"Oh my God, what a night of terrible suffering and anxiety. Eight men in a mere shell in a bed of sunken rock, a heavy sea rolling over the adjacent reef and rocking us to and fro, the volley of every heavy wave exposing the hideous surface of the rocks, and eight miles away from land. If the night was a long and terrible one, these 8 miles to land were most perilous. Every moment we were in a position to be dashed against a sunken rock or rolling waves threatened to overpower and swallow us. Five hours of hard work brought us to land. Prayers of gratitude went up to heaven from our trembling hearts, while hot tears of joy trickled from our eyes and dropped on the land upon which at last we stood. The feelings experienced during these 12 hours, during every moment of which death threatened us, are simply too awful to

Father Chrysostom Schreiner, O.S.B.

209

describe. An attempt seems sacrilegious. More so when I see that only the Hand of God could have safely landed us on that shore. On any other supposition I am convinced that if 100 vessels were wrecked in a like place the lives of all on board the ninety-nine would be lost." [71]

During the harrowing hours Father Chrysostom spent in the life boat, he made a vow that if his life was spared he would remain in the Bahamas for the rest of his days as a missionary. Schreiner held this vow as sacred, although a religious with solemn vows could not canonically make such a solemn promise independently of his superior. When he returned to Nassau he entered with renewed vigor into his lonely apostolate. Father Paul returned to Minnesota, and Abbot Bernard was hard-pressed to send further assistance. But he came down to the Bahamas for a visit in November of 1892 and stayed during the Christmas season. He brought with him Father Rupert Kiefer, O.S.B., who was suffering from tuberculosis and left him with Father Chrysostom. The abbot, like thousands of tourists in the years ahead, found the climate at that time of year unsurpassed. The picturesque character of Nassau, the beautiful tropical plant and marine life, but most of all the winning ways of the natives, made the Bahama venture attractive. On Christmas day the first Solemn High Mass was offered in Nassau with Father Chrysostom as celebrant, Father Rupert Kiefer as deacon, Frater Melchior Bahner as subdeacon and Frater Bartholomew Rebholz, O.S.B., as master of ceremonies. Abbot Bernard preached the sermon and in the afternoon dedicated St. Benedict's Hall, a stone school to be used as a free kindergarten for colored children. The two clerics, Fratres Melchior and Bartholomew, were in the Bahamas for seven months to recover their health.

During his administration Abbot Bernard never made a definite decision about St. John's support of the Bahama undertaking. He supplied what assistance he could to Father Chrysostom, and even sent two newly ordained priests, Fathers Gabriel Roerig and Melchior Bahner, to the Bahamas on 4 June 1894. But there was little sympathetic understanding among the majority at the abbey for this missionary endeavor. The summer heat of the islands was believed to be overpowering; the lack of any financial support whatever from the islands themselves made the project insecure. Most significant, however, was a lack of appreciation for the need of foreign missionary work among members of the community. Abbot Bernard sent Father Alexius Hoffmann, professor of dogmatic theology at St. John's, to the Bahamas to view the field, and though he enjoyed the experience, he was completely unimpressed by the potential of the undertaking. Hoffmann even made the statement that St. John's should not be in this work because each nation had the obligation to bring itself to Christianity. Hoffmann's viewpoint was not exceptional for his times, however. Among American Catholics in the late nineteenth century there was little if any interest

210

in foreign missions. The problems of assimilating and caring for the waves of Catholic immigrants to the United States occupied ecclesiastical attention. The struggle to organize an apostolate for the American Indians and Negroes during these years received little enough support. Finally the nationalistic spirit so rampant in the United States at this period was a real barrier to any form of international effort or support.

The tenacity and determination of Father Chrysostom thus emerge all the more distinctly. He deserves unqualified recognition for first implementing foreign missionary work at St. John's and developing the opportunity obtained for the community by Abbot Alexius. The Reverend Carl Thomas Albury, '26, a native of Nassau and at present pastor of Ladysmith, B.C., Canada, summed up the impression made by this pioneer American Benedictine foreign missionary on the people of the Bahamas when he said: "Father Chrysostom was the biggest man I have ever known in every sense of the word and nothing can shake my confidence."[72]

But at first the achievements of Father Chrysostom were far from big. His advances were little steps. He sold the first rectory on Queens Street and through the mediation of Major Ayde-Curran was able to secure at public auction one of Nassau's oldest and finest buildings. It was situated on a height adjacent to St. Francis Xavier Church and was the former residence of the governor, recently used by the Imperial Government as a military hospital. This building, renamed 'The Priory,' became the center of parochial and missionary work. Additional property was purchased and the school buildings improved. Such advances were made possible by the generosity of Archbishop Corrigan, Monsignor Michael J. Lavelle of New York, Bishop Charles E. McDonnell of Brooklyn and a large number of eastern clergy who began to visit the Bahamas on vacation trips. Father Chrysostom journeyed to the States to collect money, especially in New York and Brooklyn, and Corrigan made arrangements to obtain funds for the Bahamas from the annual American collection for Negro and Indian missions.

The free schools operated by the Sisters of Charity flourished and at once became known as the best educational centers on the island of New Providence. By 1894 there were 325 students enrolled in these schools. Father Chrysostom opened a small school at the priory in 1893 in which he, Fathers Rupert and Melchior taught Latin, English and mathematics to boys. This educational effort did not survive, however, because Father Rupert returned to the States, and the cleric Melchior was only temporarily in the Bahamas for his health. Father Chrysostom made himself known throughout the colony through articles in the papers, public disputations with Anglican ministers, and formal lectures on Catholic doctrine to which he invited the officials and leading citizens of Nassau. Within a short time he became a major force in Bahamian affairs. Conversions were slow but consistent; in 1892 he

211

had 37 baptisms, almost as many as the total Catholic population when he arrived the previous year. In 1893 there were 82 Catholics in Nassau. The first out-island mission was opened on Andros Island on February 25 of that same year, and a catechist, James Martin from Brooklyn, was stationed there for five years. When the newly ordained priests, Fathers Gabriel and Melchior, arrived in June of 1894, Father Gabriel went to this first mission at Andros and built by hand St. Saviour's Chapel at the Salvador Point settlement. Father Melchior was stationed at Sacred Heart Chapel in eastern Nassau and had a stone church completed there by 1897.

For thirty years the Bahama mission work was of this nature. Catholic life centered around these three parish centers. Additional mission stations were established, but lack of priests prohibited permanent advance in such mission areas. The hope, as Archbishop Corrigan reported, was in the schools where the great majority of the colored children were not Catholic. Support had to come from the United States as the colored Catholics of the Bahamas were few and extremely poor. Hardship and self-sacrifice were the lot of the Benedictine monks and the Sisters of Charity. The official colonial governmental set were Anglicans, and there was much prejudice against Catholicism to be overcome among both the ruling White minority and the Colored Protestant majority. But the Catholic missionary group of three Benedictines and eight Sisters of Charity did not lose heart, as Father Chrysostom reported:

"The growth of Catholicism in the Bahamas is slow but constant and sure. We are now beginning to have Catholic families, which place the work on a surer basis and make it possible to hold converts. Where there have been isolated conversions from Protestant families, a few have become backsliders owing to the many obstacles placed in the way of practicing their religion, but where whole families or a majority of the members of a family have been converted, there is little danger of this occurring." [73]

Meanwhile back at the abbey, Abbot Bernard was pushing forward with the main concern of his life, enhancing the public worship of God and perfecting the observance of the *Rule* of St. Benedict. Hoffmann explained why this was necessary:

". . . A fine liturgical tradition did not exist in the American Cassinese Congregation, and Abbot Alexius was not much of a liturgist, though he could wrangle on ceremonies or rubrics. In those days, i.e., previous to 1890, the *Opus Dei* was considered the canonical *Onus diei*. The tendency was to consider the recitation of the Brevery — as they called it — the substance of that *Onus*, and they hurried through it, even in choir, as if they were paid according to the speed they were making. *Es muss von Fleck gehen*, as the Germans say. The recitation

212

was sufficiently *unisono*, but the tempo was speedy and hardly any pauses were observed." [74]

Abbot Bernard began his reforms by insisting that in the monastic church no function be omitted, and he fitted out Abbot Alexius' church with vestments and other requirements for dignified celebration of the feasts of the Church Year. He pontificated on all major feasts, and his discourses were never more eloquent than when he spoke of divine worship. For him the distinctive mission of a Benedictine community was the promotion of the liturgical life, the *Opus Dei* of St. Benedict's *Rule*. Abbot Bernard soon became recognized as an authority on liturgy, but it appears that his emphasis was in great part on rubrical exactness. He was punctilious as to bows, ordered the monks to touch the floor when mistakes were made in carrying out the divine office, and inaugurated Lenten reading of the Missal rubrics after which he commented on mistakes made by members of the community in celebrating Holy Mass. He insisted that all candidates for the priesthood be trained in liturgy and ecclesiastical chant.

In directing that the mind of the Church be carried out in regard to church music Abbot Bernard made a real contribution to the community. While not musically talented or trained, he did appreciate its liturgical role. St. John's had previously participated in the national movement for Cecilian music. Gregorian chant, or what was accepted as such, was heard only at Requiems. Now the new abbot wanted only Cecilian and Gregorian music at the abbey, and in pursuit of this end he sent the Reverend Otto Weiser, O.S.B., to study organ and chant directing under the famous Dr. Franz Xavier Haberl in Regensburg, and to visit Beuron Abbey and Bayreuth studios. New musical scores were purchased through the abbey of Metten. Father Stanislaus Preiser was called home to direct music, and the simplified Gregorian chants, known as the Ratisbon style of Gregorian chant, were introduced at all functions. One of the abbot's main dreams was actualized in 1891 when the organ loft was extended twelve feet and a large organ, built by Philip Odenbrett and William Schuelke of Milwaukee, was installed. It was modeled on the organ in the Green Bay cathedral and was pronounced a piece of superior workmanship by experts.

Although the Divine Office continued to be recited in the choir chapel, the abbot's main attention was directed to its perfection. The monastic cucullas, previously worn only at profession and burial, were now ordered for choir on major feasts. Those who missed attendance at the morning choir not only had to excuse themselves, but also could not attend that community's afternoon *haustus*. Silence and clausura were strictly enforced, and the abbot humbly and patiently led his community primarily through his own good example. He did not like travel or public functions, and his retiring nature was the best counterpart for these reforms he was advocating. The Conrad brothers, Frowin and Ignatius, of Conception Abbey were his close friends and advisers. Abbot Bernard had a special admiration for the observance of the monks of Conception, asked Abbot Frowin to conduct the first retreat of his administration, and was in close contact with him throughout his life.

Resignation And Reform

The externals of divine worship were not Abbot Bernard's only object, however. He worked through conferences and circular letters for an increase of religious spirit both at home and on the missions. One of his first acts was to ask all the missionary monks for their schedule of meditation, spiritual exercises, and spiritual reading. His aim was ever to remodel his monks according to their ideals. "Living alone outside the monastery," he stated, "*paulatim* diminishes love of monastic life and fervor of religious spirit." Abbot Bernard definitely held that monks should serve the Church in her needs, especially in America where priests were scarce. Because this was the tradition at St. John's, the Benedictines were enabled to contribute their services to the Northwest. But he also realized that the effect of his endeavor would have been more complete if more of the monks had been at home or in new monastic foundations. Peace and good will flowed from Abbot Bernard's sincere and zealous program. In previous years the material and financial security of the house had been amply provided for. Now, at least at home, there was a spiritual quickening, deepening and perfecting along lines of family worship, based on a growth in study and virtue. For Abbot Bernard was a dedicated student of theology and spent long hours in prayerful study.

He was also particularly zealous in encouraging popular religious movements, and in this spirit obtained permission from Pope Leo XIII to establish in America an Archconfraternity of Perpetual Adoration of the Blessed Sacrament for the relief of the souls in Purgatory under the patronage of St. Benedict. This pious confraternity was modeled upon one in the abbey of Lambach, Austria. The confraternity soon grew into a movement of national scope, was incorporated in many parishes, and continues to the present day. The abbot, as national director, could often be found far into the night on his knees in silent adoration before the Blessed Sacrament.

While Abbot Bernard was thus promoting monastic and interior life at St. John's he found himself faced with the major problem of his administration. The beginning of his abbotship coincided with the erection of the diocese of St. Cloud. Bishop Otto Zardetti, first ordinary of the diocese and former vicar-general of Bishop Marty in Dakota, stated at the beginning of his administration that "he would be a friend of the Benedictines and would not be run by Archbishop Ireland." [75] Bishop Zardetti actually clashed with Archbishop Ireland several times during his St. Cloud years over the German question, in which

214

Zardetti was an ardent defender of gradual assimilation of foreign-born Catholics, and also favored the parochial school system during the Faribault-Stillwater school experiment of the archbishop of St. Paul. But Abbot Alexius had forewarned what actually came to pass when the first bishop of St. Cloud turned to the development of his new diocese: "I would not be surprised if several of the missions would be taken from St. John's as the result of the Visitation." [76] The missionary Benedictines who had joined in opposition to Abbot Alexius and his program found within one year that their effort had the unexpected result of achieving just what their resigned abbot had predicted.

Bishop Otto Zardetti

Bishop Zardetti described his approach to this situation:

"On coming here I found the diocese existing by name and *de jure,* but otherwise yet the confusion of a vicariate existed. The diocese was nearly in the power of the Benedictines. There were but 15 secular priests in the poorest missions. . . . From the beginning I strove to build up a diocesan clergy, to educate young men and to provide the secular clergy with missions so that I could hope to attract a new generation of priests and destroy the prevalent impression that the St. Cloud diocese was but a dominance of the Benedictines. Already when Abbot Bernard took up the administration he by my request gave over to the secular clergy the following missions: Holding Ford — St. Anna — St. Stephen — Belle River — Perham — St. Nicholas — Lake Henry — Spring Hill — Kraintown — Kimball Prairie — Alexandria.

"The missions, however, being poor, most of them only stations and yet nearly all regular and perfect parishes in their possession, so that I was greatly embarrassed when obliged to make changes, that the secular clergy justly complained, etc., I resolved to take steps toward securing some good missions to the secular clergy. In a memorial to Rome of 40 Pages I stated the condition of affairs, asked for at least six perfect parishes out of 10 they had, went personally to Rome pleading my cause. Although my claims were found just by the authorities, still they after asking information from St. John's hesitated to do anything." [77]

During the first year of his administration Bishop Zardetti, in pursuit of the policy he described had negotiated with Abbot Bernard to turn over fourteen missions to the diocese. His requests included Perham, Belle River, Alexandria, Buckman, Holdingford, St. Anna, Avon, Krain, St. Stephen, Maples, St. Nicholas, Spring Hill, Lake Henry and Logering (Eden Valley). The bishop had at first a sufficient number of clergy to fill only seven of these missions. Requests to St. John's from other bishops had to be turned down because the Benedictines were caring for missions which the bishop had taken from the abbey. But while this condition continued Bishop Zardetti instead requested that at least six of the well-organized Benedictine parishes of Stearns

215

County also be turned over to the new diocese. Abbot Bernard then felt obliged to question this new demand. He wrote a memorial of his own to the Holy See, and explained his case in person at the Propaganda while in Rome for the dedication of the new buildings of the International Benedictine College of Sant' Anselmo. Locnikar was supported in this move by the new president of the American Cassinese Congregation of Benedictines, Bishop Leo Haid, O.S.B., who enlisted the support of Abbot Smith in the case:

". . . All the Abbots of our Congregation are in perfect sympathy with Abbot Bernard, but for the present, I tho't it sufficient to send his statement of facts. Should you desire full personal information, I would request you to see Rev. Prior Adalbert of S. Anselmo's — as he is acquainted with all the facts concerning the foundation of St. John's Abbey, the heavy sacrifice of men and means which the building up of Catholicity in Stearn's Co., Minn., cost our Order and especially the monastery there. Bp. Zardetti is certainly making extravagant demands. Besides Stearn's Co., settled and Catholicized by the Bened., there are other counties in his diocese to which he can well direct his Episcopal zeal and leave alone the work already done by the Benedictines there! Excuse my blunt way of putting it." [78]

Cardinal Ledochowski, new prefect of Propaganda after the death of Cardinal Simeoni, after hearing both sides in this matter, delegated Archbishop Ireland, the metropolitan, to effect a compromise between the bishop and the abbot. As a result, on 8 June 1892 Ledochowski recommended to Abbot Bernard that six Stearns County parishes, as requested by Bishop Zardetti, be relinquished to the diocese of St. Cloud. Ledochowski also counselled that Benedictines who had labored in the missions for more than ten years be called back to the monastery for at least one year. [79]

Abbot Bernard acceded to these requests in a reply to the cardinal prefect which was forwarded to Rome by Bishop Haid in the name of the American Cassinese Benedictines. Because it so clearly expresses the prudence and charitable approach of the abbot in this issue, the memorial is included in Appendix VI. Abbot Bernard asked that the Stearns County parishes of Richmond, Cold Spring, St. Martin, Farming, Meire Grove, New Munich, Freeport, Albany, St. Joseph, and the Immaculate Conception in St. Cloud be placed in care of the Benedictines in perpetuity. On 23 June 1893 Cardinal Ledochowski granted this petition, and the ten parishes were assigned to St. John's.[80] The Benedictines, in turn, withdrew from Luxemburg, Melrose, Millerville, St. Augusta, Rich Prairie (Pierz), and St. Lawrence (Rush Lake).

Bishop Zardetti wrote after this decision:

". . . Thus a question was settled which I had not opened in a sentiment of passion, but which had caused me considerable annoyance, much trouble over unpleasant judgments on the part of those religious

216

who looked on me as a robber of their possessions. The Rt. Rev. Abbot, however, was always fair and just. Thus the condition of the diocese is now satisfactorily and permanently settled. The secular clergy can no more complain. They have now a good number of good missions. Small and new ones will grow and multiply. All counties except Stearns are free from the religious. Now and more later, the sec. clergy is master — on the other hand it is only natural that the Benedictines who were the pioneers of this territory retained a certain limited strength. They are now in sure possession of their 10 missions which in our country like daughters surround the monastery, the mother, which, however, in every spiritual and temporal way are subject to the Bishop's orders." [81]

Benedictine Parishes

The program which Bishop Zardetti promoted to organize the new diocese of St. Cloud on a solid basis under control of the diocesan clergy was normal and traditional in every way. The ordinary operation of the Church had always been of such a character. The history of the Church is replete with similar examples of religious clergy establishing missionary territories which were then turned over to a diocesan clergy. Permanent diocesan work was obviously and primarily the domain of diocesan priests under the direction of their respective bishops. The missionary Benedictines who found the action of Bishop Zardetti difficult to understand were the same who opposed Abbot Alexius' program of expansion through new monastic foundations in other needy areas. The Benedictines, in the service of the Church, had never done any one work exclusively without suffering decline and decay. Permanent parish activity had no traditional claim on monastic allegiance. It was, moreover, to Abbot Alexius' varied religious, educational and social projects that the community turned when the diocesan clergy took up most of the parochial work the monks had inaugurated in the region. At the same time the Holy See had authorized continued Benedictine pastoral work in ten parishes surrounding the abbey itself, so that St. John's was not divorced from the unique Catholic colonization endeavor its pioneers had so successfully developed.

That the Benedictines were still needed in less developed dioceses became obvious even while these events were transpiring. Bishop James McGolrick of Duluth had asked the abbey to take charge of the Thief River Falls parish late in 1893. When a church congregation in Red Lake Falls was organized in June of 1894, this parish was also entrusted to the Benedictines. Thief River Falls was then attended from Red Lake Falls until a resident priest was appointed in 1901. The growing state of Washington was also in need of priests, and Bishop Aegidius Yuenger of the diocese of Nesqually, subsequently Seattle, requested St. John's to take charge of the recently organized German congregation of Our Lady of the Holy Rosary at Tacoma, the most flourishing city in Washington. Abbot Bernard, accompanied by

Father Valentine Stimmler, visited the Pacific coast in 1891, studied the proposed field of labor and recommended it to the chapter. The capitulars accepted the proposal on 3 August 1891 and Father William Eversmann was sent to inaugurate another undertaking. For eight years Father William cared for this Tacoma parish, and after 1892 was assisted by Father Wolfgang Steinkogler, who attended a number of missions in the area. These two monks felt that if the Benedictines wished to establish a permanent monastery in Washington, land for a monastery and school must be secured. With this in mind a tract of 570 acres was obtained twenty-eight miles from Tacoma and about four miles from the city of Olympia. But Abbot Bernard was not to see the inauguration of the Benedictine community there known as St. Martin's Priory.

*Resignation
And Reform*

For the abbot, always frail and far from healthy, began to evidence signs of declining health in 1894. His heart was weak and he had difficulty breathing. Then, on the evening of June 27 a violent tornado passed over St. John's which was a severe shock to his constitution. There had been oppressive heat in the upper midwest region for several days in late June of 1894, and a storm was expected for days. On this evening eleven tornadoes formed in Minnesota and eastern South Dakota and at 8:30 one tornado came over Lake Sagatagan. It had formed from two air currents meeting east of Cold Spring, rushed over the grasshopper votive chapel and strewed the beautiful pioneer shrine down the hill. At Pearl Lake the church was deposited in the middle of the road, while at Jacobs Prairie the church was demolished, leaving only the sacristy. At St. John's the funnel-shaped cloud touched the north corner of the cemetery and swept in a northeasterly direction across the monastery grounds. The old laundry on the lake shore was struck, the trees surrounding the abbey were broken off like so many matches, and the roofs of barns and shops lifted up into the air like pieces of cardboard. When the tornado reached the main buildings, the entire southern half of the south wing was blown away. Father Roman Homar, director of the Indian Industrial School housed in this building, saw the storm coming across the lake and rushed into the wing to direct the students into the main quadrangle. He remembered that some of the smaller boys had gone to bed early, and he rushed into the attic dormitory to check under the covers of each bed to be sure all had fled. It was none too soon, for the tornado struck as he was ready to leave, and the floor sank at a forty-five degree angle. Father Roman crawled to safety on all fours and headed for the cellar of the main quadrangle.

Then the tornado threw itself against Abbot Alexius' main quadrangle. Windows were sucked out, chimneys pulled off, shingles pulverized and the main turret damaged. But the buildings gave not an inch, and when the storm subsided they were there as usual, mighty and indomitable. Icehouse, greenhouse, bakery, boilerhouse, corn mill, butchershop, pigsty and shoeshop were all damaged, while the barn was demolished to the stone foundations.

Abbot Bernard, who had rushed from his room at the first impact of the storm, found the vice-president of the school, Father Alexius Hoffmann, at the end of the corridor looking out of one of the large windows at the havoc. The abbot was completely unnerved and sobbed, *Alles ist verloren*, as Father Alexius led him away from the window. Abbot Bernard described what followed:

". . . We came from our shelter after a short time, only to be met with another dread. There seemed to be a smell of something burning! Alarmed, we went from room to room, thinking that perhaps a lamp had been overturned. Thank God, we found no fire. The smell came from the knocked-down chimneys. In the search for the fire, we got some idea of the great destruction the wind had caused in such a few minutes. Scarcely a room was left intact. In all, 225 windows were broken, allowing the rain to pour in. With each report of destruction, I felt as though a knife were cutting out my heart. But what could one have done about it? *In Gottes Namen.* He sent it to us. I went to church. Here I found peace and quiet. It seemed that the church was left intact." [82]

As soon as the storm had passed over St. John's some of the monks followed its path to see if they could be of any help to the farmers in the vicinity. They found wrecked farm buildings and dead livestock, but all the farmers had escaped injury, as had everyone at St. John's. The schoolhouse on the other side of the Watab had been demolished. Although the Cold Spring–St. John's area was the only part of the region hit by this tornado, severe storms were reported from all sides. Abbot Bernard stated:

". . . Wherever I turn my eyes I see nothing but desolation and destruction. . . . Only God knows how long it will take us to recover from this catastrophe. And yet we should not complain. We must thank God in many respects because it could have been much worse. In many places people lost their lives; he spared all here. Some of our neighbors lost everything; we still have a house to live in, although it is severely damaged. And what has been destroyed will, with the help of God, be built up from the ruins." [83]

The community set to work during that summer of 1894 to repair the damage and rebuild as quickly as possible. Damage was estimated at from $60,000 to $70,000. Abbot Ignatius Conrad of New Subiaco Abbey sent a donation of $10, and Theodore Loebmueller, district schoolteacher at Farming, gave $5 from his $40 a month salary. These donations moved Abbot Bernard deeply and he read the donors' letters in chapter. But at the same time he told his community that they must live up to their founder's ideal of self-sufficiency and rebuild their monastic home through their own labors. The abbot was personally convinced that the cyclone had been a direct punishment of God for the recent controversy which led to Abbot Alexius' resignation.

Abbot Bernard never fully recovered from the shock of the night of the tornado. In September he undertook a tour of inspection of the missions. Early in October he reached Duluth where he preached his last sermon. When he arrived in St. Paul his physician advised immediate medical treatment and ordered that he take a complete rest. The abbot then entrusted the government of the monastery to Prior Pancratius Maehren, and went to the abbey's parish of St. Mary in Stillwater to stay with the pastor, his classmate Father Alphonse Kuisle. Here he failed rapidly and treatments were ineffective. It was discovered that he was suffering from Bright's Disease, a liver malady with consequent uremic poisoning. His patience and serenity of soul were edifying during these days. He wrote to Prior Pancratius:

". . . if the heart does not change I will surely have to make myself ready to go. I thank you for your faithful prayers for my full restoration. Well, if it be the will of God He will hear you — if not His will be done. I hope everything is all right at home. . . . I am almost ashamed to be absent so long and doing nothing whilst I expect everybody else to be at his post. I hope God will help me, that I may soon be able to be at my post too." [84]

But there was no sign of improvement and he informed Father Alexius he intended to come home on Wednesday, November 7. His condition had been declared hopeless and he wanted to be brought back to his monastery to die. Actually his announcement that he would come home on November 7 was somewhat prophetic, for at eight o'clock on that morning he quietly yielded his soul into the hands of God. Although suffering intense pain, his mind was bright and active during the last hours, and he spoke affectionately to the members of the community around his bedside. He commissioned Father Peter, who had come from the abbey, to thank his brethren at St. John's for everything they had done for him and to impart to them his last blessing. His dying wish was that they remain worthy sons of St. Benedict, above all in conscientious observance of divine worship. His final words to his community were: "How beautiful, how grand is the choir chant of devout monks."

Not only the monastic community but all who knew the abbot and St. John's were shocked at his sudden death. He was but forty-six years old, had served as abbot for four short years, and was the first abbot of St. John's to die.

The first Solemn Requiem was sung at Stillwater by Abbot Frowin and the body was then escorted to St. Paul. A large throng was waiting at the Union Depot in St. Paul to escort the remains of their former pastor to the venerable Assumption Church, while people lined the streets in silent prayer as the cortege passed. The body was placed in the sancturary for two days while clergy and laity passed in steady processions to pray for the 'good Abbot's soul.' The final obsequies were held at St. John's on November 14, the day on which all deceased Benedictines are commemorated. Abbot Alexius came back from New York to officiate, Bishop Shanley preached again as he had on the occasion of Abbot Bernard's blessing, and then the 2,000 people who had assembled at Collegeville accompanied the body to cemetery hill where the deceased abbot was interred in a temporary vault in front of the main cross. Before the casket was closed Father Alexius had been instructed to remove the abbot's pontifical insignia. He testifies that as he unfastened Abbot Wimmer's cross, which Abbot Bernard wore, and drew off the ring, he did not realize the presence of death by any odor. This impression moved him deeply.

The faithful people around the abbey began at once to visit Abbot Bernard's grave and pray for their needs. It was a living tradition among them for years that many petitions, especially in regard to rain and crops, were answered after his intercession was sought. While such conclusions were subjective opinions of individuals, it was universally acknowledged that St. John's had been favored at this time with an exemplary monk and abbot. His devotion to Christian virtue and the interior life had brought unity and peace to a seriously divided community at a critical point in its development. He was, as Hoffmann said:

". . . a very devout man, and a scholar, a highly esteemed theologian. His brief administration of 4 years did not permit him to develop extensive activities: he had all that he could do to keep running what his predecessor had built up. He did not believe in external expansion; rather advocated the cultivation of religious spirit; he disliked travel, and amusements. In spite of his frail constitution he was always cheerful among the brethren. He did not read promiscuously but studied much. You would call him unworldly. He was a good monk and tried to lead his flock aright." [85]

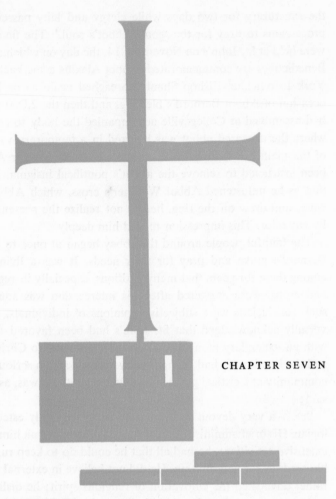

CHAPTER SEVEN

AND THE ROCK WAS PETER

Three days before his death Abbot Bernard predicted to Father Peter Engel that he would be elected as his successor and asked the subprior not to refuse because he would otherwise be acting against the will of God. Three weeks after the third abbot's death the assembled members of the St. John's chapter, on 28 November 1894, proceeded on the fourth ballot to elect Father Peter. For three ballots a close contest had taken place in voting between the subprior and Father Edward Ginther, who at that time was pastor of Assumption Church, St. Paul. At no time were there more than seven votes separating the two leading candidates. Father Edward, who had spent all of his priestly life as a Benedictine on various missions, was the candidate of the missionary members of the community, while Father Peter had spent his entire monastic life at the abbey in educational and administrative work. According to the statutes of the American Cassinese Congregation, if an election is not

222

attained with a two-thirds majority in the first three ballotings for an abbot, an absolute majority of votes will suffice in succeeding ballots. On the fourth ballot Father Peter received 30 votes; Father Edward, 17; and Fathers Meinulph and Alfred one each. Forty-nine of the sixty-two qualified electors were present at the chapter. Those members of the community in Washington, New York and the Bahamas were prohibited from attending because of distance, and a revision of the Congregation's statutes at that time excluded proxy voting.

Abbot Peter Engel

Father Peter protested strongly and gave way to tears when the tabulation was completed. He had made up his mind even before the election not to accept if he should be chosen. Four short years before he had been eliminated from consideration, and the election now indicated that there was still a strong sentiment unfavorable to the loyal supporter and personal preference of Abbot Alexius. But Bishop Leo Haid, O.S.B., president of the Congregation who presided at the election, said: "Now you just accept. The community has called you and you must respond." So Father Peter submitted in obedience, but with sincere conviction of his unworthiness, as he wrote Abbot Frowin:

". . . Please God may my election not be detrimental to the Order! How gladly would I take the last place. Now I must be leader for so many to monastic perfection, I who have not yet learned to guide myself, and possessing hardly more than the externals of religion. If I could only now prove myself an obedient instrument in God's hand. Then everything would be all right. For God likes to choose the weak." [1]

Abbot-elect Peter felt himself too young, too inexperienced in parish affairs, and unpopular with a number because of his attachment to Abbot Alexius. But at the time of his election no other member of the community had behind him the years of experience and service in monastic administration and education that Father Peter had. When Father John Katzner left the election hall and went over to the students' side to break the news, the big smile on his face was indicative of the joy throughout the house. "Well, Father Peter is our new abbot," he told the waiting boys. It was not a surprise to the community, its friends and the general public that the subprior had been chosen. It was rather accepted on all sides as a natural step in the development of St. John's. The man who had done the most to build up the institution under the two previous and markedly dissimilar regimes was now to head the Collegeville community. During the next twenty-seven years he would, moreover, quietly fulfill the trust that a majority had originally placed in him.

The Holy See ratified this election on 11 January 1895, but the abbot-elect postponed his benediction and installation until the summer time. Six months later on the Patronage of St. Benedict, 11 July 1895, his abbatial blessing was given by Bishop Martin Marty, O.S.B., who had just been transferred from his diocese of Sioux Falls to succeed

Bishop Zardetti as second bishop of St. Cloud. As Abbot Peter stood on the front porch after the ceremony, he even looked the part of St. Benedict's abbot. Dressed in full pontificals, the tall mitre giving him more height than nature had, he left the impression of paternity. Perhaps his heavy, black beard, which he kept except for a short period throughout his entire administration, helped to fix this impression. Once on his way to Rome in later years he was told on board ship that he must be a Jewish-Russian patriarch. But Peter Engel was not only the first American-born abbot of St. John's. He was also thoroughly American and a typical product of the late nineteenth century Western frontier. In 1904 he wrote in his masterly script a synopsis of his life which is both a personal chronicle and an example of his realistic humility:

"I, Peter Engel, was born February 3, 1856, in the parish of St. Nicolas, Town Belgium, Ozaukee Co., Wis. My father, a native of Bausendorf, Rhineprovince, Prussia, came to American in 1848. My mother, Margaretha (nee) Weiskopf, born in Kinheim on the Moselle, arrived in Wisconsin about 1853.

"Five children were born to my parents — I being the first-born. My only brother and my sister Eva died in their infancy; my sister Catherine died, aged twenty years, as an aspirant of the Sisters of Notre Dame. My older sister, Mary Gertrude, joined the Sisters of Notre Dame in Milwaukee, and for the last twenty years has been teaching in Jordan, Minnesota.

"When little over five years I attended the district school which was quite near our house, and my first school teacher, Peter Schneider, lived in our house. In the spring of 1856, we came to Minnesota and settled on a farm near St. Michael's, Wright Co.

"My parents soon noticed that I showed no liking for the work on the farm, but some aptitude for study, and consequently, after I had attended for four winters the poorly managed district school, and had received first Communion at the hands of Rev. George Koering, I was brought to St. John's College and placed in charge of the Benedictine Fathers in September, 1869, Rev. Wolfgang Northman being at the time director of the College.

"I had at that time no clear idea about my vocation, but it was the oft-expressed wish of my parents that I should become a priest. My first thought about joining the Order of St. Benedict was given me by Rev. Alexius Edelbrock, who on the closing day of 1872 called me to his room and asked me whether I did not like to become a Benedictine. I answered that I had no particular objection, and I might do so provided my parents approved this step; still it was not before Christmas, 1873, that I finally made up my mind to join the Order.

"In July, 1874, I was sent, together with Ludger Ehrens and George Hepperle to make the novitiate in St. Vincent Abbey, Penn. During

224

the first four months of my novitiate I was at times tempted to go back to the world, but these temptations ceased entirely, and the year of my novitiate became the happiest of my life. July 19, 1875, I made simple vows before Abbot Boniface Wimmer, and remained after that a few months longer in St. Vincent's to study physics and chemistry under Rev. Adalbert Mueller, O.S.B., the newly-elected Abbot Alexius Edelbrock, O.S.B., so worked it.

"In September, 1875, I returned to St. John's Abbey where I was appointed Bookkeeper of the College and taught several classes, studying at the same time philosophy, dogmatic theology and Church history.

"September, 1878, I began to teach philosophy, and on December 15th the same year, I was ordained priest together with Rev. Ludger by Rt. Rev. Rupert Seidenbusch. My first Mass I celebrated at St. Michael's in the church where I had received my first Communion. Rev. J. A. Schroeder, the rector, preached the sermon. Rev. Ulric Northman and Fr. Othmar Erren assisted.

"August 15, 1879, I was appointed subprior in place of Fr. Norbert Hofbauer, who was at that time made Prior. . . . I resumed my work as teacher. I ordinarily taught philosophy, physics, chemistry and, off and on, Latin, Greek, Evidences of Religion, Algebra, Geometry and Astronomy. From 1883 to 1894 I was Director of Studies. My spare moments and free time from 1881–1894 were mostly taken up with work in the photographic gallery. In 1887 I was appointed Master of Novices, which I retained one year after I was elected abbot; during most of that time I also gave *culpa* and instruction to the Brothers.

"After the untimely death of our saintly Abbot Bernard Locnikar, I was elected November 28, 1894, to succeed him as abbot of St. John's. I never cared for any office, much less did I desire the responsible one of Abbot, and I only accepted the latter in submission to God's will." [2]

From this chronicle, crisp and simple as it is, emerge the qualities and achievements which made Abbot Peter the most beloved of the abbots who served during St. John's first century. He was a man of broad knowledge, generosity, love of study, and spiritual depth. In fact, the first abbot primate of the Benedictines, Hildebrand de Hemptinne, declared during his tour of the United States in 1910 that Abbot Peter was "an excellent man and monk." [3] He appeared to be a simple man, and yet in reality was highly skillful. His manner was matter-of-fact, even at times distant; his leadership quiet but firm. Long years of scientific study had endowed his mind with clarity and balance. Beneath it all as a solid base, rock-like, was his love of the spiritual life which enriched his character with stability and understanding. Abbot Rupert had been the pioneer, Abbot Alexius the imaginative frontier-builder, Abbot Bernard the spiritual molder. With Abbot Peter the community received a leader of the extreme center, a quiet, reasonable man who knew what was possible for the day. His training and idealism were rooted in the spirit of Abbots Wimmer and Alexius, and with him the Alexian spirit was restored to St. John's in a more mature synthesis.

Abbot Peter directed community affairs as St. John's passed from the nineteenth into the twentieth century. American society was dominated by the ideals of progress and the possibility of a reasonable solution of existing problems. Peter Engel had experienced this idea of progress and perfection in two ways: on the frontier it dominated, and he was a child of frontier society. Secondly, he had studied long and carefully in scientific fields. He well understood science's dogma at that time, of reason conquering all, and was student enough to grasp the mixture of truth and error in this thesis. He did not turn his back on the technological age, but rather accepted and strove to understand it. He used what was good in method and system in order to contribute to the Church's effort to create a synthesis of reasonable progress with faith and tradition. His ideals were both modern and ancient, European and American. The monastic community which had grown up in Minnesota's 'Indianbush,' and the new foundations it would establish under Abbot Peter, strove to preserve faith in God, truth about man, and St. Benedict's ancient way of life in an untraditional but idealistic nation. In all ventures and policies Abbot Peter had too much of the Alexian spirit in him to allow the community to become reactionary. As growth and development was nature's law, so too a Christian community, he felt, must root its life in both tradition and development. One of his favorite words when commenting in his diary on some happening was *crescat, crescant* (may it grow). This was his concern and goal. It would be unhistorical, or 'unscientific' as Abbot Peter would say, to picture him as possessed of a master plan which he carried through from 1894 to 1921. No postfactum pattern can be created where it did not exist. He and his administration were too inductive, casual and even haphazard at times for that. The synthesis, integral and sound, was the result, not a master cause. The cause was, perhaps, his understanding of the perennial applications of St. Benedict's monastic system. And Abbot Peter gave this system life and form in his times.

The union under Abbot Peter of Benedictine tradition with American practicality was achieved first and foremost in the abbey's educational work. The new abbot was a dedicated teacher and of St. John's abbots the most interested in developing its school. He had studied and taught natural philosophy, physics and chemistry; developed a physics laboratory; opened a meteorological station in the college tower on the fourth centenary of the discovery of America; installed, with Father Francis Mershman, a wireless telegraph station the following year; and opened an astronomical observatory on top of the water tower as early as 1880. Engel did not pursue these interests alone but always integrated them as community activities and trained younger monks to assist and eventually take over from him, as Father Agatho Gehret, O.S.B., did in telegraphy, and Father Fridolin Tembreull, O.S.B., in the weather station. The St. John's weather station was associated with the U. S. Signal Service, and daily weather observations have been forwarded to the Minneapolis Weather Bureau without interruption from its inception. When Engel became abbot he pushed to completion the present observatory, and supervised the installation of its instruments. His reputation as an astronomer brought him consideration as director of the Vatican Observatory in 1888, a position which was filled by the Reverend John George Hagen, S.J., of Georgetown University. In the late 1880's he was also considered as a professor of natural philosophy at the International Benedictine College of Sant' Anselmo in Rome, but could not be spared at St. John's.

Besides pursuing the above sciences, Engel had as a first love the field of photography. Beginning with a meagerly equipped photographic shop in the corner of his chemistry room, and with a camera which he had made himself, Father Peter and his associates next set up more spacious quarters in the old frame house. Everything from sensitizing the plates to polishing the mounted photographs was done by this group, and experiments were made with color photography. When the new library building was erected in 1900, a large and complete photographic department was installed on its third floor. Throughout these years thousands of prints of the institution's life were made under Engel's direction which have been preserved and today supply a valuable and unique pictorial history of St. John's. The galleries were also placed at the service of the people of the region for family sittings on important occasions like baptisms and weddings, and for innumerable individual pictures of clergy and laity.[4]

When he became abbot, Father Peter did not abandon these interests. He was determined to continue as a student of science, taught a class in physics for four years, studied ornithology privately, and developed pictures. He took steps to electrize the institution, and Hoffmann commented on this development:

"Little by little the electrical era began to manifest its presence: there were electric bells, electric clocks, the telegraph, the telephone, even some demonstrations with wireless telegraphy and X-rays had been made, but the most substantial accomplishment was the introduction of the electric light. Owing to the isolated location of the institution, it was necessary to build a power house for the dynamos and engine, and to 'wire' the vast buildings, not forgetting the laundry, observatory and stables. Work was begun during the summer, and on October 10th [1899] the service was tested. The study-halls were now brilliantly lit up by dazzling clusters of lamps: in the church the old Bailey reflectors with their oil-lamps made way for scores of incandescent bulbs arranged artistically about the capitals of the pillars and along the walls of the sanctuary and shedding a light that lent new charms to the soft colors and gleams of gold in the decorations."[5]

By 1909 Abbot Peter and the community had decided to proceed with plans for a new science building. The site of the old carpenter shop was chosen, and a three-story, 60x100 foot brick building to accommodate all the sciences was erected. Classes were held in the new building in the fall of 1909, with mechanical and electrical engineering in the basement; biology and physics on the first floor; chemistry on the second; an art and drawing department and a semicircular demonstration hall on the third floor. The weather station was placed on the very top of the building and remained there until 1942.[6] Almost fifty years later this same science building is being used for a greatly expanded school, and while proving too small for present needs, stands as a testimonial to the early interest in the natural sciences at St. John's.

More important than these advances was Abbot Peter's gradual realization that the monks needed professional and competent training for their educational endeavor. He was not satisfied just to operate a school in connection with the abbey, but wanted it to be as good a school as possible. Accordingly in 1898 he sent the Reverend Anselm Ortmann, O.S.B., to take graduate courses in physics at Johns Hopkins University in Baltimore. Father Anselm was the first member of St. John's to do graduate work at a recognized secular university, and when he returned did much for the improvement of the physics department, laying particular stress on experimental work. He was soon followed by the Reverends Bernard Kevenhoerster, O.S.B., and Albert Erkens, O.S.B., who studied chemistry and zoology at the University of Minnesota, and the Reverend Charles Cannon, O.S.B., who took English courses at the same institution. Father Polycarp Hansen, O.S.B., studied mathematics at Columbia University; Father Virgil Michel, O.S.B., obtained a doctorate in English at the Catholic University of America, as did Father Basil Stegmann, O.S.B., in theology, with emphasis on Scripture studies, and Father Cuthbert Goeb, O.S.B., a masters degree in history. Abbot Bernard had sent Frater Michael Ott, O.S.B., to the International Benedictine College of Sant' Anselmo in Rome, and Abbot Peter continued this practice desired by Pope Leo XIII, as a means of unifying the Benedictine Order and attaching it more closely to the Holy See. Abbot Peter sent Fratres Bruno Doerfler, O.S.B., Bede Mayenberger, O.S.B., Alcuin Deutsch, O.S.B., Alphonse Sausen, O.S.B., and Ulric Beste, O.S.B., to study philosophy and theology at Sant' Anselmo and to receive doctorates according to the Roman system of conferring such titles. Fathers Innocent Gertken, O.S.B., and Wilfrid Partika, O.S.B., were sent to Conception Abbey to study chant under Father Gregory Huegle, O.S.B., one of the pioneers in the American Gregorian chant movement. Upon their return, they

228

trained the monastery and college choirs. Father Gregory also came to St. John's to deliver Gregorian chant lectures to the community in July of 1908. These moves were made to comply with Pope Pius X's famed *motu proprio* four years earlier which inaugurated the modern revival of Gregorian chant. Gradually this ancient form of sacred chant known as the Vatican chant and cultivated by the monks of Solesmes Abbey in France, was introduced at divine worship except for Vespers. The new Roman vesperal was not as yet prepared, and for Vespers the Ratisbon chants were used. Father Stanislaus Preiser had been teaching and propagating this simplified variety of chant after his return from Germany, and in 1901 he had edited and published a *Vesperale Romano-Monasticum* at St. John's for this purpose. Father Stanislaus had labored for over twenty-five years in parishes and at the abbey, first for Cecilian music and then for Ratisbon chant.

Abbot Peter's progressive efforts were also directed toward improving the library situation, which was much in need of attention. The library was housed in a section on the second floor of the main quadrangle where facilities and accommodations were at a minimum. In 1901, a new library, the abbey's first fireproof building, was erected south of the main quadrangle. It was again a three-story brick structure and was the first building at St. John's to be erected under building contract. Adequate space was now available for the rather good collection of books. The second floor was devoted to a museum while the third was given over to photography and the music department. The apparent incongruity of a music department being attached to a library did not present practical difficulties during these years. With Father Alexius Hoffmann as librarian, the sanctum of the library was a walled preserve which students did not enter either to study or browse and which members of the community used only by appointment. It was not until the advent of a more developed college program in the late 1920's that the building was gradually given over to full library uses.[7]

Other physical additions during Abbot Peter's time besides the astronomy, science and library buildings, included a gymnasium in 1901, new shop buildings, a home in 1904 for the Sisters who did the institution's cooking, an infirmary in 1908, a laundry building and a three-story classroom and kitchen extension of the main quadrangle in 1914. The church was twice redecorated, in 1898 and 1908, with new main altar, canopy, choir organ and choir stalls added. The five-bell chimes and eight-dial clocks were raised in the twin towers in 1897.[8] Finally an improved electric light plant, hydraulic ram for water, the Watab turbine and steam heating plant rounded out the modernizing steps taken under Abbot Peter's direction. Cement pavements were placed between the buildings; the three-mile road from the Collegeville station past the abbey to the Watab dam was levelled and improved in 1907. The same year a beginning was made in reclaiming the old north cranberry bog as an extensive athletic bowl and baseball diamond.

These buildings of Abbot Peter betray their transitional character in several ways. The main quadrangle erected by Abbot Alexius represents in architectural line the European and Benedictine roots of St. John's, as well as the early mediaeval beauty of the quadrangle technique. The buildings that Abbot Peter put up were attached to it in all directions, apparently without plan. They were utility buildings, hastily erected in great part by community direction and labor. They have the air of the American West about them. Artistic and architectural principles, traditional in Benedictine endeavor, gave way to the needs of a growing Catholic community in a rapidly expanding society. In his last year in office St. Benet's residence hall was begun, and this structure inaugurated another period in St. John's building history. Here, as with the auditorium and power house, which were built under his successor, an effort was made to utilize Romanesque architecture.

Hasty additions to the physical plant were made necessary by a steady increase in the student body. In 1896 there were 234 students at St. John's, and at the end of Abbot Peter's administration, in 1920, the total had risen to 486. This enlarged student enrollment was in the high school, college, seminary and commercial departments because the abbey's unique Indian Industrial School had to be closed in 1896 after eleven years of work in this interesting educational experiment. In 1890, after an inspection by government investigators, the St. John's Indian School had been highly praised by Indian Commissioner Morgan. A new contract with the abbey was then issued in which permission was given by the Bureau of Indian Affairs for enrollment of any number of pupils the abbey could accommodate to be taken from any reservation desired. Direct contact with the Indian Bureau, rather than through the Catholic Indian Bureau, was readily granted. The monks of St. John's at that time preferred direct negotiation with the Indian Bureau of the Department of the Interior because of unsatisfactory experiences with the Catholic Indian Bureau in the past.

In the early 1890's a campaign was begun, as has happened so consistently in many American developments under liberal influences, to effect a separation between religious Indian work, or 'sectarian' as it is called, and governmental grants. The original $150 per capita allowance for training of Indian pupils was first reduced to $125, and then in 1896 to $62.50. This last amount, furthermore, was to be granted only if nonsectarian schools could not be provided. Under these circumstances it was impossible to continue the St. John's Industrial School, as well as its counterpart for girls at St. Benedict's in St. Joseph, and the Indian children left, "never to return," as Abbot Peter sadly recorded. After that the abbey expended facilities for their spiritual and educational care in the Indian missions of northern Minnesota.

79 Homeplate: where St. Benet Hall's
telephone booth now stands.

80 Roman Dworschak and Gerhard Zankl
(Fr. Angelo, O.S.B.), interested radio students.

81 Caught in the air:
shotput in 1909.

82 Biologist, psychologist, James Hansen, O.S.B.

83 To World War I heroes, a shrine.

84 *Bruno Doerfler, first abbot of St. Peter's.*

85 *The plains of Saskatchewan: original St. Peter's foundation.*

86 *Abbots Alcuin Deutsch (St. John's), Severin Gertken (St. Peter*
Justus Wirth (St. Bede), at St. Peter's Abbey in Canada.

87 *Michael Ott, second abbot of St. Peter's.*

88 *St. Peter's Abbey, Muenster, Saskatchewan, Canada, from the*
today.

89 St. Martin's, Olympia, Washington: St. John's first foundation.

90 Oswald Baran, St. Martin's first abbot.

91 Air view of St. Martin's Abbey.

92 James Trobec, third bishop of St. Cloud.

93 *An air view, 1924: campus and lakes.*

94 *An early air view.*

95 *Expansion of St. John's as envisioned by Abbot Alcuin Deutsch.*

96 *Abbot Alcuin at laying of cornerstone for St. Boniface's Church. Minneapolis.*

97 *Abbot Alcuin and community welcoming the apostolic delegate, Archbishop Pietro Fumasoni-Biondi, to St. John's in 1928.*

98 *The present apostolic delegate to the United States, Archbishop Amleto Giovanni Cicognani in St. Cloud with Bishop Joseph Busch, Abbot Alcuin and clergy.*

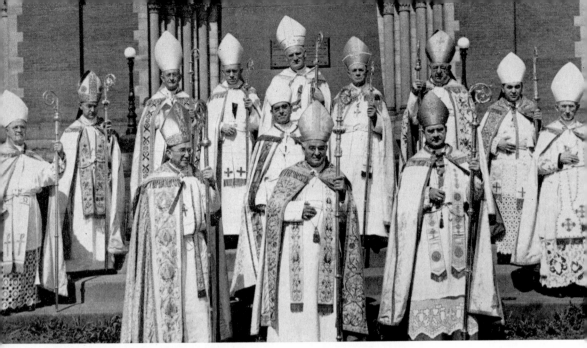

99 *American Cassinese abbots at St. Vincent's centennial celebration, 1946: L. to R. Back: Abbots Bertrand Dolan (St. Anselm's); Cuthbert Goeb (Assumption); Severin Gertken (St. Peter's); Mark Braun (St. Gregory's); Leonard Schwinn (Holy Cross); Vincent Taylor (Belmont); Boniface Seng (St. Bernard's); Theodore Kojis (St. Andrew's); Patrick O'Brien (St. Mary's); Front: Alcuin Deutsch (St. John's); Cuthbert McDonald (St. Benedict's); Archabbot Alfred Koch (St. Vincent); Lawrence Vohs (St. Bede).*

100 *Coadjutor Bishop Peter Bartholome welcomed to St. John's in 1942. With him: Bishop Busch and Abbot Alcuin.*

101 *Bishop Busch, Archbishop John Gregory Murray of St. Paul and Abbot Alcuin.*

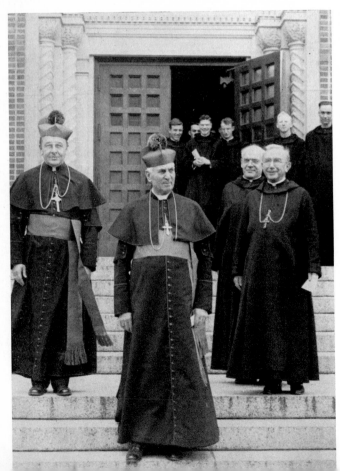

102 Father Virgil Michel:
liturgist, philosopher, educator.

103 Father Alexander Korte
observing Father Oliver Kapsner
at work cataloguing.

104 Fathers Walter Reger and
Theodore Krebsbach, college and prep
deans in the early '30's.

105 Father Gilbert Winkelmann:
a new interest in architecture.

106 *The Fathers' recreation room.*

107 *Jubilarians, Fathers Thomas Borgerding and Roman Homar dictating their memoirs.*

108 *Musician, Father Innocent Gertken, with artist, Father Anthony Unterhoefer of Seitenstetten Abbey.*

109 *"Hearken my son to the precepts of your Master." Father Placid Wingerter at monastery gate.*

Abbot Peter often visited these Indian missions, gave as many permanent pastors as possible, encouraged improvements and schools, checked accounts, and suggested means of financing. The Alexian Indian apostolate was thus made an integral part of St. John's life by Abbot Peter, and Pope Benedict XV gave him special commendation for this service. Indian work was carried on in the diocese of Duluth, and when the diocese of Crookston was erected in 1910, also in that jurisdiction. The first bishop of Crookston, Timothy J. Corbett, desired St. John's to establish a monastery in the vicinity of Crookston, dedicated primarily to Indian work, but this proposal never materialized.

During his years as abbot, Peter Engel strove to strengthen the academic program at St. John's by modernizing it and organizing the curriculum according to existing practices. Besides broadening scientific programs and beginning advanced training of the monks, he inaugurated in 1897 an intensified six-year divinity program of two years of philosophy and four of theology. Two years later Father Alexius Hoffmann attended the first conference of American Catholic Colleges held in Chicago from 12–13 April 1899. There discussions centered on ways to unify and improve college courses as distinct from academy or high school curricula, which a large majority of Catholic educational institutions taught together in an indeterminate program.

At St. John's, a new division was made as a result of this study. After 1899 the classical course embraced a seven-year program with three years of high school or academic work distinct from four years of collegiate studies. Scientific, commercial and preparatory departments were continued as separate study programs. The majority of the students were enrolled in the high school and commercial departments during these years. In 1901 a Winter School was begun for boys of the region who could not attend school except during the winter months of the year. Courses in this department were practical in character and were offered to boys who had finished grade school and who desired some commercial and business training. This department was popular with the farmers of the area and was a practical Benedictine adaptation of a traditional classical program in order to serve the needs of the region in which the monastery was located.

At the turn of the century organized athletics and competition between teams representing different schools became popular. This new spirit of extramural athletic competition spread to St. John's. The traditional recreational activities of 'duck-on-the-rock,' 'prisoner's base,' 'lost-sheep-lost,' which were played through the whole woods around the school; outdoor bowling; croquet; boating; and walking — all were soon outmoded. The Reverend Louis Traufler, O.S.B., formed the first Athletic Association at St. John's in 1900 and collected $50 from the students for footballs, basketballs and baseballs. This money was deposited with the bookkeeper, Prior Herman. But whenever the association wanted to withdraw any of this money, they had great difficulty in obtaining it from the prior, who lectured them on the 'important things' that could be purchased with these funds. But a baseball team was fielded during that first year of 1900, and two games were played, both with the St. Cloud High School, with St. John's winning the first 12–11 and losing the second 14–4.

The younger monk-professors such as Fathers Louis Traufler, O.S.B., Pius Meinz, O.S.B., Robert Wewers, O.S.B., and Theodore Kevenhoerster, O.S.B., then prevailed upon Abbot Peter to formulate a policy in regard to athletics at St. John's. The abbot called a chapter meeting on 31 January 1901, and he kindly and simply defended the innovation of an organized athletic program with extramural competition. In reply to one of the dissenters who was skeptical of such an untraditional move, Abbot Peter replied: "Well now, we have to be up with the times, Father." After further discussion of the inadequate facilities for athletics in the basement of the main quadrangle, the chapter approved the erection of a separate gymnasium building. Father Alexius drew the plans for it. This first gymnasium, which cost $30,000, was a major addition to student life at the institution. Although it at first had only a dirt floor, there was an elevated running track, and a physical education director was hired. This first athletic director at St. John's was Louis Mockenhaupt from St. Cloud whose forte was gymnastics and Indian club swinging.

At the same time Father Louis pushed ahead with a football team. The institution's first team in 1900 lost its two-game schedule with the St. Cloud High School, but during the following year things were quite different. The same team was back, mostly boys from Stillwater and St. Paul who were in good condition after practicing on the gravel in front of the main quadrangle. They included the captain, John O'Leary, who had played before at Monroe High School in St. Paul; William Kilty, "a deer at end"; Ignatius O'Shaughnessy at tackle, whom Father Louis characterized as "one of the team's outstanding players"; Joseph O'Brien, Charles Houska and Fred Hinnenkamp, who later became a priest of the St. Cloud diocese. This team defeated the St. Cloud High School twice, the St. Cloud Normal School and as a season's finale played St. Thomas College in St. Paul for the first time. This Catholic college for men had been established by Archbishop Ireland in 1885, and from this first game of 1901, a traditional rivalry developed between St. John's and St. Thomas. Father Louis described what happened:

". . . I had a time to obtain permission for that game from Abbot Peter. Everyone was antagonistic to extramural games. The students were allowed to go home only at Christmas and Easter, and it was extraordinary to get a 'per' to go to St. Joe. If anyone went beyond the observatory a quarter of a mile, was caught, and repeated, that was

232

cause for expulsion. Abbot Peter left the decision to Father Bruno [vice-president] and myself, and if there was any disorderly conduct, all would be finished. So we received permission to go to St. Paul. We left on the 'dinky' from Collegeville and arrived in Minneapolis the night before the game. The pastor of St. Boniface Church, Father Timothy Vaeth, had offered to accommodate the boys for the night. He had wooden barracks at the parish for a recreation center and the boys were given cots there. The ladies of the parish furnished supper and breakfast. All went to Mass and Communion the next morning, and then took the streetcar to Lexington Park. The game started at nine a.m. on Thanksgiving morning. A large number of alumni were there. We were called 'the hay seeds,' so the boys came on the field with hay seeds in their caps. One of the men from St. Thomas had written a poem and set it to song: 'When Rueben comes to town,' and they were to sing and play it during the half. They were a foregone conclusion to win and had a paid coach. Our boys had no equipment except canvas jackets and shorts (out of that $50), and no head gear. We led in the first half and won the game (15–6). The boys ran over each other for touchdowns. They made a human pyramid so they could run over each other. We returned on the midnight train and had no trouble controlling the boys, nor was anyone missing." [9]

The college catalogue as well as Father Alexius' jubilee history of the school in 1907 called this undefeated team of 1901 "the collegiate champions of Minnesota," although such a title was inconclusive as such colleges as Carleton and Hamline were not played. During these years before the Minnesota College Conference was formed, St. John's regularly played baseball, basketball and football with neighboring high school teams from St. Paul, St. Cloud, Elk River, Little Falls, Sauk Centre, Melrose, as well as St. Thomas College, St. Cloud Normal, St. Cloud Business College, North Dakota Agricultural College and the University of Minnesota freshmen. The won-and-lost record was comparatively good with the St. John's teams winning better than two-thirds of their games during these first ten years.

In many ways these years at the end of the nineteenth and the beginning of the twentieth century were the halcyon days at St. John's. With Abbot Peter at the helm, peace and quiet were the prevailing norms. The pioneer days were over; the 'brick and mortar' era was slowly receding, and the labors of the first fifty years had begun to take effect. The monastery and its school were located in a place of withdrawal where the community could live sufficiently away from the rush and noise of a booming American industrial society. First and second generation Catholic immigrants were gradually but consistently sending their sons to St. John's for training. The student body was never large, and the monks in the monastery, with the aid of a handful of dedicated laymen, were not overly pressed with the problems of administration and teaching in a school with less than 500 students enrolled. Life was colored by the absence of large numbers so that relations could without effort be personal and individual. As younger members entered the monastic family, they shared religious community life with the older Benedictines. Together they also shared the twofold experience of learning the spiritual, liberal and manual arts, and then transmitting them in school, parishes and missions. Father Walter Reger, O.S.B., has characterized this traditional Benedictine atmosphere of respect for the freedom of the person which develops in a monastery following the *Rule* of St. Benedict:

"To the achievement of the aim of Christian education Benedictines bring first a healthy sense of freedom born of the saintly wisdom of our Founder, who thoroughly understood human nature and made moderation, discretion, flexibility and versatility characteristic of the *Holy Rule*. According to psychologists, the development of mature personalities demands essential freedom by all the laws of being. Without being able to define accurately this freedom, I should suggest that it means freedom from subjection to arbitrary authority — authority used selfishly or unreasonably or for ulterior motives — the kind which inhibits or in some way interferes with the normal productive faculties of persons to love, to reason, to will and to feel. It is this generous and noble respect for the dignity of the human person which distinguishes the Benedictine approach to education in a special way.

"If we examine the prescriptions and regulations as they come to the monks in the teaching accents of our Holy Founder, we find that all of them are full of the breath of warm solicitude and human understanding. St. Benedict wants no bruised reed to be broken, no flock to be overdriven, nothing done but what will benefit another, a seeking of love rather than fear, on the part of the abbot and superiors. All of this suggests an environment of voluntarily elicited obedience and humility, which at least Catholic psychologists assure us are proper aids to the further acquisition of freedom by fortifying free will against the surrender of it, and thus promoting inward growth of the person. Benedictine discipline is firm, but not military or harsh or unreasonable. At least ideally, therefore, in the monastery there is a wonderful blending of virtues which ensure soul-satisfying conditions of security, generally characterized as the *Pax Benedictina*. In this atmosphere everything favors the development of mature personality and opportunity for creative endeavor. Education becomes a high adventure before it becomes a tedious exercise." [10]

In this spirit several steps were taken during these years toward the development of interesting and original research projects. A number of the monks were able to combine the pursuit of individual fields of interest with their monastic and teaching responsibilities. Abbot Peter set the pace himself with his various scientific projects and his example

234

of consistent habits of study. Father Severin Gertken prepared a *Catechism of Chemistry* (Baltimore, 1905) and Father Anselm Ortmann edited a *Catechism of Astronomy* (Baltimore, 1905) when he succeeded Abbot Peter in astronomy. When Father Anselm was in turn succeeded by Father Polycarp Hansen, O.S.B., in 1911, the latter applied his knowledge of astronomy to meteorology and devised a system for predicting the local weather.[11]

Father Polycarp's brother, Father James Hansen, was also of a scientific bent. Although a victim of tuberculosis, in the course of thirty-two years he collected, classified and mounted thousands of plants. Father James did for biological sciences at St. John's what Abbot Peter accomplished in his fields of interest. Both initiated sound departmental programs, and then went on to perfect their original investigations, while inspiring several generations of students, both clerical and lay, to follow in their footsteps. Father James and his students, through field trips and exchange programs, built up an impressive insect collection containing some 30,000 specimens, and over 7,000 mounted slides for use in microscopic work. At the time of his death his herbarium, consisting of over 900 species of flowering plants, 300 of mosses and 50 of ferns, was recognized as one of the best in the region. By his work and example Father James was a living refutation of the supposedly irreconcilable conflict between religion and science of that time. This monk-scientist not only refuted that canard so typical of late nineteenth century liberal confusion; more important, he was one of the pioneer American Catholic scientists whom a chairman of the department of history at the University of Minnesota has characterized as "a true naturalist in the best tradition of Father Mendel."[12] He was a charter member of the Entomological Society of America and a Fellow of the American Association for the Advancement of Science. Not satisfied with existing scientific textbooks, he prepared a *Catechism of Botany* (Baltimore, 1905); texts on *Animal Tissues; Plant Tissues; Evolution, Its Present Standing*; as well as two studies, *Psychology Notes* (Ann Arbor, 1928) and *The Evolution Controversy* (Ann Arbor, 1928).

Literary and research efforts were not confined to the natural sciences. Father Alexius Hoffmann published a jubilee *History of St. John's University* (Collegeville, 1907) on the occasion of the fiftieth anniversary of the establishing of the school. At the same time he prepared a 400-page manuscript history of St. John's Abbey, continued Father Xavier White's abbey chronicle, collected voluminous data in notebooks and essays on all aspects of St. John's past, and the history of the Church in the Northwest. He wrote continually on these topics for European and American magazines and newspapers. Father Francis Mershman collected sixty-five volumes of newspaper clippings on St. John's. He also wrote *A Handy Manual of Pontifical Ceremonies*

235

(Collegeville, 1904) and compiled the *Ordo* for the Congregation for twenty-five years while solving moral cases and writing liturgical advice to priests throughout the country during his forty-seven year professorship in the major seminary. Father Francis wrote 120 articles on liturgical and historical subjects for the first edition of the *Catholic Encyclopedia*. Fathers Alexius, Michael Ott, and Chrysostom Schreiner also contributed many articles to the *Catholic Encyclopedia* on the doctrine, discipline, philosophy and history of the Church.

But perhaps the most significant contribution of this period was made by Father John Katzner. For some thirty years he had been teaching string, wind and percussion instruments in the music department. He had customarily devoted up to ten hours a day to music classes besides his monastic duties. When his nerves gave out in 1905, Dr. Louis Pinault, St. John's physician, ordered him to spend as much time as possible out of doors. Then Father John decided to turn his energies to horticultural pursuits. For years he had been experimenting with wild plums, grapes, crab apples and cherries of the region, which because of the cold climate were deficient in sugar content. Now he earnestly began fruit experiments, collected and catalogued seeds from all the world, and when the procurator would bring a basket of apples into the community recreation room, Father John would even ask everyone to save the seeds. He first raised the seedlings in his room, which had a southern exposure on the second floor of the main quadrangle. In the spring he would then move his pots to the nursery on the Watab shore; when the seedlings were two or three years old he started grafting with cuttings obtained from different regions. Soon he was growing an apple which he called 'translinda.' All this was done with money he obtained from sale of his fruits, with the help of some of the Brothers in their spare hours, and on unused land where the present major seminary building stands. Within a short time he had introduced the hearty up-state New York apples to Minnesota. He developed and named the 'Alpha grape,' which was a cross between the region's wild grape and the Concord variety. Its bunches grew as large as seven inches in length and four inches in width, and the vine could withstand a cold of forty degrees below zero without protection. Not only did the Alpha grape spread throughout the area, but his cuttings were distributed by the thousands in the United States and abroad. Later Matt Reisinger of Collegeville took over the distribution of this Alpha grape.

Father John also experimented with pears as early as 1901. Trials with American and European species failed because of blight and the cold of Minnesota's winter. Fifteen hundred seedlings raised from German pear seeds also froze in the winter, but the roots were hardy and sprouted each spring. Katzner then tried forty new varieties of Chinese pears, but all succumbed except two wild pears from Siberia which were sour in taste. He now, however, had a pear tree on which he could graft other varieties to test their hardiness. This was in 1914 and after experiments with over 150 varieties of pears. Then his friend, Charles G. Patten, horticulturist of Charles City, Iowa, sent him a new variety which he grafted onto the German pear stumps. They developed into healthy trees which produced a small, slightly gritty pear of good quality for eating and preserving. Generations of St. John's students have found it in pickled form at their meals. Other varieties were also developed by Father John by grafting onto the Siberian pears and then grafting again onto the German pear roots. Professor N. E. Hansen of the South Dakota State College of Agriculture at Brookings also worked with Father John, and gave him samples of his pears obtained during five trips to Russia and Asia. Although the resulting fruit was small it was hardy, and pears were grown in the region. Father John thought his pear orchard was blight resistant, but after his death in 1930, blight hit the trees and impaired to some degree his years of work. Brothers Ansgar Niess, O.S.B., and Julius Terfehr, O.S.B., continued Father John's horticultural efforts after his death.

Horticultural Experiments

In all, Father John painstakingly experimented with over 200 varieties of apples, 60 of plums, 35 of grapes, 10 of cherries and was working on the raising of peaches in Minnesota. As his fruits gained recognition, he was praised for his contribution, and horticulturists visited St. John's to study his work. He was elected vice-president of the Minnesota Horticultural Society in 1907, and appointed superintendent of that society's Trial Station established at St. John's during the following year. In a tribute to Father John, Roy D. Underwood declared at the 1926 meeting of that society: "Father Katzner has for years rendered splendid service to the cause of Minnesota horticulture as a plant breeder, experimenter and disseminator." [13]

Meanwhile Father Adrian Schmitt was conducting similar experiments with evergreens and continuing the work begun in this field by Father Urban Fischer. Tamaracks grew in abundance only around Collegeville, and Father Adrian noted that the constant use of wood for building and heating was making heavy inroads on the forest reserve around the monastery. His relatives were governmental foresters in Baden's Schwartzwald, and Father Adrian sent land samples to his father and brothers who advised him on indigenous evergreen and needle wood. He then started a nursery beside Father John's on the Watab. Father Adrian had also been ordered to spend as much time as possible out of doors because of throat trouble. Since he could not do much teaching, he devoted his energies to forestry and care of the sick as infirmarian. With the assistance of Father John, fifteen varieties of evergreens were raised in the nursery plots. Thousands of these trees were planted each spring by the novices around the buildings, on observatory hill and the beautiful *dreizehn linden* on the knoll beyond Adrianople bridge. Father Adrian's reforestation efforts were the beginning of a tradition for the preservation of the woodland areas around the abbey which is continued to the present day. He, like Father John, received recognition for his work from the state's department of forestry.

Besides horticultural and reforestation efforts, work was done during these years to develop a fish hatchery at St. John's. Father Bruno Doerfler obtained for the institution exclusive fishing rights on Lake Sagatagan in 1901, and in 1906 Father Hilary Doerfler began the erection of a fish hatchery on the shore of the Watab, where numerous springs supplied up to 144,000 gallons of water a day. This water was comparatively warm; when the air temperature was zero, the temperature of the springs was fifty-four degrees. Water cress grew in a rich green carpet over the pond during the winter months, while clouds of vapor rose from the open pools. The fish hatchery and its surrounding woods abounding in rare plant life soon became the main beauty spot of the campus. The ponds filled with numerous specimens of rainbow trout, and the feeding of live frogs to these fish became a favorite pastime. By 1909 the hatchery was operating full force and approximately 50,000 trout-fry were being placed in the lake each season. A shortage of water during the dry seasons as well as theft of the fish eventually hampered the development of this fish culture, however. The tanks have disappeared, the surrounding woods have been partially destroyed, and the beautiful Watab park is overgrown. Like so much of the scientific pioneering done at St. John's during Abbot Peter's time, this venture was not encouraged during the administration of his successor.

In a less scientific but equally important way, many of the Benedictine missionaries in the parishes of Stearns County were advising their farmer parishioners on seeds and rotation of crops. When a crop suffered from rust, pastors such as Fathers Anschar, Benedict, Meinulph, Pancratius, Andrew and Clement would write to Europe or send a delegation to Canada for new seeds. The same was done for fruit seedlings. These pastors taught thrift and economy from their pulpits, and encouraged rotation through fertilizers, corn, wheat, oats and potatoes in successive years. A pastor like Father Meinulph would visit the farms of his congregation at Meire Grove and offer minute agricultural and medicinal advice which descendants of those families can still recall at the present time. Even Abbot Peter himself, on trips to the Indians of White Earth and Red Lake, would go out to the plots of the Indians to advise and encourage them. Wherever these Benedictines served the Catholic farmers in parish or mission they closely united cultivation of the soil with the worshipping life of the Church through the traditional Rogation and Corpus Christi processions through the fields, pilgrimages for protection against insects, and harvest festivals.

In these several ways the processes of transition thus became evident in St. John's life. The distinctive features of the Benedictine way of life were preserved, yet adapted and given new application at the beginning of the twentieth century. The Benedictine revival, begun less than a century before, was maturing. One example of it was the way the influences of St. Benedict's *Rule,* Europe's Western heritage and the American frontier were combining to mold St. John's in Stearns County. This Benedictine institution was, like thousands before it, gradually evolving a harmony of the past in sound perspective. August C. Krey has again commented in this regard:

Agricultural Projects

". . . How much Minnesota owes to those early Benedictines for the rapid transformation of so much of the central and northern part of the state from wilderness to cultivated land can probably never be exactly determined. As those Benedictine Fathers and Brothers wandered back and forth between the scattered missions and St. John's they placed at the disposal of the pioneers any helpful information they possessed or could obtain. We know that they experimented with plants and soil seeking to find out what was best adapted to this region, and they made their findings available to the people. And we can be quite certain as we ride over this country-side amid the well tilled fields, neat farm houses, and the lovely little towns crested with those beautiful little churches — and some not so little — that all reflect the very real help and advice of the Benedictine Fathers and Brothers. . . .

"I remember clearly the impression of my first visit to St. John's. As we turned off the main highway through the well cleared woods, so symbolic of the forest that once covered all this region, so serene in its quietness, screening off all signs of human activity — 'apart from the world, yet of it' — suddenly there burst upon our view the monastery and the church, the college, the service buildings, and the well tilled fields beyond. I had an unconscious feeling that I had been there before, though I had not. This feeling became more pronounced as my acquaintance grew. The cordial hospitality to the stranger within the gates was very familiar. It was exactly like my historical visits to all the Benedictine monasteries I had known from Monte Cassino to Cluny." [14]

In regard to parish and mission work, Abbot Peter was a loyal son of Abbot Wimmer and his American Benedictine program. He accepted this role as laid down, and made the community's work in parishes and missions his constant concern. Perhaps he entered so wholeheartedly into this responsibility because he "loved that work" so much himself. He had served as pastor of the Collegeville parish off and on for many years, even after becoming abbot, and only abandoned that post in 1917 when he realized that his close friend, Bishop Trobec, and the monks felt he should not be doing so much. His zeal for the local people is still a living memory. There was not a morning when he was home that he did not spend half an hour in the parish confessional; he brought Holy Communion on foot to Thielmann's, Gretch's or as far as Kucera's on the Big Watab. He knew by name all the Collegeville children, sons and daughters of the farmers and workers around the abbey, always had a little candy in his pocket for them and "enjoyed their innocent mirth." At the end of a year's entry in his diary he would record the number of confessions, sermons, Forty Hours, etc., which he had contributed to the apostolate.

During his last years in office one of his keenest regrets was that he couldn't go over to 'St. Joe' more often to hear confessions, or give a Forty Hours in one of the parishes under the care of Benedictines, diocesan alumni or friends of St. John's. Throughout his abbotship he kept visiting all of the abbey's parishes in regular cycles. Upon his arrival he was accustomed to enter the confessional and take his turn, examine the children in the school, preach to the people who would have felt greatly slighted if 'good Abbot Peter hadn't said a few words.' In the towns neighboring the abbey he was serenaded on his name day. When a dignitary or foreign guest came to St. John's he would personally conduct him 'on the rounds' from St. Joseph through St. Cloud, Cold Spring to Meire Grove and home by way of Albany so the visitor could see the Stearns County parishes. Not infrequently these trips extended over more than one day, and the spirit of hospitality shown on those occasions is also legendary. He guarded his monks on the missions and in the parishes with care. His pastoral letters to them are many, simple and consistent: prudence, zeal, patience, humility and poverty are their keynotes.

Bishop Marty lived only two years after being transferred to the diocese of St. Cloud, and his successor in that episcopal office was the Most Reverend James Trobec. The third bishop of St. Cloud had been trained at St. Vincent for the archdiocese of St. Paul, and after pastorships at St. Felix parish in Wabasha, and St. Agnes parish, St. Paul, was named by the Holy See as Bishop Marty's successor on 5 July 1897. During his seventeen years as spiritual leader of the diocese of St. Cloud, he quietly worked to deepen Catholic life throughout his jurisdiction. Abbot Peter and Bishop Trobec were not only close personal friends who worked harmoniously together, but were even strikingly similar in personality and ideals.

During these years, moves were made to build more parochial schools in the diocese of St. Cloud. The St. Cloud parishes of St. Mary's and Holy Angels, and St. Paul's parish in Sauk Centre had begun parochial schools in 1856, 1887 and 1896 respectively. In all the other parishes and missions of Stearns County, Catholic children were attending district schools. Bishop Trobec explained this development:

"Catholic parochial schools are not as numerous in Stearns County as the great number of parishes would justify. This, however, is not owing to any lack of appreciation of such schools. Catholic settlers of Stearns county, mostly Germans, trained themselves under Catholic

240

auspices, were no less profoundly imbued with the idea of the necessity of Catholic parochial schools than had been their parents and grandparents of preceding generations. They brought with them to this new country their old faith and love for their native tongue which they were bound to preserve at all cost in their children and children's children. The school alongside the church was the motto of the first settlers, and in several places both church and school were built together to serve the double purpose. However, in settlements composed of people of the same creed and language, there was not much danger for either, in making use of the existing public schools in charge of Catholic teachers. Where, however, there was a mixture of people of different creeds and tongues, Catholics, if sufficiently numerous and able, establish as soon as possible, their own private parochial schools." [15]

Pioneer Catholics of central Minnesota had entered upon the interesting and valid democratic experiment of using their district schools under the charge of Catholic lay teachers. But now the supply of these capable and dedicated lay apostles was running out. With the growing control over public instruction by state teachers colleges and a centralized state department of education, secular ideas of education became the vogue in American educational circles. It thus became apparent that the Stearns County experiment would have to be abandoned and Catholic parochial schools erected as quickly as possible so that Catholic children would continue to have their natural right to religious as well as general education. Thus at Eden Valley, St. John Cantius parish in St. Cloud, Albany, Melrose and St. Joseph, parochial schools were begun in the years after the turn of the century down to World War I. The Benedictine Sisters from St. Joseph with much sacrifice and dedication responded to this need of the diocese at the invitation of Bishop Trobec. Abbot Peter cooperated in the Benedictine parishes in every way possible, as did most of the Catholic people of the region, although a minority found this added expenditure of money and the necessity of abandoning their district schools and lay teachers hard to understand. Bishop Trobec and Abbot Peter, as would be expected, moved prudently, and slow progress was made.

During Abbot Peter's years the abbey also continued to serve the Church in the other Minnesota, Dakota, Washington and New York dioceses where it had previously labored. Some changes were made. St. Mary's parish in Bismarck passed from the care of the Benedictines, and became the cathedral for the newly erected diocese of Bismarck. Mandan and Garrison in Dakota, Thief River Falls, Detroit Lakes and Mahnomen in Minnesota were organized or supplied with permanent Benedictine pastors. In St. Paul the venerable parish of the Assumption, served by the Benedictines for fifty-five years, had been several times divided because of the increasing Catholic population of that city. It was slowly becoming a downtown parish, and Archbishop

Ireland in 1912 decided to place the large St. Paul parish of St. Bernard in charge of the Benedictines, and assign a diocesan priest to the Assumption. St. Bernard's parish had been originally organized by Father Bernard Locnikar in 1890 just before he was elected second abbot of St. John's. When Archbishop Ireland was arranging for the Benedictines to leave the Assumption church and to take up the care of St. Bernard's parish, he stated: "I should be extremely sorry if circumstances should ever arise to counsel the Benedictine Fathers to withdraw from St. Paul. They have here rights of equity and traditions that should not be broken." [16] Abbot Peter's relations with Archbishop Ireland were cordial, and he desired here, as in every other instance, to allow the events of the late 1880's to be forgotten as much as possible. In fact, during his years as abbot there was a conscious effort at St. John's to remain apart from all of the American Catholic issues which centered around Archbishop Ireland's Faribault-Stillwater school experiment, the Cahenslyism furor and the famed 'Americanism' controversy. When, in the 1890's, Father Alfred Mayer, pastor of the Assumption parish, took public issue with Archbishop Ireland's Faribault-Stillwater school plan and ardently defended parochial schools, Abbot Peter immediately complied with the archbishop's request for his removal and assigned him in 1899 to St. Clement's parish in Duluth.

Meanwhile at St. Anselm's parish in New York Abbot Alexius was, despite his strong constitution, beginning to feel the effects of old age. He was also suffering from diabetes and needed assistance in his growing parish. Father Rupert Kiefer was with him as assistant, and Fathers Louis Traufler and George Scheffold were also sent by Abbot Peter to relieve the aging abbot. The old affection between Abbots Peter and Alexius never dimmed during the years, and Abbot Peter did everything possible to assure his former superior that his work for St. John's had not been forgotten. From Abbot Alexius' parish venture in New York, another field besides the mission in the Bahama Islands had opened for the monastery at Collegeville. His first assistant, Father Gerard Spielmann, had gone over to Long Island in the diocese of Brooklyn and was serving as pastor of St. Kilian's parish in Farmingdale. Father Edmund Basel, O.S.B., assisted him there. Bishop Charles E. McDonnell of Brooklyn, former secretary of Archbishop Corrigan, was as friendly to the Benedictines as was the metropolitan of New York, and he desired St. John's to branch out from this parish and establish a monastery on Long Island which would conduct both a retired priests' home and a men's college for the diocese. Two other parishes were entrusted to St. John's in the Brooklyn diocese: St. Pancras' at Glendale, under the charge of Father Luke Fink, O.S.B., and St. Martin's at Amityville with Father Benno Ferstl, O.S.B., as pastor. Father Gerard had made initial moves for this foundation by choosing forty acres on Lake Ronkonkoma in Nassau County as a site for a proposed Long Island monastery, in a rural district on the fringe of the nation's largest concentration of Catholics.

But the prolonged indecision over the eventual status of Abbot Alexius' foundation in the Bronx militated against another undertaking in neighboring Long Island. Abbot Alexius was now physically incapable of making moves toward beginning a monastery there, even if he were inclined to do so. Many felt that priority should be given to St. Anselm's as a monastic site, although the Fathers in Brooklyn continued to press for permission to begin a foundation which appeared to have such a bright future. After Abbot Alexius' death, the chapter at St. John's did take preliminary steps on 15 March 1909 to establish a Brooklyn abbey if there were a sufficient number of volunteers. But Abbot Peter did not assume positive leadership in the project and it was eventually dropped. The Fathers were withdrawn from all the parishes and this early opportunity to begin a New York Benedictine monastery was abandoned.[17]

Abbot Alexius' final years in his parish at St. Anselm's were spent peacefully in prayer and reading. He was not able to pray his Divine Office toward the end, but sat in his chair fingering his large rosary. Previously he had spent long hours reading from his good collection of historical works, and whenever he had a visitor he always turned the conversation to historical topics. Archbishop Corrigan's successor, Archbishop John Farley, desired a parish school to be erected at St. Anselm's as early as 1906, but Abbot Alexius still had his heart set on completing the basement church. At first, consideration was given to the possibility of having Father Chrysostom come back from the Bahamas and take charge of St. Anselm's so that the dying abbot could be assisted and the school started. But Abbot Peter decided to send Father Bernard Kevenhoerster, rector of the seminary at St. John's, as administrator of St. Anselm's. He, with the assistance of Father Louis, built the parish school in 1908 with parish money Abbot Alexius had been saving for his last church.

For years Abbot Alexius had obtained assistance at St. Anselm's from French Benedictines coming from Europe, especially those going to Sacred Heart Abbey in Oklahoma. Since his relationship with St. John's was so indefinite it was believed that he might turn St. Anselm's over to the monks of Sacred Heart Abbey. But Abbot Alexius at the end did not do this. Moreover, he agreed to leave the money he had personally acquired during his New York years to 'his folks' at St. John's. Father Louis, who had been his companion and assistant during the last years, described how this took place:

"I brought him Holy Communion on the last day. He was sitting in his chair and was very restless. . . . Later in the day I went down to his room, got down on my knees beside his chair and put a book on his knees. . . . He said: 'Give me my pen.' He used to hold his pen between the second and third fingers, put his glasses on, and take his old gold pen. He said: 'I'm shaky, Louis.' 'Should I hold your hand,' I asked, and he said yes. And with my hand he signed those checks." [18]

In the early afternoon as he grew weaker, Father Bernard asked him what he wanted them to tell everyone in Minnesota. He answered: "That they should pray for me." When the end came all of his New York confreres were at his bedside along with Monsignor Edwards and Bishop Leo Haid, who had come up from Belmont to be with his old friend as he breathed his last. As this group was reciting the rosary, he slept away at four o'clock in the afternoon of 18 May 1908. Abbot Alexius had often said that he wanted to be buried at St. John's, and arrangements were made to fulfill this request. Abbot Hilary Pfraengle of St. Mary's Abbey, Newark, sang the first Requiem at St. Anselm's on May 20 and Bishop Haid preached. In his funeral oration he said: "People sometimes misunderstood him, but those who knew him best will bear me out when I say that his was a most affectionate character, a strong character, a justice-loving man." Fathers Bernard and Rupert then accompanied the body back to St. John's. There again on May 23 funeral obsequies were held in the abbey church he had raised in the Indianbush, and Bishop Trobec delivered the sermon. Then the community bore the body to his cemetery overlooking Lake Sagatagan and placed him to rest beside his fellow worker, Bishop Seidenbusch. His grave was marked with a granite slab, stone like that which he had used for the foundations of his buildings throughout the area. Father Alexius Hoffmann summed up his many writings on Abbot Alexius with this final tribute: "He was in many ways a phenomenal man; he has more monuments in Minnesota than any other man. He was a good man, a rough diamond. God knew his heart; men often misinterpreted his actions." To which August C. Krey has added: "He was one of that iron age of strong men in Minnesota, the age of James J. Hill, Archbishop Ireland and Bishop Whipple, with all of whom he was well acquainted and among whom he occupies an honorable place." [19]

Although neither the Bronx nor Brooklyn parishes on the Atlantic seaboard had served as initial steps toward monastic foundations, across the country on the West Coast such a development did take place during these years. There, at Holy Rosary parish in Tacoma, Washington, Fathers William Eversmann and Wolfgang Steinkogler had made early moves under Abbot Bernard to establish a monastery and school which eventually became St. John's first daughter abbey. Abbot Peter went out to Washington to examine the property and location chosen for a new Benedictine house on a wooded hill four miles outside the city of Olympia, and called 'Woodland.' As in every other undertaking of his administration, Abbot Peter declared that the com-

244

munity would proceed carefully and slowly in developing this under-taking. But Father Wolgang expressed the spirit of the monks in Wash-ington when he told the abbot:

"... You say in your letter: we will go slow, but sure — that is the correct and the only reasonable way to begin in order to succeed; but let the 'slow' begin once and not suffer it to be referred to the Com-mittee on Procrastination. About the prospects that await us out here in regard to a College and Missions I can say that they are neither very bright nor are they discouraging by any means. *Es herrscht hier wie auch anderwo noch immer ein grosser Ueberfluss an Geldmangel.* We can hardly hope to escape going through the mill of hardships and dis-appointments, and that's the best foundation for a new house. Educa-tional institutions take better with the people than even churches and though we may not have crowded studyhalls in the beginning we may expect a fair number to begin with. *Deus providebit,* if we do not neg-lect to do our share in this noble undertaking. St. John's ought to have a grown-up daughter by this time. The Abbeys of Newark and North Carolina have already grown-up daughters. N. C. has already an Inde-pendent Priory and another new colony in view somewhere in Mary-land. Considering the poverty of N. C. we ought no longer to hesitate to found an institution in the much-promising West. There is everything here to make this country flourish in the near future, it only needs de-velopment — let us help it along and we will be right in the swim after a little while." [20]

St. Martin's Abbey

Animated by such determination, the far western colony of Bene-dictines achieved monastic maturity for their foundation at a pace which was reminiscent of Abbot Wimmer's earlier achievements. Their monastery, dedicated to St. Martin, was inaugurated in 1895, became an independent priory in 1904, and was raised to the status of an abbey by the Holy See on 18 April 1914. This rapid advance was not ac-complished without serious hardships and discouragements, however. The story of St. John's pioneer days, and of most religious undertak-ings, was repeated in the far Northwest. When the full history of this undertaking is prepared, the sacrifices and devotion of that band of Benedictines will emerge as an integral part of the history of Christian effort in the Pacific Northwest.

Abbot Peter appointed Father Oswald Baran, director of the com-mercial department, as first prior of St. Martin's, and sent the cleric Frater Benedict Schmitt with Brothers Francis Zwiesler, Herman Krell, and St. John's seasoned cook, Brother William Baldus, to begin monastic and educational life. Father Demetrius Juenemann had pre-ceded them in March of 1895 to supervise the construction of the first frame building, 100 x 60, and Father Wolfgang left the parish at Tacoma to assist in beginning the new school. In May of the following year St. John's pioneer, Father Cornelius Wittmann, obtained permission to join the new foundation where he intended to spend his declining years. But he was both too old to adjust himself to a new venture and handicapped by failing eyesight. After nine years, during which he landscaped 'Peter's Acre' on the monastic grounds, he returned to St. John's, where he lived to celebrate his golden jubilee as a Benedictine. Other St. John's Benedictines who served at St. Martin's during these years include Fathers Clement Staub, Matthew Britt and the deacon Mark Wiechmann who went West in 1900, and Father Ulric Scheffold, who joined them during the following year to take charge of commercial classes. Monks from several other American religious houses and candidates of the foundation itself year by year helped to increase personnel. One of these pioneers, Father Matthew Britt, distinguished himself by early efforts in popularizing the liturgy of the Church through his books, *The Hymns of the Breviary and Missal* (New York, 1922), and *A Dictionary of the Psalter* (New York, 1928).

St. Martin's began with one student in its abbey school in 1895, and slowly built up enrollment by training Catholic and non-Catholic young men, until at the time of its abbey status 135 students were enrolled in its high school and junior college. From the very beginning St. Martin's College, as it was called, acquired a reputation in the Northwest because of the standards maintained by its pioneers, who were intent on developing a good educational program. Father Oswald begged Abbot Peter to relieve him of the office of prior after five years, and when the abbot finally complied with his request, he served as pastor in Port Angeles and then at Holy Rosary parish in Tacoma. Abbot Peter then appointed Father Wolfgang as prior for a three-year term, at the end of which the community of St. Martin requested independent status. The request was granted by the Holy See and Father Demetrius was elected as first independent prior in 1904. He was followed by Father Justin Welz as second independent prior from 1909 until the abbatial election in 1914, when the community recalled Father Oswald from its parish in Tacoma to serve as first abbot of St. Martin's. Throughout this entire period Abbot Peter constantly supported the Washington enterprise, and rallied the community at St. John's whenever difficulties arose. At one point in 1898 when Prior Oswald wrote him a sharp letter reminding him of St. John's responsibilities to their foundation, he replied characteristically, "Great Jupiter, what a letter," and sent immediate assistance and fatherly encouragement. His sympathetic backing was an important factor in bringing St. John's first daughter house of age.

The story of the second monastic establishment during Abbot Peter's years runs in the same vein. Here the historical parallelism with the beginnings of St. John's is even more striking. What was undertaken in central Minnesota in the mid-nineteenth century by Benedictine monks was repeated at the beginning of the twentieth century on the plains of

246

Saskatchewan Province in Canada. When the Canadian Pacific Railroad and Canadian Northern Railroad had been completed to the West Coast, thousands of immigrants streamed into the Canadian Northwest territories and homesteaded along these railroad lines. A large number of Catholic settlers from the United States were among these new American pioneers after the turn of the century. German Catholics from the Minnesota River Valley and central Minnesota were prominent among the immigrants, and they requested their former pastors to help them obtain priests for these new Canadian settlements. Such requests reached, among others, Father Conrad Glatzmeier, O.S.B., at Albany, and he sought the aid of Abbot Peter. The abbot of St. John's then sent Father Bruno Doerfler, O.S.B., vice-president of the school, to investigate Canadian conditions with a view to selecting a location for a Catholic colony which eventually would have a Benedictine monastery as its center. As Benedictine monks had contributed to the making of European civilization by an identical process in the early middle ages, so now national boundaries were crossed anew to carve out a Christian commonwealth on the virgin plains of Western Canada.

A Canadian Undertaking

Father Bruno was accompanied to Canada during August, 1902, by three Catholic laymen of Stearns County: H. J. Haskamp of St. Cloud, Moritz Hoeschen of Freeport and Henry Hoeschen of Melrose. They traveled by rail and wagon into Saskatchewan, but on reaching Saskatoon, Henry Hoeschen decided to turn back. Undismayed, the other three investigators moved on through the regions of Rosthern and Cudworth to the present location of Muenster. There was no habitation, only beautiful virgin prairie spotted with small lakes and poplar groves. Here they found what they had come in search of: a vast expanse of fertile land. Father Bruno wrote in the *Record* of their impressions:

". . . As we proceeded, our enthusiasm increased over the found treasure, for we found the soil to improve continually. When we finally arrived at the summit of the slope, we were greeted by a gently rolling plain, studded with beautiful groves and crystal lakes. The soil of this plain was the very choicest, for it was deep black humus." [21]

When the observers returned in September with their glowing reports, the chapter at St. John's decided to take over the spiritual care of settlers who would move into a colony in that area. This information was all that was needed; Haskamp and Hoeschen formed the German American Land Company and purchased about 100,000 acres of railroad land in the district. A Catholic Settlement Society was also created in St. Paul to advertise the undertaking and assist the settlers in filing and locating on homesteads which they could obtain under Canadian law for $10 a quarter section. Father Bruno and the Hoeschens returned with Prior Herman and Father Conrad to Saskatchewan during the same month to make a thorough examination of the projected colony as far east as the present Mount Carmel. All were agreed on its potential and in the late fall of 1902 the project was definitely approved.

And The Rock Was Peter

At this point the precarious condition of another Benedictine priory in southern Illinois was the occasion for solving the problem of personnel for a Canadian undertaking and at the same time resolving the difficulties of a floundering monastic foundation. St. Vincent had established a priory named Cluny near Wetaug, Illinois, in 1892, of which the literary Benedictine, Father Oswald Moosmueller, was prior. After his sudden death in 1901, Abbot Innocent Wolf, in his capacity as president of the Congregation, presided over the election of a new prior. When two monks of St. Vincent, Fathers Maurus Hartmann and Leo Eichenlaub declined the position, Abbot Innocent petitioned the Holy See to appoint a prior to Cluny, and Father Alfred Mayer of St. John's was recommended. He accepted charge of the small community of eleven members, but Prior Alfred became convinced within a year that Cluny had no future. The small number of monks, lack of unity among the capitulars, a non-Catholic neighborhood, and especially the unhealthy climate due to marshes and resulting malaria, all militated against the success of this undertaking. The Cluny community considered moving to Caseyville, Illinois; Knight's Valley, California; Pueblo, Colorado; to St. John's Long Island site; Cottonwood in the Boise, Idaho, diocese; and then finally decided to transfer to the projected monastic site in Saskatchewan upon the invitation of Abbot Peter.

Seven Benedictines set out in mid-May, 1903, to initiate the new undertaking. Under Prior Alfred were the former members of Cluny who had decided to transfer their vows, along with Fathers Bruno Doerfler, O.S.B., Meinrad Seifermann, O.S.B., and Dominic Hofmann, O.S.B., of St. John's, who had volunteered for the new foundation. One of these Cluny pioneers, Father Peter Windschiegl, O.S.B., the present prior of the monastery which developed in Saskatchewan, has written an informative memoir history of the trials and accomplishments of this Catholic colonization venture on the great wheat plains of North America.[22] There he has detailed the stirring New World chronicle of the establishment of a monastery which was dedicated to St. Peter in memory of Abbot Peter's support of the project, of the beginnings of Catholic parishes for the settlers, and of perseverance in spite of the rigors of a northern climate. The settlers called Saskatchewan the 'Promised Land' because of the bountiful crops, but the project became a success only after years of hardship and toil. The Benedictines of St. Peter's shared the experiences of pioneering with the Catholic people of their colony, and sustained them by bringing the joys and graces of the Church's life as a stable part of this community venture. The vicar apostolic of Prince Albert, Bishop Albert Pascal, O.M.I., welcomed the monks into his vicariate, entrusted fifty townships to

248

their spiritual care, and remained a firm friend of St. Peter's Colony during these years.

When Father Alfred's five-year term as prior had expired, the monks elected Father Bruno as second prior, and Mayer returned to Minnesota. Three years later, and only eight years after the move to Canada, the priory was ready for abbey status. Monks from Europe, Minnesota and several other American Cassinese monasteries had joined the monastery in sufficient numbers to insure stability and self-sufficiency, and Pope St. Pius X granted the request for abbey status on 3 June 1911. Prior Bruno was elected first abbot and served for eight years, when he died suddenly on 12 June 1919 of a heart attack. Under his successor, Abbot Michael Ott, former professor of philosophy at St. John's, St. Peter's Colony in 1921 was erected by the Holy See, at the request of the abbey's friend Bishop Pascal, to the status of an abbey *nullius*. The abbey and colony were to be directly subject to the Holy See with the abbot of St. Peter's possessing powers of an Ordinary over the territory. Under Abbot Michael the membership of St. Peter's Abbey increased from fifteen to forty-four. The second abbot, however, did not enjoy good health and determined to resign after seven years in office. The community then chose Father Severin Gertken, O.S.B., who had been active in school work as professor of chemistry at St. John's and he was appointed by the Holy See as abbot-ordinary of St. Peter's. Since 1926, Abbot Severin has been the spiritual director of the abbey and colony. Sons of Catholic families from several of the parishes established by the Benedictines have entered the monastery at St. Peter's, and a further step has thus been taken in making Saskatchewan's abbey an indigenous Canadian product. Throughout the years the relationship between St. John's and St. Peter's has been of a personal, family nature, and the Benedictine clerics from Canada have continued to receive their philosophical and theological training at Collegeville. Father Alfred summed up this relationship when he wrote to Abbot Peter:

". . . No one can or will deny that St. John's has kept its promise made when the Cluny community accepted the offer of taking charge of the colony to be established in Canada, and has rendered this twig of a community every possible assistance. Indeed without the aid of St. John's it would have been nigh to impossible to assume charge of this colony or carry on the work we are now doing. For this reason this community as established in Canada may regard itself as a quasi-foundation of St. John's, and look up to the latter as its foster father and protector. We therefore also appreciate the favors bestowed on us by St. John's, and certainly no one appreciates this more than I do." [23]

The lasting contributions that Abbot Peter made to St. John's itself during his long administration are more difficult to measure. These so-called intangibles were the values, the spirit and the atmosphere that

St. Peter's Abbey

249

gave character to his term of office and continue on at the abbey and school to the present time. This lasting contribution was, perhaps, best summed up by the monks, students and friends of St. John's who so often declared that he was deeply loved. He has been called 'charity personified,' and a 'grand Father.' He was a man of both intellectual attainment and pronounced emotional feeling which he carried beneath an external calm. Long years of self-discipline made it possible for him to live the Benedictine life as though it were a simple and easy experience. More than that, he brought to his monks spiritual confidence and inspiration through his own example. To those who lived under him in the St. John's religious family, he was not a figure of large proportions but an ideal because of his sympathy with the joys and sufferings of his community, because he was so broad in understanding and temperate in action.

Abbot Peter wanted the St. John's family to grow in charity and knowledge through generous living according to the precepts of St. Benedict's *Rule*. Wisely and kindly he strove for this by example and counsel. If this ideal was at times lost by one or the other, he strove meekly and patiently to win him back to his first fervor. Those who too often missed morning choir could expect to have Abbot Peter knock at their rooms on his way to the choir and say: "Father, we are just about to begin Lauds." He ever strove for reconciliation of differences and advised submission, as he would say: "Now I don't want to put the whole blame of this condition on you, but knowing that even a little step on your part would bring about a reconciliation, I ask you to make this soon. There is no humiliation in the sense of degradation, but one that is honorable."

He was also reluctant to cause pain. He asked his monks to look at the bright side of developments "and then everything will be all right." Before giving a command or making a correction, he would prepare every word in advance, write a letter by hand and correct it, hold off and rechart his course. He claimed that he never mastered the art of expressing his thoughts so as not to offend. At least he was correct to the extent that his brief and halting public speeches were undistinguished. He possessed an open mind, however, and did not expect his men to agree with all his views: "I am the last man that would expect such a thing from my subjects." He wrote in this vein to one of his priests: "I am sorry that my remarks made you feel sore. I did not intend that; in fact, it is not in my nature to cause pain for others without feeling it myself." [24]

This policy won the majority to sound ideals and deep trust, but it also led to some abuses, especially in the last years of his long administration when he was no longer able to keep in contact with a growing community. His admonitions did not hold in some cases. He himself wrote: "How little are my well-meant admonitions understood. That it

250

were my lot to obey and not to command." He was accused of being "too good." This slowness to act, this democratic urge of his, did have its drawbacks, but in the long view was perhaps the reason he did maintain, as Pope Benedict XV stated on his twenty-fifth abbatial anniversary, "high standards of religious life among those in your care." [25]

The incidents, tales and stories are myriad of the fourth abbot's humanity and spiritual depth. If it is his charity, there was that day of 13 July 1898 when he ran down to the shore of Lake Sagatagan, upon hearing that Brother Paul Noll had drowned, and dived repeatedly and in vain for the Brother. If it is his humility, there was the time after a pontifical high Mass when one of the monks proceeded to correct him on his rubrics "as not being up to his predecessor's." Abbot Peter thanked him quietly, although he said "the admonition stung me," and promised to amend. Once when playing billiards in the community recreation room, and he was a good billiard player, he ripped his cue through the table-covering in disgust after missing an easy shot. Instantly he was on his knees before the Fathers asking their pardon for this act, and he never played billiards again as a penance. If it is his love of children, for whom he always carried candy in his pocket, there is the precious incident of his falling into conversation with a little girl on the train from Minneapolis to Collegeville. "What's your name," she asked. "Peter," he replied, and for the rest of the trip the child entertained him and the entire coach by singing loud and long: "Peter, Peter, pumpkin-eater." Or the day the school children came over from 'St. Joe' for an outing at the abbey, Abbot Peter playfully pushed one of the boys into the Sagatagan. It was immediately evident that the boy could not swim and Abbot Peter, in his religious habit, had to go after him. At alumni reunions the 'old boys' always are ready to talk about Abbot Peter's taking an evening swim after choir during the summer season, or of his chopping and trimming trees below the observatory or at the cemetery. He was a confirmed woodchopper; he cut twenty-four cords of poplar during the winter of 1919. To the consternation of the community he climbed twenty feet into a tree in 1920 to cut a branch, and was out in the woods cutting timber during his last week at St. John's.

It was during that year of 1920 that all began to notice Abbot Peter was failing in health. He had been abbot since 1894 and had been deeply affected by World War I as he watched so many of St. John's boys go off to Europe, some never to return. As soon as the war was over he at once began a charitable campaign of donations and goods directed toward the needy in all European countries, irrespective of national boundaries. But he realized in June of 1920 how old he was getting when he met at Father Cuthbert Goeb's first Mass, in his home town of St. Michael, Mrs. Conrad Friedrich, the bride of his first Mass, now herself a grandmother. He had headed St. John's for over a quarter of a century, and for half of that time had been president of the American Cassinese Congregation of Benedictines. When he had been elected in 1894 the community numbered 115, including 65 priests. Now the total, apart from two new foundations, was 164, with 113 priests.

And The Rock Was Peter

Abbot Peter could not have chosen a more ideal novice master to introduce all of these new monks to Beneditcine life than Father Athanasius Meyer. For forty-four years he taught Church history and general history at St. John's and as novice master for thirty-two years inculcated the distinctive spirit which Abbot Peter was fostering. The abbot and his novice master complemented each other ideally, and the differences over Benedictine principles and traditions which had harassed the American houses in their formative years evaporated at St. John's during this period. As the American Cassinese Benedictines grew to maturity, time confirmed the wisdom of Wimmer's original blueprint. The New World houses took their place in the international Benedictine family as a young but valid manifestation of living monastic development in modern times. Father Athanasius knew his Church history well enough to appreciate the nature of the opportunity presented to the Church and her religious in the free atmosphere of American life. He did not turn his back on this distinctive phenomenon and look only into previous centuries or to contemporary European Benedictine practices, valuable in themselves and in special national frameworks, but scarcely exportable without modification. As Abbot Boniface had consistently advocated adjustment to American circumstances and temperament without sacrifice of Benedictine essentials, so now Abbot Peter and Father Athanasius strove to combine tradition with a response to the needs of the Church as existing at the moment. The English, French, German, Spanish, Italian, Swiss, and Austrian Benedictines were formulating revived Benedictine procedures during these decades. The American Benedictines too began slowly to discover that their branch of the Order had taken root and was flourishing as a healthy and sound member in the service of the Church. Among the young Benedictines trained by Father Athanasius in this spirit were those monks who later initiated the projects at St. John's which are now accepted as its unique present contribution.

Abbot Peter's silver abbatial jubilee was observed on 26 August 1920, and Bishop Leo Haid was on hand to evaluate the significance of the occasion:

"As we stand on the banks of the beautiful lake, we admire the solid magnificent buildings of the abbey and university — proofs of the taste, talents, industry and sacrifice of the sons of St. John's. Our vision broadens and beholds church upon church raising cross-crowned steeples over an extensive part of the State of Minnesota. The Indian wigwam, once the only home of the devoted missionary, has given place to comfortable dwellings; schools and churches have replaced unsheltered sanctuaries. . . . Beyond the Dakotas St. Peter's Abbey, a daughter of St. John's, graces the plains of Saskatchewan, and St. Martin's, another daughter, brings joy to the virgin forests of Washington and holds aloft the Cross of Christ and the torch of education. Our hearts expand with gratitude to God for all these visible proofs of His bounty, for all these testimonials of the successful labors of the Benedictines of St. John's Abbey. Could we visit the towns and cities of Minnesota, and many other states, we would be greeted by busy, successful merchants and professional men, by God-serving priests and prelates who proudly call St. John's Alma Mater. . . .

Death of Abbot Peter

"If the guiding hand of the Rt. Rev. Abbot is seen in the education of laymen and priests, in the building of churches and schools, in the missionary activities of devoted men, it is more especially felt in the public service of God in the abbey, the holiest and most pressing duty of the Benedictine monk. . . .

"In joyous gladness we unite with the children of the abbey in offering our sincerest and heartiest congratulations to the Rt. Rev. Jubilarian, rejoicing with him and admiring the great work which he has guided and directed for twenty-five years."[26]

Abbot Peter did not often enjoy the privilege of wearing his new *cappa magna* given him by the Holy Father at the time of this celebration. The shadows were closing in around him. His good friend Bishop Trobec had resigned his see and was in his last illness. Since 1904 the abbot had chronic kidney trouble, but in 1920 he began to suffer from acute nephritis. He now began more and more to lean on his prior, Father Alcuin Deutsch, whom he had appointed in 1917 to succeed Father Herman Bergmann, who had faithfully filled that position for twenty-two years. In the fall of 1921, the abbot's condition was such that he was advised by local doctors to undergo examinations by the Mayo Brothers in Rochester. The community assembled to wish him a speedy recovery; he tried to muster his energies so as to appear "not so bad," as he wrote in his diary, but it was evident that he was suffering much. As he was helped into the car he cast a long glance at the monastery and school which he had headed for so many years. The abbey chronicler recorded that all felt it was a last look, and the reports Prior Alcuin sent back from Rochester confirmed this opinion. A diverticulum had developed in connection with his kidney trouble. He rallied from an operation on November 22, but a sudden suppression of the kidney function set in, another operation failed, and on the afternoon of November 27 his sons at home received a telegram that their abbot was slowly dying at St. Mary's Hospital. That same night, at 8:45, he passed into God's hands after receiving the last Sacraments of the Church. He was sixty-five years of age.

Prior Alcuin brought the body home on the following day, and pontifical obsequies were held on December 1 by Bishop Joseph F. Busch,

Bishop Trobec's successor in St. Cloud. Then he was laid to rest in the cemetery under a spruce he had planted years before. From all sides testimonials were received of the love and esteem in which he was held. His name was secure in the annals of the upper midwest, and yet shortly before he died, Abbot Peter had written with deep personal conviction in his diary:

"I feel more and more that I am not the right man for the place. May God, who has called me against my will to this responsible office, not forsake me on account of my sins, but assist and strengthen me to perform my duties as superior for the good of the community and His greater glory. I have so little courage and no confidence in myself. But let me trust in Him who strengthens the weak and does not disdain to use the most unworthy as instruments for good." [27]

CHAPTER EIGHT

NO TASK REFUSED

Sixty-five years had followed rapidly one upon the other from the humble beginnings of Benedictine life in Minnesota to the end of Abbot Peter's administration in 1921. In that period, short in monastic annals, the activity of St. John's had broadened out in circular patterns from central Minnesota down the Mississippi and Minnesota River Valleys, across the Dakotas to Washington, and north into Canada. Those years were filled with missionary and pioneering educational efforts for Catholic settlers of the upper midwest. Most of the Benedictine missions had become parishes and St. John's had contributed to the establishment of the St. Paul archdiocese and its suffragan sees of St. Cloud, Duluth, Crookston, Fargo, and Bismarck. At the same time two daughter abbeys had been established in the state of Washington and in the province of Saskatchewan, Canada, while a missionary apostolate was begun among the Indians of northern Minnesota and the na-

255

tives of the Bahama Islands. At Collegeville a physical plant to serve the needs of the abbey, seminary, college and high school was erected, and stable monastic and educational life firmly established. In many ways the years from the War Between the States to the First World War were ideal for the growth of a monastic organization. Three generations of St. John's family, under the community's first four abbots, had enjoyed the opportunity of developing traditional Benedictine endeavors for religion and society in the free atmosphere of expanding American life.

This period had been missionary in character and design. Like the Church in the United States, which had been designated as missionary territory by the Holy See down to 1908, St. John's Benedictines had entered heartily into the common effort of organizing and stabilizing Catholic life in the nation. Abbot Peter's successor was now about to inherit a monastic community which had been brought to this stage of development through sacrifice and dedicated work, a large religious body which was on the threshold of its maturity.

The story of that final phase of St. John's first century embraces thirty years, from 1921 to 1951, and in its details fulfills to a marked degree the plans and designs which Abbot Wimmer and his pioneers had so ardently hoped for when they transplanted Benedictine life to the New World. The critical history of this last period, with full evaluation of character and events, must await future treatment at a time which does not embrace the life span of those who have been contemporaries of the persons involved. The general outlines of the period are apparent, however, and serve to round out the picture of the first century of an American Benedictine house.

The capitulars of the community who gathered on 28 December 1921 for the election of Abbot Peter's successor evidenced, in the names they advanced during the *scrutinium,* a desire to choose an abbot who would bring their monastery to full maturity. For seven hours during that afternoon and evening, discussions centered around the prior and subprior, Fathers Alcuin Deutsch and Alexius Hoffmann, each of whom had received an equal number of 42 *scrutinium* votes. Both of these monks had devoted their lives to monastic, educational, and especially in the case of Father Alexius, literary pursuits. Also considered were two monks engaged in parochial work, Fathers Bernard Kevenhoerster, successor of Abbot Alexius in his church of St. Anselm, New York City, and Father Alfred Mayer, former prior of St. Peter's monastic foundation in Canada, and successively pastor of Assumption Church, St. Paul, St. Mary's Church, St. Cloud, and St. Joseph's Church, Moorhead. The opening session was terminated at eleven o'clock on the first evening and resumed the following morning. By noon a two-thirds majority had been reached on the third ballot and Prior Alcuin was returned as abbot-designate. While Bishop Joseph

Busch was coming from St. Cloud to join the community in the *Te Deum,* Abbot-elect Alcuin rose to speak to the community. At first he wept and protested his lack of strength to bear such a burden. He then proceeded to announce his motto which he had ready. It was to be *Non Recuso Laborem,* taken from the well-known deathbed words of St. Martin, bishop of Tours: "Lord, if I am still necessary for your people, I will not refuse the work: Your Will be done."

The election of Alcuin Henry Deutsch as fifth abbot of St. John's illustrates better than the most elaborate thesis on democratic theory the opportunity for advancement afforded in the Catholic Church in the United States. He was born of German parentage in the Hungarian village of Valla on 13 February 1877, and was brought to the United States by his immigrant parents in early childhood. His father was a hard-working day laborer in St. Paul with a large family to support. Henry had a deep admiration for his father which he retained throughout life. The abbot left among his personal effects after death a touching tribute to his father in verse, which in Victorian fashion he often and hastily composed.[1] Young Henry received his elementary education along with his brothers and sisters in the parochial school of the venerable Assumption Church in St. Paul. The Benedictine priests and nuns there soon recognized the gifts of Henry and encouraged his parents to send him to St. John's as a candidate for the priesthood. From the fall of 1890, when he enrolled in the classical course, until his ordination to the priesthood Henry received his complete education gratis from the Benedictines. In later years as abbot he was ever sensitive and particularly sympathetic to the needs of poor boys who applied for assistance. Young Deutsch at once evidenced the drive and determination to excel which characterized his entire life, and year after year he took satisfaction in winning scholastic honors and premiums. Even at this early date there is evidence in the school records of keen competition between Henry Deutsch from St. Paul and the son of another German immigrant from Minneapolis, Bernard Kevenhoerster, with each receiving a good number of the awards for academic achievement.

Henry Deutsch entered the novitiate at St. John's in 1896 and received the name of Alcuin in religion. After one year of study in the seminary at Collegeville, Abbot Peter sent him to the International Benedictine College of Sant'Anselmo in Rome to complete his studies for the priesthood and pursue the major course in philosophy at that institution. His six years in Europe were a period of growth in capacity and stature as he met young Benedictines from all parts of the world at Sant'Anselmo, toured through various European countries and visited many of the ancient cloisters of the Order during summer vacations.

His scholastic career was not as enjoyable as the experiences of life abroad, however, and he had to work hard to master his philosophical studies. He failed in his first attempt at the bachelors degree, but continued to make progress after that, although he confessed to Abbot Peter: "That doctorate has been the bug-bear of my course here." [2] He wrote his thesis on the topic *De Origine Potestatis Civilis*, and when it was accepted in 1903 he returned to teach philosophy and act as prefect at St. John's. The young priest professor was soon being called 'doctor confusus' by the students who did not find his lectures well-organized, or his teaching technique easy to follow. But Father Alcuin had administrative ability, and Abbot Peter appointed him rector of the major seminary from 1907 to 1909, and then vice-president of the school from 1909 to 1913. The character traits which made him an abbot of international reputation were not, however, acceptable to a number of his confreres when he was acting in a subaltern position. Abbot Peter was forced to remove him from the office of vice-president in 1913 after he had acted hastily in expelling a large group of students for disciplinary reasons, and Father Alcuin was sent as assistant to the aging Father Othmar Erren at St. Joseph's parish in Minneapolis. Here he remained for two years, and throughout his long life always looked back with fond memories on this interlude of spiritual work among people in parish life. When Father Francis Mershman began to fail in health and his work had to be distributed during 1916, Abbot Peter recalled Father Alcuin to teach moral theology. Deutsch informed his superior that he submitted to this decision that he must return to St. John's, and wrote: "I am not coming up to dictate, but to obey." [3] During the following year Abbot Peter finally acceded to repeated requests which the community at home had made to him as well as to the triennial visitators and the general chapter, that Prior Herman Bergmann's twenty-two year term of office be terminated. He proceeded on 9 September 1917 to appoint Father Alcuin as claustral prior as further testimony of his personal confidence. During the next four years as he declined in health Abbot Peter relinquished more and more of the actual administration of the community to Prior Alcuin, who continued in that position until the time of his election as abbot.

The blessing ceremonies of Abbot Alcuin were delayed until the spring season for the convenience of alumni and friends of the institution, when on 3 May 1922 the local ordinary, Bishop Busch, was the officiating prelate. The new abbot associated with his administration Father Alfred Mayer as prior and retained Father Alexius Hoffmann as subprior. The abbey's chronicler observed that a strong spiritual undercurrent was evident from the very beginning of the new regime, and the events which rapidly followed confirmed the accuracy of this view.

Abbot Alcuin was ready to inaugurate an extensive program of spiritual synthesis at St. John's. Abbot Peter by slow evolution had developed a simple, easy and flexible relationship between the abbot and community; his successor aimed at broadening and deepening monastic life along lines which he had observed during his years in Europe. At Sant' Anselmo and during visits to cloisters on the continent he had come in contact with the vigorous Benedictine revival which had been developing in the nineteenth century. Abbot Alcuin was not the first abbot of St. John's who studied in Europe, as the community's first abbot had received his early education in his native Bavaria. That, however, had been before the influence of Abbot Prosper Gueranger at Solesmes Abbey in France, and of the Wolter brothers, Maurus and Placid, at Beuron Abbey in Germany and Maredsous Abbey in Belgium, had been felt throughout the Catholic world. In these monastic centers a new environment of idealism had been created through an emphasis on liturgical life and Benedictine principles. The Holy See supported a Gregorian Chant revival, and monks trained in this spirit became the first two abbot primates, namely, the Right Reverends Hildebrand de Hemptinne and Fidelis von Stotzingen. Abbot Alcuin was likewise filled with the conviction that the Benedictines, in their ancient and traditional Christian family life, could offer to contemporary society both meaningful and attractive standards of conduct.

The new abbot's first years in office were crowded with projects for implanting these ideals in his own religious community. During the 1920's a series of new customs and procedures were introduced in quick succession. As prior he had given indication of what was coming when he was instrumental during January of 1918 in introducing a Solemn High Mass as the Conventual Mass on Sundays. This was an innovation, for the liturgical renaissance then developing in Europe had not yet reached American shores. The community's chronicler recorded that this act could be considered as the beginning of the liturgical movement at St. John's. Ten days after the documents approving his election as abbot arrived from Rome he, for the first time, on 26 March 1922, wore rose-colored Gothic vestments on Laetare Sunday designed by one of the monks, Father Ignatius Wiltzius. A new horarium for the Divine Office and educational life was also established in 1922: Vespers and Compline were to be at 5:30 in the afternoon; Matins and Lauds at 7:30 in the evening; Prime, Conventual Mass and Little Hours at 4:30 in the morning. Classes were to meet from 8 to 12 o'clock in the morning, and from 1 to 2:45 in the afternoon. At first the practice of reciting the Divine Office in the choir chapel within the monastic enclosure, was continued, but Abbot Alcuin ordered that his throne be moved into the center of the choir. Gradually parts of the Divine Office were chanted in the main abbey church, and solemnly on the major feasts, until by 1928 the entire daily official prayer of the Church was recited in the abbey church. The choir stalls were enlarged, an abbot's throne installed, and in 1929 the sanctuary was deepened. The main altar was moved forward from the rear of the apse and the apsidal area of the church redecorated in the Beuronese style of art similar to the abbey church at Maria Laach, Germany, by Brother Clement Frischauf, O.S.B., a monk of Seckau abbey.[4]

The monastic enclosure was carefully laid out and workmen who had formerly lived within the monastery were provided with separate quarters in 1924. Rooms were prepared for the abbot at the front entrance of the monastery during that same year, and eventually Abbot Alcuin had the chapter room, community recreation room and office of the procurator placed in the same immediate area adjoining his rooms. The refectory had been the object of his attention from the very beginning. Simple oak tables and chairs were designed and made by the Brothers from abbey lumber; a separate table for the abbot with accommodation for guests was provided; traditional monastic meal prayers were introduced along with a weekly blessing of table waiters and reader. A martyrology was now read at table in English, commemoration of anniversaries of deceased members of the community and major historical events of the community's past were announced after the reading at meals was concluded. Brother Clement painted a series of murals illustrating Benedictine life on the refectory walls and when the work was completed this room was accepted on all sides as the most artistic area at Collegeville. In this way the importance of the community refectory, second only to the church, was stressed, and its spiritual association with the Eucharistic life of the Church more clearly emphasized.[5]

In order to foster the Gregorian chant revival more effectively the Gertken Brothers, Fathers Innocent and Norbert, were sent in 1922 to Mother Gregory Steven's Pius X School of Liturgical Music at Manhattanville College of the Sacred Heart in New York, where they studied under the famed Dom André Mocquereau of Solesmes Abbey. When they returned, Father Innocent was appointed director of the monastery choir, which he faithfully led while acting also as organist for twenty-four years. Father Norbert directed the students' choir, and trained the clerics in vocal technique. After the liturgical movement was launched he devoted his energies to training parish choirs throughout the region in Gregorian chant, advising organists and advancing an understanding of liturgical music. When Abbot Alcuin returned from his European trip of 1925 he brought with him Dom Ermin Vitry of Maredsous Abbey. Expert in both secular and ecclesiastical music, Dom Ermin desired to contribute to the Gregorian chant revival in the United States, and during these years he likewise trained parish choirs throughout the country.

Prior Alfred was simultaneously supporting activities toward deepening spiritual and Benedictine life. During the summer of 1923 the spiritual retreat movement for laity, which was developing during these years under the leadership of the Society of Jesus, was introduced at St. John's.[6] Two retreats for men were held in the month of August under Prior Alfred's direction, and sponsored by Bishop Busch of St. Cloud. One retreat was in English conducted by Father Alfred and the other by Father Augustine Brockmeyer, O.S.B., in the German language. Only fourteen Catholic men attended the first retreats, but a beginning had been made. In 1926 and 1928 summer lay retreats were again held, and in 1931 the undertaking became an annual event at St. John's, with 13,316 having made annual retreats to date. Father George Scheffold also was interested in conducting parish missions. His initial efforts in 1919 were continued in a more organized fashion in 1926 when he and Father Method Porwoll began missions in parishes throughout the country. Father Celestine Kapsner joined in the work in 1928, and after the liturgical movement was launched a program of liturgical missions was prepared.[7]

In 1925 Abbot Alcuin and Prior Alfred began fostering an interest in the Institute of Oblates of St. Benedict. This ancient association of laity wishing to enter into a spiritual relationship with a particular monastery had been revived in the United States in 1894 by Archabbot Leander Schnerr of St. Vincent. Pope Leo XIII had fostered the development of this religious confraternity of people who desired to mold their lives according to the principles and ideals of the *Rule* of St. Benedict and share, as members of the monastic family, in the spiritual work of the monks. Sixty Oblates were received by Abbot Alcuin on the Feast of St. Benedict, 21 March 1925, and the movement was fostered in the parishes attached to the abbey. The Solemnity of St. Benedict on July 11 was designated as annual Oblates' Day at St. John's, and the original *Manual for Secular Oblates* first issued by St. Vincent in 1923 was revised and re-edited under the abbot's direction. Students, alumni, friends and interested laity began to join. A director of Oblates was eventually appointed, a monthly paper was first issued on 22 January 1927 prepared by clerics of the abbey for members, and a lending library of spiritual books was arranged. In the thirty years since the movement was launched 2,400 Oblates from all parts of North America have affiiliated themselves to St. John's, and in 1956 there is a total membership of 1,600. A strong spiritual bond was in this way created between these Oblates and the abbey and its activities, while an understanding and devotion to St. Benedict's way of life was given a fresh impetus in modern times. Other American abbeys also developed Oblate programs during these years, and one of the main spheres of cooperation between American abbeys of all Congregations has been the heartening unity of approach worked out by directors of this undertaking.

While fanning out with these ideas during the enthusiastic first years of his administration, Abbot Alcuin found himself in a position to undertake one of his most cherished projects. He was a loyal alumnus of

Sant' Anselmo and was personally convinced that individual abbeys throughout the world should send young monks there for undergraduate and advanced studies whenever possible. Studying in the capital of Christendom young Benedictines could view at first hand the full life of the Holy See, grow in affection for the Holy Father, and appreciate

the universal character of the Church at its font. At the International Benedictine College young monks could meet and become acquainted with fellow Benedictines from cloisters throughout the world, and in this way learn the ancient and diversified traditions of individual houses and congregations which were following the *Rule* of St. Benedict. In this way he felt that his young Americans would be broadened, and a decisive step would be taken toward an eventual closer bond of unity between Benedictine families.

Abbot Alcuin had inherited a large religious family from Abbot Peter. It was as well a Benedictine community which was financially sound as a result of the achievements and sacrifices of Abbot Alexius and the pioneer monks. Moreover, during the 1920's large classes of novices entered the monastery at Collegeville. Thus the new abbot was in the enviable position, which many contemporary American abbots and bishops did not share, of being able to spare personnel for extended periods of study. The dedicated work of the pioneers of St. John's had begun to bear fruit, and a first manifestation was this opportunity for a somewhat leisurely pursuit of academic disciplines which the largely self-trained educators and missionaries of the first three generations did not enjoy.[8]

Fratres Roger Schoenbechler and Reinhart Koll were the first to go to Sant' Anselmo in October of 1922, but the latter cleric died during the following year at the monastery of Ettal. Father Virgil Michel, O.S.B., after completing his doctoral work in English at the Catholic University of America, was sent to Sant' Anselmo and Louvain University in 1924 for advanced philosophical studies. Two years later the clerics Dunstan Tucker, Jerome Simmer, and Marcellus Leisen were sent as a group to Sant' Anselmo, as were Fratres Paschal Botz and Godfrey Diekmann in 1928. Abbot Alcuin encouraged his clerics to travel during summer months to various countries and to visit different abbeys as he had done. Monks were also sent to other traditional European academic centers by the abbot during these years. Father Conrad Diekmann studied theology and art at Munich; Father Paschal completed his advanced work in theology at Tuebingen University under Dr. Karl Adam; Fathers Godfrey and Method attended the Liturgical Academy at Maria Laach Abbey; Father Basil Stegmann attended classes at Sant' Anselmo after finishing his theological degree at the Catholic University of America; and three clerics, Egbert Goeb, Severin Lauer and Alexander Korte, were sent to the ancient Benedictine University of Salzburg in 1929 after Abbot Alcuin had been asked to support its restoration.

Abbot Peter's policy of sending members of the community for graduate work in various fields at American universities was also continued. Fathers Severin Gertken, Sylvester Harter, Theodore Krebsbach and Damian Baker worked in chemistry, English, and classics at the University of Chicago; Fathers Christopher Bayer and Oliver Kapsner took library science at Notre Dame, where Father Angelo Zankl also studied art. Fathers Mark Braun and Arthur Danzl enrolled in education and mathematics at Columbia University; Father Clarus Graves pursued courses at Columbia and the Sorbonne. Fathers Matthew Kiess and Walter Reger studied chemistry and history at the University of Minnesota; while Fathers Damian Baker and Aidan Germain worked in the fields of classics and history at the Catholic University of America. The interesting experiment of sending five clerics and two priests to the University of Minnesota during the summer of 1928 was also made. In the 1930's and '40's this liberal policy of graduate training for his monks was continued by Abbot Alcuin at the same pace as it was begun in the 1920's. During his twenty-nine year administration a total of 101 monks were sent to forty-six universities in Europe and America, with twenty-eight receiving doctorate degrees, and thirty-seven masters degrees. The long-range effect of this generous interest in professional training and advanced study soon had significant effect on the academic life of the school and the volumes of original studies which slowly began to appear in the coming years.

Graduate Studies

While Abbot Alcuin gave the basic impetus to these projects, his central position cannot be stressed as isolated from his contemporary religious brethren. No person was ever left alone to lead a cause, and in the case of Abbot Alcuin he too was surrounded by groups in the community who actively and intelligently supported each undertaking. Sometimes it is difficult to distinguish precisely where the movements originated, and more often the true pattern can be found in the intriguing phenomenon of a whole community forging a project together. The effort for a fuller monastic life was unquestionably advanced, as Abbot Alcuin often stated himself, by those monks who had studied and observed Benedictine life abroad. The program of giving young Benedictines the best possible professional training at recognized university centers was not only begun by his predecessor, but defended and repeatedly recommended to the abbot by such members of the community as Fathers Severin Gertken, Mark Braun, Walter Reger, Matthew Kiess, Damian Baker and Virgil Michel who were actively concerned with the educational effort of St. John's.

A mention of the name of Father Virgil Michel opens the complicated story of what was, perhaps, the most significant development of Abbot Alcuin's administration. The relationship between the abbot and Father Virgil, with its aspects of cooperation, dependence and opposition, had effects on the life of the Church throughout the whole of the United States and in varying degrees throughout the English-speaking world. For in the mid-1920's an organized movement was brought from Europe and launched at St. John's by Michel with the support of his abbot which Theodore Maynard in his *Story of American Catholicism* has termed the most significant aspect of contemporary religious life. It is called the liturgical movement, or more correctly the liturgical revival. The full story of this development is now being exhaustively studied and prepared for publication. In this way adequate treatment will be given to one of the vital movements of our times. The broad outlines of the undertaking are given here only as an introduction.[9]

No Task Refused

Father Virgil George Michel, like Abbot Alcuin, had been raised in the environment of the abbey's Assumption parish in St. Paul. Father Alcuin took an early interest in George Michel when he became a student at St. John's in 1903. He once asked the promising young man if he ever thought of becoming a priest. Michel replied: "Father Alcuin, if monasticism were what it once was, I would enter St. John's Abbey." On 4 July 1909 he did decide to enter the novitiate at St. John's, received the name of Virgil in religion, and during the next seven years followed a traditional program preparatory to the priesthood. Then in 1916 Abbot Peter sent him to the Catholic University of America for doctoral studies in English. While there he evidenced more interest in his minor work in philosophy, and in the field of education during two summer sessions at Columbia University. His thesis topic, *The Critical Principles of Orestes A. Brownson,* opened to him the world of this nineteenth century journalist-convert's controversial and expansive thought. Unquestionably Michel was deeply influenced by his thorough study of Brownson's writings. Although his doctoral thesis was not particularly distinguished, much of Brownson's courageous approach can be seen in Father Virgil's later efforts. They were, like Brownson's, primarily journalistic and embraced the intellectual, social, educational and philosophical ramifications of the relationship between religion and society. As the Reverend James P. Gillis, C.S.P., editor of *The Catholic World,* told Michel on 23 February 1927: "My experience is that Brownson's profound philosophical thought seems to have cast its shadow upon all who study him."

During these years he was also sensing that American Catholic life was coming of age, and wondering what part the Benedictines could play in that endeavor. Michel wrote to Abbot Peter in this vein:

"I am glad to hear that the question of colleges is still alive. In a few years we shall be going more and more into that kind of work and that of giving missions; and the time for preparing for these fields is present.

I often admire the foresight of Abbot Alexius in starting the large building at St. John's, and the large parish house at St. Anselm's, which is now hardly too large. . . . Goodness knows how we need good Catholic writers in this country, and I am of the Benedictine tradition. On the contrary, I think that the time has arrived when some of the Abbeys can devote more energy to work of giving missions and of being leaders in sound thought. So far there was too much necessity in other fields, fields that are closer to the heart of the servant of the Lord. But soon the time will come when we shall commence to emerge from that state which I always like to compare with the glorious work of converting Europe in the first centuries of our existence; and our attention must be directed elsewhere soon if we do not wish to deteriorate. I think the best thing for us, especially with the nervous American spirit, is to see ahead of ourselves at all times and at least double the work we can manage." [10]

Father Virgil Michel

When he returned to St. John's in 1918 he taught English literature as well as one course in history of philosophy. In 1921 he took charge of seminary philosophy, but his prime interest in modern philosophy dominated the course. Abbot Alcuin, after his election, sent Father Virgil to Rome to study under his own former mentor, Father Joseph Gredt, O.S.B., at Sant' Anselmo, where the abbot believed the young priest could obtain a thorough grasp and appreciation of scholastic philosophy. After an impatient semester there, Michel spent an enjoyable year in philosophical study at Louvain University, and two summers of travel on the continent and in the Middle East. At Sant' Anselmo Father Virgil came in contact with Dom Lambert Beauduin, Benedictine of Mont Cesar Abbey, who was teaching ecclesiology and liturgy there. This Belgian pioneer in the modern liturgical revival stimulated Michel's interest in the renaissance of sacramental, liturgical piety based on a realization of the nature of the Church as the Mystical Body of Christ. At this point in his development Father Virgil looked upon himself as primarily a philosopher who would do liturgical translations as a hobby. He began to write letters to Abbot Alcuin encouraging him to make St. John's a center where European liturgical works already issued might be translated and introduced to American Catholics, and liturgical writing be begun by the monks of the abbey. Further contact with the liturgical work of Benedictines at such abbeys as Montserrat, Solesmes, Maredsous, Saint André, Maria Laach and Beuron deepened this conviction, and the young monk who went to Europe to learn more scholastic philosophy soon was offering himself to his abbot as the organizer and editor of a liturgical magazine and a 'Popular Liturgical Library.' He had caught the vision of the potentialities of worshipping Christians realizing their oneness in the Mystical Body of Christ, actively participating in the liturgical and corporate life of the Church and carrying this spirit over into American society.

Father Virgil also saw that social problems are rooted in spiritual problems. A vigorous support of the liturgical movement, he felt, would be, as Pope St. Pius X had so fervently advocated, the providential means not only of counteracting current paganism based on individualism, naturalism and secularism. It would also be the primary and indispensable source of the true Christian spirit, the best way of reviving Western Christian society in modern times.

While studying at Louvain he was already translating European liturgical publications and asking Abbot Alcuin to consider the possibility of St. John's beginning an American liturgical review. He wrote:

"And our Popular Liturgical Library has kept pace with time, except that it still awaits your approval (in its general lines). But before that comes I must frankly warn you. While the whole thing may get to be one of the biggest events that struck the Catholic U.S. since the NCWC [National Catholic Welfare Conference] (I believe that very sincerely), it also may mean what every big thing means — WORK and manpower. The prospects for its growth as a movement of liturgical restoration are so big that I sometimes feel like backing out of the whole matter. And still there is the urge to go on, which apparently can only be checked by your word. Which way will your decision fall? There are many indications that a liturgical movement will be well received in the U.S. in many quarters — and that means going ahead once the start is made. That again means on our part the giving over of a few men to that work. . . ."[11]

At the same time the Reverend William Busch, professor of Church history at the St. Paul Seminary, was also encouraging Abbot Alcuin to undertake the work that Father Virgil was advocating. Father Busch, brother of the bishop of St. Cloud, was a leader among the little band of pioneers who endeavored to organize a liturgical awakening in the United States. Father Busch had pleaded during 1925 for a return to a liturgical consciousness as the reservoir of Christian spirituality in the columns of two national Catholic weeklies, the *Commonweal* and *America,* as well as at the annual convention of the National Catholic Educational Association at Pittsburgh. He had read the works of such European theologians as Abbot Prosper Gueranger, Johannes Moehler, Josef Scheeben, Josef Kramp, S.J., Romano Guardini, and Dom Gerard van Galoen of Maredsous. The popularizing efforts of the *Ecclesia Orans* series emanating from Maria Laach was also an inspiration to him.

Another pioneer in liturgical work in the United States was the Reverend Martin Hellriegel, chaplain to the Sisters of the Most Precious Blood in O'Fallon, Missouri. Together with the Reverend Anthony Jasper, pastor of the local church there, he was striving through articles, a pamphlet, and experiments with the dialogue Mass to begin a revival.

266

The Reverend Leo F. Miller, professor of theology at the Pontifical College Josephinum, was also a pioneer, and with Father Busch prepared translations of Kramp's *Eucharistia* and *Opfergedanke und Messliturgie.* The Jesuit scholastic, Gerald Ellard, also began writing letters on the liturgy to the editor of *America* in 1925, and visited liturgical centers in Europe in 1927.

Two American Benedictines had been working to arouse interest in an American liturgical apostolate. The Reverend Bede Maler, O.S.B., of St. Meinrad Abbey, had labored for over thirty years through the columns of his Eucharistic monthly, *Paradiesesfruechte,* earlier called *St. Benedikts-Panier,* for an increase of liturgical piety, but was unable to exert any influence on his successors as editors, as he informed Abbot Alcuin. Dom Augustine Walsh, one of the founders of St. Anselm's Priory in Washington, was the other Benedictine who had called for such a movement in 1924, and was even about to formulate plans for an organized effort when he heard of St. John's intentions. He then withdrew from the field, while promising to collaborate in the common endeavor.

These seven priests were, accordingly, working as early as, if not before, Abbot Alcuin and Father Virgil began the organized liturgical movement in the United States. They not only supplied invaluable assistance and support throughout the formative years, but as firm friends joined in the common venture.[12]

Abbot Alcuin was receptive to these urgings because he saw in the projected undertaking a further means of deepening Benedictine spirit in the abbey at Collegeville. He had been influenced by the Beuronese monk-brothers, Pius and Hildebrand Bihlmeyer, Dom Ursmer Berlière and Germain Morin of Maredsous. He had met Dom Columba Marmion of Maredsous during his years in Europe, as well as Aidan Cardinal Gasquet and Abbot Cuthbert Butler of Downside, and was a classmate at Sant' Anselmo of two monks who were now the abbots of Maria Laach and Saint André, Ildefons Herwegen and Theodore Nève. He had been giving liturgical homilies to his clerics and was now ready to inaugurate in the United States what these European Benedictines were developing. Father Virgil returned to Collegeville in the autumn of 1925 as a carrier of an ancient Christian deposit which was stirring the spirit of modern man. Father Hans A. Reinhold wrote of his arrival:

"It is almost beyond human comprehension to grasp the completeness with which he absorbed everything that Austria, Belgium, and Germany had to offer. But greater yet was what he did with it. Instead of dragging his find across the border as an exotic museum piece, he made it as American as only an American mind can make it. He had seen the high sweep of German ecclesiology and sacramentalism; he had admired the Belgians for their clear grasp of a new spirituality and their critical awareness of all that stood in the way of liturgical, ecclesiastical piety from traditional carry-overs; he had learned in Austria what the common people could gather from the Church's treasures without fright, but he did not come back to force these foreign and incoherent moulds on the American Church. Besides, his clear realism and his burning apostle's heart had one urge none of the great masters in Europe seemed to see; the connection of social justice with a new social spirituality. For Virgil Michel the labor encyclicals of Leo XIII and the liturgical reforms of Pius X did not just by accident happen within one generation, but were responses to cries of the masses for Christ, who had power and gave the good tidings. They belonged together." [13]

No Task Refused

In one busy year from the fall of 1925 until the fall of 1926, Father Virgil, with an energy which would become legendary, prepared to launch the American liturgical movement under a twofold program. A monthly review, to be called *Orate Fratres,* was to be issued from Collegeville with himself as editor and a board of associates representing the broadest possible collaboration from the English-speaking world. Secondly, a 'Popular Liturgical Library,' consisting of pamphlets and paperback booklets, was to be inaugurated by a Liturgical Press. Since there was no tradition of publishing or printing at St. John's, the amount of study, planning and contact accomplished in these months is worthy of a separate study in itself. Father Virgil's capacity to enlist and release the energies of all around him was at once apparent. St. John's entered upon a period of vitality, creativity and live ideas which aroused an imaginative response on the part of the community reminiscent of the days of Abbot Alexius' ventures of the 1870's and 1880's. Several of the monks actively joined in the movement; translations were undertaken; open discussions of liturgy and its role in the life of the Church were held; monks in the abbey's parishes were encouraged to work with their people; clerics entered into the new field of study with energy. Those members of the community who collaborated with him most actively through the years included Fathers Cuthbert Goeb, Rembert Bularzik, Basil Stegmann, Ermin Vitry, Dunstan Tucker, Roger Schoenbechler, Godfrey Diekmann and Paschal Botz.

While leaflets, brochures and circulars were being prepared to explain the liturgical apostolate, and announce the 'Popular Liturgical Library,' and *Orate Fratres,* arrangements were made with the abbey's good friend Joseph Matt of the Wanderer Publishing Company in St. Paul for major publishing undertakings. Piece work and smaller jobs were to be done in Collegeville, although in later years some larger works were done at the home printshop. Father Virgil and Father Louis Traufler, pastor of the abbey's parish of St. Benedict in New York, jointly prepared the first pamphlet entitled *Why the Mass.* In quick succession Michel's translations of Dom Lambert Beauduin's and Abbot Emmanuel Caronti's works on liturgical principles appeared under the titles of *Liturgy, the Life of the Church* and *The Spirit of the Liturgy*. Father Cuthbert Goeb drew up a lay *Ordo* and published a pamphlet called *Offeramus*, a dialog Mass booklet with explanations which was spread across the country as one of the first means of developing active participation by Catholic congregations in the Sacrifice of the Mass. Father Alexius Hoffmann prepared a *Liturgical Dictionary*, and entered with relish into this new undertaking which had come to his beloved St. John's. His long years of teaching dogmatic theology and recording the chronology of the institution had never embraced such literary production as he now witnessed, although he had for years labored alone in his own way and ardently desired such a development.

These were the first publications on the liturgy emanating from Collegeville, the first in a long series which continue to the present day in increasing number. Father Virgil and his collaborators were determined that they would be printed as artistically as possible, and began the tradition of preparing all publications according to distinctive standards of liturgical and sacred art as a hallmark of the Liturgical Press.

Simultaneously Father Virgil was organizing his staff of associate editors and trying to contact possible collaborators for the liturgical review, *Orate Fratres*. He was determined to begin on as broad a basis as possible, not to stigmatize the American liturgical endeavor, as had happened too often in Europe, with a predominant monastic or Benedictine flavor. He hoped to include all clergy, religious and laity who were interested. He evidenced his practicality and common sense in determining to steer clear of highly technical and narrowly scientific dogmatic and liturgical controversies which had likewise plagued European developments. Since Father Virgil was not a professional theologian he could scarcely at any rate have directed such a professional magazine. Through private study and natural zeal he had come in contact with the European liturgical movement, and now was going to attempt a positive and popular explanation in journalistic form. The Reverend Leo R. Ward, C.S.C., of Notre Dame University declared that he knew of no one who had more intellectual courage and enterprise.[14] Father Virgil, despite his wide reading and exhaustive study, was not a profound scholar. He produced no original research study based on primary sources in his short and overcrowded life. He was primarily a synthesizer who read all available literature on a topic and then created, sometimes hastily, essays from these varied sources. Perhaps his journalistic bent was one of the main reasons he so successfully chartered the original course of the American liturgical movement. He avoided negative and sterile criticisms of existing Catholic pious practices, archaic or dilettante hobbies of enthusiasts, or literal insistence on a return to the past without recognition of legitimate historical development and present needs of the Church.

Father Virgil carefully invited collaboration for the delicate undertaking.[15] He prepared a foreword or statement of principles for the first issue of *Orate Fratres* on 28 November 1926 which because of its vision and key importance to the whole effort is included in Appendix VII.[16] The cover design was executed by the English Catholic artist Eric Gill, and the first issue was mailed to 800 subscribers who were mostly from the midwest and western sections of the country. The subscription list was doubled after seven numbers, and by the end of the first year the magazine had circled the globe.[17] During the first years requests for the magazine and Liturgical Press publications came in from over thirty countries. Gross volume was never large, however, and thirty years later the magazine has not attained a circulation of 10,000, with its average total for the period being much closer to 5,000. The *Catholic Journalist* commented on this development on the occasion of the magazine's twenty-fifth anniversary:

"In proportion to its circulation no Catholic magazine ever exerted so great an influence on American Catholic life. And it's true that you can trace the remarkable growth of the liturgical movement in the United States directly to the editorial leadership of *Orate Fratres*. The efforts of the late Fr. Virgil Michel, O.S.B., and of the present editor, Fr. Godfrey Diekmann, O.S.B., prove that it's sometimes possible to do a great work for the Church with a miserably small circulation." [18]

The laity often evidenced almost as much interest in the movement as the clergy. During the year 1954, for example, the magazine's circulation was divided as follows: clergy, 38.8% ; laity, 26.72% ; institutions, 22% ; nuns, 11.6% ; and publications, .88%.[19] One of the most pleasant and encouraging experiences through the years was the amount of steadily increasing interest in all publications of the Press on the part of Protestant ministers, seminarians and publishing houses. The possibility emerged of the liturgy forming a bridge, as it had already become in such countries as Germany, between American Catholics and their separated brethren of the Christian community. The Baltimore *Catholic Review* as early as 1930 took editorial notice of the missionizing possibilities of the liturgy and observed:

"For this progress much credit is due the Benedictine Fathers. The world over they are teaching a love of the Mass, the love of sacred music and an appreciation of religious art and architecture.

"If all of us could catch the enthusiasm of the Benedictines in making known the meaning of the Mass, of making liturgical music appreciated by revealing its beautiful lessons, of arousing a greater appreciation in artistic statuary and captivating architecture, the Catholic Church would be more admired and appreciated by our non-Catholic

No Task Refused

270

friends. Admiration and appreciation, you know, often lead to investigation, and investigation often leads to Truth. Indeed, the liturgical movement, as fostered by the Benedictines, is opening to tens of thousands of our Catholics vistas of which they had not known before." [20]

*Orate
Fratres*

Pierre Pourrat likewise declared in his monumental *Christian Spirituality*:

"Catholic theology in modern times has been largely a work of reaction. It had to combat heresy refusing to lay down its arms. It constantly defines its doctrines in opposition to Lutheran and Calvinistic errors. An analogous tendency is manifested in the sphere of spirituality. The faithful have to be put on their guard against Luther's quietism, and against illuminism and private inspiration. In this direction the reaction, perhaps, went too far." [21]

With a liturgical revival stirring through the Catholic world the unknown beauties and truths of a worshipping Christian community could be unfolded, the whole area of controversy emanating from the sixteenth century by-passed, and a way opened for an orthodox return to the primary fonts of Christian living. The subjectivism and individualism which had dominated modern piety could thus be subordinated. St. Pius X was the first pope in modern times to invite the Christian world to return to traditional Christian piety when he said that if the people were well-instructed and celebrated the feasts of the Church in the spirit intended by the Church, there would be a notable revival in faith, piety and religious instruction: the entire life of the Christian would thereby become better and stronger, for the liturgy is the fountainhead of Christian life.[22] Abbot Alcuin grasped this vision from the beginning and often stated that the very term 'liturgical movement' was in many ways not a happy one. He wanted to call it a return to the full Christian life of the ages of faith, with liturgical ideals incorporated into the regular organizations and life of the Church. To a priest who criticized an article in the *Oblate* as 'unliturgical,' because it had stated that the laity need not pray all the prayers of the Missal as they are primarily for the celebrant, Abbot Alcuin replied:

"I submit that the great purpose of the Liturgical Movement is to teach us Christian living, life in and with Christ, and not primarily to have us use the Missal. . . . The trouble with you, my dear Father, as with some of my older men is that you have not yet caught the true spirit of the Liturgical Movement. You try to popularize the use of the Missal and you quite forget that, unless you teach the people to penetrate into its inner spirit, you are merely getting the people to substitute one form of prayer for another, and that, in the course of time, they will tire also of this new form. And they surely will, if you do not lead them gradually into a deeper meditative understanding of its text and spirit. But this is impossible if you want to urge them to say all the prayers, especially with a rapid fire priest." [23]

The veteran missionary Henry Borgmann, C.Ss.R., wrote in to congratulate Abbot Alcuin on the fact that "the great Order of monks which throughout the history of the Church stood for liturgy, has presented our country with a review dedicated to the great cause of liturgy." He was also enthusiastically advancing the idea that the opportunity must now be seized of reorientating Christian instruction along traditional lines of Bible, liturgy, and catechism, and added:

No Task Refused

"The liturgical movement will get nowhere with conventions, associations, reviews, academies, etc., etc. Those things do not reach the kitchens where real movements centre. The lower strata, the man in the street, the *hoi polloi*, the common people must be reached. They can be reached through the children in our schools and Sunday schools. Children are the levers of society and once we get the liturgical movement into the lives of the children, then we have scored success en masse." [24]

To which Abbot Alcuin replied:

"What a glorious period on which the Church is now entering! This is bound to come if the children are fed on Liturgy, the Bible and the Catechism. No doubt at all: you are right; it is the only reasonable way. But, as you fear, it is going to take some time to put it over. Yet perhaps not so long a time! The Spirit of God has evidently breathed over the country and on all sides there is a stirring of dry bones." [25]

These two correspondents were typical of the large number of people who began after 1926 to write to Collegeville as one focal point for liturgical ideas and their implications. The majority supplied helpful suggestions, but as always with new movements there were persons with fixed ideas, fringe elements with extremist tendencies who rushed into the endeavor anxious to advance their personal cure-alls for the solution of religious and social ills. Both Abbot Alcuin and Father Virgil were determined to keep such extremists at arm's length, not allow them to use the magazine as a vehicle, nor to mark the liturgical effort as a suspect undertaking. There was enough misunderstanding on the part of priests who confused liturgy and rubrics, and of antiquarians who reveled in Gothic vestments or table altars for purely aesthetic reasons. J. J. Murphy records that a priest from the eastern section of the country had termed the liturgical conference "a meeting of a bunch of Germans out in the Midwest," while the author of a story of the Sisters of St. Joseph in St. Paul characterizes the attitude of Sister Antonia McHugh, president of the College of St. Catherine, on liturgical efforts:

"The Liturgical Movement centered at St. John's, which aimed to diffuse social charity and understanding through increased lay participation in the official worship of the church, was something with which

272

Sister Antonia would have nothing to do. 'Why, I have been in all the churches in Rome,' she would say, 'and I never heard a Missa Recitata. What is good enough for the pope is good enough for me.' The Psalms were beautiful poetry and she taught them vigorously, but the thought of connecting the Psalms with the Divine Office for socially activated prayers was too irritating to be considered. To her mind the whole commotion was doubtless of German origin, reminiscent of Cahensly-ism. She accorded little consideration to the Gregorian Chant, whatever Pius X had to say. Polyphony was prettier and better suited to women's voices." [26]

The most pressing duty of Christians, as Pius XII would later declare in *Mediator Dei*, is to live the liturgical life. With prudence and obedience to the directives of the highest authority of the Church the pioneers in the liturgical movement aimed at broadening its scope from intelligent and congregational participation in worship to include a return to the sources, the Bible and the Fathers, a revival of dogmatic preaching, catechesis and pastoral methods based on the reality of each parish as a miniature Mystical Body.[27] Abbot Alcuin's close friend and Roman classmate, the eminent liturgist-abbot of Maria Laach, encouraged and advised him in this spirit: "I wish you success with all my heart for the initiative which your abbey has undertaken for the liturgy in the United States. You will experience that you will have to have much patience due to a lack of understanding. But good will emerge, and the result for the Church of Christ will not be without significance." [28]

Fifteen bishops wrote in supporting the undertaking in its initial stages. Bishop Busch, the local bishop, called it a 'meritorious undertaking' and declared:

"I hope all our priests will soon be inoculated with the new interest in the liturgy, and I am happy to know that our seminarians are privileged to live in this atmosphere, as they no doubt will of necessity absorb enough to influence their entire life, to their own as well as the advantage of those to whom they will be called to minister." [29]

The metropolitan, Archbishop Austin Dowling, wished the movement the full measure of success, as did Bishop John Cantwell of Los Angeles and San Diego who asked for a Benedictine in 1929 to teach Gregorian chant to parish choirs and in parochial schools throughout his diocese. Archbishop John Glennon of St. Louis declared: "We welcome with all our heart a liturgical movement." Two other midwestern bishops were firm supporters from the very beginning. Bishop Joseph Schlarmann of Peoria identified himself with the movement, wrote articles, made his retreat in 1934 at St. John's and declared the abbey's "splendid work in the liturgical line has a special attraction for me." Bishop Joseph Schrembs of Cleveland likewise lent his support because he felt, as he told Father Bede Maler:

273

"The faithful must be brought into a living participation with the liturgy of the Church, to which today, as a matter of fact, they are practically strangers.

"The trouble with the faithful today is that they know nothing of the liturgical life of the Church and their public participation is practically limited to the recitation of the Rosary and the singing of a few hymns like 'Mother Dear Oh Pray for Me,' or 'On This Day,' and the like. . . . St. John's Abbey in Minnesota stands out head and shoulders over all the others in this matter." [30]

On a trip to Rome in 1929 Abbot Alcuin presented the first three volumes of *Orate Fratres* to Pope Pius XI as a gift and a testimonial of devotion on behalf of all engaged in the liturgical apostolate. On 21 November 1929 he received a most welcome letter from Pietro Cardinal Gasparri, Secretary of State:

"The Holy Father is greatly pleased that St. John's Abbey is continuing the glorious Benedictine tradition, and that there is emanating from this abbey an inspiration that tends to elevate the piety of the faithful by leading it back to the pure fountains of the sacred liturgy.

"Wishing the movement a most abundant harvest of fruit, the Sovereign Pontiff is thankful for the expression of homage, and imparts to you, Right Reverend Father, and to all who collaborate with you in the publication of the review, the Apostolic Blessing." [31]

Encouraged by these approvals Father Virgil and his associates pushed ahead with the difficult task of furthering the liturgical apostolate. Liturgical retreats were given to diocesan clergy, religious communities of men and women, seminarians and lay groups throughout the country. Parish choirs were assisted and trained, and liturgical missions given in parishes. Abbot Alcuin listed twenty members of the community who participated in these activities at varying times in the 1930's. Religious communities of Sisters and Brothers were assisted in improving their recitation of the Divine Office and a liturgical calendar was prepared yearly for the Brown and Bigelow Company of St. Paul which has enjoyed wide distribution. Abbot Alcuin himself spoke on the liturgy at national meetings such as the Priests' Eucharistic Convention at Buffalo in 1927, and at both the New Orleans and St. Paul National Eucharistic Congresses in 1938 and 1940. St. John's was asked to direct programs of diocesan teachers' institutes, and as an example of the growth of the movement, one of the monks, Father Dominic Keller, was invited to conduct classes in Gregorian chant at the University of Minnesota in the summers of 1946 and 1947. The works published, the sacrifices and generous cooperation in the common effort by St. John's many friends form a stirring chapter in the history of American Catholicism which is receiving full and separate treatment by Father Paul Marx, O.S.B. Its details are beyond the scope of a general history of St. John's.

274

Father Virgil continued writing letters, initiating projects, lecturing across the country, receiving visitors, while at the same time acting as prefect of clerics from 1927 to 1929 and teaching seminary philosophy and college religion. In the summer of 1929 the first liturgical summer school was held at St. John's from June 24 to August 13 with seventy-five in attendance. On July 25 a National Liturgical Day was held for four hundred people. The project was not deemed successful enough to make it an annual event, however, and was discontinued.

Father Virgil had been moving at a feverish pace for five years when in 1930 his eyes and nerves gave out and he suffered a near nervous collapse in April of that year. This apostle of the liturgy was ordered by his doctor not to offer Holy Mass for two months nor to pray the Divine Office for two years. Abbot Alcuin sent him first to Cass Lake and then to White Earth to regain his health while working among the Indians on St. John's missions in northern Minnesota. Michel loved this work and entered into it with a zest he had evidenced for every Christian activity during his life. In 1933 he was recalled to St. John's to assume the deanship of the college since Father Mark Braun had been appointed the abbot of St. Gregory's Abbey in Oklahoma, and Father Virgil's name and ability were needed to help that division of the abbey's educational activity.

Upon his return he was at once back in the center of an ever-broadening field of activity. In 1935 he resumed the editorship of *Orate Fratres,* which had been continued by Father Joseph Kreuter, O.S.B., in his absence. He then began to write and lecture more and more on the social implications of a liturgical consciousness. Father Virgil's approach was that of a social philosopher, not of an empirical sociologist. The American depression of 1929 with its accompanying disillusionment brought forth ideas and plans throughout the nation for a new social order. Father Virgil's social suggestions were in this spirit experimental. His main concern, however, was to advance the principles found in the encyclicals of Popes Leo XIII and Pius XI. Michel stressed the necessity of Christian social action and the liturgical movement mutually stimulating one another. He constantly maintained that the Mystical Body of Christ is the true basis of Christian solidarity, and that a renewal of the 'true Christian spirit' must be a prerequisite of social justice. With this in view he organized a stimulating seminar in the college on Catholic backgrounds and current social theory in which the cooperative order, distributist-agrarian movement, money, and Marxian theories were analyzed.

With the encouragement of Joseph Matt and his son Alphonse, '22, of St. Paul, the Minnesota Branch of the Catholic Central Verein offered to cooperate in 1935 in sponsoring an Institute for Social Studies at St. John's. For six years this early Catholic adult education program was conducted on weekends for members of the Central

Verein, and after 1936 was incorporated also in the Catholic Action program of the St. Cloud diocese. Under the title, *The Social Problem*, series of lectures were printed in four paperbacks from 1936 to 1938 and sponsored as study-club material by the Central Verein, St. Cloud diocesan Catholic Action program, and the Young People's Social Guild of the archdiocese of St. Paul. Just as members of the community responded to the first liturgical effort ten years previous, now a group of younger monks and lay professors cooperated with Father Virgil in applying principles of Christian social teaching to modern problems.

Several individuals came to Collegeville to discuss the implications of these ideas, to address the student body, and to integrate the ideals of the liturgical apostolate in the movements they were advancing. Peter Maurin and Dorothy Day of the Catholic Worker Movement were visitors, and as the editor of their newspaper, the *Catholic Worker*, informed Abbot Alcuin:

"We have been trying from the start of our work to link up the liturgy with the Church's social doctrine, realizing the doctrine of the Mystical Body of Christ is at the root of both. . . . We have included in our Catholic Workers' School several courses in the liturgy, emphasizing its social implications. As Father Busch wrote us recently, we need a union of the forces between the liturgists and sociologists for the sake of both." [32]

The Baroness Catherine de Hueck likewise came and lectured. When she was looking for Catholic colleges in 1939 to enroll her first two Negro boys and girls from Friendship House in Harlem, St. John's and St. Benedict's welcomed them. Among others who came were A. B. McDonald and Father M. M. Coady of the Nova Scotia cooperative movement, along with Ralph Borsodi, the advocate of family living from Suffern, N. Y.; the artists Graham Carey, Ade Bethune and Maurice Lavanoux of the Liturgical Arts Society; the sociologist Eva Ross of Trinity College, Washington; and the philosopher Mortimer Adler of the University of Chicago. All of these people were working in their several ways to find a solution to the crisis of Western Civilization during the worried 1930's as economic collapse, totalitarianism, and Communism prepared the way for World War II. The emergence of this thinking and searching for a Christian synthesis among the Catholics involved was a welcome manifestation of the coming of age of Catholicism in the United States. Although some of the movements these people championed have been attacked as visionary and transitional in character, yet they had imagination and a vitality which was a living refutation of the assertion so often made in the previous three centuries, that Catholicism had lost contact with the needs of society. It was the privilege of St. John's to be associated with this revival. As a result St. John's in turn found that its influence, which for two-thirds of its first century had been regional in character, was now joined with contemporary endeavors on a national scale. Edward Skillin, Jr., editor of the *Commonweal*, expressed his opinion of this development when he told Abbot Alcuin:

"In a day when the great mass of American Catholics are in appalling ignorance of their religion and its fullness, unaware of the real dangers of Communism . . . you are holding up to our gaze the riches, the deeps, the inspiration to be found by the laity in the Mass and the Divine Office — making asceticism no longer dread. . . .

"When young people are thrown into contact with the Liturgy, as they do in such rare churches as Our Lady of Mercy at Whippany with Rev. Cornelius Clifford, they are fascinated. And if they were only presented with truths of the Liturgy Sunday in and Sunday out, and if the Mass were said slowly and distinctly etc., they would gradually build up a Catholic viewpoint, and then they would see all shortcomings in their proper light. The earthen-vessel concept will be real to them.

"For these reasons and because the priests that are coming out of the seminaries now are Liturgically minded due to your influence and because of your attitude on the social question and the general impressions of your excellent work of various kinds, from my vantage point I believe you are the greatest hope in the United States today for the Church. . . .

"There seems to be so few places where Catholics are aware of their responsibilities and their opportunities but St. John's gives me the strong impression that I am in a place where in large part people know where they are going and how to get there." [33]

It was the special gift of Father Virgil Michel to attract people to the cause. Although he was not a dynamic speaker, and his writings were from the very first and repeatedly criticized for their dryness and laborious periods, whatever he undertook attracted dedicated listeners. Then, in the late fall of 1938, before the community or his legion of friends could realize what had happened, he died suddenly in his forty-eighth year after thirteen short years of liturgical endeavor. While shaving one morning he had cut his lower lip, and this instead of healing developed into a carbuncle. Often in his younger years he had suffered from repeated boils on the neck. On November 19 he went to the local infirmary where his condition, aggravated by his rundown physical state, became serious after pneumonia and a streptococcus infection of the throat developed. Since it was before the days of the discovery of penicillin, only sulfanilamide was available. He was prepared for death by his confrere and co-laborer Father Joseph Kreuter, and early on the morning of November 26 he died with complete resignation to God's will. His bodily remains were interred at the end of one of the long white line of graves in the abbey cemetery. It took Abbot Alcuin months to acknowledge the letters of condolence. Abbot Martin Veth of St. Benedict's Abbey, for example, told Abbot Alcuin:

"I can't get over the death of Father Virgil. Although I could not warm up to his style in the beginning, I liked his later writings, especially his 'Timely Tracts' in the *Orate Fratres*. . . . More of our Fathers ought to dig in, as he did, and produce something. His death is a loss for the Order in the United States. But God knows best: His will be done!" [34]

At his weekly conference to the community on the afternoon before Father Virgil died, Abbot Alcuin talked about his approaching death and stated:

"I saw Father Virgil this afternoon and he asked me to request pardon from the community for anything that he might have done in his life. As you all know, Father Virgil and I could not see eye to eye on many things. But I wish to state here that after the difficulties were over he never bore a grudge and was always respectful to superiors. If there is any one characteristic of his life which stands out it was the way he always made proper use of the time given him in his life; he even would write articles while riding on trains. I recommend him to you as an example in this. Through his writings and his work Father Virgil made this abbey known as no member has ever made it known. Let us all unite in accepting God's pleasure." [35]

It was often expressed in the months following Father Virgil's death that the liturgical movement in America had suffered a serious setback and that it would be impossible to find successors to continue the work. But just as it was not accidental that the organized effort had begun in a region where such pioneers as Archbishop Ireland, his colonizing associates, and the Benedictines had labored to establish Catholic colonies where the full Christian life could be experienced, so now a seedbed had again been implanted. Young monks who had come from families in those parishes had been sent to Europe by Abbot Alcuin at the urging of Father Virgil to study Scripture, theology and liturgy at such places as Rome, Tuebingen and Maria Laach. Father Virgil had broken the ground and assisted in awakening an interest in the liturgy which was beyond the most sanguine hopes of 1925. In the period since his death, especially under the farseeing leadership of Pope Pius XII, major liturgical reforms have been introduced for the universal Church which mark this pontificate as one of the most significant revivals of Christian piety in the history of the Church. In quick succession a new edition of the Psalter based on the original Hebrew has appeared; encyclical letters have been issued on the true nature of Christian life and worship; the celebration of certain sacramental rites has been permitted in vernacular languages; the Eucharistic fast mitigated and Holy Mass allowed to be celebrated in the evening on specified occasions; and most dramatic of all, first the ancient

278

110–114 Brothers Maurus, Clement, Innocent, Hubert, John: at work on their crafts.

115 Brothers of St. John's Abbey: 1956.

L. to R. First Row: Brothers Paul Crone, Conrad Zimmermann, Victor McMahon, John Anderl, Hubert Schneider, Edward Zwak, Gabriel Bieniek. Second row: Brothers James Hugues, Peter Enright, Leo Bettendorf, Gerald Ihrig, Boniface Selander, Matthew Holiday. Third row: Brothers Martin Rath, Aloysius Davis, Maurus Luchy, Alcuin Weinand, Urban Pieper, Otto Thole, Sylvester Kinney. Fourth row: Brothers Gerard Wojchowski, Kevin Brush, Bonaventure Watson, Felix Neussendorfer. Fifth row: Brothers Anthony Lucking, Samuel Lickteig, Meinrad Burnett, Gregory Eibensteiner. Sixth row: Master of Brothers Father Paschal Botz, Brothers Ronald O'Donnell, Jude Kish, Anselm Bawek, Henry Daverveld, Ansgar Niess, Francis Peters, Pius Ethen, Augustine Keel, Paschal Brisson, Leslie Kartes.

116 *"That he who is today made abbot, by the imposition of our hands": blessing of St. John's sixth abbot, Baldwin Dworschak.*

117 *Ordinations to the priesthood in the abbey church.*

118 Coach Joe Benda, with St. John's athletes,
Vedie Himsl, '38, and Charles Carlin, '38.

119 Ted Schreiner of the Porter's Office.

120 St. John's first experience with military life.

121 World War II: Air Force Cadets march at Collegeville.

122 *Ground breaking ceremony: Bishop Peter Bartholome, Prior Baldwin Dworschak, Bishop Joseph Busch, Father Peter Lorsung, '33, Abbot Alcuin Deutsch.*

123 *Bishop Peter Bartholome speaks at seminary cornerstone laying.*

124 *Seminary dedication: Edward Cardinal Mooney presides at Pontifical High Mass celebrated by Bishop Leo Dworschak, '26.*

125 *Overlooking Lake Sagatagan: St. John's Seminary of the Diocese of St. Cloud.*

126 Church of the Holy Name of Jesus, Humacao, Puerto Rico.

127 Puerto Rico: San Jose school.

128 Monasterio San Antonio, Humacao, Puerto Rico.

129 Colegio del Tepeyac, Mexico City.

130 Prior Clarus Graves with Fathers Burton Bloms,
Adrian Fox and lay professors at Tepeyac school.

131 Civilian garb in compliance with Mexican law:
Fathers Placid Reitmeier, Raphael Haller, Edmund Hall, Burton Bloms,
Adrian Fox, Brother Philip Heitkemper, Prior Berthold Ricker.

132 Candidates for the Mexican foundation in 1956.

133 *Benedictine Fathers of St. Maur's:*
Harvey Shepherd, Wendelin Luetmer,
Alexander Korte.

134 *Chanting Divine Office in Shakers'*
'Center House' at St. Maur's Interracial Monaste
South Union, Kentucky.

135 *Air view of St. Maur's*
priory and seminary.

136 *Abbot Baldwin and Tokyo Benedictines.*

137 *Exterior of St. Anselm's Church.*

138 *Interior of St. Anselm's Church.*

139 *Model of exterior: St. Anselm's Parish, Tokyo.*

140 *Archbishop Peter Tatsuo Doi and Father Aloysius Michels,*
laying cornerstone of St. Anselm's.

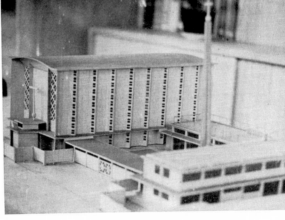

custom of the Easter Vigil was restored, and then in 1956 the ancient observances of Holy Week were restored to parochial life.

At St. John's the liturgical apostolate was continued in magazine and press, with greater emphasis on the dogmatic and scriptural basis of Christian piety. Father Godfrey Diekmann, O.S.B., succeeded Father Virgil as editor of *Orate Fratres,* which after its twenty-fifth anniversary was given the vernacular title of *Worship.* Steadily broadening cooperation of clergy and laity was realized. Several of the monks directed the Liturgical Press through the years, and after 1951, under the management of Father William Heidt, O.S.B., widespread and popular dissemination of liturgical publications was achieved at an accelerated pace.

While the liturgical movement was being launched another undertaking was inaugurated at St. John's as a corollary. When the Feast of Christ the King was introduced by Pope Pius XI during the Holy Year of 1925, Father Joseph Kreuter went to Abbot Alcuin with the idea of publishing a review for the Sisterhoods in the English language which would stress ascetical and interior life. Father Joseph explains his intentions in this matter:

"I realized that Sisters who were working so hard in active, educational, charitable, and domestic works needed more ascetical training. I had been teaching mysticism in the seminary and felt that the world needed more asceticism, the spirit of sacrifice, more interior living and recollection.

"The word, idea and title came from the Feast of Christ the King. I used to give an old German instruction and prayerbook for young ladies, *Die Koenigsbraut,* as spiritual reading material. Then the title of the feast was combined with this book and we got *Sponsa Christi* which we adapted to *Sponsa Regis* because it was Christ the King.

"This movement and the liturgical movement came at the proper time. Religious life in the United States was not as authentic as it could be because there was a little too much worldliness. There was not a tradition of solid spirituality as well as a lack of theological background. It was necessary to arouse religious to deep spirituality. Naturally a person cannot do much in the world without it. The influence of the Sisters on the future is tremendous, and there was a tendency to activism. This was a counteraction to that heresy of the age, namely that the more active you are the better you are. What is needed is solid spiritual living, sacrificial living. This is the real following of Christ. We must be active spiritually. World War I did a great deal and World War II did more to convince modern man of this fact. Priests and religious were in too much activity, and the *Sponsa Regis* movement was to make this action more fruitful. In this way religious and priests could be prepared for what the Holy Spirit has in preparation for them in the future." [36]

Abbot Alcuin granted permission and here again showed his breadth

279

of vision and initiative. The abbey was actively engaged in liturgical work, but the abbot agreed that this ascetical emphasis was also needed. After three years' preparation, Father Joseph in 1929 began with a sixteen page monthly review for Sisters called *Sponsa Regis*. Brother Clement designed the first cover, and writers were slowly obtained from other religious societies of priests and Brothers, as well as Sisters who in this way developed talent for writing. Subscriptions came in rapidly as there were 100,000 Sisters in the United States at that time, and it was not long before the subscriptions totalled 8,000 in forty-five countries. This was a high rate, since orders were in great part for convents, institutions and libraries. The magazine was read in convent refectories and for spiritual reading, and Father Joseph encouraged his subscribers to bind the issues and reread them at stated intervals. All bishops in the country also received the magazine, and Father Joseph often declared that it was one of the most widely read of Catholic magazines besides being the first publication devoted to the interior life of the Sisterhoods in the English-speaking world.[37]

The first aim of the magazine, to point up the ascetical life and bring about a greater degree of union with God, was augmented by a secondary purpose, which was to spread a love and understanding of the liturgy of the Church. Father Joseph insisted that the liturgy was a means to the end of union with God. Through an ascetical life, liturgically orientated, the best possible spiritual background could be offered to the Sister for participation in Pope Pius XI's call for Catholic Action. The *Sponsa Regis* program also had a third aim, an outgrowth of the other two called the Way of Victimhood. It was for those persons who wanted to do more than the ordinary program offered, to follow Christ more closely, through interior life and recollection based on sacrificial living in the spirit of Christ. There were a number of such associations in the Church, one of which was centered in the houses of the Daughters of the Heart of Jesus. Any Sister or person who desired with proper approbation to declare herself a Victim Soul out of love of Christ was enrolled by Father Joseph in the lists at a convent of the Daughters of the Heart of Jesus at Hall near Innsbruck in the Tyrol. These voluntary members were quite unknown to their associates in daily life, and in the period since the American movement was begun through *Sponsa Regis*, the names of over 10,000 generous souls have been sent from St. John's to convent registers of the Daughters of the Heart of Jesus. These unsung and unknown heroic souls are offering their lives in special sacrifice to God for the welfare and conversion of the world.

The German Jesuit, Max Schmid, had issued a manual for such victim souls in Germany in 1920 which was issued in English by Loyola Press in 1933. Father Schmid gave Kreuter permission to publish his own *Guide For Victim Souls* at Benziger Brothers in 1939. It was revised in pamphlet form by Father Paschal Botz in 1951 under the title of *Way of Victimhood in the Sacred Heart*. This literature as well as other ascetical and mystical publications were issued from the Abbey Press for the use of the Sisterhoods. Father Joseph continued directing these activities until 1946 when he spent a year in Germany assisting in postwar charities, and then was appointed pastor of St. John's Church, Meire Grove. He was succeeded by Father Paschal Botz as editor of *Sponsa Regis*.[38]

The editing of two magazines as well as the writing and publishing connected with the Liturgical Press, Victim Soul and Oblate movements initiated Benedictine literary activity at St. John's on a scale unknown before the late 1920's. At first only a limited number of priests participated in these new activities, but a broad base of cooperation was stimulated and encouraged among the clerics and younger members of the community. It was evident that this type of activity, as well as more scholarly research, would occupy a growing number in the future.

The missionary work of the Benedictines in the upper midwest was no longer expanding. The dioceses of the province had developed to the point where an increasing number of diocesan clergy were caring for existing parishes and opening new missions and parishes for the growing Catholic population. The parish activity of St. John's was, accordingly, stabilized around the number of thirty-five in the archdioceses of New York and St. Paul, and the dioceses of St. Cloud, Crookston and Duluth. St. John's continued parochial work in conjunction with St. Cloud diocesan priests among the descendants of the German Catholic pioneers of central Minnesota who had come into the area with the Benedictines. A large percentage of these people remained on their farm lands and developed Stearns County, through thrift and industry, into the largest butter-producing county in the United States. Traditional Catholic life was preserved in these large families of Stearns County, which had become proportionately one of the most Catholic counties in the United States. Foreign visitors to the area often noted this phenomenon.[39] Archbishop John Gregory Murray of St. Paul, in his centennial sermon at St. Mary's Cathedral, St. Cloud, on 7 September 1955, likewise cited the work of clergy and laity in developing "the most Catholic area of any part of the United States," and stated that this zeal and devotion was a challenge to future generations.[40]

Simultaneously the abbey's Indian mission work was continued in the dioceses of Crookston and Duluth, and former missions there were given Benedictines as permanent pastors. Moreover, Abbot Alcuin was always ready to assist any bishop who asked him to supply a priest temporarily. Bishop Aloisius Muench of Fargo expressed his appreciation for this assistance, when he wrote:

"I cannot tell you how grateful I am to you that you helped me out again and again when I was in need. God reward you for it."[41]

Many pastors also began in the 1930's to ask for week-end assistance in their growing parishes from the teaching Benedictines at St. John's, and Abbot Alcuin supplied here as well. The priests went to these parishes on Saturday and returned on Sunday evening. When diocesan priests were called into service as chaplains during World War II, requests for this week-end assistance increased rapidly although St. John's itself had given fourteen chaplains to the services. Nor did requests slacken after the war was over, due to the rapidly increasing Catholic population and the new parishes erected for their spiritual needs throughout the area. At present around thirty of the monks supply in this manner each week end of the year.

In 1933 the interior of the Holy Angels Cathedral, which had been erected by Bishop Seidenbusch, was destroyed by fire, and Bishop Joseph F. Busch of St. Cloud requested St. John's to transfer St. Mary's Church, the mother parish of St. Cloud, to the diocese as its cathedral. A large Romanesque basilica had recently been completed at St. Mary's under the direction of Father Luke Fink, O.S.B., which was well suited to cathedral functions. After prolonged negotiations the Holy See requested the Benedictines in 1934 to withdraw from St. Mary's where they had served since the parish's inception in 1856, and Bishop Busch in turn entrusted the parish of St. Augustine in East St. Cloud to the charge of St. John's.

The main activity of St. John's continued during the last period of the first century to be, as before, its educational effort. At the beginning of Abbot Alcuin's administration some four hundred students were following courses in seminary, college, commercial, and high school departments. The largest department was the high school, but as more public and parochial high schools developed in the region, and the college movement gained momentum, St. John's began to place more emphasis on the development of its college. Unlike many other pioneer institutions St. John's did not abandon its college preparatory school, however, but retains it to the present time with an enrollment of around 250 students. Concentration in the high school department continued to be on a classical and scientific curriculum in preparation for college work. At present over half its students are preparing for the priesthood, while the remaining students, many of whom are sons of alumni and friends of St. John's, are planning professional careers. As a private boarding school, high scholastic standards are maintained as a means of developing the individual capacities of future Catholic leaders. In the academic year 1953, for example, 50 of the 51 graduates from the Prep School entered college. Up until the end of the 1930's the majority of the preparatory school's faculty was composed of Benedictine clerics, but as the community grew it was possible to build up a permanent core-staff of Benedictine priests and laymen.

282

The major educational development at St. John's in the last thirty years has been the emergence of the college department of the school's academic program. Classical and liberal arts programs had been offered since 1857 to both priesthood and lay students, but before the 1920's emphasis was placed on the School of Theology, preparatory and commercial departments. In the nineteenth century the training of priests, and a business and high school education were the primary needs of the Church in the United States. The Catholics who had come to American shores in the great waves of immigration from the 1820's through 1910 struggled to make a living, learn the English language and American customs, and give their children the opportunity of at least a basic education. After World War I, however, a growing number of the Catholic population were in a position to give their sons and daughters a higher education. Catholics then joined in the college movement which mushroomed after the turn of the century and Catholic colleges for men and women multiplied across the country. Abbot Peter in his gradual and careful way had taken some steps to develop the college department at St. John's. When Fathers Mark Braun, Severin Gertken, Virgil Michel, Walter Reger, Matthew Kiess and Damian Baker had returned from graduate training in the 1920's, and Abbot Alcuin had succeeded Abbot Peter as president, much thought and planning was begun toward improving the arts and science programs on the college level. Father Virgil informed a friend at this time:

"As to our condition here, we Benedictines are just emerging out of the days of strenuous pioneer life as missioners, and still have much of the rough-and-ready mentality of the pioneer about us. We are only now beginning to head in other directions; so far the mission work of building up parishes and dioceses drained all our forces." [42]

The main task was to strengthen departments and expand the teaching staff so that senior college work could be offered in all areas of the sciences and humanities. The staff was capable, with experienced personnel in such fields as philosophy, chemistry, biology, astronomy, languages, history, art and architecture, music, mathematics, English, and drama. But deepening was needed in these areas as well as development of economics, and social and political science departments. In the 1920's and early 1930's a constant effort was made to improve the college faculty from community resources. Fathers Mark, Virgil and Walter as deans of the college led in this endeavor. The task was all the more difficult because St. John's had no large endowment fund to draw upon for the hiring of an expanded lay faculty. The contributed services of the Benedictine faculty was the institution's only sure endowment. Since year after year over two-thirds of the student body was being assisted by whole or partial scholarships and grants-in-aid, which were given by St. John's itself, income from contributed services was cancelled. When a committee on education of the Minnesota State Legislature asked for information concerning the state's private liberal arts colleges in the 1930's, Abbot Alcuin pointed up this fact:

"I do not know what I should present for the consideration of the legislative committee regarding our institution except the great fact that for seventy-five years its presidents and faculty have labored without compensation, except lodging, food and clothing for the education of the young men of this state, thousands of whom have received their education entirely gratis or at a minimum cost."[43]

No Task Refused

Abbot Alcuin cooperated to a marked degree in sending young monks to graduate schools in Europe and America for advanced training in college work. But trained faculty members were also needed in theology and philosophy for the major seminary, with no financial aid forthcoming from the dioceses. Then in the late 1920's several of the monks who had received advanced training were sent to other American Benedictine abbeys that St. John's was bolstering or supporting, and three of them, Fathers Severin, Mark and Cuthbert were named abbots of those communities. Soon after this assistance was given, the abbot began six new monastic foundations from St. John's itself which further drained available manpower. Nevertheless, rapid advance was made in developing the college department at St. John's. Invaluable advice and direction was given by members of the Senate Committee on the Relations of the University of Minnesota to Other Institutions of Learning who came to St. John's to inspect departments for accreditation. Among these university professors were Dean Royal R. Shumway, and Professors Martin Ruud, Aubrey Castell and St. John's close friend and advisor, August C. Krey. In 1931 St. John's students from individual departments, beginning with history, philosophy, chemistry, and psychology-education, were accorded unqualified admission to the university's graduate school, and the other departments of the college were recognized in succeeding years.

Abbot Alcuin was not enthusiastic over the need of gaining recognition for St. John's from any source or accrediting agency. He repeatedly stated that he was 'of the old school' in educational theory, and held to definite and traditional views on the subject. He told his monks that he did not want St. John's to become a large school, but a 'model school,' and the institution's reputation would then be self-evident. He had no time for educational fads, premature specialization, the elective system or 'progressive' educational theories in any form. His frame of reference was the Benedictine educational experience of fourteen centuries and the discipline of his own classical-philosophical education of the Roman schools. When, for example, John W. Studebaker, U. S. Commissioner of Education, inquired from him if St. John's was offering appreciation of radio or movies in its teacher training course, he replied unequivocally:

"I beg to state that I think such special courses an unwarranted waste of time and money. If the general education that the future teacher gets does not fit him to give his pupils sufficient education and instruction to appreciate the radio and motion picture, then it is not likely that a special course in appreciation of radio and motion pictures will equip him." [44]

The abbot ever insisted on the protection of local and individual rights in education. He informed his close friend Senator Henrik Shipstead of Minnesota that the elimination of the private schools would spell the gradual elimination of our liberties, and in the same vein told Congressman Harold Knutson of Minnesota's Sixth District: "The indiscriminate higher education of so many who are unable to profit by it has become a menace to the welfare of our country." [45] He felt that any governmental interference or the supervising procedures of an accrediting association would create a 'dictatorship of agencies.' For these reasons he steadfastly refused to seek recognition for St. John's from the North Central Association of Colleges and Secondary Schools. He believed that Catholic colleges which were joining their regional accrediting associations in large numbers were by this move destroying the opportunity of developing a distinctive Catholic educational system in the United States. He even asked Archbishop John McNicholas, O.P., chairman of the executive board of the National Catholic Welfare Conference, to support a move for an effective Catholic educational accrediting association, but the great mapority of Catholic educators did not share his enthusiasm for such an idea. Sister Antonia, president of St. Catherine's College, also disagreed with the abbot's position on joining national accrediting associations, according to the author of *On Good Ground*:

". . . St. John's University at Collegeville, Minnesota, perhaps came in for the least favor; the principal thorn was its complete indifference to the emoluments of accreditation by the North Central Association. This was sheer suicide, she [Sister Antonia] predicted, but somehow St. John's held on as successfully as the other colleges in the same fields and in addition its officers worked out with President Hutchins and Mortimer Adler of the University of Chicago a program integrating philosophy and theology which vitalized their own purposes." [46]

President Lars W. Boe of St. Olaf College, Northfield, a Norwegian-American Lutheran institution with which St. John's has continually enjoyed friendly and understanding relations in the common endeavor of Christian higher education, felt differently about this question. He informed Abbot Alcuin he was pleased that some colleges were growing restive under agency controls, and stated:

"There are some men that I meet that I do not care very much whether I meet them again or not. Others I am drawn to. From the very

285

first acquaintance with you and your institution I have been interested in the work you are doing.

"I think of the hurry and scurry of our day and age. Every group that contributes to the quietness of the spirit is making a real contribution. I think so often of what is said in the 46th Psalm: 'Be still and know that I am God.' I wonder if that is not the message that our day needs, and institutions like yours are a strong exemplification of this thought." [47]

With the advent of World War II the question of belonging to the North Central became critical when St. John's men were not accepted as eligible for commissions in officer training programs because the school did not appear on official lists of recognized accrediting agencies. Fathers Martin Schirber, O.S.B., and Arno Gustin, O.S.B., as dean and registrar of the college, recommended that St. John's join the North Central in order, among other reasons, to obviate this difficulty. Abbot Alcuin told Senator Shipstead:

"I don't want to be tied down by a lot of red tape. I want our school to develop freely and not according to direction from outside and distant agencies. But of course such cases as the one presented to you bring pressure to bear upon us that is hard to resist, if we want to survive. But unfortunately the freedom of individual initiative which we used to boast of, is vanishing more and more from our country.[48]

Application for admission of St. John's was, accordingly, made to the North Central Association in 1948, and the institution was accepted in 1949. The fears of former years were proved groundless since the association, according to its present policy, actually encouraged institutional development along characteristic lines as the best means possible of realizing its potential. At the same time certain minimum educational requirements were safeguarded through membership.

Abbot Alcuin was personally interested in the school, as he repeatedly stated, and desired in his characteristic way to supervise all of its activities. With this in mind he changed the administrative organization of the university in 1925. The office of rector or vice-president, which had been in existence for sixty-eight years, was eliminated, and three deans, of the seminary, college and high school, were made responsible to the abbot as president. But the school continued to grow while the abbot became more and more occupied with large-scale commitments in the Benedictine world. As early as 1932 he admitted that his "great personal interest in the school is almost submerged by other interests, the care of which I cannot throw upon others as I can the school. Briefly, my life has been an exceedingly busy one." [49] He found it difficult to keep abreast of educational developments, although he spent much of his available reading time in studying educational publications. He never lost his interest in new and exploratory ideas, and was ever enthusiastic in supporting a program which might open challenging possibilities in Catholic education. His main interests, to say the least, were not in natural sciences or social sciences.[50] Classical, philosophical and theological questions occupied his attention. For this reason, perhaps, he was more receptive to sending young Benedictines for study in philosophy, theology, patristics, liturgy, Church history and Christian archeology. After he had read one of Abbot Herwegen's books he congratulated his old friend and stated again how much he wished he too could study:

Research and Writing

"I think about the time when we were together at Sant' Anselmo. I dream of our former literary work. But that is far from things as they are now and the years have flown by in other works. I cannot consider such a possibility. But as God wills."[51]

Abbot Alcuin respected high standards of scholarship, and on 7 July 1934 told F. J. Lang, who sought his advice concerning a proposed book on Church history: "Publish the absolute truth, regardless of any and all considerations." The Redemptorist, Father Henry Borgmann, told him that the American Benedictines were long overdue in producing some studies of their history, and the abbot replied:

"You are quite right. We American Benedictines have been neglectful of our own history. Some of the neglect may be due to a sort of traditional reluctance on the part of the monks to blow their own horn. But some of it is due to other causes, connected mainly with our condition as pioneers. I am happy to say that these conditions are gradually disappearing, and that there is a growing interest in our history. With a little more leisure, which will come in the course of time, I think we American Benedictines too shall be coming forward with some story of monasticism. Of course, you and I may not live long enough to taste the fruit of such work."[52]

In this spirit he encouraged his monks to do research and write, and the surprising development was that a number of them did find time to do so in the midst of increasing teaching and administrative schedules in an enlarging school. The tradition of research and writing, so integral to European Benedictines, which had been planted by such St. John's pioneers as Fathers Michael Ott, Alexius Hoffmann and John Katzner, was nurtured during these years. The issuing of two monthly magazines involved several members of the community in original writing and editing responsibilities, while the publications of the Liturgical Press brought forth a constant stream of pamphlets and books, both translated and original, on liturgical, ascetical, Benedictine and Gregorian chant subjects. Faculty members, both religious and lay, wrote studies and textbooks during this period in the fields of library science, canon law, modern languages, sociology, philosophy, education, history and religious education. Translations have been made of scriptural, classical and Benedictine literature. The tradition of scientific experimentation inaugurated in the nineteenth century was continued. An agricultural experimental station has been in operation for sixteen years, and studies made on use of fertilizers, temperature and sunshine averages. Relative yields of corn, alfalfa, legumes, and hay have also been evaluated and recorded.[53]

St. John's was repeatedly requested to expand into organized agricultural work along the lines of this experimental station. Bishop Peter Bartholome, Monsignor Luigi Ligutti and other members of the National Catholic Rural Life Conference thought of Collegeville as a possible center for an agricultural school. Bishop James E. Walsh, M.M., vicar-general of Maryknoll, asked for the establishment of a school where future missionaries could be trained in agricultural sciences. Abbot Alcuin favored the idea, as did several members of the hierarchy. St. John's attention to college preparatory and liberal arts programs in the center of the large Catholic rural population of central Minnesota did not meet the pressing needs of these people for more formal education combined with agricultural science, even as a part time winter program. The ever increasing demands in existing educational departments as well as lack of personnel and funds prohibited any development along these lines. However, when the National Catholic Rural Life Movement developed in the 1930's under the leadership of Bishops Edwin O'Hara of Kansas City, Aloisius Muench of Fargo, Vincent Ryan of Bismarck, William T. Mulloy of Covington, Monsignor Luigi Ligutti, and Father James Byrnes of St. Paul, several Benedictines took an active part in its programs. The first rural life summer school for priests and leaders was held at St. John's in 1939. Father Martin Schirber, O.S.B., of St. John's, assumed directorship of these schools, and sessions were held throughout the country in the 1940's. At St. John's rural life schools were held from 1941 to 1944, in 1946 and 1953. Agricultural leaders from the fields of government, education and state agencies participated, and the sessions served as a rallying point for all groups concerned with rural problems.[54]

At different times during these years Abbot Alcuin gave consideration to new educational programs. One of these programs was the opening of a school at St. John's for the training of church musicians and choir directors because, as he said, so few Catholic musicians had any training in Gregorian chant or found themselves capable of handling music according to the mind of the Church. Although a program was not developed for the yearly academic course, the Gregorian Institute of America, under its director Clifford A. Bennett, began summer schools of liturgical music at St. John's in 1949. In 1955 the schools were continued under the direction of St. John's University.

288

A second educational experiment was the entrance of the Benedictines of St. John's into Newman Club work. As early as 1928 the Federation of Catholic College Clubs had asked St. John's to supply teaching materials on the Mass and liturgy in Newman Clubs during that year. When the abbey's friend, Bishop Joseph Schlarmann of Peoria, asked Abbot Alcuin in 1939 to take over the Newman Club on the campus of the University of Illinois, he accepted and sent Fathers Roger Schoenbechler, O.S.B., Gerald McMahon, O.S.B., and two younger monks who could assist there while taking graduate degrees in the university. At Champaign they had charge of the large St. John's Chapel as well as Newman Hall, a residence building for 324 Catholic men students which their predecessor, Father John A. O'Brien, had erected. Under Father Roger's direction a distinctive religious education program was worked out along lines of the liturgical revival. In the same way as Benedictines in Germany were teaching courses and directing Catholic students at state universities, an opportunity was now offered for American Benedictines to contact the growing number of young Catholics who either could not afford it or were unable to find room in Catholic colleges. At Illinois University, for example, the four Fathers were able to work among 1,400 Catholic youths and deepen their appreciation of the truths and worshipping life of the Church, while at St. John's less than half that number were enrolled. During this period American Catholic leaders began to recognize more fully that existing Catholic colleges could not alone care for youths seeking education, and came to accept the fact that large numbers were attending and would continue to attend the private and state universities of the land.

Not only were the religion courses taught at Newman Hall accepted for credit by the university, but Father Roger was also able to have courses in scholastic philosophy granted academic recognition. Newman Hall was ranked as a private institution of higher religious education accredited to the University of Illinois. Lectures on liturgical art, music, as well as medical, legal, and business ethics were given; inquiry classes were regularly conducted; a choir was trained in Gregorian chant, and High Mass was broadcast on Sunday over the university's radio station. Full participation in the *Missa recitata* and parts of the Divine Office was encouraged. An All-Catholic Boys Cooperative House was formed under the title of Urban House and approved by the university.

In 1943 when the armed forces wished to take over Newman Hall for training purposes, Abbot Alcuin decided to recall the men from Champaign, although they wanted to stay on at the chapel. Bishop Schlarmann begged the abbot to reconsider and not abandon the experiment so precipitously, as he said:

"The Fathers have done a magnificent job. I believe they did as

289

much good there as they could in any place you might assign them. Furthermore, I am convinced that Father Roger and his associates love the work. . . . I still believe your men are best fitted to do it." [55]

There were many others who also felt that the Benedictines were fitted for Newman Club work, but Abbot Alcuin said he needed the monks for other projects. In 1942 Bishop Aloisius Muench of Fargo asked the abbot to send assistance to the Newman Club of the University of North Dakota at Grand Forks. Fathers Gerald McMahon, O.S.B., and Cassian Osendorf, O.S.B., were sent for a three year period when this second venture into the field was also abandoned. A beginning in Newman Club work had been made, however, and the possibility opened for future development of the idea, since the abbot and all involved found the experience strikingly congenial to Benedictine ideals. The possibility, for example, had only been opened of introducing the liturgical life of the Church to a large segment of future leaders who do not attend Catholic colleges, and of associating Benedictine community life with the main educational currents of the nation.

Another intriguing educational venture which was contemplated in this period came out of the association of Father Virgil and Professor Mortimer Adler of the University of Chicago. Adler, along with President Robert M. Hutchins of that university, had electrified the academic world in the 1930's with their valid criticism of the proliferation of collegiate curriculums. The irrelevant aims of social contacts, athletics, extracurricular activities, vocational training, preparation for business, and credit requirements had made a country club, trade school, or finishing school of too many American educational institutions. They wished to return to the traditional educational processes of apprehending, understanding, and knowing. Humanities, liberal arts, philosophy, and theology were their concern. To Father Virgil these sentiments had the familiar ring of a traditional Benedictine educational program of the early middle ages. Adler worked out a program of returning to the 'Great Books' of Western civilization, and basing the educational process on the patterns of the medieval *trivium* and *quadrivium*.

Such an experiment was being made at St. John's College, Annapolis, Maryland, and in 1938 Professor Adler and Father Virgil, who was then dean at St. John's, carried on correspondence about a similar educational experiment at St. John's in Collegeville. The four year program was to be divided into two parts: the reading of the classics with seminars and public lectures; and a sequence of proficiency in the liberal arts consisting of reading and writing, science, mathematics and Greek tutorials. The program was to run apart from, but simultaneously with, the regular academic schedule at St. John's, and to be opened to about twenty qualified students a year beginning in 1939. Father Virgil saw in this experiment, purely humanistic in itself, an opportuni-

290

ty to develop the intellectual virtues at a Benedictine school in combination with the development of the moral virtues through community participation in the liturgical life of the Church. Adler visited Collegeville, gave the commencement address in 1938, and continued to correspond with Father Virgil on the proposal. On 13 September 1938 he sent a complete work schedule for the projected undertaking and stated: "I hope it is not too late to be of some help." Two months later Father Virgil was dead, and the program, which he did not have time to work out with the faculty, was not undertaken.

Such ideas found a receptive hearing at Collegeville because several of the faculty, as they developed their departmental programs, were not satisfied with the existing liberal arts program of American colleges which some Catholic colleges were uncritically adopting. Professor James Gray, in his history of the University of Minnesota, characterized the American liberal arts college as:

". . . an imitation of an imitation — out of England, by way of New England, with certain borrowings from Germany. Its traditions of specialization had become sterile and many a student who escaped from an arts college in the teens of the century presently found that he had no whole garment to his back. He was a creature of educational 'shreds and patches' snatched up at random from catalogues of history, science, and English departments. If he took the trouble to evaluate his experience he was inclined to be profoundly dissatisfied with it. A product of the English system of the same period listed for the benefit of *Who's Who* the schools that he attended and added with engaging irony, 'largely self-educated.' " [56]

At Collegeville theology had been taught in close connection with the various liberal arts since 1857. A favorable climate for integration of the theological, philosophical, and liberal disciplines was in this way created. The great divorce in education following the Renaissance and the Protestant Revolt, crowned by the French Revolution, had its origin in the separation of classical and liberal humanities from scriptural, dogmatic, and moral theology. Catholic educational practice since the Council of Trent had served to accentuate this divorce by the separate education of clerics and laity, and the ending of a layman's education with philosophical studies. At St. John's there was never any question of theology's position as the queen of the sciences, and in the 1930's and 1940's the institution was spared those endless educational experiments of specialists, social reconstructionists, pragmatists, and conformists. Instead, several positive steps were taken to reintegrate theology with liberal arts as an effort to restore the sense of the sacred through a reverent study of natural and social sciences. It was, in short, an attempt to revive in modern dress the traditional medieval synthesis of the abbey school and university. As early as 1923 a course in Church history was open to all college seniors, and St.

John's thus helped to restore Church history to the college course. A course was at the same time offered in the history department in American Church history, and this at a time when religious history was, to say the least, not stressed in historical circles.

With the coming of World War II St. John's student body was drastically reduced, and Abbot Alcuin took this opportunity to advance the suggestion that a theology school for lay Catholic leaders be introduced. The normal four-year liberal arts program was to be supplemented by two years of theological studies in the vernacular as a training for Christian leaders. Special programs in church architecture, liturgical arts, Church music, journalism, and original writing were to be arranged in conjunction with the theological school. This program, however, could not be worked out on the practical level from either a faculty or student standpoint, and it did not materialize in its original form. But from the proposal came a department of lay theology which was incorporated into the regular collegiate program after World War II. In the university's bulletin this theological program is characterized as an attempt:

". . . to answer the growing need on the part of the laity for a deeper grasp of Catholic truth. The increasing opportunities (and obligations) of the lay apostolate and Catholic Action in a secularized civilization demand a corresponding training. Less technical than the seminary course, theology for the laity is no less penetrating or complete a synthesis. It should produce leaders of profound conviction and vigorous action in applying revealed truth to all spheres of professional and social life." [57]

Courses taught by both seminary and college faculty are offered in early Christian literature, dogmatic theology, Sacred Scripture, moral theology, liturgy, Church history, the Church year, and Catholic social thought. They are open as electives to students in all departments of the college. Further organization and additional faculty personnel are needed, but the step had been taken.

All of these ideas came to Collegeville as an outgrowth of the modern liturgical revival after the 1920's. The educational implications have only been tapped of a worshipping student community working, as a supernatural and natural overflow, at creating the arts of a Christian civilization. Every effort was expended to create an atmosphere hospitable, as Father Virgil stated:

". . . to teaching the truths of our religion in their practical relation to that living religion, to the actual living out of these truths in the Church both by the Church as a whole and by each member as an active participant. It means that the truths in their interrelation of dogma and worship must also be taught in their mutual relations to the everyday life of the Christian, which must ever be but an extension of the sacrificial dedication of himself to God at the altar. It means that

292

the truths must be taught with all the interrelations that they have in the living liturgy itself, psychological, emotional, intellectual, volitional, natural, and supernatural." [58]

Visitors to St. John's have repeatedly commented on the spiritual program of the school. The age-old Benedictine program of training the whole man, strengthened by modern liturgical consciousness, is aimed at awakening American youths of the twentieth century to the richness and beauty of sacramental living. Attendance at daily Mass or reception of the sacraments is not obligatory, but each Mass is either a *Missa recitata* or a *Missa cantata* with the student community singing the Gregorian chants. On individual floors of student halls, Compline, the official evening prayer of the Church, is frequently recited by groups in common, while in the major seminary parts of the Divine Office are recited by the seminarians in public. Leagues of the Divine Office are voluntarily formed among students who share the responsibility of reciting the Short Breviary in the vernacular.

In a small way these efforts to study and act on the implications of the theology of the Mystical Body of Christ opened educational vistas at a time when the physical interdependence of men and nations made the reality of the family of mankind more apparent. Thornton Wilder said at Harvard University that one of the profound changes of this century would be a growing feeling of human kinship. A realization of the spiritual, intellectual, and moral interdependence of mankind had also to be enlarged. The Benedictines were given an opportunity, in an age when Communism had captured the minds and imaginations of large sections of the world, to contribute to a realization in the West of the spiritual character of every community. On the occasion of the second centenary of Columbia College, Dean Lawrence H. Chamberlain spoke in this vein and declared that the college of the future will lay greater stress on development of morals and character than on the intellect:

"Most of the unhealthy conditions which afflict society today cannot be attributed so much to a lack of technical competence as to moral deficiency. And no matter how excellent the technical training at the professional level may be, all of this specialized skill will accomplish little unless these schools are supplied with the right kind of human product. One cannot ignore the futility and the danger of turning out highly skilled moral vacuums. . . .

"With all its excellence the college program is incomplete — hence one-sided. While we have talked about the whole man we have made systematic provision for training only part of him, taking it more or less for granted that the other part would take care of itself. . . .

"Columbia college, like all American colleges today, is getting young men whose social, moral, and spiritual qualities are under-developed. If we concentrate exclusively upon their minds, later we may have to face the realization that our investment has been partly wasted because the individual in question is in default on social, moral, or ethical grounds. . . . It seems to me that the college should provide intellectual training for good citizenship, but it should also lay the groundwork for effective citizen participation and build logical bridges between student preparation for life and life itself. I hope that in the years ahead Columbia college can pioneer as constructively in this area as it has in the academic field. If it does we will truly be educating the whole man." [59]

Enrollment in the three sections of the abbey's school rose rapidly in this period. In the 1920's and 1930's total student population remained around 460; by 1940 it was up to 668. With the advent of World War II normal academic life was interrupted. St. John's joined in the war effort as a member of the college training program for aircrews of the Army Air Forces Training Command. From February of 1943 until July of 1944, 1,500 air forces personnel received training at Collegeville at the rate of 300 every four months. Among the cadets in this program was Jack Webb, 'Sergeant Friday' of the current television program, Dragnet. While at St. John's he directed variety shows which have been continued each year as a traditional part of the homecoming program.

When the war was over and students had returned to Collegeville, St. John's was invited to accept a Branch General unit of the army's ROTC program. Under this new type of ROTC training, devised by civilian and military educators in 1952, all cadets pursue a uniform program of military science without concentration on any particular branch. At the end of four years of instruction they are commissioned in various army branches. Colonel Benjamin J. Chapla inaugurated this program in the summer of 1952.

By 1950 students numbered 1,203. In 1956 there were 1,400 students enrolled at St. John's of whom 176 were major seminarians, 1,000 collegians and 250 in the college preparatory school. There is a faculty of seventy-five Benedictines and twenty-five laymen. Over 85% of the students reside on the campus at Collegeville, and a growing number of applications for admission cannot be accepted. The forecasts for increasing students, particularly on the college level, present major problems for St. John's and other American educational institutions whose policies and ideals cannot be realized by unlimited expansion.

Student activities at Collegeville continue in the same general patterns established by 'Johnnies' of earlier years. Musical organizations, literary publications, and dramatics are emphasized as previously, and campus clubs hold regular meetings, although the present-day student is not as much of a 'joiner' as his earlier American counterpart. The university orchestra is in its seventieth year, a men's chorus, under the

294

direction of Father James Kelly, O.S.B., is gaining recognition, and a yearly opera is presented jointly by St. John's and St. Benedict's. A Minnesota Intercollegiate Athletic Conference was formed in the scholastic year 1919-20, and has continued to flourish since that time among Minnesota's liberal arts colleges. Its original membership included the colleges of Carleton, Concordia, Gustavus Adolphus, Hamline, Macalester, St. Olaf, St. Thomas, and St. John's. Augsburg, St. Mary's, and Duluth Branch of the University of Minnesota have since joined this conference, while the two Northfield colleges of Carleton and St. Olaf have withdrawn from membership. St. John's has throughout the years fielded representative teams which have consistently finished in the upper divisions of the various sports competitions. George Durenberger, '28, who succeeded Edward Flynn in the athletic directorship, does not place emphasis on St. John's intercollegiate sports record, but rather concentrates on offering the students recreational skills they can use in their mature lives.

Diocesan Seminary

Durenberger sums up the program this way: "We make every effort to provide an activity to satisfy the interest of every student. We are constantly on the watch for the need of additional sports and recreation to meet the demands of a changing student body. With our vast natural facilities we feel we are in a position not only to satisfy their interests but to provide them with instruction in outdoor activities that will carry over for years in benefits after they leave school." [60]

St. John's continued its major seminary program along traditional lines until 11 April 1949 when a singular arrangement was entered into between the abbey and the diocese of St. Cloud. At the suggestion of Coadjutor Bishop Peter W. Bartholome, the ninety-two-year-old St. John's Seminary was to be jointly operated by the abbey and the diocese. A diocesan house of studies, incorporated as 'St. John's Seminary of the Diocese of St. Cloud,' was established on the campus by the people of the diocese for 100 seminarians of the St. Cloud diocese and other dioceses. The spiritual and temporal administration of St. John's Seminary is under the authority of the bishop of St. Cloud, who appoints the rector, spiritual director of the diocesan seminarians and bursar. Monsignor William Renner was appointed as first rector. St. John's continues to conduct the school of divinity, which serves both diocesan and Benedictine priesthood candidates. Father Gregory Roettger, O.S.B., former rector, continues as dean of the school of divinity. The Benedictine clerics remain under the direction of the master of clerics, while the diocesan and monastic seminarians attend classes together as formerly.

In this way the original intent of Abbot Wimmer was retained, namely that the future diocesan and religious priests study together and cement ties of fraternal understanding. At the same time Bishop Bartholome's proposal opened the possibility of a closer association between the diocese and its abbey. At the breaking of ground for the diocesan house of studies for St. John's School of Divinity, Abbot Alcuin said:

No Task Refused

"We Benedictines differ from other Orders in that we may be said to belong more permanently to the place where we settle than other Orders. This monastery is the home of its members. We do not belong to a province, but to an independent monastery modelled on the family pattern, and rooted in the surrounding community more deeply and permanently than other religious. And so we hope to go on with the work that we have begun in this diocese for many, many years — centuries, if God wills it, as monasteries in Europe have gone on for a thousand years and more. And may it please the good Lord to let the Seminary of the Diocese of St. Cloud continue for as many years and be productive of many good priests who will make this diocese of St. Cloud one of the most outstanding dioceses in the United States.

"Of course, I look upon the realization of this project, and I am sure my community shares my view, as a token of good will, which the diocese has always had towards us, and which we hope will continue. I hope it will bring the diocese and the abbey even closer together than they have been, and I trust that this bond between the diocese and its people will grow ever stronger." [61]

During the years these monastic, liturgical and educational developments were taking place, the abbey was called upon to assume several heavy external responsibilities. In quick succession Abbot Alcuin was named apostolic administrator of three Benedictine houses in the Western world which were in need of assistance and direction. Insecure beginnings, overoptimistic expansion and lack of adaptation were the three causes of imminent collapse which moved the Holy See to request St. John's intervention in the affairs of these independent houses. In the Benedictine Order each individual monastery, although united to a congregation of several monasteries, is, according to centuries-old traditions of autonomy, ultimately responsible only to the Holy See. In the wake of world-wide financial collapse in the 1920's some Benedictine houses were on the point of extinction. At this time the Holy See turned to larger and more financially secure abbeys to assist in their preservation. Thus Abbot Alcuin found himself, as a result of the pioneering sacrifices and vision of Abbot Alexius, as well as the solid religious foundations laid by Abbot Peter, requested soon after his election to assume burdens for the welfare of the Order and the Church.

The first of these three apostolic administrations was for the Abbey of the Sacred Heart in Oklahoma, which was a French foundation of the Congregation of the Primitive Observance. This abbey was detached from its original congregation and joined to the American Cassinese Congregation in 1923. Abbot Ernest Helmstetter of St.

Mary's Abbey, president of the congregation at the time, asked Abbot Alcuin to send one of his monks as administrator to Sacred Heart Abbey, Sacred Heart, Oklahoma, who would also act as rector of that abbey's college located at Shawnee. Father Alphonse Sausen, who had been vice-president at St. John's, was sent in the autumn of 1924, and three years later three other members of the community, Fathers Kilian Heid, David Yuenger, and Hilary Doerfler, who had taught at Collegeville for years, were also sent to bolster the Shawnee staff. In the meantime, Bishop Francis J. Kelly of Oklahoma City was taking an active interest in reviving this Benedictine abbey in his diocese. The abbey was dwindling in numbers, and needed an infusion of new blood, particularly of American monks, as the French founders had not developed along American lines. Candidates, scarce enough in Oklahoma, had not joined the house. Bishop Kelly stated that he took a *Catholic Directory* in hand and sought out a large American abbey to take over direction of Sacred Heart, and in this way came upon St. John's. When the Congregation of Religious would not allow the Sacred Heart community to elect an abbot from their own members, Bishop Kelly recommended to Rome that the abbot of St. John's would be best able to place men in Oklahoma. Abbot Alcuin told the abbot president that he would not accept the responsibility unless the Holy See absolutely commanded him, and on 28 May 1928 he received documents appointing him as apostolic administrator of the abbey.

Father Alphonse continued as prior, and in 1931 Abbot Alcuin sent two other St. John's monks, Fathers Sylvester Harter and Raymond Basel, to assist in the restoration. Bishop Kelly cooperated in every way possible in finding a solution to the abbey's problems. He suggested that the Benedictines might move to Oklahoma City where he was ready to offer them the cathedral parish where they could start a high school; or the abbey might be moved to Shawnee and operate a boarding school there, possibly even the major seminary for his diocese; or the school at Sacred Heart could be closed and a novitiate and scholasticate begun instead; or the preparatory seminary at Tulsa could be given to the monks if they moved there; or he was even ready to discuss the possibility of an abbey *nullius* at McAlester. Kelly told Deutsch that prospects were financially bright. The Oklahoma oil development was moving steadily closer to land around Sacred Heart and Shawnee, not to mention the prospects of oil on abbey property in California, where the monks had two parishes, one dedicated to St. Benedict at Montebello and another to Our Lady of Lourdes in Los Angeles.

After careful consideration of all prospects Abbot Alcuin and the Oklahoma monks decided in 1929 to move the abbey to Shawnee, where their college was, change the corporation's name to St. Gregory's Abbey, and continue monastic and educational life there. Three years later Abbot Alcuin felt the community was ready to have its own abbot, and asked the Oklahoma chapter to express its choice by submitting three names. The monks presented the names of three St. John's monks, Fathers David Yuenger, Basil Stegmann, and Mark Braun in that order of preference. Abbot Alcuin favored the advancement of the dean of the college at St. John's, Father Mark Braun, and he petitioned Rome to appoint an abbot. Deutsch informed Kelly that Father Mark was "able, prudent, sanely progressive and financially conservative. I am sure you will find him an easy man to work with. We greatly regret to lose him . . . but I willingly make the sacrifice if he proves an asset to St. Gregory's and to Your Excellency's diocese, as I am confident he will." [62] The large majority at St. John's would have preferred to keep Father Mark at home, as he was leading the effort to establish the college on a sound basis. But he was appointed abbot by the Holy See on 18 October 1932, and in the next twenty years charted a prudent and safe course of development for this new member of the American Cassinese Congregation.[63]

No Task
Refused

While Oklahoma affairs were pressing, another apostolic administration was given to Abbot Alcuin. St. Mary's Abbey, a monastery of the Swiss-American Congregation, located at Richardton, North Dakota, was dissolved in July of 1924 and involuntary bankruptcy proceedings were opened against the abbey corporation in the fall of that year. St. Mary's had been established by the first bishop of Bismarck, Vincent Wehrle, O.S.B., who came to Dakota in 1887 as a missionary.[64] Wehrle began at once to plan for a monastery in western Dakota which would be a missionary and educational center for German-Russian immigrants. By 1894 he had obtained permission from Bishop John Shanley of Fargo and the Holy See to open a priory dedicated to St. Gall at Devils Lake. Five years later the small community was moved to Richardton. Here Prior Vincent began building. After four years of struggle the priory was changed in name to St. Mary's and was raised to abbey status, with Prior Vincent as first abbot, on 25 November 1903. During the next six years Wehrle continued his building program which included the erection of a large church, a fine example of the Romanesque style, at Richardton. Then in 1910 Abbot Vincent was appointed first bishop of Bismarck, though he continued as abbot of St. Mary's for five years while residing in Bismarck. The day after he did resign his abbatial office the community elected one of their members, Father Placid Hoenerbach, as second abbot. Abbot Placid inherited debts of $315,000 from his predecessor who had borrowed heavily during the previous years and lived in the expectation that Dakota lands, on which he had members of the community living as squatters, would go up in value. Not only did these lands go down in value, but Abbot Placid was forced to borrow money to pay interest rates of from 8 to 12% on Bishop Wehrle's debts, meet current expenses and make necessary repairs. All the time he was making new investments so that within two years the abbey's indebtedness stood at $400,000.

During the years from 1915 to 1924 affairs at Richardton rushed toward a tragic ending. Abbot Vincent at least left buildings with his debts, while Abbot Placid instead of retrenchment and economy to meet the abbey's obligations, entered upon a series of additional loans, incredible investments and grandiose 'air castle' plans, as Bishop Wehrle called them. He spoke in glowing terms of shares in prospective oil wells, and had multimillion dollar plans drawn up for an abbey and university at Mandan, where he envisioned moving the community. He was a friend of the future Archbishop Francis J. Beckman of Dubuque and Bishop Michael J. Gallagher of Detroit, and travelled the country making contacts and obtaining loans from a large number of individuals. To Abbot Placid's credit it must be recorded that he was faced with a most difficult situation. Wehrle had placed the abbey in a small prairie village in an unprotected semi-dry belt where for the past decade there had been partial or total crop failures. There was no other source of sufficient income and Bishop Wehrle, who had not favored the advancement of Abbot Placid, rendered no help to his foundation, while taking away parishes and missions from the community. A future for the abbey's school at Richardton looked dim at the time because the poor farmers in a thinly populated area were not in a position to send their boys to school, and the place was remote from Catholic centers of the upper midwest region.[65]

Abbot Placid was convinced that if given time he would solve these problems. But rumors of conditions reached the Swiss-American abbots, and some members of the Richardton community petitioned the Apostolic Delegate to the United States to examine developments. During these years the aging Abbot Frowin Conrad of Conception was acting as president of the Swiss-American Congregation, and although official visitations were made of the Richardton abbey, no steps were taken. Abbot Athanasius Schmitt of St. Meinrad Abbey was elected president of that congregation in 1922, but he was hospitalized for nine months and resigned his office, to be succeeded as president by Abbot Philip Ruggle of Conception Abbey. Abbots of the Swiss-American Congregation meeting in Chicago, with the Apostolic Delegate presiding, on 24 September 1924, held that their congregation was not legally responsible for Richardton's indebtedness, as a later decision of an ecclesiastical tribunal confirmed, and that they could not take over the debts in charity without grave danger to themselves.[66] Abbot Placid was suspended from office and one of the monks, Father Edward Lippert, was appointed administrator. But since he resided at Devils Lake, and only periodically visited the community, something further had to be done. Bishop Wehrle pleaded with the community to

299

remain together and become a dependency of another monastery, like St. John's, for a few years until religious and economic stability could be achieved. The chapter of Richardton unanimously rejected Bishop Wehrle's proposition on 16 July 1924. Some of the monks remained in Dakota parishes, while others temporarily went to other monasteries such as St. John's, along with several candidates and students for St. Mary's. The abbey buildings and properties were in the hands of receivers, and for four years prairie winds were the only sounds heard in the empty corridors of St. Mary's Abbey.

*No Task
Refused*

In the meantime the Congregation of Religious, the Abbot Primate, the Apostolic Delegate, and Bishop Wehrle were endeavoring to re-establish abbey life at Richardton. Overtures were made to Abbot Alcuin that St. John's make Richardton a dependent priory, but the abbot, with the approval of his chapter, recommended that the responsibility for administering St. Mary's be entrusted to himself personally to carry through his recommendations for rehabilitation. After his 1925 trip to Rome, Abbot Alcuin was appointed administrator by Pope Pius XI on 10 July 1926 and his proposals were embodied in the decree *Lacrimabilis* of 7 April 1926. Monks who had been Richardton students at the time of the breakup returned from St. John's, along with those Fathers and Brothers who wished to return from other abbeys or Dakota parishes. Abbot Alcuin's secretary, Father Cuthbert Goeb, was sent to Richardton as prior on 1 September 1928 with the major task of redeeming the church, buildings, and property, as well as to pay off mortgages and creditors at reduced rates on the dollar. St. John's assumed no financial responsibility for St. Mary's Abbey, but only administered the monastic affairs of the community so that it could eventually be self-supporting and independent. Father Cuthbert went to Dakota, accordingly, with only $2,000 in his possession which represented the money with interest collected for the services of the Richardton Fathers during the years 1924–28.

Father Cuthbert soon won the confidence of the capitulars of St. Mary's, restored monastic life, developed discipline and good will through economy and dedicated labor.[67] Within three years the chapter at Richardton was in a position to petition the Holy See for full restoration of abbey status, and on December 15 of that year Prior Cuthbert was appointed third abbot of the community. Bishop Wehrle was overjoyed and called Prior Cuthbert 'a special gift of God for Richardton.' He told Abbot Alcuin:

"I use this occasion to thank you and your Abbey for all that you have done to bring Richardton Abbey back into existence and, we can truly say, into a very promising condition. May God bless you and reward you and your whole community."[68]

Abbot Cuthbert was blessed by Bishop Busch on 13 April 1932 amid the general rejoicing of the Catholic people of North Dakota that the

300

Benedictines had returned to stay.[69] On October 17 the abbey was transferred to the American Cassinese Congregation at the request of the community's chapter, and the name of the monastery changed to Assumption Abbey. In 1938 the last mortgage was paid off, and during the following years new buildings were erected by the monks, their school developed, and young monks given advanced training. By 1955 the community had grown to seventy-eight members. Abbot Cuthbert, who had directed all of this growth while suffering from chronic ill health, requested the Holy See in 1954 to allow the election of a coadjutor, and on 14 July 1954 Father Ignatius Hunkler was elected by the community as coadjutor abbot of Assumption.

The third apostolic administration which was entrusted to Abbot Alcuin was for the Abbey of Santa Maria di Montserrat in Manila, Philippine Islands. In 1940 Abbot Anselm Catalan of Nuova Norcia Abbey in Australia informed Abbot Alcuin, after making an apostolic visitation of the Manila abbey, that this Benedictine house would have to be closed if American professors could not be obtained for San Beda College, which was attached to the monastery. The Manila monastery, of Spanish origin and belonging to the Primitive Observance Congregation, had mortgaged all of its property to secure a debt of $225,000. Income from San Beda College was not sufficient because the faculty was Spanish in orientation while the Filipino students wanted American teachers and techniques. There would be no shortage of students, nor lack of sufficient income, if American assistance was forthcoming, and Abbot Catalan asked the abbot of St. John's to take over the monastery and incorporate it into the American Cassinese Congregation. If this were done loans could be readily obtained in Manila, and the school would not only escape foreclosure but would flourish. The Archbishop of Manila, as well as Abbot Immanuele Caronti, abbot general of the Primitive Observance Congregation, concurred in this request.

But Abbot Alcuin answered that this offer could not be accepted because the General Chapter of the American Cassinese Congregation, which alone could admit new monasteries to its union, would not accede to the request because of St. Mary's debts. Deutsch suggested instead that an apostolic administrator be appointed by the Holy See. After its affairs were in order, the Manila community could decide to remain aggregated to its own congregation, join some other, or form a new Oriental Congregation of its own. He agreed that the community must not emphasize its Spanish traditions and way of life to such a pronounced degree, and went on to say that it must not only Americanize its school but, most important, work vigorously for native Filipino vocations to the monastic life, a program that had not been followed up to that time.

Abbot Alcuin felt he had too many pressing responsibilities at hand

301

without assuming another. But in October of 1940 the Holy See requested him to become apostolic administrator of the Manila Abbey and he accepted the burden "from a sense of duty to the Holy See and of interest in the Order." [70] As in the case of Richardton, the St. John's community was not involved financially in this commission. In February of 1940 two monks from St. John's, Fathers Owen Tekippe and Boniface Axtman, were sent to Manila. Abbot Alcuin's good friend, Abbot Martin of St. Benedict's, answered his appeal for help from other American Cassinese abbeys by giving one of his men, Father Alfred Koestler.

No Task
Refused

Abbot Alcuin made a hurried trip to Manila early in 1941 to study the situation at firsthand and to take steps to save the abbey and its school. He and the prior, Father Owen Tekippe, whom he appointed as his delegate, accepted coreceivership for the abbey, and by refinancing as well as by rejuvenation of San Beda through the influence of American teachers, the impending foreclosure was prevented. Although the Manila community first asked St. John's for a loan of $75,000 and later for a loan of $10,000, it was not necessary to comply with these requests, although the chapter of St. John's had voted in favor of the second request. After his return to St. John's, Abbot Alcuin selected five additional members of the community to assist at San Beda College. Arrangements were made for their trip to Manila in July of 1941, but at that time the State Department cancelled all passports. It was only after the close of World War II that three additional monks of St. John's could be sent to Manila.

The history of the strengthening of San Beda College, as well as the story of the internment of the American monks by the Japanese after their occupation of the Philippine Islands, await future treatment. Despite his advancing age Abbot Alcuin again visited the Manila abbey in the spring of 1946, accompanied by his secretary, to discover whether the community was sufficiently re-established to administer its own affairs. The Holy See accepted his recommendations, and his apostolic administration of the Manila abbey was terminated in December of 1946. The community voted to remain attached to the Primitive Observance Congregation, and Abbots Alcuin and Martin recalled the American Benedictines by April of 1947.

"Well, they are certainly keeping you on the jump," Abbot Ernest Helmstetter of St. Mary's had told him as early as 1930. But Abbot Alcuin seemed to thrive on work, and he consistently evidenced as the years wore on that he was an ecclesiastic with insight, energy, and courage. In ordinary affairs he sometimes made hasty and shortsighted decisions, but he repeatedly showed vision in his major decisions. Nor did he refrain from expressing his opinions when he considered it a matter of principle or for the welfare of the Order. For example he

302

wrote unequivocally to Abbot Ernest, the president of the American Cassinese Benedictines, in 1930:

"Permit me to express to you a thought that has been with me before . . . . You are not giving us the leadership that we should and must have in the difficulties by which we are confronted, and you are not keeping us sufficiently informed as to things that concern the congregation. We have been summoned to meetings and little was accomplished because we were not prepared. . . .

"You are very courteous and considerate at our meetings. You let everybody talk as long as he pleases and you do not impatiently interrupt him, when he rambles into subjects not pertinent to the discussion. You have more patience than I would have; I get impatient with our rambling procedures and would like to get something concrete and tangible. That is why I sometimes take more action in our meetings than I should, usurping in a measure your privilege as chairman to direct the deliberations. I do not do this unconsciously and I do it reluctantly. But it irks me to arrive at nothing.

"We are in a critical period of our history with Holy Cross and the University of Peking on our hands. We must be more wide awake, organized and active. We must have more contact with each other and we must be kept informed. We must get suggestions from our President as to what will make for the welfare of our houses severally and as a congregation. All this requires time and labor. Perhaps you are too old for this and handicapped by your poor sight, but this should not jeopardize the welfare of our communities and our good name and that of the Order.

"You will pardon me if I have spoken boldly. I mean no offense. I send this letter with much hesitation and only because I feel it a duty to do so." [71]

Abbot Ernest received this missive with his customary gentleness and humility, and two years later, at the next general chapter of the congregation, Abbot Alcuin was elected president of the American Cassinese Benedictines, a post which he held from 1932 to 1944.

With this responsibility, as all others, he entered seriously and with determination upon the business at hand. He supported the collection of a monastic ritual for the congregation which was prepared by Abbot Cuthbert Goeb and Fathers Roger Schoenbechler and Jude Koll of St. John's. An American Benedictine Educational Association had been in existence since 1917 as a coordinating agency for the educational work of the respective abbeys. Abbot Alcuin was never enthusiastic about this organization, and in 1947 was instrumental in converting it to an American Benedictine Academy. Modelled after a similar organization among Bavarian Benedictines, the Academy was aimed at stimulating original research as well as historical and literary pursuits among American Benedictines of both congregations. A journal, the *American Benedictine Review*, is issued quarterly, and a series of monographs is projected.

No Task Refused

Abbot Alcuin's large correspondence was extended again by the office of abbot president, and he managed the affairs of the congregation with dexterity, common sense, and justice. When asked for advice concerning discipline, admission of young monks to vows, or monastic procedures, he was not slow to give it. He always quoted Benedictine principles, and never tired of recommending fear of God, reverence, humility, patience, and self-control. He possessed definite ideals and standards of monastic life which he introduced in his own abbey, and as president and triennial visitor of other abbeys of the congregation he recommended them for adoption elsewhere. Abbot Alcuin's penchant for changing whatever he put his hand to appears again in this instance. But the American Cassinese Congregation had solid traditions that were deeply rooted in its Bavarian beginnings and had stood the test of time. He was, for example, not successful in altering such customs as the daily *haustus* in some houses, or the tradition of maintaining parishes, a practice which he opposed in his first years as abbot and as strongly defended in his later years. With innovations emanating from modern American society he would have no part. He stood in opposition to golf, radios, cameras, cigarettes, and especially vacations for Benedictines. His own tastes for Italian cigars, wines and tours, which he had acquired during his years in Europe, were left outside the pale of such restrictions, however. In fact, Bishop Busch of St. Cloud referred to him as 'Alcuin of Tours,' although he made trips throughout his long years as abbot only when required by duty. On these trips he always selected the cheapest mode of travel, and would frequently forego his regular meals or sit up at night in a day coach. Abbot Alcuin was not slow to reprove a community for those practices which he personally disliked when he came among them as a triennial visitor. Sometimes his gruff exterior and imposing presence did not especially endear him. Yet he was always respected.

This fact was confirmed in 1937 when Justin Cardinal Seredi, O.S.B., wrote to Abbot Alcuin concerning the impending election of an abbot primate for the Benedictine Order during that year. The cardinal stated that in his twenty-three years of close association with Rome, monastic life had not advanced as an influential part of contemporary Church life to the degree that it should have. Seredi told Deutsch that many of the abbots were thinking of him for the office of abbot primate and he requested him not to refuse the sacrifice but accept it as the will of God. Abbot Alcuin replied that he did not consider himself competent but would gladly make whatever sacrifices the office might entail.[72] As the abbot prepared to leave for Rome on 15 August 1937 and bade farewell to his community it was understood on all sides that there was a strong possibility of his being elected abbot primate. But at the sessions in Rome Abbot Alcuin expressed himself strongly in favor of giving the abbot primate more jurisdiction, and of greater centralization in the Benedictine Order, a policy which he supported in practice whenever it did not affect his own affairs. The assembled abbots then proceeded to return Abbot Fidelis von Stotzingen for a second term as abbot primate. Abbot Alcuin told his community upon his return to Minnesota on November 9 that he had spent the whole of the return trip on board ship in his cabin, making a retreat, and added: "Well, you will have to accept me as your abbot for as long a time as the Lord will give me." [73]

As abbot president of the American Cassinese Congregation Abbot Alcuin was faced with two major problems which had been growing more serious for some years. The first concerned the financial status of Holy Cross Abbey at Canon City, Colorado, a foundation of St. Vincent Archabbey which was made in 1886 and raised to the status of abbey in 1925. A building program was begun under the community's first abbot, the Right Reverend Cyprian Bradley, O.S.B., which through a combination of unforeseen and unpredictable circumstances brought the abbey corporation to the brink of insolvency by 1931. Water was found at a four foot depth on the building site of the main monastic unit, and costly pilings and repairs on the superstructure had to be made. The architect underestimated total costs by one-half; the contractor had to be dismissed; income from abbey enterprises did not materialize; and worst of all, the financial crash of 1929 cut off pledged support by benefactors of that abbey. Interest payments on indebtedness were soon four times the net income of Holy Cross Abbey. When Abbot Cyprian explained this situation to the assembled abbots of the congregation at Chicago in September of 1930 they promised to assist if he would resign and an apostolic administrator be appointed. On 4 February 1931 the resignation of Abbot Cyprian and the appointment of a monk of St. Vincent, Father Leonard Schlimm, O.S.B., were announced.

Abbot Alcuin succeeded Abbot Ernest as president at this juncture and at once vigorously entered into plans to save the Colorado community. Father Leonard Schlimm served as administrator for two years, and then Abbot Alcuin's friend Abbot Martin of St. Benedict's came to the assistance of the congregation and gave one of his most able monks, Father Leonard Schwinn, O.S.B., as second apostolic administrator. The total debt was over $700,000, and a committee appointed by the general chapter recommended that the individual houses of the congregation finance $427,000 of this amount. Several of the bondholders threatened foreclosure, and Father Leonard had the unenviable and difficult assignment of meeting these obligations, saving the parishes from foreclosure proceedings, while continuing

305

the ordinary operation of the abbey and its school. Abbot Alcuin encouraged him, gave direction, requested and obtained permission from the St. John's chapter to send $50,000 if 50 cents on the dollar was to be paid on the bonds, or $100,000 if the full amount had to be repaid. Father Leonard declared in later years that if Abbot Alcuin had done nothing else in his career he made a major contribution to the Church by this one act alone. "Like a little Napoleon he stood up and fought, and his success lay in winning support for the cause." St. John's sent around $65,000 to Holy Cross in the following years, and at a time when, in the aftermath of the depression, cash was scarce, to say the least. Nor was the Collegeville community alone in this support; St. Mary's Abbey in Newark under the leadership of Abbot Ernest gave proportionately more for its size. St. Benedict's Abbey in Kansas, and St. Anselm's Abbey in Manchester, generously joined in the cause, while small Benedictine houses like St. Andrew's Priory in Cleveland and Assumption Abbey in Richardton generously contributed. For example, Richardton sent $1,500 at a time when that community, struggling for existence, had to borrow the money and pay interest on their contribution. Several convents of Benedictine Sisters also donated, and slowly the debts began to dissolve. The devotion, integrity, and honesty of the Holy Cross community, with the support of the American Benedictines, turned the tide. By February of 1952 all creditors had been paid at full rate of their original bonds, the abbey and parishes saved, and the Colorado community and its buildings actually enlarged. What looked like a tragedy of the 1930's became one of the success stories of American Catholicism in modern times. A near casuality of one of the American houses was averted, and the American Cassinese Congregation was more closely united by this common experience in cooperation. In 1937 Father Leonard was nominated as second abbot of Holy Cross and blessed on August 10 of that year.[74]

The second impending collapse which came to a head during the years that Abbot Alcuin served as abbot president concerned the Fu Jen Ta Hsueh or the Catholic University of Peking, China. Since his and St. John's connection with this complicated phase of twentieth century Benedictine history came late in the development of this project, only a cursory treatment can be given here. One volume of a multivolumed history of The Catholic University of America has been devoted to a corresponding period in that institution's history. At a time more properly removed from contemporary events the noble and farseeing story of this abortive pioneer effort will offer stimulating research.

In brief, Archabbot Aurelius Stehle, O.S.B., of St. Vincent, with the encouragement of the Right Reverend G. Barry O'Toole, an American educator and Oblate of St. Vincent Archabbey, took the lead after

No Task Refused

306

World War I in establishing a Catholic university at Peking in northern China. St. Vincent, with the assurance of moral support from the other abbots of the American Cassinese Congregation, answered the urgent invitation of Pope Pius XI to increase the effectiveness of a native apostolate by establishing a center of Catholic higher education at Peking for training Chinese Catholic leaders, rejuvenating the ancient culture of China, and introducing the scientific knowledge of the Western world. The projected institution reflected the missionary ideals of Pius XI, and he called upon the American Benedictines, in the same way as popes have repeatedly erected university centers, to take up this work in the Far East. "You can do nothing dearer to us," Pope Pius XI had stated, "or more useful for the Holy Church of God, or more honorable to noble sons of your Father St. Benedict than that, exerting the whole effort of your wills, you should supply the University at Peking on the one hand with the men best fitted to govern, to teach, and to bring up souls in piety, and on the other hand to provide the equipment and instruments to teach the sciences properly, as well as with funds and revenues." [75]

Peking Catholic University

The university was established in 1922. Two monks of St. Vincent went to China in 1924 to prepare for the foundation of a Benedictine community, and in the following year Archabbot Aurelius and Dr. O'Toole arrived in Peking to buy property for the future institution. They purchased the ducal palace and grounds of Prince Tsai Tao, uncle of the deposed Chinese emperor, and Father Adalbert Gresnigt, O.S.B., designed buildings for the compound which were acclaimed as achievements in native architecture. A number of monks were sent from St. Vincent and other American Benedictine houses in the next eight years to augment the staff. Six Benedictine Sisters from St. Benedict's Convent, St. Joseph, went out to China in 1930, and two years later opened the Women's College of the university, the first Catholic college for women in China. Three university colleges were established in Arts, Natural Education, and Education with nine departments; an Upper and Lower Middle School; and a fine arts course in Christian art along Chinese lines. A governmental recognition of the university was obtained in 1929, and the original student body of twenty-three increased to over a thousand. The large share of this teaching load was carried by Chinese professors, and through this native contribution real and distinctive progress was made in removing the foreign character of the Christian mission to China.

But the fundamental problems of the university increased with its growth. There was a critical shortage of funds, no assured source of income, no organized plan of soliciting funds among the American Benedictines, and all the while the debts mounted. Archabbot Aurelius, Dr. O'Toole, and the chancellor, Father Francis Clougherty, O.S.B., exhausted every energy in the cause, and Archabbot Aurelius proceeded to borrow money to preserve the institution. His untimely death on 12 February 1930 brought the whole issue to a head. For in his enthusiasm Stehle had been carrying the burden of the university almost alone among American Benedictines. The American abbots then voted that they did not wish to withdraw from the undertaking, but to stand, as Abbot Alcuin told Archabbot Aurelius' successor, the Right Reverend Alfred Koch, O.S.B.:

". . . wholeheartedly and courageously by that decision and support the university to the best of our ability with well-trained teachers who are at the same time good monks. Let us make this known to the Holy See, but let us make known also the financial condition of our monasteries and our inability to finance the university with our own funds." [76]

In 1932 Archabbot Alfred asked Abbot Alcuin to send his prior, Father Basil Stegmann, O.S.B., as prior of the monastic family at the university with the hope of bringing cohesion among the monks who were from several different houses. Upon his arrival in China Prior Basil called the endeavor a providential missionary undertaking, and stated that its abandonment would be "a reproachful blot on the pages of American Benedictine history." [77] Monastic and educational centers were unquestionably the major need of the Church in the Far East, rather than isolated missionary activity as had been emphasized in the previous hundred years or so. But Prior Basil felt that the monastic community at Peking was too much of an aggregation from different abbeys, unprepared for its task, with authority divided between the abbots in the United States, the chancellor and the prior in China. The whole endeavor had been built too rapidly, and as Abbot Alcuin said, not along traditional Benedictine lines of humble beginnings dedicated to the establishment of a native community as a chief work.[78] The American houses were themselves struggling to train a sufficient number of professors for their schools which were slowly developing during the same years, and could not supply men. The Holy See declared on 28 July 1932 that support of the Peking University should be an all-American Benedictine affair of both the Swiss American and American Cassinese Congregations, but the Swiss abbeys maintained that they had never been approached directly or officially by Rome and their abbeys could not afford to add another burden during the hard times of the 1930's. Archabbot Alfred felt that St. Vincent was being left in great part alone to maintain the work at its necessary high level, that most of the eleven monasteries in the congregation were small and struggling with their own problems, and that the archabbey could not indefinitely continue the project under those circumstances. He, accordingly, felt forced to ask Rome to transfer control of the university to another religious body of the Church, and in April of 1933 the Holy See commissioned the Society of the Divine Word, with special reliance on the American Province, to take over direction of the institution in August of that year. Prior Basil recommended that the Benedictines return from China and await a better opportunity, although both the apostolic delegate to China, Archbishop Celso Constantini, and the prefect of the Congregation of the Propagation of the Faith, Pietro Cardinal Fumasoni-Biondi, requested that they remain and begin a new foundation.

Abbot Alcuin, as president of the congregation, had to go to Rome that spring of 1933 to explain the American Cassinese side of the Peking question to the officials at the Holy See. Abbot Martin told him before his departure:

"So the matter with China is coming to a head. I think it is providential and that we are thereby spared a more scandalous winding up of affairs there. As a Congregation we are not in a position to undertake such a work. We recognized that when we turned China over to St. Vincent's; of course, as it happened, this only made more trouble for us. In view of conditions the world over and reflected in our Abbeys, no one can justly find fault with us in failing to make things go. We simply have not the money. . . . Techny has the machinery for missionary work; we have it not. May they succeed with the project! I doubt whether you will succeed in clearing up the 'black eye' we already have in Rome. Still, we must do what we can and then leave the rest to God." [79]

The abbot of St. Benedict's was correct in his surmise that Abbot Alcuin would have an unpleasant visit in Rome. Although the details of his interview with Pope Pius XI were never documented, he stated afterwards that it was the most difficult thing he ever had to do, that Pope Pius XI was, as he could be in such cases, severe and stated in the course of the interview that the Benedictines were indeed an "Order without order."

In this instance the centuries-old autonomy of separate Benedictine houses was pointed up as militating against common effort such as the establishment of a Chinese university demanded. From the time of Pope Leo XIII contemporary popes have worked to bring about more centralization among Benedictine houses. As a first step the Abbey of St. Anselm with its international college in Rome was established, an Abbot Primate to be elected by the Benedictine abbots of the world was created, and Pope Pius XII inaugurated a Confederation of Benedictine Monastic Congregations in 1952 to expedite "in a manner suited to the circumstances of the present day . . . fraternal assistance among the Congregations, whether this be by persons, money, or work." [80] The foresight and vision of Archabbot Aurelius stand forth in his attempt to join Benedictine effort, according to the desire of the Holy See, to the missionary needs of the Church. Archabbot Aurelius' farsighted but unilateral plans were ahead of their time, the means were not at hand, and the traditions of Benedictine procedure ran in opposing lines.

But the Chinese experience did have its effect on the future course of Abbot Alcuin. From the time of the American Benedictine withdrawal from the Far East it is clear that he began formulating plans for re-entry into the missionary life of the Church as soon as it was feasible. This development is especially apparent in the renewed interest he showed in the frequent requests coming into his office in the 1930's and 1940's for St. John's to start new monasteries. For example, the former Columbus College in Sioux Falls, South Dakota, was offered in 1927 and again in 1940. St. Gregory's Abbey offered to sell their Montebello property in California in 1932 as a possible foundation. A military school in Jackson, Mississippi, was offered in 1940. Father Peter E. Dietz, pastor of St. Monica's parish, offered fifteen acres on Whitefish Bay, Milwaukee, for a monastery and school which would be a cultural center dedicated to fine arts, liturgy, music, painting, carving, sculpture, and metal arts to offset the exclusive intellectual pursuit of higher learning in Catholic circles. Both Patrick Cardinal Hayes and his consultors showed interest in 1937 in the establishment near New York of a monastery by St. John's which would have the two New York parishes of St. Anselm and St. Benedict, and perhaps even the Bahama Islands mission as part of its active work. None of these projects materialized despite the fact that the community chapter had even approved of some of them. There was ever a shortage of personnel. In 1937, for example, two St. John's monks had transferred to St. Gregory's in Oklahoma and four were working there; three were serving in parishes attached to Assumption Abbey, Richardton; one was assisting at St. Peter's Abbey in Saskatchewan, Canada; and twelve monks had been sent to the Bahama Islands.

More influential than this shortage of personnel, however, was Abbot Alcuin's interest during his last years in the foreign missions of the Church. He had a strong admiration for the mission work of the St. Ottilien Benedictines of Bavaria, and of Saint André Abbey in Belgium. Thus when requests came in for a monastery and school in Santiago, Chile, in 1941; for a monastery and normal school in Peru in 1944; or for a monastic foundation after World War II in Bombay, India, he was always interested. He was convinced that St. John's was growing too large. Many of his monks kept reminding him that the abbey had not made a monastic foundation of its own during his entire administration, and that the missionary period of the Church's life in the upper midwest was over.

Thus in the last six years of his administration, in quick succession, and at the rate of almost one a year, four new foundations were made in mission territories, and two others were attempted. It was a series of dramatic moves reminiscent in many ways of the days of Abbot

310

141 *Indian Congress at Grand Portage with Minnesota's
oldest church in background.*

142 *Indian Congress at Cass Lake.*

143 *Holy Family Mission Church, near Cloquet, one of the oldest
missions in Minnesota.*

144 *The Jacobs Prairie 'grasshopper Shrine' became a permanent monument in granite during the Marian Year at Cold Spring.*

145 *Seminarians and clerics at St. Maur's Seminary, Kentucky.*

146 *Father Thomas Borgerding, oldest priest in the United States, 'at home' with Fathers and Brothers on Red Lake Indian Mission.*

147 *Red Lake Indian Mission.*

148 *The Priory, Nassau, Bahama Islands.*

149 *Early Benedictines in the Bahamas.*

150 *Patrick Cardinal Hayes and Bishop Bernard Kevenhoerster.*

151 *Abbots Vincent Taylor (Belmont) and Alcuin Deutsch in the Bahamas.*

152 *St. Benedict's Hall, Bahama Islands, in 1892.*

153 Consecration of Bernard Kevenhoerster, first vicar apostolic of the Bahama Islands, in St. Patrick's Cathedral, New York.

154 Bishop Bernard and Father Quentin Dittberner about to visit Bahama mission.

155 Bishop Bernard praying at grave of Father Chrysostom on San Salvador.

156 Bishops Leonard Hagarty and Stephen Donahue (auxiliary bishop of New York)

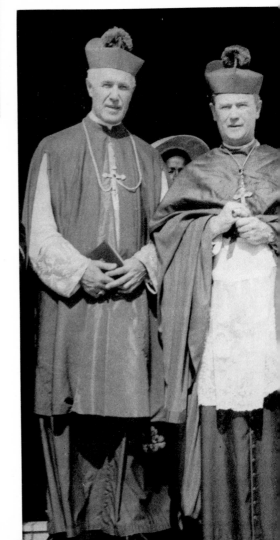

157 Laying of cornerstone of St. Augustine's Monastery, Nassau,
by Abbot Alcuin on 11 July 1946.

158 Rampart on Cat Island, Bahamas: hermitage of
Monsignor Jerome Hawes, T.O.S.F.

159 Bishop Bernard and Abbot Alcuin with the Roerig brothers,
Fathers Gabriel and Leander.

160 Blessing of St. Augustine's Monastery and School, Nassau, 11 March 1947.

161 Bahama nuns: Native Sisters and Sisters of Charity.

162 Native Sisters with the Bahama's most popular vehicle.

163 In Puerto Rico: Monsignor Luigi Ligutti, Prior Owen Tekippe,
Bishop James Davis (San Juan), Mr. Anthony Roig, Father Juan Rivera.

164 Before the election of St. John's sixth abbot.

165 Abbot-president of American Cassinese Congregation, Mark Braun,
and Abbot Alcuin Deutsch congratulate Coadjutor-abbot Baldwin Dworschak.

166 Forty-three years of sterling service in the kitchen of St. John's:
The Sisters of St. Francis of Collegeville.

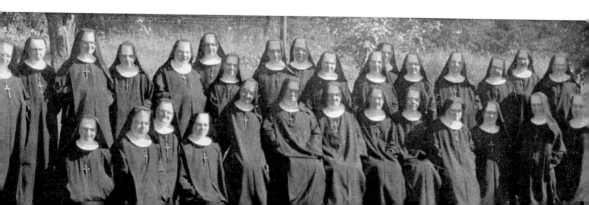

L. to R. First Row: Fathers Romuald Bloms, Cyprian Seitz, Andrew Winczewski, Peter St. Hilaire, Landelin Robling, Kilian McDonnell, Jude Koll, Philibert Harrer; second row: Ferdinand Schreifels, Vernon Miller, Sixtus Steuber, Valerian Thelen, Hubert Dahlheimer, Quentin Dittberner, Bernard Watrin, Augustine Strub; third row: Method Porwoll, Demetrius Hagmann, Stephen Wagman, Joseph Kreuter, Athanasius Fuchs, Barnabas Laubach, Oliver Kapsner.

167–168 *The community of St. John's, 1956.*

L. to R. First Row: Fathers Adalbert Unruhe, Edward Botzet, Odilo Kohler, Constantine Thelen, Alphonse Sausen, Hildebrand Eickhoff, Norbert Gertken, Herbert Buerschinger, Louis Traufler, Pius Meinz, Victor Ronellenfitsch, Basil Stegmann, Lambert Weckwerth, Wendelin Luetmer, Theodore Krebsbach, Severin Lauer; second row: Fathers Bruno Schmid, Alban Fruth, Lawrence Schmidt, Marion Roth, Benno Watrin; third row: Fathers Justin Luetmer, Pirmin Wendt, Roger Schoenbechler, Othmar Hohmann, Elmer Eisenschenk, Columban Kremer; fourth row: Fathers Denis Parnell, Angelo Zankl, Burchard Arnheiter, Jordan Stovik, Blaise Schumacher, Cassian Osendorf, Linus Schieffer, Oswald Johannes, Osmund Jacobs.

Alexius. Now in Collegeville people were talking about and preparing to go to Mexico, Puerto Rico, Utah, Kentucky, and Japan. It was a unique development in contemporary American educational circles as well, for from one school separate faculties on seminary, college, and high school levels had to be drawn for these undertakings. Over forty Benedictines who could have been teaching at Collegeville, assisting in developing individual departments when expansion was badly needed, or being trained in graduate schools to bolster the faculties of St. John's, were sent instead to areas where educational institutions were needed. These monastic and educational institutions were pilot projects of international understanding, and were undertaken without government or foundation grants from American sources. As the nation assumed its role in international cooperation during the same years, American monks moved to meet the needs of religion and society in critical areas. Abbot Alcuin repeatedly stated that if St. John's sacrificed in this way the community would be blessed. To Collegeville as a consequence came students from these new monastic and educational centers to study in high school and college. Some followed liberal arts programs, others took preprofessional courses with the aim of returning to their homeland. A large number of candidates both from the United States and abroad began to apply for admission to the monastery with a view to going to these new foundations, and within a short time the clericate of the abbey took on a certain United Nations character.

The first of these monastic foundations was made in Mexico City. In 1944 a Catholic Mexican organization know as the Centro Cultural del Tepeyac secured two Benedictine priests and three Benedictine Sisters from St. Benedict's Abbey, and St. Scholastica's Convent, Atchison, Kansas, to take charge of the Colegio del Tepeyac, a school for boys and girls in Mexico City. This was the former well-known American School of Mexico which had been directed by Mrs. Florence Bush. The Atchison monks asked Abbot Alcuin to allow Father Clarus Graves, O.S.B., professor of modern languages at St. John's, to assist them at the Colegio del Tepeyac.[81] When the chapter at St. Benedict's decided not to continue their work in the Tepeyac school, Father Clarus appealed to the St. John's chapter to take up the undertaking. Abbot Alcuin journeyed to Mexico City to study the situation, and Archbishop Luis M. Martinez invited him to make a monastic foundation in the archdiocese. The proposition of accepting the control of Colegio del Tepeyac with the ultimate aim of establishing a Benedictine monastery in Mexico was presented to the St. John's chapter on 17 December of 1946 and approved.

During the following January Father Clarus, as prior, led the first group of St. John's monks to Mexico City. They were Fathers Burton Bloms, O.S.B., Adrian Fox, O.S.B., and Brother Philip Heitkemper, O.S.B., and in the following years their numbers were augmented by

311

others from Collegeville. Although forbidden by existing Mexican laws to wear religious garb in public, these monks carried on monastic life within their cloister. The school was favored with a good reputation and its growth was rapid. From an original enrollment of 500 it has grown to a total of over 2,000 students in 1956. While most of the teaching is done by Mexican personnel, the Benedictines have charge of the religion and English classes. Father Burton acts as director of a three department curriculum: primary, secondary, and university preparatory. With this school a challenging opportunity is being offered to train an educated and apostolic laity so badly needed in the service of the Church in Mexico.

Prior Clarus, in the Benedictine tradition, at once began a monastic training program for Mexican candidates. The first of these candidates, Father Hildebrando Garza Gonzales, was ordained in 1954, six are studying at Collegeville at present, and there are thirty postulants at the priory in Mexico City. When Father Clarus returned to St. John's in 1950, to become claustral prior a year later, the same program of building up a native community was continued by his successor, Prior Berthold Ricker, O.S.B. On 12 October 1955 the chapter at St. John's voted to purchase a portion of the Rancho Santa Cruz which is situated near the Colegio del Tepeyac, and plans are being formulated for the building of a monastic home at that site. In 1955 several citizens of Poza Rica, an oil city on the Gulf of Mexico, with Señor Jaime Merino at their head, invited St. John's to take over a newly constructed school in their community. Father Berthold began administration of this school in February of 1956 and also serves the spiritual needs of the people there. Poza Rica opens the possibility of a second Benedictine foundation in Mexico, and all within a ten year period. Meanwhile Father Raphael Haller succeeded Father Berthold as prior in Mexico City.

St. John's second foundation of the late 1940's came in response to a unique invitation from Puerto Rico. Don Agripino Antonio Roig, sugar planter from Humacao, was moved as early as 1939, to establish a religious foundation in Puerto Rico along the lines of a 'Boys' Town' for poor boys of the island's Humacao and Yabucoa districts. He was actively supported in this plan by the scholarly and farseeing pastor of the Holy Name parish in Humacao, Padre Juan Rivera Viera. Overtures were first made to the Salesians in Turin, Italy, but they could not accept the offer because of the losses in personnel during World War II. Father Rivera was not to be discouraged, however, and when the Most Reverend James P. Davis became bishop of San Juan in 1943, he prevailed upon him to invite some Benedictines to undertake the work, because of "the Benedictines' experience in winning native recruits wherever they go." [82] Bishop Davis took out a *Catholic Directory* and looked up the largest Benedictine monastery, and in this way, like Bishop Kelly of Oklahoma before him, came upon St. John's. Mr. Roig planned to establish an industrial and agricultural school where young Puerto Ricans, especially from rural areas, could have an opportunity of learning manual arts, cultivation of land, and technical skills. In such a trade school he desired also that pupils learn a sense of responsibility, a desire for work and the principles of Christian living.

A Puerto Rican Foundation

Abbot Alcuin, as well as representatives of the chapter at St. John's, journeyed to Puerto Rico to talk to Bishop Davis, Father Rivera and Mr. Roig concerning this invitation. Arrangements were completed, and on 27 February 1946 the St. John's chapter accepted the Puerto Rican offer. It was to comprise a grant from Mr. Roig of ninety-two acres outside Humacao, as well as the erection of buildings, and the endowment of an agricultural and trade school. Bishop Davis invited the Benedictines to make a monastic foundation in connection with the school, and turned over to the projected priory the Holy Name parish in Humacao with its four mission stations which Father Rivera generously desired to place in the hands of the new community. Father Basil Stegmann, as prior, along with Father Julian Simon, arrived in Humacao on 1 July 1947 and took up residence with Father Rivera. By mid-September Fathers Jordan Stovik, Edmund Hall, and Brother Joel Blekum had joined them there, and plans were formulated to establish the school and priory of San Antonio outside the city. Father Cloud Meinberg went to Puerto Rico in December to sketch the preliminary plans for the first building which was completed in 1949. Four Sisters of St. Benedict from St. Joseph also joined the group in the following year to operate a ten room parish school which was built in connection with Holy Name parish. Other monks were sent to the foundation, Father Julian became pastor of the 37,000 soul parish upon Father Rivera's retirement, and the school, called Escuela San Antonio Abad, was opened in September of 1950. It was a free school for one hundred poor boys of the region. Fathers and Brothers offer academic courses with a choice of prevocational training on the junior high school level in mechanics, carpentry, and agriculture. All the students are enrolled on scholarships established by Mr. Roig and other Puerto Ricans whom he continues to interest in this sole Catholic trade school on the island.[83]

Prior Basil and Prior Owen Tekippe, his successor after 1951, worked from the beginning to encourage native vocations. While progress has been slow, the Benedictine colony at Humacao has the best record to date of any religious group in Puerto Rico. Many candidates have applied for the Brotherhood, and at present there are a dozen Brothers, novices, and candidates, of whom one has taken perpetual vows, and two temporary vows. There is one cleric at St. John's, and two Puerto Rican boys are enrolled in the preparatory school at Collegeville. One of St. John's alumni, Alphonse A. Laporte, '21, lawyer from New Rochelle, New York, visited Puerto Rico in 1954 as an advisor to the Government Development Bank of Puerto Rico. He recorded his impressions of a visit to San Antonio at that time and stated:

"It is truly a work worthy of the Benedictines — an industrial school where boys are taught to use their brains and their hands, where the grounds, not too large in a tight, little island of scarce land worth $5,000 an acre on the average, must support the community and the boys in so far as possible. There your monks, priests and brothers are striving mightily to make St. Anthony's self-sustaining, a truly difficult task in the light of the poverty of the people from whom the boys come and the land size of the foundation.

"As we drove into Humacao, the town which lies approximately as close to St. Anthony's as St. John's lies to St. Joseph, Minnesota, the Bishop turned to me and said, 'Al, these Benedictines are changing the face of the earth here.' We stopped at the rectory of the ancient parish church, which the Benedictine Fathers took over by bidding of the Bishop and pastor at the same time that they came to St. Anthony's. A mission was in progress and I learned that the people being singularly blessed without clocks, the missioners went at 5:30 each morning with a hand bell and a group loudly saying the Rosary and collecting the somnolent faithful for the services held in the Plaza because the church would not hold them all.

"After Bishop Davis had visited Father Simon, who was ill, we went on to St. Anthony's. Father Prior Owen met us, dressed in white as they all are, and I could see, as he and his brethren kissed the Bishop's ring, that they loved him and knew how much he loved them and appreciated the work they do.

"There was a certain amount of harmony and a certain amount of cacophony coming from the school as we went in. Father Rupert, a mere youngster whom I had met the first time I saw St. Anthony's, was conducting the band. I didn't recognize the music but the Bishop pointed out to me that the drummer boy had bare feet. They were little Spanish speaking boys learning from a white robed, perspiring Benedictine monk, a Nordic if you please, from far away Minnesota. I was reminded of the French nuns in Africa who taught the heathen children of the brave military exploits of 'les Gaulois,' and I realized that this was indeed the Church of God. . . .

"Humacao is a foundation for Benedictines and their boys, past, present and future to be proud of because the sacrifices and hard work of the Benedictine Fathers and Brothers are contributing to the future of America. Puerto Ricans are American citizens and are coming to the mainland in vast numbers. The Benedictine foundation at Humacao will train American citizens in Puerto Rico. I am proud to be a Benedictine boy." [84]

The third St. John's foundation of the late 1940's was a challenging revival of what Abbot Wimmer in 1885 had called his favorite idea, the conversion of the colored race in the United States through monasteries as Catholic educational centers. The monasteries and schools he inaugurated in the southern states of the Union stand as testimony to his pioneering in this work. At St. John's there had also been over fifty years of work for the Negroes of the Bahama Islands. Any Negro who applied was admitted to the school at St. John's. In 1941 the first Negro candidate, Frater Prosper Meyer, was admitted into the monastery's novitiate. Within two years there were three Negro clerics and one Brother, and as the word spread across the country that St. John's was accepting Negroes into the monastery on an equal basis with all other candidates, applications increased rapidly. Fathers Basil Stegmann and Alexander Korte, novice master at St. John's and chaplain at St. Benedict's Convent respectively, began to discuss and plan, with the encouragement of Abbot Alcuin, for an interracial monastic foundation. Father Basil made initial investigations of such a possibility in Louisiana, while Father Alexander considered Chicago, Texas, Florida, Alabama, and Mississippi. In one of his many letters on the subject Father Alexander described the over-all project as follows:

". . . At the Abbey here we have a large College and find it impossible to do justice to the kind of apostolate we contemplate for the Negro and so we are compelled to look elsewhere. We have even been considering some place near Chicago (since Chicago also has a large Negro population though not many Catholics) but we are more interested in the rural type of Negro. . . . In broad strokes our plan is this: To buy some land (about a quarter or half section) with farm buildings on it if possible, and to begin a small monastic foundation on this land. To open such a foundation there would be about 3 or 4 priests available equipped to teach Seminary courses, plus the Negro clerics who are already members of our community and who could continue and finish their course at the new foundation. We would also take a few lay brothers along to take care of the farm. We would plan eventually to start a small school chiefly for the candidates who might apply for reception into the community and perhaps later on a small industrial school. We are not much interested in parochial or mission work since the monastery itself would be our mission project. We conceive the plan somewhat after the fashion of the Benedictine monasteries in Europe and England in the early Middle Ages and later. We wish to begin on a small scale and develop gradually and organically without a heavy initial outlay of money." [85]

Father Alexander continued to make plans, drew up a prospectus of the undertaking, along initial lines of Booker T. Washington's famed

Tuskegee Institute, and contacted prominent national figures in interracial work. The Catholic interracial leader, Father John LaFarge,
S.J., was most helpful, and in one letter stated:

*No Task
Refused*

"The idea of a Religious community which would be professedly
interracial is an old notion of my own and I have given a lot of thought
to the possible structure of such a community both from the purely
spiritual as well as from the practical point of view. Of course, it would
have to be worked with tremendous care. There would have to be great
explicitness as to what its aim is and what is expected of the members,
and of course the selections would have to be made with no small
degree of prudence.

"I suppose you know of a quite remarkable instance in this respect
in Alabama, the Contemplative Dominican Sisters who established an
interracial community near Montgomery. This is a very bold venture
for the deep South and is only feasibly done there because of its entirely
cloistered character.

"I agree with you and your Father Abbot that it would not be a very
practical thing to start such an interracial community in the deep South.
You would have such a terrible lot of lost motion in combating the
surrounding prejudices and obstacles that it would detract a good deal
from the tranquility and vitality of the community itself. . . .

"It seems to me that a community of that sort might set as its great
goal a profound spiritual aim, namely prayer for the unity of His Mystical Body, to be exemplified in our lives and, secondly, as an expiation
for the innumerable crimes that have been committed against the same
Mystical Body. There is a great theology and ascetic spirituality which
can be developed and on thoroughly sound and spiritually fruitful lines.
It would not be an experiment in good will but it would be the exemplification of the very essence of Catholicism. Furthermore, it would be
necessary to train both groups equally in the virtues needed for such
a task.

"These are just my casual impressions. Turning, then, to the practical
side, it seems to me your idea of starting out with a very small number
and building up from some small active work would be better than an
elaborate plan in the beginning. However, there is such a demand for
mission work that you would have to be careful as to the steps to be
pursued. It is so easy to merely immerse yourself in the sea of parish
problems and lose sight of your original plan. It should be *monastic*
right from the beginning, and be of the contemplative rather than the
active side." [86]

The first favorable episcopal response to Father Alexander's requests for permission to begin such an undertaking came from Bishop
Francis R. Cotton of the recently erected diocese of Owensboro in
western Kentucky. After several refusals, Bishop Cotton's invitation
was all the more welcome because it was so enthusiastic. Father Alex-

316

ander received his letter on the Feast of St. Scholastica, 10 February 1947, and learned that the bishop would welcome an interracial monastery as a religious foundation in his diocese, that the large majority of the clergy as well as the bishop himself had been trained at St. Meinrad's Abbey, and that the bishop felt all of the clergy and laity of the diocese would favorably receive the foundation. Negotiations were opened and, although Abbot Alcuin was pressed on every side with his other new foundations, he supported the undertaking with the typical interest he ever manifested in bold ventures. Archbishop Joseph Ritter of St. Louis, who had taken a firm stand for unsegregated parochial schools in his archdiocese, also encouraged Bishop Cotton to make the move. Bishop Cotton suggested that the Benedictines should settle near St. Denis' Church, a country mission six miles from Fancy Farm, Kentucky, in the westernmost tip of the state. The pastor of St. Jerome's Church at Fancy Farm, Father Edward J. Russell, was cooperative and helpful in every way, and Father Alexander presented the proposal to the St. John's chapter in May of 1948. Fancy Farm was only forty miles from the old Cluny Priory in Cairo, Illinois, and some fears were expressed that similar malarial conditions might exist at St. Denis, situated as it was on a ridge between two swampy valley bottoms. But the chapter was informed that an extensive control system was enforced in that area by the Tennessee Valley Authority.

St. Maur's Priory

The chapter swung solidly behind the undertaking. One of the young Negro Benedictines, Father Harvey Shepard, was ordained in June of that year, and joined Father Alexander at Fancy Farm. At first it was planned to make the mission parish of St. Denis a permanent monastic home, but the remote, hilly location did not prove feasible. Then Father Russell acquainted the community with available property that appeared to be a direct answer to the foundation's needs. Some 130 miles to the east, near South Union, Kentucky, the abandoned buildings and property of an earlier flourishing Shaker community, now owned by Oscar S. Bond of Louisville, Kentucky, were up for sale.[87] Mr. Bond wished to sell at least 635 of the total 1,763 acres, but this was too large a section for the small community to consider. Abbot Alcuin visited Kentucky in May of 1949 and he was able to reach a satisfactory arrangement with Mr. Bond, who agreed to sell fifty acres of the excellent blue grass land with its buildings for $60,000.

On 9 August 1949 the little group of monks and their first candidates left Fancy Farm, where the people had already grown attached to them, and moved into the historic Shakertown buildings fourteen miles west of Bowling Green. The new monastery was to be called St. Maur's, a name chosen for it by Abbot Alcuin. It was approved canonically by the Holy See on July 26 as a dependent priory with permission for its own clerical and Brothers' novitiate. The monks found three substantial and beautiful colonial brick buildings, the remnant of the

317

old Shaker village, which were in many ways ideally suited for their purposes. Over one hundred rooms in all were available in the three buildings which included the large Center House, with its long hallways and graceful twin staircases, Preserving House, and Wash House. Each of these buildings stood as a monument to Shaker workmanship. A large barn, constructed by Bond in 1922, was also on the property.

At first the community made the Center House its priory, and established conventual life where 132 years before them the one hundred Shaker seniors had lived. Both colored and white recruits came from St. John's, candidates joined the priory, the farm was cultivated, buildings repaired, and improvements made. The Wash House was converted into a monastery in 1954, while the Preserving House became a high school building during the school year and a retreat center during the summer months for clerical and lay retreatants. Bishop Cotton supported the undertaking at every turn, and in 1954 designated St. Maur's as the major seminary for his diocese. Augmented by personnel from St. John's, first-year theology classes for white and colored students were begun in September of 1954, and the Center House was entirely devoted to this work. Students for the archdioceses of Louisville and Sante Fe, the dioceses of Owensboro, Wichita, Belleville, and the Vicariate Apostolic of the Bahama Islands have been sent to St. Maur's by their bishops. In 1956 there are fourteen students enrolled in the major seminary. Although rapid strides have been made, much remains to be done both in enlarging the community, which at present has fifteen members, and in perfecting an adequate seminary faculty. But the need is urgent, as Pope Pius XII told the hierarchy of the United States in 1939, for increased interest in the American Negro apostolate. Mary J. Matthews, in an interview-article on St. Maur's in *Interracial Review*, summed up the challenge and responsibility of this Kentucky project:

"The need is made urgent by these rancid facts: that out of every fifteen thousand American Negroes, 14,650 are non-Catholics; that white priests outnumber colored priests 1000 to one, that forty-seven diocesan seminaries, two hundred and eighty-five religious seminaries and two hundred and nine congregations of nuns can't make up their minds whether or not they should admit Negro candidates. . . .

"St. Maur's still faces tremendous problems. More specifically, it faces the problem of growing up. There is yet to be accomplished the renovation of the buildings, the seeking of candidates, the working out of the monastic rule, and the stripping away of race prejudice in the surrounding areas. But these ideals and hopes, little more than the idle dreams of a college professor a few years ago, are crystallizing steadily, and they will in time become one solidly molded force.

"Recognition of St. Maur's has already come from numerous Catholic and secular sources. Important figures, including [former]

318

Governor Youngdahl of Minnesota and Clare Booth Luce, former congresswoman, have personally congratulated the establishment. Many Catholic collegians believe with Father Alexander that a black-white monastery on the border of the South will by education and example be a most effective means of furthering interracial understanding and good will.

"Christians rejoice at this news from St. Maur's: 'In a quiet way, we have already, through our small beginnings, changed the attitude of many Catholics and non-Catholics in our neighborhood on the race question. We hope to expand our influence and to penetrate more deeply into areas which have an even greater need of some powerful force to leaven the whole race.'

"Childlike faith and tireless zeal assure the fulfillment of Father Alexander's words: 'It is God's work, He will see it through.'" [88]

The fourth St. John's foundation of the late 1940's developed after the ending of World War II. At the time when there was much discussion abroad of the possibilities of the Japanese people accepting Christianity in greater numbers, Father Hildebrand Yaiser, O.S.B., came to the United States. He was a Benedictine from the archabbey of Beuron, Germany, who with fifteen other Beuronese monks had endeavored to establish the Chigasaki Priory south of Tokyo from 1931 to 1940. This establishment had not survived because of financial difficulties, lack of adjustment to Japanese customs, and the coming of World War II. Father Hildebrand was in the United States in 1946 at the order of his abbot, to find an American abbey which would take over this Benedictine foundation. He visited abbeys of both congregations, and on his third visit to St. John's Abbot Alcuin and the community resolved to support a Japanese foundation. The abbot wrote to Archbishop Peter Totsuo Doi of Tokyo for permission to start a parish in that city which would be the beginning of an eventual Benedictine monastery. The archbishop gladly granted permission for the establishment of a monastery in his archdiocese. On 28 November 1947 he erected a new parish dedicated to St. Anselm and gave it to the Benedictines in the hope that this nucleus would develop into a monastery with a school for boys. Father Joseph Schmerbach, one of the Beuronese missionaries of Chigasaki Priory, stayed in Japan with Father Hildebrand. In 1948 Father Aloysius Michels, who had been one of St. John's chaplains serving in the Pacific during the war, volunteered for the foundation. The little group was joined by Father Emile Butruille, a monk of Saint André Abbey who had been driven out of China in 1953, and Fathers Hildebrand and Joseph transferred their monastic vows to St. John's in 1952.

The parish of St. Anselm quickly evidenced "a great conversion record," as the Denver *Register* stated on 23 April 1954. From an original number of eight converts the parish has become one of Tokyo's largest, with over 1,250 souls, all converts, in a seven year period. The missionizing methods employed at St. Anselm's have aroused widespread interest. There the Fathers have stressed the living reality of the Mystical Body of Christ with prime emphasis on the liturgical life of the Church, and their results attest to the validity of the modern liturgical revival as basic in the mission work of the Church.

The St. John's chapter underwrote a loan of $112,000 to the new foundation for the building of a parish church, instruction building and auditorium which were completed at the end of 1955. St. Anselm's architect, Antonine Raymond, donated his plans for the parish unit which are a striking combination of functional and native Japanese forms. Moves are now underway for the second step in the development of this Japanese foundation, the finding of available property where the monastery may be established. Father Hildebrand explained these plans to the chapter at St. John's as follows:

"There are at present fifty to sixty different Orders and Congregations working in Japan. After having lived and worked among the Japanese for the last twenty-four years and seeing the work and methods of all these Orders, I am still of the opinion that our Order will have the greatest possibility and the deepest attraction for the Japanese. In fact, it is just our way of life and our way of education which are still lacking in the Church in Japan. Many Japanese who have visited Benedictine abbeys abroad came again and again through the years asking for such a foundation. May I only mention in this connection the late Admiral Yamamoto, a prominent Catholic, who up to his death was our intimate friend and wished nothing more ardently than a Benedictine abbey in the outskirts of the capital. He knew many abbeys abroad and his idea was that a Benedictine abbey, with our solemn liturgy, and a school, with our typical Benedictine education, would be one of the greatest mission forces in Japan." [89]

Father Hildebrand conceives the work of this monastic center to include the teaching of philosophy and theology, giving liturgical retreats and lectures, conducting an academy of Gregorian chant and church music, opening of a Benedictine boarding school, reception of guests, and the revival of the Japanese liturgical quarterly *Phos Christou* of which he was editor from 1938–44 and which the bishops of Japan have asked the Benedictines to reissue. Candidates have already entered the St. John's community with the intention of going to this Japanese foundation, and of these, one Japanese-American priest was ordained in 1955.

St. John's made moves during the period that the four foundations in Mexico, Puerto Rico, Kentucky, and Japan were begun, to establish another monastery in the state of Utah. This undertaking was actually the first of the foundation efforts of the late 1940's, and was carried on for seven years, from 1943 to 1950, when the project was aban-

320

doned. Bishop Duane G. Hunt of Salt Lake City asked the Benedictines, because of their experience with Indian work in Minnesota, to come to the Uintah basin to take over from the Paulist Fathers the parish of St. Helen in Roosevelt, Utah, with its eight missions among the Indians of the Uintah Reservation. Father Wendel Luetmer, O.S.B., professor of biology in the college, was sent as pastor, with Father Blase Schumacher, O.S.B., as assistant. At the same time they were commissioned by Abbot Alcuin to look around for a possible monastic site in Utah. Through the offices of Monsignor Wilfrid Giroux, pastor of St. Joseph's parish, Ogden, who had attended St. Mary's Abbey school in Newark and was a close friend of the Benedictines, steps were taken to make a monastic and educational start in Ogden. Twenty acres, ideally located, were offered for the foundation by the city of Ogden and private donors including several Mormons of that community. Monsignor Giroux offered to make a division of his parish so that the Benedictines might have a parish in Ogden attached to the proposed monastery. He was successful in obtaining a government grant to assist the Sisters of St. Benedict from St. Joseph in the erection of a hospital in Ogden whose chaplaincy would be given to one of the monks. At the monastery itself a high school and later a college for Catholic boys was to be established, the first in the state of Utah and surrounding region. At the same time pastoral work in the Uintah valley was to continue. Bishop Hunt and Abbot Alcuin signed a formal agreement to this effect on 13 January 1945 which was confirmed by the Holy See.

The Ogden monastery never materialized, however, for in the following year Monsignor Giroux died and the project was dropped. Father Wendel, who had preferred to make the foundation in the Uintah valley, continued to investigate possibilities in that area. In 1949 a non-Catholic rancher, Horace Coltharp, offered his half of a jointly owned 1,600 acre ranch seven miles out of Roosevelt, and the chapter at St. John's again voted to purchase the other half of the property. Here Father Wendel hoped to start a monastery with a small school, and eventually to establish a regional minor and major seminary there for students from Utah, Idaho, and Nevada. But the other half of the Roosevelt ranch could not be purchased from its owner, while back at St. John's Abbot Alcuin was hard-pressed to supply priests and Brothers for the other foundations in Mexico, Puerto Rico, and Kentucky which had been started in the meantime. In 1950 Father Wendel was sent to St. Maur's Priory in Kentucky as prior, and the Utah undertaking was abandoned.

When Abbot Alcuin assumed office the abbey had been engaged for thirty years in mission work on the Bahama Islands. One of his first acts was to visit the islands to discover conditions at firsthand, and the culmination of his efforts in this field was the establishment of St. Augustine's Priory in Nassau which was the sixth and last monastic foundation of the 1940's. Abbot Alcuin found four abbey priests working on New Providence, Andros, San Salvador and Harbour Island in 1923 under the direction of the venerable vicar forane of the Bahamas, Father Chrysostom Schreiner. Abbot Alcuin determined to send more Benedictines to the Bahamas, and also to relieve Father Chrysostom in 1924 of active charge of the mission. Father Hildebrand Eickhoff, O.S.B., with the title of prior, succeeded Father Chrysostom and the latter retired to Watling's Island, the landfall of Columbus, now called San Salvador through his instrumentality. There he worked until 3 January 1928 when he died suddenly in his sleep at Riding Rock after a missionary career of thirty-seven years.

Father Hildebrand added two more churches in the capital at Nassau, began the tradition of evening devotions and took an interest in establishing a native Sisterhood on the islands. The other Benedictines working in the Bahamas included Father Bonaventure Hansen, who had been sent down by Abbot Peter in 1920, the two Roerig brothers, Fathers Leander and Gabriel, Father Arnold Mondloch, and Brother Bede Seither. They were assisted by two Sisters of Charity from Mount St. Vincent on the Hudson, New York. Father Hildebrand was succeeded in 1928 by Father Hugo Tell, O.S.B., who stayed for fourteen months, and then Abbot Alcuin turned to Father Bernard Kevenhoerster, O.S.B., pastor of St. Anselm's parish in New York City. During his pastorate there a parish church had been built and beautifully decorated by European monks in the Beuronese style of art. Father Bernard was a close friend of Patrick Cardinal Hayes, archbishop of New York, and the Bahama Islands were still under the ecclesiastical jurisdiction of New York. Through the years the archbishops of New York had been instrumental in obtaining a grant for the Bahamas from the Board of Catholic Indians and Colored People. Cardinal Hayes had, along with St. John's, given yearly subsidies to the missionaries in the Bahamas and assisted in the building of churches, schools, and clinics. Before his departure for the Bahamas in 1929 Father Bernard was given the title of vicar forane by Cardinal Hayes, and negotiations were begun for the erection of the Bahamas as a prefecture apostolic. On 21 March 1929 the apostolic delegation in Washington received bulls for the erection of the Bahamas as a prefecture apostolic under the Sacred Congregation of the Propagation of the Faith. When he was informed that the prefecture he desired had been established, Cardinal Hayes highly recommended Father Bernard to Archbishop Pietro Fumasoni-Biondi, apostolic delegate to the United States:

"It has occurred to me that I should let your Excellency know what a very able, apostolic, saintly man Father Bernard is. He has been in New York some twenty years, and is revered and, I might say, beloved of our clergy and the people who know him.

322

"I do not know what the mind of the Abbot may be; but, should Father Bernard's name come up for consideration with regard to appointment to the prefecture, let me assure your Excellency no one more worthy could be presented." [90]

The mind of Abbot Alcuin was, unquestionably, along definitely different lines. Since the missionary personnel of the Bahamas was Benedictine, he as abbot felt that the ecclesiastical and religious superior should be the same person. He desired that an abbey *nullius*, an abbey with ordinary jurisdiction, be established in the Bahamas with the abbot-ordinary being named a titular bishop. The St. Ottilien Benedictines had proceeded along these lines in their African missions, and he wanted a similar arrangement to go into effect in the Bahamas. Abbot Alcuin journeyed to Rome to explain his position to Guglielmo Cardinal von Rossum, prefect of the Congregation of the Propagation of the Faith, and in the meantime the bull of erection of a prefecture in the Bahamas was held up for three years. Cardinal Hayes, Father Bernard, and the missionaries in the Bahamas at that time felt that the prefecture, which Rome had already authorized, would be more desirable. In this way the Bahamas could advance through gradual steps to the state of a diocese, and the prefect, by being named a bishop, could more easily make the indispensable mission collections in the dioceses of the United States. A bishop would lend more prestige to the Bahamian Church, they maintained, especially since the Anglicans in this British colony had a bishop stationed in Nassau.

While this impasse continued Abbot Alcuin next suggested that the Dominicans take charge of the Bahamas, and a representative of the Order of Preachers came to Nassau to examine conditions. But all of the Benedictines in the Bahamas wanted to stay on the mission, and when the abbot presented the question of retaining the Bahamas to the St. John's chapter after the close of the second retreat on 22 August 1930, a large majority favored retaining the mission. Abbot Alcuin then informed Rome that St. John's would continue Bahama mission work, but that he desired the establishment of an abbey *nullius* there. Cardinal Hayes was in close correspondence with Father Bernard at the same time, and the former apostolic delegate to the United States, Archbishop Fumasoni-Biondi, was now a cardinal and acting as secretary of the Congregation of the Propagation of the Faith in Rome. On 9 June 1931 it was announced from Rome that Father Bernard, with the title of Right Reverend Monsignor, was named first prefect apostolic of the newly erected prefecture of the Bahamas.

Cardinal Hayes journeyed to Nassau to install his good friend on 7 February 1932 in the presence of William Cardinal O'Connell of Boston who along with Hayes spent winter vacations in the Bahamas. The very next day Cardinal Hayes informed the apostolic delegate in Washington that he was convinced it was important that Monsignor

Bernard should have the episcopal character as soon as possible.[91] On November 24 of the following year Monsignor Bernard was elevated to the rank of vicar apostolic, and Hayes happily consecrated him in St. Patrick's Cathedral, New York, December 21. Archbishop Murray, Bishop Busch, and Abbot Alcuin came from Minnesota for the elevation of the second son of St. John's to the episcopacy. Abbot Alcuin informed Abbot Martin of St. Benedict's that he had first learned of the appointment in the newspaper.

No Task Refused

From 1933–49 Bishop Bernard advanced Catholicism in the Bahamas through his personal kindness and interest in the poor and needy; through the new parish schools he built, as well as through his marked success in collecting funds each year for the mission throughout the United States. He appointed Father Bonaventure Hansen as his provicar, and the two missionaries worked together in building up the Church. When Bishop Bernard first came to the islands there were 3,200 Catholics among a population of 55,000. Father Bonaventure had wanted more active convert work among the natives of the islands, as well as the establishment of a native Sisterhood on the islands, and with the support of Bishop Bernard major steps could now be taken in this direction. Abbot Alcuin continued to send more missionaries from St. John's so that a steadily increasing number of stations could be established on more of the out islands, and the Sisters of Charity greatly expanded their educational work. By 1943 Catholics had more than doubled in numbers to 7,122. In the 1954 government census this figure had risen to 13,054 Catholics in a total population of 83,060. In an eleven year period Catholics had increased by 86%, and the Congregation of the Propagation of the Faith informed Father Bonaventure that this record was one of the best in the entire mission field of the Church.[92]

One of the most interesting missionizing techniques of the Benedictines in the Bahamas is their constant stress on active participation of all the faithful in the public worship of the Church. The Negro people naturally respond to any invitation to take an active part in divine services, and Father Bonaventure describes how this worked out on Harbour Island:

". . . The people in Harbour Island had been Protestant. They were all converts and had to learn the prayers. From the very beginning we had them learn the *Gloria* and *Credo* by reciting them slowly until they knew them. The people liked this and it was a means of conversion.

"Bishop Bernard knew that I had a fancy for the *Missa Recitata* and he did not discourage it. Father Arnold [Mondloch] made a great improvement in our technique by having a leader besides the priest. The leader would recite some of the Mass prayers with the people in English while the priest would say them at the altar in Latin. I had

324

public participation before Father Bernard came. The Sisters stayed in the Bahamas during the summer months and instead of summer school I gave them liturgical books to start them out. I typed out the Latin pronunciation for the people. Those who could not read it could get it by sound. We tried it Sunday after Sunday. Then we took the *Gloria* and got that down. Before very long we knew the whole Mass. We used Abbot Cuthbert Goeb's *Offeramus* to get it going, and it went fine. When people from New York would come into our churches while in the Bahamas it was the experience of their lifetime. We had English and the children and people were answering. The Sisters would give books to the visitors and they prolonged their visit. They told Bishop Bernard that the experience they had was wonderful. Never in their lives had they heard anything like that. Then Bishop Bernard wrote me a letter and told me to introduce public recitation of the Mass prayers in all the parishes." [93]

St. Augustine's Priory

As Abbot Alcuin continued sending more Fathers and Brothers to the Bahamas he was anxious to establish a permanent monastery where traditional Benedictine community life could be carried out, including public praying of the Divine Office of the Church. In 1946 this aim was achieved with the establishment of St. Augustine of Canterbury Monastery outside of Nassau on an imposing site overlooking the ocean. St. Augustine's is a dependent priory of St. John's with Father Frederic Frey, O.S.B., as prior. Prior Frederic had for years been encouraging the opening of a first-class boys' school for the training of native Bahamians in preuniversity and preprofessional programs. This was accomplished with the beginning, during the same year, of St. Augustine's College, a preparatory school for ninety-three boys, which quickly established its reputation in the annual Cambridge examinations. Fra Jerome Hawes, T.O.S.F., a renowned English priest-architect, who had joined in the mission work and resided on Cat Island in a hermitage designed and built by himself, drew the unique plans for the monastery and school buildings which the Fathers and Brothers erected in great part by themselves.

As Abbot Alcuin and Bishop Bernard began to realize in the late 1940's that their careers were drawing to a close, the subject of an abbey *nullius* in the Bahamas was renewed. The abbot requested the bishop in 1947 to join him in a request to the Propaganda for an abbey *nullius* with Bishop Bernard to be the first abbot-bishop. But Bishop Bernard felt that the Bahamas were still in a missionary condition which limited the possibilities of native vocations in sufficient numbers to sustain an independent Bahamian abbey, as he told Abbot Alcuin:

"Our 10,000 Catholics are surrounded by a decided, strong and active Protestant culture on all sides, and we cannot expect to have many vocations to the religious life, nor the priesthood. This condition is apt to last for the next forty or fifty years." [94]

When the bishop died on 9 December 1949 the Holy See appointed as his successor Father Paul Leonard Haggerty, O.S.B. The new vicar apostolic, Bishop Leonard, had been working in the Bahamas since 1937, and assisting Bishop Bernard in his annual collections. Five years to the day after the bishop's death his vicar, Father Bonaventure, died quietly in his sleep, and the second period in the Catholic history of the Bahamas came to an end.[95]

Bishop Leonard has continued his predecessor's policies with added emphasis on the building of more schools, and the preparation of Catholic laity to make Christian social principles an integral part of Bahamian life. In a short period of five years he has directed the building of three new parish schools, doubled capacity in three more, and aided in expanding the facilities of the high school for boys at St. Augustine's and that for girls at St. Francis Xavier's. Eleven islands have Catholic spiritual care. There are twelve schools in operation, and forty-four churches and chapels with regular services. The large majority of these buildings are constructed from native stone by the Benedictines themselves. Twenty-seven priests and Brothers serve under Bishop Leonard, of whom twenty-three are Benedictine, three members of the Scarboro Foreign Missionary Society from Toronto, Canada, and one diocesan. This latter priest is Father Arthur Chapman, an Anglican convert who was with the R.A.F. in the Bahamas and was received into the Church at St. Francis Xavier parish by Father Brendan Forsyth, O.S.B., in 1949. After studying at St. John's and then at the Beda College in Rome he was the first priest to be ordained in the Bahamas when he received priestly orders from Bishop Leonard during the Easter Vigil service of 1955. Twenty-three Sisters of Charity and twenty-eight native Sisters, novices and postulants of Blessed Martin de Porres also serve in the vicariate. A growing number of active Catholic laity are assuming leadership in Bahamian affairs, among whom are two St. John's alumni, the Dupuch brothers, Etienne, '28, editor of the Nassau *Daily Tribune*, and Eugene, '34, Member of the House of Assembly and of the Governor's Council.

The five monastic and educational foundations of St. John's in the Bahamas, Mexico, Puerto Rico, Kentucky, and Japan were the last major effort of Abbot Alcuin. He was occupied with their establishment at a time when his former strong constitution was steadily weakening. He suffered from a heart condition, but he would rise from his hospital bed and be off again to his farflung foundations for visitations. In the midst of this activity Aloysio Cardinal Maglione, Vatican secretary of state, accorded him the privilege, on 17 July 1943 in the name of the Holy Father, of wearing the violet biretta and skull cap as recognition of his work for the Church. But Abbot Alcuin told no one of this honor, and proceeded to put the document and insignia away in his filing cabinet where they were found after his death.

Abbot Alcuin Deutsch had unquestionably in his twenty-nine years in office achieved much of what he initially proposed. His aim of putting first things first had been attained to a marked degree. He had assisted in bringing the Benedictine institute to maturity in the United States, and incorporating its full traditions in American observance. The American Benedictine monastery, as Abbot Wimmer had originally planned, was striving to be a worshipping, educating and missionizing center in the service of the Church. No one aspect of this program was emphasized to the exclusion of the other two. From the monastic life of worship flowed both an educational and missionary apostolate. By preserving this traditional balance, which was the original intent of St. Benedict, the vigor of early Benedictinism was revived in modern times.

Benedictine Integration

Abbot Alcuin did not attain these goals alone, however. The American liturgical revival had been fostered by Father Virgil and his circle of dedicated pioneers; Abbot Alcuin supported the movement but was not its leader. Educational work was advanced by future Abbots Mark and Severin, and Fathers Walter, Theodore, Matthew, and Damian; Abbot Alcuin sent monks for advanced studies in diversified fields but was not a leader in the educational world. The missionary Benedictines in the Bahamas, as well as St. John's monks like Fathers Clarus, Basil, and Alexander, had pushed for active participation in the missionary life of the Church; Abbot Alcuin was greatly aided by them as well as by the willingness of the community to accept heavy farflung responsibilities. In each of these endeavors, liturgical, educational, and missionary, Abbot Alcuin's contribution was, rather, that he acted as a balancer. These activities were integrated into one Benedictine program under his direction, but need further planning and organization. But the integration was attempted, and there his true historical position would probably be found. In that integration as well was the source of increasing vocations to monastic life, and the characteristic contribution which a Benedictine abbey was able to offer to modern society.

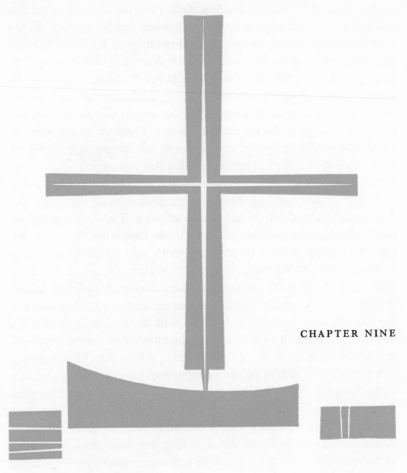

CHAPTER NINE

SERVICE NOT RECOGNITION

In the late 1940's Abbot Alcuin began to decline noticeably in health. Throughout his long administration he had enjoyed excellent health, but as old age overtook him he suffered continually from poor circulation of blood. He had difficulty in breathing and could not sleep at night. The widespread involvements of the community's undertakings made demands upon his energy at a time when he needed rest and release from administrative pressures. He admitted this development to his Roman classmate, Father Albert Hammenstede, O.S.B., the prior of Maria Laach, when he said: "I am feeling the burden of the work more and more in this constantly growing community." [1] During his long years as abbot he had with marked success practiced the technique of indefinite jurisdiction, and now found it difficult to delegate major responsibilities to subordinate officials.

But in 1947, 1949 and 1950 his doctors placed him in St. Paul and

328

St. Cloud hospitals for periods of treatment. Abbot Alcuin then realized that he could not continue as before, and unknown to the community, he petitioned the Holy See in the autumn of 1950 for a coadjutor with right of succession. In a letter of 19 October 1950 the Congregation of Religious praised his long and varied service to the Church, and informed him that the Holy Father had accepted his resignation. Authorization was given to proceed with the election of a coadjutor abbot who would have both the right of succession and power to rule the community from the time of his election and approval. On 28 December 1950 the community elected the prior of St. John's, Father Baldwin Dworschak, O.S.B., as Abbot Alcuin's coadjutor, and the new abbot was blessed at Collegeville, 29 March 1951, by Bishop Peter Bartholome, coadjutor bishop of St. Cloud.

Death of Abbot Alcuin

When Abbot Alcuin's resignation was announced, messages and letters came in to him from all corners of the world. They included the great and small of many countries who had been the recipients of assistance and charity from St. John's while he was abbot, or those who knew of his labors of the previous twenty-nine years.[2] For example, Bishop Simon Landersdorfer, O.S.B., of Passau, Bavaria, wrote that under him St. John's had become "unquestionably the greatest cloister of our Order," while Archbishop Mar Ivanios of Trivandrum, India, congratulated him:

". . . for all the achievement of your great and extensive work for such a long period and the progress that the great Abbey has made under your benign care and advice. A glorious crown is awaiting you. May I say that you have already achieved it in some measure."[3]

Abbot Alcuin at first hoped that he might regain enough health and strength to go to the Bahamas where, as he said, "I may be able to do a little work yet since we are short of men there." But his doctors discouraged even the thought of such a possibility, and he then moved across the corridor from his abbatial rooms to a simple monastic cell where he hoped to enjoy long hours of leisurely reading, meditating, and, as he had long desired, "closer communion with the realities that really count."[4] For seven months he did enjoy such a schedule. Then, on the Vigil of Pentecost, 12 May 1951, shortly after making his weekly confession and assisting with the monastic and student family at Saturday Benediction of the Blessed Sacrament, he was stricken with a fatal heart attack as the community was chanting Matins of the Feast of Pentecost. Abbot Baldwin was called from the choir and Abbot Alcuin died at 8:50 p.m., after receiving the sacrament of Extreme Unction, on the same feastday of Pentecost as his namesake Blessed Alcuin had died.

St. John's close friend, Archbishop John Gregory Murray, metropolitan of the province of St. Paul, delivered the funeral eulogy on May 17, and in the course of his tribute to Abbot Alcuin he stated:

"... Father Abbot realized that all of his subjects must be perfect monks before they became apostles. Therefore he did everything in his power in order that they might have the maximum opportunity to be sanctified to the utmost in order to be qualified to exemplify in their own lives those qualities they hoped to develop in their flocks no matter whether they were out on the Atlantic Ocean, or out in the Pacific Ocean, or whether they were on the vast stretches of the Western prairies, or whether they were down in the Caribbean Sea.

Service Not Recognition

"And so we pay tribute to him today because of his zeal and because of his apostolic spirit in carrying out the tradition of St. Benedict who was not only dedicated to the perfection of the individual without necessarily making reference to the priesthood, but also to the tradition of St. Benedict in spreading the spirit of Christianity through those who were ordained priests in his community for the sanctification and the salvation of the earth. Even as the tradition of St. Benedict became the outstanding influence in the Christianization of Europe, so the spirit of St. Benedict must be extended today in order to counteract the vicious evil influences that have been marshalled in the last thirty years in order to neutralize the influence of Christianity. And while some may look with dismay at the disaster that has spread so far and wide, Father Abbot Alcuin Deutsch saw only another challenge for all those who had the heritage of Christianity to exert themselves all the more in the spirit of sacrifice in order to meet every need, no matter what it might be, in the cause of Christ for the salvation of souls and for the perfection of the individual. . . ."[5]

At the time of Abbot Alcuin's resignation and death there was constant reference in the newspapers and magazines not only to his accomplishments, but to the fact that St. John's had become the largest Benedictine monastery in the world. One of the new abbot's first acts was to discourage this emphasis on size and numbers, so typical of the American penchant for bigness, and to warn against a spirit of gigantomania taking hold in any form. By this act and the motto he chose, Abbot Baldwin established the spirit of his administration. In chapter sixty-four of his *Rule* St. Benedict admonished the abbot to be of service to his brethren rather than to preside over them, and the new abbot chose that motto to be placed on his coat of arms. The phrase, *prodesse magis quam praeesse,* was as well the guiding spirit of policies enacted in the first five transitional years of Abbot Baldwin's administration.

The phrase was indicative also of the new abbot's monastic career before his election as sixth abbot of St. John's. He had come to St. John's in 1920 at the age of fourteen and was enrolled in the junior department of those years. The name of Dworschak was well-known in the St. John's family, as two of his uncles had received their complete twelve-year education for the priesthood at Collegeville. They are Very

330

Reverend Roman P. Dworschak, '23, pastor of St. Mary's Church, Dazey, N. Dak., and the Most Reverend Leo F. Dworschak, '26, auxiliary bishop of Fargo, N. Dak. Wilfred Dworschak was the son of Matt Dworschak and Catherine Waters, and was born at Arcadia, Wisconsin. Abbot Alcuin gave Wilfred the religious name of Baldwin when he entered the novitiate at St. John's in 1927. After pursuing the customary spiritual and academic program of a Benedictine clericate, Father Baldwin was ordained on 5 June 1933. He was sent to the University of Minnesota for graduate study in English, and after returning to St. John's he taught in the English department and acted as prefect in St. Benet Hall. Like Abbot Peter before him, Father Baldwin was interested in photography and moderated the school's yearbook, *The Sagatagan*. Abbot Alcuin named him prefect of clerics in 1945, and prior of the community in 1947. During these years Father Baldwin also gave retreats and contributed to *The Week With Christ*, which had been inaugurated by Father Emeric Lawrence as a student weekly spiritual bulletin, and during the years of World War II was sent to many American army camps for the use of chaplains and soldiers. When the community elected him as coadjutor abbot, Abbot Alcuin informed Abbot Boniface Woehrmueller of St. Boniface Abbey, Munich:

Abbot Baldwin Dworschak

"It was an excellent choice and I am happy that the community elected him whom I appointed Prior four years ago on the Feast of the Epiphany. The new abbot has been an excellent monk and priest; he has had wide experience in various appointments, and he has governed the community wisely during my illness in these last three years. He has had experience with our new foundations and will be able to continue their development." [6]

Abbot Baldwin declared after his blessing that he intended to continue the policies and traditions established by his predecessor. He has worked to build up the monastic foundations in Mexico, Puerto Rico, Kentucky and Japan so they will be able to advance as rapidly as possible toward independent abbey status. Personnel has been added in these places, as well as in the Bahama Islands; native young monks destined for these foundations have been sent to Rome for training; and the monastic setup of these dependent houses has been better organized and strengthened. At home in Collegeville the new abbot planned to integrate the ideals of the liturgical revival more fully in community observance, and as a first step daily sung Vespers was introduced.

His years of experience in the abbey school had convinced the new abbot of the importance of St. John's educational effort. Besides taking an active part in explaining the ideals and needs of a Christian liberal arts college to the public, he has served as president of the Minnesota College Fund Association which, together with thirty-eight similar organizations of the country, is presenting the needs of the small liberal arts college to American industrial and business men of the nation. In line with this effort a development fund office has been established at St. John's under the direction of Father Walter Reger, O.S.B., secretary of St. John's Alumni Association. At the invitation of the College of St. Benedict, and under the auspices of Bishop Bartholome, St. John's joined in an adult education program in 1955 in the city of St. Cloud in which a winter program of studies is offered to the people of central Minnesota. In this way an important step has been taken to bring Benedictine educational work into closer contact with the people of the region, as it was in the first years after the abbey was founded. The educational needs of central Minnesota are met on this level as a first move in a program which has potential for varied development. In 1954 summer workshops on mental health for clergymen of all faiths were begun with Father Alexius Portz, O.S.B., as director, and Bishop Bartholome as sponsor. Authorities in the field of psychiatry have served as visiting lecturers, and the Hamm Foundation of St. Paul has given yearly grants to finance this undertaking in interfaith study of pastoral care and psychotherapy. The summer retreat program has been broadened to include week-end retreats for married couples, and the summer school of Gregorian chant has been developed as an academic program of the university, with both Catholics and non-Catholics in attendance.

Service Not Recognition

In 1950–51 moves were made to establish a department of sacred art at St. John's which, while being the first academic sequence of its kind in the United States, was the development of an idea that had been discussed since the early years of the liturgical movement in the country. When the Liturgical Arts Society was formed in 1930, the architect L. Bancel LaFarge told Abbot Alcuin:

"During the past two years a number of professional men — architects for the most part — have been discussing ways and means of improving the art of the Church. While we know that Christianity, or more specifically the Church, was during the centuries the most enlightened patron of the crafts, we feel that conditions are not so favorable in this country today. On the one hand there exists, on the part of the public, an imperfect understanding of what the architect, the painter and the craftsman are trying to do. On the other hand, we ourselves realize how utterly unsuited much that passes for 'religious art' is to the worship of God and the liturgy of the Church." [7]

Two years later this Liturgical Arts Society proposed to St. John's that a college of liturgical arts and crafts be established in connection with its school, to be jointly operated by the society and the university. Abbot Alcuin received a constant stream of similar requests to make St. John's a focal point in the pioneer field of liturgical art and architecture in the United States, and artists and architects offered themselves for the cause. The abbot always said he desired to undertake such a project, but it never materialized during his administration. Perhaps the main unfulfilled desire of Abbot Alcuin was to build an abbey church, and for over twenty years he planned and obtained designs for this pressing need which were submitted to the chapter but never accepted both because of other immediate building needs and because there was no common agreement on the separate church plans. He invited the Beuronese artist, Brother Clement Frischauf, O.S.B., who had worked on the crypt of Monte Cassino, with the Benedictines in Sao Paulo, Brazil, and on St. Anselm's Church in New York City, to come to Collegeville to do the art work on his proposed church. Brother Clement, while never being able to fulfill this assignment, did contribute much to artistic development at St. John's by transplanting the Beuronese style to the United States and by painting a number of areas such as the infirmary chapel, monastic refectory, apse of the abbey church and porter's office entrance.

At the same time Father Gilbert Winkelmann, O.S.B., was teaching church architecture at St. John's, and during thirty years he trained a group of young Catholic architects who are today designing many churches and schools in the region. Father Gilbert also designed several churches himself along neo-Romanesque lines, among which are St. Benedict's Church in Avon, Minnesota, and St. Mary's Church in Foxhome, N. Dak. The tradition of offering courses in drawing and crafts which had been begun by the pioneers, Fathers Cornelius Wittmann, Vincent Schiffrer, and Raphael Knapp, was continued during Abbot Alcuin's time by Fathers Ignatius Wiltzius, Angelo Zankl and Joachim Watrin. Father Anthony Unterhofer from Seitenstetten Abbey in Austria spent the years after Hitler's *Anschluss* assisting in the art department at St. John's. Father Joachim applied geometric principles to the creation of liturgical symbols which have received wide circulation in the United States, and continue to be copied and adapted at the present time, graphically, on cloth and in stone. Fathers Angelo, Dunstan and Baldwin also assisted in the editing of the *Catholic Art Quarterly* during the same period.

In 1950–51 a move was made to coordinate these efforts of former years through the establishment of a department of sacred art with programs in architecture, painting and sculpture. In the school bulletin this undertaking is described as follows:

"The specific contribution of the arts to Christian education is a creative attitude toward the whole of life. The liberal arts deal mainly with ideas in their abstract and universal forms, whereas the fine arts seek to express them creatively in a form that is concrete and individual. Thus the whole purpose and nature of art is sacramental: to mirror outwardly the inner essence of things, to picture and embody in matter the world of spirit and of truth. A process of experimentation is the means employed in developing the power of creative intuition. For art

333

will only be worthwhile and ring true if the ideas it tries to convey are not arbitrarily imposed on the materials at hand but drawn out of them. Once awakened, this creative self-expression tends to spread to other fields of making: man, created in the image and likeness of God, is naturally a maker.

Service Not Recognition

"The primary purpose of the Department of Art is to foster contemporary sacred art. It is in this field that the sacramental principle can find its highest and noblest expression; for sacred art seeks to restate in the form and style of the present day the magnificent truths of Christian doctrine. Hence the department stresses accompanying instruction in the visual arts with a strong formal background in theology and philosophy and active participation in the sacramental life of the Church. The Church's traditions, her needs and norms, are examined in courses on archaeology, iconography and liturgical norms with a view to providing a fresh and vital approach to sacred art and revealing its many possibilities." [8]

While the initial creative work of the department was received with mixed reactions varying from high praise to unqualified rejection, it was evident that an attempt was being made to revive the creative artistic spirit so integral to Christian culture. This was noted by three observers among others. James M. Wells, custodian of the Newberry Library in Chicago, stated to Frank Kacmarcik of the department:

"I'm quite impressed with the amount of activity going on in Minnesota. It is encouraging to see how alive liturgical art is. . . . It seems to me to combine dignity with utility in a way all too rare in academic circles." [9]

The Catholic philosopher, Jacques Maritain, said:

"I like your illustrations very much — they are perhaps, to my mind, a little too hieratic and stylized, but this is, I think, a technical necessity with wood engraving, and in any case, they present us with genuine, deeply inspired and authentically living art." [10]

In the same vein the English type-expert, Beatrice Warde, wrote:

"You are doing a great work there. To me it would be thrilling beyond words if the long-overdue typographic renaissance in America were to start, as it started in England, mainly as an effort amongst the Catholic intelligentsia. I mean the sort of radical reform that starts with the *radices*, good type faces." [11]

Professor Josef Albers, head of the Yale department of art, had in a student convocation pointed up the necessity of reviving the fine arts in contemporary academic programs. He stated that the prevailing educational system is antiquated because it is arranged for a few intellectuals, while the hands, eyes and ears have to be developed if modern society is to have producers and creators. Albers went on to say that the Benedictine cloister schools of the mediaeval period produced the best-known integration of truth and beauty through creative develop-

334

169 A visit with King Paul and Queen Frederika of Greece at Kremsmuenster Abbey, Austria.

170 Benedictine abbots of the world and Christ's vicar, Pius XII.

171 Meeting the Archbishop of Tours, His Excellency Louis Gaillard.

172 Loyal to their Alma Mater: 'Old Timers' Alumni Reunion of 1955.

173 Blessing St. Mary's residence hall in August, 1951.

174 College Graduation: 'Let us put on the armor of light.'

175 Homecoming: Father Walter Reger; alumni president, Herbert Adrian, '29; Abbot Baldwin, and former alumni president, Fred Hughes, '31.

L. to R. First Row: Francis Sadlier (retired, St. Leo); Bertrand Dolan (St. Anselm's); Severin Gertken (Abbot-Ordinary, St. Peter's); Denis Strittmatter (Archabbot and Abbot-President Amer. Cass. Cong.. St. Vincent); Bernard Kaelin (Abbot Primate of Benedictine Order); Columban Thuis (Abbot-President Swiss Amer. Cong., St. Joseph's); Ignatius Esser (Archabbot, retired, St. Meinrad); Cuthbert Goeb (retired, Assumption); second row: Baldwin Dworschak (St. John's); Raphael Heider (St. Martin's); Gerald Benkert (Marmion); Cuthbert McDonald (St. Benedict's); third row: Damian Jentges (Mount Angel); Lawrence Vohs (St. Bede); Paul Nahlen (New Subiaco); Stephen Schappler (Conception); fourth row: Bede Luibel (St. Bernard's); Philip Berning (St. Gregory's); Charles Coriston (St. Paul's); Father Lambert Dunne, secretary to Abbot Primate (St. Mary's).

176 Benedictine Abbots of North America with Abbot Primate Bernard Kaelin at Sant' Anselmo in 1953.

L. to R. First Rows Fr. Novices Roy Carrere, Leon Pilon, Clarence Weber, Rene McGraw, Joel Stockert, Brian Jerabek, Alvin Fong Ben, Fr. Waldemar Reese, Fr. Felix Tang, Fr. Nov. Simeon Thole; second row: Fraters Peregrin Berres, Lanfranc LeMay, Theophil Brown, Gordon Tavis, Kenneth Russell, Cletus Rausch, Mederic Pease, Ildephonse Wenninger, Daniel Durken; third row: Fraters Mathias Spier, Otto Weber, Chrysostom Kim, Myron Kasprick, Neal Lawrence, Caedmon Wahl, Urban Steiner, Jonathan Fischer, Xavier Reichert, Nov. Paulin Blecker, Wilfred Theisen, Fr. Nov. Finian McDonald, Fr. Augustin Cerezo Murillo, Fr. Juan Tirado; fourth row: Kieran Nolan, Olaf Skjolsvik, Warren Kulas, Alberic Culhane, Anselm Pedrizetti, Aurelius Burns, Robert Blumeyer, Eugene McGlothlin, Conan Mawhorr, Jerome Coller; fifth row: Fraters Alcuin Siebenand, Meinulph Schmiesing, Andre Brissett, Wenceslaus Plotnik, Ansgar Rosen, Isidore Botz, Raban Tingerthal, Brice Howard, Corwin Collins, Donald McGinnis; sixth row: Fraters Diego Jimenez, Canute Anderson, Aldo Cadena, Thomas O'Connor, Ermin Bell, Leonard Dosh, Titus Thole, Melchior Freund, Timothy Kelly; back row: Fraters Meinrad Dindorf, Mario Shaw, Boswell Davis, Innocent Neikirk.

177 Novices and clerics of St. John's, 1956.

178 Clerics from several parts of the world.

L. to R. Front Row: Fathers Rembert Bularzik, Philip Bahner, Roman Homar, Prior Clarus Graves, Abbot Baldwin Dworschak, Subprior John Eidenschink, Thomas Borgerding, Leo Hoppe; second row: Fathers Sylvester Harter, Gerald McMahon, Gregory Roettger, Cosmas Dahlheimer, Benjamin Stein, Dominic Keller, Conrad Diekmann, Celestine Kapsner, Lancelot Atsch, Joachim Watrin, Fabian Wegleitner; third row: Christopher Bayer, Bede Michel, Odo Zimmermann, Martin Schirber, Ernest Kilzer, Matthew Kiess, Vincent Tegeder, Aldrich Huhne, Godfrey Diekmann, Paschal Botz; fourth row: Walbert Kalinowski, Jerome Docherty, Engelbert Dufner, Aubrey Zellner, Dunstan Tucker, Walter Reger.

179 The community of St. John's, 1956.

L. to R. First Row: Fathers James Kelly, Cuthbert Soukup, Boniface Axtman, Emeric Lawrence, Adelard Thuente, Alfred Deutsch, Bertram Niggeman, Mark Schneider; second row: Fathers Omer Maus, Benedict Avery, Caspar Keogh, Ronald Roloff, Vitus Bucher, Michael Marx, Alexius Portz, Florian Muggli, Francis Studer; third row: Fathers Gerard Farrell, Gunther Rolfson, Virgil O'Neill, Richard Eckroth, Germain Loeber, Jeremy Murphy, Eric Buermann, Colman Barry, Gilbert Tarlton, Henry Anderl; fourth row: Fathers Arnold Weber, Stanley Roche, Hugh Witzman, Kilian McDonnell, Gervase Soukup, Roland Behrendt, Bartholomew Sayles, Fintan Bromenshenkel.

180 *Heavy winter, the pines of St. John's.*

181 *Breaking ground for new monastery wing.*

182 *St. John's Branch General ROTC Unit.*

*183 Prior Clarus Graves and Subprior John Eidenschink
on stairway of new monastic wing.*

184 Entrance to new monastery.

185 *Interior of proposed abbey church.*

186 *New monastic wing completed in 1956.*

ment of mind, will, heart and senses. Education today, he maintained, has been changed from belief to knowledge, from a spiritual to an intellectual orientation.[12] Over one hundred years earlier Abbot Boniface Wimmer had said the same things in a striking declaration of principle for his American Benedictine abbeys:

"I am determined to have our monasteries not only schools of religion and of the sciences, but also nurseries of the fine arts, in order to develop a better taste for these things and to keep from our people the American mercenary spirit which thinks of nothing but how to make a living, because necessity demands it, and example encourages it. . . .

"Art must go hand in hand with religion, to give the exercises of religion that external splendor, dignity, and sublimity which make them more meaningful to sensuous man who cannot enter deeply enough into their inner spirit and therefore does not feel attracted to them. . . . It is the duty of monasteries to foster, to promote, and to spread art, especially religious art. . . . I am fully convinced that a monastic school which does not promote the fine arts as well as science and religion is very incomplete, and that, in the beginning, the want of scientific learning is more excusable than neglect of the arts. Heretics have not often been converted by learned men, but rather by the beauty of the Catholic Church, by the holiness of her ministers and members, and by her prayers. It will most probably not be different in America: *nil novi sub sole*. Perhaps I am mistaken, but observation and experience favor my view." [13]

Abbot Baldwin had been interested in art from his early years at St. John's, had done metal work, and designed and executed his own chalice at the time of his ordination. Shortly after becoming abbot he was faced with a major problem which had been discussed by the community for the last thirty years and not resolved. It was the question of building badly needed additions to the physical plant, a difficulty which was augmented by the rapidly growing monastic and student family. The farsighted building program of Abbot Alexius had served the community well for over fifty years. Abbot Peter had erected separate units when they were needed, while Abbot Alcuin's over-all building plans had never advanced beyond the discussion stage. In his long administration only three buildings were erected; an auditorium-music hall in 1928, a power house in 1945, and St. Mary's Hall for students in 1951, which was built through the generosity of alumni and friends. When the gymnasium, which was a fine building for its time, became too small in the 1930's, Abbot Alcuin would agree only to its being enlarged. The building was moved on rollers one hundred and fifty feet to the west and an addition of twenty-five feet added, which had to be enlarged again by another thirty-two feet in 1949. At the time of the dedication of the first addition to the gymnasium Father Virgil, as dean, stated in his address: "We owe this building to Abbot Alcuin alone."

There was, accordingly, no comprehensive solution of the community's building problems during the last years of its first century.

Service Not Recognition

When Abbot Baldwin faced the immediate need for additional space he decided, rather than making plans himself or seeking architectural advice of his own tastes, to seek consultation and joint discussion from the community at all stages of the undertaking. As an initial step, he appointed a building committee in August of 1951 composed of six members of the community to study existing facilities and make recommendations. This committee, with the subprior, Father John Eidenschink, as chairman, met in weekly sessions for a year and a half, and gradually came to the conclusion that an over-all plan was necessary to provide for present and future needs. These needs were listed in their order of priority and a report submitted to the community. The senior council and the building committee in joint session then decided on 3 March 1953 to solve the over-all problems in a dramatic and decisive way, as Father Virgil Michel had indicated in the 1920's. Abbot Baldwin sent a letter to twelve outstanding architects of Europe and America, inquiring if they were interested in preparing a comprehensive plan for St. John's which would embrace a hundred-year period. The architects, who were chosen on a basis of reputation, experience in comprehensive planning, and ability in contemporary architecture, included Richard J. Neutra of Los Angeles; Walter A. Gropius of Bauhaus fame and former dean of the Harvard School of Architecture; Eero Saarinen of Bloomfield Hills, Michigan; Thomas W. Sharp of Oxford, England; Marcel L. Breuer of New York City; Barry Byrne of Evanston, Illinois; Pietro Belluschi of the Massachusetts Institute of Technology; Professor Rudolf Schwarz of Cologne, Germany; Herman Baur of Basle, Switzerland; Robert Kramreiter of Vienna, Austria; A. Bosslet of Wuerzburg, Germany; and Joseph D. Murphy of St. Louis.

In the course of his letter of invitation to these twelve architects Abbot Baldwin stated:

"We have been working on a master list of needs and find that among the principal requirements are: a much larger church, additional monastic quarters, a library, a guest house, and an administration building. Once a successful master plan has been achieved, we will go ahead with a considerable part of it. The church, we feel, would probably be given priority.

"Although this present proposal concerns the comprehensive plan only, we are most interested in building a church which will be truly an architectural monument in the service of God. Sheer over-crowding forces us to expand our present facilities and we do not want the mere material exigencies of the situation to determine our achitecture. The

Benedictine tradition at its best challenges us to think boldly and to cast our ideas in forms which will be valid for centuries to come, shaping them with all the genius of present-day materials and techniques. We feel that the modern architect with his orientation toward functionalism and honest use of materials is uniquely qualified to produce a Catholic work. In our position it would, we think, be deplorable to build anything less, particularly since our age and our country have thus far produced so little truly significant religious architecture." [14]

To everyone's surprise all the architects who received letters answered with considerable interest, and all but two, who were too busy to accept, applied for the assignment. Five of the architects were then invited to come to Collegeville to confer and to see the problems at firsthand. These five were Gropius, Neutra, Byrne, Murphy and Breuer. Their visits during that spring of 1953 and the resulting discussion were a liberal and educating experience in architectural concepts for the community. On April 20–21 open meetings were held in which the relative merits of the different architects were discussed, and on the following day the building committee and senior council were asked by the abbot to list the five architects in their order of choice. A large majority selected Marcel Breuer because, as Abbot Baldwin stated: "He struck us as being not only an outstanding architect, but a simple, straightforward, sincere and rather humble person."

Marcel Breuer, Hungarian-born architect, made his studies in the Art Academy of Vienna and was attracted to the new Bauhaus at Dessau, Germany, where he became a professor in 1925. His analysis of the modern furniture problem led to his invention of the tubular steel chair in its original form. During his private architectural practice after 1926 in Berlin, he began his well-known studies of prefabricated, low-cost housing. By 1935 Breuer was in England, and two years later he was acting as research professor at Harvard in partnership with Walter Gropius, former director of the Bauhaus, at present in private practice in New York City. Among his more recent significant contributions is the design for the UNESCO building in Paris.

On 28 January 1954, after eight months of preparation, Breuer brought the drawings, models and books for the St. John's comprehensive plan before a meeting of the chapter. The news that St. John's intended to begin the first unit of this comprehensive program, a monastic addition, in the spring of 1954, was released to the public.

There was an immediate reaction from all sides. While there was considerable unfavorable private reaction to some features of the contemporary and functional designs, the public and professional response both in the United States and abroad was enthusiastic in support. Maurice Lavanoux, editor of *Liturgical Arts*, called Breuer's comprehensive plan "truly a milestone in the evolution of the architecture of the Catholic Church in this country," and went on to say:

". . . Even an inkling of these plans is sufficient to induce joy and hope for the future of the arts in the United States. . . . And the fact that all this should happen at Collegeville is significant, since the background of sound liturgical scholarship and practice at the Abbey is known throughout the world, particularly through its monthly publication, *Worship*, long known as *Orate Fratres*, of which Father Virgil was a founder and which Father Godfrey Diekmann now ably directs. Here we have the logical sequence: the liturgy first, in all the daily splendor of the ceremonies and of loving observance; then the arts closely integrated to the liturgy and practiced by those who take part in that liturgy, from which it draws its inspiration and substance.

Service Not Recognition

"When I first heard that Abbot Baldwin had invited a number of well-known architects to interviews at the Abbey to discuss their ideas concerning a thorough overhauling of the building plant, I felt it providential that such a creative approach should come to us from Collegeville precisely because of Saint John's strong liturgical background. Here, at last, is a plan, a dream, which might well have a great and beneficent influence in breaking that negative roadblock which so long has hindered a constructive approach to such problems." [15]

Sister M. Madeleva, president of St. Mary's College, Notre Dame, Indiana, wrote:

"I am looking at and dreaming of the new monastery which the future holds for you. . . . The interior of your Church delights me, particularly the placing of the altar. I am glad that your buildings are close to one another but not in the sequence of box cars. Your areas and quadrangles provide lovely and attractive cloisters but not distances that interfere with quick changing of classes and the like. The architecture which seems extreme to us may be the proper language of our day a hundred years from now. I am very glad indeed to have this opportunity to look with you into your future." [16]

Monsignor George Higgins of the Social Action Department, National Catholic Welfare Conference, wrote in the same vein:

"I am happy to be able to tell you that the reaction of our many friends to the plans for your proposed Abbey Church has been enthusiastically favorable. I haven't heard a word of criticism. Personally I thought that the announcement of your plans was a thrilling indication of cultural progress in the American Church. I do hope that the Abbot and his Council will have the courage to go through with the program up to the hilt. . . ." [17]

Another expression of approval came from Joseph D. Murphy, St. Louis architect, who declared:

"The design for your new church and monastery by Marcel Breuer is beautiful. I have studied the reproduction and the article in *Liturgical Arts* with great care and reviewed my impressions of your problems

338

and your magnificent site. I believe that its design is a very striking solution of the problem, beautifully situated and most expressive. . . . I feel confident that the resultant construction according to this design will be a contribution to architecture, and a tribute to the courage of the Abbey in making this important decision." [18]

The Breuer plans and designs were featured in fifteen magazines in the United States, France, Italy, Spain, Cuba and Japan, while the models have been displayed in New York, Boston, Denver and St. Paul exhibitions.[19] Marcel Breuer had as consultants for his St. John's plans the Italian architectural engineer, Pier Luigi Nervi, and two acoustical specialists, Sidney Wolfe and Walter Holtkamp of New York. The comprehensive plan calls for the eventual replacement of seventy-five percent of the present plant and is envisioned as a full century undertaking, depending on the financial resources of the community. Nineteen new buildings are designed and grouped in functional areas clustering around a central quadrangle. A system of 'shadow building' would permit the community to carry on its organic work without interruption over the long building period. A building would be erected in the shadow of an existing one, and when completed, the new building would be occupied and the old building could be razed whenever it ceased to be useful.

In this pattern, the first building, a monastic wing, was begun in the spring of 1954, and Fathers, clerics, and Brothers moved into the completed structure at the beginning of the centennial year. In this way the most immediate need for additional monastic space was met. The second step is a proposed abbey church, seating 1,400 and designed to meet the needs of full participation in divine worship by the whole monastic, student and parish community. To date the community chapter has authorized only the first building of the comprehensive plan, as *Time* magazine stated:

"The whole project may cost about $8,000,000, and since the sum is far beyond St. John's likely early means, its completion may be far in the future. But Abbot Baldwin and his black-cowled brothers are in no mad rush. 'After all,' he said last week, 'what are a few generations to the Benedictines?' " [19]

The proposed abbey church is conceived, as the French periodical *L'Architecture d'Aujourd'hui* stated, not only to express its own function but also the spirit of the Church. As described by *Architectural Forum*, Breuer plans to:

". . . bend a thin cowl of concrete into walls and roof over this monastic church, creased into folds for structural stiffness. And in front of the church will stand a symbolically modern bell tower for this 1,400-year-old client — a pierced banner of reinforced concrete.

"The structural system sought by Architect Breuer was one with which he could return to the clarity and honesty of the Romanesque

339

which he admires above all other historical styles ('Gothic already hides and fakes'). He found his opportunity in a continuous concrete slab, molded and dented into a kind of modern groining, a simpler version of the UNESCO structure with the same acoustical advantages (especially important to the chanting of the monks' offices). There will be no hung ceiling, no plastered finish. This concrete will be faced with granite on the outside, but inside will be left with the scars of the framework still on it to contrast ruggedly with a gilded ceiling and red brick floor.

Service Not Recognition

"Breuer's bell banner is no mere architectural whim, but is the product of a serious approach on several levels to the problem. 'Why build a tower?' he asked. The medieval reason supplied by church historians was as a lookout and bastion of defense. Today's reasons: a structure to carry the electrically operated bells so they can be heard by the monks at work, a symbol, a distinctive silhouette to be carried in the mind.

"Then the architect asked himself a philosophic question: what can be used today as a real architectural symbol, a form which structurally is as characteristic of our times as a dome was in the sixteenth century? His answer: the cantilevered concrete slab. He turned a slab on end so it is cantilevered vertically, broke slots in it to make it more emphatic, and he had his symbol.

"Behind the philosophy are also plenty of good workaday reasons for the concrete banner of St. John's: it provides a continuous calm surface in relation to the corrugated rhythm of the church itself. It is a notable entry for the church, suddenly revealing the glass end wall. And it permits this glass wall to be orientated north, virtually a requirement of the site, yet retain reflected south light. But more than anything else, says Breuer, it will be a 'strong statement before you come to the church.'

"The symbolism of this church starts in the plan. The Benedictines of St. John's, world famous as liturgical authorities, were confident enough to disregard some current church-planning practices and return to 'the originally correct' church-planning practices. The most prominent example of this is in the placing of the baptistry at the entrance, squarely on the central axis. This, Breuer points out, is like the original atrium, the outdoor baptistry in front of some early European churches. Glass-walled, gardened, with a skylight above, this baptistry will be as open to the outdoors as Minnesota's climate permits. More important, its location will symbolize the steps of entry into the Church: first baptism, then admission to the church and the Eucharistic sacrifice. The plan symbolism continues: the stalls of the monks who have not been ordained are on either side before the altar, while the seating for the monks who are priests is around the altar, dominated by the abbot's throne in the center. . . .

340

"The program is not one of real expansion. Says the abbot: 'This whole plan is a containment program, a program which permits us to give our present numbers the facilities they need. We don't want at all to give the impression we want to be bigger. We want to be more effective. . . .' " [21]

In commenting on this whole proposal, Robert J. Cerny of the Minneapolis architectural firm of Thorshov and Cerny, and professor of architecture at the University of Minnesota, wrote to Abbot Baldwin:

"I would like to take this opportunity to tell you that, as an architect, a professor of architecture at the University, and a Catholic, I am pleased to see the Catholic Church again taking the lead in creating great architecture. My pleasure is increased because the Architectural Renaissance will emanate from this region. . . . Marcel Breuer's designs represent one of the finest projects under consideration in the world today, and we are honored to have them in Minnesota, particularly since we have few structures of national significance to display for our visitors." [22]

At the close of its first century the St. John's community was thus absorbed in this major architectural undertaking. At the same time it was continuing the spiritual, intellectual and social works which had developed in the previous one hundred years. On the threshold of its centennial observance, Abbot Baldwin told the community:

"During the year 1956 I beg of you to make a daily memento of gratitude to Almighty God for the blessings that have been granted to the community of St. John's for the past century. Ask God to bless our efforts in the future and to guide them for His greater honor and glory. The purpose of the centennial celebration is to *rededicate ourselves* to our ideals as Benedictines, rather than to invite recognition. At the same time, let us not fail to remember those pioneers who have made great sacrifices to keep alive the true religious spirit in our community, and particularly the abbots and superiors. Our spirit as religious is what we *want* it to be, no better. Let us repeat frequently, daily, 'Raise up in us the spirit wherewith our holy Father the Abbot Benedict was animated.' " [23]

WORSHIP AND WORK

APPENDIXES, NOTES, AND INDEX

ARTICLE OF THE REVEREND BONIFACE WIMMER, O.S.B.,
concerning the Missions of America in the Augsburg *Postzeitung,* 8 November 1845

Every Catholic who cherishes his faith must take a deep interest in missionary labors; but religion as well as patriotism demands that every German Catholic should take a special interest in the missions of America. To us it can not be a matter of indifference how our countrymen are situated in America. I, for my part, have not been able to read the various and generally sad reports on the desolate condition of Germans beyond the ocean without deep compassion and a desire to do something to alleviate their pitiable condition. Hence, I have given much thought to the question how they might be practically assisted. It is not difficult to understand what should be done — more German-speaking priests should be found laboring for the spiritual welfare of our countrymen in America; the only question is how to get priests and what kind of priests will do the work most successfully. The answer to the second question will also give the solution for the first. I do not wish to offend anyone, but my opinion is that secular priests are not the best adapted for missionary labors; history shows that the Church has not availed herself of their services to any great extent in missionary undertakings. I do not mean to say that a secular priest can not labor effectually within a limited territory in America, for there are many who labor successfully even at the present day; but they cannot satisfy themselves; they themselves are in great danger of becoming careless and worldly-minded. I can not agree with Dr. Salzbacher when he says that the spiritual wants of our countrymen can be provided for by perambulating missionaries, who go about like the Wandering Jew from forest to forest, from hut to hut; for unless such a missionary be a *saint* not much of the spiritual man would remain in him, and even then by such transient visits not much lasting good could be accomplished. The missionary, more than any other priest, stands in need of spiritual renova-

345

tion from time to time, consolation and advice in trials and difficulties. He must therefore have some place where he can find such assistance; this may be given by his bishop but he will find it more securely in a religious community, in the midst of his confreres.

He should also have a home to receive him in his old age or when he is otherwise incapacitated for missionary labors; he should have no worldly cares, otherwise he might neglect or even forget his own and others' spiritual welfare. All this can be had only in a religious community. It is apparent, therefore, that religious are better adapted for missionary work than secular priests. In a community the experiences of the individual become common property; all have a common interest, stand together and have the same object in view. A vacancy caused by death or otherwise can be filled more readily, and having fewer temporal cares, they can devote themselves more exclusively to the spiritual interests of themselves and others. Hence, all other things being equal, a religious priest in a community should be able to work more effectively on the missions than the secular priest, who stands alone.

The next question is: What religious Order is most adapted for the American missions, not to convert the native Indians but to provide for the spiritual necessities of German immigrants?

As far as I know the only religious in the strict sense of the word now found in America are the Jesuits and Redemptorists. The missionaries of the Middle Ages, the Benedictines, Dominicans and Franciscans are not yet represented in the New World, except by a few individuals who do not live in monasteries. The Jesuits devote their energies principally to teaching in colleges; their students are mostly from the higher classes of society and many of them belong to Protestant families. Many Jesuits are also doing excellent work among the Indians, and others have charge of congregations in cities near their colleges. But while they accomplish so much in their sphere of labors, they can do little for Germans, because few of them speak their language. The Redemptorists are doing noble work for our countrymen in the States; in cities and thickly settled country districts they have large congregations, and also do what they can for others as travelling missionaries. Some secular priests likewise go about among the scattered Catholics doing good, but they naturally and necessarily concentrate in cities where there is a large Catholic population.

We see therefore that much is being done in America; very much indeed when we consider the small band of priests and the difficulties under which they labor. But as yet nothing has been done for the stability of the work, no provision has been made for an increase of German-speaking priests, to meet the growing demand for missionary laborers. It is not difficult to see that secular priests, whose labors extend over a district larger than a diocese, can do nothing to secure reinforcements to their own number. But why have the Redemptorists and Jesuits not accomplished more in this line? By his vows neither the Jesuit nor the Redemptorist is bound to any particular place, but he must always be prepared to leave his present position at the behest of his superiors, and may also request, if not demand his removal for weighty reasons. This has many advantages, but for

America it seems to me to have also disadvantages. For the successor of one who has been removed will require a long time to become acquainted with all the circumstances with which his predecessor was familiar, and even the uncertainty as to how long he will remain at any particular place will be an obstacle in his way. Moreover, the fact that Jesuits generally receive only the children of richer families, many of whom are Protestants, into their institutions, because they depend upon them for sustenance, and that the Redemptorists are by their statutes required to devote themselves to missionary work, and can therefore not be expected to take charge of seminaries, gives us no reason to hope that the spiritual wants of Americans, particularly of German-Americans, will be provided for by native German-speaking priests. And in case that the mission societies of Europe should unexpectedly be rendered incapable of supplying money or reinforcements in priests the situation would become even more serious. But even supposing that everything remains as it is, we can not hope to have an efficient supply of priests as long as we have no means of securing a native clergy for the United States of America. For the number of those who are educated at Alt-Oetting or elsewhere in Germany is not in proportion to the continually increasing emigration to America, not to speak of the natural increase of Germans in America itself. Jesuits and Redemptorists are therefore doing noble work in America and their number should be increased as much as possible; but they will scarcely be able to remove the chief cause of the deficiency of German-speaking priests. We need not speak of the Dominicans and Franciscans; there are very few German Dominicans, and the present social condition of America seems not to call for Mendicant Friars.

We now come to the Benedictines, who are not as yet represented in the United States. In my opinion they are the most competent to relieve the great want of priests in America. In support of my opinion I will adduce some facts. But I must again state that I have not the remotest intention of belittling the efforts and successes of other religious Orders, but on the contrary I am desirous of seeing them labor in the same field, side by side with the Benedictines.

History abundantly proves:

1. That we owe the conversion of England, Germany, Denmark, Sweden, Hungary, and Poland almost exclusively to the Benedictines, and that in the remaining parts of Europe Christendom is deeply indebted to them.

2. That the conversion of these countries was not transient but lasting and permanent.

3. That this feature must be ascribed to the fact that the Benedictines are men of stability; they are not wandering monks; they acquire lands and bring them under cultivation and become thoroughly affiliated to the country and people to which they belong, and receive their recruits from the district in which they have established themselves.

4. That the Benedictine Order by its *Rule* is so constituted that it can very readily adapt itself to all times and circumstances. The contemplative and practical are harmoniously blended; agriculture, manual labor, literature, missionary work, education, were drawn into the circle of activity

which St. Benedict placed before his disciples. Hence they soon felt at home in all parts of Europe and the same could be done in America.

When we consider North America as it is today, we can see at a glance that there is no other country in the world which offers greater opportunities for the establishment and spread of the Benedictine Order, no country that is so much like our old Europe was. There are found immense forests, large uncultivated tracts of land in the interior, most fertile lands, which command but a nominal price; often for miles and miles no village is to be seen, not to speak of cities. In country districts no schools, no churches are to be found. The German colonists are scattered, uncultured, ignorant, hundreds of miles away from the nearest German-speaking priest, for, practically, they can make their homes where they please; there are no good books, no Catholic papers, no holy pictures. The destitute and unfortunate have none who would offer them a hospitable roof, the orphans naturally become the victims of vice and irreligion — in a word, the conditions in America today are like those of Europe 1000 years ago, when the Benedictine Order attained its fullest development and effectiveness by its wonderful adaptability and stability.

Of course the Benedictine Order would be required to adapt itself again to the circumstances and begin anew. To acquire a considerable tract of land in the interior of the country, upon which to found a monastery, would not be very difficult; to bring under cultivation at least a portion of the land and to erect the most necessary buildings would give employment for a few years to the first Benedictine colony, which should consist of at least two or three priests and ten to fifteen Brothers skilled in the most necessary trades.

When the colony is once self-supporting, which could be expected in about two years, it should begin to expand so that the increased number of laboring hands might also increase the products and revenues to be derived from the estate. A printing and lithographing establishment would be very desirable.

Since the holy *Rule* prescribes for all, not only manual labor and the chanting of the Divine Office, but also that the monks should devote several hours a day to study, this time could be used by the Fathers to instruct the Brothers thoroughly in arithmetic, German grammar, etc., thereby fitting them to teach school, to give catechetical instruction and in general to assist in teaching children as well as grown persons.

Such a monastery would from the very start be of great advantage to German settlers, at least to those who would live near it. They would have a place, where they could depend upon hearing Mass on Sundays and hear a sermon in their own language; they would also have a place, where they could always be sure to find a priest at home to hear their confessions, to bless their marriages, to baptize their children and to administer the last sacraments to the sick if called in time.

Occasionally the superior might send out even the Brothers two by two to hunt up fallen-away Catholics, to instruct children for their first Communion etc. All subsequent monasteries that might be established from the motherhouse would naturally exercise the same influence.

So far, the services rendered by Benedictines would not be extraordinary; any other priests or religious could do the same, except that they would not likely be able to support themselves without assistance from Europe, whereas a community of Benedictines, when once firmly established, would soon become self-sustaining.

But such a monastery if judiciously located would not long remain isolated; all reports from America inform us that the German immigrants are concentrating themselves in places where churches have been erected or where a German-speaking priest has taken up his residence. This would also be found, and to a greater extent, if there were a monastery somewhere with a good school. In a short time a large German population would be found near the monastery, just as in the Middle Ages, villages, towns and cities sprang up near Benedictine abbeys. Then the monks could expect a large number of children for their school, and in the course of time, as the number of priests increases, a college with a good Latin course could be commenced. They would not be dependent upon the tuition fee of the students for their support, which they could draw from the farm and the missions (though these would not be a source of much income in the beginning) and hence they could devote their energies to the education of the poorer classes of boys who could pay little or nothing. Since all these boys would daily come in contact with the priests and other monks, it could scarcely be otherwise but that many of them would develop a desire of becoming priests or even religious. I am well aware that to many readers these hopes and expectations will appear too sanguine, since all efforts at securing a native American clergy have hitherto failed so signally. But we must remember that the annals of the missions as well as the oral reports of priests who have labored in America, inform us that these efforts were more theoretical than practical, that there was a desire of making such efforts but that they were not really made, and that those which were really made were more or less restricted to the English-speaking clergy, and that in general there were neither sufficient means nor sufficient teachers to train a native German-speaking clergy. It is said that the young American is not inclined to devote himself to the sacred ministry, because it is so easy for him to secure a wife and home; that the American has nothing in view but to heap up the riches of this world; that fathers need their sons on the farms or in the workshops and therefore do not care to see them study. But, let me ask, is it not the same here in Europe? Are the rich always pleased when their sons study for the priesthood? Are all Germans in America well-to-do or rich? Are they not as a rule the very poorest and to a certain extent the menials of the rest? Moreover, is the first thought of a boy directed upon matrimony? Is it any wonder that he should show no inclination for the priesthood when he sees a priest scarcely once a year; when divine services are held in churches which resemble hovels rather than churches, without pomp and ceremony, when the priest has to divest himself of his priestly dignity, often travels on horse-back, in disguise, looking more like a drummer than a priest, when the boy sees nothing in the life of a priest but sacrifice, labor and fatigue?

Projected Monastery

349

But all this would become quite different if boys could come in daily contact with priests, if they received instructions from them, if the priest could appear to advantage, better dressed and better housed than the ordinary settler, if young men could learn from observation to realize and appreciate the advantages of a community life, if they could learn to understand that while the life of a priest requires self-denial and sacrifice, his hopes of a great reward are also well grounded. Yes, I do not doubt but that hundreds, especially of the lower classes, would prefer to spend their lives in well regulated monasteries in suitable and reasonable occupations, than to gain a meager livelihood by incessant hard labor in forest regions. Let us remember that here in Bavaria from the year 740 to the year 788 not less than 40 Benedictine monasteries were founded and the communities were composed almost entirely of natives from the free classes, who had enjoyed the advantages of freedom in the world and could have chosen the married state without any difficulty or hindrance. Why should we not reasonably expect the same results in the United States where the conditions are so similar?

But such a monastery in North America would not draw its recruits exclusively from the surrounding country, but also from the great number of boys, who either during the voyage or soon after their arrival in America lose their parents and thereby become helpless and forsaken. An institution, in which such unfortunate children could find a home, would undoubtedly be a great blessing for that country. And where could this be done more easily than in Benedictine monasteries as described above, in which young boys could not only attend school, but also do light work on the farm or in the work shops and according to their talents and vocation become priests or at least educated Christians and good citizens. Surely, many of these would gladly join the community as Brothers or priests, and thus repay the monastery for the trouble of educating them.

In this way a numerous religious clergy could soon be secured, and then some of the Fathers might be sent out to visit those Catholics who scarcely ever see a priest; occasionally at least they might preach the word of God and bring the consolations of religion even to those who live at a great distance from the monastery; small congregations could be established, and the seminary could soon furnish a goodly number of secular clergy.

But where could the Benedictines be found to establish such a monastery in North America, and where are the necessary means for such an undertaking? The writer is informed that there are several Fathers in the Benedictine Order here in Bavaria, who would gladly go upon such a mission, and with regard to Brothers there would be no difficulty whatever; within a few years not less than 200 good men have applied for admission into one of our monasteries. It is a well known fact that of those who are studying for the priesthood, many are joining the Redemptorist Order simply because it offers them the hope of becoming missionaries in America.

The necessary funds could easily be supplied by the *Ludwig Missionsverein*. Bavaria annually pays 100,000 florins into the treasury of this

350

society. Would it be unfair to devote one tenth of this sum to the establishment of monasteries in America, especially since just now hundreds of our own nationality are seeking homes in the United States? Consequently the money contributed would be used to further the interests of Germans in general and our countrymen in particular. Could a better use of such contributions be made or could anything appeal more loudly to our national patriotism? Is it right that we should continually look after the interests of strangers and forget our own countrymen? Moreover, whatever would be done for the Germans would advance the well-being of the entire Church in America. We must not stifle our feelings of patriotism. The Germans, we hear it often enough, lose their national character in the second or third generation; they also lose their language because like a little rivulet they disappear in the mighty stream of the Anglo-American populace in the States. Is this not humiliation for us Germans? Would this sad condition of affairs continue if here and there a German centre were established, to which the stream of emigration from our country could be systematically directed, if German instruction and sermons were given by priests going forth from these centres, if German books, papers and periodicals were distributed among the people, if German boys could receive a German education and training, which would make themselves felt in wider circles?

Immigrant
Needs

Let us therefore no longer build air castles for our countrymen in America. Let us provide for their religious interests, then their domestic affairs will take care of themselves. Benedictine monasteries of the old style are the best means of checking the downward tendencies of our countrymen in social, political and religious matters. Let Jesuits and Redemptorists labor side by side with the Benedictines; there is room enough for all and plenty of work. If every Religious Order develops a healthy activity within its sphere, the result will be doubly sure and great, and North America will no longer depend upon Europe for its spiritual welfare, and the day may come when America will repay us just as England, converted by the Benedictines, repaid the continent of Europe.

APPENDIX II

LETTER FROM BROTHER WOLFGANG BECK, O.S.B.
to Archbishop Gregor Scherr, O.S.B., of Munich, The Indianbush, 7 November 1858

Most Reverend Archbishop:

I hope that you do not take it amiss that I should presume to write to you. It is now more than eleven years since I left you, and many times have I remembered the words of advice you gave me when I was taking my departure from you in Baden.

I am now in a place where educated people are beginning to settle, and where also, it seems, God has decided that the Order of St. Benedict should spring up for His honor.

351

Well, then, the lot fell to me to come here.

In May, 1856, a Father and two young clerics who had been professed in St. Paul were sent here. The bishop of St. Paul showed them their land, but they did not care for it. Then God sent two old brothers to me. Each had made a claim of 160 acres, and they offered to give the claims to the monks as a location for a monastery. The land lay along the Mississippi River, and in the eyes of the world it was very precious, since it adjoined the city. The transaction was carried out, and the land was bought for about a hundred dollars; the two old brothers, one fifty-five and the other fifty-seven, were taken care of for the rest of their lives.

But the Malicious Enemy, who sought to bring this business to a halt, raised up a man who also had claims to this land, and so there were court proceedings. The two old brothers had to admit that, since the land was not their own possession, they could not sell it. By this time the two brothers had changed their minds, and wanted to retain the land themselves, because the Jealous One had spoken many things to them, such as: "What use would these old priests have for such a precious piece of land?" and so forth. They valued it at about $8,000. In the same proceedings we would have had to lose not only the land but also a debt of $1,500, if God had not changed the brothers' minds on this point.

So, like all the other settlers, we were forced to make claims, and for that purpose the prior had to send other men, for each person is allowed to take possession of only 360 acres. But since there was no land left in the vicinity of St. Cloud, we had to go to the Indianbush in order to get such a large section in one piece. It is fifteen miles from St. Cloud, in a spot where a German community has settled (i.e. St. Joseph). Fr. Bruno Riess, who was born in Augsburg, is pastor there. The people have built a rectory and church there. Adjoining it are 120 acres of farmland, from which we now get our food. We had to go four miles from there to claim our land. Since there was no road leading to it, we had to go through forest and brush where we often left pieces of skin hanging alongside bits of torn clothing. Going ahead with a compass, Fr. Bruno had to be doubly careful, because there are still bears and wolves around. We Brothers came behind with axes to mark the trees. Many days were spent in this way in order to prepare a place for those who come later to build a monastery. In this manner we have claimed more than two thousand acres of fine land. On our claims are several hundred lakes filled with splendid fish. The largest of these lakes is over two hundred acres in area, the others ranging from five to forty acres. A stream runs through a great part of the excellent meadowland just as it does at Metten. In order to give you a clear picture of it, I must compare it to Oberalteich: three or four hundred acres of even meadow to the north and east, the rest hilly country.

All trifoliate plants grow well here, but as yet there are still no fruit trees. We have not as yet earned very much because for the past two years grasshoppers have eaten everything. The hay crop was fairly good, but until the harvest there was great need; and besides, there is a money shortage in Minnesota. Many people had nothing to eat but potatoes.

We built the first cabin in '57, on His Eminence's nameday, and on that

352

day I thought often of you and Metten. The snow was four or five feet deep. The cabins were made of bare logs piled one upon the other, and the cracks were closed with ordinary dirt. They are fourteen feet wide, sixteen long, with a few planks laid on top. I had to make a fire within the room in order to soften the earth before I could dig it out with ease. At night I had to live in it, and it was too bad that I was not an astronomer, because I did not even have to climb out of bed to watch the course of the stars.

In this manner I lived, during the week, with one other Brother in my beloved solitude. I did this for two years in order to make a beginning. On Sunday I had to make an hour-and-a-half trek to the place where we gathered together, like the hermits of old. On Monday I would again take my bread and coffee (but without sugar or milk) and go back to the woods. On the way I shot a young hare and so had some flesh meat for dinner. I did not encounter any bear or deer, although there are plenty. Fr. Clement has seen some of them. He is a native Swiss who comes weekly to read Holy Mass. We (there are eight of us Brothers) built a house recently: 30 feet long, 20 wide, and two stories high, although only made of logs and mud. We still have quite a way to go to finish it, however. Because five or six of the Brothers are often at work on the land, bread is sent out from the rectory, where Joseph Vill is cook. Once a Brother was coming through the woods, bringing us bread loaded on two oxen, when ten wild Indians grabbed the sack with the bread in it and began to divide it up. He gave them to understand by means of signs that they should not do this. They were not angry, and so took only three loaves, giving him money in a Loebi and went their way. They are good people, but uncivilized. Another time one of them came into my house demanding brandy and whiskey. I showed him a bottle filled with water, at which he laughed heartily. I gave him a piece of bread, but he did not eat it. Instead he told me in sign language that he had children and would divide it up when he got home. Their houses are like a bunch of hop-poles put together, as they are in Bavaria.

There are now five priests and nine Brothers in St. Joseph, where the rectory is located (i.e., when we are all there at the same time). Benedict Haindl is prior, and there are also Clement Staub, Bruno Riess and Alex Retzer, who studied at Metten and now teaches the children here all week long. On Saturdays he goes out to a mission station, as do also Fr. Prior (to St. Cloud) and Fr. Clement (to Richmond).

Ever since the last chapter meeting, which was held in September, we have been independent from St. Vincent's. So we are in our pioneer territory without any support: among a Catholic population, it is true, but one which is poor and in great need and want. We are supposed to erect a monastery sometime in the future, but we scarcely know what will come of this plan. Still, our trust is in God, and we hope that we shall receive support from our German benefactors, the thought of whom gives us strength to go on. If we want to purchase our fifteen claims we have to pay $3,000, and where shall we get that much money? Or even pay the rent? We could not even make use of all the land at present because we do not have enough men for all that work.

Therefore I ask you to remember from time to time the seed of the Bene-

353

dictines in the New World of Minnesota. And do not send it [money] through St. Vincent's, because they tax it too much.

We got a small bell from Bavaria which was sent to Brother Benno Muckenthaler, and it is very pleasant to listen to it chime in the wild woods, heard by more animals than men.

As far as the climate is concerned, it is very healthful. I am always in tip-top condition and happy, even though more a hermit than a cloistered Brother. At St. Vincent's I worked mostly on the farm.

Many Germans are living in Minnesota, with more settlers coming right along, so the German language is spoken throughout this part of the country. Many of our neighbors are from Bavaria, or from the Black Forest, but they are all from two to five miles distant. There is still a lot of land which could be settled, and about eight miles from us there is a beautiful stand of cedar. I have not seen it myself, though, because there is no road approaching it. You just have to follow a compass. According to reports there is a fine little lake cutting through it.

Fr. Pierz, septuagenarian who has lived in these wilds for twenty years, says that where he is working the land is even better. He comes to visit us frequently (although he lives 200 miles away), and always wants to get a priest for an assistant. Our Most Reverend Bishop promised that he would let Fr. Alex go to him, at which he was elated; unfortunately, however, he can no longer be spared.

Fr. Pierz has converted many of these wild people and shown them how to farm. It is wearisome labor, though, and he has been forced to spend many nights out in the snow under the open sky. But God is certainly showing mercy to the Indians, and is sending them help through the Order of St. Benedict, which is more or less our intention.

I close this letter with trust in God and hope that my expectation will be richly blessed by the love and affection that Your Eminence has for the Order of St. Benedict, and I beg your pardon for my terrible handwriting.

> Because my eyes are weak with age,
> My labored hand at the tired stage;
> I very gladly end this page.

APPENDIX III

THE CHARTER OF ST. JOHN'S
granted by the Territorial Legislature of Minnesota, 6 March 1857

WHEREAS, It is highly important, that the youths of this new, but flourishing Territory, be not only instructed in the elementary sciences, but moreover, be also educated by sound, moral principles;

And, WHEREAS, It is very desirable, that there be a corporation formed, in order to establish a scientific, educational and ecclesiastical institution;

In consideration thereof,

Be it enacted by the Legislative Assembly of the Territory of Minnesota:

354

Section 1. That the members of the religious order of St. Benedict, Demitri Marogna, Cornelius Wittmann, Bruno Riss, Alexius Roetzer and their associates and successors in office, which order is instituted for scientific, educational and ecclesiastical purposes, be a body corporate and politic, to be known by the name and style of "Order of St. Benedict," and by that name shall have perpetual succession.

Section 2. The principal object of this politic and corporate body shall be the promotion of the instruction and education of youths, to the acquirement of which end the corporators named in this act shall be hereby authorized to establish and erect an institution, or seminary, in Stearns County, on that portion of St. Cloud City, surveyed, platted and recorded as Rothkopp's Addition to St. Cloud, to be known by the name and style of "St. John's Seminary."

Section 3. This institution shall be under the supervision of said order of St. Benedict, in Minnesota, and shall be conducted by a president, secretary and procurator, which offices the corporators shall hold for the first time themselves, after whose retirement from office the new officers shall be appointed by the superiors of said order in Minnesota. The herein named officers shall also always act as trustees of said seminary.

Section 4. This politic and corporate body shall be empowered, by its representatives, with the rights as such, of suing and being sued, of contracting and being contracted with, of purchasing, holding and selling real and personal estate, of making and using a common seal, and altering the same at pleasure: Provided, that such property, including real, personal and mixed, shall not exceed the aggregate sum of one hundred thousand dollars.

Section 5. The above named corporators, and their successors in office, shall be managers of said sums of money, real estate or goods, that may be donated or willed for the purposes of this corporation.

Section 6. The proceeds of all donations of whatever nature and whatever source, shall be and remain a perpetual fund, and shall be called "the St. John's Seminary fund." The trustees of this seminary are authorized and empowered to expend such portions of the fund as may come under their control, in the erection of suitable buildings, and for the purchase of every kind of scientific apparatus, such as they may deem expedient for the object of said institution.

Section 7. The said trustees shall have power to enact by-laws for the government and regulations of the said seminary, to appoint and employ teachers, to define their duties, and to determine the amount of their respective salaries; and no student shall be required to attend the religious worship of any particular denomination, except as specified by the student, his parent or guardian.

Section 8. That the real estate and personal property of said corporation shall be exempt from taxation, as long as the same shall be used, conducted and employed for the purposes defined in this act.

Section 9. That the Catholic Bishop Cretin, of St. Paul, and his successors in office, shall exercise according to the rules of the Catholic Church the right of inspection of said institution.

Section 10.   This act shall take effect and be in force from and after its passage. Approved 6 March 1857.

An act to amend an act to incorporate the St. John's Seminary, approved 6 March 1857.

Appendix III

Be it enacted by the Legislature of the State of Minnesota:

Section 1.   That section two of an act to incorporate the St. John's Seminary be and the same is hereby amended so as to read as follows:

Section 2.   The principal object of this politic and corporate body shall be the promotion of the instruction and education of youths, to the acquirement of which end the corporators named in this act shall be hereby authorized to establish and erect an institution, or seminary, in Stearns County, to be known by the name and style of St. John's Seminary.

Section 3.   This act shall take effect and be in force from and after its passage. Approved 6 February 1864.

An act to authorize the Trustees of St. John's Seminary to confer degrees and grant diplomas.

Be it enacted by the Legislature of the State of Minnesota:

Section 1.   That the board of trustees of St. John's Seminary shall have the power to confer such degrees and grant such diplomas in their discretion as are usual in colleges and universities.

Section 2.   This act shall take effect immediately.

Approved 5 March 1869.

An act to amend Section four of an act entitled An Act to Incorporate the St. John's Seminary, approved 6 March 1857.

Be it enacted by the Legislature of the State of Minnesota:

Section 1.   That section four of an act entitled An Act to Incorporate the St. John's Seminary, Approved 6 March 1857, be and the same is hereby amended so a sto read as follows:

Section 4.   This politic and corporate body shall be empowered by its representatives, with rights as such of suing and being sued, of contracting and being contracted with, of purchasing, holding and selling real and personal estate, of making and using a common seal and altering the same at pleasure; provided always, that the annual income of said corporation shall not exceed the sum of sixty thousand dolllars.*

Section 2.   This act shall take effect and be in force from and after its passage. Approved 29 February 1872.

*By virtue of the provisions of Minnesota Statutes 309.07, the limitation of this section of the Articles of Incorporation have been removed. MS 309.07 read as follows:

"Any educational institution created and existing under or by virtue of any law of the State or Territory of Minnesota is hereby authorized and empowered to take, hold, receive, and enjoy all property and money given, bequeathed, devised, conveyed, or transferred to it and to hold, use, and enjoy the profits, rents, and income therefrom, notwithstanding any limita-

356

tion in the laws or charters by or under which such educational institutions were incorporated, or any amendments thereto."

An act to amend the act entitled An Act to Incorporate the St. John's Seminary and the acts amendatory thereof.

Be it enacted by the Legislature of the State of Minnesota:

Section 1.   That the act entitled An Act to Incorporate the St. John's Seminary, Approved March 6th, 1857, as well as the several acts amendatory thereof, and the title to the original act of incorporation, be and the same are hereby amended as follows:

That whenever the word "seminary" occurs in either thereof, the same be stricken out and the word "university" be substituted in lieu thereof.

Section 2.   That all acts and parts of acts inconsistent with this act be and the same are hereby repealed.

Section 3.   This act shall take effect and be in force from and after its passage. Approved 17 February 1883.

APPENDIX IV

PARISHES, MISSIONS AND STATIONS
served by monks of St. John's Abbey 1856-1956

P–Parish: a formally organized congregation having its own church and a resident pastor.
M–Mission: a congregation having its own church but not a resident pastor.
S–Station: a group of Catholics having neither a church nor a resident pastor. A station usually is visited at irregular intervals, Mass being offered in a private home, store or town hall.

CALIFORNIA

1. Los Angeles, Our Lady of Lourdes Church. P–1930–1938.
2. Montebello (Los Angeles Co.), St. Benedict's Church. P–1925–1926, 1930–1936.

MINNESOTA

1. Ada (Norman Co.). M–1902–1909; P–1912–1917.
2. Albany (Stearns Co.). S–1868–1870; M–1870–1883; P–1883–present.
3. Alexandria (Douglas Co.). S–1867–1870?; M–1882–1890, 1894–1895, 1899–1901.
4. Arban (Stearns Co.). S–1873–1875; M–1875–1893.
5. Arlington (Sibley Co.). P–1894–1904.
6. Avon (Stearns Co.). S–1869–1879; M–1879–1895; P–1900–present.
7. Barnesville (Clay Co.). P–1894–present.
8. Beaulieu (Mahnomen Co.). S–1895–1896; M–1896–1900; P–1900–present.
9. Becker (Sherburne Co.). S–1856–1859, 1869–1872.
10. Bejou (Mahnomen Co.). S–1913–1916; M–1916–present.

11. Belgrade (Stearns Co.). M–1890–1891.
12. Belle Plaine (Scott Co.). S–1858–1860; M–1860–1861.
13. Belle River (Douglas Co.). M–1883–1890.
14. Bowlus (Morrison Co.). P–1911–1914.
15. Browerville (Todd Co.). St. Joseph's Church. M–1884–1886.
16. Buckman (Morrison Co.). S–1880–1881; M–1881–1893.
17. Callaway (Becker Co.). S–1906–1908; M–1908–1911, 1912–1917; P–1911–1912, 1917–present.
18. Carver (Carver Co.). S–1857–1860.
19. Cass Lake (Cass Co.), St. Charles' Church. P–1930–1931, 1945–present.
20. Cedar Lake (Scott Co.). S–1857–1859; M–1859–1863.
21. Chanhassen (Hennepin Co.). S–1859–1862.
22. Chaska (Carver Co.). S–1857–1858; M–1858–1865.
23. Clear Lake (Sherburne Co.). S–1857–1859?, 1869–1872.
24. Clearwater (Wright Co.). S–1870–1875.
25. Cold Spring (Stearns Co.). S–1877–1878; P–1878–present.
26. Collegeville (Stearns Co.). P–1876–present.
27. Cologne (Carver Co.). S–1859–1860; M–1860–1865.
28. Credit River (Scott Co.). S–1859–1862.
29. Crystal (Hennepin Co.). S–1862–1863; M–1863–1865, 1876–1886.
30. Darwin (Meeker Co.). S–1861–1870.
31. Delano (Wright Co.). S–1861?–1862?; M–1872–1873.
32. Detroit Lakes (Becker Co.). P–1900–present.
33. Diamond Lake (Kandiyohi Co.). S–1860, 1868–1870.
34. Dilworth (Clay Co.). P–1910–1917.
35. Duelm (Benton Co.). M–1886–1887; P–1907–1910.
36. Duluth (St. Louis Co.), St. Clement's Church. S–1885–1887; P–1887–present.
37. Elmer (St. Louis Co.). M–1914–1923.
38. Euclid (Polk Co.). S–1897–1899.
39. Farming (Stearns Co.). S–1879–1880; M–1880–1894; P–1894–present.
40. Felton (Clay Co.). M–1902–1917.
41. Fletcher (Hennepin Co.). M–1858–1862.
42. Forest City (Meeker Co.). S–1857–1866; M–1866–1870.
43. Frazee (Becker Co.). M–1900–1906; P–1906–1917.
44. Freeport (Stearns Co.). S–1881–1883; M–1883–1890; P–1890–present.
45. French Lake (Wright Co.). S–1861–1863.
46. Gaylord (Sibley Co.). M–1895–1904.
47. Georgetown (Clay Co.). S–1883–1887; M–1887–1896, 1913–1914; P–1896–1913.
48. Glencoe (McLeod Co.). S–1858–1865; M–1865.
49. Glyndon (Clay Co.). S–1884–1886, 1890–1892, 1895–1906; M–1906–1917.
50. Grand Marais (Cook Co.). M–1907–1933; P–1933–present.
51. Green Isle (Sibley Co.). S–1859–1862?

52. Greenleaf (Meeker Co.). S–1868–1870; M–1870.
53. Hastings (Dakota Co.), St. Boniface Church. M–1869–1872; P–1872–present.
54. Hawley (Clay Co.). S–1884–1888.
55. Heidelberg (Le Sueur Co.). M–1857–1860.
56. Helvetia (Carver Co.). M–1859–1863.
57. Holdingford (Stearns Co.). S–1884–1886; M–1886–1891; P–1891–1893.
58. Holy Name (Hennepin Co.). M–1863–1873?; P–1912–present.
59. Hovland (Cook Co.). S–1939–present.
60. Jacob's Prairie (Stearns Co.). M–1856–1873, 1878–1930, 1952–present; P–1873–1878, 1930–1952.
61. Jessenland (Sibley Co.). S–1858?–1863?
62. Jordan (Scott Co.). M–1858–1863.
63. Kandiyohi (Kandiyohi Co.). S–1869–1870.
64. Kimball (Stearns Co.). M–1873–1894.
65. Krain (Stearns Co.). S–1873–1874; M–1874–1893.
66. Lake George (Stearns Co.). S–1857–1859.
67. Lake Henry (Stearns Co.). S–1857–1859; M–1882–1886; P–1886–1894.
68. Lake Minnetonka (Hennepin Co.). S–1859.
69. Lake Park (Becker Co.). M–1900–1917.
70. Lake Reno (Pope Co.). M–1884–1887.
71. Lexington (Le Sueur Co.). S–1859–1863.
72. Litchfield (Meeker Co.). S–1859–1870.
73. Loggering (Stearns Co.). M–1877–1892.
74. Long Lake (Hennepin Co.). M–1916–1948.
75. Lutsen (Cook Co.). S–1939–present.
76. Luxemburg (Stearns Co.). M–1859–1875; P–1875–1894.
77. Mahnomen (Mahnomen Co.). S–1895–1896; M–1896–1908; P–1908–present.
78. Manannah (Meeker Co.). S–1867–1870.
79. Marseilles (Sherburne Co.). S–1857–1859.
80. Marystown (Scott Co.). M–1857–1871.
81. Meadowlands (St. Louis Co.). M–1914–1923.
82. Medicine Lake (Hennepin Co.). S–1860–1863, 1886; M–1912–1917.
83. Meire Grove (Stearns Co.). S–1859–1864; M–1864–1874; P–1874–present.
84. Melrose (Stearns Co.), St. Boniface Church. M–1878–1879; P–1879–1894.
85. Melrose (Stearns Co.), St. Patrick's Church. S–1868–1872; M–1872–1880, 1884–1894.
86. Miesville (Dakota Co.). M–1874–1881.
87. Millerville (Douglas Co.). P–1882–1895.
88. Minneapolis (Hennepin Co.), St. Boniface Church. M–1858–1861; P–1861–1865, 1873–present.
89. Minneapolis (Hennepin Co.), St. Elizabeth's Church. M–1876–1882.
90. Minneapolis (Hennepin Co.), St. Joseph's Church. P–1875–present.

91. Moorhead (Clay Co.), St. Joseph's Church. P–1883–present.
92. Morrill (Morrison Co.). M–1914–1918.
93. Murdock (Swift Co.). S–1880–1881.
94. New Market (Scott Co.). S–1859–1861; M–1861–1863.
95. New Munich (Stearns Co.). S–1857–1862; M–1862–1864; P–1864–present.
96. New Prague (Scott Co.). M–1858–1861.
97. Oakdale (Washington Co.). S–1869–1870; M–1870–1885.
98. Ogema (Becker Co.). S–1910–1911; M–1911–1912; P–1912–present.
99. Osakis (Douglas Co.). S–1869–1870, 1884–1899; M–1899–1905; P–1905–1907.
100. Padua (Stearns Co.). M–1868–1880.
101. Park Rapids (Hubbard Co.). P–1916–1918.
102. Pearl Lake (Stearns Co.). M–1889–1894.
103. Pelican Lake (Wright Co.). S–1859–1862; M–1862.
104. Perham (Ottertail Co.), St. Henry's Church. M–1886–1887; P–1887–1890.
105. Pierz (Morrison Co.). P–1878–1893.
106. Radium (Marshall Co.). S–1906–1907, 1912–1913.
107. Ramey (Morrison Co.). P–1914–1918.
108. Red Lake Falls (Red Lake Co.). M–1893–1894; P–1894–1917.
109. Rice (Benton Co.). M–1884–1887.
110. Richfield (Hennepin Co.). M–1878–1886.
111. Richmond (Stearns Co.). S–1856–1860; M–1860–1862; P–1862–present.
112. Rockville (Stearns Co.). M–1912–1921.
113. Roscoe (Stearns Co.). P–1898–1920.
114. Rush Lake (Ottertail Co.). P–1886–1894.
115. Sabin (Clay Co.). S–1910–1913; M–1913–1917.
116. St. Anna (Stearns Co.). M–1889–1893.
117. St. Augusta (Stearns Co.). M–1856–1873; P–1873–1893.
118. St. Benedict (Scott Co.). S–1857–1860; M–1860–1861.
119. St. Bonifacius (Hennepin Co.). S–1858–1859; M–1859–1865.
120. St. Cloud (Stearns Co.), Immaculate Conception Church. M–1858–1861; P–1856–1858, 1861–1937.
121. St. Cloud (Stearns Co.), St. Augustine's Church. P–1937–present.
122. St. Francis (Carver Co.). S–1857–1858; M–1859–1865.
123. St. Henry (Le Sueur Co.). S–1857–1859; M–1859–1862.
124. St. Hilaire (Pennington Co.). M–1898–1909.
125. St. John (Sibley Co.). M–1859–1862?
126. St. Joseph (Scott Co.). M–1858–1864.
127. St. Joseph (Stearns Co.). P–1856–present.
128. St. Martin (Stearns Co.). S–1857–1860; M–1860–1872; P–1872–present.
129. St. Michael (Wright Co.). M–1856–1862.
130. St. Nicholas (Stearns Co.). S–1858–1866; M–1866–1881; P–1881–1892.
131. St. Patrick (Benton Co.). S–1857–1860.

132. St. Paul (Ramsey Co.), Assumption Church. P–1858–1912.
133. St. Paul (Ramsey Co.), St. Bernard's Church. P–1912–present.
134. St. Rose (Stearns Co.). S–1898–1901; M–1901–1906; P–1906–1923.
135. St. Stephen (Stearns Co.). M–1875–1893.
136. St. Thomas (Le Sueur Co.). S–1857–1859; M–1859–1860.
137. St. Wendel (Stearns Co.). S–1868–1877; M–1877–1890.
138. Sauk Centre (Stearns Co.), St. Paul's Church. S–1864, 1866–1871; M–1871–1872, 1878–1883.
139. Sauk Rapids (Benton Co.). M–1856–1878.
140. Shakopee (Scott Co.), St. Mark's Church. P–1857–1869.
141. Spring Hill (Stearns Co.). S–1858–1864; M–1864–1880; P–1880–1891.
142. Springmount (Carver Co.). S–1863.
143. Stillwater (Washington Co.), St. Mary's Church. P–1880–present.
144. Thief River Falls (Red Lake Co.). S–1893–1894; M–1894–1901; P–1901–1916.
145. Tilden (Polk Co.). S–1897–1903.
146. Two Inlets (Becker Co.). M–1916–1918.
147. Union Hill (Scott Co.). S–1857–1860.
148. Victoria (Carver Co.). M–1857–1863.
149. Viding (Clay Co.). S–1898–1903.
150. Waconia (Carver Co.). M–1859–1863; P–1863–1866.
151. Watertown (Carver Co.). S–1858–1863; M–1863–1865.
152. Waubun (Mahnomen Co.). M–1910–1919; P–1919–present.
153. Waverly (Wright Co.). S–1858–1861; M–1861–1862.
154. Wayzata (Hennepin Co.). M–1916–1925; P–1925–present.
155. West Union (Todd Co.). P–1881–1909.
156. Wild Rice (Norman Co.). S–1885–1898; M–1898–1917.
157. Winnipeg Junction (Clay Co.). S–1900–1902.
158. Young America (Carver Co.). S–1859–1865.

MINNESOTA INDIAN MISSIONS [1]
159. Ball Club (Itasca Co.). S–1896–1906; M–1906–1934; P–1934–present.
160. Beaver Bay (Lake Co.). S–1907–1911.
161. Bena (Cass Co.). S–1905–1923; M–1923–present.
162. Big Elbow Lake (Becker Co.). S–1910–1914, 1925–1942;M–1942–present.
163. Big Bend (Clearwater Co.). S–1900–1927.
164. Bowstring Lake (Itasca Co.). S–1912?–1940.
165. Brookston (St. Louis Co.). S–1896–1912; M–1912–present.

[1] It is sometimes difficult to distinguish strictly Indian missions, because white settlers are moving into some of the churches in increasing numbers. The places listed here are those which are still predominantly or characteristically Indian missions, while some of those which began exclusively as missions for the Indians have now changed to such an extent that they are listed above with the ordinary parishes.

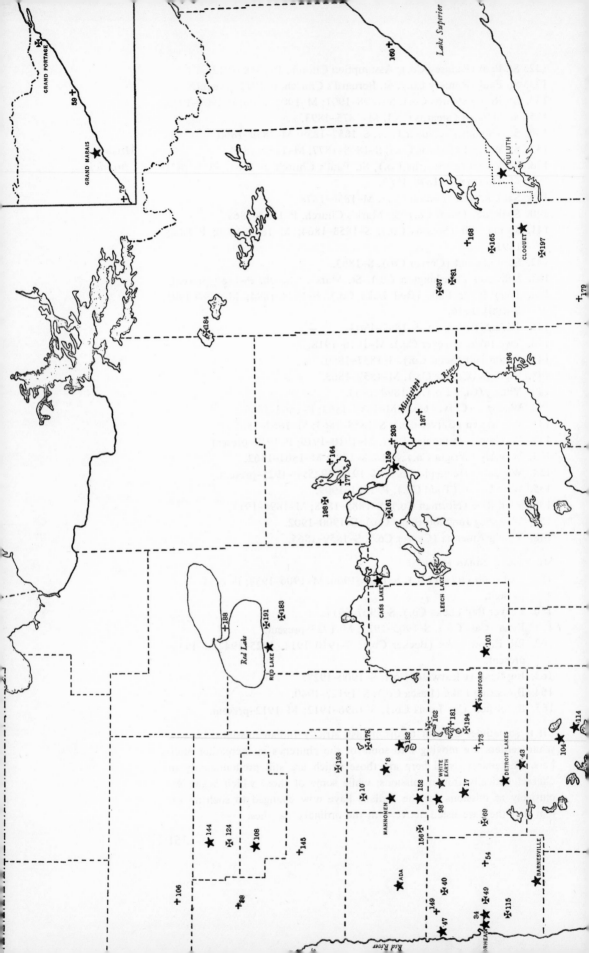

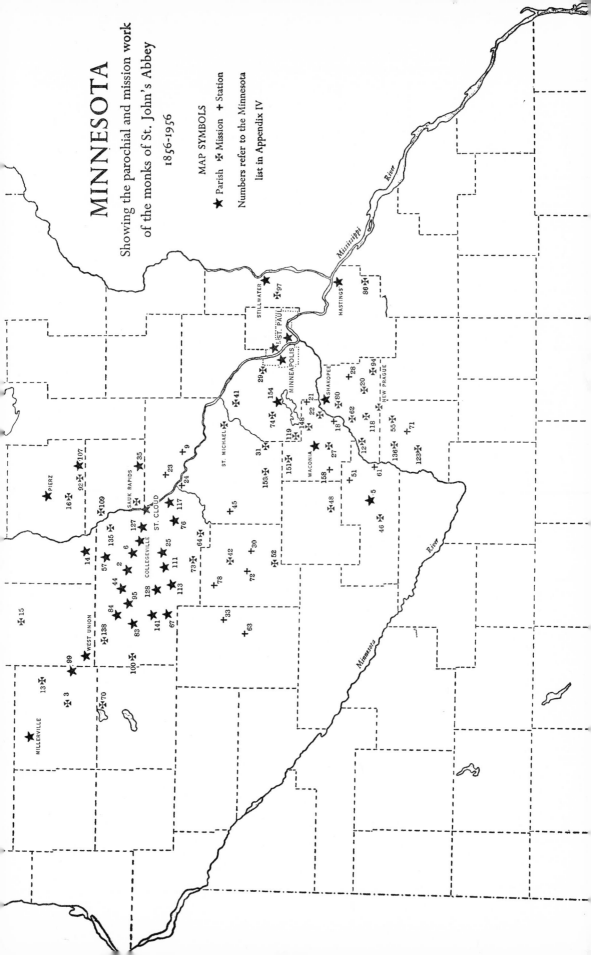

MINNESOTA

Showing the parochial and mission work
of the monks of St. John's Abbey
1856-1956

MAP SYMBOLS

★ Parish ✠ Mission ✛ Station

Numbers refer to the Minnesota
list in Appendix IV

Mississippi River

STILLWATER ★
97 ✠

HASTINGS ★
86 ✠

ST. PAUL ★
29 ✠

MINNEAPOLIS ★
154 ★
74 ✠
41 ✠

SHAKOPEE
80 ✠
28 ✠
94 ✠
20 ✠

NEW PRAGUE

21 ✛
22 ✛
62 ✠
18 ✠
12 ✠
118
55 ✠
71 ✛
136 ✠
123 ✛
61 ✛
51 ✛
5 ★
46 ✠
48 ✠

WACONIA
158 ★
27 ✛

148 ✛
119 ✠
151 ✠
153 ✠
31
45 ✛

ST. MICHAEL ✠

9 ✛
23 ✛
24 ✛

SAUK RAPIDS ✠
35 ★

ST. CLOUD ✠
117 ★
76 ★
25 ★
111 ★
113 ★
64 ✛
73 ✠
30 ✛
52 ✠
78 ✛
72 ✛
33 ✛
63 ✛
42 ✛

COLLEGEVILLE
127 ✠
6 ★
2 ★
57 ★
14 ★
44 ★
95 ★
128 ★
84 ★
188 ✠
83 ★
141 ★
67 ★
135 ✠

PIERZ ★
16 ★
92 ✠
107 ✠
109 ✠

WEST UNION ✠
15 ✠
99 ★
100 ✠

MILLERVILLE ★
13 ✠
3 ✠
70 ✠

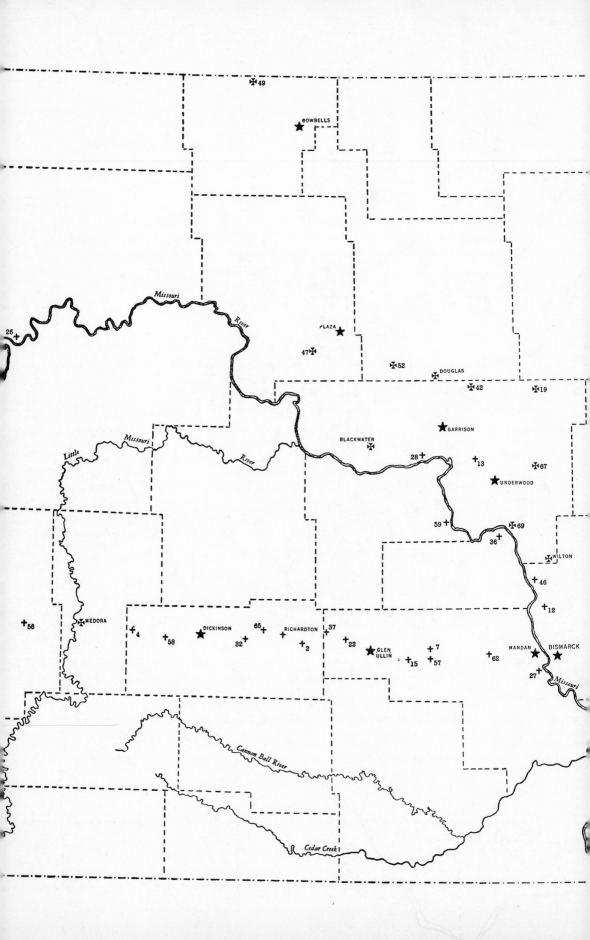

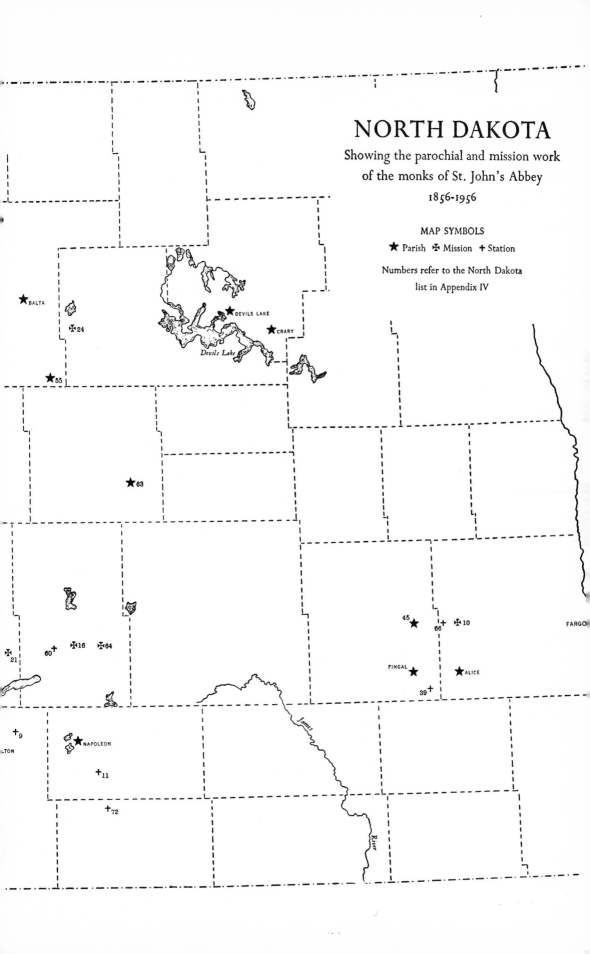

166. Cass Lake (Cass Co.), St. Catherine's Church. S–1885–1923? M–1923?–present.
167. Cloquet (Carleton Co.). M–1893–1898; P–1898–present.
168. Columbia Junction (St. Louis Co.). S–1895–1904.
169. Cramer (Lake Co.). S–1939–1953.
170. Cutfoot Sioux (Itasca Co.). S–1912?–1940.
171. Daigles Mill (Clearwater Co.). S–1950–present.
172. Duane (Mahnomen Co.). S–1910–1927.
173. Flat Lake (Becker Co.). S–1910–1924.
174. Fond du Lac (St. Louis Co.). S–1893–1911.
175. Good Harbor Hill (Cook Co.). S–1939–1953.
176. Grand Portage (Cook Co.). M–1907–present.
177. Inger (Itasca Co.). S–1940–1953.
178. Island Lake (Mahnomen Co.). S–1915?–1928; M–1928–present.
179. Kettle River (Pine Co.). S–1895–1904.
180. Lake Winnibigoshish (Itasca Co.). S–1884–1885, 1893–1901, 1936–1940.
181. Many Point Lake (Becker Co.). S–1910–1924.
182. Naytahwaush (Mahnomen Co.). S–1892–1918; M–1918–1950; P–1950–present.
183. Nebish (Beltrami Co.). M–1953–present.
184. Nett Lake (Koochiching Co.). S–1915–1917; M–1917–1923.
185. Onigum (Cass Co.). S–1883–1896; M–1896–present.
186. Park Rapids (Mahnomen Co.). S–1910–1911; M–1911–1927.
187. Pokegama (Itasca Co.). S–1884–1885, 1898–1901.
188. Ponemah (Beltrami Co.). S–1945–present.
189. Ponsford (Becker Co.). S–1895–1903; P–1903–present.
190. Red Lake (Beltrami Co.). M–1883–1888; P–1888-present.
191. Redby (Beltrami Co.). M–1937–present.
192. Rice Dam School (Clearwater Co.). S–1945–1950.
193. Rosebud Township (Polk Co.). S–1900–1901; M–1901–1908.
194. Round Lake (Becker Co.). S–1901–1915; M–1915–present.
195. St. Joseph (Beltrami Co.). M–1934–1953.
196. Sandy Lake (Aitkin Co.). S–1884–1885, 1896–1904.
197. Sawyer (Carleton Co.). S–1895–1922; M–1948–present.
198. Squaw Lake (Itasca Co.). S–1939–1953; M–1953–present.
199. Thief River ("On Red Lake Reservation"). S–1893–1905.
200. Tofte (Cook Co.). S–1950–1953.
201. Uran School (Clearwater Co.). S–1945–1950.
202. White Earth (Becker Co.). P–1878–present.
203. White Oak Point (Itasca Co.). S–1884–1885, 1893–1901.
204. Wild Rice Reserve (Clearwater Co.). S–1950–present.

NEW YORK

1. Amityville (Suffolk Co., L.I.). M–1897–1909.
2. Farmingdale (Nassau Co., L. I.). S–1896–1897; P–1897–1909.
3. Glendale (Queens Co., L.I.). P–1904–1909.
4. Lindenhurst (Suffolk Co., L.I.). M–1901,

5. Massapequa (Queens Co., L.I.). S–1897–1907.
6. New York City, St. Anselm's Church. P–1891–present.
7. New York City, St. Benedict's Church. P–1923–present.
8. Wantagh (Queens Co., L.I.). S–1897–1907.

NORTH DAKOTA

1. Alice (Cass Co.). P–1927–1928.
2. Antelope (Stark Co.). S–1884–1890.
3. Balta (Pierce Co.). P–1919–1927.
4. Belfield (Stark Co.). S–1884–1890.
5. Bismarck (Burleigh Co.), St. Mary's Church. P–1881–1910.
6. Blackwater (McLean Co.). S–1910–1913; M–1913–1928.
7. Bluegrass (Morton Co.). S–1884–1887.
8. Bowbells (Burke Co.). P–1917–1922.
9. Braddock (Emmons Co.). S–1908–1912.
10. Buffalo (Cass Co.). M–1915–1916, 1927–1930.
11. Burnstad (Logan Co.). S–1908–1912.
12. Burnt Creek (Burleigh Co.). S–1883–1888.
13. Coleharbor (McLean Co.). S–1908–1910.
14. Crary (Ramsey Co.). P–1929–1940.
15. Curlew (Morton Co.). S–1884–1887.
16. Dawson (Kidder Co.). S–1883–1906; M–1906–1909.
17. Devils Lake (Ramsey Co.). P–1928–1939.
18. Dickinson (Stark Co.), St. Joseph Church. S–1884–1887; P–1887–1890.
19. Dogden (McLean Co.). S–1910–1913; M–1913–1922.
20. Douglas (Ward Co.). S–1908–1913; M–1913–1922.
21. Driscoll (Burleigh Co.). S–1906–1908; M–1908–1910.
22. Eagles Nest (Morton Co.). S–1884–1890.
23. Endres (McLean Co.). S–1904–1907; M–1907–1922, 1926–1927.
24. Esmond (Benson Co.). M–1927–1928.
25. Fingal (Barnes Co.). P–1917–1930.
26. Fort Buford (Williams Co.). S–1884–1887.
27. Fort Lincoln (Morton Co.). S–1884–1887.
28. Fort Stevenson (McLean Co.). S–1883–1888.
29. Fulda (Pierce Co.). M–1919–1921.
30. Garrison (McLean Co.). S–1904–1906; M–1906–1907; P–1907–1928.
31. Gatey (McLean Co.). S–1898–1899.
32. Gladstone (Stark Co.). S–1884–1890.
33. Glen Ullin (Morton Co.). S–1884–1886; M–1886–1890; P–1896–1904.
34. Haymarsh (Morton Co.). S–1896–1898; M–1898–1904.
35. Hazelton (Emmons Co.). M–1904–1912.
36. Hensler (Oliver Co.). S–1884–1887.
37. Knife River (Morton Co.). S–1884–1890.
38. Livona (Emmons Co.). S–1895–1904, 1908–1912.
39. Lucca (Barnes Co.). S–1917–1918.

40. Malcolm (McLean Co.). S–1908–1909.
41. Mandan (Morton Co.). P–1884–1887, 1910–1947.
42. Max (McLean Co.). S–1908–1913; M–1913–1922.
43. Medora (Billings Co.). M–1884–1890.
44. Napoleon (Logan Co.). S–1894–1897, 1902–1905; M–1905–1907; P–1907–1912.
45. Oriska (Barnes Co.). P–1915–1916, 1927–1930.
46. Painted Woods (Burleigh Co.). S–1883–1897.
47. Parshall (Mountrail Co.). M–1916–1927.
48. Plaza (Mountrail Co.). M–1910–1917; P–1917–1927.
49. Portal (Burke Co.). M–1917–1922.
50. Richardton (Stark Co.). S–1884–1890.
51. Rutten (Ramsey Co.). M–1929–1940.
52. Ryder (Ward Co.). M–1910–1927.
53. St. Boniface (Logan Co.). S–1905–1906; M–1906–1912.
54. St. Joseph (Grant Co.). M–1903–1904.
55. Selz (Pierce Co.). P–1927–1928.
56. Sentinel Butte (Golden Valley Co.). S–1884–1890.
57. Sims (Morton Co.). S–1884–1887.
58. South Heart (Stark Co.). S–1884–1890.
59. Stanton (Mercer Co.). S–1884–1887.
60. Steele (Kidder Co.). S–1904–1909.
61. Sterling (Burleigh Co.). S–1908–1910.
62. Sweetbriar (Morton Co.). S–1884–1887.
63. Sykeston (Wells Co.). P–1925–1927.
64. Tappen (Kidder Co.). S–1895–1908; M–1908–1910.
65. Taylor (Stark Co.). S–1884–1890.
66. Tower City (Cass Co.). S–1915–1916.
67. Turtle Lake (McLean Co.). S–1905–1906, 1911–1912; M–1920–1926.
68. Underwood (McLean Co.). S–1905–1906; M–1906–1913; P–1920–1926.
69. Washburn (McLean Co.). M–1902–1913.
70. Williamsport (Emmons Co.). S–1883–1904.
71. Wilton (McLean Co.). S–1900–1904; M–1904–1912.
72. Wishek (McIntosh Co.). S–1908–1912.

OKLAHOMA

1. Harrah (Oklahoma Co.). P–1929–1932.
2. McLoud (Pottawatomie Co.). M–1930–1932.
3. Meeker (Lincoln Co.). M–1929–1932.
4. Mishak (Oklahoma Co.). M–1929–1932.

WASHINGTON

1. Elina (Grays Harbor Co.). M–1901–1904.
2. Frances (Pacific Co.). S–1898–1900; M–1900.
3. Lake Park (Pierce Co.). S–1896–1900; M–1900–1904.
4. Long Beach (Pacific Co.). S–1898–1900; M–1900–1904.

5. Montesano (Grays Harbor Co.). M–1902–1904.
6. Oakville (Grays Harbor Co.). S–1901–1904.
7. Oysterville (Pacific Co.). S–1898–1900.
8. Shelton (Mason Co.). S–1896–1900; M–1900–1904.
9. South Bend (Pacific Co.). M–1898–1900.
10. Steilacoom (Pierce Co.). M–1896–1904.
11. Tacoma (Pierce Co.), Holy Rosary. P–1891–1904.
12. Tacoma (Pierce Co.), Visitation. M–1896–1904.
13. Tenino (Thurston Co.). S–1897–1900; M–1900–1904.
14. Willapa (Pacific Co.). S–1898–1900.

WISCONSIN

1. La Crosse, St. Joseph's Cathedral. P–1877–1878.
2. Prairie du Chien (Crawford Co.), St. Gabriel's Church. P–1877–1880.
3. Wauzeka (Crawford Co.). S–1877.

BAHAMA ISLANDS, BRITISH WEST INDIES

Andros Island

1. Bastian Point. M–1933–present.
2. Behring Point. M–1898–1914? 1930?–1939, 1952–present; P–1914?–1930?, 1939–1952.
3. Calabash Bay. M–1925–present.
4. Fresh Creek. S–1924–1938; M–1938–1952; P–1952–1955.
5. High Rocks. M–1932–present.
6. Kemps Bay. S–1932–1934; M–1934–present.
7. Little Creek. S–1934–1946; M–1946–present.
8. Man O' War Sound. S–1911–1946; M–1946–present.
9. Mangrove Cay. M–1920–1934; P–1934–present.
10. Mastic Point. M–1936–present.
11. Salvador Point. M–1893–1894; P–1894–1914?
12. Stanyard Creek. S–1924–1930?; P–1930–1939; M–1939–present.

Bimini Islands

13. Holy Name. S–1942–1954; P–1954–present.

Cat Cay

14. S–1942–present.

Cat Island

15. Baintown. M–1951–1956.
16. The Bight. P–1951–1956.
17. Devil's Point. S–1948–1956.
18. Old Bight. M–1951–1956.
19. Port Howe. M–1951–1956.

Eleuthera Islands

20. The Lower Bogue. S–1933–1947; M–1947–1954.
21. The Upper Bogue. M–1952–1954.
22. Gregory Town. M–1926–1954.

23. Hatchet Bay. S–1926–1935; M–1935–1954.

Grand Bahama Island

24. Gold Rock. S–1949–present.
25. Pine Ridge. S–1941–present.
26. Station Hunter. M–1940–present.
27. West End. M–1940–present.

Harbour Island

28. Dunmore Town. P–1922–1954.

Inagua Island

29. S–1940–present.

Long Island

30. The Bight. S–1937–1955; M–1955–present.
31. Buckley's. M–1950–present.
32. Clarence Town. S–1930–1936; M–1936–1937; P–1937–present.
33. Clements. S–1935–1937.
34. Deadman's Cay. M–1948–present.
35. Dunmore. M–1942–present.
36. Hamilton. S–1930–1941; M–1941–present.
37. Hard Bargain. S–1933–1941.
38. Mortimer. M–1930–present.
39. Salt Pond. S–1947–present.
40. Taits. M–1930–present.
41. Wood Hill. S–1935–1941.

New Providence Island

42. Nassau. Our Lady of the Holy Souls Church. M–1926–1931; P–1931–present.
43. Nassau. Sacred Heart Church. M–1902–1925; P–1894–1902, 1925–present.
44. Nassau. St. Anselm's Church. S–1933–1935; P–1935–present.
45. Nassau. St. Bede's Church. P–1948–present.
46. Nassau. St. Francis Xavier Church. P–1891–present.
47. Nassau. St. Joseph's Church. P–1932–present.
48. Nassau. Ss. Peter and Paul Church. M–1927–1931; P–1931–present.
49. Nassau. St. Thomas More Church. P–1950–1955.

San Salvador Island

50. Harbour Estate. S–1925–1927; M–1927–1935.
51. Riding Rock. P–1921–present.
52. United Estates. S–1925–1930, 1936–1939; M–1939–present.

JAPAN

53. Tokyo. St. Anselm's Church. P–1947–present.

PUERTO RICO

54. Humacao. P–1947–present.

Statistics for typical years:

1860: Parishes, 3; missions, 28; stations, 22.

1875: Parishes, 13; missions, 12; stations, 3.

1885: Parishes, 26; missions, 23; stations, 37.

1900: Parishes, 38; missions, 22; stations, 30.

1925: Parishes, 47; missions, 19, stations, 11.

1956: Parishes, 50; missions, 33; stations, 10.

Summary, 1856–1956: Parishes, 113; missions, 146; stations, 102.

Total number of different congregations: 361.

APPENDIX V

ABBOT ALEXIUS EDELBROCK'S
farewell letter to the community of St. John's Abbey, Rome, 27 November 1889

V. Rev. dear Prior Norbert Hofbauer, my dear Fathers, and confrères of St. John's Abbey in Minnesota: Today I passed the spot in this holy City where SS. Peter and Paul bade each other an eternal farewell in this world. The memorable spot awakened many thoughts in me, as we were also taking leave of each other. Today I handed in my *resignation* to the Holy Father [Leo XIII]. I did so unrequested by any one: the act is one of my own free will. This my action means an *ultimum vale*. I am your superior no longer. Yet you all are dear to me and, *Deo volente,* shall remain so. I part from you with a bleeding heart, because I still sincerely love you. I pray you not to blame my course. I may have hurt, at times, the feelings of the one or the other of you, not intentionally indeed, but by accident or under trying circumstances. In as far as I may be blamable, I ask pardon of you all, and I too pardon you. May we all reach our heavenly home. I can say before God that intentionally and to the best of my knowledge, I have wronged none of you. I have ruined nobody. Most of you have grown up under me: I received you into the Order: I cared for you: I toiled for you day and night: I crucified my life for my people and for the welfare of our community. My ambition was the growth of our Order in the Northwest. St. John's University — the education of youth was my pride, and you, my dear *Confratres,* were my glory. I had no selfish end in view. I shared with you all trials and difficulties and sufferings, — yes, I have borne more hardships than any of you: you had a place to rest your head on. I have been, as it were, homeless during the last fourteen years. I felt the bitterness of my position, and on my lonesome travels in the burning heat, in rain and sunshine, in snow and bitter cold, I shed many a silent tear: I felt as the children of Israel in the Babylonian captivity — far away from the house and the cell that I love so well. I went wherever my duty called me. There is scarcely a recreation trip in my whole official life. Often, yes generally, even in poor health, I bore up ready to lay down my life for you, my flock. I

371

expected no recompensation in this world except your love and loyalty. It was always my endeavor that we proceed *viribus unitis* in order to make our efforts pleasing to God and a success in this world. The words of Sallust: *Concordia parvae res crescunt, discordia maximae dilabuntur,* as also the Saracens of Spain were well-known to me. When peace had departed and when factions had arisen, then the great Roman Empire fell; when relatives had fought against each other, then Spain was seized by the enemy and almost annihilated. *Qui potest capere capiat.* History always repeats itself. Like causes produce like effects. Shall St. John's Abbey cease to exist? Shall its honored and honorable position among the Abbeys of the world be a thing of the past? The answers to these questions I must leave to you, as all will depend on your course. My parting advice is: stand together firmly, say some earnest prayers, leave all personal rancor and ill-feeling aside, look to the Commonweal and do your full duty; stand by each other, stand faithfully by your superiors, pray for them, honor them, bear with their faults, as they also bear with yours. Criticizing superiors will not build up any institution: criticizing superiors will not preserve any institution; criticizing superiors will not draw down God's blessing on you; criticizing superiors will not open heaven for you. A good monk looks to his own faults, reveres his superiors and avoids the *Vicovaroites.* Nothing has hurt my feelings as much as the assertion that a majority of my folks were opposed to me. *This is the main reason of my resignation.* I might have been able to swallow calumnies and detractions. I might gain a victory over their infernal machinations: but what would such a victory amount to without your love and firm attachment? I could not work in the future: my days would be bitter as gall. This consideration has caused me to step aside. I thank every one of you for every act of kindness ever shown me. God reward and bless you for it. No one will have reason to regret the fidelity and the love he has borne his superiors. There is a just God who notes down our acts: the *serve bone et fidelis* will in due time receive his reward. I cheerfully lay down the burden piled onto me 14 years ago, but to part from my monastery forever seems impossible to me. I purpose to remain a *Capitularis* of St. John's Abbey, and when peace shall have returned to its sacred halls, then, too, do I hope to see you, my dear *Confratres,* once more. *Interim valete! Deus vos benedicat et custodiat. Orate pro me sicut et ego pro vobis. In visceribus Jesu Christi.*

ABBOT BERNARD LOCNIKAR

to Miceslaus Cardinal Ledochowski, Collegeville, 24 March 1893

Your Excellency,

The letter (1455) Your Eminence sent me I received recently, delivered under the prudent care of Archbishop Satolli. My greatest thanks to you because you recognize and celebrate with such praise the labors of the Benedictine Fathers for the propagation of the faith in the regions now part of the diocese of St. Cloud. Such things move me with singular joy! We freely accept everything that will be prescribed in the future and whatever, after it has been carefully examined, Your Eminence considers must be enjoined for the good of Religion or this diocese. Therefore, that Your Eminence may the better examine all things in his directing our affairs, I reverently and humbly beg leave to clarify and add to the propositions.

There are three main propositions in the above-mentioned letter which Your Eminence inculcates or recommends for our consideration. 1. Six of our missions should be handed over to the bishop to be cared for by the secular clergy. 2. The Mass stipends collected in the missions in the St. Cloud diocese should be given to the bishop if the Masses cannot be celebrated in the missions or in the monastery of St. John's. 3. The Fathers who have labored in the missions for more than ten years should be called back to the monastery for at least one year. Permit me to add a little comment on each proposal.

1. That six of the missions cared for by the Benedictine Fathers be given to the bishop. I think we have more than fulfilled this proposal of Your Eminence because we have recently given not six, but fourteen, missions to the bishop. The missions cared for in the diocese of St. Cloud at one time were part of the diocese of St. Paul, and later a part of the Vicariate of Northern Minnesota. In both instances these missions were left to the care of our Fathers, and the bishop of St. Paul as well as afterwards the Vicar Apostolic, Bishop Seidenbusch, even gave us new missions as well as some old ones which for various reasons were being neglected, e.g. Millerville, Rich Prairie [Pierz], Perham, and others.

However, when the Most Rev. Otto Zardetti became Bishop of St. Cloud, he gave himself to the duties of his diocese with a zeal not witnessed before. He turned his attention to the flourishing missions in our care and he began to negotiate with us to give him some of them. We put our own wishes aside and handed over some of our missions as he wished, and a little later he wrote me a letter stating his satisfaction in this matter. After a while other missions were constantly added to this number, and finally, when we took count on January 8, 1891, no less than fourteen missions were designated to be given to the bishop: 1. Perham, 2. Belle River, 3. Alexandria, 4. Buckman, 5. Holding Ford [sic],

373

6. St. Anna, 7. Avon, 8. Krain, 9. St. Stephen, 10. Maples, 11. St. Nicholas, 12. Spring Hill, 13. Lake Henry, 14. Loggering.

In previous years we gave to the bishop of St. Paul no less than fifty-two missions which he has given over to the secular clergy, while we still take care of some in his diocese.

Appendix VI

I have set forth these things with an open mind. Allow me to take this opportunity to ask a favor of Your Eminence. Keeping in mind the above restrictions, please confirm that the missions we now have in our care be under the authority of our monastery at St. John's, so that in the future we may be able to conduct them well and enjoy peace.

When the Benedictines came here at the invitation of the Most Rev. Bishop of St. Paul, they found a vast prairie for the most part occupied by savage Indians. Some of the devout families had congregated into villages where the Fathers forthwith received temporary aid and were able to enjoy continual peace. Our Fathers looked after these country places from the beginning and nothing hindered them. Amidst many hardships, in the greatest need, in danger of death, but with indefatigable zeal, they wandered through this vast region — the diocese covered the whole territory at that time. Since there was scarcely a single church at this time, they celebrated Mass and administered the Sacraments in the homes of the faithful. They gathered the dispersed Catholics together and instructed them, so that in the course of time at least small chapels of wood were built. God, however, so blessed their labors that in the whole United States perhaps nothing can be found comparable to Stearns County where they have sown the seed of their labors, and all the bishops know that it is completely Catholic. Because God blessed us so abundantly in the diocese of St. Paul and in this new diocese we were able to give fourteen missions to the bishop as he requested. Thus if there is any reward for furthering the cause of religion, allow us to keep those missions which now are in our care, especially those that are in Stearns County where the monastery of St. John's is located. Situated in the center of the county, it may be considered their father, as it were, their mother in the midst of her daughters whom the superior is able to visit in two or three days' journey from the monastery.

The Benedictine Fathers conduct a college and a seminary where at least thirty-five young men are pursuing a liberal training and are preparing for the priesthood. Their needs are for the most part supplied by the monastery, for, since they are very poor, they would otherwise never be able to become educated. Of these, some will enter the Benedictine Order and others will become diocesan priests. Furthermore, we also reduce twenty-five percent of the expenses of all the seminarians in theology.

Lately four of our Fathers have been working in the missions among the Indians who have no means of support. In the mission now called White Earth in the diocese of Duluth, the monastery built a church and a house for the missionaries for $25,000 (125,000 lira), not counting the free labor of the lay Brothers. Besides furnishing money for erecting

374

fifty buildings in the diocese of St. Cloud, the Fathers in the missions, where they have been working with the diocesan priests for the last thirty years, must give a part of their salary each year for building an episcopal residence. The good of religion will suffer from such things. Our missions are taken care of in accordance with the instructions the Ordinary sends out. The secular clergy have enough work to care for the missions outside Stearns County, whereas almost all our missions are found in the county. There are fifteen other missions in the county which are now being quickly settled so that many villages want more priests than can be supplied. As a result, of the fourteen missions we have handed over to the bishop, he has been able to give only seven to the care of the secular clergy. The rest are still left in our care, much to our inconvenience. And since these are no longer our missions, we could put these Fathers to the care of the many missions scattered far and wide that are given to us by other bishops. We would be willing to take care of these missions for the common good and the good of this newly-erected diocese. We are confident that Your Eminence will generously grant some of the request we humbly beg for. May you at least grant that the missions we now have be left to our care in the future so that we may have peace. Then with a deep sense of gratitude we will work with a greater zeal for souls, for God, and for Mother Church.

2. Your Eminence suggests that the Mass stipends collected by the Benedictine Fathers in the missions of the diocese be given to the bishop if the Masses cannot be celebrated in the missions themselves or in the monastery of St. John's. However, it must be remembered that the stipends are not so numerous as Your Eminence supposes. Furthermore, the faithful who offer the stipends often insist that the Masses be celebrated in their own church so that they may be able to assist at these Masses. As for those sent to the monastery, and I speak truly, there are not enough for a fourth part of the year for the Fathers staying here.

3. We must highly commend Your Eminence for his suggestion that the Fathers who have labored outside the monastery for more than ten years be called back to live in the monastery for at least one year. This to me as a superior seems the most important of the proposals and I thank you very much for communicating these instructions to me. Hence I have your approbation to introduce this practice as soon as possible. If the bishop would give the missions we have given him to the secular clergy, this practice could be begun immediately. But he does not have many priests who can give themselves over to the care of souls, and within the past two years I have called back some whom I considered less suited for such work.

As for the rest, I hope that these instructions were not meant for censure or punishment. Though some things have been done by way of exception (contrary to the instructions proposed), the religious spirit in our community has not been relaxed up to this time. Last year at the triennial canonical visitation, the visitators congratulated me both by word and in writing, on the good spirit prevailing in our community.

375

Within the past two years I heard the bishop, who for obvious reasons is a most strict judge in his dealings with us, at least five times publicly commend us for our good community spirit. Furthermore, very frequently those outside the monastery are excellent religious, while some negligent ones can be found in the monastery.

Finally, I wish to thank Your Eminence again for your paternal solicitude toward us by all the favors we have received and will receive in the future, especially during these times when religious families are more or less troubled. I promise that the community will always remember you in their prayers.

APPENDIX VII

A STATEMENT OF PRINCIPLES

by the Reverend Virgil Michel, O.S.B., in *Orate Fratres,* 28 November 1926

For some time the phrase "liturgical movement" has been entering with increasing frequency into current speech. Now the term "liturgical apostolate" bids fair to supersede it. In all cases, even where the significance of the phrases is of the vaguest for those employing them, the words are meant to stand for some sort of liturgical awakening among the Catholics of the country. It is for the furtherance of such an awakening that we, the editors of *Orate Fratres,* are herewith launching a liturgical review upon the stream of Catholic life among the English-speaking peoples. In this first number of the review, it will not be out of place to say a word about our aim, our hopes, and the general outlook as it appears to us.

The Aim. Our general aim is to develop a better understanding of the spiritual import of the liturgy, an understanding that is truly sympathetic. This means that we are not aiming at a cold scholastic interest in the liturgy of the Church, but at an interest that is more thoroughly intimate, that seizes upon the entire person, touching not only intellect but also will, heart as well as mind. Should we choose, we could express this aim in words borrowed variously from the different pronouncements of recent popes, from the first encyclicals of the saintly Piux X down to the recent encyclical on the feast of Christ the King, the entire context of which shows how intimate a concern its subject-matter is to the heart of its author, the reigning Vicar of Christ, Pius XI.

A sympathetic understanding of the liturgy is one that will affect the actual life of the Catholic. The liturgical life is essential to the Catholic, for without a minimum participation in it he can not be a faithful child of the Church. This participation in the liturgical life of the Church admits of increase in its intensity as well as in its individual and corporate extent. An increase in all of these ways is our aim in promoting the liturgical apostolate; and should prove a natural result of the efforts expended

376

on *Orate Fratres,* if these efforts will be at all blessed with success. A better understanding of and participation in the liturgical worship of the Church, should affect both the individual spiritual life of the Catholic and the corporate life of the natural social units of the Church, the parishes, so properly called the cells of the corporate organism which is the entire living Church, the mystic body of Christ. Growth in all of these is included in the aims as we have set for ourselves in bringing out *Orate Fratres.*

The Hopes. What are our hopes, and on what are they based? Our hopes are simply that our efforts may be blessed with some success. We hope that the interest aroused in the liturgy will be primarily spiritual; that the liturgy may be recognized more universally as being what Pius X so happily called it when he characterized it as the primary and indispensable source of the true Christian spirit. Our hopes are therefore based, like our efforts, on the possibility that many persons may find in the liturgy the first answer to the intimate need of their souls for a closer contact and union with the spiritual and the divine.

Our hopes, indeed, do not exclude other aspects of the liturgy, all of which may combine and should combine to emphasize its essential function in the spiritual life. Many and varied interests meet in the liturgy. The latter is a great mine of the widest cultural life. There are the literary, musical, artistic, historical, even ethnological and archeological aspects, all of which are worth fostering, and all of which are replete with interest and value in life. Our hopes are also for a better appreciation of these aspects of the liturgy, but always in subordination to the more fundamental aspect, that of the spiritual import, which is its true essential nature. Should any of the secondary aspects and interests break away from their proper relation to the real nature of the liturgy, that is, should any one of them cease to be a way of leading to the latter or of revealing the latter, and should that result occur by reason of our efforts, we should have to confess to the keenest disappointment of our hopes, if not of complete failure.

Our hopes are not based on any exaggerated appraisal of our own powers or endeavors. A liturgical awakening must come through a sympathetic understanding on the part of the general faithful. All we can do is to present the liturgy in the way in which it appears to us, and in the way in which it has made its impression on other Catholic minds both of the past and of the present. Beyond this we can not go. Further results depend on others. A liturgical awakening is necessarily a collective event, and therefore needs the co-operation of many. One of our hopes is to furnish a common medium of exchange, and to present to all the faithful the opportunity of an active exchange of views and impressions. To this end we extend a cordial invitation to all who feel sufficiently interested, to join us in the expression of their beliefs and hopes, to offer their suggestions, or to ask for the experiences of others. For some time there has been a spiritual leaven at work among our Catholics, which has developed in many isolated localities into a growing appreciation of the liturgical life. These experiences are valuable to all inquiring Catholics, and can furnish the basis of a general co-operative endeavor, such as alone will produce tangible results.

Principally, however, all hopes of success must rest on something higher than human effort. There must be no delusion about that. The essential aim having to do with the spiritual life of the Catholic soul, all human effort is fruitless unless it is blessed by Him who alone gives the increase. That He may give an increase, where we and those joining us shall in all modesty try to plant and water, is our great hope — a hope based primarily on the fact that our endeavors are trying to fulfill the inspirations that have so repeatedly come from the mouth of the visible representative of Christ here on earth.

The Prospect. Another question: What prospect of success has our undertaking? We must say frankly that it is impossible to make any predictions. Success in our undertaking, we have indicated, depends on the co-operation of the faithful in general, and particularly on the readers of *Orate Fratres.* If that is not forthcoming, our efforts may not extend beyond the year which for the present marks the goal of our planning. We do not doubt in the least that the cause as such will triumph in time. The cause, as has been well said, is "much greater than any individual" or body of individuals. Ultimately the liturgical movement is bound to come, even should our own efforts not be the means of bringing about an approach to it — a possibility that we are for the present not contemplating.

On the contrary, it seems very probable to us that our efforts will answer a more permanent need of the Catholic soul, and then, with the grace of God, *Orate Fratres* may continue indefinitely. Should there be a real increase of the seed that we in conjunction with all joining the liturgical apostolate in word and action, are planting, the means and instruments of the good work should likewise increase. In that case there might be a good field for more reviews like ours, or rather for liturgical reviews that are more specialized and profound in their study and endeavor. Again there should be a fair prospect, then, of seeing a liturgical column or question-box become a regular feature of all Catholic periodicals, which would be a great step ahead.

Which of these possibilities will come true, it is now impossible to say. No human tongue can tell what are our prospects of success. Only one thing we know, and that suffices. The voice of Peter has spoken, and spoken repeatedly. And our effort in response to it shall be made as best we know how. Further questions of hope and success are distracting and useless.

NOTES

CODE TO ABBREVIATIONS

Archives AAB — Archives of the Archdiocese of Baltimore
AAMe — Archives of the Abbey of Metten
AAMi — Archives of the Archdiocese of Milwaukee
AANY — Archives of the Archdiocese of New York
AAP — Archives of the Abbot Primate, Rome
AASB — Archives of St. Benedict's Abbey
AASJ — Archives of St. John's Abbey
AASM — Archives of the Archabbey of St. Meinrad
AASP — Archives of the Archdiocese of St. Paul
AASPOW — Archives of the Abbey of St. Paul Outside the Wall
AASV — Archives of the Archabbey of St. Vincent
ACA — Archives of Conception Abbey
ACMSV — Archives of the Convent of Mount St. Vincent on the Hudson
ACSB — Archives of the Convent of St. Benedict, St. Joseph
ADR — Archives of the Diocese of Richmond
ADSC — Archives of the Diocese of St. Cloud
ALMV — Archives of the Ludwig Missionsverein
AMHS — Archives of the Minnesota Historical Society
ASCC — Archives of the Stearns County Courthouse
ASCHS — Archives of the Stearns County Historical Society
ASMA — Archives of St. Mary's Abbey
NA — National Archives
Periodicals AD — *Acta et Dicta*
AVG — *Annalen der Verbreitung des Glaubens*
BLS — *Berichte der Leopoldinen Stiftung*
CE — *Catholic Encyclopedia*
CHR — *Catholic Historical Review*
MH — *Minnesota History*
OF — *Orate Fratres*
SM — *Studien und Mitteilungen des Ben. Orden*

NOTES TO CHAPTER ONE

1 August C. Krey, *Monte Cassino, Metten and Minnesota* (St. Paul, 1927), pp. 11–12. Dr. Krey has graciously allowed the title of his masterful address delivered before the Minnesota Historical Society on 16 June 1927 to be used for the first chapter of this work.

Chapter I of this work was published in advance in CHR, XLI (October, 1955), 272–296, under the title

379

"Boniface Wimmer, Pioneer of the American Benedictines."

2 *Fulgens radiatur* (Lisle, Illinois, 1947), pp. 11–12.

3 Two of the more basic studies of Benedictine monastic history are Philibert Schmitz, O.S.B., *Histoire de l'ordre de Saint-Benoît* (6 vols: Maredsous, 1949); Stephan Hilpisch, O.S.B., *Das Benediktinertum im Wandel der Zeiten* (St. Ottilien, 1950).

4 C. P. Higby, *The Religious Policy of the Bavarian Government During the Napoleonic Period* (New York, 1918); H. Brueck, *Geschichte der Katholischen Kirche in Deutschland im Nuenzhenten Jahrhundert* (2 vols.; Mainz, 1889).

5 Wilhelm Fink, O.S.B., *Entwicklungsgeschichte der Benediktinerabtei Metten* (Munich, 1926–28), passim; *Alt und Jung Metten*, IV (1926), 3–64.

6 Printed sources on Wimmer include Oswald Moosmueller, O.S.B., *Erzabt Bonifaz Wimmer, O.S.B.* (New York, 1891), and *St. Vincenz in Pennsylvanien* (New York, 1873); Sebastian J. Wimmer, "Biographical Sketch of Rt. Rev. Arch-Abbot Wimmer, O.S.B., D.D., Patriarch of the American Cassinese Benedictines," *Records of the American Catholic Historical Society of Philadelphia*, III (1891), 174–193; Bernhard Lester, "Erzabt Bonifaz Wimmer, Das Bild eines deutschen Mannes in Amerika," *Frankfurter zeitgemaesse Broschueren*, XII (1891), 397–424; Willibald Mathaeser, O.S.B., "Koenig Ludwig I. von Bayern und die Gruendung der ersten bayerischen Benediktinerabtei in Nordamerika," *Studien und Mitteilungen*, XLIII (1925), 123–182, and *Bonifaz Wimmer, O.S.B., und Koenig Ludwig I. von Bayern* (Munich, 1937).

The Reverend Felix Fellner, O.S.B., of St. Vincent Archabbey has devoted a lifetime to the study of the career of Wimmer. He has an authoritative biography of Archabbot Boniface in manuscript and has published a number of separate studies, including: "Archabbot Boniface Wimmer, O.S.B.," *Dictionary of American Biography*, XX, 370–371; "Archabbot Boniface Wimmer As an Educator," *National Benedictine Educational Association Bulletin, XXV* (December, 1942), 85–114; "Archabbot Wimmer and Historical Sources," *Records of the American Catholic Historical Society of Philadelphia*, XXXVII (December, 1926), 299–304; and *Die St.*

Vincenz-Gemeinde und Erzabtei (St. Vincent, 1905).

Cf. also Baltimore *Katholische Volkszeitung*, 17 December 1887, and 7 January 1888; Gerald Bridge, O.S.B., *Illustrated History of St. Vincent's Archabbey* (St. Vincent, 1892); "Sportsman's Hall and St. Vincent Abbey," *St. Vincent's Journal*, 15 February 1893–15 May 1894; Louis Haas, O.S.B., *St. Vincent Parish and Archabbey* (St. Vincent, 1905).

7 *Album Benedictinum* (St. Vincent, 1889), p. 53.

8 A translation of this article first appeared in *St. Vincent's Journal*, II (15 February 1893), 171–174; II (15 March 1893), 202–208.

9 "Archabbot Boniface Wimmer as an Educator," *National Benedictine Educational Association Bulletin*, XXV (December, 1942), 89. Because of its central importance as establishing the spirit and aim of Benedictine effort in America this article is included in Appendix I.

10 Cf. Severus Brandus, *Die katholisch-irisch-bischoefliche Administration in Nordamerika* (Philadelphia, 1840), for an exaggerated but typical German attack in the United States; and Joseph Salzbacher, *Meine Reise nach Nordamerika im Jahre 1842* (Vienna, 1854), for a European opinion of religious conditions on the American scene.

11 Oswald Moosmueller, O.S.B., *St. Vincenz in Pennsylvanien* (New York, 1873), pp. 128–30. The papal approval was delayed, however, by the Italian revolution of 1848, and was not received until 1852. Thus during those first years Wimmer had the further trial of being in the anomalous position of acting as "superior" without canonical jurisdiction for himself or for receiving the vows of his monks.

12 ALMV, Wimmer to Mueller, 13 April 1849.

13 AAMi, Mueller to Henni, Munich, 1 March 1847.

14 ALMV, Wimmer to Von Reisach, St. Vincent, 1 May 1855.

15 At St. Vincent no beer was brewed until Christmas of 1860. In later years temperance fanatics attacked the Benedictines for this practice and the initials, O.S.B., were even interpreted "Order of Sacred Brewers."

16 AASPOW, O'Connor to Smith, Pittsburgh, 13 August 1852.

17 Wimmer to Ludwig I, St. Vincent, 13 February 1852, in Willibald Math-

aeser, O.S.B., *Bonifaz Wimmer, O.S.B., und Koenig Ludwig I. von Bayern* (Munich, 1937), p. 34.

18 Oswald Moosmueller, O.S.B., *Erzabt Bonifaz Wimmer, O.S.B.* (New York, 1891), p. 164. Cf. also pp. 149–180 for an interesting contemporary account of the controversy by Moosmueller who was then prior of St. Vincent. O'Connor's position is found in several letters to Abbot Bernard Smith, while Wimmer's is detailed in numerous communications to Abbot Angelo Pescetelli. The Smith and Pescetelli documents are preserved in the archives of the Abbey of St. Paul Outside the Walls, Rome. They have been microfilmed and complete copies of both collections are on file in the archives of St. John's Abbey.

19 Archives of the Archdiocese of Dubuque, Wimmer to Loras, St. Vincent, 8 February 1856. When Bishop O'Connor was informed of the decision he wrote to Abbot Boniface:

"I congratulate you on your safe return and on the success of your efforts. You must be aware that, though I considered the erection of the monastery into an abbey somewhat premature, I gave my candid consent to the measure, if the Holy See thought it prudent to proceed to that step, and I considered it at all times only a question as to when it should be done. At present it was more prudent than when it was first mooted, and I have every confidence that whatever dangers may yet be apprehended will be counteracted by your tact and prudence. To your being attached to the Congregation of Monte Cassino and consequently entitled to the exemption granted such congregations, far from regretting it, it affords me pleasure. It is in accordance with the course which the Church has sanctioned in all such matters, and is naturally the best guide for any one who wishes to see all things right" (AASV, O'Connor to Wimmer, Pittsburgh, 14 December 1855).

20 Archives of the Abbey of St. John's, Wimmer to di Marogna, Munich, 5 September 1855. Cf. also January 28, April 9, July 29, August 22 and 1 October 1855. Hereafter all letters and documents quoted from the archives of St. John's will be listed without archival identification.

21 AAMi, Henni to Gall Morel O.S.B., Milwaukee, 28 April 1847, copy. As late as 1875 Henni was still trying to persuade Abbot Martin Mar-

ty, O.S.B., of St. Meinrad's Abbey, to establish a Benedictine house as soon as possible in the Archdiocese of Milwaukee. Marty asked the Benedictines of St. Boniface Abbey in Munich to assist him since a college was to be started at once. But this project did not materialize either (AAMi, Marty to Henni, Covington, 8 November 1875). The Benedictines did not come to Wisconsin until 1946 when Abbot Richard Felix, O.S.B., began the establishment of Benet Lake Monastery in the Archdiocese of Milwaukee, 100 years after Henni's original request.

22 Felix Fellner, O.S.B., "Boniface Wimmer," *Dictionary of American Biography*, XX, 370. Cf. also Boniface Wimmer, O.S.B., "Beiträge zur Geschichte des Benediktiner-Ordens in den Vereinigten Staaten von Nord-Amerika," *SM*, VII (1886), 459.

23 Wimmer to Ludwig I, St. Vincent, 4 July 1853, in Mathaeser, *op. cit.*, pp. 52, 54.

24 ALMV, Wimmer to Mueller, St. Vincent, 12 December 1858.

25 *Ibid.*

26 Pescetelli to Seidenbusch, Rome, 7 November 1865.

27 Wimmer informed Pescetelli and Mueller that Cretin had pleaded with him to send monks to Minnesota (AASPOW, Wimmer to Pescetelli, St. Vincent, 21 March 1856; ALMV, Wimmer to Mueller, St. Vincent, 9 June 1856); Wimmer was in correspondence with Bishop Frederic Baraga during this time (Archives of the Diocese of Marquette, Baraga to Wimmer, Sault Ste. Marie, 19 March 1856, copy); Wimmer had been invited several times by Bishop John Martin Henni of Milwaukee (Cf. fn. 20); Wimmer wrote to Bishop Loras of Dubuque: ". . . A religious order stands in need of the confidence and benevolence of the Bishop, and in return a Bishop will earn a great deal of advantage from a well organized religious corporation); still there are regards for both of them, that must be kept in view, which, Sir, I do not think hard, if you want to know the men, who would come to be your assistance in the vineyard of the Lord. Therefore I thought it necessary to speak frankly and to say what is our practice now and what may be our practice afterwards. *Nil nisi quod traditum est*. We enter only into the paths of our fathers of old. We are Germans, but not so obstinately as not to conform to the

genius of the country if it be a good Catholic one; we have our countrymen, but not exclusively; we serve willingly the Bishops, whilst we try to observe our rule; and ᴣrant slowly the preference to other orders, already established here, but try not to be behind them" (Archives of the Archdiocese of Dubuque, Wimmer to Loras, St. Vincent, 8 February 1856). Bruno Riess, O.S.B., one of the clerics accompanying Prior di Marogna to Minnesota, wrote in his memoirs of the trip west: ". . . Our trip to St. Louis covered two weeks. There we encountered some tempting inducements. The archbishop of St. Louis [Peter Richard Kenrick] was one of the six applicants for Benedictine priests, and, when we arrived, thought we had come in response to his request. He would not have us go any further. At the same time congregations at Germantown and Highland, Illinois, had been informally promised a Benedictine priest, and from these quarters no efforts were spared to detain us" (*The Record*, February, 1889). Riess also stated that six bishops requested Benedictines at the time the colony was sent to Minnesota, but indications of requests or interest from only five bishops are extant. Riess, moreover, painted a romantic description of the procedure employed by Wimmer and his monks in choosing the diocese for their first daughter abbey. He recorded these memoirs late in life, and there is no factual authorization for the following recollection: "It happened in January, 1856, that six American bishops sent petitions to the late Archabbot Wimmer for the introduction of the Benedictine Order and erection of monasteries in their dioceses. This movement caused some perplexity. Widely divergent opinions and proposals were brought to the front in a chapter in which these applications were considered—one favored acceptance of this, another of that post. The Abbot listened, no conclusions were reached. Finally he arose and said: 'We will commit the whole affair to the hands of God—may He decide where we should make the beginning. I shall,' said he, 'write to each of the bishops and tell him our needs, i.e., the conditions upon which we will be able to correspond with his request. All of these letters I will mail at the same time and the first bishop who will reply satisfactorily shall have our priests.' And behold, the voice of God

came from the West, from St. Paul, the most distant point which the mails only reached via Dubuque and thence per stage; from St. Paul came the first unconditioned call for Benedictine monks" (*The Record*, February, 1889).

28 Wimmer to Ludwig I, St. Vincent, 30 May 1856, in Mathaeser, *op. cit.*, p. 81.

29 A biography of Pierz was prepared for the observance of the centennial of his activity in central Minnesota: William P. Furlan, *In Charity Unfeigned* (Paterson, N. J., 1952). Cf. also John J. Miller, "Letters of the Reverend Francis Xavier Pierz (1854-1865)," (M. A. Dissertation, St. Francis Seminary, Milwaukee, 1930); Sister Grace McDonald, O.S.B., "Father Francis Pierz, Missionary," *Minnesota History Bulletin*, X (June, 1929)ₚ 107–25; John Seliskar, "The Reverend Francis Pierz," *AD*, III (July, 1911), 66–99.

30 'Squatting' was a common term for settlement in the United States on new or unorganized land without right or title. Delegate Henry Rice of Minnesota Territory sponsored and saw through the U.S. House of Representatives an Act of 4 August 1854 granting the privileges of pre-emption rights to all settlers on unsurveyed lands in Minnesota. The same privileges had been granted during that year to settlers in the territories of California, Kansas, Nebraska, Washington and Oregon.

31 (St. Louis, 1855). Cf. Cincinnati *Wahrheitsfreund*, 4 March, 8 June 1854; 3 May 1855; 6 June 1861; 9 and 16 April, 28 May, 30 July, 8 October, 26 November 1862; 19 August 1863; 2 November 1864; 26 April, 5 July, 11 October 1865; New York *Katholische Kirchenzeitung*, 10 May 1855.

32 Furlan, *op. cit.*, pp. 250–51, 255–56. This English translation was made by the Reverend J. B. Tennelly, S.S., present director of the Bureau of Catholic Indian Missions, Washington, D.C.

33 Wimmer to Ludwig I, St. Vincent, 30 May 1856, in Mathaeser, *op. cit.*, p. 81; Moosmueller, *op. cit.*, p. 297.

34 Wimmer to Ludwig I, St. Vincent, 29 November 1856, in Mathaeser, *op. cit.*, p. 86. Throughout his life Abbot Wimmer refused to believe that he was a successful missionary, or that he had accomplished much, despite

the fact that he had spread the Benedictines into every area of the country. Twenty years after his first monastery had been established in Minnesota he wrote, with characteristic humility: "Often it seems to me that I have been living too long, already. My habitual sins — taking everything easy — I used to commit often enough yet, and the consequence thereof will be, I am afraid, a great lack of order and regularity, or bad discipline. Of course, you speak only in a complimentary way, if you call me an ornament to the Order. I ought to be one: indeed, every Abbot ought to be one: and those thousands of Saints of our Order were mostly all of them Abbots, and as such, ornaments to the Order and to the Church. But alas, after a 45 year-long life in the Order, I am farther away from the lowest grade of perfection than I was when I joined. Therefore it is, that I cannot do anything in the administration of the Abbey and its Dependencies, for which I am not more or less sharply censured: certainly for the reason that I never hit the nail on its head. Of course, I don't mind this, nor do I wonder at it, but often the thought comes into my head, that I am not the man for the office. To be sure, an Abbot's duty is not to please people, but to rule them; still as he ought to rule so that they gain thereby, it is to be feared, they are not well ruled if they complain about me, and this fear

is a grave one. In a few days I am going into the 70th year of my life. Only one of those 12 Fathers who joined the Order in Metten in its first period, is living yet, besides me — P. Xavier Sulzbeck. Of course, I am aware that the end of my career must soon be here. I am not attached to life so much, that I would not gladly die any day it may please God to call me home, but for the fear of judgment. A certain success and prosperity or good luck is no sign of Predestination. It is a poor consolation for me, that I succeeded in getting up one monastery aided by the Mission Society, by King Louis and other good friends. The great question will be, if in that Abbey, and in the abbeys descending from it, the spirit of St. Benedict is at home or not, or only little, perhaps very little.

People may think I have done great things, and God may judge I have greatly failed in doing what I chiefly ought to have done! Not to speak at all of my private life as a priest and a Religious and an Abbot! I often think, I should not have undertaken such a work at all, because to do it right, would require not only an energetic, assiduous and wise man, but a holy man. I am none of that. For this reason I am afraid of death, but likewise of long life, since it is very doubtful, if I can or will do much better." (Wimmer to Alexius Edelbrock, St. Vincent, 29 December 1877).

NOTES TO CHAPTER TWO

1 *The Record,* February, 1888. The Reverend Alexius Hoffmann, O.S.B., pioneer librarian and archivist, tirelessly assembled during his lifetime available data concerning the members of St. John's community. With devotion he preserved these materials in numerous note books, folios, chronicles, etc., in the archives of St. John's Abbey, while writing a large number of articles for papers, magazines, encyclopedias. He wrote the only published historical study of St. John's on the occasion of the fiftieth anniversary of the school, *St. John's University* (Collegeville, 1907), and also prepared a manuscript history of St. John's Abbey which is preserved in the institution's archives.

2 Cf. Callistus Edie, O.S.B., "Demetrius di Marogna," *The Scriptorium,* IX (Easter, 1949), 7–31; "Bruno

Riess," *The Scriptorium,* X (Easter, 1950), 5–39; Brother Thomas Whitaker, O.S.B., "Brothers of St. John's Abbey; 1856–1866," *The Scriptorium,* XIII (April, 1953), 38–53.

3 AASV, di Marogna to Wimmer, On Board the 'Paul Anderson', 9 April 1856. As these Benedictines were moving down the Ohio they passed within a few miles of another group of pioneering Benedictines from Einsiedeln, Switzerland, who had come to America in 1854. Prior Demetrius mentions passing through Cannelton, Indiana. Ten miles below Cannelton, at Troy, these Swiss Benedictines made their first stop, and settled eventually at St. Meinrad, Indiana, fifteen miles from Troy. This foundation developed into the large and flourishing archabbey of St. Meinrad, motherhouse of the Swiss Ameri-

can Congregation of Benedictines. For an historical account of St. Meinrad's developments, prepared for that institution's centennial in 1954, cf. Albert Kleber, O.S.B., *History of St. Meinrad Archabbey*, (St. Meinrad, 1954).

4 *The Record*, February, 1889. Father Bruno wrote these memoirs of Benedictine missionary contribution to Minnesota Catholic development in 1888 at the request of the Reverend Alexius Hoffmann, O.S.B. Father Alexius in turn translated them from German into English, and entered his translation in the columns of *The Record*, official paper of St. John's University and organ of the alumni association. The original mss. and translation are preserved in the abbey archives.

5 Dubuque *Herald*, 28 April 1856.

6 Minnesota *Pioneer and Democrat*, 1 May 1856.

7 William Watts Folwell, *A History of Minnesota* (4 vols.; St. Paul, 1921), I, 360.

8 Minnesota *Pioneer and Democrat*, 26 April-3 May, 1856. The New Hampshire *Patriot* of 20 April 1856 reported that in Chicago during a forty-eight hour period nearly 9,000 immigrants passed into the West from fifteen railroads terminating in Chicago.

9 Minnesota *Pioneer and Democrat*, 19 May 1856. Cf. Also St. Paul *Daily Times,* 15 May 1856.

10 AASV, di Marogna to Wimmer, St. Paul, 7 May 1856. The diocese of St. Paul was erected by Pope Pius IX on 19 July 1850 upon the recommendation of the American bishops at the Seventh Provincial Council of Baltimore in May 1849. The diocese embraced the area between Lake Superior and the Missouri river, and from the Iowa state line to the Canadian border. The vicar general of the diocese of Dubuque, Joseph Cretin, was named first bishop of St. Paul. A native of the diocese of Belley, France, he had come to the United States in 1838 to serve as a missionary in the diocese of his friend Bishop Mathias Loras, first bishop of Dubuque.

11 *Ibid.*

12 AASV, di Marogna to Wimmer, St. Paul, 7 May 1856.

13 AASV, Riess to a confrère, St. Cloud, 4 July 1856.

14 *The Record*, February, 1889.

15 *Ibid.* The original "Cash Book" employed by the Minnesota Benedictines, preserved in the abbey archives,

lists the travelling expenses of the five pioneers from St. Vincent to Sauk Rapids. Totals were: from St. Vincent to Pittsburgh, $4.75; steamer fare for the party from Pittsburgh to St. Louis, $60; from St. Louis to St. Paul, $75; from St. Paul to Sauk Rapids, $44; freight charges on both the 'Paul Anderson' and 'Minnesota Belle,' $22.84. The expedition thus cost $206.59. Articles the Benedictines purchased en route included two saddles and bridles at $48.50, carpenter tools, two clocks, and several books among which were four antiphonaries.

16 *The Record,* February, 1889. Prior Demetrius kept a diary of the first days of the Minnesota foundation, and Father Cornelius recorded memoirs of these events late in life.

17 German Catholic immigrants were concerned in great part not only with their material well-being in the new world, but primarily with their spiritual life. This may be deduced from the fact that among their first interests was the erection of a church and school. Fresh from Germany and feeling isolated because of their language differences, these German Catholics in the United States from the outset insisted that separate churches were an absolute necessity for themselves. The German Catholics settled together in colonies wherever possible, often by their own choice, more often under the direction of zealous German missionary priests. They desired to have churches of their own in which their traditional religious observances and customs could be carried out, where they could hear sermons in their mother tongue, go to confession as they had learned to confess from early childhood, and take an active part in parish life through their beloved societies. They wanted the order and discipline of parish life as they had known it before coming to the United States. Cf. Emmet H. Rothan, O.F.M., *The German Catholic Immigrant in the United States (1830–1860)*, (Washington, 1946).

18 *The Record,* February, 1889.

19 *The Diocese of St. Cloud,* III (June, 1893), 1.

20 There were other opinions, more exact, regarding the quality of land in central Minnesota. One of the first settlers in Mankato visited the region in 1854 on the recommendation of Bishop Cretin, but decided to advise his friends in Missouri not to settle in central Minnesota because the soil

was too sandy. A number of settlers who had first intended to settle in Stearns County homesteaded in the Minnesota River Valley, although there was a steady stream of Germans moving into Hennepin, Wright, Benton, and Stearns counties. Father Benedict reported to Abbot Boniface after his first visit to central Minnesota: "The location of St. Cloud pleased me very much. I do not consider the land to be very good. It is sand prairie, although a few parts of it are somewhat better. St. Joseph appears to me to be a poor farming community. On the prairie I saw a three story deep cellar which had been dug and lined with tamarack wood. It is destined for lager beer. I noticed that the black soil is somewhat mixed with sand, one foot deep; it might also be fifteen inches. Then there is eighteen inches of sand mixed with a little humus. Then comes the nicest sand I have ever seen. It appeared as clean as gold. It cannot be good farming land. The place where they made their claims or want to make them, pleases me more. The soil is without doubt better and the country is more beautiful" (AASV, Haindl to Wimmer, Shakopee, 14 July 1857).

21 The Minnesota *Pioneer and Democrat* for 15 May 1856 carried an editorial praising the Society for Promoting Catholic Settlements which had been organized at this time. The *Pioneer and Democrat* felt that such an organization was far more practical and direct in its agencies than fanciful philanthropies such as the Fourierites in Iowa, the Socialist phalanx in Texas, or the Octagon settlement in south Kansas, which all looked to the West "for a realization of the dreams which have floated through the philosophers of all ages, and which appear only now to meet with an accomplishment." At the very time that the Benedictines were helping to establish Catholic colonies in Minnesota, which in time were among the most successful in the history of the Church in the United States, Bishop Michael O'Connor of Pittsburgh was encouraging just such an effort. O'Connor stated that something systematic must be done for the thousands who were moving West by supplying them with information, acquainting them with difficulties and the means to overcome them, while arranging with the bishop of the place to have a priest for the immigrants.

He pointed out that Catholics usually go where there is a church, which means to the somewhat densely populated areas, and thus they cannot afford the price of land. The majority then remain for life at the lowest rung of the ladder as drudges of the community. If the Catholic immigrant goes to areas where land is not settled and population sparse, then he is isolated from kindred and creed with serious consequences to his faith following as a result. Accordingly, societies must enable the immigrant to take his church with him into the wilderness. If Catholic immigrants would move from the crowded cities to the soil because of the persecution of the Know Nothings and other nativistic bigoted organizations, they would then be but following the course of those who made the nation what it is. They would thus eventually reach the position which the descendants of the latter now enjoy. O'Connor concluded: "It will be but another instance of good growing out of evil, and hate working to the advantage of those whom it wished to injure."

22 Abbot Wimmer described the Minnesota monastery as "built in a rather odd style: seventy-two feet long, twelve feet wide and one story high. One part was constructed of stone and the other part of boards. It has three cells, a refectory, a kitchen, a small chapel, a carpenter's work shop, and a guest room. All the doors open directly on the outside. The barn, a rectangular building, has stone walls ten feet high. The roof is formed by wooden rafters crossing the frame of the building. On top of the rafters straw and hay are piled. There two horses and two oxen are housed. There are no doors, and there is absolutely no room for a threshing floor" (ALMV, Wimmer to Archbishop Gregor Scherr, St. Vincent, 3 November 1856). Cf. also Boniface Wimmer, O.S.B., "Die Gruendung Eines Benediktiner Priorats in Der Dioezese St. Paul," *AVG*, XXIV (1856), 519–40.

23 AASV, di Marogna to Wimmer, St. Cloud, 13 October 1856.

24 AASV, Riess to "Rev. Confrère," St. Cloud, 4 July 1856.

25 The original "Cash Book" carries many entries indicative of the expenses involved in launching the new monastery. Purchases included 1,000 feet of boards; 400 feet of scantlings; 843 feet of joists, flooring, etc.; a

yoke of oxen and wagon from the settler Ostendorf; $6 worth of mosquito bars; three horses and one wagon for $350. Food was bought from Tenvoorde's store.

Father Bruno asked Abbot Boniface, while comparing the beginnings of St. Vincent's and St. John's: "If for example there would not have been in St. Vincent anything in the beginning, no cultivated land, no tools, no house, no drafting cattle, no clothes, no food, and on top of this two crop failures, what would they have done?" (AASV, Riess to Wimmer, St. Joseph, 5 January 1858).

26 AASV, Haindl to Wimmer, Shakopee, 8 September 1857.

27 Father Pierz deeded his St. Cloud properties to Bishop Cretin after repeated requests from the bishop that he transfer title to his ordinary. The position of Cretin and Pierz respectively in this matter is found in letters of both parties to the *Ludwig Missionsverein* in Munich. (ALMV, Report of Central Committee, 15 February 1856; Pierz to Reverend Secretary, Crow Wing, 25 June 1856). Bishop Grace in his turn deeded these lands to the Benedictines in 1861 for $100. Cf. also ASCC, Office of Register of Deeds, Plat 79, Book 81, 86, 87, 88; E 417; F 147, 622; G 490, 493; S 79. Pierz also accumulated other valuable tracts of land, viz. six lots in Sauk Rapids, ten acres as a gift from the parishioners in Jacobs Prairie, and one hundred *joch* in St. Augusta. A *joch* was computed as a tract of land plowed by a yoke of oxen in one day.

28 *The Record*, February, 1889.

29 AASV, Riess to Wimmer, St. Cloud, September 1856.

30 Gilbert J. Garraghan, S.J., *The Jesuits of the Middle United States* (2 vols., New York, 1938), II, 53–65. Weninger was conservative in outlook and determined to spread traditional and orthodox Catholicism in America. He feared minimists, who he felt wanted to reduce papal infallibility to a minimum, and Heckerites, who he claimed wanted a church along parliamentary lines and of a temporary form (AAMi, Weninger to Henni, Gardenville, 24 May 1869). He made frequent reports to the Holy See concerning conditions in the United States, such as the fanaticism of temperance advocates, unequal treatment of Germans and their schools, annual

collections, etc. (AAMi, Weninger to Henni, Wheaton, Illinois, n.d.).

31 *AVG*, XXV (1857), 533–34.

32 *The Record*, March, 1889. Father Bruno also records that "one of the Brothers was busy plowing on a very warm day. Overcome by the heat he took off his coat and hung it upon the fence. When he was about to return home for dinner the coat was missing. I was working near by. He came to me and told me his coat had been stolen. We searched about the place where the coat had been placed and were astonished to find nothing save the buttons and some shreds of cloth, and even these were beset by the omnivorous little beasts. A few days late we encountered a similar experience."

33 *Ibid.*

34 *Ibid.*

35 AASV, Young to Wimmer, Erie, 21 November 1856.

36 *The Record*, April, 1889. Cf. Appendix II for the full text of Brother Wolfgang's picturesque account of the hardships and endurance of the pioneer Brothers who lived in these cabins to prevent claim jumping and until the community could obtain money to purchase the land.

37 William Bell Mitchell, *History of Stearns County, Minnesota* (2 vols., Chicago, 1915), II, 1343. Father Cornelius had to support this first St. Cloud school entirely by voluntary collections from his congregation. On 27 September 1857, the XVII Sunday after Pentecost, he announced at Mass: "Today after Mass the contribution for the teacher will be taken up. I encourage you to be generous for a community without education of its children can hardly be called Catholic. At our last meeting we decided that the church and school room floors should be tiled. Contributions have already come in and we can begin to buy materials. The rest of the parishioners must contribute money or labor." Apparently the collection was not up to his expectations, for on the following Sunday, XVIII Sunday after Pentecost, 4 October 1857, he announced: "The collection last Sunday for the teacher was not good so will you please give more again today. I hope no one plans to hang the school on a nail. As the weather is cold and we cannot hold school in unheated rooms, you are asked that all those who intend to contribute would

do so today, because tomorrow the wagon is going to collect the wood" (Announcement Book, St. Mary's Parish, St. Cloud).

38 Hamline University, St. Paul, under the direction of the Methodist Church, was established by a Minnesota Territorial Charter of 3 March 1854, and opened a Preparatory Department at Red Wing on November 16 of that year. Its first college class was graduated in 1859, and Hamline continued in existence for fifteen years in Red Wing until 1869. The institution was then moved to St. Paul and, after the interruption of eleven years, classes were again resumed in that city in 1880.

A charter for a University of Minnesota was enacted by the U. S. Congress on 19 February 1851. A Preparatory Department was begun in 1851 and carried through until 1855. It was re-opened in 1867, and the first college classes were begun on 15 September 1869, eighteen years later.

39 AASV, di Marogna to Wimmer, St. Paul, 16 February 1857. Territorial Governor Willis A. Gorman was a native of Kentucky, born in Flemingsburg on 12 January 1816, and died in St. Paul on 20 May 1876. He was trained in law, served in the Mexican War and appointed governor of the Territory of Minnesota in 1853 by the Democratic administration. He was also a delegate to the State's constitutional convention, member of the state legislature, colonel of Minnesota's First Regiment in the War Between the States, and city attorney of St. Paul from 1869 to the time of his death.

40 John L. Wilson, "Notes on Passing St. John's Charter," and "For the Record." Cf. Appendix III for the text of St. John's original charter of 1857.

41 AASV, di Marogna to Wimmer, St. Paul, 16 February, 7 March 1857.

42 AMHS, *Journal of the House of Representatives of the Territory of Minnesota.* (St. Paul, 1957), 76–201. Cf. Also Minnesota *Pioneer,* 19 and 21 February 1857.

Prior Demetrius informed Wimmer further: "Since our charter, of which I sent to you a copy, will only be in force thirty days after the signature of the governor, I had to conduct myself quietly these thirty days. It seems there were no objections made. After the expiration of this time I was able to take further steps for the incorporation of the Order. I sent a copy of the bill and a little chart of the two claims here to the delegate of the Territory in Washington (Henry M. Rice) with the request to take the necessary steps to confirm by charter the two claims besides the fraction and the two islands to the St. John's Seminary fund so we could begin construction of the seminary. Then I also wrote to the new president (James Buchanan). I told him about the plan of the late bishop in regard to our mission, how we were called here, and his wish to have the Chippewa boys educated. I asked him to allow us to choose two sections of unclaimed land on the Watab River as a fund for the incorporated Order for which $200 were to be paid annually for the first eight years. I also asked him to effect our obtaining a grant in the form of a township in the vicinity of the Chippewas whom we are to convert. I also told him what I had written to the delegate" (AASV, di Marogna to Wimmer, St. Cloud, 5 April 1857). There is no documentary evidence that either Rice or Buchanan took any steps in this matter. But the episode was told and re-told, written to Europe, etc., and the ever-growing fable developed that President Buchanan had given the Minnesota Benedictines 5,000 acres of land in that state in 1858 with the stipulation that they begin a college there as soon as possible. The story persisted down to the present. Cf. Wilhelm Winkler, "Koenig Ludwig I. von Bayern und die deutschen Katholiken in Nordamerika," *Historisch-politische Blaetter fuer das Katholische Deutschland,* CLXIX (Munich, 1922), 717.

43 "Original of H. of R., No. 70 With Remarks by Hon. J. L. Wilson." In an additional document, titled "For the Record," Wilson itemizes aid which he supplied to early settlers and institutions of central Minnesota. He lists the different claims he purchased for around $4,000; $3,200 for expenses during the legislative sessions in St. Paul during 1856–57; $17,000 expended for relief of the settlers during the grasshopper plague. He wrote: "A portion of the ten acres given for the erection of the (Stearns County) Court House sold for about $23,000 for which he received $7,000 in unsalable Bonds, the largest part of which was disposed for provisions and other necessities for destitute settlers

during the Locust Raid of 1857 and Eight . . . *Some people cannot see of what use such Democrats* can be to a community or benefit to the county at large."

Mitchell characterized Wilson as the 'Father of St. Cloud' and the patriarch of Northern Minnesota pioneers. He was of New England background, born in Maine on 24 February 1820. His family moved several times, and Wilson secured different employment including printing, contracting, construction of saw and flour mills. He came to Minnesota in 1851, erected a saw mill and house at Sauk Rapids, completed another mill at Little Falls and built the first saw mill of Stearns County at St. Augusta. He platted the townsite of St. Cloud, encouraged settlement, while serving as first president of the city council, alderman, city justice, chairman of Stearns County commissioners, judge of probate of Benton County, member of the territorial and state legislatures during four sessions. He died at St. Raphael's hospital, St. Cloud, on 3 January 1910. Mitchell stated: "John L. Wilson was a born optimist. Everything looked good to him. He was always cheerful and hopeful, as happy when he had but a nickel in his pocket as when he had a roll of bank bills. He was open-hearted and generous, perhaps too much so for the good of himself and his family. Many men with his opportunities would have accumulated a fortune, but during his last years he had to depend on others to show him some of that kindness he had so willingly shown to those who needed it during his years of prosperity. He was wholly free from malice and his motto was to do good rather than evil" (*op. cit.*, I, 645–46).

44 AASPOW, Wimmer to Pescetelli, St. Vincent, 15 June 1856. During the same session of the Minnesota Territorial Legislature, eight academies, seminaries and universities were incorporated, of which St. John's is the only surviving institution. The other newly proposed and chartered institutions included an Anoka Academy, Brunson Seminary at Hamilton, Fremont City University, Hastings City University, Hobart University at Spring Valley, Lake University in Freeborn County and Northfield Literary Institute.

45 "Cash Book, Number I," 6 May, 14 May, 25 July 1857. Prior Demetrius paid $40 to the Stearns County surveyor and $8.35 to the Recorder of Deeds for platting and registering the lots.

46 NA, Waite to Hon. Cyrus Aldrich, St. Cloud, 18 March 1862. Brott was employing the Postal Pre-emption Act of 3 March 1855 which provided mail contractors with the privilege of occupying stations at the rate of not more than one for every twenty miles of route on which mail was carried. The mail contractor acquired pre-emption right if the public land were unclaimed, up to 640 acres, to be taken contiguously and to include improvements.

47 Sister Mary Regina Baska, O.S.B., *The Benedictine Congregation of Saint Scholastica: Its Foundation and Development, 1852–1930* (Washington, 1935), passim.

48 The Panic of 1857, begun by a collapse of credit in New York, spread across the country with extreme violence. In Minnesota Eastern banks and creditors recalled their loans, exchange rose ten percent, everyone was in debt and the territory was literally emptied of money. Folwell records that: "Business ceased, banks closed their doors, merchants suspended or assigned. Holders of property desiring to realize dropped their prices. City lots became virtually valueless. The lawyers were busy with foreclosures, the sheriffs with attachments and executions. The floating population of speculators began to look for other scenes of operation and left the cities and towns none the worse for a numerous exodus" (*op. cit.*, I, 364).

During that same year of 1857 central Minnesota settlers were afflicted with a second grasshopper invasion. The congregations at St. Cloud, St. Joseph, Jacobs Prairie and St. Augusta vowed to make an annual pilgrimage on September 6, feast of St. Magnus, patron invoked against noxious vermin, if the plague was lifted. It was abated in July but the settlers suffered much throughout the following winter from lack of food, no money because of the panic and the loss of crops. Stories of the courage, faith and patience of the pioneers during this trial of 1857 have been proudly handed down in the families of central Minnesota.

Nor did they forget their promised pilgrimage of thanksgiving. They held a first one on July 4, with the congregations of St. Cloud and St. Augusta proceeding on the road to St. Joseph until they reached the Sauk river. There the people of St. Joseph, St. James and Richmond met them, and a Solemn High Mass was offered under the open sky with Father Alexius as celebrant and Father Clement as preacher. There was no bridge across the Sauk river, so a line of wagons was placed in the shallow bed of the stream, and the procession filed across, all the while continuing the recitation of the Rosary which along with hymns and other prayers was uninterrupted along the entire route.

The second pilgrimage held on 6 September was even more solemn. A correspondent in the New York *Kath. Kirchenzeitung* for 31 December 1857 describes the event:

". . . at 7:00 in the morning the congregations at St. Joseph and Richmond were assembled in their churches, where Holy Mass was celebrated; then the procession was organized; after the cross-bearer came the school children, then the church banner, followed by the men, the Brothers of the Benedictine monastery at St. Joseph with the pastor, and these were followed by the women. Prayer and song alternated during the procession. In this order the great and splendid array of people walked to the church at St. James, eight miles distant from St. Joseph, while the congregation of that church came out to meet us and escorted us to the mission cross. In the meantime the procession from Richmond arrived.

"A neatly decorated altar had been erected at the foot of the mission cross, and by means of wreaths and garlands had been changed into a field chapel. Unfortunately the weather was so unpleasant that it was necessary to celebrate the Mass within the church, which could not accommodate even one third of the multitude. After the solemn Mass Fr. Clement preached in German and Fr. Alexius in the English language (since there are a few Irish and French families at St. James). After a short pause, the Litany of the Saints was chanted before the Blessed Sacrament, after which Fr. Bruno delivered a sermon. In conclusion the *Te Deum* was chanted and benediction given with the Blessed Sacrament, after which all returned to their homes, praising God. I saw many a tear of joy flowing that day. Many persons who have been in this country twenty or thirty years told me they felt as if they had been transported to their old home in Germany, for they had seen nothing of the kind since they had come to America." Cf. also Cincinnati *Wahrheitsfreund,* 23 September 1858.

49 When Wimmer learned of this action he requested Bishop Young to retain those Sisters still in Erie as part of the foundation there.

50 The pioneer Minnesota Benedictine nuns were Sisters Willibalda Scherbauer, O.S.B., superioress; Gertrude Casper, O.S.B., Gregoria M o s e r, O.S.B., and Evangelista Kremeter, O.S.B. Sister Grace McDonald, O.S.B., of the department of history of St. Benedict's College, St. Joseph, Minnesota, is at present completing a centennial history of St. Benedict's Convent for publication in 1957.

51 AASV, di Marogna to Wimmer, St. Cloud, 12 August 1857. Contributions for support of the Sisters and the school continued to be difficult to obtain. Father Cornelius announced on the XX Sunday after Pentecost, 10 October 1858: "Nothing has been paid toward the school for the last five months. The people are now reminded to keep their promise. It costs only $2.00 a year for each student. That is accordingly a half dollar for each quarter, and a dollar for each half year. That is certainly not much and for this reason it is painful that nothing is being paid. I hope that I shall not have to say this again from the pulpit" (Announcement Book, St. Mary's Parish, St. Cloud).

52 AASV, di Marogna to Wimmer, St. Cloud, 12 August 1857.

NOTER TO CHAPTER THREE

1 *The Record,* June 1888. Peter Maus, who served as cook at the 'Old St. John's' near St. Cloud, left some diary notes of his memories of the first days of the community. These notes were collected and translated by the Reverend Celestine Kapsner, O.S.B. Peter Maus, a native of Trier, came to America in 1851, bringing with him a statue of St. Wendel. He made a promise to St. Wendel that he would erect a shrine in his honor if he would arrive safely. He records that the crew joined him in his prayers during a storm, and they reached shore unharmed on December 8. He worked first in Pittsburgh and Ohio, but he heard that the West offered better opportunities for a young man. He came to Minneapolis with an immigrant party, and was given

work by a contractor in a small saw mill at St. Cloud. He then continues: "At this time three Benedictine Fathers, Demetrius, Cornelius and Bruno, arrived in St. Cloud and made their headquarters near the Mississippi River where the present orphan asylum is now located. They toured the neighborhood in search of Catholic people, and it came about that Mr. Maus kept the home fire burning and always had a warm meal for them on their return. He asked, in return for his work for them, that they erect a chapel in honor of St. Wendel as he had promised. The Fathers experienced difficulties in securing a right to the land on which they were situated, and added to this, the rough camp life was not conducive to establishing a monastery there. This induced them to look for a better location, and so they went out to the heavy woods known as the Indianbush. Mr. Maus then filed for a homestead near what is now the town of Luxemburg, Minnesota. He kept in touch with the Benedictine Fathers and they came out to visit that territory. Thus Mr. Maus was instrumental in having his chapel built in what is now the church of St. Wendel, the present title of the church of Luxemburg, Minnesota. Here Mr. Maus taught school for three years and did the janitor work for the church free of charge. The Reverend Omer Maus, O.S.B., is one of his grandsons and a member of St. John's Abbey."

2 There are neither complete nor authentic student enrollment records of the first students of 'Old St. John's'. Their numbers included such Minnesota pioneers as the Duerr brothers from St. Joseph, Henry and Joseph, who became school teachers and taught in various parts of the state; Conrad A. Marschall, also a schoolteacher; the Edelbrock brothers, Anthony, later abbot of St. John's, and Joseph, a businessman; the Emmel brothers, Louis, a druggist in New York City, and Henry J., a representative in the Minnesota State Legislature, 1878 and 1909; the long line of St. Cloud Mockenhaupts, August, Paul who became a merchant in Chicago, Robert who entered business in Los Angeles, and Gustav who became a priest and served as pastor of Centralia, Illinois; numerous St. Cloud business men such as Frank Minar, Frank Molitor, Henry Robbers, Edward Goerger; and, for pioneer times, a surprising number of leading men of the surrounding communities such as

Stephen Ethen of Cold Spring, Stephen Fiedler of St. Joseph, Andrew Stalberger of Lake George, Henry Klostermann of Richmond. The student Valentine Stimmler entered the St. John's community.

3 Alexius Hoffmann, O.S.B., *St. John's University* (Collegeville, 1907), pp. 9–10.

4 The centennial history of St. Benedict's Abbey and College, Atchison, Kansas, which was established as a monastery in 1857, became an independent priory in 1858, and was raised to abbey status in 1876, is being prepared for publication in 1957 by the Reverend Peter Beckman, O.S.B., of the department of history at St. Benedict's College.

5 AASV, "Recessus Capituli Generalis Congregationis Benedictino-Americanae Habiti Abbatia St. Vincenti, 20–21 Sept. 1858." The election of independent priors by this general chapter was approved for three years by the Holy See on 23 December 1858. The Augsburg *Sion* of 28 August 1859, in commenting on this expansion of Wimmer, stated that perhaps nothing like it could be found in the world. "The Benedictines are in eight states of the Union planting the Cross, building churches, erecting schools and sowing the seed of the Word of God." *Die Katholischen Blaetter aus Tirol* of 17 November 1858 likewise praised the vision of establishing these new communities in Minnesota and Kansas. Wimmer himself informed the abbot of Metten with unmitigated enthusiasm: "Truly, Minnesota can be entirely Benedictine" (AAMe, Wimmer to Utto Lang, St. Vincent, 16 September 1857).

6 "Memoranda: Haindl, Benedict," n.p.

7 This log structure was to serve as center for the farming enterprise Prior Benedict began in the Indianbush. This house, called the 'Old Farm,' was located a short distance northwest of the present Collegeville railroad station in the Watab meadow. Here it was that the first death in Minnesota's monastery occurred. On the morning of 29 March 1859 Brother Benno Muckenthaler, O.S.B., one of the pioneering band that came West in 1856, was found dead of apoplexy in his bed at that farm house. His remains were first buried in St. Joseph and later removed to the abbey cemetery.

8 On 11 May 1858 the Territory of Minnesota was admitted to the Union.

Confidence in the future potentials of the new state was at high tide. A German Catholic correspondent from central Minnesota expressed this frontier optimism: "We are still suffering from the effects of the financial crisis of 1857. Since we have no railroads as yet, we are practically cut off from the rest of the world during winter. As soon as the river opens, however, conditions will improve, for we had a splendid crop last year, and our farmers have wheat, oats, corn and even potatoes in abundance. This is an odd world: during the early years we had money enough, but nothing to eat; now we have enough to eat, but no money . . . Believe me, Minnesota will be a fine country in a short time. *Minne* is the old German word for love, and where love of God and neighbor is to be found, all is well. The soil is very fertile, so that the words of Our Lord, 'Seek first the kingdom of God and all these things shall be added unto you,' present no difficulty. Notwithstanding the scarcity of money, the settlers are content . . . Eight new churches are being built. There are at present eight Benedictine priests, twelve Brothers and eight Sisters with us" (New York *Katholische Kirchenzeitung,* 10 February 1859).

9 Wimmer to Ludwig I, St. Vincent, 12 December 1858, in Mathaeser, *op. cit.,* pp. 106–10. Cf. also AASV, Mueller to Wimmer, Munich, 15 March 1859.

10 *Ibid.,* 5 April 1859.

11 Sister Benedicta in the meanwhile went to Europe to plead her case. She first protested against Wimmer's mode of procedure to the Bavarian king, *Ludwig Missionsverein,* archbishop of Munich and bishop of Eichstaett. Then she presented her case at Rome to the Congregation of the Propagation of the Faith concerning the right of granting admission to candidates, power of judging qualities of Sisters for temporary and solemn vows, authority to preside at meetings at which superiors were elected or Sisters transferred to priories, and the restoration of her good name. The Propaganda transferred her case to the Congregation of Bishops and Regulars since it concerned the validity of vows. The bishops of Pittsburgh and Erie were also consulted, and on 6 December 1859 the decision was handed down through Giovanni Cardinal della Genga. Wimmer's plea was rejected to have the Sisters' foundations of Erie, Newark, and Marystown approved

by apostolic authority and raised to the rank of priories while being incorporated into his congregation. The Sisters were placed under the jurisdiction of the ordinaries of the dioceses in which they were located. These prelates could in turn delegate Abbot Wimmer to govern the Sisters, and appoint Benedictine priests as confessors of the Sisters, if they so chose.

The Sacred Congregation instructed Bishop Young of Erie to send Sister Benedicta back to Eichstaett, since she had in the meantime returned to the United States. But because of illness she was dispensed from that regulation. She went to the convent of St. Cloud where she sent an apology to Wimmer. The entire unfortunate incident ended in this way. Sister Benedicta, whose major contribution to American Benedictine development, apart from this celebrated incident, awaits careful and worthy treatment, died in Minnesota on 15 March 1862.

12 Ludwig I of Bavaria abdicated in 1848, spent the greater part of his time in Rome, and died at Nice, France, in 1868.

13 Abbot Boniface, in his capacity as Visitator of the American Cassinese Congregation, also established regulations concerning the observance of the vow of poverty, monastic enclosure, three days of abstinence each week, and abstinence from meat at breakfast except when one of the monks was travelling on the missions.

14 "Minutes of the Meeting of the Minnesota Chapter, 11–12 April 1861." Cf. also the manuscript memoirs of the Reverend Magnus Mayer, O.S.B.

15 Bishop Thomas L. Grace, O.P., was born in Charleston, S.C., on 16 November 1814. The family moved to Ohio and Thomas entered the Order of St. Dominic at St. Rose Priory there. He studied at the Minerva College in Rome and at Perugia where, five years after his ordination, he received the Dominican S.T.Lr. degree. He first taught on the faculty of St. Rose, then served as assistant and pastor of St. Peter's Church, Memphis, Tennessee. When the Reverend Anthony Pelamourgues, priest of the diocese of St. Paul, declined the office of bishop of St. Paul, Grace was appointed as Cretin's successor on 21 January 1859. He served as second bishop of St. Paul until his resignation was accepted on 12 August 1884 in favor of his coadjutor, Bishop John Ireland. He lived in retire-

ment in St. Paul from 1884 until his death on 22 February 1897.

Bishop Grace made his first visitation and confirmation tour through central Minnesota, accompanied by Vicar General Ravoux, on 19 September 1859. He toured all of the missions of the Benedictines, approved wholeheartedly of their work, and became a close friend of the monks working in his diocese. On 23 June 1860 he sent the Benedictines $300 contributed by the *Leopoldinen Stiftung,* Austrian mission society in Vienna. On 26 November 1859 he appointed Father Demetrius as vicar general of the diocese for all German Catholics.

16 AASP, Wimmer to Grace, St. Vincent, 16 October 1861.

17 AASV, "Actus Capituli Secundi Generalis habetur in St. Vincentium die 15–18 Septembris 1862." Cf. also "Minutes of the Meeting of the Chapter, St. Cloud Priory, 15–16 October 1862."

18 It is recorded in the "Annales Abbatiae S. Joannis Bapt." that Brother Placidus Brixius, O.S.B., was drafted into the Union army on 4 August 1864, and that the community paid the customary $300 commutation fee which exempted him from service. On June 21 and October 11 of the same year the Benedictines contributed $275 toward a fund to release persons drafted for the Union army from St. Joseph township.

St. Joseph was involved in a fantastic incident at the conclusion of the War Between the States which focused national attention on this frontier hamlet. On the morning of the day that President Lincoln was shot, 14 April 1865, fourteen hours before the event took place, people met on the street of St. Joseph Village and discussed the news that the president had been assassinated by pistol shot. Later no one could even suggest where the news originated, and all this in a community without railroad or telegraph connection. Citizens of Manchester, N.H., also were discussing the assassination during that same morning previous to the event. Subsequent investigations revealed nothing concerning either of these coincidents, except that the people were discussing rumors. Yet the story that the Catholic people of St. Joseph, Minnesota, knew of Lincoln's death before it happened never died down, and was used during the bigoted attacks of the American Protective Association as an argument against the Catholic Church in the United States. Cf. an example of this in *The Boston Investigator* for 19 March 1890. Under the title of "The Murder of President Lincoln," the ridiculous canard was repeated that Catholic priests were accountable for the deed, and that "priests of St. Joseph" were aware of the fact of the assassination fourteen hours before it took place. The story of St. Joseph and Lincoln's murder appears even at the present time in sensational journal circles, as for instance in the February, 1953, issue of *True* magazine.

Archbishop Francis Patrick Kenrick of Philadelphia and Abbot Boniface appealed to the War Department for exemption of Benedictines from military duty because of their religious profession, and this petition was granted on 28 November 1862. As the draft laws were altered Wimmer appealed to both President Lincoln and Secretary of War Stanton for extension of the original privilege on 10 and 11 June 1863, and the exemption was sustained. Wimmer's letters, preserved in the *Official Records of the War of Rebellion, Series* LLI, III, 333 ff., are typical of his usual lengthy explanations of every aspect of his American Benedictine establishments. What were the reactions of Lincoln and Stanton to these picturesque, detailed accounts of Benedictine ideals and purposes, all in broken English, by this sincere immigrant who had sacrificed everything for the advancement of religion in the United States?

19 *The Record,* February, 1890.

20 N. H. Winchell, Edward D. Neill, J. Fletcher Williams, *History of the Upper Mississippi River Valley* (Minneapolis, 1881), p. 148. Cf. also pp. 137–55; Folwell, *op. cit.,* II, 109–302.

21 *The Record,* March, 1890.

22 "Minutes of the Meeting of the Chapter, St. Cloud Priory, 22–24 January 1863." Cf. also Grace to Wirtz, St. Paul, 17 April 1863.

23 Bishop Grace expressed his delight that more Benedictines were coming into his diocese: "I am happy to learn of the arrival in the diocese of the new recruits you speak of from St. Vincent's. They are greatly needed and indeed if the number were quadrupled there would be found enough to occupy them advantageously in this new field of religion" (Grace to Wirtz, St. Paul, 1 June 1863).

24 Grace to Wirtz, St. Paul, 27 April 1863.

25 NA, RGLO, Waite to Aldrich,

St. Cloud, 15 March 1862. Waite was concerned, as one of the early promoters of central Minnesota development, that the Benedictines might possibly transfer to Shakopee if they received an adverse decision. At the same time Brott's lawyers collected testimony in favor of his position from Yankee supporters including the Reverend Thomas E. Truman and John G. Mervin.

26 "Notes on the Rothkopp case," n.d. The General Land Commissioner, on 9 June 1863, awarded these seventy-five acres to Prior Benedict as administrator of the Rothkopp estate.

While challenging the Rothkopp claims, Brott was simultaneously contesting claims, all under the preemption laws, of several other persons to lands along the Mississippi river. They included Moses R. Brown, Joseph F. Noel, Charles F. Stearns, John Ball, Romanza A. Smith, Regis H. Noel and Newton N. Smith, with whom he entered into agreement for separate settlements in order to obtain continuous title to the entire area as a town development site.

For documents *in re* the Rothkopp case cf. S. A. Smith to Rev. M. Alig, Washington, 2 February 1860; Commissioner Joseph S. Wilson to St. Cloud Register and Receiver, Washington, 9 May 1860; Register Thomas C. McClure to Clement Staub, St. Cloud, 19 June 1863; John Dowling to Benedict Haindl, Washington, 22 April 1862; Affidavit of Demetrius di Marogna, subscribed and sworn before Notary E. H. Barritt, St. Paul, 8 July 1858. Cf. also NA, RGLO, Secretary Caleb B. Smith to Commissioner J. Edmunds, Washington, 30 August 1861; Commissioner Joseph L. Wilson to St. Cloud Register and Receiver, Washington, 15 March 1861; Commissioner J. M. Edmund to Col. M. Thompson, Washington, 18 April 1861; Smith to E. F. Drake, Washington, 23 October 1861; I. Pusher to Edmunds, Washington, 28 June 1862; Nathaniel Wilson to General Land Office, St. Cloud, 10 March 1864; Waite to Edmunds, St. Cloud, 7 July 1864; Nathaniel Wilson to Commissioner Joseph L. Wilson, St. Cloud, 24 September 1866.

27 The original charter of 6 March 1857 had authorized the Order of St. Benedict "to establish and erect an institution or seminary in Stearns County or that portion of St. Cloud city, surveyed, platted and recorded as Rothkopp's addition to St. Cloud." A permanent change of location could not be made, it was felt, unless some modification was petitioned in the charter. Prior Othmar submitted this petition for an amendment to the original charter which was granted by an act of the Minnesota state legislature on 6 February 1864.

28 AASV, Wirtz to Mayer, The Indianbush, 22 May 1865.

29 Cf. Wimmer to Wirtz, Rome, 27 August 1865; Wimmer to Confrères in Minnesota, Rome, n.d.; AASV, Wirtz to Mayer, St. Joseph, 26 December 1865.

30 In 1926 Father Alexius Hoffmann began work on a manuscript titled "The Natural History of Collegeville, Minnesota," which he finished on 12 March 1934. In these one hundred and twenty-four pages he traces with devotion and affection the geography, geology, hydrography, and botany of Collegeville, and adds two appendices on the inhabitants and neighbors of the township. He includes invaluable facts, traditions, and records data of local history which he had collected.

31 After Abbot Alexius had built the main quadrangle Brother Benno's bell was hung in the north turret of the college buildings, and served as class bell for years. It was stored in the museum with the advent of the first electric bell system, but again came into its heritage in 1948, when Abbot Alcuin gave it to St. John's foundation priory in Humacao, Puerto Rico. There today it rings forth again as of old.

In Prior Benedict's "Account Book" are found for the first time several names of pioneer workmen, family names which reappear continually in St. John's records during the first century. They contributed not only service but also loving devotion to the development of St. John's family. Many of them settled around the abbey, as lay people had done for centuries in Europe, established families of their own, and laid the foundations of Catholic community life in Collegeville township and parish. They included Peter Eich who fastened a thousand feet of lumber for the 'Old Stone House' at $.025 per foot; Theodore Pierz who pried up and hauled stones at $4.50 per ox cart load; George Fruth, Andreas Fuchs, Damien Schwinghammer, John Obermiller, Nickolaus Dahmen, Anton Bock, John Dietrich, all of whom worked as stone splitters, hod carriers, masons and carpenters at the rate of

$1.25 a day. Prior Benedict's itemization of costs for the building totalled $1,150, but not all accounts were entered.

32 The document enclosed in the cornerstone of the community's first building on its permanent site was as follows:

B†D

"A.D. Nostri Jesu Christi 1866 die 19. Julii, huius aedificationis lapis primus positus est a Reverendissimo Toma Landon Grace, Episcopo S. Pauli, regnante Pio IX, Papa, Reverendissimo Bonifacio Wimmer O.S.B. Abbate ad montem S. Vincentii, Praeside Congregationis Americano Cassinensis, Reverendo Benedicto Haindl, O.S.B., Priore hujus monasterii, Andrea Johnson, Praeside civitatum foederatarum.

Nomina Patrum conventualium sunt: P. Clemens Staub, P. Demetrius Marogna, P. Cornelius Wittmann, Anscharius Frauendorfer, Georgius Scherer, Othmarus Wirtz, P. Meinulphus Stuckenkemper, P. Wolfgangus Northman, P. Antonius Casper, P. Joseph Vill.

Adnotatio: Die 4 Junii hujus anni supradictus Prioratus a Sancta Sede in Abbatiam erectus est; sed propter temporis brevitatem Abbas eligi nondum potuit."

33 PP. Pius IX, Apostolic Brief, 3 August 1866, copy. While in Rome at this time Abbot Boniface attempted to have the solemn vows of the Brothers cancelled and classified as simple perpetual vows. All Brothers who had made profession before 1859 had taken solemn vows, but Wimmer thought they should be relieved of some of the obligations of solemn vows since they were without exception assigned to manual labor duties in all of the monasteries at that time. But Pope Pius IX would not permit a change to be made. The Brothers who had taken solemn vows were to remain bound, but in the future all Brothers were to make simple perpetual vows.

34 AASP, Wimmer to Grace, Rome, 21 June 1866.

35 The parish missions served from these three centers of operation were:

1) St. Cloud Priory: St. Mary's Church, St. Cloud; St. Augusta; St. Wendel, Luxemburg; Clearwater; Sauk Rapids; Big Meadow (St. Patrick); Clear Lake; Forest City.

St. Joseph: St. Joseph's Church, St. Joseph; Richmond; Spring Hill; St.

Martin; New Munich; Meire Grove; Jacobs Prairie; Lake Henry; Lake George; St. Nicholas.

2) Shakopee: Shakopee; Marystown; Jordan; Belle Plaine; St. Joseph; St. Benedict; Cedar Lake; Credit River; New Market; New Prague; St. John; St. Scholastica, Heidelberg; St. Henry; St. Thomas; St. Bonifacius; Chanhassen; Victoria; Chaska; Carver; Waconia; Cologne; Young America; Watertown; Helvetia; Jessenland; Glencoe; Green Isle; Waverly; Delano.

3) St. Paul: Assumption Church, St. Paul; St. Boniface Church, East Minneapolis; St. Michael; Fletcher.

Counties traversed by the pioneer Benedictines included Stearns, Benton, Sherburne, Meeker, Scott, LeSueur, Carver, Sibley, McLeod, Ramsey, Hennepin and Wright.

36 The Benedictines preached solely in German at first to the Catholic German groups, and whatever English they could muster to the mixed congregations. Father Benedict reported that "the Irish here in Minnesota are not as demanding as they are in Pennsylvania. They are satisfied if they merely hear English" (AASV, Haindl to Wimmer, Shakopee, 8 September 1857).

John Flynn of Forest City in the 'Big Woods' along the Crow River, and his neighboring settlers John Whalen, Andrew Sullivan, Bryan McNulty, Edward Campbell and John Murray, came to the priory in St. Cloud in 1856 asking the Benedictines to bring them spiritual care. At first visits were made twice a year, but gradually as personnel increased, mission stations and parishes were established in Meeker County. The monks continued to serve the settlers until 1870, and Mary Clare Pfeffer, a granddaughter of John Flynn, wrote an account of this pioneer spiritual effort, interviewed early settlers and surveyed the effects in that region. She wrote: "It is difficult to conjecture what would have occurred at Meeker County during the twelve years of its infancy had the Benedictines not ministered to the spiritual welfare of the settlers. Would the Catholic immigrant have ceased to continue, or would the settlers there have been without instruction for twelve years, and thus have been lost to the Faith? Would the lack of religious services have retarded or have obliterated Catholicity as it did in some nearby places? Beyond a doubt, the early Benedictines here as well as in other parts of Minnesota did much good, and the story of one group is the story of them all — the same hardships, sufferings, and privations; but, it must be said that in the life of the true Benedictine there is that peace and happiness that comes to him who lives his entire life for the greater glory of God." ("A Modern 'Deserted Village'," *St. Benedict's Quarterly*, VIII [April, 1934], 9–12).

37 *The Record,* March, 1889. The St. Cloud *Journal* of 4 March 1875 reported another evidence of these missionaries' dedicated service to the region: "We regret to learn that last Saturday while Fr. Benedict (Haindl), formerly in charge of the church here, now located at New Munich, was making sick calls some distance from the village, he lost his way. When found by parties who went in search of him, he was in a snow bank and his hands, feet, and nose, were badly frozen. He was able to return home Sunday. This misfortune is severe, as Fr. Benedict is quite an old man."

38 AASV, Wittmann to Wimmer, St. Cloud, 6 March 1857. The St. Cloud *Democrat* for 26 September 1861 announced: "Up street hangs the first church gong bell in the march of civilization. It hangs in a pyramidal shed in the yard of a convent kept by a company of Benedictine nuns, and is regularly rung for matins and vespers by the lady abbess who is a small, slight, graceful and accomplished lady as you could meet in any circle." The bell of St. Mary's Church, St. Cloud, was likewise the first church bell, according to the *Northwestern Chronicle* of 5 January 1867, hung in a church belfry west of the Mississippi River. Care and attention was given to every church building erected throughout the area. The St. Cloud *Journal* of 4 October 1866 describes the new church at Richmond as a substantial structure, 88x50 feet, with a 75 foot tower, 2,200 pound bell and a fine organ. "The building reflects great credit on William Wolke, the master builder." The bell for the new church at Richmond was declared to be the largest in the state when it passed through St. Cloud (*Democrat,* 29 June 1865). Cf. also Cincinnati *Wahrheitsfreund* of 26 July 1865.

38 Set over against this first Corpus Christi procession at Shakopee was the infamous Corpus Christi caricature enacted by Freethinkers and 'Forty-Eighters' a short distance down the Minnesota River at New Ulm in 1861. Con-

temporary religious writers often associated the sacrilege performed on that occasion in terms of cause and effect with the Sioux Indian massacre at New Ulm in the following year. Father Pierz, for example, related the incident to the *Leopoldinen Stiftung* in Vienna: "This (massacre) was evidently a chastisement of God, for the most of them were apostates who refused to hear anything of religion or priests . . . Last year on Corpus Christi they created a great scandal. The atheists conducted an ox, which they had ornamented with garlands, around the city honoring him by music and dance at four different places. At last they roasted him as if in sacrifice. No wonder that the savage Sioux as a chastisement have murdered those people" (*BLS,* XXXIII [1863], 32–33). Cf. Also Mathaeser, *op. cit.,* p. 156.

40 St. Cloud *Democrat,* 21 November 1861. By 1865 a fair held on January 5 at the courthouse in St. Cloud for the new Catholic church realized $1,000, and a three day fair from 11–14 December of that same year totalled receipts of $1011.

German Catholic papers in Europe and America described the processions, feasts, statistics, buildings and growth of the Church in these missions. Cf. Cincinnati *Wahrheitsfreund,* 6 September 1858; 6, 13 and 28 October 1859; 19 January 1860; 12 February, 11 April, 9 May, 5 December 1861; 22 October 1862; 16 December 1863; 17 January, 3 February, 5 April, 4 May, 14 December 1864; 15 February, 16 August 1865. *SM,* II (1881), 266; III (1882), 42–65. New York *Kath. Kirchenzeitung,* 24 July 1856; 14 August 1856; 14 April 1859.

41 From January through May of 1954 the Reverend Louis Traufler, O.S.B., pastor of St. Augustine's Church, St. Cloud, generously gave a series of week-end interviews concerning the early developments of St. John's, events and trends of the institution's life, regional social history, as well as his own personal memoirs.

42 Professor August C. Krey of the University of Minnesota has noted this phenomenon when he wrote: "Visitors to St. Paul are usually shown what is called 'the old German church,' the Church of the Assumption, as one of the most picturesque of the older sights of that picturesque city. And tourists, as they drive along the highway that leads westward out of St. Cloud marvel

at the church of St. Joseph, which seems too large for the little village that clusters about it. They are yet more puzzled by the church steeples that peer out over the trees four miles beyond, at Collegeville. Yet all three and many more spots in Minnesota and the Northwest serve to establish the connection between Minnesota and Metten and Monte Cassino" (*Monte Cassino, Metten and Minnesota* [St. Paul, 1927], p. 7).

43 Noteworthy among these families was that of Lucas Gertken of which seven daughters and four sons became Benedictines at St. John's and St. Benedict's. All musically talented, they in turn had an influence on the development of Church music wherever they have moved. The Reverend Innocent Gertken was organist and directed choirs at St. John's for 47 years, from 1899–1946; Sister Urban Gertken has served as choir director at St. Benedict's since 1921; the Reverend Norbert Gertken was professor of music at St. John's for thirty years, and then travelled to parishes and religious communities as one of the first priests in this country to offer parish training in congregational singing and Gregorian chant; Sisters Veneranda, Cecilia and Gemma Gertken have taught Church music and directed choirs in parish schools and churches throughout the northwest. One brother, Frater Alban Gertken, died as a deacon at St. John's, and another brother, the Right Reverend Severin Gertken, is present abbot-ordinary of St. Peter's Abbey, Saskatchewan.

Other Benedictine sons of these school teachers include the Reverends Conrad and Godfrey Diekmann, professors, respectively, of English and theology, sons of John Conrad Diekmann; Cyril Ortmann, pastor of St. Martin's Church, St. Martin, son of Theodore Ortmann; Othmar Hohmann, pastor of St. Boniface Church, Cold Spring, son of Jacob Hohmann; Odo Zimmermann, professor of classics at St. John's, son of Anton Zimmermann, who, after the death of his wife, entered St. John's as a Brother, and received the name of Conrad in religion; Berthold Ricker, son of Herman Ricker, in charge of St. John's latest foundation at Posa Rica, Mexico.

NOTES TO CHAPTER FOUR

1 Alexius Hoffmann, O.S.B., "How St. Louis Abbey Got Started," pp. 1–7. The pioneer, Father Bruno Riess, had left Minnesota before Abbot Rupert's election, and Wimmer sent him to work at St. Mary's parish, Newark. After a full life of missionary activity in several parts of the country, Father Bruno died in Illinois on 2 February 1900, and is buried in the community cemetery of St. Bede's Abbey, Peru, Illinois.

2 *Acta Capitularia,* 12 December 1866. Abbot Boniface informed the abbot of Metten, Utto Lang, of these events: "I presided over the election. Fr. Rupert was elected unanimously by the twelve capitulars in a large house in the midst of a forest of 2,600 acres which belong to the monastery. This was on December 12. The weather was very cold, but we sang the *Te Deum* very enthusiastically in the neat chapel. Last summer, about half an hour's walk away, a new and large building was constructed which was not yet finished. It will be the abbey. The location is excellent. The lake is about 600 acres and has many fish in it. I did not remain longer than necessary" (AAMe, 27 January 1867).

3 Seidenbusch to Haindl, St. Vincent's, 19 December 1866.

4 AASV, Rome, 9 November 1865; Munich, 15 August 1866. Abbot-elect Rupert had a brother who was also a Benedictine, the Reverend Dr. James Seidenbusch, professor at St. Stephen's College, Augsburg, Bavaria. Another brother was a practicing physician in Newark, N.J.

5 AAMe, Wimmer to Lang, St. Vincent's, 19 April 1868.

6 *Ibid.,* 28 January 1867.

7 Niccola Cardinal Paracciani-Clarelli to Abbot-Elect Rupert Seidenbusch, O.S.B., Rome, 16 March 1867.

8 Baltimore *Katholische Volkszeitung,* 15 June 1867.

9 "Varia Notes," n.d.

10 ALMV, Seidenbusch to Scherr, St. Louis Abbey, 18 September 1867.

11 ALMV, Report of the *Ludwig Missionsverein,* 18 April, 10 November 1868; 17 November 1870; Seidenbusch to *Ludwig Missionsverein,* St. Louis Abbey, 9 October 1868; 21 October 1869. Actually this mission society gave considerably more to the abbey during Abbot Rupert's administration than the promised yearly grant of $860. Abbey

records show over $12,000 donated by the Bavarian mission society from 1867 to 1875.

12 Frater Alexius pronounced his solemn vows on 1 September 1867 at St. Louis Abbey before Prior Benedict, was ordained by Bishop Grace in St. Paul on September 29, and offered his first Mass in Richmond on October 6. His sister, Elizabeth, wife of Henry Broker who later became Collegeville postmaster, was then living there. His father was at this time living in St. Joseph, Missouri, where he had gone in 1861 after shooting a Michael Reedes in defense during an altercation in the Edelbrock's St. Cloud store.

13 On the south shore of St. Louis Lake there was a small island especially favored by Dr. Aylward. Here during the summer of 1872 the clerics decided to build a chapel to the Blessed Virgin under her title of *Stella Maris* which would replace a rude one that had been erected a few years previously. Frater Vincent Schiffrer, O.S.B., directed this enterprise, and all materials were brought to 'Doctor's Island' by boat. The chapel, 16x20 feet, was Gothic in style with ornamental brickwork and a wooden spire. Although the interior was not finished until 1889, and Mass was not offered in it, this first shrine of the institution was a favorite terminus of lake-side strollers. It was destroyed by fire in 1903, re-built by clerics twelve years later, strengthened and restored anew by clerics in 1944 under the direction of Frater Cloud Meinberg, O.S.B. Today the student community participates in an annual Marian Mass there during the month of May. In 1880 Dr. Herman Zschokke, imperial chaplain at the Austrian court and later rector of the University of Vienna, lectured at St. John's. In a travelogue account of his tour of America he wrote of this chapel: "On the other shore of the lake there stands a small chapel surrounded by trees — *Stella Maris* — built by the students in honor of the Mother of God. It was a sunset picture so exquisite, that one could not imagine anything more perfect. The sun, which had just disappeared below the horizon, poured a flood of orange-hued light over the western sky; the placid lake caught and mirrored the glorious light which transfigured the thick foliage of the forest. From its height the abbey looked calmly upon the scene; and when finally the bell sounded the *Ave Maria* and its voice was wafted over the quiet, peaceful landscape, finding many an echo in the woods, I found myself transported in spirit back into the early centuries, when the sons of St. Benedict penetrated with holy zeal into the wilderness, enkindling everywhere the light of faith and bringing civilization to Europe" (*Nach Nord Amerika und Canada* [Vienna, 1882] p. 501).

14 Cf. Baltimore *Katholische Volkszeitung,* 6 July 1867; St. Cloud *Journal,* 25 July 1867; *Northwestern Chronicle,* 13 July 1867.

15 Abbot Rupert received, for example, vestments from the English Franciscans, a chalice from the abbot of Augsburg and two relics, which were labelled as fingers of St. Benedict, from the bishop of that same city. He did not go to Rome on this trip because of lack of money and time, and also, as he wrote to Abbot Boniface because "you did not want me to and I had no business there anyway" (AASV, Augsburg, 25 September 1867, 30 January 1868). Cf. also Haindl to Wimmer, St. Louis Abbey, 26 October 1867, 8 January 1868. Abbot Rupert also made contact with the Society for the Propagation of the Faith in Lyons, France, and received chasubles, stoles, albs, paintings, antependiums sewn by hand by members of this organization.

When Abbot Rupert returned to Minnesota he was welcomed along the way with parades, bells and salutes in the parishes at St. Paul, St. Cloud and St. Joseph. The last stage of the journey through the Indianbush was less dignified. The community, both monks and students, had moved on 7 April 1868 in procession to the foot of the hill to await his arrival, while the brass band stood poised in the turret of the Stone House. When the heads of the horses appeared at the turn of the road the signal was given with a shot gun; bonfires were lighted, and the band burst forth. To everyone's amazement, behind the horses strode Father Anthony, while the carriage, abbot and luggage were stuck fast in a marsh one mile back in the woods. When the abbot was finally rescued and brought into the Stone House, which was decorated with garlands and transparencies, the welcoming program was successfully concluded.

16 The community lost three men during this same period; Fathers Demetrius di Marogna died in 1869; Othmar Wirtz in 1874; and Brother Placidus Brixius in 1871. All were buried in the

first abbey cemetery which was a hundred feet northeast of the buildings.

St. John's founding prior, Demetrius di Marogna, died on Holy Saturday, 27 March 1869, in the rectory of Assumption Parish, St. Paul. He had been failing in health since 1868, had gone to Florida, returned to resign the parish and act as chaplain at St. Joseph's Academy until the spring of 1869. Requiem Masses and public processions were held in St. Paul, St. Cloud and at the abbey.

17 The basement of this addition was divided into two dining rooms with kitchen; the first floor included two parlors and several classrooms, while the abbot's apartments and rooms of the officials were on the second floor. The third story was originally about thirty feet high and intended for a church, but was never used for that purpose and served continually as another student dormitory. When this building was remodelled after the tornado of 1894 the dormitory space was divided into rooms and the mansard arranged for dormitories. From the peak of the roof rose a small cupola surmounted by a cross. Cf. Andreas, *Illustrated Atlas of the State of Minnesota* (St. Paul, 1874), p. 113, for a lithograph of these additions. Here the full building plans of the first years are sketched. They include two projected buildings, one of brick and one of stone, to flank the main building on the north, as exact counterparts to those adjoining it on the south. The second abbot abandoned this design when he began his major building program.

Frater Vincent Schiffrer designed the first and second brick additions. Some of the workmen who helped the monks and scholastics labor on the second addition included Wenzel Wolke (carpenter) and Charles Creven (brick burner) of St. Cloud, August Leivermann (painter) of Chaska, and Peter Eich (teamster) of Collegeville.

While this building was going up Abbot Wimmer asked Abbot Rupert to pay a bill of $571.42 to cover charges, at the rate of $1 a week, for training of the abbey's novices at St. Vincent. Wimmer also asked Seidenbusch to begin payments of another bill of $2,475 which had been running since the time the St. Cloud Priory had been founded, and represented the amount spent by St. Vincent to establish the foundation in Minnesota. Wimmer stated: "As things are, it cannot be expected that you ever will be without debts because

necessary and desirable buildings will consume what could be saved in the best of cases. Therefore, there is no sense in waiting for payment until such time as St. Louis will have nothing else to pay. I would not mention this at all if I were not burdened by considerable debts, as for instance only recently I had to post bail for more than $6,000 and even had to assume the responsibility for its interest for Atchison" (St. Vincent, 30 July 1871).

18 "Memoirs of the Reverend Alphonse Kuisle, O.S.B.," n.p.

19 Father Alexius Hoffmann wrote of these mills: "Both mills at the Watab dam were soon in operation, the power being generated by a water wheel overshot, that hung between the mills. The rumbling of the gristmill and the singing of the sawmill added romance to the spot" ("The Abbey of St. Louis on the Lake," p. 8). Farmers of the region came to the gristmill where Brother Andrew ground bran for their cattle, flour for cooking, shorts for pigs and the much used '50/50,' composed of bran, flour and shorts. The wheat was ground on two soft or 'pipe stones' with square ribs and surrounded by iron bands. It was at this time that Brother William Baldus, O.S.B., abbey cook, introduced the first form of what has come to be known as 'St. John's black bread.' The earliest type of bread at the monastery had been a *Schwartz Brot*, which was dense like pumpernickel. It was customarily eaten along with another slice of white bread. Then Brother William originated the whole wheat dark bread which was not quite as dense, but heavier than the present-day form of the community's bread which now includes rye and white flour. Brother William insisted that this bread be baked in an oven built entirely of brick. The finished loaves were eighteen by eight inches, and were cut into slices five-eighths of an inch thick.

20 The Kneipp Cure included submerging the patient in cold water, then wrapping him tightly in sheets and blankets, after which he was put to bed and allowed to come to a heavy sweat. The victim was then unpacked and again placed in cold water, after which he was allowed to return to regular body heat in bed. This procedure was employed to obtain good circulation of the blood. Father Adrian had his own specialty for rheumatism. It consisted of collecting hay seeds from the barn floor and putting them into tea in a

bathtub. The patient would then lie in this ingredient, and many persons insisted that they had been cured by this procedure. For the common cold, herbs were cooked into a tea which was poured into a milk pail, and the sufferer would hold his head over the pail while inhaling the steam. Heated bricks would periodically be placed in the pail to increase the steam.

21 ASCHS, Dean Nelson, "Review of Physicians and Surgeons in the History of Stearns County," 27 April 1938. Father Clement continued these medical practices during his pastorate at the Assumption Church from 1863–1875. During 1874 some local doctors began to oppose Father Clement on the ground that he was cutting into their clientele. A German Free-Thinker paper, *Das Volksblatt,* which ridiculed everything Catholic, made a special target of Father Clement, and Bishop Grace advised him to discontinue the practice of medicine. Father Clement did not follow these instructions, and the bishop asked that he be removed from the parish. The complicated and dangerous financial position of Assumption Church, following Father Clement's elaborate building adventure, also necessitated his removal, and the second abbot recalled him to the abbey, while appointing him prior. Here he continued 'doctoring' until 1877 when he returned to his first love, parish work, at St. Joseph. There he took up his medical advising again and continued in much demand until his death in 1886.

22 Wimmer to Seidenbusch, Rome, 7 January 1870.

23 Christmas Matins in Abbot Rupert's second year were chanted at eleven o'clock in the evening, followed by a solemn high Mass at which Prior Benedict officiated, assisted by Fraters Valentine and Alphonse. The same celebrants officiated at a late high Mass at nine o'clock on Christmas morning. For New Year's Day, only two priests, the abbot and the prior, were in the monastery, and as no organist was at home, only low Mass was offered. St. Benedict's Day was observed with as much pomp as possible. A novena was begun on March 12 and the abbot pontificated on the feast at eight-thirty in the morning. On this day the abbot always dispensed from the Lenten silence. Holy Week services began on Palm Sunday with a solemn high Mass. The 'palms' were branches of tama-

rack or willows and could not be distributed during Mass because the chapel was too small for any movement, but everyone was permitted to take one after the services. The Passions and Lamentations of Holy Week were chanted by those with the best voices, usually the two Northman's, Wolfgang and Ulric, and Fraters Louis and Simplicius. Tenebrae was chanted with organ accompaniment daily at four o'clock in the afternoon. The master of ceremonies informed the monks that, by order of the abbot, all were, according to ancient custom, to rap on their breviaries at the end of Lauds, when the taper was brought back from the rear of the altar, or, in this instance, from the sacristy. On Holy Thursday there was a simple pontifical high Mass, and the Blessed Sacrament was carried to the altar in the sacristy for reposition. During the afternoon the students adored, and at six o'clock the clerics, two by two, continued until midnight, when the Brothers took their turns until morning. On Holy Saturday the prior would officiate at all functions in the morning, and the ancient German 'Resurrection Service' would be held at five o'clock in the afternoon, but without procession. The abbot pontificated on Easter Sunday.

24 *The Northwestern Chronicle* for 27 March 1869 reported: "The professors and students of the college, together with the Brothers of the abbey celebrated St. Patrick's Day by attending high Mass in the morning, dispensing with study and labor during the day and indulging in the thoughts and memories that spontaneously spring up as the hallowed associations of the past or the fond hopes for the future presented them to view. At 4 P.M. all sat down to an entertainment gotten up expressly for the occasion by the faculty of the institution and which was in every way worthy of the day, the place and those who presented it. During the feast the college band discoursed sweet music and the choir burst forth with most rapturous songs, the joy of the college students celebrating, the eloquent and appropriate remarks of the speakers, the feast of reason and flow of soul of the professors, taken altogether served to transplant all into an enchanted place, where a spring of perpetual youth washed away all the ills that flesh is heir to." Father Alexius Hoffmann commented on this account: "Which report, incidentally, bears wit-

ness that in those cradle days there were some scribes possessed of no mean skill in blarney."

Der Wanderer of 16 June 1869 carried 'Spectator's' account of the St. Boniface Day celebration on June 5 of that same year. The forty members of the newly formed St. Boniface Literary Society were in charge of arrangements. The entire student body participated in a solemn high Mass and members of the association received holy Communion. The afternoon was spent at a picnic with music and declamations on the Eirenesos (Isle of Peace), known later as the 'British Isles.' *Der Wanderer* was a St. Paul German Catholic newspaper founded in November 1867 at the instigation of Father Clement Staub. It was already paying for itself with 2,008 subscribers and no agents in the field within one year (AASV, Staub to Wimmer, St. Paul, 24 January 1868). Father Clement was joined in this publishing venture by several German laymen of the Assumption parish, St. Paul. They organized the Wanderer Printing Company and Father Clement was president of the firm until 1875. This weekly acquired a national reputation during the editorship of the convert Hugo Klapproth (1883–99), and has been ably edited since that time by Joseph Matt, a prominent Catholic layman of the Northwest, and close friend of St. John's.

25 Among the students during these years were William Tenvoorde, '69, St. Cloud business man; Severin Corrigan, '69, St. Paul physicist and astronomer; Otto Dreher, '69, teacher and organist at St. Joseph's church, Chicago; George Mitsch, '69, druggist and Fire Commissioner of St. Paul; Anthony Moosbrugger, '69, Stearns County official; Gustav Beaulieu, '70, deputy U. S. marshal and known as 'the watchdog of the Chippewas' in the Indian country; William Markoe, '70, Catholic author; the Chippewa Indian Chief, Ignatius Hole-in-the-Day, II, '70, who was baptized at St. John's; James Kelly, '74, Minnesota State Senator; and such future priests as John Abb, '69, of Green Bay; Max Wurst, '73, of Wabasha; Vincent Reitmeyer, '69, California Jesuit.

26 The Reverend Louis Traufler, O.S.B., stated in an interview on 21 February 1954 that this commercial school developed into one of the best of its kind in the midwest. St. John's was the only school offering a distinct commercial course at that time in Minnesota.

27 Some other alumni prepared in this department included John Zapp, '84, and Edward Zapp, '89, of St. Cloud's Zapp State Bank; John Hoeschen, '78, an early merchant of Freeport; Christopher Borgerding, '77, of the Bank of Belgrade; Herman J. Terhaar, '91, of the State Bank of New Munich; Frank Hausdorf, '88, St. Paul financier; Frank Gross, '89, president of the German National Bank in Minneapolis; Judge Alois Himsl, '87, of St. Cloud; George Meinz, '02, of American National Bank in St. Cloud; Ignatius O'Shaughnessy, '01, of the Globe Oil Company, St. Paul; Urban, Thomas and Joseph Powers, '18, of building construction, Gardner and Powers Hotels in Fargo; Anthony Hoenninger, '98, financial advisor to the Kolping House in New York, and his brother John, '99, New York lawyer; Joseph and Louis Wachter, '97, LaCrosse brewers; William Bohmer, '95, of the Melrose Granite Company, St. Cloud; John Boyd, '02, retail clothing merchant in Langdon, N. Dak.; John and Matthias Kotschevar, '86, furniture merchants in Breckenridge; Alfred Knaeble, '00, St. Paul furniture merchant; Charles Moos, '95, of Joyce Insurance Company and former postmaster of St. Paul.

28 St. John's alumni who became members of the hierarchy include the Most Reverends Alexander Christie, '74, archbishop of Portland; James J. Keane, '77, archbishop of Dubuque; John Shanley, '70, bishop of Fargo; Joseph B. Cotter, '70, bishop of Winona; John Bernard Kevenhoerster, O.S.B., '97, vicar apostolic of the Bahama Islands; John H. Peschges, '99, bishop of Crookston; Louis B. Kucera, '05, bishop of Lincoln; John L. Paschang, '21, bishop of Grand Island; Leo F. Dworschak, '26, auxiliary bishop of Fargo; and Paul Leonard Hagarty, O.S.B., '36, vicar apostolic of the Bahama Islands.

29 All students followed the same schedule: rising at five o'clock in the morning; morning prayers and Mass at 5:30, followed by breakfast and recreation until 7:00; classes and study until 11:00; dinner, short visit to the chapel and recreation until 1:00; classes until 3:00 and then lunch which consisted of a slice of dry bread; 4–6:00 classes; supper; recreation until 7:30; one hour of study and bed time at 8:30. Thurs-

day and Saturday afternoons were free, except for study from 2:30–3:00 and 5–6:00. On Sundays and Holy Days all rose a half hour later; Mass and sermon at 6:00; study from 10–12:00; Vespers at 2:30 and religious instruction from 5–6:00 in the afternoon. During Lent of 1873 Abbot Rupert decided that the diocesan seminarians should attend choir, or the public chanting of the Divine Office, with the monks. This practice was shortly discontinued, however, probably because it was impractical and over-taxing for seminarians to rise at 3:30 in the morning. On feast days both the monastic and student communities would be awakened by the booming of the institution's two cannons and music by the brass band.

30 *Annual Report of the Superintendent of Public Instruction for the State of Minnesota for the Year ending September 30, 1872* (St. Paul, 1873), pp. 200–01. Carleton College, the only other Minnesota private collegiate institution mentioned during these years, was founded at Northfield in 1866 by the Board of Trustees of the Minnesota Conference of Congregational Churches with preparatory school opening in 1867, and first college classes formed in 1870. The institution was first known as Northfield College, but was changed to Carleton College in 1872 in honor of an early benefactor, William Carleton of Charlestown, Mass.

31 *Sixteenth Annual Report of the Superintendent of Public Instruction for the State of Minnesota for the Year Ending September 30, 1875* (St. Paul, 1876), pp. 57–59. Other early descriptions of St. John's College appeared in the Cincinnati *Wahrheitsfreund* of 17 June 1868, and in the *Einsiedler Kalender fuer 1870* (New York, 1870), p. 63. Abbot Rupert appealed for financial help in Catholic publications during these years. He announced that two perpetual Mass foundations were being established, on March 19 and November 2, for the intentions of all those who donated five dollars. He also set up prize lotteries (with tickets to be forwarded by mail on receipt of money) for plots of land: 160 acres in Anoka County; 160 acres in Stearns County; four lots in St. Cloud; five acres in Shakopee; one house and lot also in Shakopee; sixteen lots in St. Joseph; twelve in Richmond; and two lots in Scott County. Cf. The Boston *Pilot*, 21 May 1870, and Baltimore *Katholische Volkszeitung*, 18 May 1870.

32 Minnie Mary Lee was the pseudonym of Mrs. Julius A. Wood, one of the first Catholic writers in the Northwest. She was born 13 April 1825 at New London, N.H., received a literary and classical education in the state schools there and married W. H. Wood who died in 1870. From 1851 the Woods published the *New Era*, weekly newspaper in Sauk Rapids, and Mrs. Woods was a frequent contributor to magazines. She was a convert to Catholicism and wrote several popular novels of an apologetic character, including *The Heart of Myrrha Lake, Hubert's Wife, The Brown House of Duffield, Strayer From the Fold, Story of Annette*. She died at St. Raphael's Hospital, St. Cloud, on 9 March 1903. Father Alexius Edelbrock always made a practice of giving away copies of Mrs. Wood's books as premiums on commencement day, as well as other works such as Cardinal Manning's *Lectures, The Statutes and Teachings of the Society of Jesus,* Chateaubriand's *Martyrs,* or DeSmedt's *Indian Sketches.*

33 *The Northwestern Chronicle,* 24 June 1874.

34 *Sixteenth Annual Report for 1875,* p. 58.

35 Hoffmann, *op. cit.,* pp. 22–23. The first of a long line of institutional pets, which have included deer, horses, dogs, a blue heron, and a crow, was a bear called Murro which Father Wolfgang and the student Gus Beaulieu trained in 1867. This pet bear was gentle and had full run of the institution, sleeping in students' beds, begging food from Brother William in the kitchen, or ambling into study halls and classrooms much to the delight of the students. On 2 June 1869 the history of Murro took a tragic turn when Sylvester Sheire, student from St. Paul, was teasing the animal by throwing sticks at him. Murro lunged at the boy who ran down to the lake and jumped into a boat. The bear followed and when the boy hit him with an oar the animal jumped into the boat, threw his forelegs around the boy and bit him in the neck. Father Wolfgang arrived on the scene too late to save the boy's life. The bear was tied to a nearby tree and immediately shot.

36 Edelbrock to Trobec, St. John's, 4 March 1874, copy. If students acted irresponsibly, such as destroying property, Father Alexius promptly charged

401

them. Thus William Kilian was fined $1.75 "for breaking the door to the shoe room" on 30 June 1874, as was James J. Keane, future archbishop of Dubuque, assessed $.40 for breaking a chair on 6 December 1874.

37 Edelbrock to "My Dear Madar," St. John's, 10 December 1874, copy.

38 ALMV, Seidenbusch to "Dear Friend and Benefactor," St. Louis Abbey, 28 November 1872.

39 George N. Shuster, "Catholic Culture in America," *Today,* VIII, (March, 1953), 12–13.

40 Cf. Timothy Majerus, O.S.B., *The Church of St. Joseph, St. Joseph, Minn. 1871–1946* (Collegeville, 1946). The Assumption Church in St. Paul was consecrated on 18 October 1874, with Bishop Grace again consecrating and Abbot Rupert pontificating, before Minnesota's governor, senators, Twin City mayors, and one of the largest crowds in St. Paul's history up to that time.

41 Folwell, *op. cit.,* III, 73.

42 In a statement, typical of the narrow and distorted North European bias of this nationalistic period of United States development, the federal commissioner of statistics congratulated Minnesota on its accession of "the best blood of Europe:" honest and laborious Scandinavians who had sympathy for popular institutions; Germans "with an intellectual organism in which the massive properties and the tough Saxon fibre needed for laborious research are mingled with the finer qualities of the musician and the prophetic spirit of the poet"; and the Irish "with their muscular power and gifts of a warm and impassioned nature" (Commissioner of Statistics, *Reports* [Washington, 1870], pp. 125–27, quoted in Folwell, *op. cit.,* III, 59).

43 Individual priests, especially in the East, were in contact with Abbot Rupert concerning available land in central Minnesota for their parishioners (Rev. Bonaventure to Seidenbusch, New York, 20 May 1879). From the Cold Spring-Richmond area the Benedictines wrote to the Cincinnati *Wahrheitsfreund,* on 15 February 1865 that the Sauk River basin was filling up with German Catholics, and then added: "It can be the basis of Catholic life in the whole Northwest." Father George Scherer announced that wooded land was going for from $3–$5 an acre, that the climate was ideal, that the Benedictines were supplying priests and schools throughout the region (*Wahrheitsfreund,* 3 February 1864). The Baltimore *Katholische Volkszeitung* announced in its 31 August 1872 issue that central Minnesota presented an opportunity for community settlement to all who wished to establish secure homesteads. Continual news releases were also sent to these papers on all abbey, college and parish developments (cf. *Wahrheitsfreund,* 24 February 1859, 2 January, 17 April, 5 June 1867; 21 January, 17 June, 1 July, 16 September 1868; 3 March, 13 October 1869; 21 December 1870; 14 June 1871; 20 August 1873; 1 March 1876; and *Katholische Volkszeitung,* 31 August 1872, 18 June 1878. On 23 March 1878 Bishop Rupert and Abbot Alexius together wrote a letter to this latter paper in which they announced Minnesota as the land of the future, a home for the poor and a safe retreat for Catholics.

44 The settlers moving into the region at this time were not only from Europe, but also in large numbers from such eastern states as Maryland, Pennsylvania, Ohio, Michigan, Indiana, Illinois and Wisconsin. These latter homesteaders were second-generation offspring of immigrants, and thus had already begun the process of Americanization before their arrival in Minnesota. Their sons who attended St. John's were looked upon as 'Americans,' and included John Traufler who received the name of Father Louis. His father, Nicholas Traufler, had been an engineer in the copper mines at Calumet, Mich., for ten years before deciding to take up some of the cheap land around Luxemburg, Minnesota, and in this way find the security that a craftsman could never hope for in American industrial society of that period. John Heid, barrel maker also from Calumet, moved with his wife Barbara to Stearns County, and their son Kilian entered St. John's as Father Kilian, as did the Henry Hansen family whose son John became Father Bonaventure. The WPA Stearns County Historical Project was devoted to collecting and recording the memoirs of typical pioneer families of central Minnesota, as well as accounts of housing, tools, amusements, marketing, prices and community customs. This documentation is preserved in the Stearns County Historical Society Museum, Court House, St. Cloud.

45 AAMi, Grace to Henni, St. Paul, 17 December 1871.

46 AAMi, Heiss to Henni, La-Crosse, 26 December 1871.

47 The Holy See also at this time erected the see of Peoria, and elevated the Vicariate of Kansas into the diocese of Leavenworth. When Bishop Grace learned that the most energetic and promising young priest of his diocese, the Reverend John Ireland, was appointed to the Vicariate Apostolic of Nebraska, he hastened to Rome. There he requested that Father Ireland rather be made his own coadjutor with right of succession to the diocese of St. Paul. At Lourdes he learned that the Holy Father had granted his request; in the meantime Father Ireland had returned his apostolic brief of appointment to Rome. Bishop Ireland was consecrated in St. Paul on 21 December 1875 as coadjutor to Bishop Grace. It was in this way that John Ireland was retained in the upper midwest where he would in the succeeding years have a major influence on the development of the Church in so many distinctive ways.

48 Hipelius to Seidenbusch, St. Mary's, Pa., 24 February 1875; 16 April 1875.

49 *The Catholic Directory*, 1876. The Franciscan Sisters at Belle Prairie were established in 1873 by Mother Mary Ignatius (Elizabeth Hayes), a convert of Edward Cardinal Manning in London, and foundress of the Missionary Franciscan Sisters of the Immaculate Conception. With the permission of Bishop Seidenbusch she established herself in the parish at Belle Prairie and laid the foundation for a motherhouse and novitiate. She then travelled throughout the United States and Europe establishing other houses, while her community taught Indians and in the parochial school at Belle Prairie. This convent burned down in 1888 and was not rebuilt until 1911. In the meanwhile the majority of the Sisters moved to Little Falls and there, under Mother Mary Francis Beauchamp, established a diocesan Franciscan community which continues today to serve the Church in schools and hospitals throughout the diocese of St. Cloud.

50 Alexius Hoffmann, O.S.B., "The Abbey of St. Louis on the Lake," pp. 21–25; Norbert Hofbauer, O.S.B., "Electio Abbatis, 1875," 8 April 1889. Abbot Boniface explained to Abbot Utto Lang of Metten why he had proceeded in this manner at the election: "Now I must make the new abbot of St. Louis on the Lake in Minnesota, as you did in Scheyern; partially because he is young (33); partially because he is sharp; partially because he is the *factotum* in the college. Because his elevation to the abbacy would have infringed on his college activities a small minority did not elect him, but rather my Prior Innocent with 13 of 24 votes, and in spite of my having stated from the very beginning that I would not consent either to Fathers Oswald (Moosmueller) or Innocent (Wolf) as abbot if they would elect one of them. I cashiered the election and gave them Father Alexius Edelbrock who received eight votes on the first and eleven on the third ballot. Two young and one old Father protested. I forwarded their protest to the Holy Father, together with the acts of the election and my report. The Holy Father 'approbavit et confirmavit' my procedure, and now everyone is satisfied. The new abbot is Westphalian. As a child he came to America, and as a boy to Minnesota. He was a rather wild boy until our Father Alexius Roetzer of happy memory, from whom he took the name Alexius, taught him manners. Then he ran away from his father who was a rugged man in order to study at St. Vincent. He has great talents which he developed with unceasing industry, and after finishing his studies he returned to Minnesota. Under Abbot Rupert he contributed most to the development of the foundation and college whose director he also was. He is healthy, strong, smart, and will accomplish much for the honor of God and our Order, I hope in God. Abbot Rupert bequeathed to him a great deal of work. He brought along from Europe a plan for a church drawn up by Riedl which was supposed to be and was built in St. Paul. The plan was exactly executed despite my repeated warnings orally and in writing. The church is all of stone with two beautiful towers and a basement church for winter. It is a magnificent structure. But debts, debts! So you may immediately send another 50,000 florins. Well the 'plan maker' is still an unusual person" (AAMe, St. Vincent, 16 December 1875).

51 Wimmer then wrote to Abbot-elect Alexius, after Edelbrock had once again expressed his reluctance to assume the office: "and so you are not

grateful to me that I made you an abbot. Well, frankly, I didn't make you. You had at least the relative majority, and so if I had made someone else abbot, I would have had the right to do so. But in that case I would have had to ignore the majority of Innocent and yourself. That I could not well do. But the vote of your supporters was in any case also mine, and so I chose you. My motives were not at all any part of friendship . . . you are not obliged to me. You did not mean that. You meant not to thank me for the election because it is no *bene*, and because you have not gained anything by it but trouble. So what you really meant is that the abbatial dignity is no gift worthy of thanks. But you said that without much thought; really and with due consideration you would and should not have said so. To repeat, you are not of my making. You are elected by your confrères. Your office is your *bonum* and you should be grateful for it because it is from God. Besides all this, the cares of an abbot are no obstacle to sanctification. Proof of this is

that so many abbots did become saints, that the Church gave them their own *Commune Abbatum* in the Breviary and Mass, and that the abbatial state was received into the ecclesiastical hierarchy, which means that individual abbots have set the pattern for individual centuries. In their totality they have influenced to a large part the destiny of the Western world.

"I am an abbot not because of the honor, which is insignificant, but because of the opportunity to do more good than any number of bishops together. Our nobility goes back to St. Benedict. We should not be ashamed of our ancestors. To be an abbot and to do nothing, to suffer nothing, not to meet with adversities, that would not mean anything. But in our days to be an abbot, to build one's monastery from the ground up, not finding anything to work with, and yet to accomplish something, that is what makes it rewarding. At least you should thank God that you are an abbot" (St. Vincent, 4 January 1876).

NOTES TO CHAPTER FIVE

1 Bishop Louis Fink, O.S.B., told Abbot Alexius that he hoped his elevation would be "a source of happiness and blessing to yourself and the Community, that it will last at least fifty years — to start with — and after that we will see what is further to be done" (Leavenworth, 1 October 1875). Three alumni, the Reverend J. Bassler of St. Joseph's College, Dubuque, together with E. A. Kenney and J. J. Nelson, wrote on October 27: "It is with feelings of profound respect that we recur to your untiring efforts for the promotion of the welfare of St. John's College. You rocked it in the cradle, you looked with anxiety upon its first steps and today you behold it in the prime and vigor of its manhood." Father Edward Hipelius, O.S.B., of St. Vincent, who had been secretary at the abbatial election, wrote that he knew the abbot would rule properly, but he feared trouble ahead for him and offered help in any way possible: "I don't felicitate you; in fact I would sooner see you a poor hermit than abbot of such a chapter. There is more poison among them than you may be inclined to suspect. *Sed Deus sit auxiliator et susceptor tuus in omnibus viis tuis, ut inoffenso pede deambules super aspidem*

et basiliscum. If I am wrong I will retract every word I wrote" (St. Vincent, 2 October 1875).

2 Wimmer reprimanded A b b o t Alexius rather sharply for these sentiments, and then went on to advise him: "Be glad that you are an abbot. You can learn and merit much. Maybe men will not know, but God certainly will. You will need much patience, but you will learn that step by step. Also much prudence in judgments because one is easily deceived or will become deceived if he does not consider duly and observe the *audiatur et altera pars*. Besides, an abbot should leave the impression as little as possible that he is an abbot unless there is need for some severity because in any case he will be envied and even hated. But honestly we are not to be envied. In spite of this, it is a great thing to lead a column of brave, pious and educated men, who, if well used, will together accomplish much good, and in spite of all weaknesses they may have, will still possess many precious gifts and complement each other. The worst thing was and is that the means are out of proportion to our desires, and this is going to last until only a little has been accomplished. In all these forty years I have

not even finished building one monastery. But even for this cross the only remedy is patience and humble submission because we realize that we can call ourselves happy only if God makes use of us as a tool for the accomplishment of one little work of His mercy" (St. Vincent, 13 February 1876).

3 AASV, Edelbrock to Wimmer, St. Joseph, 23 February 1876.

4 Interview with the Reverend Louis Traufler, O.S.B., St. Cloud, February, 1954. A number of the personal anecdotes included in this chapter were recalled by Father Louis, who was assistant to Abbot Alexius at St. Anselm's Parish, New York City, during the abbot's last years, and who spoke often with him about his career.

5 The *Ludwig Missionsverein* had donated 20,260 marks ($5,065) to the monastery from 1868–75 and 11,400 marks ($2,850) in 1882, while the *Leopoldinen Stiftung* gave 2,000 gulden ($800) for the Assumption Church in St. Paul. When the abbey entered the field of Indian work the *Ludwig Missionsverein* again supported this new endeavor, giving on 8 November 1880, 4,600 marks ($1,150) as an initial grant.

6 On 22 March 1877 this fire started in the corridor of the seminarians' quarters, and most probably in one of the wooden cuspidors. It was difficult in the inky darkness and smoke for anyone to enter the building. Father Aloysius Hermanutz, O.S.B., heard the noise and rushed upon the scene with a rifle, shouting: "Where are they?" for he thought robbers were sacking the building. Then the abbey chronicler records: "Father Ulric Northman, who was one of the first to discover it, quickly got a Babcock extinguisher to playing on the flames and with the aid of a few priests and Brothers, who turned on the water from the new works, soon extinguished the fire."

7 Wimmer to Edelbrock, St. Vincent, 2 November 1876. Wimmer informed Abbot Benedict Braunmiller of Metten after a Visitation of St. John's: "Abbot Alexius is an excellent manager. He has in a short time accomplished so much that one scarcely recognizes the place . . . St. Louis on the Lake has the potential of becoming a first class establishment" (AAMe, St. Vincent, 2 July 1879).

8 Shane Leslie, *Cardinal Gasquet* (New York, 1953), p. 3.

9 Cf. Albert Kleber, O.S.B., *History of St. Meinrad Abbey* (St. Meinrad, 1954), pp. 261–328. Father Albert is at present working on a biography of Abbot and Bishop Martin Marty.

10 Before Father Pierz came to Crow Wing in 1852, the Reverend Frederic Baraga, later bishop of Marquette, visited Fond du Lac, Minnesota, as early as 1837 from La Pointe, Wisconsin. Father Pierz moved out from Crow Wing to visit such distant places as Mille Lacs, Fond du Lac, Shady Lake, White Oak Point, Otter Tail and Leech Lakes. He reached Red Lake in 1858.

11 The immediate occasion of Bishop Seidenbusch's request for the Benedictines to take over White Earth arose from the conflict between the White Earth agent, Lewis Stowe, and Father Tomazin. The latter believed Catholic Indians were not being fairly treated and he proceeded to encourage Indian children to leave the reservation for their education. Tomazin also led an Indian delegation to Washington, and entered into imprudent newspaper controversy. At the same time, Tomazin had several justifiable grievances. Voluminous documentation in the National Archives, the Archives of the Minnesota Historical Society as well as the Archives of the Catholic Indian Bureau in Washington attest to the fact that representatives of both Episcopalian and Congregational religions, along with Stowe and Edward P. Smith, commissioner of Indian affairs, were anything but favorable to Catholic missionary activities and requests from White Earth. Father Tomazin was finally forcibly removed from the reservation, leaving the Catholic Indians without a priest. The Catholic Indian Bureau then took action and worked for the removal of Stowe, who was succeeded by Major Charles A. Ruffee. The Catholic Indian Bureau recommended to Bishop Seidenbusch that Tomazin should also not be returned to the reservation. The bishop was reluctant to agree to this proposal, but for the sake of peace and progress of religion on the reservation, turned to Abbot Alexius for assistance.

12 Aloysius Hermanutz, O. S. B., "Memoirs of White Earth Catholic Indian Mission." The two Benedictine nuns, Sisters Lioba Braun and Philomene Ketten, were sent along to White Earth with Father Aloysius by Mother Scholastica Kerst, O.S.B. Abbot Alexius had asked her to participate in this

work, and although short of personnel, she agreed to send Benedictine Sisters into this new field.

13 President Ulysses Grant's well-meaning 'Peace Policy' established by the federal government in the 1870's, placed the supervision of Federal Indian affairs in the hands of the various religious groups working among the separate tribes. The aim of this policy was to foster a more humanitarian treatment of the American aborigines. In actuality it fostered bigotry. Catholic Indian groups were frequently placed under the control of agents of Protestant denominations. According to one report, an agent "had the power to appoint missionaries, and to prevent the Catholic missionary from setting foot within the Indian reservation, and he could also punish the Indians for going off the reservation to attend a Catholic church if the missionary erected a chapel on free ground" (*The American Catholic Quarterly Review*, I [1876], 166). For a complete treatment of this period of Indian affairs, as well as the establishment of the Catholic Indian Bureau as a national Catholic center for Indian support and defense, cf. Peter J. Rahill, *The Catholic Indian Missions and Grant's Peace Policy, 1870–1884* (Washington, 1953).

14 Whipple stands in Minnesota history with Father Pierz, patriarch of Indian missionaries, as one of the pioneer nineteenth century religious figures who dedicated his life to the advance and care of northwest Indians. Henry Benjamin Whipple (1822–1901) was first rector of Episcopalian free churches in Rome, New York, and Chicago before being called to Minnesota in 1859 as bishop. He developed Episcopalian schools at Faribault as well as extensive missions among the Chippewa and Sioux Indians. The Indians called him 'Straight Tongue' and placed confidence in his support. Cf. his autobiography, *Lights and Shadows of a Long Episcopate* (New York, 1902). An historical picture of Indian affairs in Minnesota history may be found in Folwell, *op. cit.,* IV, 190–329.

15 Abbot Alexius was always interested in political developments, and did not hesitate to take sides in campaign issues. Ignatius Donnelly, the 'Sage of Ninninger,' who had sent his son Stanislaus, '78, to St. John's, wrote Edelbrock, while asking him for support in an election: "I well know that no man in Stearns County has more influence than you have" (Hastings, 10 December 1888). As early as 1880 the abbot was pushing actively for a new dam in St. Cloud. He was a Republican in sympathy, and that in an almost totally Democratic section of the area. He was a personal friend and supporter of the institution's old friend, Henry C. Waite, lawyer of St. Cloud. In 1882 this support brought him into an acrimonious political conflict. In October of that year Waite stood for state senator as a Republican. Abbot Alexius' sympathy was well known, and some members of the college went out of their way to speak out for his candidacy. Both the German Catholic paper of the area, *Der Nordstern,* and St. Cloud's daily, *The St. Cloud Times,* were vigorous Democratic vehicles.

The editors of these two papers, Peter Brick and C. F. MacDonald, attacked 'the powerful organization' in their columns, and when Waite was elected, the *Times* announced "Stearns County loses Senator — the 'College' gets one." (8 November 1882). Cf. *Der Nordstern* also for 28 September 1882. Abbot Wimmer warned against giving such public political support, but Abbot Alexius answered him: "I have no reason to reproach myself on account of the last election. We did not take the offensive but the defensive, and only then when it became a moral necessity for us. To write a long story about this now is hardly necessary. Our monastery has not lost anything thereby as is clearly shown. Anyhow it is somewhat odd that a Republican should be elected in a Democratic county with a majority of 561 votes, and that in spite of three newspapers, the *Times, Nordstern, Kreuzbote* opposing him. It was and still is not to my liking that we were drawn into the fray; however, we were inveigled into it by the Democratic candidate. He was an Irish dog and the Germans, he thought, ought to sell their votes. Well the whole affair is over. In the whole campaign I stayed in the background. Dozens of my friends were ready to draw the sword for me. It seems that this contest had to come. One thing makes me happy and that is that all my people stood by me as one man" (AASV, St. John's, 20 December 1882). MacDonald later admitted he had gone too far in attacking Abbot Alexius. Waite, in turn, sponsored the amendment to change the title of St. John's Seminary to St. John's University in the legislative session following his election.

16 The Reverend Benno Watrin, O.S.B., during the years 1924–52 when he was doing missionary work among the Chippewas, spent long hours recording the reminiscenses of the abbey's Indian missionaries, Fathers Aloysius, Thomas, Roman, Corbinian and Felix. He also interviewed Indians and Whites in northern Minnesota, and did research in the Archives of St. John's Abbey as background material for a history of the Benedictine labors among the Chippewa. His manuscript history of the Catholic missionary efforts at White Earth, Red Lake, Grand Portage, Fond du Lac, Leech Lake, Pine Point, Beaulieu and Mahnomen is preserved in the abbey archives. In this work he exhaustively and painstakingly collected all available material at his disposal.

17 Abbot Alexius had been directed to the Drexels by the Reverend Corbinian Gastbiehl, O.S.B., a friend and advisor. Katherine Drexel had offered assistance to Bishop O'Connor of Omaha in building Indian schools, but he had no one to undertake such a project. Gastbiehl then recommended Abbot Alexius' work at White Earth to her, while encouraging the abbot to write to the lady (Wilmington, 2 March 1886). He proceeded to do this on March 8 and stated: "I assure you before God that the White Earth Mission is worthy of a helping hand. No one, in fact, has given these Chippewa Indians any encouragement or help except the Benedictine Order. We have brought all the sacrifices in the past which our Abbey was able to bring; yet a great deal is now necessary. The Indians are well disposed and are anxious to become children of the Catholic Church; they have already repeatedly begged me for another priest, for more Sisters, for churches and schools, yet our Abbey has not and is not now able to erect the necessary buildings. I could furnish one or even two more Fathers and Benedictine Sisters, but cannot send these out to freeze or starve to death; the necessary buildings must first be put up and this requires money. Even last year I proposed to Bishop Seidenbusch that he should contribute $10,000 and that I would then also contribute $10,000 for the purpose of building a Mission House, Churches, and Schools. Alas! the bishop had no money and nothing has been done. A School and Church ought to be built for the Pembina Indians, a branch of the Chippewas, at Wild Rice River; all these Indians except two families are Catholics and have neither Church nor School. They are twenty miles distant from the White Earth Missions. A school ought to be erected at the White Earth River—also about twenty miles from the present mission. The present Agent of White Earth, Mr. Sheehan, is a Catholic, the first Catholic agent ever appointed for the Agency. He is, however, not a practical Catholic, yet well-disposed towards us; he has even requested me to start a *boarding and industrial* school on the Reservation. We had to decline for want of pecuniary means. There is a great deal to be done for our poor Indians, but alas! very few really care for them. Dear and esteemed lady, I am a stranger to you in as far as not knowing you personally. I have often heard of the munificence of your father, to whom may God grant eternal rest, also, your own charitable disposition is well known to me. All I can say is the Chippewa Indians of Minnesota have been much abandoned, they cry for bread and there is no one to give it to them. I cheerfully recommend them to your patronage and we promise to co-operate faithfully with you as far as our limited pecuniary means will allow."

The abbot's Indian efforts were detailed and praised in several newspapers at this time. Cf. the St. Cloud *Times*, 2 February 1881; St. Paul *Pioneer Press*, July 15; St. Louis *Amerika*, July 24; Cleveland *Universe Bulletin*, July 28; New York *Freeman's Journal*, July 30.

18 Father T h o m a s Borgerding, O.S.B., has dictated his memoirs several times: to Sister Laurentia, O.S.B., of Mt. St. Benedict's Convent, Crookston, Minnesota, in several interviews from 1947–49; to Dr. Charles Vandersluis for publication in the Bemidji weekly *Northern Times* from 21 January-1 June 1954; in preparation for the centennial history of St. John's during October-November 1952. The Reverend Roman Homar, O.S.B., likewise dictated his memoirs during December 1952.

19 Wimmer to Edelbrock, St. Vincent, 12 March 1881. As soon as it became known throughout the country that the St. John's Benedictines were entering into Indian missionary work, other requests were soon received by Abbot Alexius. In November, 1880, the Very Reverend Jean Baptist Brouillet, director of the Catholic Indian

Bureau, asked the abbot to encourage the Benedictine Sisters from St. Benedict's Convent to go to the Grand Ronde Indian Agency in Oregon. The Most Reverend Charles John Seghers, archbishop of Oregon City, wrote to the abbot on 12 January 1881 stating that Brouillet's invitation had his full approval and inviting the monastery to establish a new house and college in his diocese. "Here on the West Coast there is a wide field for the activity of the Benedictine Order to accomplish much for the cause of religion. I hope you will pay us a visit to look at the country and select a place for a monastery. May the Lord inspire you to take possession of this virgin soil and conquer it for Christ." Four Sisters from St. Benedict's Convent were sent out in March 1881, and in November, Abbot Alexius and Father Edward Ginther, O.S.B., journeyed via California to the West Coast. Abbot Alexius was not pleased with conditions as he saw them in Oregon; felt that it would be premature to begin a monastic establishment there before the Northern Pacific railroad reached the West Coast; could not agree to assume responsibility for Indian work alone; and since the Catholic population was so small, there was no need for Benedictines in White parishes or missions. Archbishop Seghers was disappointed in this decision and asked the abbot to reconsider, but he abandoned the project as did the Sisters who returned from Oregon in 1882. Two Swiss Benedictine priests arrived in Oregon in the summer of 1881, however, and laid the foundation for the establishment of Mount Angel Abbey at Gervais. En route home the Abbot and Father Edward visited San Francisco and Los Angeles. Vicar General James Vila of the latter diocese invited them to make a foundation in or around Los Angeles. Abbot Alexius liked the climate and prospects very much, but nothing came of this invitation. In 1887 lumberman Joseph Bruning and his wife Gertrude offered two hundred acres and $2,000 to St. John's to establish a monastery and school near Rio Vista, California. The Brunings had sponsored St. Gertrude's Academy, operated by the Sisters of Mercy, in the same place. They also wanted to leave the full estate to these two institutions since they were childless. Archbishop Patrick Reardon of San Francisco wanted the Benedictines to come, but the offer was not ac-

cepted because the abbot was by that time about to resign.

Other invitations which Abbot Alexius did not accept during his administration included offers from Bishop John Vertin in 1880 to establish a monastery in his diocese of Marquette, Michigan, and from Bishop John Dwenger, of Fort Wayne, in 1887, to come to Rensselaer, Indiana. There he was offered the Catholic orphanage as a monastery and school.

20 After establishing priories in Minnesota (1856), Kansas (1857) and New Jersey (1858), Wimmer turned south. He began St. Joseph's Priory, Covington, Kentucky, which for a time continued to conduct a small boys' school; San José Priory in 1858 near San Antonio, Texas, which had to be discontinued after 1868 because of the hardships of the Civil War and Reconstruction periods; St. Mary's Priory, Richmond, Virginia, in 1868, which conducted a school that was incorporated under Belmont Abbey, Belmont, North Carolina, when it was established in 1884; missions in Alabama which were united in 1891 to form St. Bernard's Abbey; Negro Missions in Georgia, as well as St. Benedict's Industrial School for Colored on Skidway Island, which was transferred to Belmont Abbey in 1884, as well as Benedictine Military School in Savannah, Georgia; Florida missions accepted in 1886, later given to Belmont Abbey, and in 1889 incorporated under St. Leo Abbey, St. Leo, Florida. During these same years, Wimmer was starting St. Joseph's Priory, Chicago, Illinois, in 1861; Assumption College, Sandwich, Ontario, Canada, the Diocesan Seminary of the Diocese of Detroit, which had to be discontinued because of Civil War hardships and insufficient French-speaking professors; College of St. Elizabeth, Rome, in 1865, as a house of studies for American Benedictines; St. Procopius Priory, Chicago, Illinois, in 1865 for Bohemian Catholics, which was raised to an abbey in 1894 and transferred to Lisle, Illinois, in 1914; missions in Colorado in 1886 which led to St. Leander Priory and School in Pueblo, and after 1925 Holy Cross Abbey, Canon City, Colorado; finally Bahia, Ecuador, which was taken over by Wimmer on his death bed in 1887, and transferred to the Brazilian Congregation of Benedictines restored in 1889 by Leo XIII.

21 Father Alexius Hoffmann wrote

of Abbot Alexius: "When he was at home, i.e., in the abbey, and his throat was in condition, he regularly attended all the Offices . . . The Abbot was not eager for solemn functions—his voice would give out. He officiated at pontifical High Masses several times a year, also at numerous Benedictions. The ceremonies were often very extemporaneous and undignified, for he was an impatient man and talked out loud when his patience snapped. He officiated on Holy Thursday (when his voice served him), sometimes on Good Friday, but never on Holy Saturday, leaving that to the Prior or Pastor. He found delight in splendid vestments, mitres, slippers, but only a wooden crozier. That crozier of gilded wood may still be seen in St. Anselm's Church, New York City" ("Miscellaneous Notes," n.p.). The abbot would begin pontificating on the appointed days at five or six o'clock in the morning. When he was in Rome, he was impressed by the liturgical solemnities, and was happy when ecclesiastics there told him to wear his pectoral all the time. From St. Mary's in Trastevere he wrote in 1880: "I was assisted, had a special candle—everything grand." He was particularly impressed by the fact that all dignitaries were obligated to wear rochet, mantelletta, mozetta and biretta "all at the same time."

22 Concerning these bricks, Father Louis Traufler stated in an interview on 7 March 1954: "Abbot Alexius saw the clay and wood around St. John's and he didn't see why money couldn't be saved by making bricks at home. Laborers received fifty cents a day, or twenty cents with board. The first clay was obtained along the Watab where the log house blacksmithy stood. When that became too sandy, at the time the church was built, new clay was found east of Caesar's Bay in the hollow behind Observatory Hill. It was hauled up to the grounds of the tennis courts in front of the institution where the brick yard was. The St. John's bricks were called 'slop bricks' because they were made of wet, sloppy clay slapped into a frame of four bricks. The forms were made by Bro. Francis and that is why the bricks were made in different shapes, some with round noses, etc. The kilns took two weeks to build and three weeks to burn. The burning had to be continuous and was done with wood. Thousands of cords of wood were always standing

ready on the seminarians' recreation grounds. The making of that brick was an achievement. The first two abbots broke from the tradition of building in stone because buildings were needed fast, and the cheapest building was of brick. They forgot about art and concentrated on getting a roof overhead."

23 Present were four bishops, three abbots, forty-six clergy and a large gathering of guests. Abbot Wimmer consecrated the altar of the Blessed Virgin; Abbot Innocent Wolf, that of St. Benedict. Bishop John Ireland preached a dedicatory sermon, while the Reverend Dr. Otto Zardetti, subsequently the first bishop of St. Cloud, spoke in German. Bishops Grace and Krautbauer were also present for the ceremony.

While the church was going up, Abbot Alexius also assisted the Sisters of St. Benedict's Convent, St. Joseph, to enlarge their physical plant. The Sisters had been living in a shabby frame house since 1863, despite their growth through the years and the fact that they had been conducting an academy for girls. Abbot Alexius furnished bricks, materials and assistance to raise a convent in the rear of the parish church and off the main street of the village. The community chapter on 24 November 1883 unanimously voted to cancel the $12,647.61 indebtedness of the Sisters to the abbey for this building. Abbot Wimmer also expressed his pleasure that the Sisters had been aided in this way, and explained again at great length why he had used Ludwig's money for the purchase of St. John's land rather than for the Sisters in 1857. Other assistance to the Benedictine Sisters during these years included a donation of $2,000 on 23 October 1886 for materials used in the building of the Industrial school for Indian girls at St. Joseph by Father Gregory and the Brothers; loans of $9,340.19 on 3 October 1887 for the Lamborn Hospital in Bismarck, and $34,070.83 for St. Mary's Hospital, Duluth, dedicated on 3 April 1888.

24 Three altars of white marble with wooden superstructure stood against the west wall of the apse and transept. Above the high altar was a large canvas from the Lamprecht Studios, New York, representing St. Benedict in glory and surrounded by eminent saints of his Order, which was sent to the Benedictine abbey in Seoul, Korea, when the church was renovated.

The statuary was from the Mayer Studios in Munich of which the best was a group representing the death of St. Benedict. It is preserved as a basement corridor shrine in the monastery. The windows were from the Misch Studios in Chicago. Three Catherine-wheels or Rose windows, two in the transept and one above the main entrance to the church, contained series of symbols in circular fields. The façade window contained symbols of the *Rule* of St. Benedict, while the two transept windows held Old and New Testament representations. Other nave and transept windows contained pictures of Benedictine saints and doctors of the western Church.

25 *Special Laws of the State of Minnesota* (St. Paul, 1883), p. 233.

26 Wimmer to Edelbrock, St. Vincent, 17 July 1884. Cf. Cologne *Volkszeitung*, 6 August 1883, for a complimentary appraisal of the work of Abbot Alexius.

27 ACSB, Edelbrock to Sister Gertrude, St. John's, 27 June 1878.

28 *Fourteenth Annual Catalogue of the Officers, Faculty and Students of St. John's College* (St. Paul, 1881), p. 4. In this same issue a salutatory ode to the memory of the pioneers of St. John's was entered by Hon. John L. Wilson, pioneer legislator who secured the institution's charter.

29 In an interview of 7 December 1952, Father Roman stated: "The school was successful while it lasted. The boys were good and obedient in every respect. One thing I would like to mention about them is that they were good penmen. You bet your life. In calligraphy they would write with their left hand as well as with their right hand. They were ambidexterous, that's a fact. Some of them were pretty good artists, especially in drawing animals, trees, lakes. The hardest thing was to teach them the ABC's. They did not like to go to school and it took a good deal of coaxing. The parents would ask the children if they wanted to go to school, and if they said yes, they went; if they said no, they didn't. The Indian father had nothing to say about the child. When I asked an Indian father, he said: 'You better ask the old woman'; if I asked the mother and she said no, they didn't go. But from 1900 the government made schooling compulsory . . . I had to make a monthly report on the Indians. I had to weigh them on their arrival, and in the monthly report it was almost unbelievable that an Indian boy had gained fifteen pounds. The government told me that I should be particularly careful to see that the Indians learned to speak English as much as possible. Still some of them would use their own language when playing baseball, and the inspector told me about that. Abbot Alexius used to like to see them hit the ball and run."

30 Hipelius to Edelbrock. St. Vincent, 20 February 1878.

31 In August of 1873 several Irish-born Benedictines decided to begin an English-speaking Abbey. This monastery was canonically erected as St. Malachy's Priory at Creston, Iowa, as an Irish-American house for Benedictines recruited from the existing monasteries. Father Augustine Burns, who had come west with Abbot Alexius, was the first prior. Abbot Alexius was not sympathetic with this venture because he felt that all nationalities should live together in monasteries undistinguished by nationality characteristics. But Abbot Boniface supported the undertaking, as he later encouraged the Bohemian foundation at St. Procopius Abbey, and told Abbot Alexius: "In the interest of the Order, we must give the Irish a chance . . . They will aid in spreading the Order in America, Canada, and Ireland, and after a few years bring salvation to many Irish" (St. Vincent, 29 December 1875; 13 February 1876). The Reverends Eugene Phelan, O.S.B., and Placid McKeever, O.S.B., joined the Creston priory from St. Vincent and St. Benedict's. But Prior Augustine's career was very brief; he died of apoplexy in Burlington, Iowa, on 12 August 1874. Commenting on his sudden death, the *Northwestern Chronicle* for 19 August 1874 wrote: "His life on the mission was one of trial and great hardships, for he had a vast territory to attend to (in Minnesota), and his name will ever remain a household word in the northwestern portion of the State. How the inhabitants of the scattered Irish settlements extending from Big Woods to the frontier of the State looked and longed for his coming. He was not alone their spiritual Father, but he was their kind friend, scolding, sometimes encouraging them, but never parting with them without having done some good. In many a home in this State, these poor words of tribute to the memory of one so beloved will be read through with blinding tears, and none will weep more sincerely than the converts he received into the

Church while on the mission here. Plain and simple, he still possessed a magnetism that drew people toward him and, under God, he has been the means of making many converts."

From 1873 to 1887 the monks of this priory worked in six Iowa counties. They sent their candidates to St. Vincent and St. Benedict's for training, and aimed at establishing a college at Creston. This monastic undertaking did not flourish, however, and after 1887 is no longer mentioned in the *Catholic Directory*. The parish continues today in charge of Benedictines from St. Benedict's Abbey.

32 *Northwestern Chronicle*, 18 August 1887.

33 Abbot A l e x i u s Edelbrock, O.S.B., *Association of St. Benedict* (St. Paul, 1887); *Bruderschaft des Heil. Benedictus* (St. Paul, 1887).

34 Abbot A l e x i u s Edelbrock, O.S.B., *Die 1400-jaehrige Jubel-Feier des heiligen Benedictus, Patriarchen aller Moenche des Abendlandes am 4., 5. und 6. April, 1880* (Collegeville, 1880); *The 14th Centennial Jubilee Festival In Honor of Saint Benedict, Patriarch of Western Monks. April 4th, 5th and 6th. A.D. 1880* (Collegeville, 1880).

35 The St. Paul *Dispatch* of 25 May 1879 announced the publication of a musical composition by the Reverend Leo Winter, O.S.B., of St. John's, entitled *The Beautiful Watab*, a series of waltzes published by J. A. Weide of St. Paul.

36 A handy one-volume summary of Benedictine history was prepared by the Reverend Stephen Hilpisch, O.S.B., *Das Benediktinertum Im Wandel Der Zeiten* (St. Ottilien, 1950). In the last two chapters, pp. 169–92, an up-to-date account of nineteenth and twentieth century Benedictine restoration throughout the world is outlined.

37 By 1881 Abbot Alexius had 6,000 prints on the market of St. Benedict, St. Scholastica, and the Death of St. Benedict, to retail at fifty cents each. They were the first Benedictine reproductions in the United States. He told Wimmer on 1 March 1883 that he believed they could not be surpassed, but Wimmer thought they were too large. The next year the St. John's chapter voted to establish its own novitiate at home rather than sending novices to a common novitiate at St. Vincent. Abbot Maurus Wolter, O.S.B., of the abbey of Beuron (1863), whom Edelbrock had met at Monte Cassino, ad-vised him to make this move. Abbot Alexius also felt that the growth of the Order demanded such a move, and it would be a means of deepening community spirit. He hoped that Wimmer would understand, not be offended, and not allow this move to effect their intimate bond of unity in the American Cassinese Congregation. Abbot Innocent Wolf, O.S.B., agreed with him and desired to have that abbey's novices also trained at home. Wimmer agreed to this development, but at first some monks of the motherhouse did not.

38 A pair of young trotting horses was the abbot's pleasure, and he always kept a team for his personal use. He had nine bells outside his study, and would ring one for the prior, two for the vice-president of the school, etc. Nine were for Father George to bring in the horses, and when he would come out of his room at four o'clock in the afternoon and ring those nine bells, it was a signal that the abbot was about to leave. He would sometimes take the Fathers who were going to St. Cloud down to the afternoon train at Collegeville, place them on the train, and then proceed to race the train to St. Cloud with his horses. As the train had to stop at St. Joseph for passengers, mail and cream cans, when the priests would come into the rectory of St. Mary's parish, they would find the abbot there waiting for them and laughing heartily. He was a hard driver and had a number of runaways and spills. On 8 May 1884, he had a near-fatal accident in St. Joseph when his horses ran away, throwing him out of the carriage and under the horses' hoofs. He grasped one of the wheels and held to it as he was dragged two blocks through the village. One of the horse's hoofs hit his head and the wheel went over his body. He told Abbot Wimmer: "I lost one gallon of blood and was laid up for a few days." A month later he had another runaway, but jumped just as the buggy was upset. All of his longer journeys were by train. One night because of a schedule mixup, he slept on the floor of the depot in Detroit Lakes with his overcoat under his head as a pillow. Another time he was stranded in Dakota on a stalled train during a blizzard; once he was stranded at West Union and came home, to the community's astonishment, in a box car.

39 Abbot Alexius inserted an appeal for Brothers to join the community in several papers. In this characteristic

paragraph he stated in no uncertain terms what he expected: "I have previously entered several lines in the newspapers in order to obtain Brothers for my abbey. I again send out my invitation to those who intend to join the Order of St. Benedict, and to work and worship in the same. The Brother of the Order has the best opportunity to do good by helping to spread the faith and by joining in honoring God. He can live quietly and once for all in peace leave the world. Happy is he who understands the sublimity of this state, and doubly happy is one who is called to it by God! It is necessary, however, that I state which persons have no business in the Order. There is no place here first for cripples, prattlers, lazy fellows, dissatisfied characters, those who quarrel with God and the world. Second, those who have given their best years to the world and are almost as old as Methusala. Persons are needed here who are sound of body and soul, who are able and willing to work. They should not be over thirty years or at least not over thirty-five years of age. Third, those who love prayer and God and value the salvation of their souls higher than the almighty dollar, are welcome. May God, from whom the will as well as the accomplishment comes, grant that this invitation bear abundant fruit" (*Baltimore Katholische Volkszeitung,* 3 March 1877). Cf. also Brother Thomas Whitaker, O.S.B., "The Brothers of St. John's" *The Scriptorium,* XIII (April, 1953), 38–53; XIII (December, 1953), 71–89; XIV (December, 1954), 35–55.

40 "Autobiography" n.p. Father Louis Traufler, O.S.B., remembers that candidates helped construct these buildings, and since there was a shortage of hammers, the abbot passed out axes and hatchets with which to pound nails.

41 "Miscellaneous Notes on Priests and Missions," n.p.

42 Haid to Edelbrock, Belmont, N.C., 1 May 1888; Conrad to Edelbrock, Conception, Missouri, 13 December 1886; Wimmer to Edelbrock, St. Vincent, 21 January 1886. The St. Cloud *Journal Press* for 18 October 1888 carries an article on St. John's on the occasion of a visit to the institution by the faculty of the St. Cloud Teachers College. Here the "immense buildings" are praised and it is asserted: "The Institution is in a flourishing condition, being one of the largest and

most successful of its kind in the West."

While this building activity was in progress during these years, Abbot Alexius donated to charitable causes to a surprising degree. He assisted such endeavors as the Sacred Heart Mission in Oklahoma's Indian Territory under the direction of French Benedictines; the Sisters of Charity in Ballaghaderin, County Mayo, Ireland; Father Damien's Leper Colony of Kalawao, Molakai, for which he had the students take up collections. But the most consistent charitable work carried on by the second abbot was the harboring and rehabilitation of diocesan priests who had disciplinary problems. Abbot Wimmen had agreed at the II Plenary Council of Baltimore in 1866 to assist the American bishops in this difficult responsibility, and opened the doors of his monastery to all who were sent. St. John's carried on the tradition started by St. Vincent, and during these years priests lived at St. John's from such dioceses as Brooklyn, Pittsburgh, Cleveland, Peoria, Fort Wayne, Marquette, Milwaukee, LaCrosse, Green Bay, St. Paul, Vicariate of the Dakotas, Omaha, Denver, Monterey-Los Angeles, and Dublin. Abbot Alexius took a personal interest in their problems, visited them regularly in their quarters on the third floor of his new quadrangle, and worked assiduously to have them re-accepted by a bishop. His correspondence files contain many copies of recommendations he wrote for such priests. At the same time Abbot Alexius felt that religious houses conducting schools were not the proper places for suspended priests. He recommended to Archbishop James Gibbons before the III Plenary Council of Baltimore that contemplative monasteries would be best qualified to conduct an institution for priests (AAB, Collegeville, 29 August 1884). As nothing definite was accomplished in this matter at the council, St. John's continued to supply this service.

43 ALMV, Seidenbusch to Archbishop Gregor Scherr, St. Cloud, 8 July 1875; 20 July 1877; Seidenbusch to Ludwig Lebling, St. Cloud, 15 February 1876; 27 July 1879; 2 July 1883; Seidenbusch to Archbishop Anton Steichele, St. Cloud, 20 February 1879; 20 May 1880; Seidenbusch to Otto Kagerer, St. Cloud, 5 January 1881; 8 February 1887.

44 An example of Bishop Seidenbusch's uncritical charity occurred

when he accepted the Reverend Pierre Alphonse Seguin, formerly of the Archdiocese of Montreal, from which he had been expelled by Archbishop Langevin. Archbishop Ireland, after consulting Langevin, refused to accept him at St. Paul, but Bishop Seidenbusch accepted him into the vicariate after Seguin imposed a pitiful story upon him. He immediately resumed his unpriestly conduct and Seidenbusch was forced to expel him. Seguin then became an ex-priest at Pepin, Wisconsin, and Amboy and Good Turner, Minnesota. His final act was to publish an anti-Catholic paper at Monroe, Wisconsin.

45 AASV, St. John's, 24 December 1886. Bishop Seidenbusch's trouble with the three French-speaking priests came to a head in 1887. These three priests, the Reverends John Baptiste Genin of Duluth, A. Lemay of Belle Prairie and Telesphor Vandry of Little Falls, caused difficulties in the vicariate for years. Through the medium of a fellow Frenchman, the Reverend Charles Boucher, pastor of St. Louis Church, Fond du Lac, Wisconsin, they carried their cases to Rome, and Cardinal Simeoni requested Cardinal Gibbons to investigate the difficulties and report to Rome. Gibbons made arrangements to hold this investigation at St. Paul en route to the Pacific Coast where he journeyed in October of 1887. Bishop Seidenbusch told Gibbons on July 22 that he would calmly await the arrival of the cardinal, detailed some of the wrongs he had suffered at the hands of these priests, while declaring: "A quire of foolscap would not suffice to relate all their ugly doings." Genin was the only one of the three who was incardinated into the diocese, and it was Genin who had prevailed upon Seidenbusch to admit the others on trial. Bishop Seidenbusch, in his kindness, had tried to remonstrate when their parishes were necessarily divided, etc. While Abbot Alexius was serving as administrator, Genin was summoned before an ecclesiastical court and his faculties subsequently suspended. The metropolitan, Archbishop Heiss of Milwaukee, sent Genin to New Melleray Trappist Monastery in Iowa, and when Gibbons came to St. Paul, he studied all sides of the question. In the Archives of the Archdiocese of Baltimore, box 83 is filled with documents relating to various phases of the Minnesota trouble, but no copy of Gibbons' report of his findings to the Holy See can be found. However, Gibbons did tell Bishop Haid that Bishop Seidenbusch "had succeeded in showing his innocence" (Haid to Edelbrock, Belmont, N.C., 9 November 1888). All three priests subsequently left the vicariate.

46 The Reverend Vincent Tegeder, O.S.B., has written two thorough historical essays on Benedictine effort in the north central region from 1856–90, while placing the work of these pioneers in its proper significance on the American frontier. They are used as a basic source here. Cf. "The Benedictines in Frontier Minnesota," *MH,* XXXII (March, 1951), 34–43; "Pioneer Monks," *MH,* XXXIII (Summer, 1952), 53–60.

47 Lewis F. Crawford, *History of North Dakota* (3 vols.; New York, 1930), I, 263.

48 *Ibid.,* I, 261.

49 Cf. Albert Kleber, O.S.B., *op. cit.,* pp. 261–328, for a complete treatment of the life and career of Abbot and Bishop Marty.

50 Cf. also Foffa to Edelbrock, Bismarck, 19 August 1878. During the first year after his election, Abbot Alexius had undertaken a similar project in the state of Wisconsin. Bishop Michael Heiss had offered two parishes in his diocese of La Crosse to the monastery: that of St. Joseph in the city of La Crosse and of St. Gabriel in Prairie du Chien. The chapter accepted this offer and Benedictines were sent to these two parishes from 1876–80. At Prairie du Chien the Christian Brothers also offered St. John's College to the abbey. The development of this undertaking into a monastery, school and mission area was seriously considered during four years, but was abandoned in 1880 because it was considered too difficult to maintain. On 14 March 1880 the Society of Jesus took over St. John's College and began their Campion College at Prairie du Chien, while the bishop of La Crosse placed the parishes in charge of his diocesan clergy.

51 Cf. the two maps of Benedictine mission activity on pp. 362–65 which were prepared by the Reverend Ronald Roloff, O.S.B. Father Ronald also assembled a listing of parishes, missions, and stations served by St. John's monks from 1856–1956, which is included in Appendix IV.

52 Bismarck *Tribune,* 15 April 1885. Abbot Alexius dedicated this

hospital on the Fourth Sunday After Pentecost, 1885, and noted in his diary that the Feast of the Finding of the Holy Cross fell on the same day that year. He felt that he had found and loaded upon himself another cross, and he added: "It is hard to bear the cross, yet it leads to triumph. *Ergo: fortes estote.*"

53 St. Cloud *Times,* 30 May 1888. One year after the Bismarck hospital was opened Abbot Alexius helped the same Benedictine Sisters initiate their hospital in St. Cloud, which was blessed and dedicated to St. Benedict on 25 February 1886. At first this hospital could accommodate only twenty patients. But it served a city crisis within two months, on April 14, when a tornado swept through the St. Cloud and Sauk Rapids areas. For a complete historical account of the contribution of this hospital to central Minnesota cf. Sister Grace McDonald, O.S.B., "The Benedictine Sisters and the St. Cloud Hospital," *MH,* XXXIII (Autumn, 1953), 291–97.

54 There is no extant evidence that Abbot Alexius was a close friend of James J. Hill. Hill did give an annual gold medal for excellence in scholarship for the institution's graduation exercises, but the traditions that the two men worked together or that Hill considered donating a building to St. John's have no foundation. Abbot Alexius had a pass on the Great Northern Railroad, however, and the story persists, unsubstantiated, that the abbot asked and obtained in exchange for allowing the railroad to pass across abbey property, one year's free freight to Collegeville. During that year Abbot Alexius is supposed to have brought in and stock-piled building materials. Abbot Alexius thanked Jim Hill on 5 April 1880 "for all the favors shown us," and informed the railroad magnate that he had consented to cooperate in efforts to settle central Minnesota "with decent people." Abbot Alexius and his closest friend and fellow novice, Father Ulric Northman, worked for years in arranging land contacts for settlers, and the abbey sent a steady stream of invitations to European papers for immigrants.

55 Duluth *Tribune,* Clippings XIV, 144, 145, 146.

NOTES TO CHAPTER SIX

1 "Declaratio in Cap. III," *Constitutiones,* p. 4: "Causas graviores cum toto conventu, i.e., eorum, qui in monasterio praesentes sunt et commode ad capitulum vocari possunt, capitulariter expediendas esse."

2 Alexius Edelbrock, O.S.B., "Notes on the Apostolic Visitation," Rome, 1 November 1889.

3 "Declaratio in Cap. VI," *Constitutiones,* p. 14: "Singuli annuatim subeant sacram solitudinem, i.e. Exercitia Spiritualia annua: singuli in suis cellis aliisque locis congruis per unam Septimanam agant vitam solitariam." During retreats from 1886–88, Holy Mass, Way of the Cross and devotions were held in common. Abbot Alexius stated that many of the community expressed themselves as well pleased with this type of retreat and not one had disapproved before the Visitation took place.

4 "Notes on the Apostolic Visitation," Rome, 1 November 1889. Abbot Alexius maintained to the end of his life that he never made any trip that was not for monastery business, and that he never had a vacation. Father Roman Homar stated in an interview of 5 December 1952 of Abbot Alexius: "Often he was on a train all night and Father George who was his 'taxi driver' would go after him at four o'clock in the morning. He would offer Mass after traveling all night. Another man would not have done this." Father Alexius Hoffmann also records: "He would read Mass daily in the choir chapel or in the parish churches when he was outside. After his *gratiarum actio* he would go to the refectory and break his fast with a cup of coffee and a slice of buttered bread. Then he would go up to his room, sit down aside of his table and say the Rosary (I saw this ever so many times). Then he was ready for routine work."

5 The building achievement of Abbot Alexius speaks for itself. During his fourteen year administration he inaugurated seven projects besides the new buildings and church at St. John's itself. For these endeavors he expended $257,235.28, which when broken down include $11,665.14 on Indian missions at White Earth; $34,967.75 on St. Alexius Priory, West Union; $59,048.41 on St. Clement's Priory in Duluth; $41,180.11 on real estate and

414

Lamborn Hospital in Bismarck; $54,-662.04 on new buildings at St. John's; $37,509.52 on the abbey church; $18,-199.51 on steam heat installation at St. John's. The average annual income from the university was around $9,000 and from the missions $19,000. This striking building achievement was made possible by personal enterprise of the abbot over and above normal institutional income. As Abbot Alexius told Abbot Frowin of Conception Abbey on 3 March 1886: "I have been very lucky in making investments." Such investments included the purchase of a former roller skating rink in Minneapolis; 112 acres in St. Paul which included 6 blocks along Snelling Avenue, Hague Avenue, Herschel Street and Division Street; a block and several lots in Duluth; a hotel and 24 lots in Bismarck; 8 lots in St. Cloud; and 5,433.13 acres in Stearns, Anoka, Douglas, Todd, Winona and Otter Tail counties. All profits that he realized from sale of these properties were immediately used in the establishment and construction of his far-flung charitable and educational projects for religion and society in the Northwest. Neither he personally nor St. John's utilized any of this income for other purposes.

6 Alexius Edelbrock, O.S.B., "Day Book Notes," 7 May 1889. In his defense to Cardinal Simeoni, Edelbrock stated: "The time which I spent on the different missions, the sermons which I preached there, the confessions which I heard there and the many other duties which I performed there, also go to show that the Fathers on the missions are not left to themselves. I lived and acted as every other superior, and what is here affirmed of me, might be said of every other prelate. To say that the Fathers on the missions are left entirely to themselves also gravely reflects on the respective Bishop, as the Fathers on the missions stand under the Bishop. Now, if the Bishop does his duty, they are never entirely left to themselves. But why blame the abbot for any neglect of which the Bishop may have been guilty? If this incrimination affects me in anyway, then it would also seem to affect Mgr. Ireland with equal force, because many of my Fathers were and still are in his diocese. The Archbishop is not guilty, nor am I."

7 Abbot Alexius denied the assertion that he did not give adequate attention to spiritual matters, and wrote to Cardinal Simeoni: "Do I not say my prayers, morning and evening? So I am made to appear. In self-defense I may be allowed to say, that I say my morning and evening prayers. I recite my Breviary daily, make my meditation daily, say Holy Mass daily. Besides, I have heard confessions many times and in many different churches: I have preached, on an average, from two to three times each month for the last fourteen years, both at home and in different missions; have made several converts, have conducted retreats, etc., etc. I have done all the work usually done by pastors in charge of souls; Bishops do no more. And yet it is alleged in this Visitation that I gave no attention whatever to spiritual matters. How is such a statement possible?" Abbot Alexius went on to explain that because of his throat trouble and bronchitis his attendance at choir had been irregular since 1880 and that he had offered to resign at both General Chapters of 1881 and 1884. But Archabbot Wimmer insisted that he do not resign, exempted him from attending choir, and the Fathers in the monastery had requested him in writing to save his throat by not attending choir. Despite Wimmer's dispensation, he had attended choir whenever his health and duties permitted. The abbot's correspondence reveals him carrying on religious discussions with George Eley of Monroe, Wisconsin, giving further instructions to the authoress and convert Minnie Mary Lee, and being the main inspiration for the conversion to Catholicism of Henry C. Waite, St. Cloud lawyer and state senator.

8 Wimmer to Edelbrock, St. Vincent, 2 June 1882.

9 Zilliox to Edelbrock, New Munich, 27 August 1887. Abbot Alexius was deeply hurt that his old friend should act in this manner, as he said: "I have tried to build up with the material at my disposition, did the best I could, but failed to satisfy some persons sanctimoniously inclined" (Edelbrock to Leo Winter, Collegeville, 19 November 1887). Zilliox insisted he acted as he did because Archabbot Boniface had requested him to send a report, but Wimmer's request concerned Abbot Alexius' difficulties with suspended monks, not with a general critique such as Zilliox proceeded to make. When the movement against Abbot Alexius grew in momentum Zilliox

then divorced himself from its course and expressed satisfaction that a petition of defense was drawn up by the Fathers in the monastery, although he wrote a letter of recommendation for Father Othmar Erren to Rome. He returned East and died after a lingering illness on 31 December 1890. Abbot Innocent Wolf requested Prior Norbert on 30 April 1888: "You would do me and even our whole Congregation a favor, if you would give me the facts about Abbot James' interfering in your Abbey. Abbot Alexius complained of it orally, but never mentioned particulars. I would want them to show the rest of the Abbots how careful they must be with Abbot James, who reminds me vividly of the 16th century Reformers, who spoke so much of reforming the head, the Pope, the Cardinals and those Bishops who supported the Pope. To reform radically, they proposed to suppress the monasteries, etc. Abbot James is such a reformer: instead of keeping the rule himself, and saving his own soul, he disclaims against Superiors: gets all, who like to be rid of the yoke of obedience to bring charges against the good discipline, etc. My blood boils when I think of such pharisaism, hypocrisy and malice: and yet such persons give themselves a halo of sanctity."

10 Edelbrock to Lawler, Collegeville, 2 March 1882. Often Abbot Alexius' choice of words was sarcastic, brusque and typical of frontier life. He was told at different times that he used language "worthy of a ferry-boat boy, but not a prelate" (Burchard Bauernschubert, O.S.B., Wabasha, 26 December 1884); "haughty, blaming words full of ridicule and scorn" (Urban Fischer, O.S.B., St. Cloud, 3 September 1887); "you do not ask as a priest, but as a hard-hearted business man, and at that a poor one" (John Heinz, St. Paul, 29 March 1882).

11 AASPOW, Edelbrock to Smith, Collegeville, 7 August 1888. Concerning Erren, Abbot Innocent Wolf wrote to Prior Norbert on 30 April 1888: "Am not astonished at what you say about Rev. Othmar: I am more astonished that he did not kick sooner: he abused his talents as long as I know him, to give vent to his passions and had no regard whatever for authority, but feared it. When I was there at the Dedication of the Church (1882), I expressed myself publicly to him in that sense in the Community Room: I

was thought rather severe, but I thought a warning would not hurt."

12 Cf. New York *Freeman's Journal,* "Benedictines and Beards," 2 January 1885; "Puritans Who Wink at Roller Rinks," 31 January 1885; "Borealis on Prohibition," 27 March 1885; "Borealis from Moorhead," 25 October 1885.

13 "To the Right Reverend Alexius Edelbrock," St. John's, 29 June 1887. Father Vincent repented and was reinstated; Father Ambrose, after assailing the characters of both Abbot Alexius and Bishop Seidenbusch, acknowledged that he had "committed a great wrong," and was allowed to go to Mandan. Father Bede, after several trials and re-instatements, left the Order and was incardinated into the diocese of Oregon City.

14 AASPOW, Wolf and Pfraengle to Smith, Atchison, Kansas, 6 September 1888.

15 AASM, Marty to Wimmer, Yankton, 8 August 1887, copy; AASPOW, Marty to Edelbrock, Yankton, 25 August 1887, copy. Wimmer told Zilliox: "If Bishop Marty wants to defend Lethert let him have the onus of it," as the demonstrable facts of Father Ambrose's case were overwhelmingly against him. Abbot Innocent Wolf took an even stronger position against Bishop Marty when he stated on 7 May 1888 to Abbot Alexius: "I know Bishop Marty will not be deceived again by his seeming kindness. I had to deal with him in regard to students and candidates, and know that he has no consideration for any superior. Bishop Fink had some experiences in that line too." On 26 May 1888 Wolf again wrote to Edelbrock: "It is nothing extraordinary on the part of Bishop Marty to accept any accusation, and that from anyone, although he had many a lesson already."

16 AASPOW, Wolf to Smith, Atchison, 7 August 1888.

17 Marty to Erren, Yankton, 25 July 1888. Cf. also Zardetti to Hofbauer, Yankton, 6 May 1888; Marty to Erren, Yankton, 2 August 1888; Zardetti Memorandum to Erren, n.d. Erren kept a diary account of his trip to Rome from 1 August–28 December 1888. Therein he lists those who financed his undertakings: Bishop Marty; two friends, Frank Schlick of St. Paul and George Schaefer of Albany; Father Cornelius Wittmann; and his mother from whom he borrowed $300.

On the inside of this diary under date of 26 July 1888 Erren wrote: "Bishop Marty; no canon law ever taught in St. John's. Remark in Rome. Get copy of Holy Rule with Statutes. Aug. 7. Archbp (Ireland) in correspondence with Bp. Marty will surely arrange letter of introduction to Card. Simeoni: will write to Denis O'Connell.

Alx. 'Should the monarch prove unjust and at this time —'
Queen 'Then I must wait for justice until it come and they are happier far whose consciences may calmly wait their right.'
Schiller: *Don Carlos.* Act IV Sc. 15."

In the correspondence of Monsignor O'Connell are three letters of introduction for Erren, from Marty, Zardetti and Zilliox. Cf. ADR, Marty to O'Connell, Yankton, 10 August 1888; Zardetti to O'Connell, Yankton, 31 July 1888; Zilliox to O'Connell, St. Vincent, 6 August 1888; Zilliox to Erren, Washington, D.C., 6 August 1888.

18 AASPOW, Wolf and Pfraengle to Smith, Atchison, 6 October 1888.

19 ADR, Ireland to O'Connell, St. Paul, 4 August 1888. The career of O'Connell is detailed in *The Catholic University of America. The Rectorship of Denis J. O'Connell* (Washington, 1950).

20 Cf. *The Catholic Church and German Americans* (Milwaukee, 1953), Chapter II.

21 AASP, O'Connell to Ireland, Richmond, n.d. U. S. Ambassador to Austria, Bellamy Storer, characterized O'Connell to Archbishop Ireland as a "clever, accomplished intriguer—but an imprudent and unsafe confidant; vainglorious of his own influence and personality" (AASP, Meran, 9 December 1903).

22 AAMI, Simeoni to Heiss, Rome, 3 April 1887.

23 AASP, O'Connell to Ireland, Rome, 21 December 1887; 23 February 1888. Cf. also 16 September 1887; 15 March 1888; 13 June 1888.

24 ADR, Ireland to O'Connell, St. Paul, 11 July 1888.

25 AASP, O'Connell to Ireland, Rome, 7 August 1888. Ireland told O'Connell on 18 August 1888: "I presume you have by this time met Fr. Othmar—the Benedictine envoy. *Inter nos*, I am becoming daily more than satisfied that things are wrong among those Benedictines, and something

should be done." Seven days later the archbishop again wrote: "As to the resignation, I will not meddle much in it. I have hinted to Propaganda that religion would be benefited by it. This is an evident fact. Now I leave the future to Providence."

26 AASPOW, Edelbrock to Smith, Collegeville, 26 October 1888. O'Connell wrote to Ireland on 13 November 1888 concerning this testimonal in support of Bishop Seidenbusch: "The petition about the resignation was valued at its worth. Very prompt action was taken about the resignation."

27 Lamothe to Seidenbusch, Little Falls, 29 October 1888.

28 Bishop Seidenbusch spent the greater part of the day praying and reading in his room, or in walking in the monastery garden. His assistant, Brother Prosper, continued to care for him to the end of his life, and both Abbots Bernard and Peter encouraged the bishop's old friends among the Fathers to visit him regularly and play a game of cards. When returning from the South to St. John's in June of 1895 he suddenly and quietly died at the Benedictine parish of St. Mary in Richmond, Virginia, at the age of sixty-five years. Bishop Seidenbusch had requested that he be buried at St. John's, and in his funeral oration Bishop Marty declared of Bishop Seidenbusch:

"I never saw a man more unselfish, more humble, more loving, more patient, more forgiving and more like unto Him who has said of Himself: 'Learn of me, for I am meek and humble of heart,' than the late lamented bishop. No man possessed these attributes of charity in a more intense degree than Bishop Seidenbusch . . . Bishop Seidenbusch was the chief instrument in the hands of Divine Providence to bring about the progress of Catholicity in northern Minnesota, to lay the foundations for an edifice that is to endure. He was assisted by the priests, by his brethren, by the people, but he led with the spirit with which he was inspired, and he inspired them with that courage, that charity without which there can be no success. Therefore our hearts are filled with gratitude towards our common benefactor. We feel happy in giving him a testimony of our loving devotion; his memory will be in our hearts, and will live in our prayers."

29 "Diary," 31 August 1888.

30 AASP, Mueller to Wolf, Rome,

17 September, 3 October, 24 October, 1 November 1888.

31 Even in the midst of his troubles Abbot Alexius moved ahead in the abbey's Indian apostolate and sent Fathers Simon Lampe and Thomas Borgerding to Red Lake. Abbot Innocent Wolf congratulated him on this new undertaking and stated: "You will have to get ready for another attack of the arch-enemy, because he will try to hinder you from doing more to decrease the infernal power over the Indians. I am afraid, that if you would resign, your successors could not do so much for the Indians as you can do, because you have success in establishing houses, of which others would be afraid to think. You will not have rest in this world anyhow, and rather fight it out on the field on which you started, than be pushed out by Satan and the other evil spirits into a field where you cannot make any good use of your administrative talents . . . If we read history, we find similar cases and even worse ones, when whole monasteries were against their Superiors, and when they could do nothing else, they used even force, or appealed to the civil power. As I said last time, the old Archabbot, of happy memory, was attacked in a similar manner as you are now, and that, by those whom he had raised and favored by giving them special occasions to learn more than the rest: in his case the facts were put in such a bungling way that the Cardinal saw at once that they were not possible. In your case, the devil uses also a tool, that is very ungrateful, but more wicked—a man that can by his tongue make things appear plausible" (Atchison, 17 November, 9 December 1888).

32 AASP, O'Connell to Ireland, Rome, 17 September, 8 October, 31 October, 18 November 1888. On October 17 Erren noted in his diary: "Got a letter yesterday from Bp. Marty in which he says that as soon as I get the investigation I can come home." Marty in turn wrote to O'Connell the next day: "Rev. Othmar Erren's affair seems to be in a fair way and I feel particularly obliged to you, as you were the only one to direct and recommend him. Please accept my heartfelt thanks for your favors" (ADR, Yankton, 18 October 1888).

33 AASP, O'Connell to Ireland, Rome, 21 November 1888. Bishop Marty wanted Erren to spend the win-

ter months at the bishop's mother abbey of Einsiedeln, Switzerland, before returning to the United States, both because of the advanced season for an ocean voyage and because he wished him to have a sojourn of a few months in an old, genuine Benedictine monastery "which would be for him and his monastery of immeasurable benefit and advantage." Marty told the Dean at Einsiedeln that Erren, who was "close to my heart," had just "obtained a decision from the Propaganda that he and his confrères should not any more tolerate many years of oppression from their abbot who is a thorough or rather improper financier." But Father Chrysostom Foffa, O.S.B., informed Bishop Seidenbusch that the abbot of Einsiedeln would not even allow Erren to offer Holy Mass there despite the fact that he came fortified with a document from Marty that he was *nulla censura irretitus.* Foffa said: "May God have mercy and pity on this young priest—so young yet so hard-hearted and upset. Through Zardetti who visited us we heard the entire story also what part Bishop Marty had in it" (AASM, Marty to Father Ildephonse, Yankton, 18 October 1888; Foffa to Seidenbusch, Einsiedeln, 13 January 1889). Bishop Marty's brother, Monsignor Martin Marty, Chaplain of the Swiss Guards at the Vatican with whom the bishop had directed Father Othmar to reside in Rome, also had a somewhat different opinion of Erren. He told Prior Adalbert of Sant' Anselmo of the adverse impression Father Othmar had made in Rome (Edelbrock to Hofbauer, Rome, 9 July 1889).

34 Alexius Edelbrock, O.S.B., "Visitatio Apostolica," 1 April 1889. On 25 April 1889 Ireland and Marty met in St. Paul and drew up recommendations to the Propaganda that suffragan sees be placed at Winona, St. Cloud, Duluth, Sioux Falls, and Jamestown. They alone sent on *ternae* of names for these sees. Vicar General Franz Xavier Stemper and Abbot Alexius, as consultors of the Vicariate of Northern Minnesota, were not called to this meeting. Both Stemper and Edelbrock felt that Ireland and Marty had acted against the decrees of the II Council of Baltimore in not obtaining the recommendations of the consultors of the vicariate which had not yet been decreased. Abbot Alexius wrote in his diary: "Did Mgr. Ireland purposefully put off the

Visitation to April 29 in order to have this meeting between himself and Mgr. Marty, exclusive of myself? I am still under a cloud and the Visitation is not finished and consequently his excuse for not saying one word to me about the new Bishops, etc., to be appointed. Is this fair? Does it look as if Mgr. Ireland were impartial? I feel sure that his feelings towards me are unfriendly. His *modus agendi* permits of no other interpretation."

It was all the more difficult for Abbot Alexius to realize that Archbishop Ireland was not favorably disposed toward him because years previously they had worked together on a cordial basis and Ireland had often been at St. John's. Ireland and Edelbrock had disagreed at times on parish matters, but each time they had expressed their opinions openly to one another. Nor had Ireland been unfriendly to the Benedictines. In 1885 Prior Aidan Gasquet of Downside had written a new introduction to Montalembert's *Monks of the West* in which he explained the nature of each Benedictine monastery as a family and not a regiment of an army under a general as more modern Orders were organized. Ireland wrote to Gasquet about his introduction: "How much you do say! I never before understood the grandeur, the wisdom of St. Benedict and of the Rule which he inculcated. Better far, in my opinion, for Religious Orders and for the Church, if the Benedictine Rule had remained more than it has, the type of religious life. One remark you made struck me much—when you speak of the relations of the monasteries with the Episcopate, the result of these relations being that the religious life, so acted out, was an element of activity, of strength in the Church, without assuming to be or appearing to be the Church. No one can be a Catholic without admiring the 'religious life,' and without according to it a large place in the Church's action: but there are Catholics who take objection to the religious life, when, as in the case of the Society of Jesus, it aims consciously or unconsciously to be the whole Church" (Shane Leslie, *Cardinal Gasquet* [New York, 1953], p. 34).

35 Alexius Edelbrock, O.S.B., "Visitatio Apostolica," 3 and 4 May 1889. In this protest the Fathers wanted it reported to Rome that Father Othmar had declared: "Two cents and a few lines to Bp. Marty will get me another

place if punished by the Superior of St. John's Abbey."

36 Wolf to Edelbrock, Atchison, 18 February 1889.

37 Haid to Edelbrock, Belmont, N.C., 22 April, 25 August, 22 December 1888; 12 January, 11 April 1889. Cf. also Wimmer to Seidenbusch, St. Vincent, 2 August 1887; Hintenach to Edelbrock, St. Vincent, 17 April 1888; AASB, Pfraengle to Wolf, Newark, 26 July 1889.

38 Edelbrock to Hofbauer, St. Paul, 14 June 1889. In his official memorial on the apostolic visitation submitted to Cardinal Simeoni, Abbot Alexius also wrote that Archbishop Ireland had said to him: "Rome must uphold you. It — Rome — went against the Bishop of Cleveland, against Bishop Krautbauer of happy memory, etc. If Rome went against me in one decision, I would be unable to rule my diocese. This Visitation — I admit — did you no good. The malcontents wanted just such an occasion. Do not resign in Rome, even if requested (This he repeated several times). Bp. Seidenbusch should not have resigned in Rome. If you should be asked to resign, then do so after your return. Rome ought to support you strongly, or else you ought not to return, because of the opposition of those Fathers" (Notes on Apostolic Visitation, Rome, 1 November 1889, copy).

39 Edelbrock to Hofbauer, Rome, 9 July 1889.

40 Edelbrock to Hofbauer, Rome, 22 July, 24 September, 20 October 1889. While traveling from abbey to abbey in Italy and Germany Abbot Alexius took notes on items of monastic observance for which he had been attacked. He observed that at San Callisto and Monte Cassino each monk had formerly made his yearly retreat by himself, but that a retreat master was now engaged; at Beuron the monks either made retreats by themselves or one of the community gave the retreat. The Bavarian monks had parishes attached to their abbeys, and monks assisted on weekends in diocesan parishes. St. Ottilien monks and nuns worked together in charitable and religious missions in Africa with the encouragement and blessing of the Holy See.

41 AASP, O'Connell to Ireland, Rome, 23 and 31 July 1889. O'Connell also warned Ireland that the "Jesuits have beaten Apb. Salpointe all to

pieces. They also have Mons. Bourgade in a very tight place and the Vicariate will be divided to make peace." O'Connell was referring to Archbishop John Baptiste Lamy of Santa Fe, and Bishop Peter Bourgade, vicar-apostolic of Arizona.

42 Haid to Edelbrock, Belmont, N.C., 29 October 1889.

43 *Ibid.*, 1 November 1889.

44 Edelbrock to Hofbauer, Rome, 27 October, 10 November 1889.

45 AASP, O'Connell to Ireland, Rome, 24 February 1889. Cf. also ADR, Zardetti to O'Connell, Yankton, 18 March 1889. In Munich Abbot Alexius was informed that Father Zardetti had been there on his European trip presenting himself for that episcopal see.

46 AASP, O'Connell to Ireland, Rome, 8 October 1889.

47 Edelbrock to Hofbauer, Rome, 12 November 1889. On 30 November he added: "the so-called compromise comes from Mgr. O'Connell, the mouthpiece of Mgr. Ireland and Co. From this it would appear that they also are not certain of any victory. Well, a victory for either party would be injurious to religion and to immortal souls. A victim is necessary, and I am that victim. My resignation is honorable; it is not called for by my superior."

48 Palmieri wanted all the American Cassinese abbots and a majority of the St. John's community to join in a petition to the Pope stating that Abbot Alexius had been misled into resigning by erroneous statements (Palmieri to Schreiner, Rome, 27 December 1889).

49 Wolf to Edelbrock, Atchison, 10 December 1889.

50 "Notes on the Apostolic Visitation of 1889," 22 November 1889. Abbot Alexius stated to Father Francis Mershman: "When I wrote my resignation in Rome I at first gave no reason at all. I simply threw up the ship. Then Smith said to me 'you must state a reason, for otherwise your resignation will not be accepted. But don't say anything about the Visitation since your petition will have to be presented to the Holy Father, who knows nothing of it.' If Cardinal Simeoni had made me an Abbot, he could have received my resignation also, but as the Holy Father had done the act, my resignation had to be accepted by him. And therefore Smith was anxious that I

should make no mention of the Visitation" (Newark, 29 March 1890).

51 This final document of Abbot Alexius' official life at St. John's is included in Appendix V.

52 "Diary," 30 November 1889. Both Abbot Alexius and Prior Norbert agreed to pack in boxes all of the letters and documents concerning the entire visitation and resignation affair and save them as they would be "most valuable in time to come." Father Alexius Hoffmann then preserved these documents intact in the abbey archives, and even painstakingly copied a large number of them by hand so there would be duplicates available and ready for a history of St. John's.

53 AASB, Wolf to Mueller, Atchison, 29–30 June 1890. Abbot Alexius underwent other tempests en route home when the steamer La Bourgoyne, on which he was a passenger, collided at sea with the Tarridan on 5 January 1890 at two o'clock in the morning, and on January 10 was buffeted by such a storm that the vessel was despaired of for a time.

54 AASV, American Cassinese Abbots and Priors to Cardinal Simeoni, Newark, 12 February 1890.

55 AASP, Simeoni to Ireland, Rome, 28 March 1890. Cf. also AAS-POW, "Memorandum of Abbot Smith," 18 March 1890; Engel to Smith, Collegeville, 25 March 1890; Schreiner to Smith, Collegeville, 27 March 1890.

56 Engel to Edelbrock, Collegeville, 26 November 1889. Cf. also 22 October 1889.

57 *Ibid.*

58 AASB, Wolf to Mueller, Atchison, 29–30 June 1890. Abbot Innocent had notified Father Othmar in Dakota that he could not take part in the election as he was suspended, and disregarding the censure, also canonically irregular. Father Ambrose Lethert was re-instated and allowed to vote; Father Bede Northman wrote that he was no longer a Benedictine and had joined the diocese of Oregon City.

59 Wolf to Edelbrock, Atchison, 23 June 1890.

60 AASB, Wolf to Mueller, Atchison, 29–30 June 1890.

61 Schreiner to Edelbrock, Collegeville, 1 October 1890. The Rt. Rev. John L. Zaplotnik wrote a biography of Abbot Bernard in the Chicago Slovenian paper *Novi Svet* which appeared in twenty-two installments during 1948.

In this journalistic biography much attention is given to Abbot Bernard's Slovenian ancestry and his contribution to the cause of Slovenian-Americans. Locnikar was very attached to his fatherland, worked for the spiritual care of Slovenians, and invited Slovenian students to St. John's to study for the priesthood during his administration. He strove in every way possible to continue the outstanding missionary contribution which Slovenian Catholics had made to American Catholicism; first, by caring for the Slovenian settlement of Kraintown northwest of the abbey; and secondly, by sending the Reverend Cyril Zupan, O.S.B., to Colorado at the call of a Slovenian colony there.

62 Erren to Edelbrock, Conception, Missouri, 12 September 1890.

63 *Ibid.*, 3 October 1890.

64 Locnikar to Eversmann, Collegeville, 20 October 1878; ACA, Locnikar to Conrad, Collegeville, 12 September 1891.

65 Edelbrock to Locnikar, St. Leo, Florida, 28 August 1890. Abbot-elect Bernard replied to Abbot Alexius on May 12, after his election: "Well the election is over, with the result as you know. I did as you told me. I made up my mind beforehand, that whatever may come, I will say: *Ecce adsum!* I know the trouble and burden that I will have to carry. I know that I will be almost unable to bear it, but I will try to accept everything as sent by God, and I know He will strengthen my weakness. I am sure you have been informed about the proceedings of the election, how everything went off nicely and peacefully, etc. Well, if the beginning is any *presagium* of the future it will not be so very hard. But generally after the sunshine stormy days may be expected and I am afraid there will be no exception in our case. Yet whatever may come, God's will be done."

66 Locnikar to Edelbrock, St. Paul, 23 July 1890.

67 Nelson to Edelbrock, Alexandria, 18 August 1892.

68 Abbot Alexius immediately began his well-known economies and financial enterprises. He took up collections every morning and sometimes realized five cents; building fund boxes were placed at every entrance. At the same time he did much charity among the poor of the area and never turned a beggar away from the rectory door.

Whenever he gave an alms he advised the recipient: "Now if you go from door to door they are all Catholics and by the end of the block you'll have a quarter. See how quickly you'll have a dollar." Wales Avenue behind the rectory was only a muddy hole because of a creek running through the area. The abbot would announce every Sunday at Mass that the people should pick up a stone along the creek and drop it on the pathway so that they would soon have a solid walk. He visited the sick and was untiring in his zeal as a pastor, while at the same time he developed a large clientele of friends outside the parish proper, who contributed consistently to the building of the abbot's parish. Even in New York a retired abbot from Minnesota establishing a parish in the country some seven miles from the city limits was a unique figure.

69 Locnikar to Edelbrock, Collegeville, 10 October 1890; 17 January 1891.

70 AANY, Schreiner to Corrigan, Nassau, Bahama Islands, 30 March 1891; 11 May 1891. Father O'Keefe, after returning to New York, worked to establish the first Catholic chapel at West Point, where he was buried with military honors.

Literature on the Bahama Islands include an article in the *Catholic Encyclopedia,* II, 204–206, by Father Chrysostom, and an unpublished Master's dissertation at the University of Florida by Wallace Dierckx, '41, "A Historical Geography of the Bahama Islands" (Gainesville, Florida, 1952). Cf. also Kevin McCann, O.S.B., "Catholicism in the Bahamas," *The Scriptorium,* XX (Easter, 1950), 126–35; XI (March, 1951), 14–21.

71 Nassau *Guardian and Bahama Islands' Advocate and Intelligencer,* 9 April 1892. Father Paul also wrote an account for the St. Cloud *Der Nordstern.* Although Father Chrysostom never reached Watling Island on this first journey, he was shipwrecked only a short distance from it. Father Chrysostom devoted much time and energy to having the original name of San Salvador restored to Columbus' landfall and succeeded in this endeavor. He also entered into controversy with the Chicago *Tribune* which in 1891 had erected a monument on the eastern shore of San Salvador marking the spot where Columbus was supposed to have landed. Father Chrysostom organized the first expedition investigating Co-

lumbus' landing and sailed through the same waters as Columbus had done. He arrived at the conclusion, after careful study and research, that Columbus had landed on the south side of the island where he could find a lee from the ocean swells, while on the rocky eastern shore there was no safe landing beach. In 1956 the Bahamas Legislature officially restored the name of San Salvador to the island. On 25 February 1951 a scientific expedition arrived at the same conclusion as Father Chrysostom had originally made, and erected a bronze marker on Landing Beach.

72 Albury to Virgil Michel, O.S.B., Nassau, 13 March 1927.

73 *The Record,* February, 1898.

74 Hofbauer to Edelbrock, Collegeville, 12 December 1889. A biography of Bishop Zardetti has been written as an unpublished Master's dissertation at St. Louis University by Sister Mary Mark Donovan, O.S.B., "The Episcopate of The Most Reverend Otto Zardetti, First Bishop of St. Cloud, Minnesota, 1889–94" (St. Louis, 1954). Cf. also Benjamin J. Blied, "The Most Rev. Otto Zardetti, D.D., 1847–1902," *Salesianum,* XLII (April, 1947), 54–62.

75 *The Catholic Church and German Americans* (Milwaukee, 1953), pp. 154, 169, 188, 191, 208, 213.

76 Edelbrock to Hofbauer, Rome, 4 February 1890. Bishop Zardetti also began to make unfriendly statements in public about his relations with the Benedictines. Then, when Zardetti determined to build an addition to the Holy Angels Cathedral rectory, where he resided, he suggested to St. John's that they donate the bricks for this addition: "I would like to remind the Abbey that their buildings, etc., were erected from the resources of the diocese" (Zardetti to Engel, St. Cloud, 9 May 1890). While the history of the erection of St. John's building with home-made bricks and through community labor obviously proved the inaccuracy of this statement, the monastery at once complied with his request and donated 80,000 bricks made in their kilns for the bishop's episcopal residence.

77 ADSC, Otto Zardetti, "Summary report of my administration of the Diocese of St. Cloud since Nov. 21, 1889 until May 1, 1894. To My Successor."

78 AASPOW, Haid to Smith, Belmont, N.C., 2 November 1892.

79 AASV, Ledochowski to Locnikar, Rome, 28 June 1892.

80 *The Diocese of St. Cloud,* Vol. III, 1893.

81 Cf. fn. 77. On 15 January 1894 it was suddenly announced that the bishop of St. Cloud had been named archbishop of Bucharest, Roumania. On March 4 Zardetti wrote Locnikar: "All my troubles are taken away. I have been relieved of my office. I always wanted to be a friend of St. John's, never did anything that I thought would hurt the abbey." In his farewell sermon on Pentecost Sunday at the cathedral he stated: "Others have laid the foundations. Others will build up and finish the work. I only laid the water table." Zardetti took charge of the metropolitan see of Bucharest on 8 December 1894 and by June of 1895, after repeated requests, his resignation had been accepted by the Holy See. No research has been made on the exact reasons for this development. Zardetti was then named a titular archbishop and acted as a Roman consultor until his death on 10 May 1902.

82 *Der Wanderer,* 4 July 1894. Cf. also Titus Thole, O.S.B., "Alles ist Verloren in Gottes Namen," *The Scriptorium,* XIII (December, 1953), 31–41.

83 *Der Wanderer,* 4 July 1894.

84 Locnikar to Maehren, Stillwater, 6 October 1894.

85 "Miscellaneous Notes," n.p.

NOTES TO CHAPTER SEVEN

1 ACA, Engel to Conrad, St. John's, 3 December 1894. Bishop Leo Haid said of this election: "I can well recall the earnest countenances, bowed heads and trembling hands as ballot after ballot was dropped into the urn. Every detail prescribed was carefully obeyed. At last the name of the chosen one was announced, and there was joy in every face except one. Father Peter, pale and trembling, begged his brothers not to impose the heavy burden on his shoulders. But all insisted. Bitterly weeping, almost angry, his appeal was in vain. He finally, though most reluctantly, bowed to the will of his brothers and rejoiced their hearts by acquiescing in their choice" (*The Record,* 1920). Abbot-elect Peter wrote in his diary on the night of this election: "How strange everything appears! I feel like one banished from the society of my

confrères and left all to myself — so lonesome and forsaken."

2 "Historical Sketch," 30 July 1904.

3 Archives of the Archabbey of Beuron, Germany, "Viaggio Americano 1910–11," 1 October 1910.

4 A large number of the prints in this book were made by Abbot Peter and preserved with loving care on glass negatives. The number of prints preserved in the abbey archives totals around ten thousand. Abbot Peter's work was continued by Fathers Fridolin Tembreull, Luke Fink, Edmund and Raymond Basel, Damian Baker, Arthur Danzl, Lambert Weckwerth, Angelo Zankl, Abbot Baldwin Dworschak and Henry Anderl. Cf. Hugh Witzman, O.S.B., "St. John's Studio," *The Scriptorium* XI (March, 1951), 66–73.

5 "Notes," n.p.

6 During Christmas vacation of 1914 Father Hilary Doerfler purchased a wireless apparatus, and during the following May steel towers, eighty feet high, were erected north of the science hall, as well as another tower on the science hall itself. After these towers were extended by another fifteen feet, good reception was achieved, and the time signals sent out by the federal government's station at Arlington, Virginia, were obtained. Messages were also sent out, the first being to Melrose on 18 December 1915 to inform the natives of the defeat their high school basketball team had suffered at the hands of the Johnnies. An amateur radio club was formed and messages were sent to all parts of the United States and Canada by St. John's Station 9XT. In 1923 a radio-phone was added so verbal as well as code messages could be sent, and the first program received was a concert from Schenectady, New York, which came in so loud "that the listeners could hear it distinctly fifty feet from the phones" (*The Record*, 20 September 1923).

7 For a historical, critical study of the development of the St. John's library cf. Ronald Roloff, O.S.B., *St. John's University Library: An Historical Evaluation* (Collegeville, 1953).

8 Professor John Singenberger of Pio Nono College in Milwaukee was asked by Abbot Peter to supervise the casting of these bells, examine the moulds, place the inscriptions so as not to interfere with the purity of tone, and to correct any imperfections in casting. When the work was finished, by Gardiner Campbell and Sons of Milwaukee, Singenberger stated that "I have not, in this country, heard a chime that pleased me as well as the one just completed." These five bells, cast to the notes of A, B, D, E and F-Sharp, and dedicated to the Sacred Heart, Blessed Mother, Guardian Angels, St. John the Baptist and St. Benedict, weigh 18,365 pounds. Three of the bells serve as clock chimes for the eight-dial clocks on the twin towers. Their tolling of each quarter hour across the Collegeville countryside is an institutional memory for anyone who has been at St. John's.

9 Interview of 23 May 1954.

10 "A Review of the Principles of Benedictine Education," Theological Conference at St. John's Abbey, 8 February 1955.

11 Gunther Rolfson, O.S.B., "Our Scientific Endeavor," *The Scriptorium,* V (Christmas, 1944), 38. Cf. also "Our Scientific Endeavor: Part II," V (Summer, 1945), 18–25.

12 August C. Krey, "The Heritage They Brought Us," Minnesota Centennial Convocation, St. John's University, 20 May 1949.

13 Cf. also Mitchell, *op. cit.,* II, 744 ff.

14 August C. Krey, "The Heritage They Brought Us."

15 Mitchell, *op. cit.,* I, 284.

16 Ireland to Engel, St. Paul, 28 September 1912. Cf. also Archbishop Ireland's tribute to the Minnesota Benedictines on occasion of the 25th anniversary of the St. Cloud Cathedral in *Acta et Dicta,* II (July, 1910), 272–82.

17 There were several other projects and monastic foundations under discussion during Abbot Peter's time, but they all remained undeveloped. Bishop Timothy Corbett of Crookston pleaded for years for a Benedictine monastery and college at Crookston, and Abbot Peter favored this move, but the chapter was against it. Bishop James O'Reilly of Fargo wanted a Benedictine college at Casselton or Devils Lake. Mandan and Valley City were under consideration as places for a monastic foundation at various times. The Indian Mission at Assinins near Baraga, Michigan, was offered to St. John's in 1900, as was a projected German Catholic colony at Cordele, Georgia, in 1897, and a splendid piece of property in Knight's Valley, California. None of these materialized. Abbot Alexius had dreamed of Benedictine expansion into key points of the northwest,

and then into these areas where the needs of the Church called. With his retirement these plans suffered a permanent set-back. There is no evidence that Abbot Peter had like inclination in this regard. His easy-going temperament worked against his taking dynamic steps. He definitely wanted the abbey to expand, but he had no blueprint marked out. He saw two foundations through to maturity; he would have liked more. But his prudence and patience always moved him to compromise in order to preserve unity.

18 Interview of 13 February 1954.

19 "Miscellaneous Notes," n.p.; *Monte Cassino, Metten and Minnesota* (St. Paul, 1927), p. 10.

20 Steinkogler to Engel, Tacoma, 29 March 1895.

21 *The Record*, September, 1902.

22 Peter Windschiegl, O.S.B., *Fifty Golden Years* (Muenster, Saskatchewan, 1953). One of the most significant experiments made at St. Peter's Colony was the establishment of a Catholic newspaper, begun on 11 February 1904, less than a year after the arrival of the Benedictines in Canada. It was the sole German Catholic paper in the entire Dominion. In May of 1922 an English edition, *The St. Peter's Messenger*, was founded, which later was called *The Prairie Messenger*. This Catholic weekly continues today with a wide circulation in the colony and beyond its borders, and is a representative example of good Catholic journalism.

23 Mayer to Engel, St. Paul, 16 March 1906.

24 Father Alexius Hoffmann records an incident which brings out this sincere desire of the abbot to show consideration and "avoid unnecessary worry and discouragement." "July 14: Abbot Peter informed me that he had decided to make P. Bruno Doerfler the director of the college. He was apparently quite nervous about it. I was sitting with the prefects on the north side of the building after supper on this fine evening, when the Abbot came around the corner and walked around aimlessly without seemingly noticing us. Finally he came up to us, made an obvious remark, and asked me to go with him—he had something to say. When we were alone he struggled with himself and told me of his decision to make a change in the directorship . . . He felt much relieved at seeing I was not going to make a fight . . . He thanked me for taking it that way and assured me that he did not mean to humiliate or degrade me" ("Autobiography" [1896–1904], 31–32).

25 PP. Benedict XV to Peter Engel, Rome, 24 June 1920.

26 *The Record,* September, 1920.

27 Engel Diary, 27 November 1919.

NOTES TO CHAPTER EIGHT

1   "To My Father
Nine years have passed since thou wert laid away!
Yet oft my fancy sees thee still
After the heat and toil of day
With body bent and weary feet
Plod homeward to the evening meal
And soothing rest.

Train upon train of clanging cars
Rushes by. A glance at them and then a sigh
And wearily onward thou draggest thy limbs.
'A nickel saved!' Why give it to them that millions have
As long as my feet can carry me still
And my wife and children have scarce their fill.

No envy filled thy heart. Never a covetous glance
At the rich man's palace nor all the comforts of wealth.

Thy laborer's jacket—a crust of bread,
A bit of meat, thy pipe at morn and noon and night
A cheap, clean suit to worship in God's house
Thy children fed and sent to school
Where they might learn to know and love their God."

2 Deutsch to Engel, Rome, 13 November 1902.

3 Deutsch to Engel, Minneapolis, 31 March 1916. Father Alcuin organized St. Anselm Literary Society for the junior monks when he returned to St. John's. To encourage Benedictine studies and habits of writing among the younger members of the community he inaugurated *The Benedictine Forum,* an eight-page folio which first appeared on 23 December 1916, and continued for eleven numbers to February of 1919 when it was discontinued.

4 Brother Clement and the Belgian artist, the Reverend Adalbert Gres-

nigt, O.S.B., painted the interior of the new parish church of St. Anselm in New York City in the early 1920's.

5 On 6 May 1928 the relics of St. Peregrin were solemnly transferred from the Church of St. Anselm in New York to St. John's, and the reliquary placed under the main altar of the Brothers' Chapel in the lower church. The relics of St. Peregrin were first brought to the United States in 1895 by Father Gerard Spielmann, O.S.B., a monk of St. John's, and temporarily reposed in St. Anselm's Church, New York. Father Gerard had obtained permission to bring the relics to America from Prince Karl von Loewenstein who had been given title to the Benedictine abbey of Neustadt after the secularization of German monasteries in 1803. The relics of St. Peregrin had been brought to Neustadt by Abbot Kilian Kneuer of Neustadt in 1731 who had in turn obtained permission to remove them from the catacombs. St. Peregrin, martyr, was a Roman boy who was tortured and killed in 192 during the persecutions of Emperor Commodus.

6 A retreat for laymen had been held at St. John's as early as 1914 with Father Augustine Brockmeyer as director, but the movement was not fully developed until the late 1920's.

7 Father George gave missions from 1919 until his death in 1939; Father Method worked in this field from 1926–40; and Father Celestine has continued giving parish missions from 1933 to the present. He has given over five hundred parish missions in fifteen states and four Canadian provinces, all oriented toward an increase in liturgical piety in parish life.

8 Abbot Alcuin was a loyal supporter of Sant' Anselmo, his alma mater, and he endeavored to arouse interest among other American abbots, as he wrote: "I am rather eager that all our abbeys entertain a kindly feeling toward S. Anselmo and send some of their young monks to it for study of the Sacred Sciences. I think it most important for the welfare of our abbeys. I know very well that there has been some dissatisfaction in several of our houses with the institution, because some of the men sent there have not turned out very well. But I know S. Anselmo, I dare say, better than the rest of our abbots, except perhaps Abbot Martin, and he shares my opinion, and I am satisfied that the fault lies not with S. Anselmo but with us and those we have sent there" (Alcuin

Deutsch to Abbot Bertrand Dolan, Collegeville, 20 November 1936, copy).

9 The Reverend Paul Marx, O.S.B., is at present writing a doctoral thesis at the Catholic University of America on Father Virgil Michel and the beginnings of the Liturgical Movement in the United States. For a liberal and critical evaluation of the movement cf. also Ernest B. Koenker, *Liturgical Renaissance in the Roman Catholic Church* (Chicago, 1954). Father Godfrey Diekmann, O.S.B., has viewed the development of this aspect of the American apostolate from the viewpoint of a participant: "The Primary Apostolate," *The American Apostolate* (ed. by Leo R. Ward, C.S.C.; Westminster, Maryland, 1952), pp. 29–47.

10 Michel to Engel, Washington, 15 November 1917; 3 March 1918.

11 Michel to Deutsch, Louvain, 14 March 1925.

12 Father Paul Marx, in the fourth chapter of his projected work, traces for the first time the isolated and painstaking efforts of individual American Catholics during the nineteenth century to arouse a liturgical consciousness. He discusses the contribution of Archbishop John Carroll; Bishop John England; the pastoral letter of the American hierarchy at the conclusion of III Plenary Council of Baltimore; Father Alfred Young, C.S.P.; Archbishop James Blenk; the Reverend Thomas Shields; Mrs. Justine Ward; Mother Georgia Stevens, R.S.C.J.; the Reverend John Young, S.J.; and the Reverend Herman Untraut.

The Reverend Adrian Fortescue in an article on "Americanism" discusses the general atmosphere of nineteenth century Catholicism in the United States, and states that it was characterized by an insistence on practical, natural virtue, social improvement, "and a corresponding reticence about pure dogma or theological discussion." Fortescue wrote that American Catholics unquestionably accepted the full Catholic faith, but were anxious to have the Church known as a body that does most toward solving social questions, as the poor man's friend in the fields of temperance, education, care for orphans, etc. Instead of reviving old theological disputes, a friendly rivalry of good works between religions emerged. He found among American Catholics: "a keen feeling for everything that is modern, and a great insistence on the fact that we are no longer in the Middle Ages, that we must move with the times. 'The sort of religion we want now,' says Archbishop Ireland, 'does not consist in singing antiphons in gorgeous vestments from cathedral stalls, while the nave is empty and people outside are perishing of spiritual and moral decay. We must hunt up men of the world, and talk to them in a language they can understand, not in the stilted periods of the seventeenth century.' (L'Eglise et le Siècle, p. 102)" (*Folia Fugitiva* [ed. by the Reverend W. H. Cologan; New York, 1907], p. 271).

Archbishop James Blenk, S.M., of New Orleans remarked, however, in his pastoral letter of 22 November 1907: "We have covered the land with our great churches and cathedrals, with modern and well-equipped schools . . . which are the admiration of the Christian world. Shall we allow ourselves to be baffled by the problem of organizing our solemn worship in accordance with the will of the Church, or shrink from the sacrifices involved? To what purpose is the sumptuous decoration of our temples — the marble, the stained glass, the silver and the gold — if we neglect the very act of worship itself to which all these things are but the setting?"

13 *National Liturgical Week: Proceedings (1947),* p. 11.

14 Ward to Deutsch, Notre Dame, Indiana, 28 November 1938.

15 The first board of associate editors of *Orate Fratres* included five diocesan priests, a Jesuit, a Franciscan, a Benedictine, a Dominican prioress and two of the laity. They were the Reverends William Busch of St. Paul Seminary; Martin Hellriegel, chaplain to the Sisters of the Most Precious Blood at O'Fallon, Missouri; Gerald Ellard, S.J., of St. Mary's, Kansas; Leo Miller of the Pontifical College Josephinum, Columbus, Ohio; Richard Power of the diocese of Springfield, Massachusetts; Jeremiah Harrington of the St. Paul Seminary; James O'Mahoney, O.F.-M.C., of Ireland; Patrick Cummins, O.S.B., of Conception Abbey, Missouri; Monsignor Francis Holweck of St. Louis; Mother Mary Ellerker, O.P., of Duluth, Minnesota; Donald Attwater of England, and Mrs. Justine Ward of Washington, D.C.

16 Cf. Appendix VII, page 376–78.

17 Abbot Alcuin received congratulations on the initiating of *Orate Fratres* in a steady stream after the appearance of the first issue. Father William Busch, for example, told him on 17 November 1926: "While your name does not appear in the first number, I know to what extent the work is due to you." Father John R. Volz of Waterville told him on May 17 that the liturgical effort was "the great cause of the day," while Father F. Markert, S.V.D., of Techny, Illinois, wrote on 8 October 1926: "I think that every faithful member of our Church should hail your undertaking with genuine joy and give it all possible encouragement."

18 *The Catholic Journalist,* II (November, 1950), 4.

19 "A Survey of *Worship* For 1954," prepared by Church History 32 Class, 31 May 1955.

20 Baltimore *Catholic Review,* 20 July 1930. Two Lutheran ministers, Irvin Arkin and Ernest Beck, who joined the Catholic Church in 1954, declared that liturgical life as lived in Monsignor Hellriegel's parish of the Holy Cross in St. Louis, a reading of *Orate Fratres,* and the annual proceedings of the National Liturgical Weeks led them to become Catholics. Cf. *Our Sunday Visitor,* 11 July 1954.

21 *Christian Spirituality* (New York, 1922), III, 72.

22 Cf. also Pius X, *Motu Proprio: Tra le Sollecitudini* (Rome, 22 November 1903), 5.

23 Alcuin Deutsch to Benedict Bradley, O.S.B., Collegeville, 21 September, 1935, copy.

24 Borgmann to Deutsch, Baltimore, 14 March 1930.

25 Deutsch to Borgmann, Collegeville, 26 April 1930, copy.

26 Sister Helen Angela Hurley, *On Good Ground* (Minneapolis, 1951), p. 261. The position of Sister Antonia on the liturgical movement was not necessarily representative of the Sisters of St. Joseph at that time. Cf. also, J. J. Murphy, "A Call for Irish-American Honest Self-Appraisal," *The Homiletic and Pastoral Review,* LIV (March 1954), 509–13.

Father Pierre Bouscaren, S.J., of St. Louis University, asked Abbot Alcuin in the summer of 1927 if he could come to Collegeville to observe liturgical life. Abbot Alcuin answered him on 15 July 1927: "I hope you do not entertain any high expectations. We are after all only in the beginning of things, struggling more or less successfully to emerge from the crude American way of pioneer life. We usually do not chant the Conventual Mass nor Vespers except on Sundays and feastdays, and for most of the community the Liturgical Movement is quite a new thing, except in so far as liturgical functions are somewhat more traditional with us than with some others. Yet, our tradition too has suffered, the more so since the Order was brought into this country by only one priest [Wimmer] who had only a brief monastic experience." After his visit Father Bouscaren wrote to Abbot Aluin on August 27: "I came to learn Christ better than I knew Him, by drinking in of the liturgy. I have found, not only in the chapel and church, but in the community life, that which I sought — the spirit of Christ which prays in Christ and thinks in Christ and lives in Christ. You have shown me in practice the spirit of which Abbot Marmion has written so masterfully."

27 One of the most important advances which followed closely upon the establishment of *Orate Fratres* was the publication of the Leaflet Missal by two close friends of St. John's, Fathers Paul Bussard, an associate editor of *Orate Fratres* and the editor of the *Catholic Digest,* and Edward F. Jennings, '22, both priests of the archdiocese of St. Paul. In 1930 they issued this weekly Sunday leaflet with the Mass text of the day which introduced millions of American Catholics to greater participation in the liturgical life of the Church, and brought many to the use of missals.

28 Ildefons Herwegen to Alcuin Deutsch, Maria Laach, 30 June 1928. Abbot Alcuin often stated during these years that there was a close relation between Maria Laach and St. John's. This German Benedictine center of liturgical study and life was a constant source of ideas on liturgical, monastic, artistic matters. Several St. John's monks studied at the Maria Laach Liturgical Academy, and when Prior Albert Hammenstede of Maria Laach led a small group of monks to the United States in the late 1930's, to prepare the way for a possible refuge in case Hitler's government confiscated their monastery, Abbot Alcuin assisted the group in every way possible. During his stay in the United States Prior Albert told Abbot Alcuin: "I have learned a great deal about the true monastic spirit since I came to America, and my respect for the American Benedictines has been increased enormously. Here at Mount Angel Abbey for instance I feel very much edified by the perfect harmony in which the cler-

ics of the two American Benedictine Congregations are living together. That shows that they have got a very good monastic education . . . It is my conviction that also after the war a foundation of the Beuronese Congregation in America will be absolutely useless. Only people who have never lived in American monasteries can dream of such a foolish thing. The two great Benedictine American Congregations offer all desirable possibilities and varieties for young Americans who wish to become Benedictines . . . There is so much good will just among the young American monks that our Holy Order will soon become most flourishing in this country. The Beuronese novices and clerics had never to work so hard as the American clerics and nevertheless the latter are always cheerful and happy. And above all, very grateful. One good word makes them feel happy. I like them very much" (Hammenstede to Deutsch, Mount Angel, Oregon, 3 October 1943).

29 Busch to Deutsch, St. Cloud, n.d.

30 Schrembs to Maler, Cleveland, 21 June 1927, copy. Cf. also Hellriegel to Michel, O'Fallon, Missouri, 22 August 1926; Dowling to Michel, St. Paul, 14 December 1926; Schlarman to Deutsch, Peoria, 11 August 1934.

31 In a one volume history of St. John's mention cannot be made of the many close friends and collaborators, such as Monsignor Joseph McMahon of New York and Father John J. Harbrecht of Cincinnati, to name only two, who labored unceasingly in this period to advance the cause of the liturgical revival.

Abbot Alcuin desired that the liturgical movement in the United States be as quickly as possible united with existing organizations of the Church in the United States, and not be labelled in any way as a Benedictine undertaking. The abbots of both congregations sponsored a Benedictine Liturgical Conference from 1940–43 which held annual meetings, under the direction of Father Michael Ducey, O.S.B., of St. Anselm's Priory, Washington, D. C. This organization was viewed as transitional in character. On 8 September 1943 the abbots voted to discontinue this Benedictine Liturgical Conference in favor of the National Advisory Committee founded by the pioneer liturgist, Monsignor Joseph Morrison of Chicago, and Father Michael Ducey. This organization was the forerunner of the present National

Liturgical Conference which holds annual meetings for clergy and laity throughout North America and continues the apostolate of spreading an understanding of liturgical life in our times.

32. Day to Deutsch, New York, 26 February 1934. Abbot Alcuin answered on 2 March 1934 that he was greatly interested in their venture, that it was he who had called Father Virgil's attention to their "excellent little publication," and urged him to bring it to the attention of the students.

As a practical application of liturgical and social principles a credit union was organized on 15 September 1938 by Fathers Virgil Michel, Marcel Leisen, O.S.B., and Luke Fink, O.S.B., for the Collegeville parish. Beginning with thirty members, membership has increased to 247 in 1955; assets total $80,000, and over a quarter of a million dollars was lent during that period as a service to the people of the parish and employees of St. John's. Theodore Schreiner, porter at St. John's, has acted as secretary and treasurer of the Collegeville Credit Union since its inception, and served on the Minnesota State Board of Credit Unions from 1945–51. Credit Unions were also founded at Meire Grove, Eden Valley and Luxemburg, but did not continue in existence.

In the same vein a Workmen's Guild and family salary scales were established for faculty and employees of St. John's.

33. Skillin to Deutsch, New York, 19 December 1936. Skillin also visited St. John's several times, and lectured. The Collegeville student body have not only actively supported *The Commonweal*, but when the magazine needed subscription drives at various times, students have taken up collections and even journeyed to communities of the region to conduct public appeals.

34. Veth to Deutsch, Atchinson, Kansas, 3 and 19 December 1938. In an academic convocation commemorating the centennial of the Minnesota Territory on 20 May 1949 Professor August C. Krey of the University of Minnesota stated: "When I prepared my talk for the Minnesota Historical Society at St. Cloud in 1927 on 'Monte Cassino, Metten and Minnesota,' I stated that the Benedictine Fathers, though they had done so much in other respects, had not yet given us a Venerable Bede. I should now like to modify or correct that statement. True, the volume of the world's knowledge has now grown so great that it is no longer possible for one individual to encompass all learning nor even for one individual to be singled out as the most learned man of his own time, as Bede was in his, Rhabanus in his age, and Gerbert in his. I did not realize at the time I made that statement how soon nor how near St. John's would come to meeting the challenge of my statement. In Father Virgil Michel, who knew so much in so many fields of learning and made original contributions not only in one but in several fields, St. John's has given us a scholar whom Dante would gladly have placed on the celestial planet where he found the great scholars and teachers to associate with Bede, Rhabanus, Gerbert, and the many others in mutual respect and admiration."

35. Abbot Alcuin was referring to differences, sometimes acute, which had developed during previous years between him and Father Virgil over procedures and methods of organizing the liturgical movement. Both had definite ideas on the matter, and Abbot Alcuin termed Father Virgil as "rather headstrong in matters referring to the liturgical movement" (Deutsch to Thomas Reilly, O.P., Collegeville, 20 February 1937).

36. Interview with Father Joseph Kreuter, 18-19 May 1955. Before inaugurating *Sponsa Regis* Father Joseph had worked in New York, Chicago, St. Louis, Detroit, Denver and Washington, D. C., as American representative of the "Catholica Unio" movement begun by Dom Augustine von Gallen of Emmaus Abbey, Prague, for reunion with the Orthodox Churches. In 1926 he was invited by Bishop Busch to organize the Society For the Propagation of the Faith in the St. Cloud Diocese, and he organized the diocesan mission office in St. Mary's Building, St. Cloud, introduced the Mission Association of Catholic Women and Girls founded by Catherine Schynse of Pfaffendorf, Germany, and managed the *Catholic Mission Messenger*. He was succeeded by Father Henry Frank, '25, as diocesan director.

37. Father Joseph was assisted in the *Sponsa Regis* work by Prior Rembert Bularzik.

38. When Father Joseph was moving from his room at St. John's he asked Abbot Alcuin what he should do with his large collection of manuscripts and documents concerning the early

years of the *Sponsa Regis* movement. Without consultation the abbot ordered him to destroy the whole corpus. By this decision an invaluable and singularly rare collection on the growth of the interior life in the United States was lost to future students of American Catholicism.

39 Two foreign visitors commented on the development of Catholicism in Stearns County during these years. Xavier Geyer stated that "all in all Stearns County is the finest and best developed area of German Catholic background that I saw in the whole country" (*Bei den Deutschamerikanern* [Godesberg, 1926], p. 61), while Joseph Scheben called St. John's the spiritual originator of the row on row of parishes in Stearns County ("Eifeler Amerika-Auswanderung," *Rheinische Vierteljahrsblaetter*, II [October, 1932], 272).

40 St. Cloud *Times*, 7 September 1955.

41 Muench to Deutsch, Fargo, 8 September 1944. Bishop Busch told Abbot Alcuin in the same vein on 29 December 1946: "I too appreciate the many acts of kindness shown me by you and the members of your community during these many years."

42 Michel to A. Taggart, Collegeville, 15 January 1927.

43 Deutsch to John C. Acheson, Collegeville, 14 January 1933, copy.

44 Deutsch to Studebaker, Collegeville, 4 May 1936, copy.

45 Deutsch to Shipstead, Collegeville, 6 June 1942; Deutsch to Knutson, Collegeville, 3 September 1930, copy. These sentiments were entirely in accord with Abbot Alcuin's political views, which tended to be conservative. He declared that he favored "every measure looking toward the improvement of the economic and social condition of the American people except when fraught with danger to the liberties of our people than which nothing is more important" (Deutsch to Shipstead, Collegeville, 17 February 1937, copy). Abbot Alcuin carried on an extensive correspondence with Senator Shipstead and Congressman Knutson but ever maintained that he preferred to trust their judgment and honesty to promote the welfare of the people of the country rather than to urge them to vote this or that way on measures. He felt that bombarding congressmen with letters and telegrams was more 'mobocracy' than democracy because "the representatives of the people should, after having thoroughly informed themselves of the merits of a question, vote according to their best judgment, even though that may be contrary to the majority of their constituents . . . an intelligent representative is more likely to know what is right and expedient than the masses of the voters, uneducated or thoughtless or belabored by propaganda, as they frequently are" (Deutsch to Knutson, Collegeville, 3 September 1930, copy). Yet he repeatedly stated his opinions on current issues, in which he was ever interested. He felt in the 1930's the people were thrown into confusion by economic distress and that "the conservative element must work to block the more dangerous legislation and in that way accomplish much for the country." He was against the Supreme Court packing bill, against compulsory military training, but in favor of the Farm Security Administration, the National Youth Administration, and aids for Indians and Negroes. He was far from enthusiastic over entering World War II because he felt it would spell the end of democratic government in the United States and bring "precisely that totalitarian form which we claim we must fight in Europe." He told Senator Shipstead on 17 April 1944 that he hoped the senator would "continue to watch carefully every move that is made by the Administration and do all in your power to prevent its making this country a tool of Russia and England and getting into the same totalitarian system of government that has been and is prevalent in Russia." The abbot wrote a strong protest to President Roosevelt and the Minnesota delegation in Congress against the division of Poland after the war as a betrayal of the vast majority of the American people and the principles of the Atlantic Charter. He was not sanguine about the United Nations organization, but felt as he told Shipstead on 17 August 1944: "that a gesture in that direction may not be without some value. Unless we do succeed in getting some sort of federation among the nations similar to that of our own United States, I greatly fear that we will be having another world war before long."

46 Sister Helen Angela Hurley, *op. cit.*, p. 261.

47 Boe to Deutsch, Northfield, 28 May 1937.

48 Deutsch to Shipstead, Collegeville, 16 June 1941.

49 Deutsch to Bonaventure Reitmeier, Collegeville, 22 August 1932.

50 A radio station, WFBJ, was opened at St. John's on 8 March 1925 under the direction of Father Hilary Doerfler. Weekly lectures, musical programs, and athletic events were broadcast until the early 1930's when the project was discontinued. An opportunity to spread the ideals of the liturgical movement, as well as to supply educational programs via radio for the region, was lost. Since the 1940's St. John's programs have been carried over St. Cloud radio stations, usually on a weekly schedule.

The Commercial College, or commerce department, was discontinued in 1922 when steps were made to organize an integrated college curriculum.

51 Deutsch to Herwegen, Collegeville, 23 January 1933, copy.

52 Deutsch to Borgmann, Collegeville, 23 June 1939.

53 Father Matthew Kiess, O.S.B., director of St. John's agricultural experimental station, has also carried on studies in conjunction with Dr. Robert P. Koenig, '46, in developing a simplified filter paper electrophoresis with a study of human serum proteins.

The productions of Father Virgil Michel, O.S.B., include many articles on liturgical, philosophical and sociological topics. In conjunction with Father Basil Stegmann, O.S.B., and the Marywood Dominican Sisters of Grand Rapids, Michigan, he wrote the *Christ Life Series* in Religion (New York, 1934-35), *The Christian in the World* (Collegeville, 1939), and *Our Life in Christ* (Collegeville, 1939). Independently he wrote *Christian Social Reconstruction* (Milwaukee, 1937), and *The Liturgy of the Church* (New York, 1937).

Father Ulric Beste, O.S.B., dean of the major seminary at St. John's from 1929-39, wrote a commentary on the canon law of the Church, *Introductio in Codicem* (Collegeville, 1938), which is used in a number of American and continental seminaries. In 1939 Father Ulric became rector of the International Benedictine College of Saint Anselm in Rome, since 1941 has served as a consultor of the curial Sacred Congregation of the Holy Office, and at present is also a commission member of the Sacred Congregation of Religious.

Father Oliver Kapsner, O.S.B., during twenty years of library work at St. John's, became conscious of the need for a list of subject headings expressing adequately the content, mentality, and terminology of Catholic literature. He prepared a work, *Catholic Subject Headings* (Collegeville, 1942), at the invitation of the Catholic Library Association, which was immediately acclaimed as an indispensable tool of every librarian, and the work has had three editions in eleven years. Father Oliver also prepared *Catholic Religious Orders* (Collegeville, 1948), and *A Benedictine Bibliography* (Collegeville, 1949-50) as further editions in library listings. In 1951 he was invited to become a research cataloger in the Mullen Library at the Catholic University of America. He also supervises and advises on cooperative cataloging for the Library of Congress of Catholic titles which are not included in their collections.

Father Clarus Graves, O.S.B., wrote a widely-used series of text books in classical and modern languages based upon a system of extensive repetition. His four volumes of *Latin* (Milwaukee, 1938-43) have had sixteen editions. Cf. also *German* (Collegeville, 1936); *French* (Collegeville, 1928); and *Spanish* (Collegeville, 1937).

Other faculty productions of this period include *Western Social Thought* (Milwaukee, 1954), by Father Ernest Kilzer, O.S.B., who also collaborated with Eva Ross on a social science textbook, *American Democracy* (Milwaukee, 1944); *Fundamentals of Gregorian Chant* (Toledo, 1947), by Father Dominic Keller, O.S.B.; *The Week With Christ* (Chicago, 1950), by Father Emeric Lawrence, O.S.B.; *Education in India* (New York, 1951), by Father Aubrey Zellner, O.S.B.; *Nothing But Christ* (St. Meinrad, 1953), by Father Kilian McDonnell, O.S.B.; *Survey of Christian Life* (Collegeville, 1954) by Father Lancelot Atsch, O.S.B., and Emerson Hynes.

Father Gregory Roettger, O.S.B., translated Ildefonsus Cardinal Schuster's *Saint Benedict and His Times* (St. Louis, 1951); Father William Heidt, O.S.B., translated Paul Heinisch's *Theology of the Old Testament* (Collegeville, 1950), and *History of the Old Testament* (Collegeville, 1952); Fathers Odo Zimmermann, O.S.B., and Benedict Avery, O.S.B., translated St. Gregory the Great's *Life and Miracles of St. Benedict* (Collegeville, 1949).

54 Father Martin Schirber has dis-

cussed the implications, pro and con, of the National Catholic Rural Life Movement in a provocative article, "Catholic Rural Life," *The American Apostolate* (ed. by Leo R. Ward, C.S.C.; Westminster, Maryland, 1952), pp. 133–49.

55 Schlarman to Deutsch, Peoria, 18 March 1943.

56 James Gray, *The University of Minnesota*, 1851–1951 (Minneapolis, 1951), p. 461.

57 *Bulletin of St. John's University* (Collegeville, 1955), p. 72.

58 "Liturgical Religious Education," *Orate Fratres*, XI (1937), 267.

59 St. Paul *Pioneer Press*, 6 July 1954.

60 St. Paul *Pioneer Press*, 7 February 1954.

61 On 16 September 1952 Edward Cardinal Mooney of Detroit dedicated the new seminary building. Some seminarians from the dioceses of Fargo, Crookston, Green Bay, LaCrosse continue, as before, to study at St. John's, as do seminarians from other dioceses of the country.

62 Deutsch to Kelly, Collegeville, 8 December 1932, copy.

63 Abbot Mark Braun died on 2 April 1954 and was succeeded by Abbot Philip Berning, '33, who studied as a cleric at St. John's.

64 Father Vincent Wehrle, O.S.B., was ordained at the abbey of Einsiedeln, Switzerland, on 23 April 1882, and came to St. Meinrad Abbey, Indiana, on October 9 of that year, while remaining a capitular of Einsiedeln. He was first sent to St. Meinrad's priory of St. Benedict in Arkansas, served as assistant at Jaspar, Indiana, and then joined Abbot Marty in the Dakota mission field.

65 Background materials on the history of St. Mary's Abbey, Richardton, N. Dak., were obtained through interviews and access to archival deposits kindly furnished by Abbot Cuthbert Goeb and Prior Benedict Pfaller on 3 and 4 September 1952.

66 Albert Kleber, O.S.B., *op. cit.*, pp. 460–62.

67 The late Dr. Richard Purcell was accustomed to tell his history seminar classes at the Catholic University of America about visiting his former student, Father Cuthbert Goeb, at Richardton Abbey, and of finding him and the monks, as St. Benedict had advised, working in the fields, and restoring their abbey.

68 Wehrle to Deutsch, Bismarck,

27 May 1932. Abbot Cuthbert Goeb also declared to Abbot Alcuin on 29 May 1935: "The present rehabilitated abbey owes everything to St. John's and to you, and it will be our endeavor to continue the traditions of St. John's as we learned them while there and under your direction. May God bless you and St. John's."

69 Cf. The Mandan *Pioneer*, 10 February, 13 April 1932; Dickinson *Press*, 11 February 1932; *Nord Dakota Herold*, 12 February and 22 April 1932; *Catholic Tribune*, 13 February, 20 April 1932; *Der Wanderer*, 18 February, 14 April 1932.

70 "Minutes of Meeting of the Chapter," 7 May 1941. The American Benedictines sent to Manila included Father Alfred Koestner, O.S.B., of St. Benedict's Abbey, and Fathers Owen Tekippe, O.S.B., Boniface Axtman, O.S.B., Edmund Hall, O.S.B., Clement Burns, O.S.B., and Raphael Haller, O.S.B., of St. John's.

71 Deutsch to Helmstetter, Collegeville, 31 December 1930, copy.

72 Seredi to Deutsch, Rome, 20 July 1937.

73 Abbot Alcuin was too sick to attend the next election of an abbot primate after World War II in 1947. During the years of his administration he was several times spoken of as a possible successor to different diocesan sees of the upper mid-west when they were vacant, but such a development never took place.

74 Abbot Leonard Schwinn and Father Francis Hornung, O.S.B., archivist at Holy Cross Abbey, kindly furnished, during August of 1952, background materials and interviews on that community's history.

75 Pope Pius XI to the Chancellor of the University of Peking, Rome, 20 August 1929, copy.

76 Deutsch to Koch, Collegeville, 25 February 1931, copy.

77 "Prior Basil Stegmann to Rev. and Dear Confrere," Peking, n.d. Other St. John's monks who were sent to the University of Peking were Fathers Aidan Germain, O.S.B., and Terrence Carroll, O.S.B.

78 "Notes of Prior Basil Stegmann;" Deutsch to Koch, Collegeville, 16 December 1932, copy.

79 Veth to Deutsch, Atchison, Kansas, 14 March 1933.

80 "Lex Propria Confoederationis Congregationum Monasticorum Ordinis Sancti Benedicti," 21 March 1952, numbers 21 and 22.

81 Father Clarus was already in Mexico since May of 1944. Father Alcuin Heibel, O.S.B., of Mount Angel Abbey, Oregon, had begun an agricultural school during the previous year at Sahayo, Mexico, and had asked both Abbots Alcuin and Martin to send assistance. Three monks from St. Benedict's and one from St. John's were sent to this foundation. Father Clarus was forced by sickness to go to Mexico City.

82 Rivera to Stegmann, Humacao, 2 July 1953.

83 Fathers Basil Stegmann, O.S.B., and Rudolph Baumberger, O.S.B., furnished interviews during July, 1955, on the establishment of this Puerto Rican monastery.

84 Laporte to Walter Reger, O.S.B., New York, 26 February 1954.

85 Korte to Albert Heald, S.A., St. Joseph, 7 October 1945. Father Alexander Korte, O.S.B., supplied documents and interviews during August of 1953 on the founding of St. Maur's Priory.

86 LaFarge to Korte, New York, 25 October 1946.

87 Cf. Julia Neal, *By Their Fruits* (Chapel Hill, N. C., 1947) for a study of Shaker communities in the United States. Cf. also Thomas O'Connor,

O.S.B., "Benedictines in Shaker Buildings," *The Scriptorium*, XIV (December, 1954), 55–67, and the Bowling Green *Park City and Daily News*, 18 August 1949.

88 Mary J. Matthews, "Interracial Monastery," *Interracial Review*, XIV (June, 1951), 86–88.

89 "Report and Suggestions for the Monastic Foundation in Japan," September, 1955.

90 AANY, Hayes to Fumasoni-Biondi, New York, 8 August 1929, copy. Cf. also AANY, Fumasoni-Biondi to Hayes, Washington, D. C., 8 June 1929; "Constans Apostolicae Sedis," 21 March 1929.

91 AANY, Hayes to Fumasoni-Biondi, Nassau, 8 February 1932. Cf. also the New York *Catholic News*, 13 February 1932; Nassau *Daily Tribune*, 8 February 1932.

92 Interview with Father Bonaventure Hansen, O.S.B., June, 1952.

93 *Ibid.*

94 Kevenhoerster to Deutsch, Nassau, 4 August 1948.

95 Father Silvan Bromenshenkel, O.S.B., wrote a biographical sketch of Father Bonaventure's missionary career in the *Bahama Benedictine*, Spring, 1955.

NOTES TO CHAPTER NINE

1 Deutsch to Hammenstede, Collegeville, 17 June 1946, copy.

2 For example the St. John's chapter voted after World War II to give ten per cent of the community's net income for relief and rehabilitation of the needy in war-torn countries.

3 9 January 1951; Landersdorfer to Deutsch, Passau, 9 December 1950.

4 Alcuin Deutsch to Donald Cowling, Collegeville, 13 April 1945, copy; Deutsch to Landersdorfer, Collegeville, 9 January 1951, copy.

5 Abbot Mark Braun of St. Gregory's Abbey, and then president of the American Cassinese Congregation of Benedictines, stated that he regarded Abbot Alcuin "as the outstanding Benedictine in the world. He certainly knew the Holy Rule and strove diligently to live it daily. He was most heroic also in bearing up with the pain and discomforts of his illness. I think that sometimes he did not want to be spared the pains and burdens of his illness" (Mark Braun to Cosmas Krumpelmann, O.S.B., Shawnee, Oklahoma, 10 July 1951, copy).

6 Deutsch to Woehrmueller, Collegeville, 11 March 1951, copy.

7 LaFarge to Deutsch, New York, 22 March 1930.

8 *St. John's University Bulletin, 1955–56* (Collegeville, 1955), p. 29–30.

9 James M. Wells to Frank Kacmarcik, Chicago, 27 January 1953.

10 Jacques Maritain to Frank Kacmarcik, Princeton, 31 January 1953.

11 Beatrice Warde to Frank Kacmarcik, London, 16 March 1955.

12 "Student Convocation," of Dr. Josef Albers, St. John's, 10 March 1954.

13 Wimmer to Ludwig I, St. Vincent, 23 July 1849, in Mathaeser, *op. cit.*, p. 12; Wimmer to *Ludwig Missionsverein, Annalen*, XXI (1852), 16–18.

14 Baldwin Dworschak to "Dear Sir," Collegeville, 7 March 1953, copy. Cf. also "A Benedictine Monastery by Marcel Breuer," *Architectural Forum*, CI (July, 1954), 148–56.

15 Maurice Lavanoux, "Collegeville Revisited," *Liturgical Arts,* XXII (February, 1954), 44–47.

16 Sister Madeleva to Godfrey Diekmann, St. Mary's, Indiana, 4 May 1954.

17 George Higgins to Godfrey Diekmann, Washington, 12 May 1954.

18 Joseph Murphy to Abbot Baldwin, St. Louis, 4 May 1954.

19 Cf. "A Benedictine Monastery by Marcel Breuer," *Architectural Forum,* CI (July, 1954), 148–56; "Abbaye de St. John, Minnesota," *L'Architecture D'Aujourd'hui,* XXV (July-August, 1954), 85–87;" Paul Bussard, "A Plan For A Church," *Catholic Digest,* XIX (November, 1954), 70–73; "The Planning of St. John's Abbey," *Church Property Administration,* XIX (January-February, 1955), 44–47, 144–48; "A New Abbey For St. John's," *Jubilee,* II (July, 1954) 36–39; Maurice Lavanoux, "Collegeville Revisited," *Liturgical Arts,* XXII (February, 1954), 44–47; *Time,* 26 April 1954; "Ancient Religious Ideas," *Northwest Architect,* XVIII (September-October, 1954), 34–38; Victor Drapela, "Ameriky Prehled," *Novy Zivot,* XXII (July, 1955), 159; Minneapolis Morning *Tribune,* 22 April 1954; St. Paul *Pioneer Press,* 22 April 1954; St. Cloud *Daily Times,* 22 April 1954; National Catholic Welfare Conference News Release, 15 April 1954.

Interiors magazine, CXIV (January, 1955), 10, in an editorial on "The Liturgical Art Renaissance," spoke of the "timidity and sterility of invention that has marred some of the reform efforts in liturgical art (such as the Benedictine attempt in Collegeville, Minnesota)." When asked for the basis of this statement the editor of that magazine replied: "For a completely unwarranted criticism carelessly and irrelevantly tossed into the text of a report of the work of another college *Interiors* gives. . . its humble apologies . . . St. John's College (is) one of the most enlightened of our educational institutions, not only in how and what it teaches, but in its role as a patron of the building arts" (*Interiors,* CXIV [April, 1955], 8).

20 *Time,* 26 April 1954.

21 *Architectural Forum, op. cit.,* pp. 149–54.

22 Robert Cerney to Abbot Baldwin, Minneapolis, 23 February 1955.

23 Abbot Baldwin to "Dear Father," Collegeville, 30 December 1955, copy.

Abbatial blessing, 15, 97–98, 131–132, 198–199, 258, 329; elections, 14, 93–95, 128–129, 193–198, 256–257, 329; throne, 108, 259

Academic curriculum, 57, 59, 109ff, 227–228, 231, 283, 290–291, 292, 294–295; degrees, 114, 143–144, 146; 'exhibitions,' 114ff; discipline, 57–58, 117–118

Adler, Mortimer, 276, 285, 290–291

Adult education program, 332

Alexian Philharmonic Society, 150, 198

Altoetting Shrine, 6, 7, 106

American Association for the Advancement of Science, 235

American Benedictine Academy, 303

American Benedictine Educational Association, 303

American Benedictine Review, 304

American Cassinese Congregation, 14, 19, 52, 61, 68, 84, 94, 128, 145, 156, 173, 183, 187, 193–194, 205, 216, 252, 296, 297, 298, 301, 303, 304, 305, 306, 307, 308; general chapters, 173–174, 182, 183, 187, 190, 197, 258; statutes, 173–174, 193–194, 222–223; visitations, 171, 173–174, 179, 182, 183–184, 188, 194, 258

American College, Rome, 172, 173, 174

American School of Mexico, 311

Americanism, 175, 242

Annual Report of the Minnesota Superintendent of Education, 113

Apostolic Delegate, 299, 300

Archconfraternity of Perpetual Adoration, 214

Architectural methods, 82–83, 87, 101–102, 105–106, 121–122, 141–142, 152–154, 230, 339–340

Army Air Forces Training Command, 294

Art Department, 228, 332–335

Assumption Abbey, Richardton, N.D., 298–301, 306, 310

Assumption Parish, St. Paul, 29, 30, 61, 65, 73, 74, 81, 86, 94, 98–99, 107, 111, 113, 121–122, 126, 132–133, 135, 141, 144, 160, 165, 201, 220, 222, 241–242, 256, 257, 264

Athletic Association of St. John's, 231–233

Athletic field, 229–230

Auditorium, 335

Augsburg *Postzeitung*, 7, 8, 18

Ayde-Curran, Major, 207, 211

Aylward, James P., 103

Bahama Islands, 203, 204, 205–212, 223, 242, 310, 315, 321–326, 329

Bahner, Melchoir, O.S.B., 210, 211, 212

Baker, Damian, O.S.B., 262, 283, 327

Baldus, William, O.S.B., 245

Balleis, Nicholas, O.S.B., 9

Baraga, Frederick, Vicar Apostolic of Northern Michigan, 19, 20

Baran, Oswald, O.S.B., 111, 183, 245–246

Bartholome, Peter, Bishop of St. Cloud, 288, 295–296, 329

Baseball, 118, 230, 232, 233

Bachelor of arts degree, 114

Bauhaus, Dessau, Germany, 336, 337

Bavarian Cassinese Congregation, 5, 6, 10, 14, 64, 73, 84, 94, 108, 303

Bayely, James Roosevelt, Bishop of Newark, 53, 112

Beauduin, Lambert, O.S.B., 265, 269

Beck, Wolfgang, 43, 44, 45

Beer, 13–16, 148

Belmont Abbey, N.C., 183–184, 192–193, 245
Benedict XV, Pope, 231, 251, 253
Benedictinism, missionary character, 4, 17, 18, 56–57, 60–61, 84–85, 100, 127, 137, 145–146, 165–166, 206, 207–208, 217, 226, 245, 252, 330; 19th century revival, 252, 259; oblates, 150, 260–261; spirituality, 4, 17, 42–43, 85, 93, 94, 100, 107–108, 113, 117, 150–151, 166, 201, 206, 212–214, 220, 234, 238–239, 252, 259ff, 267, 330
Beuron Abbey, Germany, 166, 213, 259, 260, 267, 319, 333; art style, 260, 333
Bigotry, 18, 47–49, 212, 230
Bismarck, N.D., 155, 157, 158, 160–161, 204; diocese, 178, 241, 288, 298
Board of Catholic Indians and Colored People, 322
Boating, 118–119
Boe, Lars W., 285–286
Boerger, William A., 46, 92
Bohnen, Aloysius, Carl, and Nicholas, 92
Bond, Oscar S., 317–318
Borgerding, Thomas, O.S.B., 140, 167, 183, 195
Borgmann, Henry, C.Ss.R., 272, 287
Botz, Paschal, O.S.B., 262, 268, 281
Bradley, Cyprian, O.S.B., Abbot of Holy Cross, 305
Braun, Mark, O.S.B., Abbot of St. Gregory's, 263, 275, 283, 284, 298, 327
Breuer, Marcel L., 336, 337ff; training, 337; principles, 339–340
Brewery controversy, 13–16
Brick making, 101, 142, 152, 153, 155, 162
Britt, Matthew, O.S.B., 246
Brixius, Placidus, O.S.B., 76
Brocker, Joseph and Henry, 88, 127, 133, 134, 135
Brockmeyer, Augustine, O.S.B., 261
Brooklyn, N.Y., diocese, 211, 212; proposed abbey, 242–243
Brott, George F., 51, 77
Brown and Bigelow Co., St. Paul, 274
Brownson, Orestes A., 264
Buh, Joseph, 124, 125, 137, 138, 154
Building programs, 99–102, 140–143, 152, 152–154, 158–159, 160–162, 227–230, 335ff
Bureau of Indian Affairs, 230
Burns, Augustine, O.S.B., 102, 103
Busch, William, 266
Busch, Joseph F., Bishop of St. Cloud, 253, 256, 258, 261, 273, 282, 300, 304, 324
Bush, Florence, 311

Cannon, Charles, O.S.B., 228
Carleton College, Northfield, Minn., 113, 149, 233, 295
Carrell, George A., S.J., Bishop of Covington, 97–98
Carrolltown, Pa., 8, 9, 11, 16
Catholic Action, 276, 280, 293
Catholic Central Verein, 275–276
Catholic Directory, 297, 312
Catholic immigration, 7–8, 11, 58–59, 110–112, 123, 155, 156, 158, 161, 206, 211, 233
Catholic Indian Bureau, 138, 146, 230
Catholic Settlement Society, St. Paul, 247
Catholic social action, 268, 272, 275–277
Catholic University of America, 175, 191, 228, 262, 263, 264, 306
Catholic University of Peking, 303, 306–309
Catholic Worker Movement, 276
Cecilian music, 116, 213, 229, 273
Cemetery, 135, 218, 221, 244, 254
Centro Cultural del Tepeyac, 311
Chapla, Colonel Benjamin, 294
Charter controversy, 47–50
Chicago and Rock Island Railroad, 21, 27
Chigasaki Priory, Tokyo, 319
Chinese missions, 306–309
Chippewa Indians, 20, 44, 69–70, 118, 119, 137ff, 146–147, 155
Choir chapel, 107–108, 259
Christian ascesis, 279–281
Churches: bells, 83, 88, 108, 229, 339–340; building, 88, 121–122, 140–143, 339–340; furnishings and adornment, 33, 87, 88–89, 229, 259–260, 340; holidays, 89–90, 238; music, 88, 90–91, 116, 213, 228–229, 259, 260, 273, 274, 288, 292, 293, 320; organs, 88, 213, 229
Cincinnati Wahrheitsfreund, 21, 35
Cluny Priory, Wetaug, Ill., 248–249, 317
Colegio del Tepeyac, 311–312
Columbus College, Sioux Falls, S.D., 310
Commencements, 114ff
Conception Abbey, Mo., 148, 154, 199, 214, 228, 299
Confederation of Benedictine Monastic Congregations, 309
Conference of American Catholic Colleges, 189, 231
Conrad, Ignatius, Abbot of New Subiaco, 214, 219
Conrad, Frowin, Abbot of Conception, 148, 154, 199, 214, 220, 223, 299
Conservation, 237–238
Contributions, donations, and bequests, 7, 8, 9, 11, 23, 33, 36, 44, 46, 50, 54,

436

62–64, 74, 88, 101, 105, 106, 133, 134–135, 139–140, 165, 206, 209, 211, 219, 243–244, 322

Corbett, Timothy J., Bishop of Crookston, 231

Corrigan, Michael J., Archbishop of New York, 203, 205–206, 207–208, 211, 212, 242

Cotter, Joseph B., Bishop of Winona, 112, 114, 189, 199

Cotton, Francis R., Bishop of Owensboro, 316–317, 318

Cretin, Joseph, Bishop of St. Paul, 17, 19, 20, 23, 28–32, 39, 45, 47, 49, 53, 86; residence 28, 29

Crow River Mission, 67

Crow Wing Mission, 20, 137

Dakota Territory, 123, 128, 137, 155, 157, 158, 171, 172, 241, Territorial legislature, 159

Dangers and hardships, 10, 27, 32, 37–38, 41–42, 54, 57–58, 69–72, 209–210, 218—220.

Danzl, Arthur, O.S.B., 263

Davis, James P., Bishop of San Juan, 312–314

de Hemptinne, Hildebrand, O.S.B., Abbot Primate, 225, 259

Democratic Party, 47–48

Deutsch, Alcuin, O.S.B., Abbot of St. John's, 228, 253, 256–258, 303ff, 327, 330; assists other houses, 296–304, 305; character, 302ff; early life and training, 256ff; ideals, aims and policies, 258ff; last days, 326, 328–329; motto, 257; projects: art, 332, building, 333, 335–336; educational, 261–263, 282ff, 287, 289–290, 296; liturgical and devotional, 259, 260, 261, 266ff, 279–280; missionary, 206ff, 281–282, 288; Bahamas, 321ff, 329; China, 306–309; Japan, 319–320; Mexico, 311–312; Puerto Rico, 312–314; Kentucky, 315–319; Utah, 320–321

Devil's Lake Indian Agency, Fort Totten, N.D., 128, 199, 298, 299

di Marogna, Demetrius, O.S.B.: abilities, 14, 23, 26, 30, 36, 37, 39, 46, 48, 49, 54, 55, 61, 65, 94, 103; aims and ideals, 26–27, 29–30, 47, 50, 52, 54–55; early life and training, 26; establishment of Benedictine Sisters, 52–54, 63–64; shortcomings, 37–38, 66–67, 80

Dialogue Mass, 266, 273, 289, 293, 324–325

Diekmann, Godfrey, O.S.B., 262, 268, 270, 279, 338

Divine Office, 10, 23, 42–43, 78, 80, 83, 91, 107–108, 142, 166, 212–213,

220, 250, 259, 273, 274, 275, 289, 293, 325, 331, 339

Doerfler, Bruno, O.S.B., 228, 233, 238, 247–249

Drexel, Katherine M., 139–140

Dworschak, Baldwin, O.S.B., Abbot of St. John's, 329ff; early life and training, 330–331; motto, 330; projects: art, 332, 333; building, 335ff; educational, 331; liturgical, 331; missionary, 331

Dworschak, Leo F., Auxiliary Bishop of Fargo, 331

Economic measures, 15, 41–42, 50, 57–58, 63–64, 66, 106–107, 119– 120, 132–135

Edelbrock, Alexius, O.S.B., Abbot of St. John's, 33, 57–58, 60, 77–78, 126, 129–130, 131, 132, 133, 134, 135–136, 143–144, 156, 167, 177–178, 184–193, 215, 221, 224–225; character and piety, 119–120, 132, 134, 141, 148, 164–165, 168–169, 186, 192, 201–202; early life and training, 102–103; ideals, aims and policies, 110, 120, 132–135, 148, 149, 156, 163–166, 169, 206, 225–226; motto, 133, 144; opponents, 129, 134, 144, 145, 164ff, 183, 184–190, 194–196, 199–200, 201–202; projects: building, 135, 140–143, 152–154, 158–159, 160–162, 218, 230, 335; abbey church 140, 143, 212–213; devotional, 150; educational, 144–147, 149, 193, 119ff; farm, 151–152, 204; historical, 150; missionary, 136–140, 155, 156–157, 158–160, 163, 164–166, 185–186, 208–209, 242; Bahamas, 208–209, 242; Dakota, 158, 160–161, 204; Duluth, 161–162, 202, 204; New York, 202–206, 242–243; musical, 150; resignation and last days, 151, 162, 163–164, 170–171, 187–188, 190–193, 202–206, 208–209, 220, 242–244; supporters, 135, 140, 145, 154, 161, 170, 180–184, 186, 190, 191, 195, 197, 201, 202–203, 223

Edelbrock, Joseph and Anton, 32, 33, 35, 46, 88, 102–103

Educational efforts and policies, 11, 12, 46–50, 52, 54, 56–60, 75–76, 100–101, 102–105, 109ff, 138, 139–140, 146–148, 208, 211, 212, 226–227, 228, 230ff, 234, 235ff, 245–246, 261–263, 264–265, 282ff, 301, 307–308, 311–312, 312–314, 318, 325, 327, 332

Electrification, 227–228

Engel, Peter, O.S.B., Abbot of St. John's, 144, 145, 153, 171, 182, 194, 195–196, 199, 200, 201, 220, 240

246, 252–253, 258, 264; character and piety, 239–240, 245, 246, 249–254; early life, 224–225; ideals, aims and policies, 225–226, 234, 240–241, 242–243, 244–246, 249–253, 258; last days, 251, 253–254; motto, 226; projects: building, 227–230, 335; educational, 338; musical, 228–229; scientific, 225, 226–228, 234–235, 238

English Benedictines, 136, 137, 190, 208, 252

Escuela San Antonio Abad, Puerto Rico, 312–314

Eversmann, William, 111, 152, 159, 218, 244

Exemption controversy, 12–14, 16

Faribault-Stillwater school plan, 76, 175, 215, 242

Fairs, 89–90, 133

Fellner, Felix, O.S.B., 7

Financial crises, 42, 132–134

Fink, Louis, O.S.B., Vicar Apostolic of Kansas and Bishop of Leavenworth, 66, 112, 127, 183

Fish hatchery, 238

Flynn, Edward, 295

Food shortages, 41–43, 57–58

Football, 232–233

Frauendorfer, Anschar, O.S.B., 60, 61, 67, 71, 94, 239

Freising Seminary, 95, 99

French Benedictines, 127, 243, 252

French-Canadian immigrants, 138, 155, 161

French-Canadian missionaries, 155–156

French immigrants, 86, 138

Frey, Frederic, O.S.B., 325

Frischauf, Clement, O.S.B., 260, 280, 333

Fu Jen University, Peking, 303, 306–309

Fumasoni-Biondi, Pietro, Cardinal, 309, 322, 323

Gahr, Eberhard, O.S.B., 61, 66–67, 71, 94

Gasquet, Aidan Cardinal, 136, 267

Genin, Jean Baptiste Marie, O.M.I., 159

German American Land Co., St. Paul, 247

German hymns and songs, 90–91

German immigrants, 7–8, 11, 12, 16, 20, 21–23, 53, 55, 58–59, 64, 66, 69, 85–92, 100–101, 109, 121–122, 123–124, 133, 149–150, 155, 164, 203, 206, 217, 233, 247, 257, 281

German language question, 148–149, 175, 203, 214–215

German-Russian immigrants, 298

Gertken, Severin, O.S.B., 235, 249, 263, 283, 284, 327

Gertken, Innocent, O.S.B., 228, 260

Gibbons, James, Cardinal, 177, 203

Ginther, Edward, O.S.B., 161, 167, 222–223

Giroux, Msgr. Wilfred, 321

Glatzmeier, Conrad, O.S.B., 167, 183, 247–248

Goeb, Cuthbert, O.S.B., Abbot of Assumption, 228, 251, 268, 269, 284, 300–301, 303, 325

Gorman, Willis A., Territorial Governor, 47, 49–50

Government Land Warrants, 63–64

Grace, Thomas L., O.P., Bishop of St. Paul, 67, 74, 75–76, 83, 84–85, 86, 97, 112, 120, 122, 124–125, 127, 132, 137, 146, 155, 175, 189, 201

Grace Literary Association, 117

Grasshopper-plague Shrine, 89, 218

Graves, Clarus, O.S.B., 263, 311–312, 327

'Great Books' plan, 290–291

Great Northern Railroad, 122, 158

Gregorian chant: Ratisbon style, 90, 213, 229; Solesmes style, 228–229; 259, 260, 273, 274, 288, 289, 293, 320, 332

Gregorian Institute of America, 288

Greil, Patrick, O.S.B., 23, 26, 29, 36, 44

Gross, Severin, O.S.B., 171, 199

Gymnasium, 59, 110

Gymnasium, 229, 232, 335–336

Haggarty, Paul Leonard, Vicar Apostolic of the Bahamas, 326

Haid, Leo, O.S.B., Bishop of North Carolina and Abbot of Belmont, 154, 183, 187–188, 193, 216, 223, 252–253

Haindl, Benedict, O.S.B., 14, 38, 55, 61–62, 63–64, 65–68, 71, 72, 74, 81, 82, 83, 85, 87, 89, 93–94, 97, 99, 100, 103, 123, 129

Hamline University, 48, 233, 295

Hamm Foundation of St. Paul, 332

Hamm, William, 111

Hansen, Bonaventure, O.S.B., 322, 324–326

Hansen, James, O.S.B., 235

Hansen, Polycarp, O.S.B., 228, 235

Haustus, 213, 304

Hawes, Fra Jerome, T.O.S.F., 325

Hayes, Patrick, Cardinal, 310, 322, 323, 324

Heider, Jerome, O.S.B., 111, 167

Heiss, Michael, Bishop of La Crosse, 125, 127, 175–176

Hellebusch, B.H.F., 90

Helmstetter, Ernest, O.S.B., Abbot of

St. Mary's Newark, 296–297, 302, 303, 305, 306

Henni, John Martin, Bishop of Milwaukee and Green Bay, 12, 16, 19, 95

Hermanutz, Aloysius, O.S.B., 138ff, 181, 195

Herwegen, Ildefons, O.S.B., Abbot of Maria Laach, 267, 273, 287

Hill, James J., 158, 161, 244

Hintenach, Andrew, O.S.B., Archabbot of St. Vincent, 183, 193, 198, 208

Hipelius, Edward, O.S.B., 7, 93, 96, 126, 129, 148

Hoenerbach, Placid, O.S.B., Abbot of St. Mary's, Richardton, N.D., 298-299

Hofbauer, Norbert, O.S.B., 111, 115–116, 144, 145, 170–171, 174, 182, 187, 194–195, 196, 199, 225

Hoffmann, Alexius, O.S.B., 38, 59, 61–62, 94, 128ff, 145, 148, 153–154, 183, 200, 210, 212, 219, 220, 221, 227–228, 229, 231, 232, 233, 235, 236, 244, 258, 269, 287

Holy Angels Pro-Cathedral, St. Cloud, 133, 155, 240; destroyed by fire, 282

Holy Cross Abbey, Canon City, Colo., 303, 305–306

Holy Name Parish, Humacao, Puerto Rico, 312, 313

Holy Name Sodality, 117

Holy Rosary Parish, Tacoma, 244, 246

Holy Rule, 4, 10, 17, 26–29, 30, 38, 42–43, 80, 117, 135, 168, 198, 212–213, 234, 239, 250, 261, 262, 330

Holy See, 14, 63, 64, 68, 93, 98, 125, 126, 129, 130, 143–144, 155, 172–174, 175–176, 177–178, 186, 188, 191–192, 193, 194, 197, 198, 199, 207, 216, 223, 228, 240, 245, 246, 248, 249, 253, 256, 259, 262, 274, 282, 296, 297, 298, 300, 301, 302, 308, 309, 321, 326, 329

Homar, Roman, O.S.B., 146, 218

Horarium, 10, 42–43, 57, 73, 85, 108, 136, 259

Horticultural experiments, 236–237, 239, 288

Hutchins, Robert M., 285, 290

Immaculate Conception Church, St. Cloud, 75, 76, 86, 88, 90, 91, 95, 99, 126, 127, 131, 133, 171, 198, 216, 240, 256, 281; becomes cathedral, 281, 282

Indian education, 138, 139–140, 146–147, 230, 238, 321

Indian Industrial School, St. John's, 146–147, 218, 230

Indian missions, 20, 45, 136ff, 146–147, 157, 172, 181, 211, 230–231, 238, 275, 281, 321

Indianbush, 44–45, 62–65, 78, 93, 95, 98, 154, 244

Insects, 32, 41–42

Institute for Social Studies, St. John's, 275–276

Ireland, John, Archbishop of St. Paul, 75–76, 132, 149, 154, 169–170, 174–177, 179–182, 184, 185, 186–189, 193–194, 197, 199, 203, 214–215, 232, 241–242, 244, 278; named Vicar Apostolic of Nebraska, 125

Irish immigrants, 101, 109, 123, 124, 138, 155

Jacobs Prairie, Minn., 39–40, 41, 45, 74, 89, 92, 124, 218

Jamestown, N.D., 128; diocese, 189, 198, 199

Jesuits, 9, 15, 17, 97–98, 140, 166, 169, 207, 260

Katholischer Lehrer Verein, 91–92

Katzner, John, O.S.B., 116, 145, 150, 183, 223, 236–237, 287

Keck, Paul Maria, 66, 81, 94

Keckism, 79, 81

Keller, George, 29, 50, 55

Kelly, Francis J., Bishop of Oklahoma City, 297, 298, 313

Kenrick, Peter Richard, Archbishop of St. Louis, 19, 27, 124–125

Kerst, Mother Scholastica, 160, 162

Kevenhoerster, Bernard, O.S.B., 228, 243, 256, 257, 322–326

Kilian, Philip, O.S.B., 146

Kirchweih Fest, 90

Knight's Valley, Calif., 248

Know-Nothings, 18, 152

Knutson, Harold, Minnesota Congressman, 285

Koch, Alfred, O.S.B., Abbot of St. Vincent, 308

Korte, Alexander, O.S.B., 262, 315–316, 319, 327

'Krainers,' 124, 128

Krautbauer, Franz Xavier, Bishop of Green Bay, 95, 112, 125, 127, 132, 141

Kreuter, Joseph, O.S.B., 275, 277, 279–281

Krey, August C., 4, 239, 244, 284

Kuisle, Alphonse, O.S.B., 106, 112, 114, 220

LaCrosse, Wis., 125, 175

LaFarge, John, 316

LaFarge, L. Bancel, 332

Lake Sagatagan, 45, 82, 114, 135, 218, 244, 251; variation in names, 119, 238

Lamborn Hospital, Bismarck, 160, 162, 178

Lampe, Simon, O.S.B., 140, 195

439

Landersdorfer, Simon, O.S.B., Bishop of Passau, Bavaria, 329
Laundry, 135, 159, 218, 229
Lay theology, 292–293
Lee, Minnie Mary, 114, 115–116
Lemke, Peter Henry, 8, 18, 60
Leo XIII, Pope, 175–179, 186, 191–192, 193, 194, 228, 261, 268, 275, 309
Leopoldinen Stiftung, 7–8, 135
Lethert, Ambrose, O.S.B., 167, 170, 172, 173, 183
Lifetime abbots, 83–84, 93
Literary organizations, 116–117
Liturgical Academy, Maria Laach, 262
Liturgical Arts Society, 276, 332, 337–338
Liturgical Press, 268, 270, 279; publications, 268–270, 281, 287
Liturgical Revival, 108, 212–214, 250, 259–261, 263ff, 289, 327, 331, 338; first fruits, 278–279, 292–293, 319–320; opponents, 272–273; proponents, 265–267, 268–269, 273–274, 275–276, 324–325; social effects, 268, 270–271, 272, 275–277
Lobmiller, Theodore, 92, 219
Locnikar, Bernard, O.S.B., Abbot of St. John's, 112, 114, 126, 143, 144, 159, 165, 166, 183, 194, 195, 196–199, 222, 242; character and piety, 213–214, 219–220, 221, 225; ideals, aims and policies, 199–202, 204, 205–206, 209–211, 213, 214–217; liturgical efforts, 212–214, 220; sickness and death, 218, 220–221, 225
Long Island, N.Y., 242–243, 248
Loras, Mathias, Bishop of Dubuque, 15, 19
Louvain University, 262, 265, 266
Ludwig I, King of Bavaria, 5–6, 8, 13–14, 17, 20, 143; charity, 11, 27, 62–64, 97, 105
Ludwig Missionsverein, 7, 8, 11, 17, 20, 53, 63, 95, 96, 100–101, 105, 106, 120, 135, 154
'Luxemburger University,' 145

McDonnell, Charles E., Bishop of Brooklyn, 211, 242
McGolrick, James, Bishop of Duluth, 189, 217
Mansard roofs, 153
Maredsous Abbey, Belgium, 259, 260, 265, 266, 267
Maria Laach, 260, 262, 265, 266, 267, 278, 328
Martinez, Luis, Archbishop of Mexico City, 311
Marty, Martin, O.S.B., Bishop of St. Cloud, 127, 137, 140, 146, 155, 158–159, 171–174, 175, 176, 179, 181, 182, 185, 187, 189, 194, 214, 223–224, 240
Mass, 8, 10, 27, 28, 30–31, 33, 57, 73, 87, 90, 94, 98, 109, 115, 117, 207, 209, 210, 213, 233, 244, 251, 259, 266–267, 268–269, 270, 275, 278, 289, 293; musical, 90, 116, 198
Master of accounts degree, 111
Master of arts degree, 146
Matt, Joseph, 268, 275
Maximilian I of Mexico, 5, 103–104
Mayer, Alfred, O.S.B., 111, 165, 167, 178, 183, 194, 223, 242, 248–249, 256, 258, 261
Mayer, Wendelin, O.S.B., 67–68, 79–80
Medicine, 106–107
Melcher, Joseph, Bishop of Green Bay, 27, 112, 125
Men's chorus, 294–295
Mental Health Workshops, 332
Merino, Señor Jaime, 312
Merschman, Francis, O.S.B., 105, 144, 145, 148, 181, 183, 226, 235–236, 258
Metten Abbey, Germany, 5–6, 7, 11, 18, 193, 213
Mexico City Priory, Mexico City, 311–312
Meyer, Athanasius, O.S.B., 252
Michel, Virgil, O.S.B., 228, 262, 263ff, 283, 327, 336, 338; collaborators and supporters, 264, 265, 266–267, 268–269, 273–274, 275, 277, 278; 'Great Books' plan, 290–291; last days, 275, 277–278; translations and publications, 268–269
Mill, 106
Milwaukee and St. Paul Railroad, 122
Minneapolis, Minn., 51, 115, 145, 155, 158, 165, 200, 233; as St. Anthony's Falls, 28, 103
'Minnesota Belle,' river steamer, 27–28
Minnesota College Conference, 233
Minnesota College Fund, 331
Minnesota Horticultural Society, 237
Minnesota Intercollegiate Athletic Conference, 295
Minnesota *Pioneer and Democrat*, 27, 28, 48
Minnesota River Valley, 21, 31, 55, 62, 66, 70, 73, 74, 78, 86–87, 120, 247
Minnesota Territory: description, 21–23; immigration, 17, 19–21, 28, 34–35, 122–123; statehoood, 68; State Legislature, Committee on Education, 284
Mission crosses, 41
Mission societies, 7, 8, 12, 17
Mission work, 7–9, 11–12, 16, 17, 19, 31–32, 33, 39, 55, 73–74, 85–89, 120–121, 122–124, 155–156, 159–160, 163, 164–166, 197, 198, 203ff,

440

206–212, 217–218, 244–249, 270–271, 306ff, 315–320, 321ff, 327
Mississippi River Valley, 73, 90, 125, 137
Missouri River, 157, 158, 159, 160
Monastery at St. Joseph, Minn., 65
Monastic choir, 220, 229, 259, 260
Monastic refectory, 260
Monastic reformers, 79, 81, 164ff
Monte Cassino, 4–5, 150, 239, 333
Montebello, Calif., 297, 310
'Morning Star' Monastery, 37–38
Motu proprio, 229
Mount St. Vincent on the Hudson, 208
Muckenthaler, Benno, O.S.B., 23, 26, 29, 36, 44, 83, 108
Mueller, Adalbert, O.S.B., 179–180, 185, 187, 190, 192, 216, 225
Mueller, Ferdinand Josef, 8, 11, 12, 18, 62–63, 95
Muench, Aloisius, Bishop of Fargo, 281, 288, 290
Murray, John Gregory, Archbishop of St. Paul, 281, 324, 329–330
Museum, 229
Musical instruments, 115–116, 150
Musical training, 115ff, 150, 229, 260, 288, 294–295

Nassau, Bahamas, 207, 210, 211–212, 322, 325
National Catholic Educational Association, 266
National Catholic Rural Life Conference, 288
National Catholic Rural Life Movement, 288
National Catholic Welfare Conference, 266, 285, 338
National Liturgical Day, 275
National problem, 149–150
Nativists, 152
Negro missions, 206, 207, 208, 210, 211–212, 315–319, 321ff
Nelson, Knute, Minnesota Congressman, 139, 146, 202–203
New proposed abbey church, 336–341; praises, 337–340
New York, N.Y., 9, 122, 193, 203–206, 208, 223, 242–243, 325, 336, 339; archdiocese, 205–206, 207, 211
Newman Club, University of North Dakota, 290
Newman Hall, University of Illinois, 289
Newman Club work, 289–290
North Central Association of Colleges and Secondary Schools, 285–286
Northern Pacific Railroad, 122, 137, 157, 158, 159
Northman, Ulric, O.S.B., 115, 116, 145, 183, 225
Northman, Bede, O.S.B., 160, 167, 170

Northman, Wolfgang, O.S.B., 60, 74, 78, 82, 94, 102, 103, 109, 113–114, 115, 119, 224
Notre Dame University, 363, 269
Nova Scotia Co-operative Movement, 276

O'Brien, John A., 289
O'Connell, Msgr., Denis J., 172, 174, 175–177, 179–180, 185, 186–188, 203
O'Connor, Bishop of Pittsburgh, 8, 9, 12–14, 15, 26, 52, 61, 191
O'Hara, Edwin, Bishop of Kansas City, 288
O'Shaughnessy, Ignatius, 232
O'Toole, Msgr. G. Barry, 306–307
Oblates of St. Benedict, 150, 261
Oblate, 271
Observatory, 226–227
'Old Stone House,' 83, 95, 99–100, 102, 115
Orate Fratres, 268–270, 274, 275, 278, 279; reviews, 270, 274; *Worship*, 279, 338
Ortmann, Anselm, O.S.B., 228, 235
Ott, Michael, O.S.B., 228, 236, 249, 287
Our Lady of the Holy Rosary Parish, Tacoma, Wash., 217
Our Lady of Lourdes Parish, Los Angeles, Calif., 297
Owensboro, Ky., 316, 318

Pacific Railroad Co., 157
Parochial schools, 46–47, 52–54, 75–76
'Paul Anderson,' river steamer, 23, 25
Pescetelli, Angelo, O.S.B., Abbot of St. Paul's Outside the Walls, 14, 19, 43, 50, 130
Pfraengle, Hilary, O.S.B., Abbot of St. Mary's, Newark, 167, 173, 180, 183, 188, 194, 208–209, 244
Photography, 227
Pierz, Joseph, 20, 21–23, 33, 39, 40, 45, 69–70, 86, 124, 137
Pius IX, Pope, 9, 14–15, 63, 84, 97, 130, 135
Pius X, Pope, 229, 249, 266, 268, 271, 273
Pius X School of Liturgical Music, Manhattanville College of the Sacred Heart, N.Y., 260
Pius XI, Pope, 274, 275, 279, 280, 300, 307, 309
Pius XII, Pope, 4, 273, 278, 318
'Plattdeutsch,' 27, 124, 128, 129
Pontifical major degrees, 143–144
'Popular Liturgical Library,' 265–268
Population growth, 123, 161
Poverty, holy, 165, 174
Power house, 147, 229, 335

441

Poza Rica, Mexico, 312
'Priester Wald,' 37
Priests' Eucharistic Convention, Buffalo, 274
Primitive Observance Congregation, 296, 301, 302
Printing plant, 147, 150
'Priory,' Nassau, Bahamas, 211
Protestant Episcopal Church, 138, 207, 208, 211, 212, 323, 324, 325, 326
Protestant Revolt, 136, 151, 291
Provincial synods, 124–125
Public schools, 52, 75–76
Puerto Rico, 312–314

Quadrangle, 152–154, 218, 229, 230
Quadrivium, 57, 110, 290

Railroads, 27, 98, 122–123, 134, 154–155, 157, 158, 161
Ramsey, Justus C., Governor of Minnesota, 49, 69, 71
Rancho Santa Cruz, Mexico City, 312
Ravoux, Augustine, Vicar General of St. Paul, 29, 53, 54, 55
Raymond, Antonine, 320
Red Lake Reservation, Minn., 139–140, 167, 181, 195, 238
Red River Valley, 122, 157
Redemptorists, 7, 9, 12, 166, 287
Redwood Falls Massacre, 69
Reforestation, 237–238
Reger, Walter, O.S.B., 234, 263, 283, 327
Religious bigotry, 48–49
Republican Party, 47–49, 77
Research and publications, 234–238, 287–288
Retreats, 260–261, 332
'H. M. Rice,' river steamer, 32
Ricker, Berthold, O.S.B., 312
Riepp, Sister Benedicta, O.S.B., 53–54, 62–64
Riess, Bruno, O.S.B., 23, 26, 29, 30–31, 32, 36, 38, 39–40, 41, 44, 45–46, 59, 62, 65, 66–68, 78, 82, 133; journal, 27, 30–31, 32, 33, 37, 40, 43, 69–70, 71, 87
Robot, Isidore, O.S.B., Prefect Apostolic of the Indian Territory, 127
Rocky Mountain locust, 41–42
Roerig, Gabriel, O.S.B., 210, 212, 322
Roerig, Leander, O.S.B., 322
Roetzer, Alexius, O.S.B., 43, 44, 45, 57, 59–60, 98–99, 102
Roig, Don Agripino Antonio, 312–313
Rome, 14, 63, 64, 68, 93, 98, 125, 126, 129, 130, 135, 143–144, 155, 172–174, 175, 179, 184, 185, 187, 188–189, 197, 198, 199, 177–178, 216, 217, 223, 224, 245, 262, 278, 304
Rosary, 10, 43, 79, 314
R.O.T.C. program, 294

Rothkopp, Louis and William, 32, 36, 51, 77–78
Rothkopp claims dispute, 47, 49, 50–52, 57, 59, 62, 66, 76–77, 83
Russell, Edward J., 317

Sacred Congregation of Bishops and Regulars, 186
Sacred Congregation of the Holy Office, 81, 186
Sacred Congregation of the Index, 186
Sacred Congregation of the Propagation of the Faith, 14, 83–84, 97, 125, 130, 167, 172–173, 174–175, 175–176, 177, 178, 179, 180, 184, 185, 186, 189, 190, 192, 207, 216, 309, 322, 323, 324, 325
Sacred Congregation of Religious, 297, 300, 329
Sacred Heart Abbey, Okla., 243, 296–298; as St. Gregory's Abbey, 275, 296–298, 310
Sacred Heart Parish, Duluth, Minn., 161
Sagatagan, 331
St. Agnes Parish, St. Paul, Minn., 120, 240
St. Alexius Priory, West Union, Minn., 151–152, 159, 204
Saint André Abbey, Belgium, 265, 267, 310
St. Andrew's Priory, Cleveland, Ohio, 306
St. Anselm's Abbey, Manchester, N.H., 306
St. Anselm's Parish, New York, N.Y., 204–205, 242–244, 256, 310, 322, 333
St. Anselm's Priory, Tokyo, 319–320
St. Anselm's Priory, Washington, D.C., 267
St. Anthony's Parish, Minneapolis Minn., 74
St. Anthony's Priory, Puerto Rico, 312–314
St. Augustine's College, Nassau, Bahamas, 325, 326
St. Augustine's Priory, Nassau, Bahamas, 321ff
St. Benedict of Nursia, 4, 108, 135, 137, 145, 150, 165, 220, 226, 261, 327, 341
St. Benedict's Abbey, Atchison, Kan., 60–61, 127, 171, 172–173, 179, 194, 196, 198, 278, 302, 305, 306
St. Benedict's Convent, Bismarck, N.D., 161
St. Benedict's Convent and Academy, St. Joseph, Minn., 76, 92, 140, 146, 152, 158, 160, 162, 181, 230, 276, 307, 315; missionary efforts: China, 307; Mexico, 311; Puerto Rico, 313; Utah, 321

St. Benedict's Mission, White Earth Reservation, Minn., 138

St. Benedict's Parish, Avon, Minn., 333

St. Benedict's Parish, Montebello, Calif., 297

St. Benedict's Parish, New York, N.Y., 268, 310

St. Benet's Hall, 230, 331

St. Bernard's Parish, St. Paul, Minn., 242

St. Boniface Abbey, Munich, Germany, 331

St. Boniface Academy, Hastings, Minn., 113

St. Boniface Day, 109

St. Boniface Parish, Minneapolis, Minn., 74, 233

St. Clement's Parish, Duluth, Minn., 162, 242

St. Cloud, Minnesota, 32–36, 39, 46, 47, 50–52, 62, 73, 74, 78, 91, 92, 94, 95, 99, 101, 102, 103, 109, 119, 122, 124, 125, 126, 127, 131, 133, 135, 143, 144, 150, 155, 160, 202, 247; diocese, 175, 176, 178, 189, 194, 198, 214–217, 232, 240, 281, 282, 295–296; location of St. Joseph's Convent, 53–54, 75, 76; Sioux War, 70–72

St. Cloud Business College, 233

St. Cloud *Democrat*, 88

St. Cloud Diocesan Catholic Action Program, 276

St. Cloud ferry, 33, 102

St. Cloud Hospital, 329

St. Cloud *Journal*, 88

St. Cloud Priory, 65, 73, 79, 83–84, 86, 97, 103, 143

St. Elizabeth's College, Rome, 103

St. Felix Parish, Wabasha, Minn, 240

St. Francis Seminary, Milwaukee, Wis., 16, 91–92, 112

St. Francis Xavier Academy, Nassau, Bahamas, 208, 209, 326

St. Francis Xavier Parish, Nassau, Bahamas, 207, 211, 326

St. Gall Priory, Devil's Lake, N.D., 298

St. Gregory's Abbey, Shawnee, Okla., 275, 296–298, 310; as Sacred Heart Abbey, 243, 296–297

St. Helen's Parish, Roosevelt, Utah, 321

St. James Prairie (Jacobs Prairie), Minn., 39–40, 41, 45, 74, 89, 90

St. Jean Baptiste Parish, Duluth, Minn., 161

St. Jerome's Parish, Fancy Farm, Ky., 317

St. John's Parish, Meire Grove, Minn., 281

St. John's Abbey, Collegeville, Minn., 3–4, 92, 104, 133, 158, 159, 161, 167, 168, 176, 193, 209; abbots, 93ff, 170, 177–178, 196ff, 222ff, 256ff, 329ff; chapter, 23, 61, 65–66, 68, 73, 128, 161, 164, 165, 169, 170, 194, 198, 206, 218, 222, 232, 247, 300, 302, 306, 310, 311, 312, 320, 321, 323, 333; disagreements, 37, 65–68, 79, 128–130, 164ff, 183, 195–198, 199–200, 214–217, 282; supports Abbot Alexius and Bishop Seidenbusch, 170, 177–178; visitation, 172–174, 179–194, 195, 197, 215, 326, 330; missions, 41, 86–87, 121, 138–140, 159–160, 163, 164–166, 181, 197, 198, 204, 205–206, 208–212, 215, 216–217, 255; monastery: arrival, 36–38, 41, 42–44,56–60, 62–64, 78–79, 81–83, 95, 100ff, 107–109, 131, 135; first growth, 140–143, 145–146, 152–154, 181–182, 218–220, 259–260; second growth, 227–230, 255–256, 282ff; third growth, 335ff; name, 65, 97, 141, 143; parishes, 86, 88, 121–122, 133–134, 155, 160, 161–162, 164, 165, 181, 198, 215–218, 239, 240, 241, 242–243, 255, 268, 281, 282, 304; projects: liturgical, 259ff, 269–261, 263ff; missionary: Bahamas, 205–212, 242, 310, 321ff; Japan, 319–320; Kentucky, 315–319; Mexico, 311–312; New York, 203–205, 241, 242–243, 244, 310; Puerto Rico, 312–314; Saskatchewan, 246–249; Utah, 320–321; Washington State, 217–218, 241, 244–246

St. John's Abbey Church: present structure, 140–143; future plans, 335ff

St. John's Alumni Association, 150, 332

St. John's Archives, 150

St. John Baptist Parish, Collegeville, Minn., 141

St. John Cantius Parish, St. Cloud, Minn., 241

St. John's Chapel, Champaign, Ill., 289

St. John's College, Annapolis, Md., 290

St. John's Commercial College, 110ff, 133

'St. John's medicine,' 107

St. John's Seminary, 47–50, 55, 56–60, 62, 78–79, 100–101, 102–105, 109ff, 178, 243, 257; diocese supervision, 295–296; name, 144

St. John's University, 46, 56–60, 62, 78–79, 100–101, 102–105, 109ff, 144ff, 168, 178, 197, 224, 227–228, 230ff, 275, 282–288; art, 332–335; chant schools, 288; 'Great Books', plan 290–291; growth, 282–288, 290ff, 294–295; lay theology, 291–292; mental health workshops, 332; name, 104, 143; rural life movement, 288; sports, 118–119, 230, 231–233, 295

St. Joseph, Minn., 23, 39–40, 41, 44, 45, 59, 62, 70, 71, 73, 76, 78, 90, 91,

94, 102, 103, 114, 121–122, 128, 134, 135, 140, 143, 160, 162, 216, 230, 232, 240, 241

St. Joseph's Convent, St. Cloud, Minn., 53–54, 62–65, 75; see St. Benedict's Convent, St. Joseph, Minn.

St. Joseph's Convent, St. Mary, Pa., 52–53

St. Joseph's Parish, Chicago, Ill., 26

St. Joseph's Parish, Little Falls, Minn., 178

St. Joseph's Parish, Minneapolis, Minn., 155, 200, 258

St. Joseph's Parish, Moorhead, Minn., 256

St. Joseph's Parish, New York, N.Y., 203

St. Joseph's Parish, Ogden, Utah, 321

St. Kilian's Parish, Farmingdale, N.Y., 242

St. Leo's Abbey, San Antonio, Fla., 193, 201

St. Louis *Herold des Glaubens*, 144

St. Louis Monastery, 63, 65, 97, 98, 101, 105, 128, 133, 143; see St. John's Abbey

St. Martin's College, Olympia, Wash., 245, 246

St. Martin's Parish, Amityville, N.Y., 242

St. Mary's Abbey, Newark, N.J., 96, 166–167, 183, 192, 206, 208, 244, 245, 297, 302, 321

St. Mary's Abbey, Richardton, N.D., 298–301, 306; renamed Assumption Abbey, 301

St. Mary's Academy, Bismarck, N.D., 160

St. Mary's College, Notre Dame, Ind., 336

St. Mary's Hall, 335

St. Mary's Hospital, Duluth, Minn., 162, 170, 178

St. Mary's Hospital, Rochester, Minn., 253

St. Mary's Parish, Bismarck, N.D., 241

St. Mary's Parish, Duluth, Minn., 161

St. Mary's Parish, Elk Co., Pa., 11, 16, 52, 61, 96

St. Mary's Parish, Foxhome, N.D., 333

St. Mary's Parish, Stillwater, Minn., 220

St. Meinrad Archabbey, Ind., 17, 127, 158, 159, 172, 267, 299, 317

St. Monica's Parish, White Fish Bay, Milwaukee, Wis., 310

St. Olaf's College, Northfield, Minn., 285, 295

St. Ottilien Benedictines, 137, 310, 323

St. Pancras Parish, Glendale, N.Y., 242

St. Patrick's Cathedral, New York, N.Y., 324

St. Patrick's Day, 109

St. Patrick's Parish, Melrose, Minn., 124

St. Paul, the Apostle, 15, 171

St. Paul, Minn., 27–28, 103, 111, 116, 118, 120, 121, 122, 125, 132–133,, 135, 141, 144, 150, 158, 160, 165, 169, 174, 201, 220, 222, 232, 241, 247; diocese, 27–28, 125; mission base, 86; archdiocese, 175–176, 184, 189, 240

St. Paul's Cathedral, St. Paul, Minn., 28, 121

St. Paul and Duluth Railroad, 161

St. Paul, Minneapolis and Manitoba Railroad Co., 143, 158

St. Paul *Northwestern Chronicle*, 113, 114–115

St. Paul's Outside the Walls, Rome, 191

St. Paul and Pacific Railroad Co., 78, 122, 143

St. Paul's Parish, Sauk Center, Minn., 240

St. Paul Seminary, St. Paul, Minn., 266

St. Peter's Abbey, Saskatchewan, Canada, 246–249, 253, 256, 310

St. Peter and Paul Parish, Richmond, Minn., 91

St. Procopius Priory, Chicago., Ill., 193

St. Rupert's College, Bismarck, N.D., 158, 159

St. Saviour's Chapel, Salvador Point, Bahamas, 212

St. Scholastica's Convent, Atchison, Kan., 311

St. Scholastica's Convent, Duluth, Minn., 162

St. Stephen's Monastery, Augsburg, Germany, 6

St. Theodore Parish, Germantown, Ill., 26

St. Thomas College, St. Paul, Minn., 232, 233, 295

St. Vincent Archabbey, Latrobe, Pa., 16, 17, 19, 43, 59, 61, 68, 72, 79, 94, 95, 99, 102, 103, 128, 129, 143, 145, 166–167, 191, 196, 198, 208, 224–225, 240, 248, 305, 306–309; beginnings, 9–11; Minnesota expedition, 19, 23, 97–98; oblates, 261; seminary, 11, 12, 13

St. Vincent College, 96, 100, 103

St. Vincent's Sanatarium, Los Angeles, Calif., 156

St. Walburga's Convent, Eichstaett, Bavaria, 52

St. Wendelin's Parish, St. Augusta, Minn., 128

St. Wendelin's Parish, St. Wendel, Minn., 124

St. Wendel's Parish, Luxemburg, Minn., 73

St. Xavier's Convent, Latrobe, Pa., 10

Salve Regina, 82
Salzbacher, Canon Josef, 7–8
Salzburg University, 262
San Beda College, Manila, P.I., 301–302
San Callisto, Rome, 173, 184
San Salvador Island, Bahamas, 208, 209, 322
Sant' Anselmo, Rome, 179, 198, 216, 227, 228, 257–258, 259, 265, 267, 287, 309
Santa Maria di Montserrat Abbey, Manila, P.I., 301–302
São Paulo, Brazil, 333
Sauk River Valley, 90
Sausen, Alphonse, O.S.B., 228, 297
Saw mill, 101–102, 135
Sbarretti, Canon Donato, 177
Scandinavian immigrants, 21, 123
Scarboro Foreign Mission Society, Toronto, Canada, 326
Scheeben, Josef, 266
Scheffold, George, O.S.B., 261
Scheffold, Ulric, O.S.B., 246
Schrerer, George, O.S.B., 65, 94, 95
Scherr, Gregor, Archbishop of Munich, 6
Schyern Abbey, Gremany, 6, 11, 18, 64
Schiffrer, Vincent, O.S.B., 103, 112, 170, 182, 183, 333; early life, 103–104
Schirber, Martin, O.S.B., 286, 288
Schlick, Frank, Jr., 111
Schlick, Frank, Sr., 50
Schlarmann, Joseph, Bishop of Peoria, 273, 289
Schlimm, Leonard, O.S.B., 305
Schmitt, Adrian, O.S.B., 107, 237–238
Schmitt, Athanasius, O.S.B., Abbot of St. Meinrad, 299
Schmitt, Benedict, O.S.B., 238, 245
Schmitt, Martin, O.S.B., 107, 159, 160, 167, 183
Schnerr, Leander, O.S.B., Archabbot of St. Vincent, 261
Schoenbechler, Roger, O.S.B., 262, 268, 289, 303
Schoenthal, 45
Scholarships, 13, 119–120, 283–284
School issue, 52, 75–76
Schools, elementary, 46–47, 52–54, 58ff, 75, 109ff, 144–145, 282; parochial, 52; public, 52, 282
Schoolteachers, 91–92
Schreiner, Chrysostom, O.S.B., 107, 145, 146, 148, 149, 181, 182, 184, 185, 186, 195, 196, 199, 236; missionary labors, 205–206, 208–212
Schrembs, Joseph, Bishop of Cleveland, 273–274
Schwinghammer's Settlement, Minn., 123
Schwinn, Leonard, O.S.B., 305–306

Science building, 228
Scripture studies, 272, 273, 278
Seckau Abbey, Germany, 260
Second Plenary Council of Baltimore, 93
Secret societies and subversive movements, 18, 23
Seidenbusch, Rupert, O.S.B., Abbot of St. John's 95–99, 122, 125, 133, 135, 138, 139, 146, 167, 171, 180, 225; abilities, 96–97, 100; aims, ideals and policies, 95, 99–101, 106; early life and training, 95–97; bishop, 125ff, 131, 142, 155; projects, 100ff, educational, 102ff, 119; missionary, 101, 120ff, 123, 124, 136, 137–138, 154–156, 161; last days, 156, 158, 174–179, 185; opponents, 174ff; supporters 177–178
Seminaries, early, 9, 11, 12, 13, 16, 47–50, 55, 56–60, 78–79, 100–101, 102–105, 109ff, 112
Senate Committee on the Relation of the University of Minnesota to Other Institutions of Learning, 284
Seredi, Justin, Cardinal, 304
Shakers, 317–318
Shanley, John, Bishop of Jamestown, N.D., 181, 189, 198–199, 221, 298
Shea, Sir Ambrose, Governor of the Bahamas, 209
Sheehan, Major T. J., 139–140
Shipstead, Henrik, Minnesota Senator, 285, 286
Shuster, George N., 121
Simeoni, Giovanni, Cardinal, 167, 172, 174, 175–176, 178–181, 182, 183, 184–185, 188, 190, 193–194, 197, 199, 207, 216
Simmer, Jerome, O.S.B., 262
Singenberger, John, 91
Sioux City Railroad Line, 98
Sioux Indian War, 58, 60, 69–72
Sioux Indians, 20, 44, 137, 155, 158
Sioux Treaties of 1851–1853, 20, 69
'Sisters' House,' 229
Sisters of Charity, 128, 208, 209, 211, 212, 322, 324, 325, 326
Sisters of Mercy, 10, 11
Sisters of the Most Precious Blood, O'Fallon, Mo., 266
Sisters of Blessed Martin de Porres, 326
Sisters of Notre Dame, 52, 224
Sisters of St. Benedict, 52–54, 62–65, 75, 128, 160, 162, 241, 307, 311, 313, 321
Sisters of St. Francis, 128
Sisters of St. Joseph, St. Paul, Minn., 29, 31, 53, 272–273; hospital, 29, 53
Skillin, Edward, Jr., 277
Slavic immigrants, 155
Smith, Bernard, O.S.B., Abbot, 13, 156,

172–173, 179, 180, 184–185, 186, 190–192, 193, 194, 197, 216–217
Soccer, 118
Social Problem, 276
Society of the Divine Word, 308–309
Society for the Propagation of the Faith, 7
Solesmes Abbey, France, 229, 259, 265
Sorbonne University, Paris, 263
South Dakota State College of Agriculture, Brookings, S. D., 237
Spielmann, Gerard, O.S.B., 181, 183, 205, 242–243
Sponsa Regis, 279–281
Sports, 118–119, 230, 231–233, 295
'Sportsman's Hall,' Pa., 9
Spunk Lakes, 119, 123; see Lake Sagatagan
Staub, Clement, O.S.B., 55, 59, 65, 66, 68, 71, 72, 81, 94, 98–99, 107, 116, 121, 129, 144, 238, 246
Stearns County, Minn., 34, 41, 51, 101, 107, 155, 167, 215–217, 238, 239, 240, 241, 281
Stegmann, Basil, O.S.B., 228, 262, 268, 298, 308–309, 313, 315, 327
Stehle, Aurelius, Archabbot of St. Vincent, 306–308, 309
Steil, Gregory, O.S.B., 141, 145, 162, 183, 195; abilities and character, 153–154, 218
'Stein,' Mr., 104
Steinkogler, Wolfgang, O.S.B., 218, 244–245, 246
Stemper, Franz Xavier, 154
Stenger, Paul, O.S.B., 43, 44
Stephan, Joseph A., 146
Stevens, Mother Gregory, 260
Stimmler, Valentine, O.S.B., 74–75, 82, 100, 103, 133, 181, 218
Stuckenkemper, Meinulph, O.S.B., 74, 76, 82, 88, 94, 95, 99, 107, 164, 183, 196, 223, 238
Studebaker, John W., U. S. Commissioner of Education, 284
'Subiaco Abbey,' 65, 143
Swimming, 119, 251
Swiss American Congregation, 17, 84, 127, 137, 298, 299, 308
Swiss Congregation, 16, 17, 84, 127, 137, 158, 252

Tailor shop, 147
Te Deum, 98, 257
Tekippe, Owen, O.S.B., 302, 313–314
Temperance movements, 13, 15–16, 169–170
Tennessee Valley Authority, 317
Tenvoorde, John, 35, 53
Times Publishing Co., St. Cloud, 150
Titular Bishop of Halia, 126
Tomazin, Ignatius, 124, 137ff
Tornado of 1894, 218–220

Totsuo Doi, Peter, Archbishop of Tokyo, 319
Transference of stability, 65–66
'Translinda,' 236
Trivium, 57, 110, 290
Trobec, James, Bishop of St. Cloud, 120, 239, 240, 244, 253; educational policy, 240–241
Trusteeism, 76
Tuebingen University, Germany, 262, 278
Tschumperlin, Alois, 135
Tuition, 54, 112, 116, 119–120, 146, 230

Uintah Valley, Utah, 321
U. S. Signal Service, 227
University of Chicago, 263, 276, 285
University of Illinois, Champaign, 289–290
University of Minnesota, Minneapolis, 228, 233, 235, 263, 274, 291, 331, 341; Duluth Branch, 295
University of North Dakota, Grand Forks, 290
University Orchestra, 150
Urban House, University of Illinois, 289

Vaeth, Timothy, O.S.B., 161, 183, 233
Vatican chant, 229
Vatican Observatory, 227
Vesperale Romano-Monasticum, 229
Vespers, Sunday, 91
Veth, Martin, O.S.B., Abbot of St. Benedict's, 278, 302, 305, 309, 324
Vicariate of the Bahama Islands, 318
Vicariate of the Dakota Territory, 127, 155, 175; suffragen sees, 176
Vicariate of Northern Minnesota, 125–126, 154, 158, 174, 175, 176, 177–178, 179, 180, 215
Victim Souls, 280–281
Vill, Joseph, O.S.B., 74, 82, 94, 100
Vitry, Ermin, O.S.B., 260, 268
Von Reisach, Graf Karl August, Archbishop of Munich, 6, 8, 11, 18
Von Stotzingen, Fidelis, O.S.B.,, Abbot Primate, 259, 305

Waite, Henry C., Minnesota Senator, 51, 77, 144
Wanderer, 129, 169
Wanderer Printing Co., St. Paul, 150, 268
War between the States, 66, 68, 76, 82, 96, 123, 157, 207
Watab, 44–45, 65, 78, 101, 114, 135, 219, 229, 236, 237, 238, 240; North Fork, 81
Water supply, 135
Way of Victimhood Movement, 280–281

Weather station, 226–227, 228, 235
Webb, Jack, 294
Wehrle, Vincent, Bishop of Bismarck, 199, 298, 300
Weninger, Francis Xavier, 40–41
Westphalians, 124, 128
Wheat, 106, 123, 152, 158
Whipple, Henry B., Episcopal Bishop of Minnesota, 139, 244
White, Xavier, O.S.B., 141, 145, 148, 183, 205, 235
White Earth Reservation, Minn., 128, 137ff, 146–147, 195, 238, 275
Wilson, John L., 34, 47–49, 102
Wimmer, Boniface, O.S.B., Abbot of St. Vincent, 14–15, 43–45, 50, 51–52, 55, 77, 79, 93–98, 103, 104, 121, 127, 128–130, 132, 133, 143, 151, 156, 164, 166–167, 171–172, 173, 188, 196, 221, 225; aims, ideals and policies, 6–8, 13, 15–16, 17–19, 20, 24, 56–57, 60–61, 84–85, 107–108, 137, 140, 206, 239, 253, 295, 315, 327, 355; character, 8, 11–12, 65–68, 80–81, 135, 140, 145, 154, 161, 183; early life and training, 6; missionary efforts: Minnesota, 17, 23, 52–54, 62–64, 83–85, 93–98, 128–130; Pennsylvania, 8–16, 83–84, 93; motto, 11–12; opponents, 18, 191; last days, 183
Wimmer, Sebastian, 51
Wimmer, Simplicius, O.S.B., 112, 114
Wingerter, Placid, O.S.B., 183, 194
Winter School, 231

Wirth, Augustine, O.S.B., 60
Wirtz, Othmar Maria, O.S.B., 68, 72, 74–75, 76, 79–81, 85, 94, 98; early life and training, 72; aims and ideals, 72–73, 78, 80
Wittmann, Cornelius, O.S.B., 23, 26, 29, 30–31, 39, 46, 53, 55, 56–58, 59, 61, 65, 66–68, 88–89, 94, 121–122, 126, 164, 173, 183, 245–246, 333
Wolf, Innocent, O.S.B., Abbot of St. Benedict's, 128, 129, 171, 172, 173, 179, 180, 182, 188, 191, 192–193, 194, 196–198, 248
Wolter, Maurus, O.S.B., Abbot of Beuron, 259
Wolter, Placid, O.S.B., Abbot of Maredsous, 259
World War I, 107–251, 279, 283
World War II, 276, 279, 286, 292, 294, 310, 312, 319, 331
Worship, 268–270, 274, 275, 278, 279, 338; reviews, 270, 274

Yaiser, Hildebrand, O.S.B., 319–320
'Yankees,' 35–36, 72, 119
Yuenger, David, O.S.B., 297, 298

Zardetti, Otto J., Bishop of St. Cloud, 172, 187, 189, 197, 198, 204, 224; policies, 214–217; quoted, 34
Zelli, Leopold, O.S.B., Abbot of St. Paul's Outside the Walls, 184, 191
Zilliox, James, O.S.B., Abbot of St. Mary's, Newark, 166–168, 181

The centenary history of Saint John's Abbey and University was composed in Linotype Times Roman, which Stanley Morison designed in 1932 for use in The Times of London. The text paper is Suede book, the plate stock Cumberland Dull. The designs and the typography of the text are by Frank Kacmarcik. The book was produced by the North Central Publishing Company of Saint Paul and completed on the feast of Blessed Alcuin of Tours in the year of the Lord one thousand nine hundred and fifty-six.